Atlas Obscura
Wild Life

AN EXPLORER'S GUIDE TO
the World's Living Wonders

CARA GIAIMO AND JOSHUA FOER

with additional research and writing by
Rachel Fritts, JoAnna Klein, and other contributors

Workman Publishing ◆ New York

This book is for my dad, Mike Giaimo, who introduced me to other species when I was very young, and made sure I understood them and was not afraid. In return, when I was six years old, I brought him a bag of old crab parts I found on the beach. I hope this is a better gift. —C.G.

To all the builders of Atlas Obscura, past and present, who have contributed their creativity, intellect, and energy to the cause of inspiring wonder. —J.F.

An Important Note to Readers

Wild Life was written in the spirit of adventure and regard for nature. Readers are cautioned to travel at their own risk and to obey all local laws. Some of the places and creatures described in this book are not meant to be visited without appropriate permissions (or at all). Remember to respect wildlife, wild spaces, and the people who live where you're visiting. Neither the author nor the publisher shall be liable or responsible for any loss, injury, or damage allegedly arising from any information or suggestions contained in this book.

Workman
Workman Publishing
Hachette Book Group, Inc.
1290 Avenue of the Americas
New York, NY 10104
workman.com

Workman is an imprint of Workman Publishing, a division of Hachette Book Group, Inc. The Workman name and logo are registered trademarks of Hachette Book Group, Inc.

Cover design by Rae Ann Spitzenberger
Interior design by Janet Vicario
Cover and chapter opener illustrations by Zoe Keller
Illustrations by Iris Gottlieb
Photo research by Sophia Rieth
Photo credits listed on page 447

Workman books may be purchased in bulk for business, educational, or promotional use. For information, please contact your local bookseller or the Hachette Book Group Special Markets Department at special.markets@hbgusa.com.

Library of Congress Cataloging-in-Publication Data is available.
ISBN 978-1-5235-1441-0

First Edition September 2024

Cover printed in Malaysia.
Interior printed in Malaysia on responsibly sourced paper.

10 9 8 7 6 5 4 3 2 1

CONTENTS

INTRODUCTION

Humans

Where to begin?

RANGE: **Worldwide**
SPECIES: **Human (*Homo sapiens*)**

◆ About 7 million years ago, a new twig sprouted on the tree of life. Over time, different animals within this lineage arose and adapted. Just one of these—our own species, *Homo sapiens*—survives to the present day. But we have, by certain measures, done very well.

Humans will go almost anywhere and eat almost anything. We are constantly developing new behaviors—finding exciting ways to use our intricately folded brains, dexterous fingers, flair for communication, and peculiar stride. Many skills we once thought were unique to us have turned out to be more widely distributed—there are birds that set fires, bees that brew perfumes, and chimpanzees that invent and use tools. However, our species is singular in our desire and ability to depict and describe the world's other life forms, which we have been doing for at least 45,500 years (the age of the world's oldest known figurative cave painting, which shows a Sulawesi warty pig).

Humans are also unusual in our depth of engagement with our fellow living creatures—the plants, animals, and organisms upon whom our lives completely depend. We are of course bound to them with every breath of air and every bite of food. But we also learn from the species around us, using our observations of them to build new understandings of how life on Earth has been, is, and could be. We take inspiration from them, paying tribute to the collaged sounds of the flute lyrebird, the sudden colors of a desert in bloom, the shocking strength of the tiny hero shrew, and the hidden relationships of trees. We catalog rare cacti, study fishing cats, help gibbons, host pseudoscorpions, and work alongside honeyguide birds.

As the success of our particular species reshapes the world, now is a good time to remind ourselves that we made that world together with many others—wild creatures big and small, familiar and unfamiliar, plant and animal and fungus and microbe. A small fraction of them are collected in these pages, this era's version of a tableau on a cavern wall. May they come alive for you here.

Humans have been depicting animals since at least 45,500 years ago, when someone on the Indonesian island of Sulawesi drew this warty pig on a cave wall.

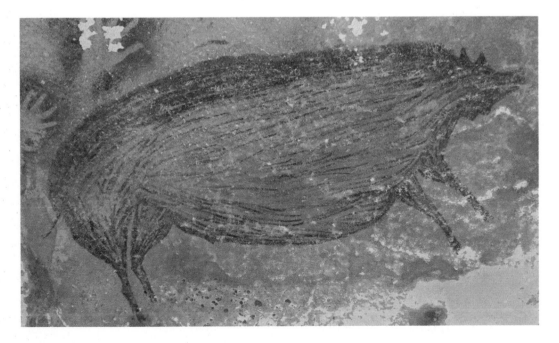

CHAPTER 1

Forests & Rainforests

I n the northwest corner of California, looming over Fog Canyon at a slight lean, there stands a coast redwood tree named Hyperion. Hyperion is the tallest known living organism. Mist tangles in its lower branches, woodpeckers nest in its hair, and black bears occasionally scratch against its ropy bark. To pluck a cone from its 380-foot-high (116 m) crown, about 60 bears would have to stack themselves shoulder to paw. The best way to gaze at its understory is to lie on your back, among the ferns and banana slugs.

Across the globe, in Borneo's Danum Valley, another tree stretches up. This one, a ruler-straight yellow meranti, reaches just more than 330 feet (100 m)—the world's next-tallest tree. Its name is Menara, Malay for "tower." The professionals who climb it sometimes bring hammocks with them, in case they need a nap break. On their way up, they pass the tree's inhabitants: tarsiers manning the lobby, epiphytes and hornbills on the middle floor, and eagles and orangutans living it up in the penthouses.

These two forests are quite different. Hyperion's temperate redwood grove is hazy and smells like spice, and the thick trunks of the redwoods absorb sound, hushing the whole grove like a cathedral. Menara's lowland rainforest is more like a nightclub, filled with dueling chatter and fragrance, with a canopy so thick in some places that it's dark at noon. But they and the world's many other forests also have a lot in common, thanks to the trillion or so trees that make them up.

In forests, trees grow and fall, lift and reach, and overlap and intertwine until they are more than the sum of themselves. They perform a kind of alchemy, transforming sunlight, water, and carbon dioxide into living material that supports even more life—around, below, and high above. Push aside that branch and let's go in.

Contributors: Ashley Braun, Christina Ayele Djossa, Lori Fox, Rachel Fritts, Natasha Frost, Claudia Geib, Ben Goldfarb, Jason G. Goldman, Vanessa Gregory, Mara Grunbaum, Myles Karp, Krista Langlois, Ella Morton, Julian Nowogrodzki, Linda Rodriguez McRobbie, Kim Thomson, Lauren J. Young

SOUTH AMERICA

Tent-Making Bats

Some bats prefer a homemade place to hang their heads.

RANGE: Central America, South America, South Asia, and Southeast Asia
SPECIES: Common tent-making bat (*Uroderma bilobatum*), Honduran white bat (*Ectophylla alba*), greater short-nosed fruit bat (*Cynopterus sphinx*), and many others

◆ Bats are known jocks, swooping around at high speeds and using echolocation to plunge and veer with pinpoint accuracy.

But some species are also artists—architects, to be precise. In tropical forests across the world, bats are building bespoke tents out of leaves. They are climate-controlled, provide shelter from the sun and rain, and even rustle when predators are near: a built-in security alarm.

More than 20 species of bat are known to make tents. Most of them are tiny fruit-eaters who perch in trees, although a few larger types, including some flying foxes, also dabble in tent-making. A male bat might build a tent during mating season in order to attract females, or a group might collaborate to pitch a family-sized roost. Bats also sometimes camp solo.

Whatever the motivation, construction usually goes the same way: The bat nibbles around a leaf's veins and stem, weakening it at strategic points until it collapses on itself. Depending on the shape of the leaves involved and the bat's particular chewing pattern, a number of different tent styles can result. Researchers have named at least eight architectural types, from the bifid tent, where two quick cuts cause a leaf to flop into a cabana shape, to the pinnate, where bats chew adjacent pairs of palm fronds until they form a long, skinny lean-to.

The most prolific builder, the common tent-making bat, can make seven different types of tents. Others specialize in one style, like Prairie-era Frank Lloyd Wrights. The Honduran white bat—a Central American species that resembles a cotton ball—makes tents only from the broad leaves of heliconias, shaping them into upside-down boats. Up to 15 white bats at a time might huddle inside one, hanging from the leaf's midrib like a fuzzy chandelier.

Honduran white bats curl up in their family-sized home.

Because so many different kinds of bats—including some from entirely different family groups—build tents, experts think the skill has evolved multiple times. More practitioners and styles will almost certainly be discovered, perhaps enough to fill a nice coffee-table book. ❯ **How to see them:** You can find tent-making bats in Peru's Manu National Park, Colombia's El Vínculo Natural Regional Park, and elsewhere.

Strangler Figs

The rainforest's worst houseguests

RANGE: North and South America, Asia, Africa, and Australia
SPECIES: Many fig species are stranglers, including *Ficus obtusifolia, Ficus nymphaeifolia,* and *Ficus aurea.*

◆ Strangler figs, like many bad houseguests, seem harmless at first. Each plant starts as an innocent seed, aerially evicted by a bird or bat onto the leaf base or canopy of an unsuspecting tropical tree. With a little luck, the seed germinates on a branch of its tree host and sprouts into a flowering epiphyte, grabbing water from the air and nutrients from soil and debris that gather on the branch.

But this stage is temporary—the sprout has plans to move downstairs.

The host tree probably doesn't find this uninvited visitor unusual—after all, it's used to guests. Monkeys are always swinging by, and more permanent residents, like ants and moss, are present full-time.

But unlike these other mostly harmless hangers-on, the strangler takes advantage of the busy tree's hospitality. The young fig sends snakelike roots down the host's trunk and into the soil, where they wrap around the host's root system, constricting its ability to get the nutrients it needs. Meanwhile, the fig also encroaches up the tree, plaiting foliage around the host's branches until it encases the canopy and blocks its source of sunlight.

Trapped in the fig's grip, the host is smothered to death from trunk to treetop. Its corpse rots away, leaving the hollowed, lattice-like fig free to claim its next victim by uprooting and toppling over a neighboring host tree. Stranglers can live this freeloading lifestyle for hundreds of years.

Not all figs are pure moochers. Researchers have found that the fig's hard exterior may help protect its host tree from cyclones and hurricanes. More important, once the fig usurps its host, it takes on the role that tree once held, providing safety, shelter, and a consistent food source for local animals. While the original host may have been a seasonal bloomer, a strangler bears its sweet, gummy fruit multiple times per year, attracting bats, birds, ants, and wasps that pollinate other plants in turn.

In fact, when loggers cut down large swaths of trees, they usually leave strangler figs alone, put off by their strange shapes and knotty wood—making them the only home left for fauna until more plants regrow. So, while stranglers may not be at the top of anyone's invite list, they at least know how to pay it forward. ❯ **How to see them: You can find strangler figs in rainforests around the globe. Special ones include the Great Banyan Tree in Haora, India, whose tendrils cover more than three acres, and several ficus trees in Monteverde, Costa Rica, that are popular tourist attractions and can be climbed from the inside.**

A strangler claims its victim.

AMAZON RAINFOREST

- The Amazon Rainforest covers 2.1 million square miles (5.4 sq km) of Brazil, Bolivia, Colombia, Ecuador, French Guiana, Guyana, Peru, Suriname, and Venezuela.

- Some researchers estimate that 10 percent of the world's total species are found in the Amazon, including 2.5 million insects, which is roughly one type of bug for every person in Chicago.

- The Amazon region has particular difficulty recovering from deforestation because much of the ecosystem's nutrients are cycling through plants rather than being present in the soil.

KEEP AN EYE OUT FOR The cerulean wings of blue morpho butterflies, so iridescent they seem to glow.

KEEP AN EAR OUT FOR The calls of male red howler monkeys, who sound like gargling giants.

KEEP A NOSE OUT FOR The rich, manure-y scent of the hoatzin, aka the "stinkbird," who ferments food in a special neck pouch.

Canopy Access

The forest floor is often quiet. But don't let that fool you. Some estimates hold that half of all terrestrial species—millions upon millions of plants, birds, insects, reptiles, amphibians, and mammals—spend most of their time in forest canopies, hundreds of feet above the average human head.

People who live in forests are often great at climbing trees and possess a solid understanding of what goes on up there. (Members of Batek communities in Malaysia climb 150-foot [46 m] trees regularly, often at night.) But those who lack these skills are left far below the action. This literal shortsightedness has meant that even forest experts have had a truncated view of canopy ecosystems—a situation akin to "going to the doctor and having them just look at your big toe," says Margaret Lowman, a researcher who has spent her career addressing this knowledge gap.

Some early attempts to answer canopy-related questions involved bringing pieces of this layer down to earth. In the nineteenth century, scientists working in rainforests would hire people who lived there to scale trees and bring back specimens. Other researchers have felled trees, knocked down branches with slingshots, or "fogged" areas with insecticides and collected the dead specimens that rained down.

Around the second half of the twentieth century, some researchers, including Lowman, developed what are now called "single-rope techniques"—methods that involve shooting a rope across a high branch with a crossbow and then using it to hoist oneself up. This allows researchers to hang out in the lower layers of the canopy, taking notes or collecting specimens.

Others have reimagined infrastructure to allow for canopy access. Some of these are simple: In Malaysia, a 15-story aluminum ladder let researchers track the daily movements of treetop animals for over a decade, until it and its tree were taken down to make room for a highway in the 1970s. Others are more complex: A French research team has surveyed the canopies of Cameroon, Australia, and elsewhere in a rainbow-colored dirigible with an inflatable raft dangling from it. And in 11 countries, including Panama, enormous construction-style cranes swing researchers from tree cluster to tree cluster to gather data.

As technology improves, broader research becomes possible. Lidar, drones, and satellite imagery now allow researchers to remotely survey the treetops, censusing large species and tracking fires and deforestation levels. Super-high structures—including the Amazon Tall Tower Observatory ❶,

which outstrips the Eiffel Tower by 3 feet (1 m)—sample air quality and clock the weather above the canopy, where the trees exhale.

But this broad information is made more useful when combined with intimate observation and the will to protect. "People need to get up close and personal with the leaves or the bugs," Lowman says. For this reason, the gold standard tools of canopy access remain relatively simple: towers and walkways.

These fixtures, now present in many forests across the world, provide what amounts to a tree's-eye view. Researchers use them to revisit spots repeatedly so they can watch the canopy change and better understand its dynamics, while visitors climb up to glimpse some of the world's most rambunctious and exciting ecosystems. Increasingly, Indigenous groups manage these towers and the surrounding research facilities, facilitating access to an area of the forest whose importance they have long understood.

How to see it: *Two great options are Napo Wildlife Center canopy tower in Yasuni National Park, Ecuador, which is run by the Kichwa Aangu community, and Lamington National Park Tree Top Walk in Queensland, Australia ❷, which is one of the first canopy walks ever built.*

Decoy Spiders

These spiders decorate their webs with spooky, supersized self-portraits.

RANGE: A region along the Tambopata River in the Peruvian Amazon and Negros Island in the Philippines
SPECIES: Two species of orb-weaving spider (*Cyclosa* spp.), not yet named

◆ Can you find the spider in the photo below? No, not that one. The eight-legged giant that seems to own the web is in fact a fake, made specifically to fool big animals like you.

The real McCoy—a tiny arachnid known as a decoy spider—is perched inconspicuously on top of her creation, which she cobbled together out of forest garbage and is about five times her size. (She's near the leg at six o'clock.) Like a low-tech mech suit, her big trash decoy protects her from predators. To complete the illusion when animals walk by, she may even waggle her web and make her double dance.

Decoy spiders weave their webs very finely so they can trap leaf bits and other rainforest debris. They then collage these materials into a spider shape, along with discarded bits of prey, their own exoskeletons, and whatever else happens to float by and get caught.

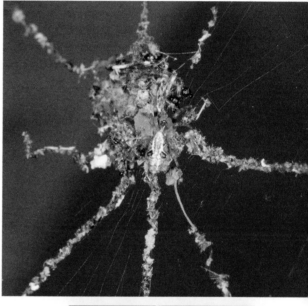

Different self-portraits have different styles. Some are more gothic, mostly made of dead things, while others might sport a floral accent or two. Phil Torres, one of the first entomologists to document the species, once found a particularly realist decoy spider: It had made one of its decoy's legs out of an actual spider leg that had drifted into its web somehow. That was "the most convincing one that I've seen," he says.

Experts think these spiders probably belong to a group called the trashline orb weavers. Other species in this group also clutter their webs with detritus in order to confuse predators. But they tend to be more abstract sculptors, making a line of rubbish and then hiding inside it, or strewing their web with small blobs and then curling into a similar shape. (One species, *Cyclosa ginnaga*, purposefully imitates bird poop by spinning white globs of web, sprinkling them with dry leaves, and plopping its brown-accented body in the middle.)

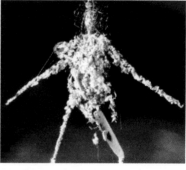

The decoy spider has the opposite strategy: Instead of scrunching up and hiding, she's "dressed up as a bigger spider," says Torres. Her actual predators—mostly damselflies and hummingbirds—see something that looks too big to tackle and move on. And if animals who eat bigger spiders, like large birds and bats, do go for the decoy, they come away with a mouthful of trash.

This tactic, which may have grown out of the simpler ones exhibited by the spider's relatives, appears to be successful: Spiders have been spotted doing it on opposite sides of the world, suggesting it has evolved repeatedly, though slightly differently. The spiders from Negros Island, in the Philippines, make decoys that have their legs splayed out like spiders in children's drawings, while those from the Peruvian Amazon make their decoys with the legs pointing down. Chalk it up to artistic license. ❯ **How to see them:** Look for a web with a big, wonky spider made of "trash" and then for the smaller sculptor who made it. They're easiest to spot at night, in the glare of a headlamp.

Decoy spiders in their uniquely tricky webs

Blending In . . .

Forests are great places to hide. While the decoy spider's ruse (page 7) is particularly elaborate, many species harness this biome's advantages: its nooks and crannies, its dappled light and shadows, and the surfeit of other creatures who live nearby and can be usefully mimicked. To pull off an effective masquerade, a creature must look like another element of the environment—something that whoever it's hiding from would normally ignore. Here are a few camouflage strategies to spot (or not).

CRYPSIS · Disguises don't have to be flashy. Animals that deploy crypsis—a classic approach—simply melt into the background. Their colors and patterns conveniently match the colors and patterns of the places where they tend to hang out, so that predators or prey mosey right on by.

In the forest, notable cryptic creatures include leaf-tailed geckos (genus *Uroplatus*), who plaster their bumpy bodies against tree limbs in Madagascar; Gaboon vipers (*Bitis gabonica*) of Africa, whose triangular heads and tan markings help them hide out in leaf piles; and elaborately textured ambush bugs (subfamily Phymatinae), which are so good at hiding in tropical rainforest flowers that they can take down prey many times their size. **❶**

COLOR CHANGE · As the forest shifts with the days and the seasons, some animals change their color along with it. They may do this slowly; for example, the coats of snowshoe hares (*Lepus americanus*) and stoats (*Mustela erminea*) turn from brown to snowy white over months to match the boreal forests where they live. Shortening days spur both species to molt their fur and grow it back in the new hue.

Chameleons are, famously, much faster. While many naturally resemble their environments, they can flood their skin cells with melanin—or pull it back again—in order to tint themselves darker or lighter, depending on the conditions of the forest. Although they're also capable of more dramatic color changes—the males of some species, including certain varieties of Madagascar's panther chameleon (*Furcifer pardalis*), can cover the rainbow—they save that for intimidating rivals and attracting mates, rather than blending in. **❷**

DISRUPTIVE PATTERNING AND EDGE DIFFUSION · Perfect matching isn't always the answer. By employing disruptive patterning, some animals trick the eye, blurring their own outlines and making themselves hard to spot. These patterns often have alternating light and dark patches, as with the coats of many wildcats, including clouded leopards (*Neofelis nebulosa*), who prefer to slip through the Himalayan forests unnoticed. This same principle underlies military camo used by humans (*Homo sapiens*). **❸**

Central and South America's glass frogs (family Centrolenidae) display a related form of camouflage called edge diffusion. Although their organs are visible through their bellies, it's their translucent backs that provide the illusion, interacting with light in such a way that the frogs visually dissolve into the leaves.

MASQUERADE · In addition to shapes, colors, and textures, a good masquerade often requires elaborate poses, all perfectly tuned by millennia of evolution.

Great potoos (*Nyctibius grandis*) of the tropical Americas are so good at mimicking branches that they can sleep all day right out in the open. Children's stick insects (*Tropidoderus childrenii*) look enough like eucalyptus leaves that their fellow stick insects sometimes try to eat them. The caterpillars of giant geometer moths (*Biston robustum*) take things one step further: Not only do they visually resemble the twigs of their host plants, they also mimic their scent. Their ant predators, who hunt by smell, walk right over them. **❹**

. . . and Standing Out

Versatile ecosystems that they are, forests are also great places to be seen. While not everyone is as dazzling as the golden poison frog (page 16), many species benefit from looks that pop against that green-and-brown background. Here are some standouts.

APOSEMATISM · Animals with good defenses—like toxins or weaponry—often advertise them visually, a strategy called aposematism. Such signals can manifest as candy colors, as with poison dart frogs (family Dendrobatidae), which brighten up the rainforests of Central and South America like jumping jellybeans.

Others are bold in a different way, like North America's striped skunks (*Mephitis mephitis*), whose high-contrast streaks warn of their audacious stink. And some split the difference between hiding and showing off—highly toxic rough-skinned newts (*Taricha granulosa*) of western North America, for example, have dull backs for camouflage and safety-orange bellies they reveal when disturbed. **❺**

AGGRESSIVE MIMICRY · To lure unsuspecting prey, some predators adopt aggressive mimicry—pretending to be something desirable, then turning on prey that comes calling. Alligator snapping turtles (*Macrochelys temminckii*) of the southeastern United States have tongues that look just like little pink worms, attracting fish that soon become dinner. Femme fatale lightning bugs (*Photuris* spp.) from North America imitate the blinking patterns used by females of other species and eat amorous males who respond.

Southeast Asia's magnificent orchid mantises (*Hymenopus coronatus*) look like soft, pink-petaled blooms and hunt by perching on real orchids. When insects visit to sip nectar, the mantises snap them up—and they're so convincing that human botanists also mistake them for flowers. **❻**

DEIMATIC DISPLAYS · When threatened, some animals will throw out deimatic displays—elaborate performances meant to surprise a predator long enough to mount an escape. (A skunk's puffery and a newt's belly flash both count as deimatic displays too.) Lowland streaked tenrecs (*Hemicentetes semispinosus*), tiny rodents from Madagascar, swell up and shake in scary situations, causing their bright yellow spines to rub together and produce a high-frequency warning sound.

Those who lack artillery can still pretend: Many unarmed flying insects, including the peacock butterfly (*Aglais io*) of Eurasia, greet danger by flapping open wings emblazoned with eyespots, as though they've radioed a huge bodyguard. One of the most theatrical bluffers is Africa's devil's flower mantis (*Idolomantis diabolica*). She whirls around and vogues at the slightest provocation, revealing brightly colored underarms. **❼**

FITNESS SIGNALS · Like loud songs or big antlers, splashy colors can telegraph fitness to mates. Researchers believe that males of many bird species must enjoy big, hard-to-gather meals full of healthy pigments in order to sport bright breeding plumage. This means their feathers—from the modest yellow uniform of the American goldfinch (*Spinus tristis*) to the bright pink costume of the lesser flamingo (*Phoeniconaias minor*)—are "honest signals": clues to potential mates about the quality of their genes and how good they'll be at providing.

But some birds might be faking it. Recent research has shown that for certain species, including the tanagers (*Ramphocelus* spp.) of the Amazon, the richness of a bird's hues may not directly relate to his fitness. Instead, brightness is amplified by feather microstructures, which seem to have evolved solely to impress females and signal nothing at all—yet more colorful trickery in the forest. **❾**

Pink River Dolphins

Rosy kings of the Amazon and Orinoco

RANGE: Amazon and Orinoco Rivers
SPECIES: Amazon river dolphin (*Inia geoffrensis*), also known as pink dolphin or boto

◆ About 16 million years ago, a warming climate melted the brims off the global ice caps and the oceans rose up, flooding the continents. It was at this point, researchers suspect, that dolphins swam into South America. For centuries they frolicked in this new sea—until the oceans retreated again, trapping some of them in inland waterways.

Fast-forward many generations, and these former strandees are right at home. Pink dolphins, also known as botos, are sitting pretty at the top of the food chain in two of the world's mightiest rivers, the Amazon and the Orinoco. They've evolved low dorsal

fins that don't snag on floating vegetation, teeth that can bite through turtle shells, and long, skinny beaks for digging snacks out of riverbank mud. They seem to delight in their rainforest surroundings—males are sometimes spotted holding lumps of clay, leafy branches, or clumps of grass in their mouths and parading them above the water, most likely to impress potential mates.

When the spring rains come and the rivers overrun their banks, the dolphins treat the newly flooded forest like an underwater jungle gym. Their broad, hypermobile pectoral fins help them maneuver, while their extra-flexible necks, which can swivel 90 degrees thanks to unfused vertebrae, let them slalom between trees. They're known as some of the world's most freewheeling dolphins, as likely to be seen swimming upside down as right side up, and fond of barrel rolls.

Male dolphins tend to be pinker than females, and pinkness is thought to increase with age—as well as with the scarring that comes from toothy male-on-male combat. As such, they can sport any number of shades: smudged eraser, dusky rose, naked mole rat.

The dolphins' facility with their inland habitat sometimes puts them at risk. Threatened, like all of the Amazon's creatures, by deforestation, climate change, and hydroelectric dams, they have gained the support of many local and international conservation organizations, which study and advocate for these playful, blushing swimmers. ❯ **How to see them:** Try a local boat tour in Colombia, Brazil, Ecuador, or Peru.

Pink river dolphins impress mates with their above-the-surface moves.

River Dolphin Dossier

Although the Amazon's flashy pink ones get a lot of attention, a few other lucky rivers boast their own resident dolphins:

GANGES RIVER, INDIA. Ganges river dolphins (*Platanista gangetica*) are almost completely blind and navigate the muddy Ganges through echolocation. They're also known as susus or shushuks for the sound they make when they surface to breathe.

INDUS RIVER, PAKISTAN. The Indus river dolphin (*Platanista minor*), or bhulan, is the national mammal of Pakistan. Slightly smaller than susus, bhulans sometimes get stuck in irrigation canals and have to be rescued.

MEKONG RIVER, CAMBODIA. Irrawaddy dolphins (*Orcaella brevirostris*) are known for their rounded, cheerful-looking faces. They like to spit spouts of water at the surface.

YANGTZE RIVER, CHINA. Champions of the stubby-headed Yangtze finless porpoise (*Neophocaena asiaeorientalis*) are turning oxbow lakes into protected reserves. They're trying to help this species avoid the fate of the Yangtze's other cetacean, the baiji (*Lipotes vexillifer*), which has likely been driven to extinction by pollution and unsustainable fishing.

AMAZON RIVER, COLOMBIA, BRAZIL, PERU, BOLIVIA. As usual, the Amazon overdoes it—the river hosts several species in addition to the pink dolphin, including the similarly ruddy Bolivian river dolphin (*Inia boliviensis*) and the stunt-loving tucuxi (*Sotalia fluviatilis*).

Flying Rivers

Above the Amazon, water is on the move.

RANGE: Most of South America
HOW TO SEE IT: Misty, diffuse, and high above the tree line, the flying rivers are difficult to see from the ground. But if you get caught in a drizzle southeast of the Amazon, you can probably thank them.

◆ The Amazon is the world's most prolific river. Every minute, it gushes about 3 billion gallons (1.1 billion L) of water into the Atlantic Ocean, enough to overfill 4,500 Olympic swimming pools.

But as this titanic volume of water makes its way through the forest, an even more impressive force flows overhead, forming an invisible yet world-changing surge—what researchers call a "flying river."

Like a supersized version of the clouds you breathe out in wintertime, the flying river is made up of the combined exhalations of the rainforest's billions of trees and plants. As they grow, transpire, and photosynthesize, these plants suck water from the ground and release it through their leaves as water vapor. Estimates suggest the forest as a whole expels close to 3.6 billion gallons of water per minute, meaning that the flying river edges out its gravity-bound cousin.

It also drives the surrounding climate. Wind carries much of the vapor south, where it bumps up against the high wall of the Andes. While some moisture manages to ford the mountains, dropping rain on Peru, most of it pushes south and east to douse southeastern Brazil.

As it falls back to earth, the water supports the Cerrado, a vast tropical savanna that is home to a rich variety of plant and animal life, from the noodle-nosed tapir to the rare blue-eyed ground dove, whose numbers hover around two dozen. It also helps farmers throughout the country's southeast grow a buffet of crops: soybeans, sugarcane, coffee, cassava, and wheat, plus wine grapes and a wide array of other fruits.

Vapor gathers above Peru's Manati River.

Northern Argentina, Paraguay, and Uruguay have the flying river to thank for much of their rainfall, too. Even northerly countries like Colombia, Guyana, and Venezuela benefit from winds that carry the water in the opposite direction.

But like many of the Amazon's driving forces, the flying river is beginning to flag. In recent years, forest-powered rainfall has decreased, sending southeastern Brazil into a series of parching droughts. While scientists are still figuring out why, the main suspects are climate change and deforestation—two threats that make it hard for trees to breathe easy.

Ghost Dogs of the Amazon

Little dogs so rare it's almost spooky

RANGE: Amazon Rainforest south of the Amazon River and east of the Andes Mountains
SPECIES: Short-eared dog (*Atelocynus microtis*)

◆ No matter how much you beg, a short-eared dog will not come when you call. Even in the dense Amazon Rainforest—a haven for rare and sneaky species—these pups are so shy and uncommon that they've earned the nickname "ghost dogs."

Until recently, the short-eared dog was almost a complete mystery to scientists. Much of what is now known is thanks to Renata Leite Pitman, a biologist and veterinarian who became obsessed with these unusual canines around 2000. Working in Peru, she started a project tracking short-eared dogs with radio collars. She discovered that the dogs are mostly loners and cleverly lazy: Rather than dig their own homes, they squat in armadillo burrows when they need shelter.

In 2009, Pitman heard that a logger had found an abandoned short-eared dog puppy and sold him at a market. The dog's buyer had second thoughts when his new puppy started eating the neighbors' chickens. With permission from the national environmental agency, Pitman adopted the puppy, whom she named Oso (Bear).

Her team started walking Oso on a leash through the rainforest, watching how he behaved. These forays attracted the attention of other short-eared dogs, allowing the scientists to observe the animals interacting for the very first time. As Oso grew, Pitman's team was surprised to hear the previously silent dog roar at people he didn't like and hoot like an owl at interested female dogs when he met them in the woods.

Oso's observers also learned that short-eared dogs are not picky: In addition to meat and fish, Oso enjoyed a variety of fruits, including Brazil nuts, forest açaí, breadnuts, and eggfruits. Pitman now believes that the short-eared dog plays an important role in spreading the seeds of many plants and trees. This discovery took on special significance in 2020, when a study confirmed that the short-eared dog is especially threatened by the Amazon's high levels of deforestation. Protecting these little dogs could be essential to maintaining the Amazon's biodiversity.

As for their accidental ambassador? Oso stayed with Pitman's team for just over a year, teaching them his doggy ways. In October 2010, Pitman removed his leash, and he trotted into the rainforest—off to do whatever mysterious things ghost dogs do. ❯ **How to see them:** Good luck! Short-eared dogs are so rare that even lifelong residents of the Amazon might never see one.

THE WILD LIFE OF A Ghost Dogsitter

■ Short-eared dogs may be mysterious, but if it weren't for biologist Renata Leite Pitman, we'd know even less about them.

• **Tell us about your first encounter with a short-eared dog.**
It was the first time I went to Peru, in 2000. I was totally sure

I was going to trap one of the short-eared dogs the first time I was there. It was a complete disappointment: There was nothing in [the traps] except a possum. That's all I got!

A friend of mine said, "Renata, chill out, stop worrying about trapping. Let's go for a walk." So we walked to a beach 10 miles [16 km] north of the Cocha Cashu Biological Station. And the first thing we saw when we arrived at the beach along this creek was a short-eared dog track.

I brought my tent there and I spent 10 days there all by myself. The first time I saw a short-eared dog was along that creek: two individuals, very dark in color. It was not a long observation, but it was like I was having a heart attack.

● **How did getting to work with Oso up close provide a perspective you couldn't have gained otherwise?**

Every morning we would walk the dog in a similar area, so that he could learn what is there and smell and we could record his reaction to everything. It was very successful. He was eating everything he was finding. I also started to hide things [to figure out what food he liked], though I was guessing. I didn't interview a short-eared dog to ask what he liked most.

We also found a female in heat, and the female started to follow him. I was able to record the mating vocalizations. That we had never heard before.

● **What's the most surprising thing you've learned about short-eared dogs?**

Their burrow behavior surprised me a lot. It explained why we do not see them much, and why we know so little about them. They spend about 50 percent of their life in burrows. They also use log holes as a refuge.

This makes you think about what this little refuge in the forest represents for them. When they don't have those places, they're much more exposed to predators. We documented two killed by jaguars and one by a puma, and one of the animals we were tracking was eaten by a 4-meter-long boa constrictor. They rely on these little burrows they find to hide themselves. That they've survived so long in a forest full of predators—I think that's amazing. ■

Ancient Arapaima

These mouth-breathing behemoths are the world's largest freshwater fish.

RANGE: **Amazon River basin, across Brazil, Peru, and Guyana**
SPECIES: **Arapaima (*Arapaima gigas*), also known as pirarucu (in Brazil) and paiche (in Peru)**

◆ The Amazon River is full of underwater toughs, from sharp-toothed piranhas to electric eels. But the arapaima makes them all look like guppies. Ten feet (3 m) long, heavier than a reindeer, and covered from snout to tail with dragon-worthy scales, the arapaima is the planet's largest freshwater fish. It's also one of the oldest—arapaima have patiently stalked the tributaries of the Amazon for an estimated 13 million years, meaning that even their strangest attributes have stood the test of time.

Arapaima will eat almost anything in the Amazon.

Arapaima are mostly slow-moving, sticking to the Amazon's calmer waters. As they mosey along between the banks, they treat the river like a buffet. They'll gulp down almost anything, from seeds, fruits, and insects to smaller fish, birds, rodents, small primates, and other creatures unlucky enough to pass overhead.

Despite their size, these fish are also excellent jumpers, capable of clearing the water's surface in pursuit of lunch. Once an arapaima has made a catch, he shreds his meal with his bony tongue, which is covered in teeth, then pulverizes it further by crushing it up against his palate—which, for good measure, is also covered in teeth. (Despite this, males carry newly hatched young in their mouths—quite carefully, obviously.)

To keep their neighbors from nibbling at them in turn, arapaima are well defended. Their scales are one of the toughest natural materials ever studied: In tests, they were strong enough to crack piranha fangs. Mineral layers cover softer collagen, making the scales hard yet flexible and extremely resistant to fracturing. Man-made body armor works the same way—if you ever find yourself wearing a bulletproof vest, you're basically imitating a giant prehistoric fish.

Arapaima show off their super-tough scales.

Thanks to a preference for lazier currents, arapaima often find themselves in low-oxygen water choked by decomposing plants. No problem: These fish evolved to breathe air and must surface every 15 minutes or so. This handy adaptation doubles as one of the arapaima's only weaknesses. Skilled Amazonian fishers can recognize the distinct sound of an arapaima breath—described as a cross between a grunt and a cough—and use it to hunt the fish down. They were once such popular eating that they were at risk of extinction, though recent changes putting fisheries back in the hands of local people are helping populations recover.

Strikingly adaptable, practically indestructible, and innovatively toothy, arapaima have survived basically unchanged for several epochs. As ice ages waxed and waned, the Amazon itself split and recombined, and other animal dynasties rose and fell, these rugged fish have kept on swimming, coming up for the occasional look around.

> **How to see them:** Look for arapaima in the Amazon's slow-moving waters. The best time to spot them is the dry season, when water levels fall and they shelter in lakes to lay their eggs— and feed on any poor fish trapped alongside them. They've also recently started showing up in Florida, probably released from exotic fish collections.

How to Breathe Air (If You're a Fish)

It's strange to think of a fish drowning. But there are actually a number of fish who would quickly perish without access to air. Although most of these obligate air breathers, as they're called, have gills, they have also recruited a number of more surprising organs into their quests for gaseous oxygen.

When arapaima surface to breathe, air enters their gas bladder, an organ most fish use for buoyancy. The arapaima's gas bladder is complexly subdivided and latticed with blood vessels, providing a large surface area for gas exchange, much like a lung. Toothy longnose gars (*Lepisosteus osseus*) breathe this way, too, as do bowfins (*Amia calva*), which can use this skill to survive on land after floodwaters recede.

Other species, including pencil catfish (family Trichomycteridae), use their stomachs to breathe. Mudminnows (*Dallia* spp.) use their esophagi, and armored catfishes (family Callichthyidae) use their intestines. Some, like the blood-red swamp eel (*Rakthamichthys rongsaw*), even use their skin. In each of these cases, the fish have evolved so that their capillaries are very close to that organ's surface, ready to pick up oxygen and bring it to the rest of their bodies.

Other fish have special organs for this purpose. The labyrinth fishes (suborder Anabantoidei), for example, have an organ—called, appropriately, a labyrinth—that is richly supplied with blood vessels and allows them to breathe air that they gulp by mouth. The labyrinth organ is located in a chamber above the gills for a double-decker breathing strategy.

Salty Clay Licks

The rainforest's most colorful snacking spots

RANGE: Western Amazonia
SPECIES: Scarlet macaw (*Ara macao*), red-and-green macaw (*Ara chloropterus*), blue-and-yellow macaw (*Ara ararauna*), and other birds, and even some mammals

◆ People in need of a sodium fix might head to the vending machine or bodega. Parrots in the western Amazon have their own salty snacking spot: Each morning, as night gives way to dawn, they gather on riverbanks to eat the finest dirt the rainforest has to offer.

In a single day, up to 1,700 birds from as many as 14 species can congregate on an Amazonian collpa, or clay lick. Clinging to the steep bank with their claws, they nibble bits of clay from the surface, pausing regularly to screech to each other like opinionated gourmands. Birds named for their colors—scarlet macaws, yellow-crowned Amazons, orange-cheeked parrots—get their beaks daubed with rusty brown, like sports cars left in a junkyard. Occasionally a recently fledged juvenile will beg for, and receive, a dollop of regurgitated clay straight from a parent's mouth.

One of the largest licks, Collpa Chuncho, is located near the northern edge of Peru's Tambopata National Reserve. Many generations of Indigenous Ese'Eja people have fished the coffee-colored waters of the Baawaja—their name for the river—in this area, so they have long known that parrots gathered each day at Chuncho and other nearby clay licks. But it likely wasn't until the mid-1990s that the wider world became aware of this colorful natural spectacle, which zoologist Charles Munn described as "a pulsing, 130-foot-high (40 m) palette of red, blue, yellow, and green."

Why supplement a diet of bright fruits and tender plants with crumbling beakfuls of clay? Researchers once assumed that the clay might neutralize toxins from rainforest plants, but according to tropical ecologist Donald Brightsmith and his team, the birds actually seek out the soil for its high sodium content. Sodium is critical for proper nerve and muscle function, but it's a scarce resource in western Amazonian rainforests, which are far from the Atlantic Ocean. Collpa soils have 40 times as much sodium as the foods in a typical parrot diet, and around 10 times more than other nearby Amazonian soils.

Activity on the collpa is especially high during the breeding season, when the parrots need extra minerals for their growing chicks. This is good news for nearby ecotourism lodges, which can virtually guarantee an amazing avian show for their visitors. And the birds themselves don't seem to mind—as long as the bird-watchers keep a respectful distance from the buffet. ❯ **How to see them:** A popular spot is Collpa Chuncho in Tambopata National Reserve. Get to the collpa early to see the birds arrive, and be patient.

Golden Poison Frogs

Yellow means stop.

RANGE: A small area of the Chocó rainforest in Colombia
SPECIES: Golden poison frog (*Phyllobates terribilis*)

◆ The golden poison frog is only about an inch long. In a rainforest full of roving snakes and hungry birds, you'd think he might be a little shy. Instead, this little frog is bold, hopping leisurely over the forest floor, often not even trying to hide. And he is bright: shiny as a polished jewel, and the kind of yellow people use on hard hats and caution tape.

That's because he knows what he's got: massive amounts of batrachotoxin—roughly Greek for "frog poison"—which he secretes from glands on his back and behind his ears. Were a bird to scarf down this frog, the chemical would leach into her bloodstream and decommission her nerves, paralyzing her instantly and killing her within minutes. It's simply not worth it. And so the frog is left alone.

Don't touch!!

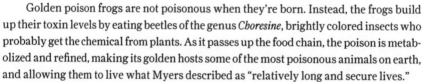

Batrachotoxin is a thousand times more poisonous than cyanide. (A truly bold spy would carry a frog in his mouth.) A microdrop the size of two grains of salt is enough to kill a person, and there is no antidote. While most scientific papers start with an introduction, herpetologist Charles W. Myers's paper on golden poison frogs, written in 1978, begins with a section called "Introduction and Warning." Myers learned about these frogs from the Emberá people of Colombia, who capture them in baskets, carefully swipe hunting darts over their backs, and then release them.

Golden poison frogs are not poisonous when they're born. Instead, the frogs build up their toxin levels by eating beetles of the genus *Choresine*, brightly colored insects who probably get the chemical from plants. As it passes up the food chain, the poison is metabolized and refined, making its golden hosts some of the most poisonous animals on earth, and allowing them to live what Myers described as "relatively long and secure lives."

But it can't protect them from all dangers. The frogs live only in a small area of the Chocó rainforest, which is being encroached upon by loggers and farmers; poison frogs of all species are also frequently poached for the pet trade. A protected area, the Ranita Terribilis ProAves Reserve, has been established specifically to support the poison frog population. Recently, researchers there began placing coconut halves around the reserve to provide safe, watery spaces for tadpoles—a helpful intervention, but not necessary for long. On an individual level, these frogs can take care of themselves. **❯ How to see them:** The Ranita Terribilis ProAves Reserve, in southwest Colombia, focuses specifically on harboring the golden poison frog and other brightly colored poison frogs.

A Burning Question

Poison frogs aren't the only animals to take advantage of batrachotoxin. Some colorful birds from New Guinea, including certain pitohuis and blue-capped ifrits, also contain this poison in their skin and feathers and likely use it to ward off predators and parasites.

In 2004, American researchers hoping to pinpoint the source of the chemical teamed up with naturalists from Herowana, a village in New Guinea. The naturalists pointed them toward beetles they called nanisani, a reference to the tingling, burning sensation that results from contact with them. (They called the blue-capped ifrit by the same name, in reference to the numbing feeling caused by contact with its feathers.)

When the researchers examined these beetles, they found many of the same batrachotoxins wielded by ifrits, pitohuis, and frogs. Because related beetles live in Colombia, they are likely the source of the golden poison frog's toxic concoction.

It's unlikely the bugs are synthesizing these chemicals themselves, however. Most animals who mix up abrasive brews get the ingredients from plants. So one last mystery remains: What in the world are the beetles eating?

NORTH AMERICA

Woodpecker Wars

Their kingdom for an acorn

◆ For acorn woodpeckers, teamwork makes the dream work. These birds spend most of their lives engaged in the relentless pursuit of acorns: finding them, eating them, and hoarding any leftovers in perfect-sized cavities that they peck into dead oaks, palms, and sometimes telephone poles and wooden siding.

Over generations, woodpecker groups can fill a tree trunk with thousands of holes, transforming it into a nut-riddled storage space known as a granary. Such a large-scale project requires cooperation rarely seen in the bird world: Acorn woodpeckers take shifts carving acorn holes and nesting holes, breed prolifically within their own groups, and even help raise each other's chicks. In the 1920s, one ornithologist described their behavior as "communism."

But there's a dark side to this loyalty. When high-up members of an acorn woodpecker group die, the neighboring groups wage brutal, days-long battles, fighting for the opportunity to take over the newly vacated spots.

It works like this: Acorn woodpeckers typically spend the first few years of their lives close to home, helping their parents raise their younger siblings. In order to have their own chance to breed, they need to shoulder their way into a neighboring group. This opportunity comes when one of those groups loses all of its breeding males or females—which can happen frequently in large forests, as old age and predators take their toll.

An acorn woodpecker adds to a granary.

When it does, news travels fast. If it's the males who have died, hopeful bands of brothers from other groups head to the newly open granary—often over a dozen different squads comprising scores of individual birds. If it's a female vacancy, bands of sisters come instead. Even woodpeckers who aren't directly involved flock from miles around to rubberneck, abandoning their chores to gain valuable intel on their neighbors.

Each squad of hopefuls stakes out a position on the granary. Then the rumbles begin. Birds scream, stretch out intimidatingly, strike with their wings, feet, and beaks, and rush each other in midair. Some break bones, get their eyes gouged out, or fall to the ground still locked together. These battles can last for hours or even days.

The granary's remaining inhabitants also attack the intruders—until one group gets the clear upper hand and drives off the rest. A new dynasty is in place, and peace is restored—until next time. ❯ **How to see them:** Head to an open oak forest and listen for a loud *waka-waka-waka*, or look for a granary tree stuffed with acorns.

RANGE: Much of Central America, along with parts of the US Southwest, California, and Oregon
SPECIES: Acorn woodpecker (*Melanerpes formicivorus*)

Gopher Tortoises

One of the Southeast's most adorable reptiles is also its premier hotelier.

RANGE: Coastal plains of the southeastern United States
SPECIES: Gopher tortoise (*Gopherus polyphemus*)

◆ The gopher tortoise is North America's only native land turtle east of the Mississippi River. It is also "scientifically the cutest turtle that exists," as Jeffrey Goessling, a biologist at Florida's Eckerd College, tells his students. The tortoises have a particularly stoic trundling style, and their ear bones are huge compared with their bodies, giving them rounded, cartoonish faces and allowing them to detect low-frequency sound vibrations and potential threats from more than 300 feet (90 m) away.

Gopher tortoises spend most of their lives underground, digging gently spiraling burrows that can reach 45 feet (14 m) in length and 20 feet (6 m) in depth—deeper than an Olympic diving pool. The tunnels protect these cold-blooded builders from extreme temperature fluctuations and are remarkably durable, making them the perfect home for an animal that can live for 70 to 100 years.

They're also the site for another role the tortoise plays: underground innkeeper. Hundreds of species in eastern North America's longleaf pine forests—including birds, other reptiles, insects, and mammals—rely on gopher tortoises for shelter, booking nooks and hideaways in the sprawling, generous structures they build.

Some animals, like the ink-hued Eastern indigo snake, use the burrows to hibernate and mate in climate-controlled comfort. High humidity levels are the probable draw for the endangered dusky gopher frog, a little amphibian with a call that sounds like snoring. Dozens of others, including coyotes, mice, skunks, and birds, like to drop by the burrow's entrance for a snack—most often when the tortoise is at home doing maintenance, because a buffet of bugs is constantly replenished as she digs.

Even the hotel's waste serves a function. One species of tineid moth feasts on tortoise poop, while the larvae of another feeds on the keratin of dead gopher tortoise shells when the tortoises pass on.

Despite their sweet faces and general magnanimity, gopher tortoises have been hunted with a vengeance; during the Great Depression, impoverished Southerners called them "Hoover chickens" and cooked them in stews. And the longleaf pine forests where they live have shrunk to about 3 percent of their historic acreage thanks to roads, development, and fire suppression. (Fire helps young pines get a leg up on faster-growing competition.)

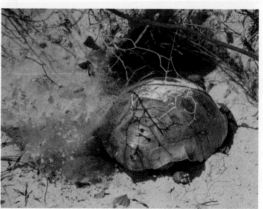

Hundreds of species find housing in the sprawling burrows dug by gopher tortoises.

But the forests and their shelled hoteliers have increasingly become the focus of conservation efforts. Goessling and others are decoding the tortoise's complex social networks, for example, and using that information to relocate isolated gopher tortoises and maximize their chances for survival. "The future," Goessling says, "is probably better than the past." ❭ **How to see them:** Florida's year-round warmth makes the state ideal for tortoise spotting. Try Egmont Key State Park, Disney Wilderness Preserve, Koreshan State Park, and Boyd Hill Nature Preserve.

Venus Flytraps

These iconic carnivorous plants grows wild in only one place.

RANGE: 75 square miles (195 sq km) in the coastal Carolinas
SPECIES: Venus flytrap (*Dionaea muscipula*)

◆ Venus flytraps loom large in the human imagination. Their yawning jaws and taste for flesh have frightened sci-fi readers, Super Mario players, and musical theatergoers for decades.

In reality, though, these plants have humble roots. When not flowering, they stand only about ankle-high. And they grow wild exclusively in "one tiny corner of the universe"—about 75 square miles (195 sq km) of boggy pine forest on the Carolina coast, says Debbie Crane, the communications director of the North Carolina chapter of the Nature Conservancy, which manages a few flytrap preserves.

Flytraps' bug-catching ability is their solution to a difficult problem: a lack of vital nutrients in the soil nearby. The "mouths," or lobes, of Venus flytraps are studded with tiny trigger hairs. If a hapless insect— usually a spider or cricket—hits two of those hairs in quick succession, the lobes will swing shut, trapping it inside. Fringes on the edges of the lobes form a kind of cage, allowing tiny captives to escape while keeping the bigger ones. (Despite their name, flytraps don't usually trap flies, which pollinate their flowers in the spring.)

Venus flytraps in Wilmington, North Carolina

As the bug wriggles around, the plant starts pumping in special digestive enzymes, liquifying its prey into a nutrient-rich soup. After about 10 days, the plant's trap reopens, an empty bug husk falls out, and the process starts again.

Humans have long been impressed by flytraps. According to information given to ethnographers by the Cherokee doctor and shaman A'yunini (Swimmer) in the late 1800s, Cherokee people would traditionally chew part of the plant and spit it onto their bait and hook, in the hope that it would help them "attract and hold the fish as the plant itself seizes and holds insects in its cup." (Cherokee people living farther west would ask their friends in the Carolinas to send flytraps their way for this purpose.) North Carolina governor Arthur Dobbs, the first British colonist known to write about the plant, called it "the great wonder of the vegetable kingdom."

A trap about to snap

Today, many people keep pet Venus flytraps, both to spook visitors and to cut down on in-home pests. Most of these plants are cloned in greenhouses. But black-market demand for wild specimens does exist and threatens the population, says Crane. In 2014, the normally acrimonious Democrats and Republicans of the North Carolina legislature came together to make poaching from the flytrap bogs a felony in the state. The vote to protect these unlikely Carolinians, she says, "was almost unanimous." ❯ **How to see them: Your best bet is at Green Swamp Preserve in Brunswick County, North Carolina.**

The Carnivorous Plant Cookbook

Venus flytraps may be the most familiar of the carnivorous plants, but they're far from alone. This survival strategy has evolved over and over again as plants in different nutrient-poor habitats find creative ways to supplement their diets.

More than 600 species of carnivorous plants are currently known. Some are impressive hunters who slake their hunger with blood and guts. Others are a bit more esoteric. Here are some of their favorite meals, and how they get ahold of them.

INSECTS • Abundant and snack-sized, insects are a staple for many carnivorous plants, which have developed a number of contraptions to catch them.

Sundews have tentacles covered with tiny hairs, each tipped with a globule of sticky mucus. When bugs wander over to investigate, they get stuck there, setting off all kinds of chain reactions. **Cape sundews** (*Drosera capensis*), which are found in South Africa, wrap around their prey, rolling it up like a bug burrito. Pimpernel sundews (*Drosera glanduligera*) of Australia catapult any bugs they catch into the center of their florets before digesting them, the same way you'd toss a peanut into your mouth.

Other plant snares are more passive but equally diabolical. Pitcher plants make insect traps that look like fluted cups. The outsides are decorated alluringly, while the insides prohibit escape. Take the **cobra lily** (*Darlingtonia californica*), a type of pitcher plant native to the northwestern United States. An approaching bug is attracted to the pitcher's entrance by a bright, fan-tailed appendage lined with sweet nectar. But once it crawls into the entrance chamber, things quickly become confusing. Translucent, window-like cells at the top of the plant trick the bug into thinking it can fly up and out. After exhausting itself trying, the bug tumbles down a chute in the hollow stalk of the plant and drowns in a pool of fluid at the bottom, where it is digested with the help of some symbiotic microbes.

WATER CRITTERS • Some carnivorous plants prefer to dine underwater. The world's many aquatic bladderwort species—including the **common bladderwort** (*Utricularia macrorhiza*), which is found in most US states—have air-filled traps that float near the surface of lakes and ponds. At rest, each trap looks like a partially deflated balloon. When something swims by and hits one of its trigger hairs, the trap snaps open, creating a pressure gradient that sucks in a gulp of water, along with the hapless prey. Then it gradually spits out the water and digests everything that's left.

Like Venus flytraps, **waterwheel plants** (*Aldrovanda vesiculosa*) have snap traps. But instead of sitting on top of a stalk, their traps are arranged in circles around a central hub, like freaky carousels. When shrimp, insect larvae, or tadpoles brush against their trigger hairs, they clamp down super fast, closing completely in a tenth of a second—10 times faster than terrestrial flytraps can.

HUGE THINGS AND TINY THINGS • Although most carnivorous plants are best equipped to deal with small prey, when a very large meal comes along, they won't say no. **Attenborough's pitcher plant** (*Nepenthes attenboroughii*), found in the Philippines, can hold up to half a gallon of liquid in its massive cup. In 2012, scientists witnessed one digesting an entire shrew that had slipped and fallen inside, probably while trying to get a drink. Mice, rats, lizards, and frogs also occasionally make this mistake. A gardener in Somerset, England,

Waterwheel plant

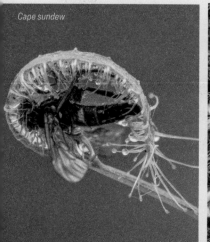
Cape sundew

Cobra lily

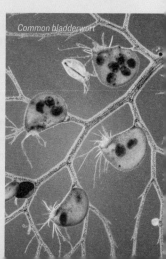
Common bladderwort

once found the remains of a great tit in a pitcher plant in his tropical nursery; presumably it died very confused.

Other species nosh on the opposite end of the size scale. **Terrestrial bladderworts** like *Utricularia blanchetii* keep their traps underground, where they slurp up pockets of water filled with microscopic worms.

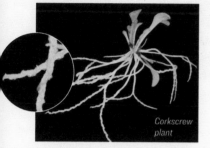

Corkscrew plant

Corkscrew plants, like *Genlisea violacea* of South America, look like unassuming herbs above the soil. But beneath it, they have hollow, spiral leaves that catch single-celled protozoa by enticing them inside with a chemical attractant. The prey quickly becomes trapped in the narrow passageways of the leaf, which are lined with sticky hairs.

POOP · It doesn't sound appetizing, but a pile of droppings or a shot of guano can be a powerful nutrition boost for a hungry plant. In Borneo, a few different members of one pitcher plant family form alliances with animals, exchanging food or shelter for regular poop infusions.

The pitchers of a young **Low's pitcher plant** (*Nepenthes lowii*) are made to capture insects. But as

the plant gets older, it modifies its design to instead attract mountain tree shrews. Each pitcher's lip is lined with sweet, sticky nectar, placed exactly so the shrews must squat over the pitcher's mouth to reach it. A predictable reaction ensues. But the plant benefits from being a toilet: The shrews provide more than half the nitrogen it needs to survive.

Another member of this family, *Nepenthes hemsleyana*, has a special relationship with the inch-long Hardwicke's woolly bats. The tiny bats roost inside the pitchers, defecating in return for a safe napping spot. The two species are so closely entwined that the bats recognize the flange that sticks out of the top of the pitcher through echolocation.

The pitcher plant *Nepenthes ampullaria*, also found in the Bornean forest, provides a home for the Matang narrow-mouthed frog, one of the world's smallest amphibians. The pea-sized frogs lay their eggs down the side of the pitcher, and when the tadpoles hatch, they swim in the water that pools at the bottom. The plant absorbs nutrients from the frog and tadpole excrement and from dead leaves that happen to fall into the pitcher.

In fact, eating waste and detritus works so well for *N. ampullaria* that the plant does not produce the super-acidic fluid that many other carnivorous pitchers use to digest live prey. Instead, it

Nepenthes hemsleyana

Low's pitcher plant

keeps its fluid mild to better harbor frogs and other creatures. You might say it's going vegetarian— just another curious adaptation from this perpetually surprising group of plants.

Low's pitcher plant and a mountain tree shrew

Nepenthes ampullaria

Synchronous fireflies illuminate the forest in Tennessee's Great Smoky Mountain National Park →

Synchronous Fireflies

The world's flashiest beetles

RANGE: North and Central America, Southeast Asia, and Japan

SPECIES: *Photinus carolinus* and *Photuris frontalis* in the United States and various species of the genus *Pteroptyx* in Southeast Asia

A single firefly is a delight; a scattering of them is charming. But a thousands-strong swarm flashing in unison, alternately illuminating the night and plunging it back into darkness, as if controlled by a mysterious light switch? As one enraptured viewer wrote in 1857, "Earth has nothing more poetic."

In parts of North America, Central America, Southeast Asia, and Japan, the males of certain firefly species gather during mating season to glow in synchronicity. It's a rare practice: Only a few of the world's 2,000-odd species engage in it, each with their special quirks of rhythm and style. Some flash in a steady beat while perched on leaves, as is the case for the famed *Pteroptyx malaccae*, frequently found in mangrove forests and along riverbanks of Thailand. Others, like North America's celebrated *Photinus carolinus*, perform their synchronized flashing while flying low above the forest floor.

Some early researchers were so bewildered by these displays that they dismissed them as illusions. Others who came across them were unsettled, describing an "uncanny" and "ghostly incandescence which came and went." Still others were more pragmatic. "The flashes were not perhaps as regular as an army officer would like to see in regimental drills," wrote Edward S. Morse in a 1918 letter to *Science* magazine, "but were so rhythmic that any one would take note of their action."

Like all fireflies, synced-up species are equipped with a special light organ, which is stocked with chemicals and supercharged by an enzyme called luciferase, after the Latin for "light-bearer." The cold, bright glow they produce is astoundingly efficient: While an incandescent light bulb loses about 90 percent of its energy to heat, and a fluorescent one loses about 30 percent, the chemical reaction in a firefly's abdomen is almost completely converted to light. A specialized flash-generating part of the firefly brain produces neural blasts that control the timing.

To align their glows, fireflies must exist in sufficient densities. Trap a single male *Photinus carolinus* in a dark tent, and he'll flash randomly rather than in a regular rhythm; only the presence of other males triggers the species' coordinated flash pattern. Tourists seek out spots known for these aggregations, settling down on picnic blankets and enjoying one of nature's finest light shows.

Of course, this spectacular, elusive display is not actually for us but for other fireflies. Researchers theorize that synchronicity helps females locate males and mate, which is an urgent task for adults who often live only a few weeks. Experiments with artificial light-emitting diodes show females won't respond if male flashes are out of sync, suggesting the behavior may have evolved to help females recognize the males of their species by reducing visual clutter—though it ended up as a choral love poem, appreciated across species lines. ❯ **How to see them:** You can see *Photinus carolinus* at Great Smoky Mountains National Park, which straddles the border of North Carolina and Tennessee in May and early June.

Firefly Folklore

Fireflies wink their way across every continent, and stories about them are told all over the world.

In Japan, two common species of fireflies—genji-botaru (*Nipponoluciola cruciata*) and heike-botaru (*Aquatica lateralis*)—are named after rival clans, the Genji and the Heike. Legend has it that the souls of samurai who died during a twelfth-century

clash between the two clans transformed into fireflies from each species.

The Ewe people of Ghana, Benin, and Togo tell of shape-shifting vampires called adze. These often take the form of fireflies, sneaking into bedrooms in order to drink the blood of unsuspecting victims. You can get an adze to leave you alone by approaching it, grasping it firmly, and

granting any requests it might make.

In one Apache story, fireflies are the only animals who can conjure flames, and they build a campfire to dance around every night. One evening, Coyote tricks his way into the gathering. He attaches cedar bark to his tail, sticks it into the campfire, and runs away, bringing fire to the rest of the world.

The Mayan myth of the Hero Twins tells the story of two brothers who defeat the rulers of the underworld. During one challenge, a messenger of Death brings them two cigars, instructing the twins to burn the cigars all night but return them in the morning intact. To solve the puzzle, the brothers put fireflies at the tips of the cigars.

Humongous Fungus

These little mushrooms are a very big deal.

LOCATION: Malheur National Forest, Oregon
SPECIES: Honey fungus (*Armillaria ostoyae*)

◆ After an autumn rain, the northern part of Oregon's Malheur National Forest is dotted with clumps of tawny mushrooms, which pop out of the ground around the trunks of some evergreen trees. Each individual mushroom isn't very big: 4 inches (10 cm) tall at most, with a cap size somewhere between a poker chip and a saucer.

But what they are part of is very big indeed. These mushrooms are the aboveground portion of a honey fungus colony known as the Humongous Fungus, which occupies just a little more than 3.5 square miles (9 sq km) of underground territory in the forest.

These mushrooms are just the tip of the iceberg.

Once considered the world's largest living organism, the fungus's crown was recently taken by a clonal seagrass meadow off the coast of Western Australia. But it still dwarfs many of its competitors from other kingdoms. Utah's famous colony of identical aspens, known as Pando, would cover just 5 percent of the same area as the honey fungus, and about 30,000 blue whales could lie nose to tail on top of it. If you dug it up and dropped it on Manhattan, it would smother everything below 14th Street.

The visible parts of the fungus—the brown mushrooms sticking out of the soil—are just its reproductive organs. They are produced when the weather is right, make spores, and then die back when they're no longer needed. The fungus's biggest and most permanent aspect is under the soil: a continuous network of thin, stringlike mycelia, which form a thick weave underground.

The mycelia are a menace to evergreen trees, attacking their root systems and creeping underneath their bark. There, they grow into thick white mats called mycelial felt, which have the texture of dried latex paint. This felt eats the trees alive, digesting the wood to feed the insatiable fungus, which grows 1–3 square feet larger each year. (Based on this pace, scientists think it's between 1,900 and 8,650 years old.)

One big happy organism

Some trees are better at fighting off the fungus than others. In the Blue Mountains of eastern Oregon, grand fir are the most vulnerable and western larch are the most resistant. One way to track the fungus's creeping march is by keeping tabs on the trees it kills.

Intertwined with the mycelia are black ropy structures called rhizomorphs, and they are likely the reason for the honey fungus's outsized success. Over time, these rootlike fingers can stretch for miles, endlessly questing for more wood. Most species of fungi don't have them and thus stay contained in relatively small, friendly patches. Experts think rhizomorphs may have evolved from mushroom stems that for some reason never emerged above ground.

Oregon's honey fungus has many huge cousins that give it a run for its money. Some of the largest colonies are in southwest Washington and Michigan, but the fungus grows in evergreen forests across the world. Next time you see a harmless-looking mushroom perched near a tree, be warned—something bigger might be lurking just below the surface. ❯ **How to see it:** Go to the northeast section of Oregon's Malheur National Forest after the first rains in the fall, then turn right on Forest Service Road 2635 and drive for about 7 miles (11 km). Check for mushrooms around the bases of evergreen trees, or look for swaths of dead trees to see how far the fungus extends across the forest.

Spirit Bears

Proof of the power of genes—and good stories

Genetically, Spirit bears are almost identical to common black bears. A single chromosomal quirk—the same type responsible for red hair in humans—changes the color of their fur from glossy black to a striking white or cream.

But this simple switch has had cascading effects. These rare, beguiling bears have helped protect millions of acres of rainforest, all because they look a little different.

Spirit bears are found only in the Great Bear Rainforest, a temperate forest distributed over the islands and rugged coast of northern British Columbia, where they fish, forage, hibernate, and play with their more traditionally hued brethren. (Because the fur-whitening mutation is recessive, a Spirit bear can have two regular black bear parents, two Spirit bear parents, or one of each.) Recent estimates put their total number around 200.

Biologists didn't start studying Spirit bears until relatively recently. But they've been observed and appreciated for hundreds, if not thousands, of years by the Kitasoo/Xai'xais and Gitga'at First Nations, who live in and around Great Bear Rainforest. They celebrate the Spirit bear, or moksgm'ol, in traditional song and dance and are the bear's most tireless advocates.

In 2016, after decades of conflict and negotiations with logging companies, 27 First Nations, including the Kitasoo/Xai'xais, enshrined the protection of 85 percent of the

RANGE: The temperate Great Bear Rainforest in coastal British Columbia, with the highest concentrations on Princess Royal Island

SPECIES: Spirit bear (*Ursus americanus kermodei*), also known as moksgm'ol or Kermode bear

Great Bear Rainforest into Canadian law. Advocacy for the bears and their habitat has been transformative for humans, too, bringing new visitors to a region historically dominated by the forestry and fishing industries.

Why white versions of black bears have endured in one small corner of Canada remains uncertain. But although stark physical variations within species are often genetic accidents, when they persist, it's usually for a reason.

Color morphs in monkeyflowers, for example, determine whether they'll attract hummingbirds or bumblebees. And cinnamon bears—another variety of black bear with a reddish-brown coat that is most common in the western United States—may avoid conflict with other animals by resembling grizzlies, whom no one wants to tangle with.

Some studies—including one in which researchers dressed in head-to-toe white and black costumes and waded into streams—have suggested that the Spirit bears' light coat helps them catch more fish when hunting for salmon in the daytime, allowing them to blend in with the sky in a way that's impossible for their dark-coated cousins.

The rest of the time, of course, they stand out. ❭ **How to see them: The Spirit Bear Lodge, in Klemtu, British Columbia, which is owned and operated by the Kitasoo/Xai'xais First Nation, is the best place to see the bears.**

A Spirit bear fishes for salmon.

THE WILD LIFE OF A Spirit Bear Advocate

■ As the stewardship director for the Kitasoo/Xai'xais First Nation, Douglas Neasloss helps plan and manage lands, waters, and resources. He's based in the remote Klemtu community, on British Columbia's Swindle Island, where he's spent years observing and advocating for Spirit bears.

• **How are the futures of the Kitasoo/Xai'xais First Nation and the Spirit bear connected?**
I would say they're really important in terms of economics for us.

They're really important in terms of culture for us. We have some really common beliefs that if we take care of the land, the land will take care of us. And if the bear does well, we do well.

• **You didn't see a Spirit bear—or even know they existed—until you started working as an ecotourism guide at age 17. Why hadn't you heard of them?**
It's always been kept quiet. The elders expressed that, during the time of the fur trade, they were

worried people would shoot the bears. And they were considered very sacred, very special. The elders didn't want people to know about them because they didn't want them hunted.

• **How do the Kitasoo and Xai'xais peoples relate to the Spirit bears?**
We just have a lot of respect for them. We've lived with these bears for thousands of years. We both share the same space, we share the estuary, we share the salmon, we share the berries.

Can you share one of the stories you tell about the bears?

In our culture, Wee'get the Raven is the creator of the world, and he also created the Ice Age. As the ice started to melt, he wanted something to remind himself of the Ice Age. So, as he was flying over, he saw a black bear and decided to turn every tenth black bear white to remember the Ice Age. And he sent them to this area of the coast, which would be their home.

What's it like to encounter a Spirit bear?

It's one of the most magical moments I think you can have. The bear just has this aura, this magical aura about it. When you see the other bears—the grizzly bears, the black bears—it feels like they're supposed to be there. They're built to blend in with their environment. And with a Spirit bear, you get a pure white bear walking out of a dark green forest. ■

World's Largest Beaver Dams

Nature's engineers outdo themselves.

LOCATIONS: Wood Buffalo National Park in Alberta, Canada, and Voyageurs National Park in International Falls, Minnesota
SPECIES: North American beaver (*Castor canadensis*)

◆ In 2007, a researcher named Jean Thie was touring Alberta from above via Google Earth, trying to keep tabs on melting permafrost in Canada's boreal forests, when something stopped him midscroll. There, through the middle of a wild expanse of wetland, ran a long, snaking wall, behind which pooled dark blotches of water. In the heart of the Canadian wilderness, miles from the nearest road, someone had built an enormous blockade, trapping so much rainfall and groundwater that the ragged, sprawling pond could be seen in satellite imagery.

The architects, of course, were beavers, nature's most prolific engineers. Thie had found the world's longest beaver dam.

The dam, located in Wood Buffalo National Park, is more than a half mile (about 775 m) from end to end—twice the span of the Hoover Dam. By examining old aerial images, Thie ascertained that beavers had been grinding away at their massive structure since the 1970s. "Several generations of beavers worked on it," Thie said when he announced his discovery, "and it's still growing."

Not only is the world's largest beaver dam visible from space, it's best appreciated that way, too. In 2014, an amateur explorer named Rob Mark became the first person to visit the behemoth. Mark spent nine days thrashing through forests and swamps, battling foot-sucking mud and helicopteresque mosquitos. When he finally arrived at

The world's longest beaver dam, viewed from the air

the dam, he seemed underwhelmed: "It was completely covered in dirt and foliage, and there wasn't much to take a photo of," he told reporters.

More impressive in person? The world's *tallest* known beaver dam. That particular colossus impounds an inlet off Kabetogama Lake, a beaver paradise in Minnesota's Voyageurs National Park.

The park is named for the French-Canadian fur trappers (*voyageurs* is French for "travelers") who once purged the upper Midwest of its beavers and turned their pelts into hats. In the twentieth century, beavers repopulated the park and returned the landscape to its former rodent-built glory. The dam, which is around 14 feet (4 m) tall and several hundred feet long, is accessible only via boat. It looms above the water like the battlement of a medieval castle. It's sturdy enough that you can walk across its rim, and high enough that you'd probably break a few bones if you fell.

Why do beavers erect such massive bulwarks? In a word: safety. Beavers are slow and ungainly on solid ground, prone to getting snapped up by cougars, bears, coyotes, and wolves. In the water, by contrast, they're powerful, balletic swimmers capable of holding their breath for as long as 15 minutes. By building dams and creating ponds, they expand their aquatic domain, improving their own access to tasty willow and aspen trees while minimizing their chances of becoming food themselves.

Although their favored building materials are wood, mud, and rock, they're not overly picky: In 2016, canoeists in Wisconsin discovered a prosthetic leg woven into a dam. They later returned the limb to its owner, who'd advertised a reward for it on Craigslist.

Beavers are beneficent landlords as well as skilled architects. A vast menagerie of critters—moose and mink, salmon and salamanders, woodpeckers and wood frogs—find food, shelter, and breeding habitat in the ponds and wetlands that beavers engineer.

We humans, too, are beaver beneficiaries. Their ponds filter our water, sequester our carbon, and store water during droughts. They even slow the spread of wildfires in the American West, helping us cope with climate change as the planet warms. The world's biggest beaver dams, then, aren't just curiosities; they're forces of profound environmental transformation. **› How to see them:** Ask a Voyageurs National Park guide to show you the tallest beaver dam. For the largest, an aerial tour of Alberta's Wood Buffalo National Park is your best bet.

Salmon Forests

Where the trees are made of fish

◆ Your kayak scrapes onto a rocky, barnacle-strewn beach on the Alaskan coast. Just beyond the high-water line is an emerald wall, broken only where a creek tumbles from the forest and into the sea. The streambed glitters with iridescent, hook-jawed fish: salmon, struggling upstream to lay their eggs.

This is the Tongass National Forest, a swath of temperate rainforest covering Alaska's panhandle. Each summer, the more than 12,000 miles (19,312 km) of streams pouring out of the Tongass seem to be made as much of salmon as water—great news for all of the other species who live here.

Tying up your kayak and following the water upstream, you find yourself in a verdant forest where moss hangs from every branch. Logs as big as SUVs rot into the earth, and a canopy of Sitka spruce, western red cedar, and other conifers block the sky, filtering out every color except green. You pause, hand on a canister of bear spray, as a brown bear wades into the stream, gobbles a few salmon, then pads back into the forest.

RANGE: Southeast Alaska, Canada's Pacific coast, and parts of the Pacific Northwest
SPECIES: Sitka spruce (*Picea sitchensis*), brown bear (*Ursus arctos*), black bear (*Ursus americanus*), Chinook salmon (*Oncorhynchus tshawytscha*), bald eagle (*Haliaeetus leucocephalus*), and many more

This ursine snack explains why trees in the Tongass are so enormous and the understory is so rich. Spawning salmon bring nitrogen, phosphorus, and other nutrients from the ocean to the forests. Bears, wolves, and other animals eat the salmon and then spread those fertilizing nutrients inland as they wander through the forest and defecate. One study estimated that a 820-foot (250 m) stretch of a southeast Alaskan river gets 176 pounds (80 kg) of nitrogen from one species, chum salmon, in just over a month. Another found that trees near salmon-bearing rivers grow three times faster than trees near rivers without salmon. Scientists can even use isotopes found in tree growth rings to determine the size of past salmon runs.

The Tongass is often called America's salmon forest, but before dams blocked salmon from their spawning grounds across the Pacific Northwest, trees as far as 900 miles (1,450 km) inland were grown from the marine nutrients carried by spawning salmon. Today, as dams like Washington's Elwha (built in the early 1900s and taken down in 2012) are demolished, salmon who have been walled off from their home rivers for more than a century are surging back, helping restore not only the rivers themselves, but the plants and animals that depend on them. ❯ **How to see it:** You can walk, snowshoe, or paddle through Alaska's Tongass National Forest all year round. If you want to see the engine of the ecosystem, try the Anan Creek wildlife observatory site near the town of Wrangell in the summer, where you can watch bears slapping fish out of the water for lunch.

The incredible growth of the Tongass (above) is powered by traveling salmon (below).

WABAKIMI PROVINCIAL PARK

- One-third of Earth's forests are boreal—high-latitude woodlands that form a ring around the top of the planet. Wabakimi Provincial Park in Ontario, Canada, is one of the world's largest boreal forest reserves, covering an area almost three times the size of Rhode Island.

- Fire—which rejuvenates boreal forests by clearing out old wood and needles, returning nutrients to the soil, spurring seed growth, and making room for new trees—is generally allowed to burn here unmanaged, hemmed in by the area's thousands of lakes.

- No roads lead into this park. It is best reached by train, boat, or floatplane.

KEEP AN EYE OUT FOR Pictographs of canoes and people, as well as moose, rabbits, and other forest creatures, drawn on riverside cliffs. The Anishinaabe people created these drawings centuries or even millennia ago with paint made from fish oil and iron oxide.

KEEP AN EAR OUT FOR Woodland caribou mothers and calves calling to each other—although the herds are generally so silent they're known as "gray ghosts."

KEEP A NOSE OUT FOR Sharply aromatic black spruces and jack pines, the conifer kings of this particular boreal forest.

THE ORIGINAL SOCIAL NETWORKS

The next time you find yourself walking through a forest, pause for a beat. You might not be able to hear it, but you're standing in the middle of one of nature's biggest, most intricate conversations. It's not in the rustling of leaves or the trilling of birdsong; it's happening under your feet.

Over the past 50 years, scientists' understanding of how trees work has undergone something of a revolution. Forestry scientists used to think of trees as individual combatants in an evolutionary tussle, perpetually scrapping for resources with their neighbors. But in the late 1970s, ecologist Suzanne Simard uprooted these beliefs when she discovered that the trees in a forest are all connected in a social community.

Simard found that, even as they competed for space and light, trees were sharing resources and information, caring for their offspring, and collaborating with their neighbors through an enormous underground network. Her discovery, and the research of others who have followed her, has placed forests in the ranks of nature's great cooperative societies: termites, elephants, whales, bees, and now trees.

How does one tree talk to another? Via a fungal mediator. The trees of a forest are connected underground by thousands of miles of white threads of fungus, or mycelia, which intertwine with tree roots at a cellular level. Together, the fungal mycelia and tree roots form symbiotic partnerships called mycorrhizae. Like an underground Pony Express, the mycorrhizae can transport water, sugars, carbon, nitrogen, other nutrients, and even messages (in the form of chemicals and hormones) from tree to tree. As their carrier's fee, the fungi get a share of the sugars the trees make through photosynthesis.

Studies of these mycorrhizal networks have found unexpected generosity, neighborliness, and even sacrifice. In some of Simard's early experiments, she discovered that during winter months, fir trees—still clothed in needles, which allow

them to photosynthesize and make sugars year-round—were sending their extra carbon to nearby leafless birch trees. In the summer months, when the fir trees were shaded by their leafier neighbors, the birch trees returned the favor. Simard and a graduate student also identified "mother trees," which have more connections within the mycorrhizal network than any other. These ancient matriarchs can actually recognize seedlings that are kin. Scientists still aren't sure how exactly they do this, but they've documented mother trees doting upon these young trees with extra gifts of carbon, water, and nutrients.

Forests look after their young. Resources, like carbon, sugars, and water, tend to flow from older trees to younger trees.

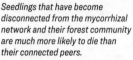

Seedlings that have become disconnected from the mycorrhizal network and their forest community are much more likely to die than their connected peers.

Mycorrhizal research has also revealed that a tree's last act is one of community service. When a tree dies, it dumps most of its reserve carbon into the mycorrhizal network, willing its worldly possessions to its family and neighbors.

In his Lord of the Rings trilogy, J. R. R. Tolkien imagined a race of talking trees called ents. As the ent Treebeard explains, it takes a very long time to say anything in Entish, "because we do not say anything in it, unless it is worth taking a long time to say, and to listen to." The trees with whom we share the Earth are in the middle of a sprawling, dynamic, slow chat—and we only just started tuning in.

When an ancient tree reaches the end of its life, it donates a substantial amount of its carbon to its neighbors. It also sends out signals that spur nearby trees to begin making defensive enzymes, protecting them against future stresses.

The mycorrhizal network also acts as an alarm bell. When a tree is attacked by pests, it sends warning chemicals through the mycorrhizal network and out into the air as pheromones. In response, the trees around it start producing bug repellent to keep the invaders away.

Mycorrhizal networks thread through the roots of many different plant species around the world. In trees, these delicate white threads form a sheath around the root tip and link up with its outermost cell layers.

THE WILD LIFE OF A Tree Eavesdropper

■ Ecologist Suzanne Simard started out working in forestry, studying competition between trees grown for lumber and those considered weeds. When she realized those trees were actually collaborating underground, she began to change how specialists from logging managers to botanists view forests.

• **What are "mother trees" and how do they shape a forest?**
These trees are the biggest trees in the forest. In making a map of the underground network, they are also the most highly connected. They have the biggest root systems, the most mycorrhizal connections, and these huge photosynthetic crowns.

They also are scaffolds for biodiversity: They have lichens, mosses, and critters living in them and on them. And those drive all the cycles in the forest: the nitrogen cycle, phosphorus cycle, water cycle.

These trees have also lived the longest and have seen the most change. As a result, climatic variations are coded in their seeds. Their seeds, compared to a younger tree's seeds, will have more genetic diversity encoded by the variations in climate. They can regenerate and produce seedlings that are more resilient into the future, as the climate is changing.

Those seedlings will be able to germinate and survive even if there is an unusual heat stress or frost. They're better poised to make it through the bumps and lumps of climate change than a seed that comes from a younger tree. But they need the right protective community, just like us—if we have our friends, our family, our community supporting us, we thrive.

• **How does what you have found through your research change your recommendations for managing trees?**
We really need to change how we're harvesting forests. The dominant way is to clear-cut them, and especially to go after the biggest, oldest trees that are the most lucrative on the market. But those are the most valuable ecologically. You can still harvest trees, but leave the big old ones there, with a neighborhood around them to protect them and let them communicate.

We also need to leave old-growth forests as intact as possible. We're still clear-cutting forests that have never been disturbed, and we need to stop doing that. They store so much carbon and are hot spots of biodiversity.

In urban environments, which is front of mind for a lot of people, one thing to keep in mind is that trees really are social creatures. They thrive in communities, but in urban environments we grow them isolated. Where we have parks with intact clusters, this is really good for the trees.

• **What do you think humans can take away from these discoveries?**
We've been on this socioeconomic model for a while that says "fight is might"—that we should dominate and earn and keep as much as we can for ourselves. But that doesn't make for very civil societies. We're social creatures ourselves, and we need to look after each other. If you look at how we treat natural resources, it's there, too—we are not very good at looking after things, and we need to change that.

And I hope that my work will help people feel closer to trees. If you feel disconnected from nature, just go sit by a tree. Get to know it. You'll start to understand more about how important they are in our lives. The serenity they provide, even the biochemistry of breathing in their smells, is good for our bodies. ■

Snowshoe Hare Cycles

This mysterious boom-and-bust phenomenon keeps the boreal forest hopping (or not).

RANGE: Boreal forests of North America
SPECIES: Snowshoe hare (*Lepus americanus*)

 The average snowshoe hare lives for only a single year. A favorite meal for many of the far north's top carnivores, from owls to coyotes to people, they also have to feed themselves in the boreal forest and tundra, where forage is poor and winter temperatures can dip to –40°F (–40°C) for weeks. Usually snowshoe hares make up for these factors by multiplying like, well, rabbits. When things are good, hare moms can produce up to four litters per season, ensuring that the forests are full of fast-living hoppers.

But every 10 years or so, things slow way down. Hare production drops by half, to about two litters per season, and predation ticks up. In these years, there are "forty- or fiftyfold" fewer hares overall than there are in better times, says University of Alberta biologist Stan Boutin, who has been studying snowshoe hare populations in southeastern Yukon's Kluane region since 1978. It's a certified hare bust.

While this cycle remains somewhat mysterious, experts are beginning to disentangle its causes. The first is what Boutin calls a "top-down" driver, closely tied to the hare's main predator, the Canadian lynx. Lynx dine almost exclusively on hare, eating an average of 1½ of them every day—about 548 hare per lynx per year.

As hare populations increase, there's more food for lynx, which leads to greater reproductive success. But more lynx need more hares, and eventually the two populations reach a tipping point: The lynx devour hares faster than they can reproduce, and the population nosedives, causing the lynx to starve or succumb to predation themselves. When the lynx population bottoms out and the pressure is off the hares, their numbers start to go back up again, beginning the cycle anew.

A second and more subtle factor is "bottom up," says Boutin. As the population of predators increases, it creates what Boutin calls "a landscape of fear" for the hares, who are essentially living in a slasher film, constantly watching their peers get killed and coming across the scents and signs of hungry lynx. This not only impacts the amount of time they spend feeding—which can affect their reproductive success—but may induce physiological changes in the traumatized hares. Once again, it takes hitting bottom, and bringing the lynx down with them, before they start bouncing back.

Climate change may also have an impact on these cycles—besides influencing the availability of food, changes in the amount of snowfall have enabled coyotes to get in on the hare-eating bonanza. Whether it's bitter winters, old foes, new foes, food shortages, or the everyday stress of being on everyone's menu, you've got to be one tough bunny to make it as a snowshoe hare. ❯ **How to see them:** Your best bet is to look for these little, well-camouflaged mammals at dawn or dusk, when they are most active. Try following hare runs—well-trafficked footprint trails they leave in the snow.

Snowshoe hares enjoy life while they can.

Wood Frogsicles

These unassuming frogs survive each winter by freezing solid.

◆ Each winter, wood frogs across North America freeze solid. These frozen frogs don't breathe, their hearts don't beat, and no blood flows through their veins. But they're not dead—they've just got a particularly dramatic way of waiting for spring.

Most animals try hard to avoid getting too cold. Water expands when it freezes; if it does that inside a cell, the cell will burst like a balloon. That's why seals pack on blubber,

Brrrr!

foxes grow thick fur coats, and bears, snakes, and amphibians spend long winters holed up in cozy caves or insulated dens.

But wood frogs are able to control where ice crystals form in their bodies and thus protect themselves from damage. Instead of fighting the cold, they give themselves over to it.

In late fall—as their amphibious peers dig burrows or bed deep down in pond muck—a wood frog prepares to hibernate by scooting under a thin blanket of leaf litter, like a camp counselor trying to prove a point. As temperatures drop, ice crystals begin forming on the frog's skin, setting off a cascade of reactions.

To begin, the frog's adrenal glands release adrenaline, which tells the liver to pump lots of glucose into the blood. The glucose is delivered to the frog's cells, where it lowers the freezing point of water, keeping the cells free of ice in the same way that salt keeps a driveway clear in winter. Urea, the main waste product in urine, serves a similar function, so the frog pumps this into his cells, too, instead of peeing it out.

At the same time, the frog's body draws special proteins into the spaces between the cells. These proteins actually encourage ice formation, leading the areas outside the cells to freeze solid as a protective barrier. The wood frog can survive with as much as 65 percent of the total water in its body turned to ice.

Why become a frogsicle? Perhaps to compensate for weak digging skills. Other land-based frogs, like the American toad, have powerful shovel-like claws that allow them to dig comfy beds below the frost line. Wood frogs' digging arms are puny in comparison, so they've made up for it with cold endurance. Wood frogs in Ohio can survive temperatures down to 21°F (–6°C), while those in Alaska can handle temperatures as low as 0°F (–17°C).

When winter ends, wood frogs can thaw out in about 20 minutes. Their hearts stutter to life again even before the last ice has melted inside their bodies. After an hour or two they can move their legs, and a day later they can move around without looking drunk. A few days later—once their brains have come online enough to remember mating behaviors—they set out for their spring breeding ponds, ready to rejoin the less hard-core species. ❯ **How to see them: During the warmer months, when they're not frozen, you might see wood frogs in shallow seasonal pools in the woods or hear their quack-like calls.**

RANGE: Northern North America, from Alaska to Labrador, and south through the Midwest and along the eastern coast to Tennessee
SPECIES: Wood frog (*Rana sylvatica*). Tiny, sonorous spring peepers (*Pseudacris crucifer*) also use this strategy—some people call them peepsicles.

AFRICA

Least American Cacti

No one is quite sure how these cacti crossed the Atlantic.

RANGE: The Americas—and, surprisingly, southern and central Africa and Sri Lanka
SPECIES: Mistletoe cactus (*Rhipsalis baccifera*)

◆ A cactus may be as big as a four-story saguaro or as small as a half-inch *Blossfeldia liliputana*; it may be round like a barrel or flat like a prickly pear. But all cacti have one thing in common: They grow naturally only in the Americas, from the edge of the Canadian Arctic Circle down to the southern tip of Patagonia.

That is, except for *Rhipsalis baccifera*, the mistletoe cactus. This plant—which has long, cascading fronds and looks a bit like a green or purple wig made of thick yarn—can be found in the wild in most of South and Central America and up through the middle part of Florida. But for as long as botanical records have been kept, it has also grown naturally in Africa and Sri Lanka, making it the only cactus species to make its home outside the Americas.

When species take hold far from where they started, we usually have some idea of how they got there—maybe they hitched a ride in ballast water or shifted range due to climate change. But the mistletoe cactus's journey has befuddled botanists for decades, inspiring impassioned papers, forum arguments, and joke headlines like "I HAVANA CLUE HOW I GOT HERE: CACTUS GOES FOR A DRINK IN CUBA, WAKES UP IN CAPE TOWN." For decades, scientists have been wondering exactly how it pulled this off.

The most popular theory is that migratory birds ate the cactus's glossy white berries in the Americas and then flew east over the Atlantic, digesting as they went. When they reached their destination and defecated, they inadvertently seeded a whole new population and set a record for long-distance cactus travel. But while flying animals do sometimes disperse plants in this way, it's unclear who the delivery bird might be in this case—there aren't any fruit-eating species that fly from South America to southern West Africa.

Another theory is that this cactus evolved before the breakup of the Gondwana supercontinent about 180 million years ago. In this scenario, as Gondwana separates into what we now know as Africa and South America, some mistletoe cacti are left on each side of the divide, slowly drifting apart until—millions of years of tectonic shifts later—they're in completely different time zones. But this is problematic, too: Most experts think cacti evolved only about 35 million years ago. And if cacti were actually around at the time of Gondwana, it's unclear why more of them didn't also get stuck on the non-American side.

Portrait of an unlikely world traveler

A third theory blames sixteenth-century merchants. Perhaps, some scientists think, sailors heading from Brazil to Africa occasionally took mistletoe cacti with them, figuring that the plant—which sips moisture from the air and doesn't require soil—could survive the journey. This theory is complicated by the fact that the plant isn't found near any African port cities, but several botanists still think it's the most likely scenario.

No matter how it got there, the mistletoe cactus is now quite at home in its unusual range—and doesn't seem too interested in explaining itself, suggesting that its story may remain a mystery. **〉 How to see them:** In the wild, you'll find these cacti hanging from the understories of trees, often in huge bunches. They're also common houseplants and are sold at many nurseries.

Chimpanzee Toolmakers

The chimps of the Goualougo Triangle are very handy.

LOCATION: Goualougo Triangle in Nouabalé-Ndoki National Park, Republic of the Congo
SPECIES: Central chimpanzee (*Pan troglodytes troglodytes*)

◆ For most of history, we humans thought our hammers, levers, and E-Z Reachers made us special. That changed in 1960, when Jane Goodall watched a chimpanzee in Gombe, Tanzania, stick a blade of grass into a termite mound and fish out some snacks. Since then, a number of animals have revealed an aptitude for tool use: Asian elephants use branches to swat flies, crows fashion twigs into grub-hunting hooks, and some dolphins carry sea sponges with them when foraging to protect their beaks from the rough ocean floor.

But chimps remain the handiest—particularly the ones in the Goualougo Triangle, a 100-square-mile (259 sq km) patch of lowland forest in the Republic of the Congo. The chimpanzees here, who have had very little contact with humans, boast a rich culture of tool use that continues to surprise researchers, says David Morgan, who co-directs the Goualougo Triangle Ape Project.

Goualougo chimps use the forest as their hardware store. To find beehives inside hollow trees, they alternate clubbing the trees with arm-sized branches and checking their progress with thin dipping sticks, an activity researchers call "honey pounding." They chew handfuls of leaves and then use the resulting mass as a sponge to soak up water. They turn leafy branches into raincoats and use individual leaves as cleaning wipes.

A Goualougo chimp pauses midtask.

They bring a whole belt's worth of tools to termite mounds: stiff twigs from one plant species for poking or widening holes, and specially selected stems from another plant for fishing out termites. Often they'll fray the stems into a paintbrush texture with their teeth, the better to catch bugs with. And they plan ahead, says Morgan: A hungry chimp will compile a kit and then head out to a mound.

Making and using these implements takes strength and finesse. Getting termites out of a ground nest involves jabbing a stiff stick into the soil, then pulling it out again and smelling the end to see if it has hit its target. Young chimps in the Goualougo tend to learn these tricks from their mothers, who will also give their modified sticks and stems to their offspring.

All chimp communities are different, says Morgan. There are many things chimps in other places do that Goualougo chimps don't, including sharpening sticks to hunt bush babies and hammering nuts open with rocks. But it's possible that remaining relatively undisturbed by humans for so long has allowed those in Goualougo to develop particularly complex relationships with tools. Chimpanzees elsewhere that experience habitat destruction, poaching, and disease are rapidly losing the toolmaking aspects of their cultures.

For now, at least, the Goualougo chimps don't have to worry about this—thanks partly to their creative gadgetry, their corner of the forest has been added to a nearby national park. ❯ **How to see them:** The journey to the Goualougo Triangle from the nearest scientific base requires a car ride, a boat trip, and then six hours on foot; the closest human settlement is 30 miles (48 km) away. Luckily, there are a lot of good videos on the Goualougo YouTube channel.

Uses of Sticks

As chimps know, a well-chosen stick can do all sorts of things. Here are a few ways that other animals use them:

BACK SCRATCHERS: Atlantic puffins (*Fratercula arctica*) have been spotted scratching themselves with sticks held in their beaks, possibly to remove ticks.

Q-TIPS: Mandrills (*Mandrillus sphinx*) use twigs to clean inside their ears and under their toenails, sometimes shredding them into splinters to better get at the grime.

SPEARS: Woodpecker finches (*Camarhynchus pallidus*) of the Galápagos Islands hunt by using sticks or cactus spines to pry recalcitrant grubs out of crevices in trees.

MUSICAL INSTRUMENTS: Palm cockatoos (*Probosciger aterrimus*) drum large sticks against the hollow trees where they build their nests, producing sonorous booms that can be heard for up to 100 yards (91 m).

BIRD TRAPS: American alligators (*Alligator mississippiensis*) and mugger crocodiles (*Crocodylus palustris*) sometimes balance branches on their snouts, potentially to lure nest-building birds—though experts are split on whether that's really their aim.

PLEASURE DEVICES: Sumatran orangutans (*Pongo abelii*) use sticks for autoerotic stimulation.

Forest Elephants

The jungle's pathbreaking maintenance crew

RANGE: West Africa and the Congo Basin
SPECIES: African forest elephant (*Loxodonta cyclotis*)

◆ Though they rank among the world's largest creatures, forest elephants are hard to find. Shier, rarer, and smaller than their spotlight-stealing cousins on the open savanna, they spend much of their time deep in the jungles of West Africa and the Congo Basin, far from most people.

But these sneaky giants make their presence known in other ways. As they tramp through the forest, searching for and harvesting the quarter ton of food they need per day, they serve as a kind of chaotic maintenance crew, clearing out some plants and encouraging others.

By eating from their favorite fruit trees and then excreting the seeds in a helpful pile of fertilizer, they spread those species throughout the forest, ensuring food and shelter for other animals. (Some plant species may even require forest elephants to survive, because their seeds are too big for other animals to digest.) Studies have shown that when forest elephants are forced out of an area, tree diversity decreases there, says Wildlife Conservation Society biologist Andrea Turkalo, who has studied them for decades.

A forest elephant reshaping her home

Other models suggest that these elephants help the forest sequester carbon—because they prefer small, tender trees and early-succession plants, they tend to wipe out younger vegetation, giving a leg up to older trees that store more carbon and keep the forest stable.

But perhaps their most enduring creations are the hundreds of paths they cut through the forest, connecting fresh water, fruit trees, and other important resources. Elephant social groups travel these paths together, calling to each other in low-frequency rumbles that are inaudible to the human ear. The sprawling trail networks have existed for hundreds of years and are "well defined from constant use," Turkalo says. They're helpful to antelopes and pigs, as well as to Indigenous people like the Bayaka, who use them to get around.

Bayaka knowledge of elephant trails is helping researchers learn more about these animals, whose populations number less than 100,000 worldwide and are declining. They're threatened by poaching, logging, and deforestation—which seems especially unfair for beings who have spent so long practicing sustainable forest development themselves. **❭ How to see them:** Try the Dzanga Bai in the Dzanga-Sangha Reserve in Central African Republic, a natural clearing in the rainforest where forest elephants and other hard-to-spot animals gather in the open.

Helpful Honeyguides

These birds form a sweet alliance with people.

RANGE: Much of sub-Saharan Africa
SPECIES: Greater honeyguide (*Indicator indicator*)

You're walking in the woods in Mozambique, humming to yourself. Suddenly, a small brown bird appears. You glimpse him in the trees ahead as he calls out: *chatter-chatter-chatter-chatter*!

Don't be alarmed. If you can, follow that bird wherever he goes. He's trying to get both of you a snack.

Across sub-Saharan Africa, and potentially over millions of years, people and greater honeyguide birds have forged a skill-sharing deal: The birds find beehives hidden in trees, and the people get the hives out. Then the humans go home loaded with honey, and the birds eat tasty grubs and wax.

It's a mutually beneficial arrangement—a total win-win. It's also almost completely unique, one of just a few known examples of communication-mediated collaboration between humans and wild animals.

While people from different cultures have different ways of interacting with the honeyguides, it generally works like this: A honey hunter enters the woods and performs a special call or whistle. If a honeyguide is near, he will call out in return, from a safe distance. The person and the honeyguide then move through the forest, sometimes for miles. They call back and forth until they reach whatever hive the bird has been eyeing, at which point he emits a softer trill and falls quiet. Then the honey hunter calms the bees with smoke, chops or digs out the hive, and fetches the honey—often, though not always, with some grubs and wax for his helpful guide. (It's thought that the honeyguide enjoys another useful mutualism with a wax-digesting bacteria.)

Honeyguides prefer to collaborate at a distance, and are not seen wing in hand with their human colleagues except in research situations.

While it's hard to tell how long this human-bird alliance has lasted, it may be "as old as our own species, or potentially even older," says Claire Spottiswoode, who studies honeyguide-human interactions in Mozambique. It could have formed any time after humans or our predecessors learned to subdue bees with smoke or plant volatiles.

Over the years, communication between the species has also become an important part of the pact. Spottiswoode and her collaborators tested the effectiveness of honey-hunter calls in Mozambique and found that by using their specific bird-summoning sound—which is traditionally passed down from father to son—they double their chances of finding honey.

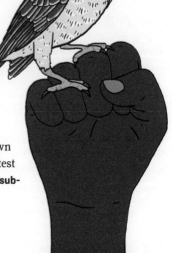

Calls and sounds vary across the continent, and honeyguides seem to learn their area's call—perhaps from older birds in their own communities, Spottiswoode says. In this way, one of the world's sweetest partnerships has stood the test of time. **❭ How to see them:** Go into the sub-Sahara African woods and make the right sound (see page 39 for tips).

THE WILD LIFE OF A Honey Hunter

■ Sylvester Gcina Dlamini is an engineering student and martial arts instructor in Manzini, Eswatini. He's also a honey hunter who follows honeyguides to find beehives—a skill he learned from his father and brothers. He is now teaching honey hunting to younger boys in his home village of Nzomane, as well as participating in international honeyguide research.

● **How does a honey hunting trip begin?**

First, we make a whistle, so we can attract the bird. We take a small fruit. We remove the inside and we make two holes. One is bigger, and the other one is very small. You use the bigger one to lay your mouth on, and the smaller one, you control with your hands or your fingers to make good music. Or instead of the fruit, we can also use the roller ball inside a deodorant stick.

● **What happens next?**

Then we sound the whistle. Sometimes, the honeyguide is not interested. But sometimes it comes. The first moment it crosses the air, it makes a louder sound. Then when you are following, the way it sings changes. We follow it, and it leads us to the beehives. If the beehives are in a tree, we make a

hole and close it after we finish, so that next time we need honey, we just go there.

We make sure we give the birds the wax, which has some larvae. We avoid giving birds the honey, because it's not good for them. If you feed that to the birds, by tomorrow, they have lost their voices.

● **What's the best time to honey-hunt?**

Early in the morning, around 5 or 6 a.m. I think most of the birds are hungry. Sometimes in the morning, the same honeyguide will lead you to four or five nests. We wait to give them food, because if it's got a full stomach, it will not show us. Then at the end we give it plenty.

But we like to do it in our free time. [In Nzomane], we are five active honey hunters. If we are there all together, we will spend our time collectively looking for honey. We enjoy that.

● **Why are so few honey hunters left in Eswatini?**

Things have changed. In my grandfather's time, they used to go into the forest looking for honey to make traditional beverages. Now we're just doing it for food. Some of the people with good knowledge, now they are grandfathers, and they don't do it anymore.

Other ones, maybe they are grown up, they're working far away. Especially my brothers, from whom I learned honey hunting—now they are not interested, because they are grown up and they are working. But sometimes on holidays we go.

There are also forest issues. Nowadays a lot of people are cutting forests. Or they set aside the land to conserve animals—then people aren't able to go into the forest, because there will be rangers. In the future, maybe there will be no more honey hunting, because of displacement.

● **What motivates you to keep doing it, and to teach other people?**

Last week I was home, and I did go into the forest. Even now, I'm grown up, I'm studying—but when I'm home, I just take my fruit whistle and I just go in the forest and hunt wild honey.

It is very good and very unique. Sometimes you can go a long way, and there's no honey—I'm very, very sad that day. But when it comes, it's something like a game. When I find myself following a honeyguide, I'm very happy. I like this bird. ■

Thanks to Jessica van der Wal for facilitating this conversation.

Honeyguide Etiquette

Across sub-Saharan Africa, people from different cultures have developed unique relationships with their local honeyguides, using a variety of calls and reward systems. Here are just a few examples.

• Yao honey hunters of northern Mozambique have a very specific honeyguide summoning call: a loud trill and then a grunt, something like "brrrrr-HMM!" Using this call to summon a honeyguide doubles their chance of finding honey.

• The Borana people of northern Kenya call to honeyguides using

whistles made out of snail shells or palm nuts or by blowing through their fists. Experienced honey hunters can tell how far away a hive is going to be just by watching how the honeyguide flies.

• In central Africa, the Baka people follow two honeyguide species: one that leads to honeybees, and one that guides to the nests of stingless bees, which also provide food. Eating either of these helpful birds is forbidden and is said to cause breathlessness.

• In a number of places, including parts of Botswana and Zimbabwe,

people are careful to reward honeyguides. It's said that birds who don't receive wax or grubs will later pretend to guide you but instead lead you to a dangerous animal, like a snake.

• The Hadza people of northern Tanzania rely on honey for their daily diet; research shows that they get 8 to 10 percent of their daily calories from honey found by honeyguides. They shout and whistle to summon the birds—and specifically do not reward them after the hunt, perhaps in order to keep them hungry for next time.

Hero Shrews

Little mammals with a lot of backbone

RANGE: Congo Basin
SPECIES: Hero shrew
(*Scutisorex somereni*)

◆ In the early 1900s, the mammologist Herbert Lang was surveying the rainforests of what is now the Democratic Republic of the Congo when his hosts, members of the Mangbetu people, introduced him to a renowned resident. As a crowd gathered, a community member brought out a small shrew. Then a full-grown man placed one foot on the shrew's back and lifted up the other, shifting all of his weight onto the animal and balancing there for several minutes.

"The poor creature seem[ed] certainly to be doomed," Lang wrote. Instead, as soon as the man stepped down, the shrew shook herself and scampered off—"none the worse for this mad experience and apparently in no need of the wild applause" she was receiving. This particular species was famous for miles around, he learned. People called it the hero shrew.

From the outside, this shrew looks like any other: pint-sized and fuzzy, with a long, pointed snout. Its secret is within, in its intricate backbone.

Hero shrew vertebrae are denser than most mammalian bones, and they're covered in a complex pattern of bumps and protrusions. In a neutral position, these articulate slightly—picture your fingers partly intertwined—reinforcing each other and providing strength and support.

But when the shrew engages special muscles between the vertebrae, they're pulled together even more tightly, locking into place like 3-D puzzle pieces. This turns the formerly bendy backbone into a rigid bar, making it much more robust than that of other species.

Although scientists are starting to understand what accounts for this super-strength, they still aren't sure what purpose it serves. One theory holds that hero shrews use themselves as wedges, lifting up rocks and prying open palm tree trunks with their bodies in order to get at fresh grubs other animals can't reach, but this behavior has never been observed by scientists. Others have suggested that having such good posture helps the shrews keep themselves clean while exploring the swampy rainforest.

The hero in the flesh . . .

. . . and bone

Recently, scientists started to study a close relative of the hero shrew, known as the Thor's hero shrew, with a slightly less jaw-dropping (but still impressive) backbone. Learning more about the intermediate steps between normal shrews and hero shrews might help us figure out how and why these tiny creatures stay strong under so much pressure. ❯ **How to see them: If you can't make it to the shrews' habitat, specimens can be found in many natural history museums, including Chicago's Field Museum.**

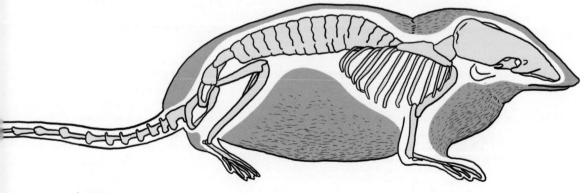

EUROPE

Scottish Wildcats

They look like sweet house cats, but don't pet them.

RANGE: Northern Scotland
SPECIES: Scottish wildcat
(*Felis silvestris silvestris* or
Felis silvestris grampia)

◆ A few traits set the Scottish wildcat apart from its more familiar relative, the house cat. It's slightly grumpier looking, with a narrow-eyed expression, and about 25 percent larger. Its tail is bushier than a domestic cat's, with a rounded, blunt tip, and unlike your average tabby, the stripes on its torso are unbroken bands. Perhaps most important: It will readily claw your face off.

The Scottish wildcat—also known as the Highland tiger—"is believed to be, weight for weight, the most aggressive cat species in the world," says Matt Binstead, head keeper at the British Wildlife Centre in Surrey. "They don't walk around their enclosure, they stalk. They don't look at you, they stare at you." Even young kittens, he says, will snarl and scratch at the slightest provocation.

Scottish wildcats are almost identical to European wildcats, which are found in various parts of the mainland, including France, Italy, Spain, and Turkey. They were separated from their continental cousins roughly 9,000 years ago, when the land bridge that connected Britain to the rest of Europe flooded.

For centuries after that, the wildcats had the run of mainland Britain, hunting rabbits and other small mammals and developing a don't-mess-with-me reputation. A number of historic Scottish clans carry the wildcat on their emblems. As far back as the thirteenth century, people knew, as the Macpherson clan motto goes, to "Touch not the cat bot a glove"—in other words, "Keep your paws off a wildcat with its claws unsheathed."

But by the end of the nineteenth century, forest clearing, fur hunting, and farmers had driven these wildcats out of England, Wales, and southern Scotland. (The farmers blamed the wildcats for eating livestock, although Binstead says they'd be unlikely to pounce on anything bigger than a small lamb.) The cats were placed under legal protection in 1988, but the damage had already been done: Estimates suggest that there are fewer than 400 wildcats roaming free in this part of the world, and they're mostly found in wooded areas of the Highlands.

Is he as soft as he looks? It's not for us to say.

The number might be even smaller. The biggest threat the species faces now comes from their domesticated doppelgängers, feral cats. Despite their differences, the two species do interbreed, producing hybrids. They're also vulnerable to the diseases that feral cats can carry, and landowners, who are legally permitted to shoot feral cats if they believe them to be predating on bird stocks, can accidentally take aim at a wildcat instead. Some groups say there are no more than a few dozen true wildcats alive.

Conservationists have considered bringing European wildcats in from other parts of the world to bolster these numbers, but they fear they might not appreciate the cold climate. Instead, efforts to resuscitate the species in the area now focus on curbing the feral cat population—and, more recently, breeding wild kittens. Wildlife centers, including Binstead's, are working with the Royal Zoological Society of Scotland to breed wild and captive Scottish wildcats and teach their offspring the skills they need to survive in the wild and keep their population going. The first youngsters were released in the Cairngorms Mountains in 2023. So if you spot a grumpy-looking kitten in a Scottish forest, you may want to keep your hands to yourself. ❯ **How to see them:** You can see wildcats (and kittens) at the British Wildlife Centre in Surrey, where conservationists are breeding them to bolster the wild population.

Hallormsstaður National Forest

Where Iceland's trees make their last stand.

LOCATION: East Iceland, near the town of Egilsstaðir
SPECIES: Downy birch (*Betula pubescens*), lodgepole pine (*Pinus contorta*), Norway spruce (*Picea abies*), and more

◆ There's a popular joke in Iceland: "What should you do when you get lost in an Icelandic forest?" The answer: "Stand up!" In a country known for grand waterfalls and simmering volcanoes, the trees—mostly short, gnarled birches that barely interrupt the landscape—can seem like a bit of an afterthought.

But it wasn't always this way. When Norse settlers arrived on the island in the year 874, at least a quarter of the land (and perhaps closer to half) bristled with tall birch trees, along with rowan, aspen, and willow.

Experts once thought that volcanic eruptions and a cooling climate caused their demise. Further research, though, has pointed at the people. The settlers chopped down forests for wood, to make space for their homes, and to clear grazing land. Constant trampling by livestock kept the trees from regenerating. By the early 1900s, forest cover in the country was down to less than 1 percent. At this point, according to the Icelandic Forest Service, "most Icelanders had never seen a tree."

This wouldn't do. In 1905, the government appointed a smattering of leftover birches in East Iceland as the country's first national forest—called Hallormsstaður after a nearby farm—and fenced in the trees to keep the sheep away.

Hallormsstaður National Forest has since expanded, both naturally and through an extensive reforestation campaign. (Tree-planting is a common summer job for Icelandic teenagers.) To bolster the native birches, the Forest Service has brought in different tree species from around the world, including lodgepole pines and Norway spruces.

Although a number of other National Forests have since been set aside, Hallormsstaður is still the country's biggest, at nearly 3 square miles (7.8 sq km). While this may seem paltry compared with the sprawling old-growth forests of the rest of Europe, it's enough to make a home for unique birds, berries, and mushrooms—and to get genuinely lost in. ❯ **How to see it:** You can visit the national forest year-round, on your own or with a guide.

Hallormsstaður was Iceland's first national forest, and it's still the biggest.

Arboreal Superlatives

Oldest (living)
White Mountains, California, USA

A bristlecone pine here, known as Methuselah, is estimated to be about 4,850 years old. One of its unnamed neighbors may be even older.

Oldest (ever)
Wheeler Peak, Nevada, USA

A bristlecone pine called Prometheus was about 4,900 years old when it was cut down here in 1964.

Oldest (challenger)
Cordillera Pelada, Los Ríos, Chile

A Patagonian cypress here may be over 5,000 years old, but this estimate has not been confirmed. Its nickname is Gran Abuelo.

Oldest (clonal)
Wollemi National Park, New South Wales, Australia

A colony of Wollemi pines here has been repeatedly cloning itself for at least 60 million years.

Oldest (individual clonal)
Fulufjället Mountain, Sweden

A Norway spruce, known as Old Tjikko, is the only tree currently growing from 9,500-year-old roots here.

Oldest (planted)
Anuradhapura, Sri Lanka

A king planted a sacred fig, called Jaya Sri Maha Bodhi here in 288 BCE.

Tallest (temperate)
Redwood National Park, California, USA

This park is home to a redwood called Hyperion that is about 380 feet (116 m) tall.

Tallest (tropical)
Sabah, Malaysia

A yellow meranti called Menara was found here, stretching more than 330 feet (110 m) tall.

Widest
Oaxaca, Mexico

A Montezuma cypress here, the Árbol del Tule, is 38 feet (11.6 m) in diameter.

Most voluminous (individual)
Sequoia National Park, California, USA

The park's General Sherman, a giant sequoia, is 52,508 cubic feet (1,486.8 cu m) in volume.

Most massive (clonal)
Fishlake National Forest, Utah, USA

A colony of genetically identical quaking aspens known as Pando has an estimated mass of 6,600 tons (6,000 t).

Most remote
Campbell Island/ Moto Hupuku, New Zealand

A Sitka spruce here, sometimes described as the "world's loneliest tree," is 170 miles (273 km) from its nearest tree neighbor.

Rarest
Three Kings Island, New Zealand

Before scientists intervened, a single specimen of *Pennantia baylisiana* was the only remaining wild member of its species; all the others were eaten by goats.

Biggest canopy
Anantapur, India

A giant banyan called Thimmamma Marrimanu spreads its branches out over almost 5 acres (20,234 sq m) here.

Squarest
Anton Valley, Panama

The cottonwood trees in this valley are the only ones in the world with square trunks.

Broadest crown
Kanchanaburi, Thailand

The crown of a local monkeypod tree, known as Chamchuri, stretches out nearly 200 feet (61 m) in diameter.

Deepest roots
Ohrigstad, South Africa

Here, a wild fig perched on top of a cave sent its roots down 400 feet (122 m) before it reached water.

Oiliest
Crete, Greece

The Olive Tree of Vouves, thought to be one of the world's oldest productive olive trees, has been bearing fruit for more than 3,000 years and has its own museum.

Sweetest
Pelham, Ontario, Canada

The Comfort Maple, now 500 years old, is believed to have been producing syrup longer than any other known tree.

Most upside-down
Bacoli, Italy

A defiant fig in this municipality has been growing the wrong way out of an ancient archway for many years.

Twistiest
Rybachiy, Russia

The trunks of the pine trees in the "Dancing Forest" do loop-de-loops, possibly due to caterpillar damage.

Most undead
Bellevue, Alberta, Canada

A limber pine here, known as the Burmis Tree, has been dead for 50 years, but local people have painstakingly kept it upright.

Homiest
Longnan, China

The world's largest ginkgo, called Li Jiawan Grand Ginkgo King, has a hollow that is said to have housed a local cattle farmer for several years in the 1970s.

Most fruitful
Syracuse, New York, USA

Tree 75, part of a project called "Tree of 40 Fruit," grows 40 types of stone fruit, including plums, cherries, and almonds, thanks to patient grafting by the artist Sam Van Aken.

Farthest traveled
Birmingham, Alabama, USA

Before one of this city's loblolly pines was planted, its seed flew around the moon on Apollo 14. Similar "moon trees" are found across the country.

Most out-of-place
Near Jebel Dukhan, Bahrain

A ghaf tree here, known as Shajarat-al-Hayat or the Tree of Life, is the only green thing for miles around. No one is quite sure how it gets its water.

Sphagnum Moss

Conqueror of space and time

RANGE: From Svalbard, Norway, all the way south to Chile and Tasmania
SPECIES: Sphagnum moss (*Sphagnum* spp.); there are 300 or so species.

◆ Sphagnum moss, also known as peat moss, is one of the world's most biologically simple plants. It has no roots, leaves, or flowers and grows no more than a few inches high.

But don't be fooled: This soft, quiet plant is deceptively powerful. It heals the sick, aids people in war and peacetime, preserves priceless artifacts of the past, and makes whisky taste better. At the moment, it's also helping to hold our fragile climate together.

Sphagnum covers 3 percent of the Earth's surface. (If all of it were gathered in one place, it would blanket an area nearly the size of Russia.) It grows from the tropics to the poles, smothering the swampy forests of Indonesia, undulating over Scotland's moors, and anchoring the Canadian tundra. This planet-conquering ability comes in part from its extremely effective reproductive strategy: An explosive dispersal system lets the moss shoot mushroom clouds of spores that can drift far distances, and asexual fragmentation helps it spread once it's established.

Thanks to this cosmopolitan distribution, sphagnum has played a role in human cultures all around the world. Alaskan settlers chinked their cabins with the plush moss, Scottish distillers use it to impart a smoky flavor to their whisky, and numerous Indigenous peoples have made mattresses, baby diapers, menstrual pads, and bandages from it.

During World War I, volunteers in the Pacific Northwest even held "moss drives," tearing up acres of sphagnum to send to the front lines to be packed into soldiers' wounds. Due to a delicate system of capillary tubes that suck up liquid like a sponge, one ounce of the moss can absorb a pound of blood—twice what a cotton bandage can hold. And

A close-up of sphagnum moss in the Canadian rockies [left] and an aerial shot of peat bogs in the Scottish Highlands [right]

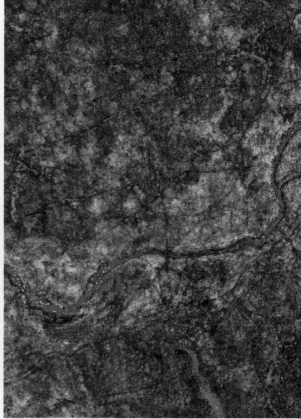

because the moss creates an acidic environment around itself by absorbing positively charged nutrients and expelling hydrogen ions, it's an ideal antiseptic dressing. In fact, injured animals are known to lie in sphagnum beds to heal.

If a person happens to die in a sphagnum bog (aka a peat bog or peatland), those same acidic, antiseptic qualities—combined with the oxygen-poor environment of the bog—keep bacteria from devouring the body, which is why some of the best naturally preserved mummies often turn up in peatlands. Scientists think that some of these people may have served as human sacrifices, intentionally interred in a place where they would be mummified for the gods. But how did ancient people know that peat would preserve human bodies? Because they also stored their meat and fish there, of course.

The future, too, depends on sphagnum. Because peatlands are made of not just living mosses but thousands of years' worth of decomposed ones, they hold an incredible amount of carbon and methane. The world's peatlands store twice as much carbon as its forests. So in a sense, the moss is preserving us as well. ❯ **How to see them:** You can find sphagnum in nearly any temperate rainforest, tundra, or boreal forest. To truly appreciate it, go for a hike in Scotland's Flow Country, home to one of the world's largest peat bogs and several Scotch whisky distilleries.

Strange Things Found in Peat Bogs

You never know what you might pull up out of a peat bog. Here are some of the most surprising things that spent centuries interred in moss.

THE LJUBLJANA WHEEL: At least 5,100 years ago, a big, blocky wheel made of ash and oak apparently rolled into the Ljubljana Marshes in what is now Slovenia. Whatever unfortunate farmer steered his pushcart over a rock that day was doubtlessly upset. More recently, though, archaeologists were overjoyed to excavate it, as the wheel is the oldest ever found.

THE PESSE CANOE: Found in a peat bog during the construction of a large highway in the Netherlands, the 9-foot (3 m) Pesse canoe was carved with an axe from a single Scotch pine log about 10,000 years ago, making it the oldest known boat. Its captain probably used it for fishing and transport.

HAIRSTYLES: Impeccably preserved, millennia-old "bog bodies" give us an unprecedented look at life in the Iron Age, including how people wore their hair. Many styles have been found, including long elaborate braids, coiled pigtails, and a twisted side bun secured with hair gel made of pine resin (on Denmark's "Osterby Man," who also had lice).

CÉIDE FIELDS: In County Mayo, Ireland, what was once an entire Stone Age farming community now lies blanketed under a giant bog. Volunteers are slowly uncovering the complex maze of stone walls, homes, and tombs by gently pushing metal rods into the peat and listening for the tap of rock.

LOTS OF BUTTER: Before refrigeration, people put butter in bogs to keep it safe and cool. Sometimes they forgot to take it out: Vats, barrels, kegs, and churns of bog butter have been found all over Ireland and Great Britain, some dating back thousands of years. And some of it still smells faintly cheesy.

Larval Couture

Young caddis flies are streambank bedazzlers.

RANGE: Worldwide
SPECIES: Thousands of species in the order Trichoptera

◆ Naked, all caddis fly larvae look about the same. Though they may belong to thousands of different species, all resemble worms crossed with silverfish: six legs sticking out near their armored heads, the rest of their bodies long and pale.

But watch what happens when they get dressed up. To camouflage themselves, caddis fly larvae construct and wear visually stunning cases: mosaics of pebbles, sand, twigs, and leaves, all glommed together with homemade silk. These cases protect the larvae from fish, birds, and other predators that would otherwise see them as quick snacks.

Each caddis fly species makes a unique kind of case. Some look like junk piles of rocks and sticks. Some are orderly, square-sided arrangements of neatly trimmed twigs, like tiny log cabins. Some are made of small pebbles, all the same size but irregularly shaped, like coarse sugar melted together on top of a pastry.

Occasionally, their disguises elicit a double take. Some caddis flies look exactly like they live inside a thinly rolled pirouette cookie. Some appear to reside inside a shower puff made of leaf shreds. Those in the genus *Helicopsyche* make cases so much like snail shells that when scientists first identified them, they misclassified them as snails.

Some caddis flies dress themselves like tiny log cabins.

The cases are both artful and functional. Caddis flies who live in fast-moving streams generally make cases out of rocks or sand, heavy enough to keep them from washing away. Those who live in still ponds or sluggish parts of rivers, where they're unbothered by currents, make cases out of lighter twigs and leaves. And caddis flies whose habitats are mucky often build wide, flat cases that act like snowshoes, keeping them from sinking into the sludge.

Others look a bit crustier.

A caddis fly larva might live in its bedazzled case for several months to two years. When it's ready to metamorphose, it does so right inside the case, capping the end with silk. The winged adult comes out skinny, brown, and nondescript—a less stylish way to blend in. ❯ **How to see them:** Look for their ornate constructions on the undersides of large rocks in freshwater streams, rivers, ponds, and lakes. Clean, oxygen-rich water often means more caddis flies.

THE WILD LIFE OF A Caddis Fly Collaborator

■ The French sculptor Hubert Duprat enlists caddis fly larvae as collaborators. In his workshop, he provides them with tiny gold flakes, pearls, and nuggets of precious stones. Duprat decides what materials they get and in what sequence, but it's up to the insects to choose the pieces they use to construct their cases—their own works of art.

• **Can you describe your process?**
I have aquariums, and the aquariums have equipment to cool down the water and to create a current, like in a river.

There's a section where the caddis flies are in cages in the water with the precious stones and gold. And I manipulate them—I take an animal, I put it in a tank with gold. Then, I put it in a tank with pearls, and after, I put it back in the tank with gold. The animal works with the materials around it.

• **Do you find that the larvae prefer certain materials, like human artists?**
Yes, of course—they prefer light materials. They like pearls. Gold is more difficult because gold is heavy. It's simply a question of

technique for them, and not an aesthetic question.

• **Where do you find your caddis flies?**
I collect them in the south of France, near Carcassonne. It's best to collect the species that habitually use pebbles for their construction, because there are other species that use twigs or leaves, and it's hard to make the caddis flies work with gold or stones when they're species that would rather build with vegetation.

- **What's it like collaborating with insects? Do they ever surprise you?**

No, not really. I'm not truly surprised. But at the same time, I do get the impression that each insect is a different individual, and that certain ones do things in a particular way, or a little differently than others.

- **What happens when the caddis fly larvae hatch?**

After a while, the case is finished, and the larva metamorphoses. Then the caddis fly leaves the case and becomes a [winged adult], leaving the tube at the bottom of the water.

So, in my experience, my work doesn't cause any problems for the caddis flies. They continue to mature. Then the [adults]— they leave, eh? They fly out the window. ■

Chernobyl Exclusion Zone

A giant accidental experiment

◆ On April 26, 1986, there was an explosion at the Chernobyl Nuclear Power Plant in Ukraine, in what was then the Soviet Union. After the accident—the worst nuclear incident in history—hundreds of thousands of people were evacuated from the surrounding area, leaving a Yosemite-sized radioactive expanse known as the Chernobyl Exclusion Zone. Houses, businesses, and even an amusement park stand empty in the zone. No one is allowed there without a permit.

But what should be a hollowed-out city is actually full of life. After the people moved out of Chernobyl, the animals moved in.

Now, visiting YouTubers interrupt owls roosting in abandoned doorways. Camera traps catch bison grazing, Eurasian lynxes sneaking around, and young moose playing in puddles. Photographers capture moments of collision: foxes posing on empty pavement, catfish swimming in the cooling ponds, and whole herds of Przewalski's horses running through the clearings and past the three-pronged "Hazard" signs.

No one expected this. Most assumed the radiation-suffused area would be unfit for animal life for hundreds of years. Instead, researchers counting mammals in the exclusion zone—as well as in the Polesie State Radioecological Reserve, just across the border in Belarus—have found that there are as many animals living there as there are in preserves elsewhere. More than 200 bird species have been sighted in the zone, along with mammals, amphibians, fish, and insects. All maintain healthy and stable population numbers.

Of course, radiation exposure isn't good for wildlife. Directly after the disaster, all the pine trees within 4 miles (6.4 km) of the plant browned, died, and had to be bulldozed under; invertebrates and small mammals perished as well. In the years since, scientists have found a significant number of asymmetrical insects, albino barn swallows, and cataracted voles in the zone, traits they have connected to the accident.

But ecologists are beginning to suspect that any such negative effects are offset—and perhaps even outweighed—by the sheer relief of not having humans around. Indeed, some species may even be adapting to the situation: Studies have shown that frogs inside the zone are darker than those outside of it, which may help them resist some of the effects of radiation. For some, at least, a tragic site is now a space of possibility. **❭ How to see them:** You can visit the zone only with a licensed guide. Walk to Folk Belarus gives tours of the Polesie State Radioecological Reserve, which covers affected parts of Belarus.

LOCATION: Chernobyl, Ukraine/Belarus
SPECIES: Eurasian lynx (*Lynx lynx*), golden eagle (*Aquila chrysaetos*), gray wolf (*Canis lupus*), wild boar (*Sus scrofa*), brown bear (*Ursus arctos*), European bison (*Bison bonasus*), Przewalski's horse (*Equus ferus przewalskii*), barn swallow (*Hirundo rustica*), eastern tree frog (*Hyla orientalis*), and more

Przewalski's horses roam the unlikely nature preserve.

ASIA

Corpse Flowers

Irresistibly stinky

RANGE: Western Sumatra
SPECIES: Titan arum
(*Amorphophallus titanum*),
also known as the corpse flower
or bunga bangkai

◆ Many plants grow modestly sized flowers every year and fill them with sweet perfume. Not the titan arum. This plant saves its energy for a decade or more before unveiling its showstopping inflorescence: a towering nighttime bloom that literally smells like death, in order to attract the carrion-loving insects—and now, the curious people—who serve as its pollinators.

The corpse flower, as it's also called, puts everything it has into its stench, which is often produced for one night only. Chemical analyses of the scent have revealed compounds responsible for more everyday wrinkled noses, including isovaleric acid (sweaty feet), trimethylamine (bad breath), and indole (feces). Emitted all at once, they make a heady mixture. Plant evolutionary biologist Kelsey Byers once spent a night alongside a blooming corpse flower in order to experience it at the height of its powers. It smelled, she says, "like a combination of really good Camembert and baby poop."

As the hours tick by, the flower's spadix—the proud yellow protrusion in its middle—heats up to about 98°F (36.7°C). This helps vaporize the scent molecules, allowing them to waft for up to half a mile. It also adds to the impression that the flower is a pile of rotting meat.

The dung beetles, carrion-eating beetles, and flesh flies of the Sumatran rainforest find this irresistible. They follow the scent like a cartoon mouse tracking a piece of cheese. When they get to the flower, they're drawn to its carcass-colored interior, hoping to lay eggs there so their babies can hatch to an incredible first meal.

Inside the flower, the bugs stomp around and get pollen on their legs. When they realize they've been fooled, they leave to find a real dead thing—and carry the pollen away, ideally to another titan arum. In this way, two titans mate, long-distance.

Certain people, too, can't resist the call of the corpse flower. When the first one flowered in captivity, at London's Kew Gardens in 1889, one newspaper described it as a "vegetable phenomenon." (The next time it bloomed, in 1926, police were apparently called to keep the crowds in line as they jostled for good sniffing position.)

More recently, gardeners have gotten the hang of growing corpse flowers indoors, and multiple greenhouse blooms now occur each year. Many name their flowers—"Putricia"; "Maladora"; "Musty"—and throw them grand, all-night parties when they finally open up. To fight a lack of genetic diversity in the species, botanists across the world are also working together to strategically swap pollen from flowers that could make good matches—so the plants' high-effort, stinky shows aren't just big whiffs.

❯ **How to see them:** Your odds of catching a wild titan arum at peak smelliness are very low. But botanical gardens worldwide treasure these plants and make a big stink about them when they're about to bloom.

Cricket Amplifiers

A little leaf engineering helps the smallest tree crickets make the biggest sounds.

◆ To our ears, a chirping cricket is a peaceful addition to an otherwise quiet night. But the cricket himself isn't going for laid-back. He wants to be seductive, debonair, and loud. That way females will hear, come over, and—to quote a human song going for a similar vibe—pour some sugar on him.

This is harder for some crickets than others, especially those that happen to be smaller than their peers. But the littlest members of some tree cricket species have hit on a solution: They use leaves to make amplifiers that help them sound much louder and bigger than they are, filling the woods with their songs and successfully impressing their potential mates.

Crickets sing by rubbing their front wings together, scraping the hard edge of one wing against the serrated ribs of the other as though they're playing the cello. But when their wings are too small, the sound waves they produce quickly overlap in the air and cancel each other out, a phenomenon called acoustic short-circuiting. Tree crickets, whose wings are about the size of your pinkie nail, are particularly prone to this problem.

When a small-statured tree cricket wants to turn up, he finds an appropriate leaf and chews a pear-shaped hole just a bit bigger than he is, right in the center. Then he sticks his head and front legs through the hole, holds the edges of his wings against the leaf, and starts sawing away. The leaf effectively makes his wings bigger, further separating the sound waves and letting them cascade across the forest—and into the ears of females—before they have the chance to short-circuit.

Through this feat of engineering, tree crickets can sing two or even three times as loudly as they would otherwise. Researchers have found that only the smallest and quietest crickets within a species tend to make leaf speakers—and that it works: Females hear an amplified cricket's way more often, and stay longer, than they would if he were playing an unplugged set. ❯ **How to see them:** Listen for a suspiciously loud cricket—and look for a telltale hole in a leaf.

RANGE: India and South Africa
SPECIES: *Oecanthus henryi*, *Oecanthus burmeisteri*, and several other tree crickets from the genus *Oecanthus*

This leaf goes to eleven.

Flying Snakes

Reptiles in the last place you'd expect: midair

◆ Say an arboreal snake is high up in a tree and wants to get to the tree next door. Lacking limbs, she has relatively few options. She'll have to slither all the way down one trunk and then up the second or seek out a place where branches overlap. What a hassle!

That is, unless she belongs to the genus *Chrysopelea*. Then she can take a shortcut. All five *Chrysopelea* species—known, as a group, as the flying snakes—can launch themselves off tree branches, wriggle through the air, and land on entirely different trees or on the ground, none the worse for wear and (presumably) having saved a good amount of time.

Flying snakes, which live in southeast Asia, are difficult to find and even harder to track. Researchers don't know much about why they fling themselves around in this

RANGE: Southeast Asia, southern China, India, and Sri Lanka
SPECIES: Flying snakes (*Chrysopelea* spp.), including the paradise tree snake (*C. paradisi*) and the ornate flying snake (*C. ornata*)

way, although it probably helps them escape hungry birds and primates.

But we do know a lot about *how* they do it. Jake Socha, a bio-mechanics professor at Virginia Tech, has spent the past few decades finding (or building) structures for the snakes to jump off—university roofs in Thailand, homemade towers in Chicago, four-story structures on campus in Virginia—and filming them with high-speed cameras in order to piece together a flight plan.

Pre-takeoff, a flying snake will slither to the end of a tree branch and hang off it "in the shape of a J," says Socha, the snake's tail gripping the bark and her head flexed upward. When the snake pushes off, she releases the branch and tightens her ribs, flattening her whole body into a long, skinny parachute.

Then, in midair, she'll start to undulate, moving from side to side, like your typical ground-traversing snake, as well as up and down, like a twanged guitar string. Research has shown that these motions grant the snake stability, so she doesn't go end over end like a flung spaghetti noodle.

When she reaches her final destination, the snake sticks the landing, either touching down softly on the ground or snagging herself expertly on another branch. Socha once saw a snake land vertically: "It smacked into the tree trunk and then just started crawling up the tree," he says.

In Socha's experiments, snakes have traveled up to 70 feet (21.3 m) in this way, taking off from a three-story perch. In the wild, they might go much farther—the trees in their native rainforests can reach skyscraper height. If you find yourself near one of them, look up: You might see a snake Superman, S-ing boldly across the sky.

> **How to see them:** Try a place like Sungei Buloh Wetland Reserve in Singapore, and look for jewel-toned bungee cords resting in sunny spots. You can also find some at the Singapore Zoo.

It's Not a Bird! It's Not a Plane!

It isn't just snakes—the rainforests of Southeast Asia are full of surprising gliders. Some experts think the unusually tall trees found here spurred the evolution of this transport mode across species. Others point to the lack of crisscrossing liana vines, which creatures in other jungles use to get around, or the relative scarcity of food, which means animals have to move far and fast to get their fill. Here are some of this region's most unusual gravity defiers.

Draco lizard

Draco lizards (*Draco* spp.) have broad, thin membranes called patagia that reach from their armpits to their thighs and are supported by extra-long, retractable ribs. Most of the time, they keep these tucked into their sides. But when a draco lizard is ready to launch, he leaps off a tree, pops open his membranes, and reaches back with his front legs to grab the top edges, like a kid with a towel pretending to be a bat. The lizard uses his arms and long tail to steer, allowing him to execute spirals, tight turns, and even barrel rolls.

While their cousins use their webbed feet to propel through the water, **Wallace's flying frogs** (*Rhacophorus nigropalmatus*) and other area tree frogs use theirs to skate through the air. Upon takeoff, they flare the membranes between their toes, which allow them to glide up to 50 feet (15.2 m) between branches. Oversized sticky toe pads help them land. Many spend all their time in the trees, coming down only to mate and lay eggs, which they position on branches that overhang puddles. When the tadpoles hatch, they fall into the water—an early taste of their soon-to-be airborne lifestyle.

Wallace's flying frog

When fully splayed, the **red giant flying squirrel** (*Petaurista petaurista*) can reach the size of a pillowcase. She spends her nights soaring around the highest parts of the canopy, often employing S-shaped flight paths that gain elevation after takeoff, and regularly traveling hundreds of feet in one glide. In this way, she can cross from crown to crown, surmounting forest gaps and sometimes highways.

Red giant flying squirrel

Parachute gecko

Parachute geckos (some members of the genus *Gekko*) blend in almost perfectly with the trees where they live, hiding from predators as they bask in the sun. When they do have to make a getaway, they often execute perfect backward dives from their vertical perches. They flip over in midair and spread out their lacy tails, their webbed toes, and the skin flaps along the sides of their bodies and faces. They then drift gently to the ground.

The superstar gliders of these forests are the **colugos** (family Cynocephalidae). Their patagia stretch from behind their ears all the way to the tips of their fingers, toes, and tails, completely enveloping their arms and legs. This huge amount of surface area transforms these cat-sized mammals into trick kites, allowing them to swoop up to 450 feet (137 m)—longer than a football field. When not in use, the wingsuit doubles as a comfy pouch for carrying young.

Colugo

Record-Breaking Tropical Trees

Yellow meranti are the reigning champs of the rainforest.

RANGE: Borneo, the Malay Peninsula, and Thailand
SPECIES: Yellow meranti (*Shorea faguetiana*)

◆ In the summer of 2016, researchers announced the discovery of the world's tallest tropical tree: a yellow meranti in Sabah, Malaysia. This stately, well-postured tree reached 293 feet (89.3 m) high, taller than the tallest buildings in eight American states. It was the best of the best, a titan among giants.

Or so people thought. By November of that year, a new winner had been found—another yellow meranti, also in Sabah. This one was nearly 309 feet (94.2 m), outstripping the Statue of Liberty. What's more, 49 other supersized trees were found at the same time—all higher than the previous record-holder, which turned out to be just a giant among titans.

These stretched-out yellow merantis live on conservation land in Sabah's lowland rainforests. There, they're safeguarded from two things that might otherwise topple them: windstorms, which merely skim the tops of the deep valleys where the tallest live, and loggers, who would otherwise fell them well before they reached such heights. Thick as well as lofty, they provide acres of prime real estate for animals and smaller plants. A thousand species can live on a single tree.

Researchers think these yellow merantis may be reaching the limits of what's possible for broad-leaved trees—at some point, the leaves are just too far away from the roots, and the trees can't pump them the nutrients they need. (Conifers, including the monstrous redwoods of the California coast, have different restrictions.)

On the other hand, those same researchers keep being surprised. In 2019, researchers passed the tallest-tree trophy to another yellow meranti named Menara (Malay for "tower"). At just more than 330 feet (100.6 m), it has the jump on Big Ben. It even sticks out of the canopy, its crown looming just above its peers—the undisputed king of the forest. At least for now.

> **How to see them:** If you want to gawk at—or even climb— a yellow meranti, consider signing up for a training with South East Asia Rainforest Research Partnership (SEARRP) in Malaysia's Danum Valley Conservation Area.

THE WILD LIFE OF A Tropical Tree Climber

■ As a field manager and wildlife photographer with the South East Asia Rainforest Research Partnership (SEARRP), Unding Jami spends a lot of time way up in the canopy. In 2019, he climbed the yellow meranti tree Menara with a tape measure, helping to solidify its standing as the world's tallest tropical tree.

• **How did you get interested in rainforest research and tree climbing?**

I was born in a logging camp in Sabah. I wanted to work to stop people from damaging the forest, and I started working with a rainforest replanting program when I was 13.

More and more, I'm understanding why all of this is very important, not just to us but for future generations.

• **What kind of tools are necessary for climbing very tall trees?**

I use a canopy access system. I have my primary line and a secondary line for backup, and a rescue system. I know one rope is good enough to hold my weight, but things can get dangerous when you're climbing with one rope—especially in the tropical rainforest, where you need to deal with many insects, animals, snakes, broken branches, and other things.

• **How long does it take to climb a tree like Menara?**

It took me nearly two hours to reach the top. Normally I climb 70-meter trees that take less than 20 minutes. With Menara, the tree was tall and very exposed, so I had to climb slowly and check every single point. Besides measuring the tree, scientists asked us to take leaf and branch samples from different heights.

The view from the top . . . I can only say it was amazing. But a bit scary to look down because you cannot see the ground. Even our team had to communicate using walkie-talkies. I know one of the tallest trees still standing is in California—that's one of my dreams, to climb that tree.

• **What's the scariest experience you've ever had in a tree?**

I was climbing a flowering dipterocarp tree. It was all fine at the beginning until a big colony of bees flew past the tree. Three of the bees attacked me. I managed to kill one and then the whole colony came to attack me!

My guys on the ground could not release me using the rescue system because I was stuck on my lanyard. Luckily I had my knife with me, and I cut the lanyard and went down. I passed out for more than 30 minutes [from the stings]. It was a good lesson for me—never kill the bees when they come to you, because the others will come to protect their friends.

• **What's the best part of climbing?**

Amazing Bornean gibbons just cross the trees when you're up there. Seeing them jump from tree to tree inspires me to climb more like them. I've always said, "Never stop climbing, and just climb like a gibbon." And, of course, the sounds of the rainforest make me feel so peaceful up there. ■

Rainbow Eucalyptus

Trees in Technicolor

RANGE: Native to Papua New Guinea, Indonesia, and the Philippines, but grown as ornamental or shade trees around the tropics and subtropics

SPECIES: Rainbow eucalyptus (*Eucalyptus deglupta*)

◆ In artistic tributes to the beauty of plants—poems about roses, paintings of fruit in bowls, photographs of fall foliage—tree bark receives little fanfare.

Flowers and fruits evolved to be beautiful in order to attract pollinators and seed-eating animals. Bark, though, puts practicality over aesthetics. Its job is to protect the tree's sensitive inner tissues from damage by pests, parasites, and the elements, and its color is generally drab.

Not so for the rainbow eucalyptus. Strips of bright green, orange, yellow, red, and blue tessellate around this tree's trunk in a pattern that recalls paint dripping down a canvas. In addition to its colors, the species is notable for its enormous height, growing to nearly 250 feet (76.2 m).

The rainbow eucalyptus's bark is paper-thin and peels naturally, like that of other eucalyptus species, as well as birch and melaleuca trees. The dizzying multicolored effect arises when the bark peels to reveal new, young layers, which are replete with chlorophyll. As these tissues age, other colorful compounds like tannins (found in grape skins) and anthocyanins (found in blueberries and blackberries) arise, adding more tints to the tree bark. It's possible that this wealth of colorful pigments helps protect the tree somehow, marrying form with function. But scientists aren't sure.

A rainbow eucalyptus stand, and a close-up of the tree's kaleidoscopic bark

The tall, striking rainbow eucalyptus is often planted as a shade or ornamental tree around the tropics and subtropics. Outside its natural range, however, the bark does not develop to be as strikingly colorful. It is native to rainforests of Papua New Guinea, Indonesia, and the Philippines, where it is used chiefly to make paper—bleached white offering a blank slate ready for new colors. ❯ **How to see them:** There are specimens in the United States, including in Miami's Fairchild Tropical Botanic Garden and on the campus of UCLA. But to see the species in its full chromatic splendor, head to its native range in the rainforests of Papua New Guinea, Indonesia, and the Philippines.

Japanese Rhinoceros Beetles

These battle-ready horned beetles are also beautiful singers.

RANGE: Most of Asia
SPECIES: Japanese rhinoceros beetle (*Allomyrina dichotoma*), also known as kabutomushi

◆ The male Japanese rhinoceros beetle is a fighter and a lover. Bulky, armor-plated, and crowned with long, forked horns, these beetles—which can grow to the size of a chicken egg—live in their adult forms for only a single summer. They spend a fair amount of this time with their horns locked, sparring with rivals over territory and the smaller, hornless females. In Japan, they are called kabutomushi—kabuto being a type of helmet worn by ancient Japanese warriors and samurai, and mushi meaning "insect."

But when combat is over, the pugnacious beetles suddenly show a softer side, singing epic, squeaky ballads to potential mates. And although their fighting prowess is the main draw for most of their human fans, research from scientists in Japan and at the University of Montana suggests it's these singing performances that actually impress the female beetles.

Japanese rhinoceros beetles mature underground as larvae for about a year. In early summer, they emerge from the ground, resplendent in tough plates colored obsidian or dark amber. They live in leaf litter on the forest floor and feed on sap that collects on trees.

As more beetles gather, the sappiest parts of tree trunks and branches quickly become battlegrounds. A male will lay claim to a particularly nutritious territory, hoping to mate with the many females that will fly there to feed. But first, other males line up to challenge him.

Rhinoceros beetle horns are some of insectdom's most impressive weapons. The larger horn, which protrudes from the front of the head, can be up to two-thirds the size of the beetle's body, and its pitchfork-shaped tip is strong enough to scoop up other males without snapping. This striking ornament has helped endear the beetles to generations of kids in Japan, who gather them from forests or buy them for a few dollars in department stores. (At one point, they were even sold in vending machines.) In some places, they're pitted against each other and bet on in street fights—facsimiles of what happens in nature.

The horns of male Japanese rhinoceros beetles can be two-thirds the length of their bodies.

Before charging in, males will size each other up. The larger a beetle is, the more likely he is to win. If a competitor thinks he can take on the current owner of the sappy spot, he horns in and the duel begins. The fighters lock together and shove before growing more aggressive. They joust, swing, and lunge. At the end, the winner may chase his challenger away—or he may lift him up and toss him off the tree, like a pro wrestler.

After this exhausting fight, the winning male faces another, more delicate challenge: seduction. When a female approaches his sap domain, he will skitter close to her and begin to purr a love song.

The warrior-turned-crooner might sing his screeching, grinding chirps for hours. Even then, the female may refuse his advances, fighting stamina and horn size be darned. Researchers think a male's song might show just how strong and healthy of a mating partner he is—or isn't. As it turns out, what's beneath that thick, pronged armor is what counts. ❯ **How to see them:** Look for Japanese rhinoceros beetles sipping sap from broad-leaved trees at night; they may still be fighting early in the morning. Visitors can also interact with them (and many other beetles) in the petting zoo at Kodomonokuni Mushi Mushi Land theme park, in Japan's Fukushima Prefecture.

Marimo Balls

As appealingly fuzzy as they are mysterious

RANGE: Found in cool lakes across the northern hemisphere

SPECIES: Marimo green algae (*Aegagropila linnaei*)

◆ The Ainu people of Hokkaido, Japan, have a special name for the balls of algae that cluster by the thousands beneath the surface of Lake Akan: *torasampe*, meaning "marsh monster." These monsters are adorable: The green, vegetal balls, some larger than a foot in diameter, rollick in the deep, sparkling with bubbles. As the sun rises, they sometimes drift up toward the lake's surface, like amiable trolls welcoming a friend; once it sets, they return peaceably to the lake's bottom. They're so cute they're celebrated on postage stamps. (In Icelandic, they're called the still more ignominious *kúluskítur*, meaning "ball muck.")

Marimo, as they're more commonly known, are velvety free-floating spheres of a common green algae growing in a deeply uncommon way. Also known as lake balls, they can be found in cool lakes in the northern hemisphere and as plant pets in many home aquariums.

For decades, the balls stumped scientists. Why were they so round? What accounted for their daily pilgrimage to the surface? More recent research has answers. The whimsical shape has nothing to do with fending off hungry fish or helping them roll back into the water when accidentally beached, as scientists once suggested. Instead, it appears to allow the species to maximize its biomass, packing more balls into a given lake.

The balls' gentle slide up and down in the water is also less mysterious than it once appeared. When exposed to sunlight, marimo photosynthesize, producing bubbles that draw them up into the shallows, as if winched up by the rising sun. As it sets, they return to the depths.

It's a simple life for what is, in the end, a simple plant. Slicing a marimo in half reveals only a dense mass of algal filaments. But seeing the balls huddle together in apparent colonies, it's hard not to feel a sense of affection for them—especially as a changing world is making it harder for them to flourish. More fish and boats, as well as changes in lake conditions, including an increase in nutrients dissolved in the water, have contributed to their decline: The balls have not been seen for at least 40 years in more than half of the places where they once bobbed, making a glimpse of these docile monsters even more special. ❯ **How to see them:** Marimo balls are especially prevalent in Lake Myvatn, Iceland, and Lake Akan, Japan, where they are protected and a festival is held in their honor each October.

Over the course of a day, marimo balls may gently rise to the surface before settling again at night.

Vegetal Festivals

Sprinkled among the world's many harvest-themed celebrations are festivals that highlight other aspects of plants—their beauty, their historical importance, or even their tendency to splat.

Marimo Matsuri
Kushiro City, Japan
Early October

This festival, run by the Ainu people, celebrates marimo balls and their home, Lake Akan. It begins with a ceremony in which the algae balls are taken from the lake by young people in canoes and ends with their return by tribal elders. In between, there's a torch parade, traditional dances, and lots of marimo-shaped sweets.

Tu BiShvat
Jewish communities worldwide
15th day of Shevat (late January or early February)

One of four traditional Jewish New Years, Tu BiShvat marks the "new year for trees"—the day that determines whether fruit borne by a tree is taxed in one year or the next. For contemporary Jewish communities, it has become an opportunity to plant trees and consider environmental issues.

Arbor Day Tree Dressing
Aston on Clun, South Shropshire, UK
Last Sunday in May

Not to be confused with the American holiday of the same name, British Arbor Day is an outgrowth of a number of older celebrations—including Oak Apple Day, which marked when King Charles II escaped angry Parliamentarians by hiding in an oak tree. The people of South Shropshire recognize the day by hanging flags all over a black poplar tree in the town center.

Infiorata di Genzano
Genzano di Roma, Italy
Sunday of Corpus Christi, mid-June

Since the eighteenth century, this town has celebrated the height of spring by carpeting its main street with intricate images made entirely of flower petals. Five tons of flowers, arranged by hundreds of artists, go into the artworks, which stretch for half an acre. At the end of the festival, children run through the delicate artwork, sending petals whirling.

La Tomatina
Buñol, Spain
Late August

Said to have been started accidentally in 1945 by youths who upset a market cart during a festival, La Tomatina is essentially a giant tomato fight. People come from around the world to spend an hour in the town square throwing squished tomatoes at each other, after which fire trucks come and hose everything (and everyone) down.

Exploding Ants

Some treetop ants protect their colonies by blowing themselves up.

RANGE: Southeast Asia and parts of India
SPECIES: *Colobopsis explodens*

◆ The more than 13,000 ant species around the globe have developed a diverse array of nest protection methods. Some spray toxic venoms; others erect rock blockades. Amid the lowland rainforests of Southeast Asia and India, however, there's a group of ants with a particularly gutsy defensive technique: They explode, showering their enemies with killer goop and sacrificing their own lives in the process.

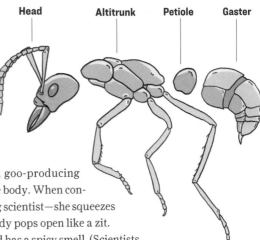

Head   Altitrunk   Petiole   Gaster

A quick ant anatomy lesson

Experts are aware of at least 15 species of exploding ants, all members of the genus *Colobopsis*. The best-studied species, *C. explodens*, forms thousands-strong colonies in and around tropical trees. The workers spend their time grazing on lichen- and moss-covered tree bark, guarding the colony's nest entrances, or patrolling and foraging way up in the canopy, often hundreds of feet off the ground.

Each worker is equipped with a pair of oversized, goo-producing glands, which extend from her head throughout her entire body. When confronted by a threat—another insect, or even an approaching scientist—she squeezes her abdomen until these glands rupture and her whole body pops open like a zit.

The ooze produced by *C. explodens* is booger yellow and has a spicy smell. (Scientists called the species "yellow goo" until 2018, when it received its much more respectable, and intimidating, scientific name.) While the gunk doesn't appear to be especially poisonous, it is extra-sticky and stops opponents in their tracks like an on-demand liquid fly trap. It's also antimicrobial, suggesting that the ants might have used it for keeping their nests clean before this deadlier function evolved.

In order to maximize impact, these mini bug bombs will strategically set themselves off after glomming onto an opponent's leg or head. For a few ambitious ants observed by researchers, this meant gluing themselves to grasshoppers an estimated 20 times their size.

This behavior—altruistically exploding to expel something harmful at an enemy—has an official name: autothysis, from the Greek for "self-sacrifice." A few other insects are known to exhibit it, including termites of the species *Neocapritermes taracua*, which live in the rainforests of French Guiana.

A member of Colobopsis explodens (at right) makes a sticky sacrifice.

These termites develop what experts have dubbed "explosive backpacks": sacs of crystals that grow increasingly toxic as the termites grow older. During battle, the oldest workers rupture these sacs, along with their salivary glands, mixing the contents of the two. This initiates a chemical reaction, producing a sticky, toxic cocktail that kills the enemy and the termite both: more bugs going out with a bang. ❯ **How to see them: You can catch a glimpse of the exploding ants at the Kuala Belalong Field Studies Centre in Temburong District, Brunei.**

Ant Arsenals

I t's not just explosives. In the millions of years ants have been around, different species have developed and honed a whole arsenal of offensive and defensive weaponry and skills. Here are some of the wild ways they've evolved to escape predators, catch prey, and fight enemies.

SNAP • When it's time for a smackdown, the long, skinny mandibles of the **Dracula ant** (*Mystrium camillae*) work like snapping fingers, with one mandible providing leverage and the other sliding quickly over it.

Mid-thwack, a Dracula ant's striking mandible reaches speeds of 200 miles per hour (322 kph)—a thousand times quicker than your fingers when you snap, and one of the fastest animal movements ever recorded. They deploy these super-snaps to stun shocked enemies and delicious centipedes across Australia and Southeast Asia.

GLIDE • **Gliding ants** (*Cephalotes* spp.) live high in the trees of South American rainforests. Their exquisite armor serves as a paragliding suit: If knocked off a branch by a clumsy monkey (or forced to jump by a hungry bird), they can swing themselves around in midair, point their back end toward their home tree, and sail toward it. They then snag the trunk with claws on their legs and head home.

CATAPULT • The mandibles of **trap-jaw ants** (*Odontomachus* spp.), most commonly found in South America, are also very special. These ants use their jaws—which are able to yawn open 180 degrees and snap shut at 145 miles per hour (233 kph)—to snare prey, carry building materials, and blast attackers away from the nest. When they're out foraging and encounter predators like ant lions, they point their open mandibles at the ground and then quickly snap them shut, catapulting themselves backward out of danger.

STING • **The bullet ant** (*Paraponera clavata*) of South American rainforests is usually not aggressive. When provoked, however, she unleashes an incredibly potent, neurotoxin-laced sting—along with a battle cry, which signals her fellows to come along and join the stingfest. Bullet ants also zap people who bother them, helping us understand how their other targets might feel. Entomologist Justin O. Schmidt put the bullet ant's sting at the top of his eponymous Schmidt sting pain index, saying it is "a tsunami of pain," lasts 12 hours, and causes the anointed part of your body to shake uncontrollably.

TUCK & ROLL • **Forest ants** (*Myrmecina graminicola*), no bigger than sesame seeds, have perfected a simple escape: When threatened by spiders or larger ants on flat ground, they freeze, wait, and hope for the best. But if they're on a slope, they tuck in their heads and legs, push off with their hind feet, and somersault downhill, into the leaf litter and out of danger.

POISON • **Red imported fire ants** (*Solenopsis invicta*) have spread from their native South America to the United States, Asia, Australia, and the Caribbean, where they form underground colonies of up to half a million workers. Some of their success comes from their necrotizing venom, which you may be familiar with—in many people, their stings cause red pustules that throb for days. This poison is so potent that fire ants often don't even bother to sting their enemies. They just dab them on the head with a droplet of venom, which quickly kills them.

ANTIDOTE • **Tawny crazy ants** (*Nylanderia fulva*), from South America, have developed an effective defense against their brutal neighbors: When attacked by red imported fire ants, tawny crazy ants produce their own slightly different chemical cocktail, formic acid, and smear it all over their bodies. This neutralizes the fire ants' venom, turning it from a burning poison into a harmless sticky substance that can be groomed off.

CAMOUFLAGE • To stay sneaky and safe while foraging, worker ants from the Central American species **Basiceros manni** are fuzzed all over with a double layer of hair. While the ants gather flies and other things to eat, their long outer "brush" hairs gather dirt and bits of leaf litter from the forest floor. Their stubbier "holding" hairs keep the soil in place, such that the ants blend in seamlessly with the dirt they're walking on—an illusion that's enhanced by their ability to freeze in place for minutes at a time.

CLIFF DIVE • *Malagidris sofina* ants of Madagascar dig nests into the faces of cliffs and build funnel-shaped entrances for approved parties. When an unapproved party—for instance, a predatory carpenter ant—tries to shoulder in, an *M. sofina* worker grabs the intruder, drags it to the entrance, and jumps off the cliff, ensuring the exclusivity of the nest like a gravity-assisted bouncer. Once the bouncer and the bounced land, the *M. sofina* ant climbs back up to the entrance and resumes her post.

TRAP • To take down enough prey to feed the whole colony, tiny **Allomerus decemarticulatus** ants reengineer one of their neighbors in the northern Amazon: the leafy *Hirtella physophora* plant. The ants strip sharp hairs off the stem of the plant and use them to build a secret structure along the stem, which they reinforce with threads of fungus and perforate with holes. They then hide inside.

When an unsuspecting wasp or grasshopper lands on the newly smooth plant stem, the ants reach through the holes and grab it with their mandibles, trapping it. More workers bite and sting the prey until it's dead, and then they all carry their prize back to the nest to feast.

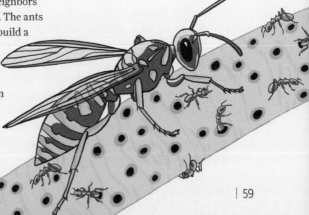

OCEANIA

Bum-breathing Turtles

These well-coiffed turtles need our help.

LOCATION: Mary River
in Queensland, Australia
SPECIES: Mary River turtle
(*Elusor macrurus*)

◆ Yes, Mary River turtles have protrusions on their chins that resemble cool piercings. And yes, some of them grow Manic Panic–style algae mohawks on their heads.

But their most alt trait is less obvious. Thanks to their cloacal bursae, Mary River turtles can engage in cutaneous respiration while submerged. In simpler terms: They can breathe through their butts underwater.

Every amphibian, bird, and reptile has an opening on its rear called a cloaca. This multipurpose orifice is used for urinating, passing waste, and mating. Mary River turtles, which grow to about 1.5 feet (46 cm) long, go one step further: Their cloacas connect to a water-storage sac system with gills. When the turtles are hanging out in the river, water gets pumped into those gills. Oxygen is extracted, and carbon dioxide is released through the cloaca.

Cloacal respiration is a power common to several of Australia's freshwater turtles, inspiring the nickname "bum breathers." In one experiment, a Mary River turtle hatchling hung out underwater for two and a half days straight—enough time to start on an algal hairstyle. Above water, they breathe the more conventional way, through their nostrils and into their lungs.

Despite this survival skill, Mary River turtles are one of the world's most endangered reptiles. They're found only in the Mary River, which squiggles through Queensland,

See you at Warped Tour.

Australia, for 181 miles (291 km), passing through forests as well as farmlands and cities. In the 1960s and '70s—before the species had even been officially described—their eggs and hatchlings were gathered and sold as "penny turtles," which nearly wiped out a generation.

They're still building back. Mary River turtles don't start breeding until they're about 20 years old, and their eggs are very appetizing to wild dogs and invasive red foxes. The eggs are also vulnerable to major floods, which are more and more common due to climate change, and turtles of all ages suffer from increasing water extraction. In 2018, after some poster-worthy photos of the species went viral, punk bands in Melbourne threw a concert to raise money for its conservation, inviting fans to "sink some beers, watch some rad bands, and come together for the punk turtle."

Less flashy, but more important, are local volunteers. They monitor the banks during nesting season, protecting eggs from hungry foxes and cattle hooves. But the other, broader threats are more difficult to counter. In recent years, surveyors have not found many young turtles, suggesting "a population crash in the decades to come," says Marilyn Connell, the Mary River turtle conservation project leader for the Tiaro & District Landcare Group—a terrible situation, and one familiar to many older punks.

❯ **How to see them:** Patient fans can use binoculars to watch these shy basking turtles, which will likely plop back into the water if you get nearer than about 100 feet (30.5 m). The Tiaro & District Landcare Group runs volunteer-based turtle patrols during nesting season, October through February.

ERRINUNDRA PLATEAU

• This cool temperate rainforest's latitude, high elevation, and high rainfall combine to support strange-bedfellow plants, with a tall layer of old-growth eucalypts sheltering a denser understory of sassafras.

• Bushfires and logging threaten nearby old-growth forests, inspiring frequent sit-ins by community members. Many of the residents of one nearby town, Goongerah, came to the region specifically to block the development of a proposed high-speed train line.

• Although it's mainland Australia's largest cool temperate rainforest, it's still quite small at 66,000 acres (27,000 ha). If it were logged at the rate of the Amazon, it would be gone in a week.

KEEP AN EYE OUT FOR Huge tree ferns, which can be found draping over almost everything and sometimes grow as large as a person.

KEEP AN EAR OUT FOR Bell miner birds, which herald each morning with echoing hammer-ping calls.

KEEP A NOSE OUT FOR The bracing scent of massive eucalypts—like the Errinundra shining gum, which is unique to these forests.

Platypuses

Neither fish nor fowl

RANGE: East coast of Australia, Tasmania, and the western half of Kangaroo Island
SPECIES: Platypus (*Ornithorhynchus anatinus*)

◆ In 1799, George Shaw, a curator in the natural history department of the British Museum, received a strange skin in the mail. It looked, he wrote, like nothing so much as "the beak of a Duck engrafted on the head of a quadruped." So unusual was this creature that Shaw suspected "some deceptive preparation by artificial means." Legend has it that you can still see scissor marks on the specimen's beak, where he checked for stitches.

It wasn't a prank—it was a platypus. But it's easy to understand Shaw's befuddlement. Even to twenty-first-century beholders, the platypus's grab bag of attributes can seem a little fudged. These animals lay eggs but nurse their young, are fur-covered but live underwater, and have fleshy bills, webbed feet, sharp claws, and venom-filled ankle spikes.

It would have been a pretty good prank.

We are beginning to see how these traits serve platypuses well in the streams and rivers where they live. They paddle with their webbed front feet, steer with their back ones, and dig ovular burrows with their claws. Females lay round, leathery eggs and lactate without nipples; when the young hatch, they lap milk directly off their mother's body. Males likely use their poison spurs to spar for dominance during mating season.

Platypuses hunt crustaceans and other prey with the help of electrosensory receptors in their beaks, which allow them to tune in to movement in the mucky water. When they walk on land, they retract the webbing on their feet to expose claws and get a better grip. A few years back, researchers discovered that they glow a soft blue green under blacklight—which may be a by-product of a camouflage strategy involving UV absorption, although it's hard to say for sure.

In other words, even as we come up with new ways to study platypuses, they continue to blur our categories and confuse our boundaries. Recent genetic analyses suggest that, along with their cousins the echidnas, platypuses are closest of all to the original mammal ancestor whose descendants branched out into the creatures we now find more familiar, from dogs to whales to humans. Strange though they may seem, platypuses may not be an anomaly but the blueprint. ❯ **How to see them:** Latrobe, Tasmania, is known as the platypus capital of Australia—try the Warrawee Forest Reserve there. Be there at dusk or dawn on a cloudy day, and stay quiet—they're very shy.

Flute Lyrebirds

Are they singing our song, or one of their own?

RANGE: Forests of the New England Tableland bioregion in New South Wales, Australia
SPECIES: Superb lyrebird (*Menura novaehollandiae*), sometimes called the flute lyrebird

◆ The lyrebirds of Australia are famous for their mimicry. In addition to their own noisy territorial songs, these birds imitate the calls and sounds of other avian species, often stringing them together to form creative mash-ups. Birds raised by people develop their own special repertoires. One superb lyrebird named Chook, who lived at the Adelaide Zoo, could do a dead-on car alarm, as well as various construction equipment sounds, which he apparently picked up when the zoo was building a panda enclosure.

And then there's the strange case of the lyrebirds whose burbling trills and scales echo over the gorges and waterfalls of the New England Tableland bioregion. The superb lyrebirds here—and nowhere else—have swapped the classic, raspy territorial song out for something much more melodic. Why they did this is one of birdsong's most enduring and divisive mysteries.

Lyrebirds have been flitting about Australia for millions of years, but the origin of the flute lyrebird is associated with a tale from the 1920s. During that time, a caged lyrebird is said to have lived at a home in the Tableland region with a man who played the flute.

Legend holds that when the man practiced his ascending scales, the lyrebird was taking notes. After the lyrebird was released into the wild, people say, he sang flute-inspired songs, influencing the birds of the area. Those birds imitated the melodies and passed them down to their offspring over the decades.

Is this really how the "flute lyrebirds," as they're now often called, came to be? The answer is a definite maybe, says Hollis Taylor, a zoomusicologist who has a research group focused on the question. They've embarked on a bit of a wild lyrebird chase, scouring old recordings and interviewing people from the region in an attempt to fact-check this account.

At this point, within the group, "half of us believe the story is true, and half of us believe the story is not true," she says. The doubters think it's just a classic animal-inspired tall tale and can't imagine why wild lyrebirds would want to learn a weird new song from a former indoor kid. The believers say they must have had their reasons.

How else might these birds have come upon such an unusual singing style? They may have been cribbing from other musicians—just not human ones. Imitations of different birds' calls, songs, and even beak snaps and wingbeats make up 70 percent of lyrebirds' vocal displays. (Basically, anything another bird says around a lyrebird is fair game for a remix.) Perhaps the so-called flute lyrebirds' tunes are actually their interpretations of other local songbirds. Or they may have improvised them all on their own.

It wouldn't be the first time we gave ourselves undue credit for the sounds these birds make. Because lyrebird territorial calls have a metallic quality, humans often think the birds are imitating our inventions, from lasers to steam trains to chain saws.

Although captive birds, like Chook, might riff on human sounds, there's no evidence of it happening in the wild. (In fact, Chook apparently never mated, possibly because the zoo's female lyrebirds found that his construction noises killed the mood.) Taylor says that whenever someone has sent her audio "proof" that wild lyrebirds are aping a machine, it's always actually a natural lyrebird song. They've been musicians for millions of years; humans are the noisy newcomers.

> **How to see (and hear) them:** Try the Lyrebird Link trail in Dorrigo National Park, New South Wales. You can also hear the songs of the flute lyrebird—and judge their provenance for yourself—at flutelyrebird.com.

A Brief History of Birdsong Notation

For centuries, ornithologists and more casual fans have struggled to pin the nuances of birdcalls and songs to paper.

Some of the earliest known English-language attempts to standardize bird sounds are embedded in the bird names themselves: chickadee, cuckoo, whip-poor-will. Others come from poems and songs. In the 1590s, iconoclastic writer Thomas Nashe tried to capture springtime by describing how "Cold doth not sting, the pretty birds do sing: / Cuckoo, jug-jug, pu-we, to-witta-woo!" Nature-loving poet John Clare spent a whole stanza of "The Progress of Rhyme" channeling a nightingale: "wew-wew wew-wew, chur-chur chur-chur, woo-it woo-it," and so on.

The polymath Athanasius Kircher was one of the first to drape chirps and twitters over the Western musical staff. In his 1650 study of music, *Musurgia Universalis*, Kircher paired illustrations of birds with transcriptions of their calls: A hen clucks in staccato *As*, a cuckoo goes heavy on the downbeat, and a parrot, maybe tone-deaf, simply says "χαίρε"—Greek for "hello." Kircher wanted more than just words because he had something to prove—he was arguing for the existence of a "cosmic harmony," composed by God and borne out by birdsong.

This project was continued centuries later by F. Schuyler Mathews, an American naturalist. In his 1904 opus *Field Book of Wild Birds and Their Music*, Mathews wrestled the songs of more than a hundred wild birds into musical notation. Like Kircher, he saw his endeavor as something of a divine calling. "I believe the birds with their music are the revelation of a greater world," he wrote in the introduction. But his chief purpose was to keep the songs "in a state of scientific preservation," he wrote, and he found musical notation to be the best possible formaldehyde.

He ran into some difficulty, though—for instance, with the tune of the bobolink, which he described as a "mad, reckless song-fantasia" and represented with the jumble of notes shown below.

As Mathews and others found, while Western musical notation is great at getting across certain aspects of sound, it leaves some important things out completely. It excludes pitches and rhythms that fall between regular intervals, and it doesn't deal at all with timbre, the quality that makes a note played on a guitar sound different from the same note played on a piano, or a robin's chirrup far from a blackbird's.

To deal with these shortcomings, the ornithologists of the early twentieth century began inventing their own notation. One type created by biology

Matthews tries to capture a bobolinks song.

teacher A. A. Saunders involved plotting swoops, chirps, and trills on a 12-by-10 grid—and led Saunders to carry a tuning fork, a stopwatch, and graph paper in his pocket wherever he went. In 1924, a pair of field biologists employed Morse Code–like dots and dashes to compare and contrast nearly 200 sparrow songs.

Then World War II began. Suddenly, the United States found super-detailed analysis of sound—the underwater chug of submarines, for example—to be a matter of national security. Beginning in the early 1940s, scientists at New Jersey's Bell Laboratories ramped up work on the sound spectrograph, a machine that could chew sound waves into data and spit them back out as images. After the war, when the technology was declassified, a company named Kay Elemetrics began making their own version, called the Sona-Graph. Birders, sensing an answer to their troubles, flocked to it.

When they started feeding their favorite songs through the machines, ornithologists discovered all kinds of details that, audible or not, had fallen through the cracks of previous notations. Pitches soared up and down the y-axis, and timbre was visible as ghostly traces, called overtones, above the main melody.

Scientists could also pursue lines of inquiry that would have been unthinkable before. Comparing and contrasting spectrograms has allowed us to learn about not just what birds sing, but how they learn their songs, how many they know, and exactly how local bird dialects vary. Since the 1950s, spectrography has only gotten more omnipresent in the bird nerd world, a vital part of studying these captivating creatures.

(right) Sparrow code

(below) Spectrograms of the songs of two birds—a chaffinch and a zebra finch

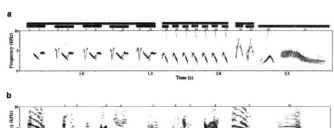

THE WILD LIFE OF A Zoomusicologist

■ When she's not sleuthing for clues about flute lyrebirds, Hollis Taylor composes and plays music inspired by her other favorite musician, the pied butcherbird, also of Australia. She describes herself as a zoomusicologist, meaning someone who studies the musical aspects of animal sounds.

• **What can you learn by analyzing birdsong through the lens of music theory?**
Music theory is indeed useful for studying the rhythms, the pitches and melodies, and even the micro and macro structure of birdsong. I've found a lot of overlaps [with] human music. You can find elements like crescendo and decrescendo, ostinato and riffs, octave leaps, truncation, alternation of patterns, contrasting themes, and much more that's really familiar to us.

But I would also say what's interesting to me are questions like, "What can birdsong tell us about the human capacity for music that nothing else might?" Because after all, they've been doing it much longer.

• **Are there common misconceptions about birdsong that you'd like to correct?**
There is a constant comparison of the least complex birdsong with the most complex human music. And that amuses me and frustrates me at the same time, because I think most human musical genres are somewhat repetitive, formulaic, and simple. So we're often comparing in the wrong direction.

• **How has studying birds and birdsong influenced your composition?**
As a composer, I understand their song to be the manifestation of millions of years of culture. So I don't feel the need to come in and try to improve on their song.

When I tried to insert licks and tricks from the other human genres that I'd studied, it never worked. It just wasn't satisfying. These birds work with their phrases all year round, and they know what works. I learned to settle for their expertise. Many of my pieces are almost direct transcriptions.

• **What about your playing?**
I play them in order to analyze them, because then I know them more intimately. But it also makes me a better violinist, and I didn't expect that at all. I would listen to the recording, and then I would transcribe it, and then I'd think, *Something's not right.* And I would realize that I need to match their gesture—it needs to be as effortless as possible, because that's the way birds sing. It needs to sound spontaneous and effortless and organic.

And so I had to foster a new physical vocabulary—maybe one I should have already had. But it made me, I think, a better violinist. ■

Giant Gippsland Earthworms

Listen up for these super-rare, super-long worms.

RANGE: About 150 square miles (388 sq km) of former old-growth forest in Gippsland, Australia
SPECIES: Giant Gippsland earthworm (*Megascolides australis*)

◆ Ah, the bucolic soundscape of Gippsland, Australia. The dueting calls of whipbirds and the sweet chirps of yellow robins; the murmur of streams and the hum of farm machinery. And beneath it all, the loud, underground gurgle-suck of . . . okay, what exactly *is* that?

Don't fret: It's just one of Gippsland's giant worms. One of the largest earthworm species on the planet, these wriggly goliaths average about 3 feet (1 m) in length but can reach up to at least 7 feet (2.1 m).

Vibrations on the ground's surface—a naive hiker's footsteps, for instance—send the worms squelching merrily through their moist tunnels, making a sound like someone's pulled the plug out of a nearby bath. "I still get excited when I hear them," says Beverley Van Praagh, who has spent a quarter of a century studying and advocating for the species.

Adult Gippsland earthworms have fleshy pink bodies and muscular purple heads, which they use to forge their sprawling burrow systems. Along the way, they feed on organic matter and leave a trail of their own nutrient-rich poop underground. Although individual worms are hermaphrodites, sporting both male and female sex organs, they couple up to mate. They then lay their young—just one per year—in translucent egg capsules, from which they emerge already 1 foot (30.5 cm) long.

Many people have found their imaginations captured by these tubular Gippslandians: The town of Korumburra, Victoria, used to hold an annual festival for the species, complete with commemorative plushies and the crowning of an "earthworm queen." But despite this widespread attention, many aspects of *M. australis*'s behavior and biology are still a mystery, including "how they meet and mate within their small burrows" and how long they live, Van Praagh says.

Our time to learn is running out. Climate change may pose a threat to the species by drying out their homes, and their habitat, once rich with old-growth forest, has been almost entirely cleared for agriculture. (They're now limited to just more than 150 square miles [388 sq km]—an area you could drive across in under an hour.) Due to their large size, the worms are vulnerable to farming equipment. Anecdotal reports from the early twentieth century tell of accidental mass killings by unaware farmers, who found the worms "hanging like spaghetti" from their plows in fields that were "red with blood," as Van Praagh once described to *Australian Geographic*.

These worms can grow 7 feet long (2.1 m).

Today, local landowners are told to listen out for worm gurgles, and some carefully revegetate their properties to lock in soil moisture and help the species. But Van Praagh thinks the invertebrates are still under-recognized. "I wish people knew how beautiful and graceful they are," she says. "They deserve our protection in the same way animals with backbones do." ❯ **How to see them:** Listen for the worms' distinctive underground squelches. Digging is discouraged, as it can harm them, but they sometimes emerge after rainstorms.

Bowerbird Bachelor Pads

These birds seduce their mates with peerless architecture and decor.

RANGE: New Guinea and Australia
SPECIES: About 20 species in the family Ptilonorhynchidae

◆ Many birds are flirtatious show-offs, using their colorful plumage or impressive singing skills to attract mates. But bowerbirds have a unique pickup method: constructing fancy houses.

Every year, a male bowerbird gathers materials from his environment to build a bower—a literal love nest, used solely for wooing and what comes after. It's meant to impress females, who spend the mating season visiting multiple bower sites in order to scope out prospective suitors. If sufficiently impressed by a bower's architecture and adornments, a female will stick around and watch the male perform a song and dance routine. If he passes that test, they'll mate; otherwise, she'll fly on to the next bower.

Like any good bachelor pad, the most effective bowers are both well built and lavishly decorated. Different species have developed distinct design types, such as "avenue bowers," in which rows of sticks fan out and upward from the ground like an upside-down archway, and "maypole bowers," stick tents rising up to 9 feet (2.7 m) around a central sapling.

When construction is finished, bowerbirds collect feathers, flowers, snake skins, snail shells, and dead bugs as ornaments. Species that live near people are known to trim their homes with human detritus, from toothbrushes to condoms. One Australian naturalist reported seeing a bower embellished exclusively with bullet shells and shotgun cartridges.

Satin bowerbirds specialize in blue objects—which are attention-grabbing due to their rarity in nature, and contrast well with the abundant straw of the habitat. Spotted bowerbirds prefer shiny things, like coins, and may prune the leaves above reflective decorations to enhance their shimmer.

A flame bowerbird (above) and a satin bowerbird (below) show off their handiwork.

Great bowerbirds arrange objects in a large-to-small gradient in what some ornithologists believe is an example of forced perspective—an illusion, commonly associated with Renaissance artists like Michelangelo, that makes the bowers and the birds themselves appear larger than they really are. And research has shown that birds with duller plumage make their bowers extra-elaborate, perhaps to compensate.

A good bower is worth the investment. Although the vast majority of bird species are monogamous, bowerbirds are highly polygynous, meaning that a successful male might mate with as many as 30 females in one season. An unsuccessful one, meanwhile, is left single—alone in a stick house decorated with condoms. **❯ How to see them:** Most species are concentrated in dense and hard-to-reach forests of New Guinea, but satin bowerbirds can be spotted right outside Sydney, especially near campgrounds and picnic sites.

Swamp Kauri

Ancient preserved wood tells the story of our planet.

LOCATION: New Zealand's North Island
SPECIES: Kauri (*Agathis australis*)

◆ Many thousands of years before human beings set foot in New Zealand, or even dreamed that such a place existed, thousands of native kauri trees, up to 200 feet in height and 40 feet in width (61 m x 12.2 m), thrived in the northernmost part of the country's North Island. Then, disaster: Sometime around 42,000 years ago, around the time of the last Ice Age, many of the trees began to die, keeling into the peat bogs that would preserve them for millennia to come.

Fast-forward to the present day. Swamp kauri, as this preserved wood is often known, is one of New Zealand's most prized—and most contentious—materials.

Many of New Zealand's Indigenous Māori people see it as a *taonga*, or sacred treasure, and have pushed for greater restrictions on the foreign investors who strip it from the land, sometimes illegally, and send it thousands of miles overseas where it's used to make everything from ornamental chopping boards to boardroom paneling. Many of the wetlands in which it lies are protected, and extracting the wood can disrupt fragile ecosystems.

A swamp kauri log dug out of a wetland

For climate scientists, meanwhile, swamp kauri's greatest value has little to do with its honeyed hue or distinctively hazy grain, like a shoal of fish making its way upstream. Each perfectly preserved tree tells the story of the time when it was growing, serving as a precious archive of long-forgotten global events. Richly detailed information can be drawn from its wood: Analysis may reveal relative humidity, rainfall patterns, and soil moisture in a given year.

More recently, researchers have been able to use swamp kauri to solve climatic mysteries. Less than 50,000 years ago, the Earth's magnetic poles suddenly flipped; they reversed back about 800 years later. But scientists had long struggled to pinpoint when this happened, and its environmental effects, until an 8-foot-wide (2.5 m) kauri was dragged out of a swamp in Ngāwhā, Northland.

Analysis of its rings and chemical makeup helped provide a timestamp for the event, and a sense of its consequences: The geomagnetic reversal took place between 41,000 and 42,000 years ago and spurred changes in the climate that led to evaporation of lakes, overturn of vegetation, and a mass extinction of large animals. (The kauri, too, experienced lean times: Its rings were noticeably thinner after the poles switched.)

Swamp kauri may yet hold other critical secrets, among them ways to improve radiocarbon dating or predict the changing climate patterns of El Niño and La Niña. But these sleeping giants, left undisturbed in their climatically controlled peat bog for tens of thousands of years, are fewer and farther between. Only careful management of their extraction can prevent these long-buried buried treasures from slipping out of our grasp. ❭ **How to see them:** New Zealand's two major museums, Te Papa and the Auckland War Memorial Museum, both hold swamp kauri in their permanent collections.

New Zealand's Anthropocene Tree

Just as swamp kauri took notes on world-altering events of the past, today's trees are keeping track of our planet's ongoing changes. In the middle of Campbell Island/Motu Hupuku, an unpopulated subantarctic island about 850 miles (1,368 km) south of New Zealand, there stands a solitary tree that some say marked the start of our current and confusing geologic era.

The tree—a Sitka spruce—is said to have been planted in the early 1900s by New Zealand governor Lord Ranfurly. Although he had meant to give it some neighbors, the story goes, no one ever got around to it. The spruce is now about 250 miles (400 km) from anything else of its kind, leading Guinness World Records to deem it the "remotest tree in the world." (Its closest competition, an acacia in the middle of the Sahara Desert, was hit by a truck back in 1973.)

Humans have also left their mark on the spruce: Back when people lived on the island, it's said, weather station employees would cut a Christmas tree–sized chunk out of its foliage each December, leaving it with an unusually lumpy crown. But our greatest impact is hidden. A group of scientists recently took core samples from the tree and analyzed the size of each of its rings. They found that one ring, from the year 1965, contains a proportionately huge amount of a particular isotope, carbon-14.

Carbon-14 has always been present in the atmosphere in small amounts. But after countries began performing aboveground nuclear tests in the middle of the 1950s, it got to levels that, say, a tree might notice. By the time 1965 came around, these high concentrations had apparently reached even this lonely spruce.

For years, scientists have been trying to decide whether we are officially in the Anthropocene: a potential new geologic epoch characterized by widespread human-driven changes to the planet. As they push the debate forward, they have been looking for a starting point, called the "golden spike," that would mark where the Holocene ended and this new epoch began. The researchers who studied the lonely Sitka spruce are suggesting that its sudden jump in carbon-14 would make for a perfect golden spike.

The spruce joins a long list of possibilities; as one researcher put it, "we are spoilt for choice." But whether or not it gets another official title, now we have proof: Even the loneliest tree in the world has been shaped by us.

Mad Hatterpillars

To keep predators off their tails, these moth larvae build up impressive stacks of heads.

RANGE: Australia (particularly the southeastern coast) and New Zealand
SPECIES: Gum-leaf skeletonizer (*Uraba lugens*)

◆ Caterpillar life is fraught. In order to transform into agile moths and butterflies, caterpillars must first survive their sluggish childhoods, eating as much as they can while avoiding hungry predators like birds, reptiles, and larger bugs.

Different species have developed ingenious strategies to make it through. Some are camouflaged or hide in leaf shelters. Others have stinging hairs or taste really bad. And still others keep their old heads, and—rather than casting them aside as they molt—wear them in a stack upon their current head to form a towering and intimidating head-hat.

The most notable of these insect Abe Lincolns is the gum-leaf skeletonizer caterpillar of Australia. (The species is named for its second-creepiest habit—its tendency to devour the soft parts of eucalyptus leaves, leaving only the spidery ribs behind.) Before it can metamorphose into a moth, a skeletonizer caterpillar must molt up to a dozen times. The second or third time is typically when it begins its spooky cranium pile. When the caterpillar starts to molt, the hard capsule that holds its head cracks open at the bottom, like an astronaut's helmet unlatching from a space suit. Then the new, slightly larger head squeezes out, pushing the capsule up from below.

The capsule gets snagged in the caterpillar's tangle of wiry hairs, which hold it in place. With each molt, the caterpillar's head gets about 30 percent bigger—and another of its former faces joins the stack.

Skeletonizer caterpillars have been known to collect up to seven empty head cases above their currently functional ones. They brandish this headgear against predators like brown soldier bugs, which try to pierce the caterpillars with sharp proboscises and suck out their insides.

A recent study confirmed that a healthy skull stack makes a caterpillar slightly less likely to be eviscerated by a soldier bug—but only if a bare-headed caterpillar is sitting next to it. It's not a foolproof defense, but given the many perils of caterpillar adolescence, they may as well do all they can to try to get ahead. ❯ **How to see them:** In spring and summer, you might find them in the forests of southeastern Australia, munching eucalyptus leaves. They're also common in the Royal Botanic Garden next to Sydney's iconic opera house.

(left) A group of the caterpillars do what they do best: skeletonizing a leaf.

(below) This gum-leaf skeletonizer caterpillar has collected five old heads to complement its current one.

CHAPTER 2

Grasslands & Tundras

I t's easy to stand in a grassland, do a quick 360, and assume there's not much going on. The human's-eye view can lull you into a real sense of sameness as you take in all that rippling grass.

But don't be fooled. Any grassland—or tundra, field, or savanna—hums with hidden specificity. A photographer who goes step by step through the prairie finds new players and dramas in every square foot. Each wildebeest born during the Great Migration, dropped onto the Serengeti among half a million other calves, knows by scent her exact mother.

Lives here are built on details like these. A wood mouse who finds a productive patch of meadow marks it with a special acorn. A dung beetle must check the Milky Way to find the perfect ball-rolling route. Prairie dogs can describe to their companions exactly who is approaching to try to eat or study them, down to the wingspan of a goshawk or the color of a researcher's shirt.

As grassland species attend to these particulars, they push forward cycles large and small. Every year, huge herds of caribou travel over the tundra, driving whole ecosystems as they eat, carve through snow, drop waste, and die. Step in one place, and a caribou might squash a brief seasonal relationship: an Arctic poppy deep into its do-si-do with the sun. Sniff in another, and she might get a bite of a potentially immortal one: a fungus and its algae joining up to form a tough, tasty lichen.

People are also are part of these cycles—for better and for worse. We tend fires that rejuvenate the land and learn to harvest plants at the right time. But we also clear the prairies of tallgrass and bison, absences the whole world now feels. Or we bring cane toads across the world, spurring an unprecedented evolutionary situation we are still trying to understand.

Understanding, too, can come from careful accumulation of detail. Let's part the grass and get into it.

Contributers: *Richard Constantine Arghiris, J. Besl, Mackenzie Breneman, Stuart Butler, Christina Couch, Elyse DeFranco, Jamie Ditaranto, Cecil Dzwowa, Kate Evans, Jonathan Feakins, Rachel Fritts, Claudia Geib, Kate Golembiewski, Mara Grunbaum, Solimary García-Hernández, Annika Hipple, Lisa Holmes, Aysha Imtiaz, Laurie Jackson, Kestrel Keller, Jacob Kuppermann, Stephanie Kyrzwonos, Pierre Le Duff, Matt Malinowski, Sam Moore, T.J. Olwig, Michael Parks, Oriana Pauli, Austin Price, Linda Rodriguez McRobbie, Holly Secon, Joshua Sokol, Jack Tamisiea, Alex Tesar, Andrew Warner*

AFRICA

The Great Wildebeest Migration

The grass is always greener . . .

◆ One of the first things a wildebeest calf learns is how to follow his mother. Within a few minutes of being dropped onto the soft savanna grass, a newborn calf can stand up; after an hour or so, he can gallop next to his mom, like a gangly satellite. He'll spend his whole childhood keeping up with her—and she'll spend it keeping up with 2 million or so other ungulates, all lifelong devotees of an endless journey known as the Great Migration.

Among the largest animal movements on Earth in terms of both distance and crowd size, the Great Migration leads a megaherd of wildebeests, zebras, elands, and other grazers on a twisted figure eight across the Serengeti, tracking fresh grass. After calving on the luxurious shortgrass plains of Tanzania in February, the group slowly moves northwest, reaching Kenya's Maasai Mara and the northern Serengeti in August. They mill around for the three-month dry season, then start heading back south in November, to graze and breed in the regreened pastures.

Blue wildebeests form the bulk of the Great Migrators—about 1.5 million of them make the cyclical trek, walking an average of 930 miles (1,500 km) per year. (This is like every single person in San Diego, California, hiking to San Francisco and back annually.) They're joined by hundreds of thousands of other grazers, including gazelles, zebras, eland, and impalas.

The movement of these herbivores, itself driven by the climate, drives most other ecological processes in the Serengeti in turn. Collectively, these herds eat nearly 10 million pounds of grass every single day, digesting it on the move. They relocate much of that nutrient content through defecation, recycled by hardworking dung beetles. And because grazing makes grass grow faster, the grazers help ensure that the landscape remains productive.

RANGE: A lumpy figure eight that connects Tanzania and Kenya

SPECIES: Blue wildebeest (*Connochaetes taurinus*), common eland (*Taurotragus oryx*), Grant's gazelle (*Nanger granti*), impala (*Aepyceros melampus*), plains zebra (*Equus quagga*), Thomson's gazelle (*Eudorcas thomsonii*), and more

About 1.5 million wildebeest make this journey every year.

The many migrators who die during this journey also feed the larger system. It's a dangerous trip—such large accumulations of animals inevitably pass around diseases and parasites, and predators from lions to crocodiles stalk the edges of what amounts to a huge antelope-and-zebra buffet. One study found that more than 6,000 wildebeests drown in the Mara River every year, the equivalent, biomass-wise, of 10 blue whales. As their bodies slowly decompose, they feed fish, crustaceans, plankton, and insects, roping these aquatic creatures into the ecological web.

Migrating wildebeest must make their way across rivers.

In this way, wildebeests and their compatriots power the Serengeti by living, eating, pooping, and dying clockwise all across it. The strangely shaped path of their migration is the true circle of life. ❯ **How to see them:** Many local operators plan tours around the Great Migration—some even offer hot air balloon rides so you can practice your herd-counting skills. If you'd like to follow the action from a distance, herd trackers are also available online.

THE WILD LIFE OF **A Conservancy Game Changer**

■ At age five, Nelson Ole Reiyia lost one of his family's goats to a leopard and was sent to school as punishment. After going on to study and work in Nairobi and Berlin, Nelson returned to the savanna of his childhood to help create Kenya's Nashulai Maasai Conservancy, the first ever Maasai-owned and Maasai-governed wildlife protection area.

• **What makes Nashulai different from most other conservancies?**
One of the problems of the standard conservancies is that the model requires the Maasai people—the landowners—to leave their land to make way for tourism. Nashulai is the first conservancy to be created, governed, and managed by the people who have actually inhabited the land for centuries, who understand it intimately, and who have sustained themselves and effectively managed their herds in harmony with the natural life of this globally important ecosystem.

We know, we see with our own eyes, the urgency of land and wildlife depletion. And poverty increases the catastrophes of ecosystem collapse and climate change. So our own interdependent

mission is "Reverse Poverty—Conserve Wildlife—Preserve Culture." Using a traditional village system, a council of elders works with conservancy managers and staff to come to decisions on how the conservancy is run. We're proud to say we're one of the only conservancies where the local people remained in their homes and on their land when the conservancy was created. We work in a manner that encourages people to live in harmony with the wildlife, as the Maasai always have.

• **Is this technique working?**
Yes. Abutting as it does the Maasai Mara, the area is a keystone area in the greater Maasai Mara and Serengeti ecosystem, a critical migratory corridor and ancient elephant nursery.

In the years since the conservancy was formed, there's been a big increase in wildlife here. Before that the land was fenced, degraded, and overgrazed by our cattle. Now, by using controlled rotational grazing practices, removing the fences that divided up people's plots of land, and employing local people to be wildlife rangers and work in the

conservancy, we have seen the land become richer and with many more animals.

• **What is it about Nashulai that you are most proud of?**
I'm most proud of our inclusive model, where the community is fully involved. The creation of balance and harmony is very important for the sustainability of people, livestock, wildlife, and tourism. I'm also very proud of how the wildlife has returned to what I remember as a small boy, and of our community work.

• **What do Nashulai and the greater Maasai Mara region mean to you personally?**
This is the land of my boyhood. The land of my people, where the bones of my ancestors are buried. And it is the land of my children. Nashulai is a critical place in the whole Mara-Serengeti ecosystem, and it was about to be lost forever. Our community rose up to save this place and become its stewards for the generations to come. ■

To learn more about Nashulai Maasai Conservancy and plan a Maasai-led safari at Nashulai, go to www.nashulai .com.

SERENGETI

• Built on volcanic soil and replenished by restless herds of ungulates, the 15,000-square-mile (38,850 sq km) Serengeti is an incredibly productive ecosystem—a wealth made most visible through the high concentrations of food-chain toppers like lions and leopards.

• The Mara River, which winds from the Mau Forest in southwest Kenya all the way to Tanzania's Lake Victoria, can more than double in volume in the rainy season, turning from a sluggish trickle to a rapids-filled obstacle course that drowns migrating wildebeests.

• Footprints made by our predecessors millions of years ago have been found in and around the Serengeti. At one site in Laetoli, Tanzania, hominin footprints are found alongside ancient impressions from mammals, birds, and even raindrops.

KEEP AN EYE OUT FOR Abandoned termite mounds, which get a second life as mammal infrastructure. Antelope use these reddish-brown dirt mounds as lookout points, and hyenas, mongooses, and other medium-sized critters co-opt them as dens.

KEEP AN EAR OUT FOR The territorial honks, splashes, and farts of congregating hippos. In super-large groups, they can reach 115 decibels, a noise level many experts consider unsafe.

KEEP A NOSE OUT FOR The fresh, grassy scent of the plains after a rainstorm.

Secrets of Serengeti Celebrities

The charismatic residents of the Serengeti are some of the most famous animals on Earth. But how much do you *really* know about them? Here's some gossip all those fawning brochures and documentaries leave out.

ZEBRAS—THEY'RE PRACTICAL! The signature stripes of a plains zebra (*Equus quagga*) or Grévy's zebra (*Equus grevyi*) are not just a bold fashion statement—they're a natural bug repellent. According to a research project that involved dressing horses in stripey coats, the contrasting bands seem to confuse flies as they come in for a landing, causing them to either veer off at the last minute or harmlessly bounce off the zebra's body.

IMPALAS—THEY'RE WEIRD! During the rutting season, male impalas (*Aepyceros melampus*) vocalize so ferociously that their

amorous calls can be mistaken for lions' roars. To confuse predators, impalas are known to "stot," jumping straight up, legs stiff, and ending the move with a can-can-like high kick.

ELEPHANTS—THEY'RE NOSY ... African bush elephants (*Loxodonta africana*) have 2,000 smell-related genes, the most known of any mammal. (Even dogs have only 800.) While the number of genes isn't as important as how you use them, scientists have found that elephants can identify an impressive array of things by smell alone, including members of their herd and the amount of food hidden in a bucket.

... AND SENTIMENTAL! Elephants have strong social bonds and seem to mourn family members—and even unrelated elephants—when they die. Researchers have seen elephants rocking back and forth near bodies of their recently deceased relatives, touching and smelling them, and inspecting and scattering their bones. Mother elephants have even been seen carrying the bodies of their calves.

GIRAFFES—THEY'RE NOT ALWAYS TALL! While most adult giraffes (*Giraffa camelopardalis*) are 16 feet (4.8 m) or taller, some can be half that size. Scientists have found at least two giraffes with a condition called skeletal dysplasia, which leaves them with uncharacteristically short legs.

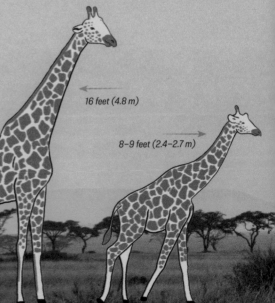

16 feet (4.8 m)

8–9 feet (2.4–2.7 m)

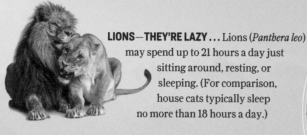

LIONS—THEY'RE LAZY . . . Lions (*Panthera leo*) may spend up to 21 hours a day just sitting around, resting, or sleeping. (For comparison, house cats typically sleep no more than 18 hours a day.)

. . . EXCEPT WHEN THEY'RE NOT! That is, until it's mating time—when a female goes into heat, she and a male partner will couple every 20 to 30 minutes for several days straight.

CHEETAHS—THEY'RE LOYAL! Many male cheetah cubs (*Acinonyx jubatus*) form coalitions that stick together for life. Members of these tight-knit brotherhoods groom one another, rest together, and share meals. Cheetah moms very occasionally adopt cubs from parents who can't take care of them, at which point they may join these coalitions.

HIPPOS—THEY CAN'T SWIM . . . Despite their well-known love of water, common hippos (*Hippopotamus amphibius*) don't actually swim. Instead, submerged hippos propel themselves forward by pushing off the river or lake bottom in a series of prancing steps, like a rotund horse trotting on the moon.

. . . AND THEY SWEAT RED ACID! Hippos on land keep cool using something called "blood sweat": a thick ooze that seeps from glands under their skin and turns red in the sun. This macabre-looking secretion serves as both a sunscreen and an antimicrobial ointment.

A Step-by-Step Guide to Giraffe Transport

In 2020, a group of rangers, community members, and nonprofit workers successfully rescued eight giraffes from a flooding peninsula in Lake Baringo, Kenya, ferrying them onto the mainland in a custom steel barge. Here's how they did it:

1. DECIDE TO MOVE THE GIRAFFE. Powerful people as far back as Julius Caesar once brought giraffes across the world, in shows of diplomacy or imperial might. Now, most giraffe transport projects are undertaken by zoos—or as rescue missions. In this case, the rising waters of Lake Baringo were trapping these giraffes on a shrinking piece of land, cutting them off from their food supply.

2. SEDATE THE GIRAFFE. As prey animals, wild giraffes see almost any approach as a threat. This team used gentle tranquilizers to sedate the giraffes long enough to put on blindfolds and rope leads.

3. UN-SEDATE THE GIRAFFE. While other large animals can handle straightforward sedation, a giraffe who stays horizontal too long risks choking on her own saliva or suffering brain damage from rapidly changing blood pressure. Veterinarians quickly provided these giraffes with an antidote so they could stand up and be led onto the barge.

4. CHOOSE A GENTLE VEHICLE. In 1829, a giraffe in an Austrian zoo died. A postmortem suggested that it had been suffering from fractures received while being hauled out of North Africa on camelback, sailing to Venice, and then walking across the Alps. Today, giraffe transporters tend to ferry their passengers on container ships or charter flights. The Lake Baringo team built a custom steel barge so that the giraffes could sail comfortably.

5. FREE THE GIRAFFE. Giraffes are masters of their own strange anatomy, with flexible arteries, strong hearts, and vertebrae the size of thermoses. After their quick barge trip, the giraffes of Lake Baringo walked onto the mainland with their heads held high.

Whistling Acacias and Ants

A mutually beneficial relationship—until things get thorny

RANGE: East Africa
SPECIES: Whistling thorn acacia tree (*Vachellia drepanolobium*) and acacia ant (*Crematogaster mimosae*)

◆ In the sprawling savannas of East Africa, whistling thorn acacia trees spend their lives under siege. Elephants, giraffes, and rhinoceroses snap their branches like Twix bars, ignoring their daggerlike spines to gobble down their small green leaves. To protect themselves from these enormous browsers, the trees rely on the devotion of some much smaller creatures: ants.

Crematogaster mimosae ants live exclusively on whistling thorn acacia trees. Once an ant colony has claimed a tree, they defend it in typical overcommitted ant fashion, greeting anyone who approaches by swarming, biting, and releasing a sharp odor reminiscent of vomit. Flipping what seems like a size disadvantage, they often bypass the tough skin of their opponents to climb up into their tender nostrils. Even rhinos will leave an acacia tree snorting in defeat.

To welcome their protectors, the trees transform themselves into leafy bed-and-breakfasts, converting some of their spines into swollen, hollow galls called domatia to house the ants and their larvae and producing a rich nectar for them to drink. The tiny entry holes ants bore into their gall condos sing when the wind rushes through—giving the trees their name, "whistling thorn acacias." The ants become attached to their specific acacia home and will battle any interloping colony to the death.

In a balanced ecosystem, both species benefit from this arrangement. But as with any relationship, context is key. When elephants, giraffes, and other grazing mammals disappear—from local extinction, declining populations, or

Ants make themselves at home in the galls of whistling thorn acacia trees.

simply getting fenced out—the trees no longer need the ants for protection and the calculus changes. The former partners turn on each other.

The acacia, once so hospitable, will try to evict the ants by cutting off the supply of sheltering galls and sweet nectar. The ants respond to their sudden status as unwanted guests by trashing their tree house: They attract damaging, sap-sucking insects to milk for their honeydew and refuse to defend the tree from disturbance. The tree begins to die, leaving the ants homeless. Without common enemies, this fragile mutualism turns into mutual destruction. ❯ **How to see them:** Whistling thorn acacias and their ants are most often found on black cotton soil in upland East Africa, especially in Kenya. Listen for the telltale whistle, which sounds like a woodwind playing a quavering note.

Another Special Ant-Tree Relationship

In Panama, Azteca ants (*Azteca alfari*) live in harmony with *Cecropia* trees, nesting inside their hollow stems, feeding off their oily leaf secretions, and defending them from chomping insects and climbing vines. They will also heal injured trees, creating poultices of the tree's own sap and fibers and using them to patch up any wounds. While this behavior likely evolved in response to claw marks made by sloths or anteaters, it was discovered by a high schooler, Alex Wcislo, who was using a slingshot when he accidentally shot a clay ball clean through a *Cecropia* trunk and, the next day, noticed that the ants had patched the hole.

African Wild Dogs

When a sneeze means more than just an itchy nose

RANGE: Arid zones and savanna of sub-Saharan Africa
SPECIES: African wild dog (*Lycaon pictus*)

◆ For humans, a sneeze between friends rarely leads anywhere significant. After a proffered tissue or a polite "Gesundheit," everyone tends to move on.

Not so with African wild dogs. For these community-oriented canines, sneezes can be quite significant. In order to make the collective decision to go out hunting or move to a new location, the pack votes by sneezing. What looks like a spell of doggy hay fever is actually a carefully tabulated poll.

Having a way to make decisions together is important for these animals, whose social order combines a strict hierarchy with group buy-in. Each wild dog pack—which these days might comprise between five and twenty dogs—has an alpha pair sitting firmly at the top. Often the alphas are the only dogs that reproduce, after which everyone collaborates to guard, babysit, and wet-nurse their pampered puppies, family-style.

After a kill, adult wild dogs patiently wait while the pups eat first. Their generosity is broad—they'll also happily regurgitate meals to feed younger or injured pack members, even though this can, in larger packs with lots of mouths to feed, result in their own malnourishment and consequent early death.

Such cooperation is worth the risk. Communal living allows the wild dogs to take down larger prey and better defend themselves against lions and other predators. Plus, it makes it easier to relax, which they also like to do as a group—wild dogs spend most of the day asleep in the shade, snuggled up into spotty piles.

That is, until someone gets the urge for a hunt or a change of scenery. A pack member with an agenda first has to get everyone else excited, which involves the same enthusiastic jumping and nuzzling familiar to anyone who has ever returned home to a dog. Then

comes the official sneeze quorum. When it's an alpha trying to rally the others, just three sneezes are required to solidify the decision, while an individual lower down in the pecking order may have to accrue 10 or more sneeze votes to get the rest of the group on board. If it works, they all head out—together. ❯ **How to see them:** Your best bet is between May and August, which is just after pup season, when the dogs tend to stay put. Recommended sites include Mana Pools National Park and Hwange National Park (Zimbabwe), Okavango Delta and Khwai Community Concession (Botswana), and Madikwe Game Reserve and Kruger National Park (South Africa).

Savanna Eavesdropping

It's a bright day on the vast plains of the South African savanna, and you're a zebra chowing down on a nice lunch of elephant grass. As you eat, your ears perk to the sound of an alarm call: One of your neighbors has spotted something that might be dangerous. But you don't react. The caller is an impala, and as you know, they're scared of pretty much everything.

Whether you're a zebra, an antelope, or a wildebeest, there are really only three goals in life: Find food, make babies, and don't get eaten. "A predator can fail at predation and he just goes home hungry, but if a prey animal fails at not getting eaten, that's the end game," says Princeton University researcher Meredith Palmer. That gives animals good reason to listen for any cue of danger.

But prey animals have to weigh potential dangers against the cost of being overly paranoid. In an experiment with a mixed group of large mammals, Palmer found

that not all species' alarm calls are as valuable as others. "Because of energy trade-offs, they have to balance that risk: Is it worth running away from a false alarm?" she says.

Palmer studied this dynamic by playing alarm calls to a group of zebras, wildebeests, and impalas while the animals grazed together in a South African national park. These three species are very different. As a result, they all face a different level of risk from predators. Put these neighbors together for a meal, and the way they react to each other reflects this.

Palmer observed that impalas were the Chicken Littles of the savanna: They reacted to everyone's alarm calls and, as a result, were the least trusted messengers of danger. Zebras, on the other hand, remained mostly cool and collected, reacting most strongly to other zebra calls. The midsize wildebeests fell somewhere in the middle, becoming more vigilant when they heard alarm calls from zebras or other wildebeests, but not from impalas.

She found this interspecies communication remarkable:

"Not only were they able to eavesdrop on other animals, but they understood essentially a different language." This tapestry of surveillance and safety, of self-preservation and paranoia, creates patterns that biologists refer to as "fear ecology."

Fear ecology does a lot more than shape whether or not an animal becomes someone's lunch. These dynamics define where animals choose to eat and sleep, the places they travel and those they avoid, the bedfellows they keep and the neighbors they snub.

Fear ecology can have such profound effects that it actually leads an animal to act against their best interests, such as when a wildebeest chooses not to go to the place with the best food because a lion might be hanging out there. The repercussions of that choice can echo outward all the way to the landscape: Places with more lions may have more plants growing around them, as plant-eaters choose to forgo a tasty lunch there to avoid becoming someone else's dinner.

Oxpeckers

A small bird and a large mammal make a blood pact.

RANGE: Sub-Saharan West Africa
SPECIES: Red-billed oxpecker (*Buphagus erythrorynchus*); black rhinoceros (*Diceros bicornis*)

◆ Red-billed oxpeckers are named after their main trade: providing cleaning services to ungulates. A typical oxpecker spends her time perched atop oxen, impalas, and other savanna ruminants, pecking bugs out of their fur and skin (and sometimes their noses). She gets to eat, and her host is freed of itchy, dangerous pests. It's a straightforward win-win transaction.

But for at least one species, the black rhino, the oxpecker's service package includes another benefit: security. Although these gentle giants are too large for wild predators to eat, hundreds—sometimes thousands—are killed every year by poachers. Quiet, solitary, and nearsighted, rhinos depend on their oxpecker ride-alongs to warn them about encroaching threats.

Settled sentry-style on a rhino's flank or horn, an oxpecker will stare at the horizon out of yellow-ringed eyes that look perpetually peeled. If she spots anything suspicious—lion, human, strange-looking cloud—she'll let out a rough-edged warning call, *tseeeee*. In response, her mount will perk up and turn his attention to the threat.

Hunters and other observers have long noted this special relationship. (The oxpecker's Swahili name, *askari wa kifaru*, means "rhino's guard.") More recently, biologists have begun to test its efficacy. It seems to be working: A 2020 study in which researchers attempted to sneak up on rhinos found that those with oxpecker lookouts were always aware of human approaches, while those without them caught on less than a quarter of the time.

Oxpeckers like this one trade information for food.

In these experiments, oxpecker-laden rhinos also noticed people from more than twice as far away as birdless ones, with each additional scout adding about 30 feet (9 m) to the detection distance. "The rhino is absolutely eavesdropping," says study author Roan Plotz.

In fact, the bird guards are so good at their jobs that they made it difficult for Plotz and his team to do theirs: They were rarely able to find rhinos with oxpeckers in the wild, he says. (They ended up focusing on rhinos that could be tracked regardless, thanks to radio transmitters in their horns.) A warned rhino will quickly turn to face downwind— more evidence that this response evolved specifically to protect from human hunters, who often approach from that direction.

In return for their vigilance, oxpeckers get meals on the job—not only ticks and other hitchhiking insects, but blood and pus from sores on the rhino's back, made by parasitic roundworms and kept open by the birds as an iron-rich food supply.

The rhino's willingness to put up with this might be more evidence that the relationship is worthwhile, Plotz says. Other large animals, like Cape buffalo, will throw themselves on the ground to get rid of an overzealously vampiric oxpecker. But a rhino doesn't seem to mind giving a little blood to his eyes and ears. ❭ **How to see them: Look for a bird with a bright red bill hitching a ride on an ungulate.**

Oxpeckers help black rhinos avoid detection, even by researchers.

Grassy Glades

Self-regenerating salad bars of the savanna

◆ Travel in East Africa's vast savannas or peer down on them in Google Earth, and you'll notice places where thorny woodlands suddenly give way to grassy fields. These openings in the scrub may seem plain enough, but some hold clues to humans' role in shaping some of the most wildlife-rich lands on Earth.

Researchers have known for decades that "grassy glades," as they're called, often occur on settlements abandoned by livestock herders. By corralling animals at night, mobile pastoralists like the Maasai concentrate huge amounts of manure in particular spots. As a result, when herders move on from a homesite, an ecological party tends to break out in their stead.

Nutrient-loving plants like manyatta or settlement grass mark the sites of some more recently abandoned homesteads. This tasty forage in turn attracts wild grazers such as zebras, wildebeests, and impalas, as well as future herders with livestock. Grassy glades also draw in abundant communities of insects, birds, rodents, and even a species of lizard, the Kenya dwarf gecko, that's scarce in nearby rangelands.

Observers of grassy glades say they're visited by wild grazers first thing in the morning. "It's like they've gone out and got their coffees and doughnuts. Then they spend the midday heat ruminating," says Stanley Ambrose, an anthropologist at the University of Illinois, Urbana-Champaign.

The upshot of all this traffic? More dung, urine, and bones pile up in the glade, until the old homestead has become a self-perpetuating nutrient hot spot. Anthropogenic glades may play a role in spectacles like the famed Serengeti-Mara wildebeest migration. They also create mosaics of habitat that likely contribute to the overall biodiversity and stability of savanna ecosystems.

How long can these glades persist? To find out, an international team of researchers, including Ambrose, excavated five sites spread across both sides of the Great Rift Valley in central Kenya. They reported that soils in places settled 3,000 years ago are still rich in nutrients like phosphorus and calcium today. Other researchers have documented

RANGE: Herder-driven nutrient hot spots occur throughout Africa (and elsewhere), but the oldest documented examples are in central and southwestern Kenya.

SPECIES: Manyatta or settlement grass (*Cynodon plectostachyus*) occupies younger glades (5 to 30 years old) in parts of Kenya, while scholars have used African foxtail grass (*Cenchrus ciliaris*) to identify Iron Age sites in South Africa.

Manyattas like this one become nutrient hot spots.

herder-driven hot spots dating back to the Iron Age in South Africa, Botswana, and Israel.

Pastoralism is the most widespread land use on the planet. As the role of prehistoric herders in shaping nutrient flows comes to light, it becomes increasingly clear that—as with most ecosystems— the "wild" savannas of nature documentaries owe a lot to people.

❯ **How to see them:** Look for opportunities to join tours or stay at lodges run by local pastoralists, who are familiar with the plant species and animals that characterize abandoned settlement sites. Some of these grassy glades can also be seen by satellite.

THE WILD LIFE OF **A Dedicated Mufudzi**

■ In the rural grasslands of Zimbabwe, the boys and men who look after grazing livestock are known as mufudzi. Thinkwell Christopher Mbindi, 34, has more than 20 years of experience in this role. Around his farm in Chiredzi, he is regarded as one of the few remaining herders who know how to safely navigate with their animals in the unpredictable savanna.

● **How long have you been a mufudzi?**
When I was at kindergarten in [my hometown near] Zaka, I sometimes accompanied my brothers and cousins to the grazing lands during weekends. By the time I was in sixth grade, it was always my duty to look after our cattle herd in the grasslands during weekends or school holidays.

● **What is your typical day like?**
I usually open up the cattle kraals [wooden shelters] just after sunrise when the vegetation still has its morning dew. I then lead the cows to the place with the greenest pastures on that particular day. I always

keep a watch to make sure that no cattle stray away from the herd.

Sometimes, I team up with herders from other farms or villages and put our cows together. The cows will graze as a large herd and we watch them as a team. At sunset, we separate the cattle and each one of us drives his herd home.

● **Besides watching the cows, what else do you do in the savanna?**
It can be quite lonely with the cows in the grasslands even if you have a guy or two beside you. You have to find something to do, something to kill the time when the animals are busy grazing. In my case, I like gathering wild fruits or bird hunting with a slingshot. I am also a fan of gathering up different natural herbs because there are many in the savanna—that is, if you know them.

● **The savanna grasslands can be dangerous. How do you stay safe?**
You have to know the food chains and even the behavior of different creatures. The presence of mice, bird nests, or even frogs at a particular place is likely to attract dangerous snakes. Dead tree trunks are favorite

habitats for scorpions. You need to know the ecosystem, and you need some luck, too.

● **What do you think is the biggest threat to the savannas?**
The world must know that the savanna grasslands are under threat just like the animals that live in them. People are building, digging, burning, farming, and applying herbicides in grasslands. The grasslands where our cows used to graze back in my village when I was a teenager are now barren grounds with almost nothing growing on them.

● **What was your worst experience in the savannas?**
I won't forget the day I was stung by a couple of wasps right on my eye. And to make it worse, I was planning to get introduced to my in-laws the following day. I had no option but to postpone the appointment because I could not meet them for the first time with a swollen eye! ■

This interview was translated from Shona by Cecil Dzwowa.

Sharp-Nosed Grass Frogs

High-performing, internationally acclaimed athletes

RANGE: Across sub-Saharan Africa
SPECIES: Sharp-nosed grass frog
(*Ptychadena oxyrhynchus*)

Sharp-nosed grass frogs, commonplace in the savannas of sub-Saharan Africa, are rather shy and unassuming. But thanks to their extraordinarily long and brawny legs, this otherwise diminutive species has propelled itself into sporting history on more than one occasion.

After Mark Twain published his hit short story "The Celebrated Jumping Frog of Calaveras County" in 1865, frog derbies became a favorite pastime of eccentric communities around the world. The main event is the triple jump, where the total distance of three consecutive leaps is recorded.

In 1954, South African naturalist Walter Rose entered a male sharp-nosed grass frog called Leaping Lena into that nation's first Frog Olympics, correctly predicting a first-place win. In fact, Lena—whom Rose described as a "perfect little jumping machine"—leaped 32 feet and 3 inches (9.75 m), smashing the world record at the time.

Believing that American bullfrogs were superior jumpers, herpetologists on the other side of the Atlantic responded with polite skepticism—until the following year, when, legend has it, an African frog (exact species unknown) upset the illustrious Calaveras County Jumping Frog Jubilee in Angels Camp, California, by leaping right off the playing field and into the crowd. The event organizers changed the rules after that, excluding all frogs smaller than 4 inches long, including *Ptychadena oxyrhynchus*.

As the sport took off in South Africa, thousands of hopeful amphibian athletes vied for gold and glory. By August 1958, a single frog on local barter markets fetched no fewer than four homing pigeons. Previously, they had traded one for one.

Meanwhile, complex regulations were drafted to protect the swell of entrants. Jockeys were forbidden from coaxing their frogs by imitating mating calls or the sound of hissing snakes. But tickling, cooing, whistling, singing, waving red flags, and playing bagpipes or concertinas were all permitted.

South African frog-jumping reached its zenith in 1977, when frog aficionado Sue Fourie entered a female sharp-nosed grass frog named Santjie into a derby in the small town of Paulpietersburg. Santjie sailed 33 feet and 9 inches (9.8 m)—longer than a stretch limo—trouncing the record and winning the much-coveted crown. (For context, the triple jump world record for humans, whose legs are roughly nine times as long as your average grass frog's, is just 60 feet [18 m].)

Today, more than 40 years later, frog derbies are a thing of the past in South Africa, meaning the savanna's sharp-nosed grass frogs are largely left to leap—and enjoy their legacy—in peace. ❯ **How to see them:** Listen for a high-pitched trill coming from the grass after it rains, and then keep your eyes peeled for an impressive leap.

Skittish and notoriously hard to catch, the sharp-nosed grass frog is just 2.5 inches (6.4 cm) long.

Stargazing Dung Beetles

To fulfill their vital role, these insects moonlight as astronomers.

RANGE: Semi-arid regions in southern Africa
SPECIES: *Scarabaeus satyrus*, a nocturnal African dung beetle

◆ Nocturnal dung beetles hold one of the savanna's most fundamental jobs. Each night, these committed insects help break down the piles of poop that giraffes, elephants, and other herbivores left behind over the course of the day. After flying to these fragrant heaps—sometimes from miles off—each beetle sculpts a scoop of droppings into a ball larger than his own body and carefully rolls it away.

But it's not just the poop shift for these guys. In addition to their deep familiarity with excrement, they are galactically inspired: *Scarabaeus satyrus* is one of the only species known to gaze at—and use—the Milky Way.

It all comes down to navigation. After his dung ball is constructed, a beetle rolls it in a straight line away from the dung pile, heading in any direction. But he must avoid rolling around in circles—if the beetle bumps into another of his kind, they might try to steal the ball.

So the beetle becomes a tiny astronomer. Before he leaves the heap, he will climb up onto his dung ball and spin around, scanning the night sky until he finds a celestial landmark. As the beetle rolls, he repeatedly refers to this landmark to ensure he doesn't go off course.

When it's available, the moon makes a good beacon. But beetles can navigate in straight lines even when the moon is not visible. This puzzled scientists, until one night a research team in South Africa investigating the question looked up and saw the blazing, sky-wide sash of the Milky Way, making them wonder if the beetles saw it, too.

Compared with human vision, which is sharp enough to resolve stars as discrete pinpricks in a black sky, nocturnal dung beetles enjoy only a blurry view of the cosmos. On the other hand, because their eyes are adapted to nighttime living, the beetles are more sensitive to the dim, cloudy pattern of the galaxy than we are. And because their eyes have a wide field of view, they see almost the entire sky, horizon to horizon, all at once. After years of experiments—some of which involved beetle-centric programming at the Johannesburg Planetarium—the research team proved it: *S. satyrus* dung beetles use the bright splotches of our galaxy as landmarks to help them go in straight lines, and they start rolling in circles when they can't see the stars.

Once properly oriented, a beetle pushes his dung ball to a special spot and buries it underground as a food stash. If he's lucky, a female may even mate with him and lay her eggs in his cached dung. And so earthly cycles continue, with a little help from the rest of the universe. ❭ **How to see them:** Wait next to a pile of dung after sunset.

Navigating by the Stars

Compared with geologic features, which erode and shift, stars can act as more or less constant waypoints over long timescales. Scientists suspect that, in addition to African dung beetles, a few other nonhuman species may have evolved astronomical navigation skills.

Indigo buntings (*Passerina cyanea*), garden warblers (*Sylvia borin*), and other migratory bird species seem to check the starry sky like a compass while traveling long distances. As chicks, indigo buntings learn to recognize the North Star, Polaris, as the only spot in the sky that stands still while Earth rotates. During spring and fall migrations, they use nearby constellations to find that part of the sky again.

Harbor seals (*Phoca vitulina*) may also look skyward over long ocean journeys. In a series of experiments in the 2000s, researchers proved a seal named Nick could see almost as many stars in the sky as humans can, and then showed that Nick and his brother Malte could learn how to swim toward the bright star Sirius.

Fluorescent Mysteries of the Animal Kingdom

Springhares, which are found on the savannas of South and East Africa, are in most ways what you might call average mammals. But just a few years ago, scientists discovered an illuminating springhare secret. Under ultraviolet light, their coats—normally a yawn-worthy beige—glow hot pink.

They're not the only animals with this mysterious property. A number of unexpected land animals display fluorescence, a physical reaction in which pigments take in ultraviolet light—which humans and many other mammals cannot see—and transform it into light within the visible spectrum.

In many cases, including with the springhare, the experts studying this phenomenon have no idea why it occurs. Here's a crayon box's worth of fluorescent animals to puzzle over.

OPOSSUMS (order Didelphimorphia) • In the 1980s, blacklight-wielding scientists roved the halls of several notable US natural history museums and brought back reports that "there was no furry area which did not fluoresce in at least one kind of opossum." Their admittedly haphazard study found an opossum species whose back fluoresced with rose and violet stripes, one whose belly glowed lavender with yellow spots, and one whose dorsal decorations were maroon while the ventral ones were peach. Unfortunately for all of us, no one has yet followed up to produce a full color table.

SPRINGHARES (genus *Pedetes*) • Researchers investigating the springhare's shocking pink fluorescent layer found that it sometimes has a patchy pattern. This may help with camouflage: If a springhare's predators are sensitive to UV light, absorbing that light and reemitting it at a different wavelength might be a better option than reflecting it directly. But that's just a theory; it might also be random or have another use entirely.

FLYING SQUIRRELS (genus *Glaucomys*) • The contemporary wave of fluorescent mammal-spotting was spurred by biologist Jonathan Martin. Martin was out with a UV flashlight in his Wisconsin yard looking for lichens—known glowers—when he caught a flying squirrel in the beam and was greeted by a flash of bubble gum pink. Further experiments revealed that all three species of North American flying squirrel display a similar hue under UV.

BUDGERIGARS (*Melopsittacus undulatus*) • Many parts of many birds—from snowy owl wings to puffin beaks—glow in various shades under UV light. As is the case for mammals, it's unclear how birds might use any information contained in fluorescence, or whether they can even see it. The best-studied avian example is likely the budgerigar, whose cheeks and crown fluoresce yellow. In 2002, researchers covered some budgies' bright spots with sunscreen and found that those birds suddenly became less attractive mates, suggesting that the birds may see (and like) these adornments.

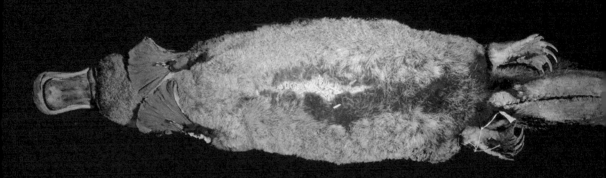

PLATYPUSES (*Ornithorhynchus anatinus*) • Platypuses officially joined the pantheon of glowing mammals in 2020, bolstering their reputation for reliable weirdness. UV light turns their fur from a staid chocolate brown to a chlorinated teal. Even before their fluorescence was confirmed by testing, mushroom hunters in Australia had occasionally come across road-killed platypuses whose coats shone in this way.

NAMIB SAND GECKOS (*Pachydactylus rangei*) • Namib sand geckos have green fluorescent patches around their eyes and along their sides, like racing stripes. These trimmings are much brighter than your typical animal fluorescence—they reflect 12.5 percent of the light they're exposed to, potentially thanks to special cells that may mirror and amplify the effects of the pigments. Researchers think the fluorescent patches might soak up and reemit moonlight, allowing the geckos to flash signals to each other so that they can more easily meet up to socialize and lick condensed fog off each other's bodies.

ORNATE JUMPING SPIDERS (*Cosmophasis umbratica*) • Like budgies, ornate jumping spiders appear to use their glowy bits to attract each other. Males of this species have special body patches that fluoresce green when they assume a particular (clearly sexy) posture: flexing their abdomens, arching their legs, and wiggling their front appendages, or palps. Females have the same fluorescence, but it's on their palps instead. A 2007 experiment found that spiders in high-UV environments courted each other with great enthusiasm, while blocking UV made them uninterested.

PAPER WASP NESTS • The current record for land fluorescence belongs not to an animal, but to an impressive secretion. Larvae of *Polistes brunetus*, a paper wasp species found in Vietnam, spin cocoons out of self-produced silk that glows three times brighter than any known land animal. Clumps of cocoons hang from trees in  the forest and shine like tennis balls even when not directly illuminated. Researchers speculate that the fluorescent compounds in the silk may act almost like blue light glasses, protecting the growing larvae from harmful UV rays while still letting in the light signals that trigger metamorphosis. But, as usual, they just don't know for sure.

POLKA DOT TREE FROGS (*Boana punctata*) • Another impressive set of glowboys is the polka dot tree frogs, South American rainforest dwellers who shine a spotty aquamarine. This is all the more impressive considering that their skin is normally translucent. Researchers have determined that the glow comes from chemical compounds known as hyloins, which circulate through the frogs' lymph systems and make them up to 30 percent brighter during twilight, when they are most active.

OCEANIA

Firehawks

Some birds just want to watch the world burn.

RANGE: Australian grasslands

SPECIES: Black kite (*Milvus migrans*), whistling kite (*Haliastur sphenurus*), and brown falcon (*Falco berigora*)

◆ Many of us consider fire making to be a uniquely human skill, like doing mathematical proofs or cooking macaroni and cheese. In the tropical savannas of Australia, though, birds of prey also start blazes, piggybacking off existing burns to commit dramatic acts of arson. While skeptics call this behavior accidental, many experts, including First Nations people and local fire managers, see it as anything but.

Birds of all types treat burning grasslands like buffets, says Bob Gosford, an ethno-ornithologist in Australia's Northern Territory. Birds that eat small insects will hover high up in smoke plumes, catching the bugs rocketed upward by the heat. Larger carnivores will chase down mammals and snakes fleeing the front, or they'll wait until the flames have passed and clean up the leftover barbecue. But a few select species seem to actually *start* fires: black kites, whistling kites, and brown falcons, which observers tend to group under the term "firehawks."

Firehawks are generally well known to First Nations people who live in these areas, and several groups incorporate their behaviors into ceremonies. In stories gathered by Gosford and his colleagues, fire brigade workers describe these birds circling high in the air, looking for smoke plumes. When they find one, they'll dive down, pick up flaming sticks in their claws or beaks, fly aways, and drop them elsewhere—generally just ahead of the burn line. As the fire takes hold in a new area and animals scatter, the birds feast.

Fire managers are often impressed by the kites and falcons and their apparently sophisticated understanding of burn dynamics. "It's pretty clear from most observers, and to me and my colleagues, that the birds do this intentionally," says Gosford. Firehawks have been seen working in groups of up to three dozen, taking turns dropping branches. They also seem to approach the job strategically, bringing the fire across creeks, roads, or firebreaks and to places that will burn quickly and drive out food. One observer reported a kite lobbing a burning twig straight into a pile of recently mown dried grass.

Their success can pose a problem for the brigades. When a new blaze flares up and no one is sure why, workers will blame birds, says Gosford: "'[Expletive] kites are at it again,' you know?"

Annoying as they may sometimes be, firehawks deserve some credit. First Nations communities have been using controlled burns to manage Australia's ecosystems for tens of thousands of years. As parts of the land currently heal from cattle ranching, these rejuvenating strategies are becoming more and more popular—and they may have been inspired by firehawks. In the 1960s, journalist David Lockwood published a book he described as the autobiography of Waipuldanya, of the First Nations Alawa tribe, in which Waipuldanya

tells of the fire-hunting techniques that may have led to this form of management as being potentially "learnt . . . from the birds" (although the account's accuracy and actual provenance are difficult to know).

Whether or not firehawks inspired humans, Gosford thinks they at least deserve credit for their own actions. "It's easy to say, 'Oh, birds don't have sentience, they don't have reason,'" he says. "But I think the more you look at how birds behave, it's easy to impute that they actually do." ⟩ **How to see them:** This behavior is rarely witnessed and has never even been filmed. Your best (and safest) bet is to accompany a fire manager during a controlled burn.

Kangaroo Grass

These unusually mobile seeds are hopping back into the spotlight.

RANGE: Africa, Asia, Oceania, and across Australia
SPECIES: Kangaroo grass (*Themeda triandra*)

◆ Like its bouncy namesake, kangaroo grass has a dramatic way of getting around. Each of the plant's seeds has a long black tail called an awn. When a mature seed falls to the ground and its awn gets wet, the awn corkscrews into a spiral. As it dries out, it straightens. That simple snakelike movement propels the seed, which wriggles and hops across the landscape until it lands in a spot where the earth is soft enough to burrow into.

A light shower or a dewy night is enough to coil up the awn again, which screws the seed further into the soil. "Over time, it will twist significantly into the ground"—a clever way to avoid getting dried out or snapped up before it can grow, says Bob Godfree, a plant scientist with the Australian government.

This survival trick, among others, may have helped kangaroo grass carpet the continent. Individual tussocks can live for 50 years and survive burning and drought.

The nutritious, springy seeds are a critical food source for browsing animals—and humans. Grindstones found at archaeological sites in New South Wales suggest that Aboriginal people have been making bread from grains like kangaroo grass for at least 30,000 years. When colonization ended their traditional management of the land and European settlers brought sheep, cattle, and invasive weeds, the once-vast kangaroo grasslands were destroyed in a matter of decades.

This grass is ready to hop.

But a reclamation is underway. Regenerative farmers are now experimenting with planting the spiky species as a perennial, drought-resistant, pesticide-free alternative to traditional pasture. And as part of a larger native foods revival, Aboriginal writer and historian Bruce Pascoe is trialing different techniques for milling the seed into a nutty, protein-packed flour that can be used in cakes, crumpets, and bread. A cultural legacy, an ecosystem keystone, sustainability potential, and undeniable tastiness—it's high time for this grass to bounce back. ⟩ **How to see it:** You can find kangaroo grass in ungrazed grasslands and grassy woodlands across Australia, or try Sydney's Royal Botanic Garden.

Seeds on the Move

Even plants and fungi that appear rooted in place often survive through mobility. Like kangaroo grass with its corkscrew tails, many seeds and spores use special appendages to hitchhike across the landscape—flying with the wind, floating down a stream, or bundling themselves into the fuzzy coat of an animal. Here are a few grassland species that have found creative ways to spread out.

BOX ELDERS (*Acer negundo*) • Some seeds need wings to fly. The box elder is a shady maple found in grasslands throughout the United States and Canada. A mature tree produces clumps of winged seeds, called samaras, that dangle from the ends of branches like handfuls of butterflies. When the samaras fall, they spin in the wind like helicopters before landing and germinating a short distance from the original tree. **①**

PURPLE-SPORED PUFFBALLS (*Calvatia cyathiformis*) • The purple-spored puffball contains billions of single-celled deep-purple spores, each just 3 to 6 micrometers in size. Scattered in pastures in temperate parts of the United States and Australia, this mushroom can become so laden with spores that its insides resemble a dense chocolate cake. By that point, any disturbance—a raindrop, the nudge of an animal, or a gust of wind—can knock the spores loose in a cloudy puff. **②**

COMMON MILKWEEDS (*Asclepias syriaca*) • Milkweed uses the wind to travel over open fields in North America's prairies, sometimes for miles. Each milkweed seed is capped by a pappus, an umbrella of downy hairs that allows it to catch a ride with a strong gust. Pappus seeds are common among grassland wildflowers—most of us have helped disperse a similar plant, the dandelion, by blowing on its seed head. **③**

WOOLLY CROTONS (*Croton capitatus*) • Other plant species must find the energy to disseminate within themselves. Woolly croton, which is found in open, grassy areas of the southern United States, disperses through a mechanism called "explosive dehiscence" or "ballistic seed projection." This plant grows a hairy, spherical capsule containing three oblong seeds. When the fruit matures, tension splits open the capsule and launches the seeds around 10 feet (3 m) away. **④**

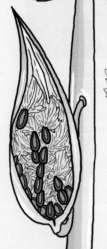

STICKSEEDS (*Hackelia* spp.) • Stickseed plants produce small, barbed fruits that stick to animal fur like Velcro, as pictured here on this black bear's fur. (In fact, the design of Velcro was directly inspired by a similar plant, burdock.) Inadvertent dispersal of seeds on the outside of animals, known as epizoochory, is a common tactic among grassland plants. Scientists in Oklahoma's Tallgrass Prairie Preserve once collected hair from a herd of about 100 bison and discovered seeds from at least 76 different plant species. ⑤

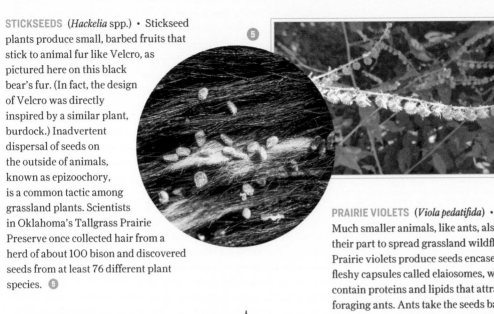

PRAIRIE VIOLETS (*Viola pedatifida*) • Much smaller animals, like ants, also do their part to spread grassland wildflowers. Prairie violets produce seeds encased in fleshy capsules called elaiosomes, which contain proteins and lipids that attract foraging ants. Ants take the seeds back to their colony, where they feed the elaiosomes to their larvae and leave the rest of the seed intact—ready to grow in the nutrient-rich soil of the ant mound. This process of ant-mediated dispersal is called myrmecochory. ⑦

WILD TULIPS (*Tulipa sylvestris*) • The wild tulip's native range extends from the Mediterranean to western China, but gardeners have brought it far and wide. Now it can be found in floodplain grasslands throughout Europe, thanks to its penchant for hydrochory, or seed dispersal via water. The tulip's floating bulb has allowed it to spread in any direction rivers flow—scientists in Germany's Aller River floodplain found that wild tulip bulbs can bob on the water for up to 11 days. When a bulb finds itself on dry land, it finally germinates. ⑥

CANDELABRA LILIES (*Brunsvigia bosmaniae*) • Each summer, on South Africa's Western Cape, candelabra lilies grow domes of fragrant pink flowers. After pollination by moths, these flowers become fruiting heads and dry in the sun. The heads then detach from the plant and tumble across the wind-swept veld like a handful of toy jacks, dropping seeds as they go. Unlike the common tumbleweed, aka the Russian thistle, which detaches from its roots and rolls across the plains, the candelabra lily stays rooted in place, sending its emissaries in all directions. ⑧

Moodjars

Parasitism never looked so good.

RANGE: Southeastern Australia
SPECIES: Moodjar (*Nuytsia floribunda*), also known as the Western Australia Christmas tree

◆ Aboveground, a single moodjar can look like a shrub, a tree, or even an entire grove. But it's actually a variety of mistletoe, and a parasite that derives its nutrition from its neighbors. Special organs in the moodjar's roots, called haustoria, entwine and penetrate the roots of nearby plants, sucking out water and sugar.

Moodjar siphons off just a bit from each helper so as to thrive without killing them. It's not picky about species, sometimes even trying to tap in to twigs, rocks, or underground cables. "You'll be on email, chatting to your parents or whatever, and the [internet or cable] goes out," says botanist David Watson. "It's like, 'Dammit! Mistletoe!'"

Thanks to this stone soup–style approach, the moodjar is the largest parasitic plant in the world—specimens can reach the height of utility poles. Success is also evident in its spectacular flowers, whose seasonal appearance inspires the plant's other name, the Western Australia Christmas tree. In local Noongar culture, recently departed souls are said to rest on moodjar branches until the plant flowers, at which point they make their way to the spirit world.

Blazing yellow orange and gesturally explosive, a flowering moodjar is large enough to be visible from space, Watson says—that is, unless the plant's roots cut the cable that runs the satellite station, as allegedly happened to an Australian NASA outpost back in the 1960s. If that's the case, you'll just have to look at it from the ground.

Cane Toad Front

A warty army advances across Australia.

RANGE: A slowly growing stripe of territory across northern Australia
SPECIES: Cane toad (*Rhinella marina*)

◆ Like many seemingly intractable problems, Australia's cane toad invasion began because someone was trying to help. In the 1930s, beetles were munching up sugarcane crops in the state of Queensland. Seeking a nonchemical intervention, the Bureau of Sugar Experiment Stations decided to gather a hundred or so cane toads overseas and release their offspring to take care of the bugs.

Ninety years later, there are more than 200 million cane toads in Australia. They did not eat the beetles, which live too high up in the sugarcane for them to reach. Instead, they began taking over the continent, colonizing about half of Queensland, then moving up and over into the Northern Territory.

These rampaging toads are poisoning native species and resisting most interventions. They're also becoming ever more powerful. The toads now leading the invasion are the fastest- and farthest-moving known, traveling—and advancing the front—more than half a mile every single night.

Cane toads are a classic invasive species: The suite of traits that allows them to survive in reasonable numbers in their home range of Central and South America makes them near-invincible in a new place. In the Americas, many predators can handle the milky poison the toads produce. In Australia, most can't. Quolls, goannas, and other reptiles and marsupials that eat the toads are particularly vulnerable to the toxin, and some species have neared local extinction when the toad front has moved through. The toads also lay tens of thousands of eggs per year, in clutches much larger than those of native frogs, and the sheer number of hungry toads out there puts competitive pressure on smaller amphibians and reptiles.

While people are trying to slow the tide, making a dent in the population has proved quite difficult. Volunteer groups called "toadbusters" often end up

> **How to see them:** In their blooming season (October through February), moodjars are hard to miss. At other times, look for gracefully bent trunks supporting fragile, tuber-like branches.

Better, faster, stronger

rounding up the louder and more densely packed males and missing the shyer females, who successfully lay eggs. So, increasingly, conservationists and concerned citizens are instead trying to help vulnerable animals learn how to live safely with the toads. One strategy involves feeding native predators bits of cane toad sausage—just enough to make them a little sick and thus put them off the taste.

It's hard to fight an enemy that's always learning. The fastest, strongest toads hop themselves up to the invasion front and reproduce with each other, producing super-skilled offspring that advance farther in turn. As the front moves forward into the desert, the toads are adapting surprisingly well to the hot, dry climate, sticking to riverbanks or hopping fast and far after rains. A smaller battalion is heading down the southeast coast, up into the cold mountains, and doing fine there as well. Experts predict the toads will reach the west coast of Australia soon—by the time you're reading this, they may already be there.

Studies have found that as the cane toads increase in vigor, they're also becoming more cannibalistic: Cane toad tadpoles in Australia eat far more of their hatchmates than those in South America. In the end, the only thing that can stop an invading cane toad might be another cane toad. **❯ How to see them:** The near-fearless toads are pretty easy to spot anywhere in their range, from Cairns in the east through to the advancing western front (which, as of this writing, was fittingly in Darwin).

Why Grasslands Get Overlooked

Australia's temperate grasslands have been compared to an old-growth forest in miniature: hundreds of delicate plant species, some of which can live for more than a century. These fields of dancing grass used to stretch across the continent's southeast; now, less than 1 percent remain. While Aboriginal people managed the grasslands for thousands of years, for modern city dwellers it can be easy to assume these islands of biodiversity are nothing more than wastelands ripe for development.

It's not that grasslands have an image problem, says Kathryn Williams, an environmental psychologist at the University of Melbourne; instead, most people simply don't see them at all. That's partly the fault of our biology: Studies show that people are drawn to landscapes with trees, flowers, and watercourses, suggesting there may be an evolutionary advantage to valuing places that provide food, water, and shelter.

Other studies suggest we prefer scenes that appear both complex and coherent and show some evidence of human management. To the untrained eye, a flat, treeless, "messy" grassland might be interpreted as "a homogeneous paddock," says Williams—which may explain why few people are chaining themselves to tussocks to protect them from bulldozers.

But worldviews are shaped by culture as well as biology, and with exposure and education, Williams says, culture can change. Protecting the last remaining fragments of grasslands will help give everyone the chance to encounter the wonder and complexity found there, which becomes so clear when we take a closer look.

EURASIA

Glacier Mice

These mysterious moss balls travel together—but why?

RANGE: Glacier mice have been found in Alaska, Iceland, Svalbard, and Venezuela.
SPECIES: Various mosses, including spiky-tipped *Racomitrium* spp., yellow-green *Drepanocladus berggrenii*, and long-nosed *Grimmia longirostris*

◆ The iced-over landscapes found past the edges of the tundra can seem as stark and empty as alien worlds. If visitors are lucky, they may even run into a glacier's version of little green men: charmingly verdant, curiously nomadic glacier mice.

Glacier mice are not actually mice. (They got their name in 1950 from an observant Icelander who wrote to the *Journal of Glaciology* describing some encounters with "jökla-mýs.") Instead, they're free-rolling balls of moss, each about the size and shape of a sourdough loaf. "You pick one up, and it's wet and mossy and squishy—kind of like a big sponge," says glaciologist Timothy Bartholomaus.

Glacier mice have been found to comprise any of a number of different moss species. They can live for many years and provide plush homes for many smaller glacial creatures: A census of glacier mice in Iceland identified everything from nematodes to tardigrades tucked into the moss.

Each blob is likely formed when a spore from a nearby forest drifts over and is lucky enough to land on a dirty patch of glacier. Combined with sun and meltwater, the thinking goes, the sediment provides enough nutrients for the moss to grow into a hefty ball—although this is merely "one of our hunches," says Bartholomaus.

But most mysterious of all is the mosses' penchant for group travel. The balls are usually found in large, loose associations, as though recently spilled out of a sack. Every single day, the whole community roams together on an extremely slow pilgrimage to who knows where.

Beginning in 2009, Bartholomaus and several colleagues tracked the movements of a few dozen glacier mouse specimens on Root Glacier in Alaska. They found that each tended to rove about an inch per day—sometimes to the south and other times to the west, but always in sync with its brethren. "They move in this schooling fashion, like a migratory herd," he says. Their movement patterns could not be explained by sun, wind, or—so far—anything at all.

Although the question of what drives these fuzzy travelers completely baffles Bartholomaus, he is confident people will continue to try to understand their culture. "They're just exceptionally bizarre," he says. "It's hard to resist them." ❯ **How to see them:** Once you make it onto a glacier, they're hard to miss. Iceland's Falljökull has a well-studied herd, as does Alaska's Root Glacier.

MAJOR MIGRATIONS

Many animals make wildly ambitious journeys every year, whether by hoof, wing, or fin. Here are some of the most notable.

❶ CARIBOU *(Rangifer tarandus)*

If you ranked land animals by migration distance, different groups of caribou would occupy the top five spots. The Bathurst herd, from central Canada, takes the gold with their 840-mile (1,350 km), lichen-fueled tromp through the snow.

❷ CONVERGENT LADYBUG
(Hippodamia convergens)

Weather radars sometimes pick up these ladybugs, which migrate from western North America's coasts and valleys to the foothills of mountain ranges in loose, miles-wide clouds.

❸ CARIBBEAN SPINY LOBSTER
(Panulirus argus)

Every autumn, populations of these spiky crustaceans march for miles from the shallows into deeper waters, lined up antennae-to-tail to reduce drag.

❺ ARCTIC TERN
(Sterna paradisaea)

The world's best-traveled animal, each Arctic tern may fly 1.5 million miles (2.4 million km) over her 30-year lifetime, taking a zigzagging path between the poles.

❹ HUMPBACK WHALE
(Megaptera novaeangliae)

Certain groups of humpbacks undertake one of the longest known mammal migrations as they travel thousands of miles from their warm equatorial breeding area to their polar feeding grounds.

⑨ GRAY WOLF (*Canis lupus*)

Non-migratory species who follow migrators can end up traveling far distances, too. In 2004, a gray wolf wearing a tracking collar set a terrestrial movement record, chasing kulan and other prey 4,503 miles (7,246 km) across the Mongolian steppe over the course of a year.

⑧ STRAW-COLORED FRUIT BAT
(*Eidolon helvum*)

In the wet season, bats from across sub-Saharan Africa sync their flight schedules and meet up in Zambia to eat fruit. Numbering up to 10 million in some years, they constitute the world's most multitudinous mammal migration.

⑩ BORNEAN BEARDED PIG (*Sus barbatus*)

The world's only migrating swine, Bornean bearded pigs travel at night through the forest on paths worn smooth by previous peripatetic pig generations, following the ripening of nuts. These journeys can stretch hundreds of miles and may include swimming between islands.

⑦ BLUE WILDEBEEST (*Connochaetes taurinus*)

Much of the action of the Serengeti is concentrated in and around this looping migration, a journey that averages 930 miles (1,496 km) per year.

⑥ GLOBE SKIMMER DRAGONFLY (*Pantala flavescens*)

These finger-length dragonflies may accomplish the world's longest migration relative to body size, riding gusts of wind thousands of miles across the Indian Ocean.

⑪ BANDED STILT
(*Cladorhynchus leucocephalus*)

Rather than migrating at predictable times, these long-legged birds travel hundreds of miles from the shoreline to breed in normally dry outback lakes right after rain fills them up. It's unclear how the stilts know when it rains so far away—they may pick up smells or low-frequency storm sounds.

⑫ ADÉLIE PENGUIN
(*Pygoscelis adeliae*)

Adélie penguins need the perfect amount of sunlight and sea ice in order to thrive. At least one population spends the year following this confluence of conditions in an 8,000-mile (13,000 km) circle off the coast of Antarctica.

Lemmings

Suicide cultists, bloodthirsty berserkers, or the most important animals in the Arctic?

RANGE: Throughout the Arctic
SPECIES: There are roughly 14 lemming species, including the brown lemming (*Lemmus sibiricus*), Norway lemming (*Lemmus lemmus*), northern collared lemming (*Dicrostonyx groenlandicus*), and Arctic lemming (*Dicrostonyx torquatus*).

◆ Despite what you might have heard, lemmings do not, as one furry mass, intentionally scurry to the edges of high Arctic cliffs and fling themselves off to perish in the waves.

Roughly every few years, though, lemmings do suddenly burst from beneath the melting Arctic snow in huge numbers. They ravage the tundra, consuming bushels of berries, acres of roots and shoots, and every smidge of lichen they can sink their sharp little teeth into. And sometimes, if their numbers become too great, they make for less cramped pastures by driving themselves over every obstacle in their path, even if that obstacle is . . . a high cliff.

Lemmings falling off cliffs is a knock-on effect of the rodent's vertiginous reproductive cycle. While researchers have only recently begun to understand exactly how it works, it bears similarities to boom-and-bust whirlwinds experienced by other prey animals, like snow-shoe hares.

During the winter, lemmings do not hibernate. Rather, they spend their very active days scampering around the warm tunnels they dig under the snow, where they have access to food—the already-formed buds of next summer's plants, mosses, and lichens—and protection from the elements.

In years with fewer lemmings, there are also fewer predators around to eat them: Migratory birds, such as snowy owls and skuas,

Norway lemmings like this one are brave beyond their size.

move on when there aren't enough lemmings, and foxes, stoats, and other toothy mammals don't tend to breed as well during low-lemming years. With the pressure off, the tunneling lemmings are free to make babies. Lots and lots of babies.

By spring and summer, "you literally have an explosion of lemmings"—as many as 100 times more than there are in slower years, says Dominique Fauteux, a research scientist at the Canadian Museum of Nature.

Subsets of these mobs are sometimes felled by poorly placed cliffs. But more lemmings are taken down by the aforementioned owls, foxes, and stoats, whose own populations are bolstered as they munch their way through the lemming buffet. The next spring, there are far fewer lemmings again, and the cycle rumbles on.

Scientists may have figured out the cliff-jumping, but some lemming behaviors during population peaks remain strange. Norway lemmings, for example, have been filmed aggressively charging animals 10 times their size when numbers are up, like tiny Viking berserkers. "It's a question mark why they do this because they're defenseless," says Fauteux. Even a fox isn't likely to be deterred by a lemming, however ferocious he appears. Though most other lemming species are pretty docile—the brown lemming, Fauteux says, is generally "just, like, chilling"—collared lemmings are notorious biters and have been known to fling themselves on their backs and scream when disturbed by researchers. ❯ **How to see them:** Look for a tiny fuzzy creature popping out of the tundra. Aim for a boom year and you probably won't be able to avoid them.

Waxcap Grasslands

A rainbow of colors springs up through the grasses, thanks to a mysterious underground organism.

RANGE: All continents but Antarctica; most common in the United Kingdom
SPECIES: Commonly spotted UK species include the snowy waxcap (*Cuphophyllus virgineus*), meadow waxcap (*Cuphophyllus pratensis*), and parrot waxcap (*Gliophorus psittacinus*).

◆ In unimproved fields close-cropped by grazing animals, you expect to see the stubbled remains of green grasses, the rosette leaves of dandelions, and here and there a mound of moss or a drifting honeybee. But look a little closer. Nearby, raising its glossy head just an inch or two above the soil, you might encounter a creature so jewel-box bright that it shocks your senses: a waxcap mushroom.

It could be a deep purple or black, or an improbably vivid red, yellow, green, or pink. You might see one or two, or a dozen growing in a ring. Get closer still and you'll find that some species, like the orange-red splendid waxcap, smell of honey. As out of place as they may appear, these shiny little fungi aren't recently landed aliens; they're ancient survivors the modern world is only just beginning to understand.

When you spot a shocking scarlet waxcap or a shiny green parrot waxcap, you are seeing only a tiny part of the entire fungus: the fruiting body that emerges to spread spores. Most of the organism lives underground as a network of fine, feathery white threads—the mycelium.

This secret underlayer explains why certain waxcaps, particularly the salmon-pink meadow waxcap, seem to grow in the evocative circles sometimes called "fairy rings." As the mycelium ages, it dies from the center outward, sending waxcaps up to grow around its perimeter.

Shockingly red scarlet waxcaps

The mycelium also holds clues to a longstanding scientific mystery: How do waxcaps thrive in marginal soil, and why do they disappear when nutrients are added? Recent studies show that at least some species of waxcap send tendrils from their mycelia into the roots of nearby plants. These waxcaps feed from their neighbors biotrophically, using them as a kind of living cafeteria.

But plants are not the waxcap's only neighbors. Underneath the verdant green of the grasslands, earthworms, larvae, and other small crawlers make their lives. When these creatures die, they contribute nitrogen to the soil. At least one study suggests that this is the form of nitrogen that the waxcap mycelium can process—and when fertilizers are added to the soil, they can eradicate this crucial underground population.

Waxcap mushrooms' sensitivity means they act as a bellwether species—their presence gives us a measurement of a wild grassland's health. Unfortunately, as people fertilize, plow, and treat soils for human uses, waxcap mushrooms' habitats are shrinking. Today, about 90 percent of waxcap species are considered threatened, and several species, including the ruffled pink waxcap and the frilly-edged yellow-gold citrine waxcap, are on the verge of extinction.

Efforts are underway to track and protect waxcaps. Conservation societies in England and Wales have enlisted the public to help identify waxcap grasslands and perform an annual count of the species found there. And scientists worldwide continue to research the diversity and habits of waxcaps, hoping to find additional ways to protect these bright and fragile emissaries from an underground world. ❯ **How to see them: You are most likely to see waxcaps in late summer and autumn, in close-cropped, unfertilized, unplowed, and well-drained grassy fields.**

Wood Mouse Waypoints

When things start looking unfamiliar, wood mice take a leaf from the scouting handbook.

RANGE: Widespread across Europe and northern Africa
SPECIES: Wood mouse (*Apodemus sylvaticus*)

If you spot a tiny pile of pebbles or shells next time you're walking in a field, try not to kick it out of the way! It could be an integral part of a wood mouse's navigation system. Aside from humans, wood mice are the only animals known to construct signposts, which help them find their way around in the fruitful yet perilous meadows where they make their homes.

Wood mice are built for night navigation. Speedy and sleek, they roam a large area for their small stature, seeking seeds, nuts, and insects. Each night's meandering might take them half a mile within their patch of territory.

But as they're searching for food, these snack-sized mice are also being sought. An attack could arrive at any moment: a tawny owl talon from the sky, a flash of weasel canine in the undergrowth. For safety, the mice follow the cardinal rule of exploration: Know your position at all times so you can scurry back home.

Wood mice's built-in equipment helps with this. Large ears perched on their heads swivel like satellite dishes, and their bulging eyes peer sideways into the gloom, giving them a wide field of view. They also form cognitive maps of landmarks like shrubs in otherwise open landscapes, and they appear to have a built-in magnetic sense that helps them orient themselves. When they stick to the well-trodden paths around their burrows, this mental map-and-compass combo enables them to take the most direct route home when danger looms.

Wood mice roam their territory looking for food like this chestnut.

But as the availability and distribution of food waxes and wanes through the year, a mouse might have to go foraging off-piste. As her nose leads her into an unfamiliar part of the home territory, the enterprising rodent does what any good scout would—she makes a waymark.

As soon as a mouse encounters an area that smells promising, she will drag a conspicuous object to the spot to mark it. She might stack shells, pile leaves, or heap up twigs. (In experiments, mice have even made do with plastic disks provided by scientists.) When she moves on, she brings the marker with her.

Why bother to mark a waypoint? Wood mice will flee to safety with little provocation if a sense of foreboding strikes, and they often sit up on their haunches to scan for danger. Meanwhile, without a distinguishing feature, patches of meadow can all look a bit same-y, even to a mouse. The structures mice build appear to save them time, allowing them to flag important areas so that if they are disturbed, they can quickly return. Using these navigational aids is probably safer than cluttering their territory with scent markers, which could be sniffed out by predators.

Knowledge of their home patch can quite literally mean the difference between life and death. By building their cairns, wood mice stack the odds a little further in their favor. ⟩ **How to see them:** Hyperalert and nocturnal, wood mice aren't the easiest species to spot, although their climbing antics sometimes bring them to bird feeders and nest boxes. But even if you can't find a mouse, you might come across her handiwork—wood mice leave ridged, circular holes in the nuts they have consumed.

Ancient Zombie Pithoviruses

Like cursed mummies, the world's largest viruses can rise from the dead.

RANGE: Beneath the Siberian tundra
SPECIES: *Pithovirus sibericum*

◆ On the Siberian tundra, where temperatures are often colder than those on Mars, the world's largest known virus lies dormant, buried deep in 30,000-year-old permafrost. *Pithovirus sibericum* clocks in at up to 2 micrometers—that's about 15 times the length of an HIV particle, with more than 50 times the number of genes. It uses its bulk to attack single-celled amoebas, sneaking into their cytoplasmic jelly and replicating until the cells split open and die.

Said amoebas have been breathing tiny hypothetical sighs of relief since the Stone Age, when changes in climate encased this pathogenic predator in a frozen tomb. But their reprieve recently ended.

In 2013, virologists Jean-Michel Claverie and Chantal Abergel placed a bunch of tasty amoebas on a permafrost sample that had been excavated years earlier by Russian scientists. When the unicellular creatures started dying, amoeba autopsies showed pithovirus particles inside—proving that "very old viruses can still be alive and well," Claverie says.

The Siberian tundra is full of them, Claverie and Abergel suspect. There, thick, unbroken layers of permafrost span an area almost twice the size of England and penetrate nearly a mile deep into the planet's crust, creating an icy soil prison that freezes microbes in time. Some of them are viruses and germs dating back a million years or more, Claverie says. A little thawing, and it's possible to create a pint-sized Jurassic Park of itty-bitty organisms that flourished long ago.

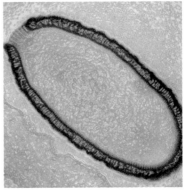

Despite having been locked in ice for millennia, Pithovirus sibericum looks remarkably similar to modern pithovirus strains.

Pithovirus sibericum may be among the largest of these microbes, but it isn't harmful to humans or animals. (Amoebas should stay vigilant, as modern variations of the virus have been found in soil and water across the globe.) Still, its resurrection raises questions about what other unfamiliar pathogens might be trapped in layers of frozen soil—and what happens as warming global temperatures melt deeper into this frozen time capsule. Claverie and Abergel have already discovered a second, completely unique giant virus called *Mollivirus sibericum* lurking in the same permafrost sample.

While some researchers have pooh-poohed concerns about resurrected viruses wreaking havoc on human and animal health, Claverie isn't so quick to dismiss them. "There is a real risk, but it is extremely difficult to assess," he says. "Maybe those viruses caused the extinction of the Neanderthal. We know nothing about this, and now we are playing with that." ⟩ **How to see it:** Might not be the best idea. But if you're dead set on it, bring digging equipment and a microscope.

Pleistocene Park

World-saving time travel, brought to you by herbivores

◆ Silhouetted by the sunset, an American bison quietly chews grass. Next to him are eight other bison—and a musk ox, a camel, and a goat. It's as though Noah's Ark ran aground and spilled out all the ungulates.

These strange grassfellows are inhabitants of Pleistocene Park, a 50-square-mile (130 sq km) experiment in the middle of Siberia. Though the park is small in size, its multispecies employees are attempting something enormous: to bring back a piece of the Ice Age and, in the process, save the global climate.

From about 2.6 million to 12,000 years ago, giant herbivores had the run of the Arctic. Their incessant chewing and tromping continually renewed the tundra's grasses and prevented trees from taking hold. This in turn protected the permafrost, a frozen layer of soil that locks a mother lode of carbon dioxide and other greenhouse gasses underground.

Over time, as humans killed off mammoths, woolly rhinoceroses, and other giant grazers, forests began creeping in, taking over territory that once belonged to the tundra and loosening the permafrost's icy hold. As it melts, the tundra is releasing a gradual, carbon-rich belch that could surpass 100 gigatons before next century. Experts fear these emissions could send the planet's climate past a tipping point and into an even more precipitous warming trend than the one we're currently experiencing.

To slow—or even, eventually, reverse—this process, Pleistocene Park has been hauling in modern-day grazers, asking them to do the work of their forebears. "We are using animals as a tool to convert from one ecosystem to another," says Nikita Zimov, the park's director.

If all goes according to plan, the transplanted animals—moose, camels, horses, bison, musk oxen, goats, and others—will set off a chain reaction that turns down the global thermostat. Their hoof-trampling will break up the insulating snow layer that covers the permafrost, exposing it to frigid temperatures and keeping it a couple of degrees cooler than it would be otherwise. By destroying trees and making room for grasses, they will aerate soil and lock up more carbon in underground masses of roots. And this

RANGE: 50 square miles (130 sq km) in the middle of Siberia, southwest of the Kolyma River
SPECIES: Moose (*Alces alces*), American bison (*Bison bison*), reindeer (*Rangifer tarandus*), and more wild and domestic grazers from around the world

Grazing horses help keep the permafrost cool.

retundrafication will tint the whole environment lighter in color, allowing it to reflect sunlight into the atmosphere instead of soaking it up.

While a simple enough idea in theory, "creation of an ecosystem is not very quick work," says Zimov, who has spent a lot of time filling out customs forms and tricking out shipping containers in order to transport small herds across the world. There are currently a few hundred herbivores in the park—a much lower density than was found during the Pleistocene. While studies so far have shown that every stomp and nibble helps, they also indicate that approximating that former density is necessary to keep things cool enough to make a real difference—and that's across the whole Arctic, not just a Fargo-sized patch.

If the scientists do reach their herbivore goals, there is more to do. A proper ecosystem needs carnivores, too. The shipping containers might eventually hold "tigers, or even African lions," says Zimov, pointing out that these contemporary savanna dwellers are genetically similar to the Siberian cave lions who once dined on grass-fed Pleistocene meat. At that point, our contemporary Noah may be able to step back, he says. "Ideally, by the time I retire, this ecosystem will not need my help."

> **How to see them:** Visiting Pleistocene Park involves a 12-hour, multi-leg flight from Moscow— or you could hitch a ride in a shipping container.

THE WILD LIFE OF A Pleistocene Rewilder

■ As the director of Pleistocene Park, Nikita Zimov has dedicated himself to bringing back the Ice Age tundra—a grand dream that, day-to-day, involves a lot of digging and hay.

• **How did Pleistocene Park start?**
It was a family hobby, to some extent. My dad [Sergey Zimov] started experiments back in the 1980s. He brought a few horses and started to keep them over the winter to see what effect the grazing has. He just wanted to return nature to its original state— that's what the motivation was. At that time, nobody was afraid of global warming; everybody was afraid that a global ice age would start soon.

And then a year later, the Soviet Union collapsed. My dad had to give away horses the very first year because we couldn't maintain them. For 20 years, the development was relatively slow. It's always been a small family project, which was maintained mostly on our labor.

• **What makes a good candidate for a Pleistocene Park grazer?**
In general, we bring small groups of animals, usually 10 or a dozen, and we see which ones do the best. For our purposes, some species are better than others. We always

wanted to get American bison. They can live on their own. It took us 20 years to reach that goal, because they are mostly on a different continent, and it is extremely complicated to bring them here.

Other animals, they need much more attention, and they've been genetically bred and changed by human activity and selection. For example, cows are good for meat and milk. They're not good at living in the wilderness. We managed to bring yaks, thinking that maybe they will be as good as bison—but no, they were not!

• **What is everyday work like in the park?**
The animals at the park are trampling down mosses, shrubs, and lichen to allow grasses to grow better. It takes time, and all that time we need to support them. For example, in the winter, some of the species get support from us because there's just not enough forage for them. So we have rangers who provide extra forage. We take care of the fencing and a generator that provides electricity for the towers and for the research equipment.

• **What is the long-term vision for the park?**

No one ever worked on creating a full ecosystem before. No one has enough information on how to do it right, so neither do I. It's like we are inventing the bike—we knew that this bike existed, and we approximately know that it had two wheels and steering. The rest, we are trying to be creative.

• **Does anyone ever come see you there?**
It's very hard to get to Pleistocene Park. We never have tourists come. Sometimes there are extreme voyagers, and they want to reach someplace in the world that is the hardest to get to. And so sometimes they appear in our town, and they call us and ask if they can visit.

• **Do you expect this project to be replicable in other parts of the world?**
I think it will take several more decades for rewilding ideas to actually become the mainstream. It's still not the general logic. The main general logic is conservation— "We need to preserve nature as we saw it three centuries ago." Rewilding says no, we need to create the nature first, and after that, we'll have something to preserve—something worth preserving. ■

Your Guide to Fashionable Horns and Antlers

Branching tiaras, tapered swoops, elegant helixes: Across the world's grasslands and tundras, otherwise humble grazers lift their heads from the ground to reveal shockingly elaborate headgear. Antlers and horns help their bearers fight predators and competitors, dig up food, show off their fitness, and generally stand out from the herd. Let's take a look—but first, we'll get our terms straight:

Antlers are found only on members of Cervidae, a family that contains more than 40 species of deer. They're made of spongy bone and are grown and shed annually during the breeding season—generally only by males, who use them to fight and court. A pair of antlers is called a rack.

Horns adorn the heads of hooved mammals from the Bovidae and Antilocapridae families. They consist of an inner core of bone surrounded by an outer sheath of keratin—the same material that makes human hair and nails. Specialized hair follicles are responsible for the lifelong growth of the structures, which are permanent and may appear in both male and female animals.

BIG • The moose (*Alces alces*), the world's biggest cervid, also pulls the trophy for largest antlers. Imagine carrying a shopping cart on your head and you'll understand how massive moose antlers can be. Spanning up to 6 feet (1.8 m) across and weighing more than 40 pounds (18 kg), these chandelier-sized racks grace the heads of mature male moose, or bulls, who invest as much energy into growing them as females do into growing calves. ❶

Greater kudu (*Tragelaphus strepsiceros*) have spiral horns that twist artfully above their heads as they roam the grassy savannas and woodlands of eastern and southern Africa. Even with these curls, which take years to grow, each horn can reach nearly 4 feet (1.2 m) in length. Indigenous people of South Africa, including the Venda and Tsonga peoples, historically used a hollow kudu horn as a musical instrument and communication tool known as a phalaphala—its low, dirge-like note can be heard across great distances. ❷

SMALL • The smallest deer in the world, South America's northern pudu (*Pudu mephistophiles*) grows tiny antlers—a pair of short, backward-arching spikes only 2 inches (5 cm) long. These thumb-sized bristles complement the pudu's overall predator avoidance strategy: At 14 inches tall (35.5 cm) and just 13 pounds (5.8 kg), this tiny deer easily

disappears in the tall vegetation of the steppe grasslands. ❸

Dik-diks (*Madoqua* spp.) are slender, house cat–sized antelope that live in the savannas of eastern Africa and eschew the typical herds to remain in mated pairs. Their 3-inch (7.6 cm) horns, which only males carry, are partially hidden by a mohawk-like tuft of fur. Males defend their territories through games of chicken: Rivals charge each other with their tiny horns displayed and jump back before they actually collide, like a pair of opposing magnets. ❹

GNARLY • Male fallow deer (*Dama dama*) grow thick, stubby racks of what are called palmate antlers, which resemble open human palms. An extra set of spikes sits at the base of each male's skull, providing additional defense as they interlock their branched crowns in open grasslands of Europe. ❺

The thick horns of African buffalo (*Syncerus caffer*) often fuse together across the animal's forehead. This elaborate unibrow serves as a protective skull cap, which comes in handy when warding off predators or wrestling other beefy bovids for mates. ❻

DANGEROUS • The giant antlers of the wapiti (*Cervus canadensis*), or American elk, can weigh nearly 40 pounds (18 kg). Male wapiti have twice the neck muscle of females to support this antler weight, which is comparable to carrying a 5-gallon (19 L) bucket of water on your head. This extra strength reduces injury during powerful conflicts for supremacy, which start when a challenger bugles to draw a rival's attention. If he takes the bait, they clash until one of them gives up or dies. **7**

The curled, sharp horns of the gaur (*Bos gaurus*), found in India and Southeast Asia, resemble those of a stereotypical Viking helmet. When threatened, gaurs form a tight circle around the weak and young in the herd and attempt to gore predators with their horns. They have been recorded killing tigers by impalement. **8**

AVANT-GARDE • Female caribou (*Rangifer tarandus*) are the only deer who consistently grow antlers like their male counterparts. Resources in the Arctic tundra are scarce and competition is fierce. Antlers give females an advantage during the harsh winters, allowing them to protect their feeding areas and uncover plants buried in snow. **9** Pronghorn antelope (*Antilocapra americana*) of the North American deserts and prairies bend the rules of horned animals, shedding the keratin sheaths of their horns annually to reveal the bony core within. Their horns are also branched, a trait more often found in antlers. **10**

HORN-ARABLE MENTIONS • The nasal ornamentations of the rhinoceros (family Rhinocerotidae) are not considered true horns: They lack an inner core of bone and are made entirely of keratin. These pseudo-horns help rhinos dig for water, defend turf, clear pathways, and protect against predators. Mother rhinos use their horns as a guide for their calves, keeping mischievous youngsters out of danger with a gentle nudge. Unfortunately, the illegal poaching and trafficking of rhino horns has brought their kind to the brink of extinction. **11**

Although small protrusions jut out of the skull of the giraffe (*Giraffa* spp.) and the males of its closest relative, the okapi (*Okapia johnstoni*), they are not considered true horns or antlers. Instead, they are called ossicones—skin-covered bones that are fused to the skull. Both male and female giraffes grow ossicones, which are used in violent, neck-swinging courtship fights. A male's ossicones may eventually grow bald on top from all the necking. **12**

DISQUALIFIED • While other deer species put all their effort into elaborate headgear, water deer (*Hydropotes inermis*), found in wetlands in China and Korea, don't have any at all. Instead, both males and females grow long, sharp fangs, almost as though they read the antler blueprint upside down. Thanks to roomy tooth sockets and a flexible jaw ligament, they're able to tuck their extravagant canines back so they can more easily graze—and move them forward again to slice at competitors during mating season. **13**

Prickly Russian Thistle

Somersaulting into infamy

RANGE: Native in southeastern Russia and western Siberia; invasive in North America, Australia, southern Africa, and Central and South America
SPECIES: Prickly Russian thistle (*Kali tragus*), also known as windwitch, salsola, or tumbleweed

◆ The town is dusty, sun-beaten, and practically deserted. Saloon doors creak in the breeze. Our hero enters from stage right, moving with a bouncy gait, a long way from home but determined to keep going. No, not the cowboy—the tumbleweed.

The tumbleweeds we know from Westerns are actually the seed-dispersing skeletons of a plant called prickly Russian thistle. When it's alive, this thistle takes the form of a gangly, branching shoot, decorated annually by cute pink flowers. Around August, after its seeds are produced, the plant begins to dry out and die; by fall, it's a desiccated, tangled mess. It soon snaps off from its root and goes for an undead joyride, bringing hundreds of thousands of seeds with it to start the cycle over.

In undisturbed environments—including much of the plant's native range within Russia and Siberia—these tumbleweeds are kept relatively well corralled by tall grass.

But let loose in a mown or otherwise altered landscape, they can keep going and going, wreaking total havoc and begetting equally chaotic offspring.

Russian thistle first arrived in the United States in the 1870s, after some seeds hitched a ride to South Dakota in a bag of flaxseed. Tumbleweeds were soon sprinting across the plains, expanding their reach by about 10 miles (16 km) per year—even faster once they started hitch-hiking on the transcontinental railroad.

By the end of the century, all of the Midwest and clear through to California was essentially a tumbleweed gymnasium. Farmers abandoned their land in order to flee what they called "the evil weed," which stole water from crops, started fires, and spiked horses in the legs until they bled. Various attempts to control the plants with pesticides, fences, moths, and even delicious Dust Bowl–era brined-and-canned thistle recipes did not succeed.

While living tumbleweeds sit quietly (top), dead ones can get up to all kinds of mischief (bottom).

As times change, unforeseen tumbleweed scenarios continue to crop up. Because tumbleweed thrives in disrupted landscapes, it gravitates not just to farmlands but also to residential areas, highways, and even nuclear testing facilities, where the seedlings suck up radioactive waste through their roots and must be pulverized before they roll off and contaminate everything. Their erratic movements even confuse self-driving cars, which tend to make emergency stops for them. This town simply ain't big enough. ❯ **How to see them:** Watch for tumbleweeds bouncing across your field of view in flat parts of the American West.

Extreme Tumbleweed Situations

As tumbleweeds roll their merry, unwanted way through the American landscape, here are some of the strangest ways in which they've piled up.

CHANDLER, ARIZONA, 1957— Every year since 1957, city workers in Chandler have gotten into the spirit of Christmas by gathering about a thousand tumbleweeds, sticking them on a chicken-wire frame in the shape of a wide evergreen, and covering them in lights and glitter.

CLOVIS, NEW MEXICO, 2014— When a storm dumped thousands of tumbleweeds on top of this small town, members of the Air Force had to come dig out the residents, some of whom couldn't see out of their windows.

COMMERCE CITY, COLORADO, 2014— A controlled burn in Rocky Mountain Arsenal National Wildlife Refuge in Colorado got slightly out of control when a fire whirl—a tornado surrounding a core of flame—sucked a horde of tumbleweeds into the air, turning them into a giant flock of flying char-balls.

RICHLAND, WASHINGTON, 2020— A windstorm sent enough tumbleweeds bounding along State Route 240 to halt traffic, and then to completely cover about a quarter mile's worth of stopped cars and semitrucks.

SIMI VALLEY, CALIFORNIA, 2023— A single tumbleweed the size of a small car briefly joined real drivers on a SoCal freeway, rolling ponderously across several lanes of traffic before finding its exit.

WICHITA, KANSAS, PRESENT DAY— Entrepreneurial people across the West sell tumbleweeds as set dressing and home décor. Custom tumbleweed chandeliers made in Wichita can go for thousands of dollars.

Indian Cobras

Charmed, I'm sure.

RANGE: Much of India, Pakistan, Sri Lanka, Bangladesh, southern Nepal, and Bhutan
SPECIES: Indian cobra (*Naja naja*), also known as the spectacled cobra, gokhra (Bengali), and nalla pambu (Tamil)

◆ Like most snakes, Indian cobras don't really want to bite. They'd rather save their energy for laying and guarding eggs and their strikes for rodents and frogs, which they swallow whole.

If pushed, though, an Indian cobra won't just nip—she may "hold on and chew savagely" while pumping as much as 60 percent of her total venom supply through her fangs, as a 2009 toxicology guide from the University of California at San Diego warns. Without proper treatment, a human victim can become paralyzed and die in as little as an hour.

This makes the skills of Pakistan's Jogi snake charmers all the more impressive. Unlike some practitioners, who may remove the snakes' fangs or sew their mouths shut, Jogi charmers do not harm the cobras they work with. Instead, as they'll tell anyone who asks, they enter into agreements with the snakes, promising food and care in exchange for their companionship.

Jogi snake charmers use a special flute, called a murli, that is made of carved gourds and bamboo. During a ritual or performance, a snake charmer sways dramatically with his flute in front of a cobra. Research into snake sensory experiences suggests the cobra perceives this instrument in multiple ways, tracking its movement with her vision, its sound with her internal ears, and the vibrations it produces through tactile sensors in her belly scales.

While there were once hundreds of thousands of Jogi snake charmers in and around Pakistan, the art is quickly dying out. Proponents of the tradition have asked the government to fund a snake charming training center, where new generations could learn the ins and outs (and back-and-forths) of this unique human-reptile relationship. 〉 **How to see them:** Indian cobras are fairly common across a number of habitats—but if you do see one, please don't approach. Jogi snake charmers exhibit their skills in street performances around the country.

Indian or spectacled cobras have eye-like patterns on their hoods.

About 80 miles [130 km] outside of Karachi, Pakistan, 50-year-old Jabal Jogi can often be found sitting with an Indian cobra around his neck, playing his murli, or flute. A member of the nomadic Jogi tribe, Jabal continues a centuries-old tradition of using music and mysticism to charm venomous snakes.

What is a Jogi, and how did you become one?

Jogis are traditional snake charmers. We're born, not made. It's our tribe's calling—and we've been doing it for as long as I, or any of my elders, can remember. The Earth and the Jogi were born together. Our art is passed down from generation to generation. We inherit ancestral wisdom allowing us to smell snakes, communicate with them, and understand them. I never considered doing anything else.

How exactly do you charm or tame a venomous snake? Where do you find them?

We find them near the jungles and undergrowth in Gadap and the Kirthar Mountains. We work with Indian cobras as well as [other snakes including] chamchur, cheingi, dumbi—even water snakes. The Indian cobra is the most popular.

"Taming" a snake is a misconception. We make a sacred pact by invoking Pirs [religious leaders of the Sufi tradition], like Hazrat Suleman. It's a beseeching request or oath. Like chanting, "In loving memory, for the sake of this Pir, come, snake. Make a pact with me."

It's a time-bound arrangement, from six months to one month, fifteen days or even five. But once you've made the pact, you could wear the snake like a necklace.

We believe there are some breeds of unspiritual snakes who don't believe in the saints we do, so we don't charm them. Commercial snake charmers don't care; they resort to cruelty, like grabbing snakes with a wooden stick, sewing their mouths shut, or extracting their venom. That makes the snake weak. It's a totally different, respectful dynamic when you have the Pir's blessing.

Can you tell us about your music and instrument?

Snakes have internal ears. We play a specific dhun [song] for them, passed down from our great-grandfathers, and sway to help them track our movement.

And we make the instrument ourselves, using male and female parts of the aak [Sodom apple or rubber bush] tree for the windpipe. Then we attach a hollowed-out gourd—an extremely bitter, inedible species—using melted honeycomb.

How do you deal with snakebites?

Some Jogis believe stroking peacock feathers on the bite draws out the venom. Some just suck it out. But we know the cure comes from the snake itself. During winter, snakes become less active and burrow underground, so the venom collects in their mouth and solidifies into a black rock.

We harvest that stone or pearl, the manka. It's incredibly potent and immediately draws the venom out, no matter what has bitten you—even a scorpion. I've never been bitten though, because I can sense when it's time for the snake to go.

How do you make a living?

Business is dwindling and unpredictable. During some seasons or festivals, we can make up to 100,000 PKR [US ~$359] in one day. But months can go by when we don't make a single rupee. We scrape together enough for "ghoray ka daana, fakir ka khaana"—the horse's hay and the man's food.

What relationship does your family have with the snakes?

Our kids think of them as best friends. Outside performances and traveling, we don't even keep them in baskets. Humans betray you; they're fickle like that—but snakes? They honor their word and won't harm you or your family after the oath if you treat them right. ∎

This interview was translated from Urdu by Aysha Imtiaz and Saqib Rafique.

Jogis and a cobra perform in Umerkot, Pakistan.

Arctic Tree Line

The tundra's receding hairline

RANGE: An 8,300-ish-mile-long (13,357 km) band circling the Arctic

SPECIES: A mixture of boreal evergreens and tundra shrubs, sedges, grasses, mosses, and lichens

◆ In the abstract, the Arctic tree line sounds majestic. The largest ecological transition zone on the planet, it divides two formidable northern biomes: the boreal forest of the taiga and the vast, treeless plain of the tundra. The wobbly halo is about 8,300 miles (13,357 km) long, do-si-do-ing with the Arctic Circle as it winds its way through North America, Eurasia, and Greenland.

In practice, though, it's a bit awkward. Despite its name, the tree line isn't a sharp boundary where tall green conifers stare down an open landscape they don't dare enter. Rather, it's a stripe that varies in size—in Canada, for example, it's 90 miles (145 km) wide on average. Inside this band, patchy trees, stunted by the cold and wind, mingle with other squat flora. It's not a wood, not yet a tundra.

Muddled as it may be close up, on a macro level, this boundary has been relatively stable for much of the past 3,500 years. But right now, as Earth's climate warms and permafrost melts, the transition zone is itself in transition. The Arctic tree line is essentially a temperature line: It marks the beginning of an area inhospitable to trees, thanks to sap-freezing average annual temperatures and root-inhibiting frozen soil.

As the climate warms and the permafrost melts, these obstacles are removed and the forest rushes in. Currently, the Arctic tree line is traveling north as fast as trees can beget treelings—their speed dependent on their environment and the seed dispersal skills of animals, wind, water, and gravity. North American forests currently migrate north a little more than 1,500 feet (450 m) per year, but to outpace climate change, they must travel about 10,000 to 16,000 feet (3,000 to 4,800 m)—six to ten times faster.

Such rapid change is both destabilizing and self-accelerating: The Arctic tundra releases methane as it warms, compounding the carbon in the atmosphere. And when permafrost thaws earlier in the spring and freezes later in the winter, runoff increases, drying soil and rendering areas more prone to wildfires.

The Intergovernmental Panel on Climate Change estimates trees will eventually take over one quarter to half of the Arctic tundra, which currently covers 4.4 million square miles (11.4 million sq km). Like the dwindling of ice caps and the desertification of grasslands, the march of the Arctic tree line is a striking example of how climate change is quickly redrawing the boundaries of our planet. ❯ How to see it: Go north. Once the taiga thins out, you're there!

Conifers encroach on shrubs in the high-altitude tundra of Denali National Park and Preserve in Alaska.

KOBUK VALLEY

- Thirty miles (48 km) north of the Arctic Circle, Kobuk Valley National Park comprises 1.7 million square miles (4.4 million sq km) of Alaskan tundra, hemmed to the north by the Baird Mountains and ribboned through with the Kobuk River.

- Thanks to the shelter of the mountains, the valley preserves qualities of the otherwise "lost ecosystem" of Beringia, a region of steppe-tundra that connected Asia and North America during the last Ice Age. In most parts of the world, climate change has reforested this land.

- Today, Kobuk Valley is one of the least visited national parks in the United States, hosting roughly half a percent as many tourists as Yellowstone does in a given year. But it's also one of the longest continuously inhabited places on the continent—people have lived and hunted caribou near the river since at least 7000 BCE.

KEEP AN EYE OUT FOR The Great Kobuk Sand Dunes, the largest dunes in the Arctic. The sand here was ground up by glaciers during the last Ice Age and blown into the valley, forming an incongruous patch bigger than Manhattan.

KEEP AN EAR OUT FOR Noisy caribou, who migrate through every spring and fall and sound like huge pigs as they snort and scratch at the ground.

KEEP A NOSE OUT FOR Sargiq, sometimes called stinkweed, which smells like extra-strong sage and is used by the Iñupiat people for everything from rash treatment to mosquito repellent.

Arctic Poppies

Soaking up the sun in the Arctic Circle

RANGE: Siberia, Canada, Scandinavia, Svalbard, and Greenland
SPECIES: Arctic poppy (*Papaver radicatum*)

◆ There are many days of darkness north of the Arctic Circle—but when the sun is out, boy is it out. In the summertime, the top of the world enjoys round-the-clock daylight as everyone's favorite energy ball grazes the horizon and lifts off again like a skipping pebble.

This is also the Arctic poppy's time to shine. This brave white or butter-colored flower is one of the world's northernmost plants, found primarily above the Arctic Circle in places like Norway, Finland, and Sweden. Of the world's numerous heliotropic, or light-following, plant species, it is perhaps the most committed, tracking the summer Arctic sun 24/7 and packing most of the year's activities into a brief six-week growing season during this window of illumination.

Like other Arctic flowers, these poppies must deal with icy winds that snatch up moisture, as well as hungry animals that snatch up plants. To cope, they grow low to the ground and boast hairy stems that may trap heat, block wind, and deter snacking. Their petals are slightly toxic, and their roots dig deep to find as much moisture as possible.

But worshipping the sun is the poppy's key adaptation. The flower's four parabolic petals cup together to form a bowl, focusing sunlight toward the center as they rotate gently over the course of the day. "Arctic poppies are the star of heliotropism because of that big satellite dish," says Paul Sokoloff, a botanist at the Canadian Museum of Nature. By concentrating sunlight 24 hours a day, Arctic poppies absorb two to three times as many sunbeams as more static plants do.

Arctic poppies come in snow white or butter yellow.

Thanks to this dedication, the small space inside the poppy can be an incredible 12.5°F warmer than the air outside—immensely helpful when even the hottest summer months are barely above freezing. The jolt of warmth extends the plant's growing season and also helps attract the Arctic bumblebee, a thick fuzzy pollinator that parks between the poppy's petals to warm up. (The plant's Inuktitut name, igutsat niqingit, means "bumblebee food.")

The brevity of the summer growing season means that poppies must flower, pollinate, fertilize, and develop seeds before the temperatures dip and the plants go dormant for the winter. Dormant poppies leave their dried-out stalks shimmying in the wind, shaking seeds loose for next summer.

It's a tenuous existence. Wind can disperse the poppy's pocket of warmth, and ill-placed clouds can throw off the heliotropism. But this cheerful survivor makes it work. Arctic poppies even eke out an existence on what is arguably the northernmost point of land in the world: Greenland's Kaffeklubben ("Coffee Club") Island, which is less than 500 miles (800 km) from the North Pole. Danish explorer Lauge Koch named the outpost after a caffeine-fueled gathering of colleagues back home—perhaps inspired by the presence of a flower equally devoted to its own energy source. ❯ **How to see them:** Take a pricey Arctic cruise to Nunavut or northern Norway. Look but don't touch: If you pluck a poppy's petals, it will no longer track the sun.

Mighty Arctic Lichens

You and I are gonna live forever.

RANGE: **Worldwide**
SPECIES: **Many, including star-tipped reindeer lichen (*Cladonia stellaris*), rock tripe (*Umbilicaria* spp.), and whiteworm lichen (*Thamnolia subuliformis*)**

◆ Despite the advance of the Arctic tree line, there's still a large swath of tundra where conifers fear to tread. In this knee-high environment, those seeking impressive organisms should look down, not up. There, encrusting weather-beaten rocks or emerging full and freakish from the soil, they may find a life form that defies harsh weather, taxonomy, and (potentially) death: the lichen.

Lichens flourish where most plants fail because they aren't actually plants. Instead, they're interkingdom collaborations: At its simplest, a lichen is a combination of a fungus, which provides form, and an algae and/or cyanobacteria, which turn sunlight into food through photosynthesis.

To shelter its partner, the fungus creates a structure that can range from luscious, lettuce-like folds laid gracefully over a boulder to a thin, precarious crust clinging to a sheer rock face. In return, the partner organism provides the fungus with food. "It's really just fungus that's transformed into a greenhouse—it's farming the algae inside," says R. Troy McMullin, a research scientist at the Canadian Museum of Nature and an expert in lichenology.

Star-tipped reindeer lichen, thriving among lingonberries in Sweden

This means that unlike plants, which generally need to root in the ground for nutrients, lichens can attach themselves just about anywhere, paving the way in difficult ecosystems. They're often the first sign of life to reappear after a volcanic eruption. They can even survive in space: In 2005, lichens collected from Spain and Antarctica were exposed to 16 days of UV radiation outside a space station before being shot back to Earth in a rocket. Twenty-four hours after their return, they were behaving as though nothing had happened.

Time doesn't seem to bother lichens much either. Certain Arctic species are thought to be thousands of years old. (It's hard to imagine living with a roommate for that long, even if they do make all your food for you.) Some scientists are investigating whether lichens are in fact "biologically immortal"—that is, unable to die of senescence—and whether this might provide clues about how to prevent aging in humans.

However, these seemingly invincible organisms have both weaknesses and enemies. Long-lived but not long-limbed, they grow a measly fifth of an inch each year on average. Arctic species grow even more slowly: It can take up to 200 years for a stand of reindeer lichen to reach its full size—and even longer when this growth is set back by reindeer or caribou, who can smell lichen through snow and gobble up to 10 pounds (4.5 kg) of it per day.

The Arctic lichen's true enemy is, predictably and unfortunately, human beings. Despite their ability to survive just about anywhere, many lichens are very sensitive to pollution, even over great distances. Indeed, lichens are often used to help monitor air quality. The US Forest Service has been collecting lichen samples since the 1990s to map and understand trends in air pollution across the country.

But the biggest threat is climate change. As the Arctic warms and the tree line advances north, larger organisms are encroaching on the lichens' domain, kickstarting further changes they may not be prepared for, such as warmer soil, reduced light access, and greater fire risk. Ironically, the adaptations that have allowed these collaborators to thrive in the harshest conditions may doom some of them as balmier temperatures arrive. And all this before we've really even gotten to know them. "I'd say we're still trying to figure what a lichen is," McMullin says. **❯ How to see them: If it looks like something threw up on a rock, it's probably a lichen. In winter, follow a hungry caribou.**

Mosquitopocalypse

Little scourges of the Arctic summer

RANGE: The Arctic, especially Greenland and Alaska
SPECIES: Arctic mosquito (*Aedes nigripes*)

◆ When entomologist Lauren Culler does research in Alaska during the summer, she wears a dense cloud of bug spray and a full rain layer, no matter the weather. She's preparing for a different kind of onslaught: Go outside in June or July, and "within a matter of minutes, there are hundreds of mosquitoes trying to find a little piece of your skin," she says.

Arctic mosquitoes—seasonal scourges of Alaska, Greenland, Sápmi, and other northern areas—are far from the tropical climes with which they're usually associated. Nonetheless, they make a huge, whining, itchy impression, thanks to their ability to work on deadline.

While skeeters in balmier parts of the world spread their mating across a whole season, or even a whole year, Arctic mosquitoes are on a tight schedule: They mate and lay eggs for just a couple of months, when temperatures are right. And there aren't a ton of mammals to go around up there, which means that every single female mosquito in the region is looking to drink from a limited quantity of warm blood. It's mosquito happy hour, says Culler. "They're *all* there."

This mosquitopocalypse also affects caribou, who spend much of the season trying to avoid bugs by pacing around or standing stoically on windy ridges—behavior that prevents them from eating and actually lessens their chance of survival. It's thought that a large-enough mosquito swarm can drink a baby caribou to death.

Uh oh

Of course, mosquitoes also pay it forward: They're a huge source of food for the tundra's birds, beetles, and spiders, which gorge on hatchlings every summer. But as the tundra warms and the ponds where mosquitoes lay their eggs melt earlier in the spring, the insects are adjusting their timelines, spending fewer days in this vulnerable state— which means Arctic summers may soon suck even more. **› How to see them:** If you really want to see them—lots and lots and lots of them—come to the Arctic during June or July.

Quotes from Annoyed Explorers

"The swarms of mosquitoes and gnats which abound on the river during the months of June and July proved a very serious annoyance.... We were obliged to wear face nets and gloves; and on one occasion an attempt to make sextant observations failed completely from this cause."
— C. P. Raymond, US Army Engineer Corps, 1869

"There is another feature in this country which, though insignificant on paper, is to the traveler the most terrible and poignant infliction he can be called upon to bear in a new land. I refer to the clouds of bloodthirsty mosquitoes."
— I. Petroff, special agent of the US Treasury, 1898

"The ferocity of these mosquitos I regard as something remarkable. The species found here is not the large, singing sort seen in the States, but a small, silent, business-like insect, sharp of bill, who touches the tender spot in a surprisingly short time after alighting."
— J. J. Rafferty, Second US Infantry, 1898

"At Salt River one could kill 100 with a stroke of the palm and at times they obscured the colour of the horses. A little later they were much worse."
— Ernest Thompson Seton, *The Arctic Prairies*, 1911

"Mosquitoes crowd on every patch of free skin. One is constantly busy repelling them. Some of us are so confused by it that our ranting never ends and breaks out into new climaxes again and again."
— excerpt from a German soldier's field diary, 1941

Remnant Tallgrass Prairies

Survivors of this once-mighty ecosystem hide in plain sight across the Midwest.

RANGE: Dotted across the American Midwest, especially in Kansas, Indiana, Oklahoma, and Illinois

SPECIES: Telltale tallgrass species include big bluestem (*Andropogon gerardii*), Indian grass (*Sorghastrum nutans*), and switchgrass (*Panicum virgatum*).

◆ In the early 1800s, settlers leaving the eastern hardwood forest peered out of their covered wagons at days and days of grass ahead and quickly dismissed some of North America's most fertile ground as "miserable," "uninviting," or "disagreeable." If you too find yourself in Kansas, Indiana, Oklahoma, or Illinois, you can avoid their mistake by taking a closer look between the corn and soybeans. There, you may find the remains of the tallgrass prairie, one of the world's most endangered ecosystems.

Before European colonization, tallgrass prairie carpeted a nearly Texas-sized swath of North America. That's 150 million acres where big bluestem, Indian grass, and switchgrass grew up to 6 feet (1.8 m) tall. Tallgrass prairie was once the world's second-most diverse ecosystem, after the Brazilian rainforest, with up to 60 species of grass and more than 300 types of wildflower, all grazed by great bison herds, danced upon by prairie chickens, and churned up by black-tailed prairie dogs.

It took only about 80 years for settlers to till away most of the tallgrass. Today, just 4 percent of its original range remains. Yet seekers of ecological ghosts can find holdout patches of this historic prairie in unexpected, seemingly mundane places: running along roadsides and railways, tucked under fence lines, or way down in ditches. Once-prolific grasses may sprout on hilltops among old cemetery tombstones, protected by fences and geography. Or they might be hiding in the middle of abandoned farm fields, having managed a small reclamation.

Even modest tallgrass prairie remnants are important—they serve as restoration benchmarks and seed sources as people doggedly try to unwind the work of the plow and the pioneers. But if you want a 360-degree tallgrass experience, there are a handful of more expansive remnants that don't require wandering railroads and graveyards. These include the Joseph H. Williams Tallgrass Prairie Preserve in Oklahoma—the world's largest protected piece of tallgrass prairie—and Kansas's Tallgrass Prairie National Preserve, harbored by the rocky, till-resistant Flint Hills.

Simply protecting plants and soil isn't enough to make the tallgrass prairie its whole self. Dense bison herds and regenerative fires, including those set by the Indigenous peoples of the Great Plains, are vital, now-missing processes that helped maintain the tallgrass. "Native people and the prairie were linked in reciprocity by intentional burning," writes botanist Robin Wall Kimmerer in *Tallgrass Prairie*. "The prairies needed their people."

Ecologists consider ecosystems like the tallgrass prairie functionally extinct: They are technically still there, but they don't work like they used to. Restoration efforts in

Few large expanses of tallgrass prairie remain, but remnants of this once-great ecosystem persist in roadside ditches and graveyards, and on protected land.

recent decades are bringing some bison and prescribed fires back to large prairie patches, marking a return to at least some of the human influence that made America's cradle of biodiversity thrive for thousands of years. **› How to see them: While traveling in their historic range, keep an eye out for gangly, tucked-away patches of grass, or pay a special visit to a protected area, like the Joseph H. Williams Tallgrass Prairie Preserve.**

Burrowing Owls

Grounded for life—well, kind of

◆ Most owls use their high food-chain status to secure penthouses with good views and solid airflow. But the burrowing owls of the shortgrass American plains prefer basement apartments. These giant-eyed owls live up to 3 feet (1 m) belowground, either digging caverns themselves or taking over leases from prairie dogs and ground squirrels. It's a strange choice, but wiser than it may seem.

RANGE: Most of the western United States, Florida, the Great Plains, Canada, Mexico, Central and South America, and the Caribbean
SPECIES: Burrowing owl (*Athene cunicularia*)

A tour of a burrowing owl home might start with the front entrance. There, the owls prepare a useful welcome mat by spreading around dried animal excrement, which they gather from livestock, horses, and other mammals. This decorative flourish attracts droves of dung beetles—the owls' favorite food. (It might also keep unwanted guests, like badgers and bobcats, from sniffing around.) Entrances may also be festooned with cigarette butts, bottle caps, and Barbie doll parts, although their purpose is unknown.

Inside the burrow, the rich sensory experience continues. On average, female burrowing owls lay seven eggs or more—one of the largest clutches of any owl species—so it's a full house. Busy parents prepare for brooding and incubation by hoarding food—in 1997, a reserve of some 200 rodents was found stockpiled in a Saskatchewan den. While the underground setting helps with climate control, it's undeniably stuffy down there. Burrowing owls deal with this problem via a high tolerance for carbon dioxide, a trait they share with diving birds.

With so much at stake, the owls have developed a security protocol: When a threat looms, they mimic the sound of a hissing rattlesnake. If that fails, families are known to "run the coop" on their featherless, roadrunneresque legs, a sight that has been compared to watching a can of baked beans sprint for dear life.

Less worrisome passersby might be greeted by the birds' trademark head bobs—like all owls, their eyes are stuck in place, so they move their heads to compensate, often in very groovy ways. Cowboys, noticing how the owls would sit on their stoops and nod as they rode by, dubbed them "howdy birds," while more recent fans have set their moves to club music.

Their domestic bliss is seasonal. Burrowing owls are among the few true migrators in the owl kingdom, and many spend the colder months in entirely different burrows farther south. One female tagged in Wyoming was recently tracked 2,200 miles (3,540 km) to a wintering spot near Acapulco, Mexico. Sometimes you just need a change of scenery. **› How to see them: Head to dry ranges or open grasslands with prairie dog towns or ground squirrel colonies. Scan the landscape carefully, and you might find a radiant pair of gumball-yellow eyes staring back at you.**

Under the Prairie

In North America's grasslands and prairies, life is hiding—not only in the swaying grass, but beneath the ground's surface. Let's take a peek.

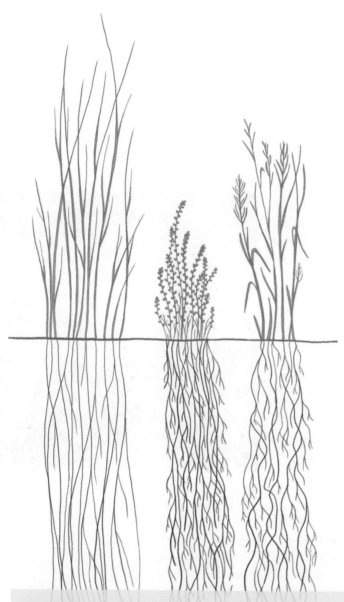

POWERFUL FUNGI • The real MVPs behind grassland productivity are arbuscular mycorrhizal fungi (AMFs). These microscopic organisms live on the surface of roots and form a symbiotic relationship with them. The AMFs' hairlike structures capture phosphorus, nitrogen, and sulfur from the soil and deliver these nutrients to the grass; in return, the roots feed the fungi sugar.

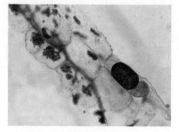

arbuscular mycorrhizal fungi

TINY DECOMPOSERS • A single teaspoon of dirt is home to thousands of species of microscopic critters, who thrive in the thin films of water that cling to clumps of moist soil. Soil microbes are found all over the world, but they play an extra-important role in temperate grasslands, where every winter sees a huge influx of dead plant material as annual grasses fall dormant. A minuscule menagerie helps break down this matter and return nutrients to the soil.

Bacteria eat decaying plants and animals, and these bacteria are in turn eaten by (comparatively) bigger organisms, like millimeter-long nematode worms, some of whom can guzzle up to 5,000 bacteria per minute. Meanwhile, the famously hardy tardigrades, aka water bears, are direct consumers of plant material and detritus; they extend their snoots, puncture plant cell walls with needlelike mouthparts, and slurp out the liquid inside.

DEEP ROOTS • The humble grassroots that tether the prairie landscape set the stage for microscopic partnerships and scientific mysteries.

Unlike trees, which have thick, woody taproots that act as central anchors, grassroots are a tangle of long, thin fibers. That extra surface area gives them more opportunities to take up water and nutrients. Some prairie grasses, like big bluestem (*Andropogon gerardii*), have roots that snake down 10 feet (3 m) into the soil. Scientists aren't sure why these roots go so deep—conventional wisdom says that it allows the grasses to reach extra water in times of drought, but research indicates that almost all of the uptake action happens in the foot of soil just beneath the surface.

red earthworm

INVASIVE EARTHWORMS •

The red earthworms (*Lumbricus rubellus*) that have wriggled into American hearts and gardens are actually an invasive species. Eleven thousand years ago, the glaciers that scraped across huge swaths of North America eroded the soil, driving many of the continent's native earthworms extinct. When European colonizers came millennia later, their ships carried soil for ballast—unwittingly unleashing European earthworms, who quickly dug themselves deep into their new home.

In the relatively brief time these invasive worms have spent in North America, they've radically changed the grasslands' soil, as their speedy tunneling and decomposition bring extra oxygen and water to the underground. They're popular with gardeners and composters, but since native plants developed their own ways of getting nutrients from the soil, the introduction of earthworms can give an edge to invasive species.

The red worms aren't the only soil invaders around—in more recent years, Asian jumping worms (*Amynthas agrestis*), named for their snakelike thrashing movements aboveground, have been making their way west across the United States. The jumping worms consume detritus even more quickly than their European counterparts, which can spell trouble for established North American ecosystems.

SURPRISE CRAYFISH •

Perhaps the most out-of-place-looking grasslands critters, prairie crayfish (*Procambarus gracilis*) live in hidden reserves of groundwater 6 feet (1.8 m) or more below the surface. The entrances to their burrows are marked by little mud chimneys, and the burrows themselves form dense networks that can be repurposed by other subterranean residents, like rattlesnakes. Prairie crayfish are pretty elusive; your best shot at seeing one is on a hot, humid night, when they emerge to feed and mate.

BIG GUYS •

Mammals have their own ways of getting comfortable underground. Badgers (*Taxidea taxus*) enlarge gopher holes into dens the size of walk-in closets and may rotate burrows or dig secret connecting tunnels to help keep their young safe. Coyotes (*Canis latrans*) burrow only during their mating season, when they tend to pups that spend their first six weeks underground, ducking briefly into this subterranean world before returning to the one above.

(left) prairie crayfish
(middle) coyotes
(bottom) badger

Prairie Dog Language

Talk is cheep.

RANGE: Colorado, Arizona, Utah, and New Mexico
SPECIES: Gunnison's prairie dog (*Cynomys gunnisoni*)

◆ In the early twentieth century, some prairie dog towns stretched for hundreds of miles. Cowboys and naturalists passing through described acres of sociable rodents, who would pop out of the ground and greet them with high-pitched chatter.

Those visitors didn't know it, but they were being described in turn. These squeaks and yips make up the most elaborate animal vocalizations we humans have yet translated. Indeed, the prairie dogs' communication system is so detailed and specific that some researchers are "comfortable calling it a language," says Con Slobodchikoff, the animal behaviorist who introduced this concept after studying prairie dogs for decades.

For a long time, Slobodchikoff himself was not a discerning listener of prairie dogs. "I thought a cheep was a cheep," he says. Then, on a tip from a colleague, he started recording the calls, using software to track slight variations: a rising pitch here, an overtone there. By combining sonic analysis with experiments, he realized the prairie dogs weren't just sounding blunt alarms with their cheeps—they were exchanging detailed bulletins.

A given call might contain information about a suspicious figure's identity ("hawk!" "coyote!"), speed of approach, and size—or, if they happen to be a nosy researcher, their height and the color of their shirt. These messages are responded to with the appropriate behavior—craning a neck for a wheeling falcon, diving into a burrow for a close-by dog. By hanging cutout shapes above a prairie dog colony, UFO-style, Slobodchikoff and his colleagues learned that the rodents can even differentiate between circles and triangles (although not, for whatever reason, between circles and squares).

"It has been unfashionable in scientific circles to refer to animal communication systems as language," says Slobodchikoff. Plenty of people consider language to be unique to our own species. But to him, the prairie dogs clear the bar, exhibiting "all the elements that linguists say you have to find," from sounds that carry distinct meanings to the capacity for expressing new combinations of thoughts.

Many other aspects of prairie dog communication remain encoded—at least for now. One mysterious communique popular with several species is the "jump-yip," a gesture-vocalization combo frequently compared to a stadium wave, in which many prairie dogs in a row cry aloud while tossing their arms (and sometimes their full bodies) into the air. An entire colony can get swept up in a jump-yip.

While it's not entirely clear what these contagious bouts are for, researchers suspect they might be a prairie dog's way of making sure everyone else is paying attention. After all, those richly drawn sentences aren't just for showing off. Talk may be cheep, but not listening can be expensive. ❯ **How to see (and hear) them: Get close enough to one and he will tell his neighbors all about you. Make sure to visit between May and September, when the prairie dogs are spending time aboveground.**

Bison Snot

The prairie's secret ingredient

◆ The American prairie once had three things in abundance: bison, tallgrass, and microbes. According to ecosystem expert Wes Olson, these three entities—from completely different kingdoms, living on seemingly incompatible scales—formed an unlikely alliance that holds the whole place together. It's glued by an equally esoteric material: bison snot.

It works like this: Like most places on Earth, the American prairie is absolutely suffused with microorganisms. These bacteria, protozoa, and fungi cling to plants, hang suspended in drops of water, and float in the air. As a bison sniffs and chews, some of these end up in her mouth, and others inside her elegant, comma-shaped nostrils, where they become trapped in snot. Every few bites, the bison digs her tongue in there to clear things out, swallowing more microscopic critters in the process.

Chewed grass, snot, and microbes are then swept down into the rumen, the first of the bison's four stomachs, where the microbes get to work breaking down the tough plant cellulose into nutrients the animal can use. The exact microbe makeup varies depending on the season and the type of grass; the prairie's microbial succession pattern allows the bison to move between foraging grounds without losing the ability to digest.

When a mouthful of grass has finished its journey through a bison, it emerges in another familiar form. A bison poops enough every day to fill a 3-gallon (11 L) bucket. This poop is generally known as dung, chips, or patties—no one seems to call it waste, maybe because it's anything but.

Insects move into the bison chips to eat the microbes still hanging out there; then bats, birds, and box turtles come to eat those bugs. People burn dried chips as fuel for warmth and cooking. And dung beetles chop some up and bury them, making them available to soil microbes, which transform the nutrients within into a form that can be used by plants. In this way, the prairie grass, after a few microbe-smoothed stops inside a ruminant, becomes itself again. **〉 How to see them:** Best not to get snot-spottingly close to a bison—but with binoculars, you can watch them get their tongues way up in there.

RANGE: Bison once roamed across North America. Indigenous-led restoration efforts are gradually bringing back small herds, especially on tribal lands in Oklahoma, Wyoming, and Montana.
SPECIES: Plains bison (*Bison bison bison*), prairie grasses, and various microbes

Death Camas Symbiosis

The survival of a unique bee species depends on a flower 10 times more toxic than heroin.

◆ One knee-high, cream-colored North American prairie wildflower has a big surprise for almost anyone who risks a bite: It's one of the most toxic plants on the continent. Unschooled humans may be incapacitated or killed by it—it sickened members of the Lewis and Clark expedition—and there is no known antidote. A grazing animal that gets a stray mouthful might vomit or go hypothermic; too much munching and they could keel over and die. Even insects who taste the plant end up with irritated tongues, which they wipe at frantically with their forelegs before becoming paralyzed and kicking the bug bucket.

The plant—helpfully named death camas in English—is scattered across central and western North America. Its weapon is a chemical called zygacine, a neurotoxin similar to the one made by poison dart frogs that interrupts the neural synapses of animals, essentially causing a brain breakdown. The toxin wards off herbivores who might otherwise graze on it and prevents precious pollen loss to generalist pollinators, who are less effective than specialists.

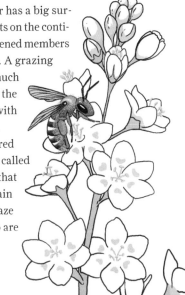

Zygacine suffuses every part of the death camas plant, causing a number of "dangerous maladies" when consumed, says toxic plant specialist Jim Cane. Death camas bulbs are hardy—plants regrow quickly after being mown or after any wildfire. Today, botanists working to restore Indigenous American food traditions cut down the plant in droves in its introduced range to prevent fatal mix-ups with blue camas, an onion-like relative with edible bulbs which appears identical to death camas before blooming.

Only one animal is not fazed by this: the death camas bee. In fact, the very survival of this bee species depends on this otherwise hostile plant.

Death camas bees are mining bees, digging underground tunnels in which to lay eggs and raise their young. They buzz between death camas plants in foraging trips, gathering dry pollen and nectar into specialized body parts called crops(also known as honey sacks) and pollinating the flowers in the process.

They lump this food into a mass "the consistency of raw cookie dough," Cane says. Then they put this toxic ball into their subterranean nest, place their eggs on top, and seal up the hole. Soon the eggs hatch, and the larvae eat the pollen. When mother bees can't find death camas pollen, they don't make eggs.

Scientists are still baffled by how this bee can overcome or sidestep the effects of zygacine. The species likely has a mutation that allows it to remain unaffected—perhaps similar to the one in koalas that helps them eat toxic eucalyptus leaves. Regardless, thanks to their dangerous diet, death camas bees likely enjoy a level of noxious protection against parasites.

However it works, the relationship exemplifies a symbiotic mutualism, a "rare exception" in bee-plant relationships, which tend to be less exclusive for the plant, says Cane. The creosote bush, for instance, is pollinated by about 20 specialist bees and many other generalists. But death camas and its bee have a uniquely codependent arrangement, relying solely on each other for reproduction. They don't need anyone else, so let the world burn—or vomit, freeze up, and die. ❯ **How to see them:** Look for a low-growing wildflower with six petals that are greenish white to cream in color, or even a little pink. Do *not* eat it—but feel free to check for unperturbed bees.

RANGE: **Western North America and across the Plains states**
SPECIES: **Death camas (*Toxicoscordion venenosum*) and the death camas bee (*Andrena astragali*)**

Death camas is filled root to tip with a dangerous toxin.

Sage Grouse Seduction Grounds

Bulbous birds use their unique habitat to put on the performance of a lifetime.

RANGE: **Mountainous areas of the American West**
SPECIES: **Greater sage grouse (*Centrocercus urophasianus*)**

◆ It's 5:30 a.m. in the high sagebrush steppe of the Colorado Rockies. The sun has just started to warm up the frosty ground. A series of loud, resounding plops echoes across the landscape. This is the awkward, otherworldly love song of the male greater sage grouse.

Sage grouse are large, spherical birds that make their home in high-elevation landscapes of states like Colorado, Wyoming, Montana, and Utah. They spend most of their time foraging for leaves and insects in the thickets of scrubby sagebrush that punctuate the otherwise bare ground. The sagebrush also gives the birds essential cover from hungry predators; at up to 7 pounds (3 kg)—that's more than three rotisserie chickens—they're a tempting target for golden eagles, red-tailed hawks, foxes, coyotes, and bobcats.

Every spring, though, dozens of sage grouse suitors risk their lives to gather in communal open areas, called leks, and strut their stuff for nearby females. They fan out their tails, pace back and forth, and puff up their chests, inflating two bright-yellow balloons of skin. Then they swish their wings against their breast feathers and thrust their heads forward, pushing the air out of the sacs like a shot from a sexy sonic weapon.

The percussive sounds that result can be heard from up to half a mile away, says Tony Apa, an avian researcher with Colorado's state wildlife agency. The purpose of this ridiculous dance is to convince females to choose them as mates, Apa explains: "They're saying, 'Look at me! I'm the biggest, best-looking guy out here.'"

In the heat of the moment, sage grouse males aren't particularly discerning about where they put on their show. They'll strut on airstrips, roads, or any other type of bare ground, says Apa, as long as it's open enough for females to see. But there needs to be sagebrush nearby for their potential dates to hide in—and for the males to scatter into if a predator interrupts the dance-off. After choosing a mate, females lay their eggs in sagebrush within a few miles of the lek.

Sage grouse may use the same leks for decades or even centuries. But their sense of tradition can backfire when humans disrupt their habitat. If an oil well, ranch, or mining operation wipes out the sagebrush around a lek, the grouse may still mate there,

but they'll be less successful at nesting. Sage grouse populations have dwindled across the western United States as a result of such developments.

Scientists like Apa are trying to determine how sage grouse choose their lekking sites, and how and when they decide to move them. That would help focus conservation efforts where they'd have the most effect and keep these iconic orbs strutting, flapping, and plopping for many generations to come. **> How to see them:** Join an organized birding trip in spring, or find a designated lek-viewing site in a state such as Colorado, Wyoming, Utah, or Montana. Many leks are protected, but certain sites are arranged to allow visitors to watch the strutting sage grouse without disturbing their sensitive habitat.

THE WILD LIFE OF **A Prairie Photographer**

■ Chris Helzer is the Nebraska director of science for The Nature Conservancy and writes about prairie ecology, restoration, and management on his blog, *The Prairie Ecologist*. In 2018, he launched the Square Meter Photography Project—a yearlong project to photograph the plant and animal life within a 1-square-meter plot of land. The resulting images were turned into both a book and a museum exhibit.

• **How did you choose your plot?**
I chose the prairie just a mile from my house. There are lots of prairies like it all throughout the Midwest and Great Plains. I thought that was going to be really important—to show people that they could do a project like this or see that same kind of diversity and dynamism.

• **What sort of routine did you maintain?**
I didn't have a set schedule; it was more driven by the light and the

wind. There were days when I was there for 10 or 15 minutes, and there were days when I was there for well over an hour just staring at this little tiny space. If you just spend time, if you really get down on your hands and knees and look, you keep finding more and more stuff.

I ended up photographing 113 species, but there were way more than that in the plot at one time or another; I just didn't get a chance to see them.

• **What do you hope people take away from your work?**

It's this idea that prairies are interesting, diverse, and dynamic, even at a small scale. I'm hoping that I can introduce people to the organisms that live in a prairie on more of a personal basis, so that rather than thinking about these sort of bland areas that are flat places they have to drive through to get to something interesting, they think about katydids or spiders catching ants.

It also has just been about paying attention to what's around you, and taking the time to sit quietly and look. You can do that in your backyard, and you can do it in the local park. You can do it anywhere there's anything green or alive. ■

Loggerhead Shrikes

North America's most vicious songbird has developed an unusual storage solution.

RANGE: Grasslands throughout North America, from southern Mexico into Canada

SPECIES: Loggerhead shrike (*Lanius ludovicianus*)

◆ North America's prairies are dotted with gruesome miniature murder scenes: grasshoppers, butterflies, and beetles impaled on barbed wire fencing and thorny branches.

The creature behind this carnage, dubbed the "butcher bird," is not a fearsome bird of prey. Instead, it's a songbird called the loggerhead shrike, whose winsome looks hide a killer personality.

Shrikes lack the gnarly talons, strong skulls, and flying prowess of raptors like hawks or falcons. But "pound for pound, they're equally powerful, equally voracious predators," says Diego Sustaita, a biologist at California State University in San Marcos who studies the biomechanics of shrikes.

To figure out how these sparrow-sized birds wreak such havoc on the plains, Sustaita and his colleagues filmed captive shrikes hunting in slow motion and broke down their kills frame by frame.

Like other predatory birds, loggerhead shrikes perch on fence posts to scan the grasses below. Their vision is aided by a dark mask of feathers, which reflects the sun's glare like the eye black of a baseball player.

Once they've pounced, shrikes induce paralysis by biting their prey on the back of the neck. Then they rapidly twist their heads from side to side, shaking their prey with a force roughly equivalent to the whiplash caused by a minor car collision—enough to snap the necks of animals as big as horned frogs, rattlesnakes, or kangaroo rats.

A loggerhead shrike and his lunch, a western fence lizard

The aftermath of most shrike attacks is not for the squeamish. While their habit of impaling prey on barbs or branches seems barbaric, it's actually quite logical: When you're a prolific predator, you're going to need somewhere to store your food. Whatever a shrike can't eat, he'll skewer for later. (The practice is also useful for consuming toxic prey, like monarch butterflies—after pinning a butterfly on a fence, a shrike will wait several days to allow the toxins to diffuse before eating his collection.)

Loggerhead shrikes are becoming scarcer, and their strange shish kebabs more difficult to find. Their population is believed to have declined by nearly 80 percent in the past 50 years. Even these ruthless feathered assassins have found it difficult to vie with pesticide-driven insect declines and shrinking prairie habitat. ❯ **How to see them:** Shrikes often perch on top of shrubs and fence posts as they survey for prey. Bring binoculars and listen for harsh trills, buzzes, and rasps.

Oh, That's Where I Put That?

You may think your roommate is strange for stuffing candy bars between the couch cushions. But many animals who hide food away for later make unusual choices about where and how to store it. Here are some with surprising habits.

Scrub jays (*Aphelocoma* spp.) are what's known as "scatter hoarders," meaning they hide caches of nuts and seeds all over their territories. If another jay is nearby while they're caching, they're more likely to pick a shady, hidden, or faraway site to prevent thievery. Some jays will even come back later and move their store in private—but only if they themselves are prone to stealing, suggesting that they are able to guess at their rival's mindset.

By contrast, many species of **moles** (family Talpidae) are "larder hoarders," gathering all their supplies in one place, dragon-style. In their case, the treasure is worms—sometimes fully dead, sometimes merely immobilized by precise or venomous bites. Moles may keep their worms in a special chamber or cram them into the tunnel walls of their underground homes, and they have been known to store hundreds at a time.

Tayras (*Eira barbara*)—large weasel relatives from Central and South America—pick green plantains and store them in high-up locations, including inside bromeliads. They'll come back a few days later to enjoy them when they're ripe.

Hyenas (family Hyaenidae) have been seen dragging meat and bones into muddy ponds, likely in order to keep other scavengers from sniffing out their leftovers.

Red-bellied woodpeckers (*Melanerpes carolinus*) stuff berries, bugs, and acorn bits deep into crevices in trees and fence posts. When it's time to retrieve these snacks, they use their sticky, barb-tipped, 2-inch-long (5 cm) tongues to pry them out. For some reason, they also use this technique to store nails, paper clips, and slivers of wood.

While **squirrels** are known for their love of seeds and acorns, many are mushroom fiends—and some, arguably, gourmands. Scientists in Canada once found an abandoned robin's nest filled with 52 air-dried deer truffles, which had been carefully stored there by a red squirrel (*Tamiasciurus hudsonicus*).

Out-of-Place Oryx

Unusual transplants make a good living on a missile range in New Mexico.

RANGE: In the Tularosa Basin and surrounding areas in southern New Mexico, and at home in southern Africa
SPECIES: South African oryx (*Oryx gazella*), also known as gemsbok

◆ In the shimmering desert grasslands and shrublands of southern New Mexico, a large antelope with a striking black-and-white face and long, straight horns can sometimes be spotted from afar. Each of these elegant ungulates is a transplant, 9,000 miles (14,480 km) away from her home on almost exactly the other side of the world.

Oryx, also called gemsbok, hail from the dry savannas and desert plains of southern Africa. They've been in New Mexico since the late 1960s thanks to one person: Frank C. Hibben, former chairman of the state's Game Commission. A big-game hunter, Hibben thought parts of the Southwest looked like the places he'd stalked oryx abroad. With the help of some donations from sportsmen and the blessing of the state's official exotic game program, Hibben captured a handful of oryx in southern Africa and brought them to the Albuquerque zoo, with the intention of using their offspring to create a safari experience right in his backyard.

From 1969 to 1977, the state released 93 oryx onto the White Sands Missile Range. A military testing ground bigger than Rhode Island, it was the site of the world's first atomic bomb, and since then it has hosted trials of a number of pointy-headed projectiles, including exotic antelope.

Despite the high concentration of ordnance, oryx have found happy circumstances. Aside from hunters, who pay to kill about 1,700 per year, they have no predators in New Mexico. (Not even mountain lions like to grapple with those horns, which the antelope wield like an aggressive forklift.) Female oryx mature fast and calve steadily every nine months. Oryx are adapted to high temperatures and limited water and have been recorded munching on more than 50 local plant species—and, in at least one instance, a military cargo parachute, which a hunter found in the stomach of an otherwise healthy oryx in the form of a 50-pound (23 kg) bezoar.

Although the wildlife biologists of the late '60s were confident that oryx would like their new home, nobody was prepared for just how much. By 2001, there were as many as 6,000 animals, and state and federal agencies scrambled to put together a management plan. The antelope were removed and fenced out of neighboring White Sands National Park, and hunting quotas were dramatically increased to prevent conflict with military operations.

Like many introduced species, oryx have developed a complex reputation in their new home. Some people view oryx as threats to native vegetation, sources of conflict with ranchers, and carriers of wildlife disease and want to quarantine them in a much smaller area or get rid of them altogether. Others see them as cherished sources of state revenue or charismatic, watchable megafauna. For his part, Hibben remained an oryx booster until the day he died. "We have more oryx in New Mexico than all of the Kalahari," he told reporters in 2001. "I'm thrilled that they're doing so well." ❯ **How to see them: Managers try to limit oryx to the White Sands Missile Range, but they can sometimes be seen outside its borders on public Bureau of Land Management land and in nearby national wildlife refuges.**

Oryx are thriving in New Mexico.

Fences

Many animals experience the territorial impulse, though their responses to it vary. Coyotes spray. Bears claw trees. Limpets shove other limpets off their little algae patches.

Humans, often, build fences. According to a 2020 study, there are more than 620,000 miles (1 million km) of combined fencing in the western United States alone, enough to wrap around Jupiter two and a quarter times.

Many of these fences are put up by property owners to demarcate borders. Others are explicitly built as conservation tools, meant to protect endangered species from poachers or predators, keep introduced species out of sensitive areas, or prevent conflict by separating wildlife from livestock or crops they might otherwise eat.

But although they're intended to neaten relationships, fences often interrupt them instead. "There are ecological winners and losers for every fence," says Christine Wilkinson, a carnivore specialist and practitioner of a new subdiscipline, known as "fence ecology," that aims to lay out these effects.

For instance, take the barbed wire fencing that crisscrosses the American West. Most of it is meant to keep domestic animals within property lines (or at least it was at one time—uncountable miles of fencing left over from past land arrangements are now just hanging out, spiky and derelict). While these fences can keep sheep from getting into trouble with wolves— and therefore keep wolves from getting into trouble with farmers—they also interrupt migration corridors for animals like mule deer and pronghorns, who may get tangled and die. To mitigate this issue, state wildlife departments counsel landowners on how to make their fences jumpable and/or duckable by large wildlife. Some government and private grants provide money to help with this.

Even fences built explicitly for conservation reasons can cause or exacerbate long-term problems. Kenya's Lake Nakuru National Park, where Wilkinson does research, is fenced off in order to mitigate poaching

and human-wildlife conflict. While it does seem to be helping somewhat with those issues in the short term, Wilkinson worries about animals becoming stuck in the park—in the very space that is meant to be a protected haven for them—as the climate changes. "There's so much drought there right now, and they can't move because of the fences," she says.

Complicating things further, animals do not usually understand when they're not supposed to cross fences. Watching how animals interact with the fence at her study site, Wilkinson found that of the 38 mammal species who routinely approached it, "27 of them crossed at least one time," she says. She's watched young hyenas slip through holes in the wire no bigger than tissue boxes, and buffalo wade through where the fence crosses a river. Good fences make good neighbors only when everyone agrees about what they're for.

Once you start paying attention to fencing, you'll see it everywhere. If you are looking to make a fence less disruptive, there are many resources available, including *A Landowner's Guide to Wildlife Friendly Fences*, written by Christine Paige and published by the Montana Fish, Wildlife & Parks department.

CERRADO

- A tropical savanna characterized by shy fauna and scrubby trees, Brazil's Cerrado lives in the reputational and aesthetic shadow of its neighbor the Amazon—it has not even been granted "national heritage" status. But it is an incredibly rich and diverse ecosystem; in the past 25 years, more than 350 vertebrates have been described here.

- It is also being destroyed at twice the rate of the Amazon, regularly losing out to soybean farms and cattle ranches. Only about one-fifth of its original extent remains.

- The Cerrado is home to more than 12,000 plant species, more than some herbaria. The first-ever plant ecology textbook, by the Danish botanist Johannes Eugenius Bülow Warming, was written based on collections made in the Cerrado.

KEEP AN EYE OUT FOR   Trumpet tree flowers, which bloom in a range of hues like lemon yellow and rosy pink and look like fireworks on the landscape.

KEEP AN EAR OUT FOR   The cricket-like chirps of tinamous—plump, secretive ground birds that are the now-extinct moa's closest living relative.

KEEP A NOSE OUT FOR   Maned wolf urine, which smells like marijuana and is used by these reclusive canines to mark their territories.

Ananteris Scorpions

These arachnids literally can't hold on to their butts.

RANGE: Brazilian Cerrado
SPECIES: *Ananteris balzanii*

◆ Carry a UV flashlight through the Brazilian savanna and you'll see two sets of constellations: bright stars above and scorpions below, glowing blue under your beam and zigzagging from rock to rock. The fastest species is *Ananteris balzanii*, a scorpion with a small body and—sometimes—a big secret.

Despite their predatory reputation, scorpions can become meals for rats, possums, and even slightly larger scorpions. If a predator grabs an *Ananteris* by the tail, the scorpion goes for a desperate gambit: He voluntarily detaches the last segments of his tail in order to escape. This behavior, known as autotomy, also occurs in other animals: Spiders may lose one or more legs, and many lizards can amputate their own tails in order to get the rest of themselves away unscathed.

But for *Ananteris*, autotomy is a bigger sacrifice. What we call the "tail" in a scorpion is more involved than the posterior appendage of a lizard, which, while nice to have, can split off with relatively little incident. A scorpion's tail includes not only his prized stinger but also the last part of his abdomen—including his anus.

A few days after the tail ejection, a scar completely blocks the back end of the *Ananteris*'s digestive system. Because his tail never grows back, a butt-less scorpion can never defecate again. He will suffer from severe constipation for the rest of his life.

To investigate the pros and cons of anus-free living, researchers have studied *Ananteris balzani* in the lab. They've found that in the short term, tail loss doesn't stop the scorpions from capturing prey, or even slow them down much overall. Scorpions can live for as long as a year after surrendering their tails. In the long term, though, the accumulation of feces limits their ability to get around, especially for males.

"How does this affect their sex lives?" you might ask. Good question. Lacking a tail (and its accoutrements) doesn't seem to interrupt courtship behavior or keep the scorpions from mating. But because constipated females have less internal space for embryo development, females without tails have fewer offspring than those who have not had to make this choice.

Overall, though, the hard moments that anus-less *Ananteris* face while running, hunting, and mating in the Brazilian savanna are compensated for by this second chance at life and reproduction—which may explain the evolution of such an extreme form of defensive behavior. If you happen to see an *Ananteris* scuttling around the Cerrado unencumbered by a tail, you can tell him the loss will be worth it—no ifs, ands, or butts.

❯ **How to see them:** Grab your UV flashlight and look for a nimble scorpion about as large as a fun-sized candy bar—and potentially sans butt.

Get Off Me

Although few go so far as the *Ananteris* scorpion, many autotomic species drop their appendages with flair.

When **leopard geckos** (*Eublepharis macularius*) autotomize to escape predators, their snapped-off tails continue to move on their own, swinging, lunging, and flipping in order to acrobatically distract the enemy.

Male **common agamas** (*Agama agama*) whip each other with their tails during battles for dominance. Those who lose theirs in the process may regenerate replacements with stubby, club-like ends, which give them an advantage in future fights.

Ground skinks (*Scincella lateralis*) often eat their own tails after shedding them to prevent the unnecessary loss of an important fat store.

A number of rodents, including **eastern chipmunks**, (*Tamias striatus*) slough off the skin of their tails when grabbed by predators, leaving only naked muscle and bone. Some species of **African spiny mice** (*Acomys* spp.) are able to regrow the skin, while others simply chew off the spooky bare appendage and move on.

Fire-Resistant Plants

To survive in fire-prone grasslands, plants have learned to burn.

◆ Imagine a desolate landscape covered with ashes. You can still smell burnt vegetation, but from the charred soil emerges a garden of wild-flowers pushing up through the gray.

Strange juxtapositions like this are common in the world's most biodiverse savanna, the Brazilian Cerrado. Here, fires sweep through every summer, razing and rejuvenating the ecosystem's plant life—a role they have played for tens of thousands of years, since long before humans arrived.

Many of the Cerrado's plants have developed protective outer structures in order to outlast the flames. Gawky shrubs from the genus *Vellozia* look like they'd scorch quickly in a blaze. (They are sometimes called "rhea's shins" because their thin trunks, triangular branches, and feathery leaves resemble the legs and feet of the ostrich-like bird.) But each *Vellozia*'s trunk is wrapped in a special leaf sheath that can burn for hours. Some members of one endangered subspecies, *Vellozia gigantea*, are 18 feet (5.5 m) tall, having survived repeated infernos for more than an estimated 500 years.

Kielmeyera coriacea, whose branches are tipped with spirally arranged, pink-veined foliage, has a thick cork layer that guards the inner part of the trunk from extreme heat. Meanwhile, its capsule-like fruits insulate their seeds against heat; in one study, seeds reached a maximum of only 140°F (60°C) in the midst of a fire burning at more than 1,300°F (704°C).

In some cases, fire even stimulates the germination of seeds that have been on the ground for years. In September 2005, a wildfire destroyed 80 percent of the ecological station associated with the Brasilia Botanical Garden, which is meant to preserve thousands of the area's endemic species. While assessing the damage, conservation scientists were astonished to find 110 different terrestrial orchid varieties suddenly blooming in the park. Before the fire, they had counted only 44. The heat from the flames cracked the previously impermeable coats of the orchid seeds, allowing them to absorb water from the soil and come to life.

Indeed, many endemic Cerrado plants are brought to life by fire—although even experts can be surprised by the rejuvenating power of a blaze. One of the quickest and most impressive is *Bulbostylis paradoxa*, says Alessandra Fidelis, a fire ecology researcher at São Paulo State University. This native sedge flourishes only after a fire, covering the newly desolate landscape with white tufts within 24 hours.

Grass species that blossom almost immediately after burning are not found in any other tropical savanna, and Fidelis and her team are still looking for the metabolic and physiological factors that drive such fast flourishing. "We often say the Cerrado is a phoenix that regenerates from its ashes," says Fidelis. "I think it is a perfect image."

RANGE: Brazilian Cerrado

SPECIES: Almost all herbaceous and grassy species found in the Brazilian savanna have developed fire-resistant traits, including the endemic *Vellozia* (*Vellozia* spp.), the jacaranda (*Jacaranda* spp.), monkey nut (*Anacardium humile*), and *Bulbostylis paradoxa*.

Bulbostylis paradoxa (top) and Vellozia (bottom) are quick to flower after fires.

❯ **How to see them:** Although the Brazilian Cerrado has lost much of its natural vegetative cover to agribusiness, fire-resistant endemic species are very common in preserved areas such as the Chapada dos Veadeiros and Serra do Cipó national parks. They are best observed three weeks after fire events, which occur during the dry season between July and September.

Pantanal Apple Snails

A snail with a snorkel saves the day.

RANGE: Throughout Brazil, most notably in the Pantanal
SPECIES: Golden apple snail (*Pomacea lineata*)

Golden apple snails spend the majority of their days floating idly in the rivers and lakes of South America, taking care to lay their eggs on vegetation lying just above the waterline. Their closest relatives among the apple snails, *Pomacea canaliculata*, are known as ravenous interlopers—following a misbegotten scheme to launch an escargot industry in Taiwan in the 1980s, these Amazonian natives invaded a large portion of the rice farms of Southeast Asia. The golden apple snail is not as well traveled as its taxonomic siblings, though. Instead, this slow and steady mollusk plays a vital role in the vast ecosystem it calls home.

The Pantanal straddles southwestern Brazil, Bolivia, and Paraguay. At about the size of Washington State, it's the world's largest tropical wetland—but only for part of the year. During the three-month-long seca, or dry period, generally from September through November, the rushing rivers that feed the Pantanal slow to lentic, lakelike bodies. Seasonal herbs and grasses quickly take over the now dry land, making the most of nutrients left over from waterfowl droppings and fish carcasses.

Then the rains begin. By early December, the season of the enchente—the flood tide—has forcefully reshaped the Pantanal. The flora that thrived in months prior are drowned. The thousands of species that call the wet-season Pantanal home, from lithe titans like the giant river otter to delicate floating flowers like the Brazilian water hyacinth, are ready to move back in.

There's only one issue. The bacterial decomposition of the dry-season plants absorbs nearly all of the oxygen in the wetland's waters, causing massive fish kills. The drier the dry season, the worse the fish death. Even detritivore fish like streaked prochilods, who normally have the job of upcycling, often can't survive long enough to consume the decaying plant matter. It's a dire situation—the nutritional riches necessary to sustain the entire ecosystem are trapped in a suffocating, anoxic brew.

That's where the golden apple snail comes in. While these snails are found in the Pantanal all year round, they spend the dry season in a hibernation-like state, shedding up to half of their body mass and biding their time, waiting for the return of the floods. When the waters finally rush in, the snails brave the harsh chemical environment to feed on decomposing plant life, allowing the nutrients contained within to move upward through the food web to snail-eaters like the snail kite and the jacare caiman.

Their trick to surviving the low-oxygen conditions of the water they graze in is deceptively simple: a snorkel. These apple snails have evolved a telescoping attachment to their lungs, an expanding siphon that sucks in air from above the surface of the water as the snail feeds below. Through the small wonder of a snail with a snorkel, the world's largest tropical wetland thrives. ❯ **How to see them:** Head down to newly flooded areas of the Pantanal in the wet season and look for snails the size of a child's fist.

A golden apple snail caught in the beak of a snail kite

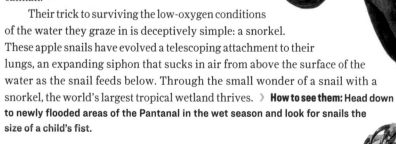

Helpful Scavengers

The animal kingdom is often divided into two categories: predator and prey. But what about the creatures who fall somewhere in between? The morbid meal choices of scavengers keep ecosystems healthy and thriving. Here's how they do it.

VULTURES · While many animals scavenge for only some of their meals, vultures (families Cathartidae and Accipitridae) are true carcass connoisseurs: All 23 species eat carrion almost exclusively. Most have great cutlery—powerful claws and hooked bills perfect for tearing apart their meals. Their unusual bald heads help them avoid getting their feathers matted with blood, and their stomachs are so acidic that they can dissolve bones and handle bacteria that cause serious conditions like gangrene in humans. At the other end, vultures excrete uric acid onto their own legs, which kills even more bacteria.

These adaptations won't win them any beauty contests but are perfect for the vulture lifestyle. Although they may seem invincible, even a vulture can't handle everything—medications for livestock and lead bullets used by hunters have been known to poison them.

HYENAS · Super-social spotted hyenas (*Crocuta crocuta*) and their more introverted relatives, the striped hyenas (*Hyaena hyaena*) trot around the African savanna sniffing out carcasses and even stealing them from other predators.

Hyenas' strong jaws help them chew up even the hardest bits of carcasses they come across. Difficult-to-digest pieces like the hooves get regurgitated as pellets, while the minerals from bones turn hyena droppings bright white. In addition to carrion, striped hyenas have gained a reputation for swiping fresh produce from croplands. They'll take a snack wherever they can get it.

AMERICAN BURYING BEETLES · American burying beetles (*Nicrophorus americanus*) are always searching for a good meal. Their cheerful orange-tipped antennae contain chemical receptors that help them sniff out carcasses from more than 2 miles (3.2 km) away. Once they've homed in, the real work can start.

Fights regularly break out between future beetle dads vying to claim a dead animal for their young. When a victor is crowned, he and his mate begin lovingly

preparing the carcass to make sure it's perfect for their offspring. The beetles bury their prize, remove hair, fur, and feathers, slather the whole thing in secretions that keep it fresh, and lay their eggs inside. When their young hatch, the parents work together to feed them, eating from the carcass and regurgitating into their little ones' mouths.

EAGLES · Majestic birds like bald (*Haliaeetus leucocephalus*) and golden eagles (*Aquila chrysaetos*) are opportunists at heart, turning to scavenging in the winter when prey is harder to find—or, for younger eagles, when their

amateur hunting skills fall flat. Their precise eyesight helps them spot carrion from miles away, and their sharp talons and beaks make quick work of fish and rodents as well as the carcasses of larger animals like elk. Eagles will even follow other birds, like ospreys, if they think they can get away with stealing their kills—unembarrassed to let someone else do the work for them.

BLOW FLIES · Most scavengers wait until an animal is fully dead to eat it. However, several species of blow flies (family Calliphoridae) are known to bend the rules. Their larvae

can nibble on feces or the deceased, but they can also take advantage of wounds on animals that are still alive—including humans. Blow fly larvae can actually help stop infection by keeping a wound clean. However, their feeding can also go too far, and severe infestations can kill an animal.

LIONS · Even the fiercest of hunters will scavenge if the opportunity presents itself. Lions (*Panthera leo*) sit at the top of the food chain, but the pack hunting they prefer takes up a lot of energy. Animals who are already dead make for the perfect lazy meal. Lions will even harass smaller predators like cheetahs to give up their own kills—savanna takeout.

Capim Dourado

All that glitters . . .

RANGE: Brazilian Cerrado
SPECIES: Capim dourado
(*Syngonanthus nitens*),
also known as golden grass

◆ Crafts made of capim dourado, whose name is Portuguese for "golden grass," shine like they're spun out of a fairy tale. Artisans in the Brazilian Cerrado use capim dourado to weave everything from gleaming hats and baskets to luminous, sun-colored jewelry. Despite its gilded look, capim dourado is a double misnomer: It's not gold, and it's not grass either.

"Golden grass" is actually the long stems of a small desert flower known as sempre viva. Lent its flash by the aluminum-rich soil in which it grows, the plant spends much of the year as a small rosette of leaves hunkered close to the ground, hidden under a canopy of taller grasses. But every July—springtime in the Cerrado—the flower stalk shoots up 2 feet (60 cm), blooms, makes seeds, and dries to a high shine in the sun. By September, it's standing tall among the other grasses, glinting until it catches someone's eye.

Capim dorado is harvested in Jalapão, Brazil.

Although it grows all over the Cerrado, capim dourado is perhaps brightest in Jalapão, where the Mumbuca community has been harvesting it for nearly a century. Husbandry of the wild plant involves regular controlled burning, which keeps the crowded grass canopy open so that sunlight can reach the rosette. The plant, which thrives in wet grasslands, does its part by trapping humid air between the folds of its leaves, which improves its chance of survival during a blaze.

This careful relationship between fire, water, plants, and people was nearly undone by the success of capim dourado crafts. When demand for the golden goods skyrocketed in Brazil in the early 2000s, a new wave of harvesters unfamiliar with the environment poured in. At that point, the local communities and government called on scientists to help maintain the balance.

A handful of gold

The researchers helped establish timing that allows the plant to complete its life cycle before it donates its stalk to beauty. "When you harvest it and it's dry, the [rest of the] plant stays on the ground. If not, you're going to take the plant with you," says botanist Isabel Belloni Schmidt. A state law issued in 2019 forbids harvesting capim dourado before September 20 each year, giving the plant enough time to mature and fully dry out.

Given an official start date, the Mumbuca community of Jalapão began a new tradition: a festival that ushers in the harvesting season. During the Festa da Colheita do Capim Dourado, people gather for three days of food, conversation, music, and demonstrations, and to be dazzled by the latest ways in which weavers have transformed this beloved material. **❯ How to see it:** This plant grows throughout the Cerrado, but handicrafts made with it are sold in Brazilian cities beyond the grasslands.

THE WILD LIFE OF A Golden Grass Weaver

■ Nubia Matos da Silva is a journalism student, a craftswoman, and a member of the Mumbuca, a Quilombo community in Jalapão State Park. Members of the Mumbuca are descended from African people who did not accept the conditions imposed on them after they arrived in Brazil, instead choosing to build their own way of life in the Cerrado. Nubia's family has been weaving with capim dourado for four generations.

• **Where does capim dourado grow?**
Capim dourado grows in the vereda, a part of the savanna where the grass grows low to the ground and the earth is very wet. It exists just before the gallery forest, an area with larger trees that grow along the river. I have heard of people who tried to grow capim dourado from seeds, but it never worked because it did not produce its golden color. Capim dourado is very mystic, very unique, full of its own identity.

• **How long has your community been harvesting capim dourado?**
There are no records of how long our community has been harvesting capim dourado, since the people here never thought about recording the times and events. But I can say that it is since the time of my great-grandmother Laurina. She was walking through the green field when she noticed something shining, and she thought that she could do something with that shining grass. She picked some of this grass and showed it to her husband. Then she made the first craft ever made with capim dourado—a hat that she gave to her husband to protect him from the sun. It was a very beautiful hat.

• **What do you make with it?**
We can make capim dourado crafts for the kitchen for decorations, charger plates for the table, or fruit bowls. We can also make jewelry like earrings, necklaces, bracelets, and much more. Capim dourado is truly versatile, and we can do a lot with it.

• **Are there risks of harvesting capim dourado?**
If it is harvested before the correct time, its seeds become sterile. That is why we need to emphasize that capim dourado can only be harvested after September 20. This practice is respected by the community.

• **What value does capim dourado have to your community?**
Every time I work with it, when making an object by hand, it takes me back to my grandmother and my aunts, and I think about everything that capim dourado gave to us. Many people walked on this grass thinking nothing of it, but my great-grandmother saw its importance and saw that that grass could give us things that would be inaccessible without it. In our community, capim dourado is one of the main sources of revenue.

Capim dourado does not only have a monetary value, it has a sentimental value and a cultural value. When I weave with capim dourado, I remember my loved ones who are not here anymore, but who have left us something so precious that it makes us remember always all the possibilities nature has to give us. ■

Giant Anteaters

Very large predators with very tiny prey

RANGE: Throughout Central America and northern South America, especially the Venezuelan llanos
SPECIES: Giant anteater (*Myrmecophaga tridactyla*)

◆ Most anteater species are what might be considered reasonably sized for creatures who subsist entirely on tiny bugs. The northern tamandua, for example, could stand shoulder to shoulder with a large raccoon, while the silky anteater is the size of a red squirrel.

Not the giant anteater. These behemoths can weigh more than 100 pounds (45 kg); with their tails stretched out, they're 6 to 8 feet (1.8 to 2.4 m) long. They fuel their shaggy, bulky bodies by hoovering up tens of thousands of ants and termites per day, thanks to an anatomy built for the job.

Giant anteaters spend many of their waking hours wandering around, snout to the ground, in search of ants and termites. While their eyesight is poor, a powerful sense of smell allows them to scope out colonies from far, far away—they can even identify different ant and termite species based on scent alone.

Once they sniff out an ant or termite nest, they shred it wide open with their razor-sharp claws, which can grow 4 inches

Body by ants

(10 cm) long. They're careful not to demolish any ant colony completely, preferring to leave their snack stashes intact so they can return from time to time.

Though they don't have any teeth, the anteater's distinctive snout conceals a secret weapon: a slender, sticky, 2-foot-long (60 cm) tongue that can flick in and out up to 150 times per minute. An anteater positions his snout near the opened-up nest and unleashes this probe, reaching into as many nooks and crannies as possible before the ants get wise and begin stinging.

Anteaters' anatomical oddities aren't just external. Because they can't really chew—remember, no teeth—their stomachs have small, muscular protrusions that contract to grind the ants and termites down to a fine pulp.

As they're pulverized, the insects release formic acid—which, ironically, they produce for self-defense in life. In anteaters' stomachs, however, the chemical helps break down the bugs' bodies even further, allowing anteaters to extract as much nutritional value from them as possible. (In fact, unlike many other mammals, giant anteaters don't produce any hydrochloric acid in their stomachs, relying on the ants to essentially digest themselves.)

Even when perfectly utilized, ants and termites don't have a ton of nutritional value—100 grams of red ants yield only 14 grams of protein. But an ant-based diet has at least one advantage: Unlike most arthropods, ants and termites are highly sociable, which means that where anteaters find one ant, they're certain to find plenty of others.

> **How to see them:** They're instantly recognizable—try Serra da Canastra National Park in Minas Gerais, Brazil.

Baby anteaters hide themselves by blending into their mothers.

CHAPTER 3

—————◆—————

Mountains

P icture a mountain from a distance. Its shape crisp against the sky, its top shrouded in clouds, a peak can seem less like a place and more like a destination—somewhere to reach for, not somewhere to be. It's no wonder communities through time and across cultures have housed their gods on mountains, giving them nosebleed seats from which to watch the world.

But the world is happening up there, too. Mortals of many sizes, shapes, and skills live in mountains—piled in dens in the foothills of the Appalachians, knitting together alpine lakes, or prowling vast territories that span the Himalayas.

For these mountain dwellers, height is not a challenge to be conquered. A mountain's escalating altitude provides a series of microclimates for inhabitants to dwell in or shift between. Mountain forests give shelter to dedicated frog parents and well-traveled monarch butterflies. Barer habitats above the tree line have other selling points: scree strewn with boulders from which pikas shriek daily announcements, or precipitous inclines where balletic goats protect their kids.

Of course, the high life can require derring-do. Himalayan jumping spiders—world record holders for altitude, found 22,000 feet (6,707 m) above sea level—may fly to their perches on gusts of wind, using balloons made of their own silk. Catfish in the Andes scale waterfalls with their fins and teeth, while female *Darevskia* lizards handle isolation in the Caucasus by cloning themselves.

But for many of these creatures, the biggest challenges come from climate change and human encroachment. As we melt glaciers, dam waterfalls, and dig elements out of mountaintops, we interrupt the mountains' carefully graded habitats. Some species are adapting—the plant *Fritillaria delavayi* is actively evolving, changing colors to better hide from human harvesters. Others, like meltwater stoneflies of Glacier National Park, will likely be lost. All underscore that mountains are worthy of our care. They are earthly places, after all.

Contributors: Ashley Braun, Ula Chrobak, Angie Drake, Kate Evans, Leah Fabel, Marco Ferrarese, Rachel Fritts, Natasha Frost, Claudia Geib, Kate Golembiewski, Mara Grunbaum, Jessica Leigh Hester, Elizabeth Hlavinka, Heather Jasper, Myles Karp, Kestrel Keller, Stephanie Krzywonos, Matt Malinowski, Jitaditya Narzary, Austin Price, Linda Rodriguez McRobbie, Julia Rosen, Ethan Shaw, Carla Silbert, Melissa Scott Sinclair, Jack Tamisiea, Kavitha Yarlagadda, Martina Žoldoš

Timber Rattlesnake Hibernacula

Ancient dens of legendary mountain dwellers

RANGE: Timber rattlesnakes are found throughout the eastern United States, from northern Florida to New Hampshire.
SPECIES: Timber rattlesnake (*Crotalus horridus*)

◆ As spring sunshine warms the Appalachian Mountains, something wakes within the rock. Golden eyes gleam. Rattles buzz. Long bodies flow from fissures and coil on stone shelves. This is an ancient ritual: the annual emergence of the timber rattlesnake.

Warm weather beckons the snakes out of their cozy dens.

Timber rattlesnakes are zigzagged with dusky colors, from tan to yellow-brown to nearly black. Those living in lower-altitude forests spend the winter tucked into individual hibernation sites, such as stump holes and animal burrows. In the mountains, however, timber rattlers have adopted a different strategy to escape the penetrating cold: They share communal, ancestral dens.

These dens, called hibernacula, are deep crevices or rock chambers to which the same population of snakes returns every autumn. The biggest dens in the central Appalachians can shelter as many as 300 snakes, their long bodies—they can stretch up to 5 feet (1.5 m)—entwined in piles. Some hibernacula have been used for 6,000 to 8,000 years, meaning snakes have been snoozing in them since Neolithic times.

Humans have destroyed all but a few of these refuges. Early settlers hated timber rattlers, as Puritans believed them to be agents of Satan. Upon discovering a den, they would stand outside it in the spring and slaughter snakes one by one as they sleepily emerged. Benjamin Franklin called rattlesnakes "Felons-convict from the Beginning of the World." "These, whenever we meet them, we put to Death," he wrote—before cheekily suggesting the snakes instead be gathered up and sent to England, to be distributed in Parliament members' private gardens.

The snakes don't deserve to be cast as villains. Although they are venomous, timber rattlesnakes "really aren't that dangerous," says herpetologist Christopher Petersen, who spent seven years tracking their movements with radio transmitters. Fewer than 1 percent of his study subjects even rattled, he says: "They're just laid-back, docile animals." And they are deeply intimate with their terrain: Males patrol home ranges of up to a square mile and may travel long distances seeking food or mates before heading back to their dens in autumn.

Timber rattlesnake populations are still declining in much of their range, mainly due to habitat loss, road deaths, and poaching. If you come across a den while hiking, just watch your step and observe with care—and keep its location to yourself, as befits an ancient secret. ❯ **How to see them:** To protect these snakes, the locations of their dens are kept under wraps. But you may encounter timber rattlesnakes in deciduous forests across the eastern United States. If you do, watch from a safe distance—the best way to ensure everyone's well-being is to leave them alone.

APPALACHIAN MOUNTAINS

- The Appalachian Mountains stretch 1,500 miles (2,400 km) up the eastern margin of North America, from Alabama into Newfoundland. They were once as high as the Alps or Rockies before erosion carved them into lower, softer peaks.

- The range's north-south orientation gives the diverse flora and fauna living there some helpful flexibility, allowing them to migrate seasonally and to easily change latitudes as the climate shifts.

- Its highest point is the top of Mount Mitchell in North Carolina, which reaches 6,684 feet (2,037 m). The peak is named for Elisha Mitchell, who fell to his death trying to measure the mountain and is now buried at the top.

KEEP AN EYE OUT FOR Different microhabitats within the mountains, including wet, boggy fens and grassy heath balds—summits that mysteriously lack trees.

KEEP AN EAR OUT FOR Adventure stories and sightseeing tips from the nearly 3 million people who hike a portion of the Appalachian Trail each year.

KEEP A NOSE OUT FOR The moldy, sweaty-socks scent of the galax, an evergreen plant whose waxy leaves cover the forest floor across this range.

Hawk Mountain

The world's first raptor sanctuary, started by a suffragist

◆ Hawk Mountain, the world's first sanctuary for birds of prey, was founded in 1934 thanks to an unlikely confluence of three elements: thermal air currents, overzealous hunters, and a bird-loving suffragist named Rosalie Edge.

Every fall, North American raptors—from lofty bald eagles to nimble peregrine falcons—migrate south from their various breeding grounds to their summer ranges, where rivers remain unfrozen and fields are hopping with food. In the spring, they come back north, riding the wind along the coast or over mountain ranges.

On the way, a whole lot of them fly by Hawk Mountain. Wind currents and thermal updrafts concentrate the flow of raptors over this sky-high ridge in the Appalachians. On gusty days, "you can get hundreds and hundreds zipping by within fifty or a hundred feet of you," says Laurie Goodrich, the sanctuary's director of conservation science.

The mountain got its name during the Great Depression, when hunters climbed up it to shoot hawks en masse. Conservation organizations failed to step in—at the time, hawks were unpopular even among bird fans, due to their tendency to eat smaller birds—and the state game commission paid $5 per head for dead goshawks. Countless raptors were killed for sport or cash on the peak.

In 1933, photographs of hundreds of shot-down raptors got in front of Rosalie Edge, a New York socialite and activist who championed conservation and women's right to vote. Horrified by the images, she made it her mission to protect the birds. The next year, she leased 1,400 acres of land on the mountain and hired the husband-and-wife team of Maurice and Irma Broun, both avid birders, as wardens to keep hunters away. Once the hunters had been dissuaded, Edge opened the area to the public, and Hawk Mountain Sanctuary was born.

It was the Brouns who began tallying raptors as they migrated past the mountain—their earliest record, from September 30, 1934, documents 128 hawks, eagles, harriers, falcons, and vultures. Today, a combination of sanctuary staff and volunteers continues the tradition, which is now the world's longest-running raptor count. They've found that between April 1 and May 15 each year, about a thousand birds of prey make their way through. Between August 15 and December 15, the average total number is 18,000.

The ongoing old-school monitoring gives scientists insights into bird populations and behaviors, which they supplement with data obtained from GPS tags. This helps us learn where the raptors go throughout the year—after they've soared safely past this checkpoint, intercepted only by binoculars. ❯ **How to see it:** Spring and autumn migration seasons are the best time to visit Hawk Mountain—aim for a windy day. The center's South Lookout is wheelchair accessible.

LOCATION: 1700 Hawk Mountain Road, Kempton, Pennsylvania
SPECIES: Sixteen raptor species fly past Hawk Mountain, including the bald eagle (*Haliaeetus leucocephalus*), golden eagle (*Aquila chrysaetos*), American kestrel (*Falco sparverius*), and peregrine falcon (*Falco peregrinus*).

A Cooper's hawk (top) and a red-tailed hawk (middle), two of the many raptor species that fly past Hawk Mountain during fall and spring migration seasons

THE WILD LIFE OF A Raptor Surveyor

■ In 1984, Laurie Goodrich became the first full-time biologist on staff at Hawk Mountain Sanctuary; today, she's the director of conservation science there. She has helped count migrating raptors at the mountain every year for more than three decades.

• **What's the view like from the top of Hawk Mountain?**

You're looking at a bowl of forested landscape. And then beyond that is farmland, and then beyond that, way in the distance, on a clear day, you can see Allentown and Bethlehem, about 40 miles [64 km] away. It's really a beautiful, idyllic kind of landscape.

• **What makes a mountaintop a good place for bird-watching?**

One of the things about being on top of a mountain that's very unique is that you can often look down on the birds. We get birds hugging the ridge, turning around right below you, and that's really a spectacular way to look at birds in flight. You just can't get that when you're at a lake or the coast or something, because then they're always going to be above you. It's a real treat.

• **What's the coolest thing you've ever seen during a count?**

I remember waking up in the middle of the night. It was so windy, the shutters on the house were banging, and I thought, "Oh, I've gotta get up there early." The sun was not even over the hillside yet, but the birds were zipping by. A sharp-shin goes *zip*, right by me, and another one goes by me here, and a kestrel's right there. I was literally in the migration. That was the coolest thing, standing there and just watching and feeling these birds going by. And all of a sudden I said, "Oh no, I gotta count them!"

• **You've been leading bird counts for more than 30 years. What changes have you seen in the raptor migrations over time?**

When I started working here, it was very rare to see a bald eagle or a peregrine falcon. We might have had 50 bald eagles go by in the year. Back in the late 1980s, everybody would applaud, because it was so rare. Now, we get more than 600 bald eagles in a season. It's a real success story, and it's a testament to banning DDT and all the effort state and federal wildlife agencies did to bring them back.

But there are other birds we're very concerned about that are declining. Some birds that used to be very common, like the sharp-shinned hawk, have been declining steadily. Nobody knows why. The American kestrel is another bird that we're doing research on—they're getting rarer and rarer. We have a grant here to do research on them, and we're trying to figure out why they're declining. So hopefully, we'll figure out what the conservation steps are.

• **You don't keep track of just threatened birds—you count common raptors, too. Why is it important to pay such close attention to birds that are doing all right?**

The time to save a species is while it's still common. If you wait until the species is rare, like the California condor, we have to take them out of the wild and breed them in captivity and put in millions of dollars just to make sure they survive. But if you can detect these declines early on, there's still a lot of opportunity for wildlife agencies to do something about it. ■

Candy Darters

North America's most beautiful fish

RANGE: Streams and tributaries in the upper Kanawha River basin, in Virginia and West Virginia
SPECIES: Candy darter (*Etheostoma osburni*)

◆ The original version of the American folk song "The Big Rock Candy Mountain" ends with a lament. "I've hiked and hiked and wandered, too," the tired narrator sings, "but I ain't seen any candy."

He should have tried snorkeling. In a handful of mountain streams in Virginia and West Virginia lives a treat of a fish: the candy darter.

Male candy darters rock a color scheme that makes them look like expensive sneakers or small clowns. Their blue and orange whorls, dots, and stripes, arranged on a backdrop of silvery scales, are so unusual for a freshwater environment that when biologist Katie McBaine first saw a photo of one, "I could have sworn it had to be a marine fish," she says. In-person encounters have since inspired her to crown the species "North America's most beautiful fish."

Loud colors aside, these fish are not splashy showoffs. Candy darters tend to hang out between rocks at the still bottoms of swiftly moving rivers, where males quietly impress females with their hot coloration. When they do come up into the current to eat insects, they use their strong pectoral fins to keep the rushing water from carrying them off. Watching them underwater involves digging your feet and hands into the riverbed and holding on for dear life, McBaine says.

Candy darters have a low tolerance for sediment, which fills up the crevices where they spend their time. As a result, their presence serves as an environmental indicator—"basically showing us that this is a clean system," says McBaine.

The proposed Mountain Valley Pipeline, which would funnel natural gas 303 miles (488 km) through Virginia and West Virginia, has been repeatedly held up by lawsuits brought by organizations seeking to protect the candy darter, which is federally endangered, as well as other fish. Other threats are more insidious—a slightly duller species, the variegate darter, has been introduced to some of the candies' streams in West Virginia, where the two species now interbreed. For the moment, though, these shy rainbows continue to sweeten up the mountains. ❯ **How to see them:** Strap on a snorkel and stick your face into one of the fast-running streams of West Virginia's Kanawha River.

Go waaaaay to the bottom of an Appalachian stream and you may get a treat.

Doomed Glacier Stoneflies

These bug martyrs are on the list.

◆ Thousands of species across the world are in mortal danger from climate change, and American legislation has had a tough time keeping up. Numerous attempts by conservation groups to put climate-imperiled plants and animals on the Endangered Species List have failed. Even the polar bear barely made it.

This trend was recently bucked by a couple of unlucky bugs. Two stoneflies native to Glacier National Park became the first invertebrates to land on the Endangered Species List specifically because of climate change—in this case, because it's literally melting away their homes.

Mountain streams house insects on a continuum: Milder, lower-altitude waters may swim with dozens of species, while the higher-altitude waters are home to fewer (but tougher) bugs. The meltwater lednian stonefly and the Western glacier stonefly are some of the only animals found up here, "where water originates," says Clint Muhlfeld, a biologist who helped survey the insects for their potential listing. A certain type of flexibility has helped the stoneflies survive just under the continent's spout, where each season brings a new challenge: dirt and turbidity in spring, fluctuating temperatures in summer, and just-thawed iciness in winter.

RANGE: Stream segments fewer than 1500 feet (457 m) beneath glaciers in Glacier National Park and surrounding areas
SPECIES: Meltwater lednian stonefly (*Lednia tumana*) and Western glacier stonefly (*Zapada glacier*)

This Western glacier stonefly needs ice and snow to survive.

"They're adapted to persist in these really harsh environments," says Muhlfeld. But climate change promises emptiness rather than chaos. Rising temperatures are whittling down glaciers and snowpack all over the world. Glacier National Park has lost 125 glaciers since 1900; according to current models, the rest will disappear by 2030.

Eventually—probably soon—these stoneflies will go with them. In their surveys, Muhlfeld and others were surprised to find small populations hanging on in snowfields and groundwater springs, even after their glaciers had melted. But as the mountains continue to warm, the stoneflies may lose those sources, too. And unlike other animals, who can chase their preferred conditions up to higher altitudes, the stoneflies are "literally at the top of the continent," says Muhlfeld. "Sooner or later there's nowhere to go."

In 2019, after over a decade of consideration, the US Fish and Wildlife Service decided to designate these two stoneflies as threatened. The listing cites "the effects of climate change," making them the first bugs with this distinction. (When the Endangered Species Act was introduced, in 1976, there were no insects on it at all.)

Under current law, the government is still not required to address the causes of climate change in order to protect these doomed bugs—but at least we've been forced to spell things out plainly. ❭ **How to see them:** Unless you're on a special collecting trip, it's unlikely you'll find yourself far enough up in the mountains to see these insects. But if you're there, look for narrow, winged bugs perched on rocks and reddish nymphs in the water.

Snow-Patch Havens

In the shaded pockets of mountains, caches of snow hang on past the springtime—and sometimes even all year long.

RANGE: Worldwide
ASSOCIATED SPECIES: Wolverine (*Gulo gulo*), gray-crowned rosy-finch (*Leucosticte tephrocotis*), icebug (family Grylloblattidae), and others

◆ Below their snow lines, as winter turns to spring and temperatures rise, formerly icy slopes melt and green up.

But if you know where to look, scraps of winter remain all year long. In cirques, gullies, and other sheltered places, caches of mountain snow persist, tucked away from the liquifying sunlight. Some of these snow patches are seasonal, lasting well into summer before melting away. Others are perennial, usually surviving until the first snow falls and thus persisting year after year.

Snow patches are ecologically assertive, their presence affecting everything from the shape of mountain forests to the behavior of large mammals. Because most plants can't grow through a snow layer, perennial snow patches delineate where vegetation can grow, while seasonal caches shorten the growing season. In some places, bands of trees act like snow fences, forming deep drifts in their lee. "Ribbon forests" may result, with tree belts—subalpine fir in the Rockies, for example, or snow gum in Australia's Snowy Mountains—separated by snow patches that prevent seedling establishment.

But snow patches help shepherd certain plant and animal species by moderating temperatures and supplying critical moisture. In wind- and sun-scorched alpine realms, for example, drought-vulnerable species like mountain sorrel and haircap mosses grow in the margins of snow patches, in the beds left after they disappear, or in the meltwater zones below.

Small predators and scavengers are also drawn to snow patches, because the same wind patterns that pile up the snow in winter bring in buggy feasts later in the year. Aerial insects and ballooning spiders are lofted upslope from lower elevations, tumble out in the eddies, and get trapped in the snow. In the high country of western North America, gray-crowned rosy-finches nest near snow and ice, ensuring a low-hassle commute to the frozen food section. Wolverines—who den in spring snowbanks—do them one better, sometimes stashing leftover meat in the drifts.

For other animals, snowy spots serve as cool-off zones, providing temporary relief from heat and biting insects. On hot summer afternoons, you might see ptarmigan, elk, or feral mustangs cooling off in them. Certain recurring snowfields have drawn caribou for millennia, often with human hunters close behind, and mountain goats are known to seek refuge from the summer swelter in the (now declining) snow patches of Montana's Glacier National Park. And, of course, as a patch slowly dwindles, it contributes to the runoff that helps hydrate the mountain and everything below.

As climate change heats up alpine habitats, out-of-season snow could be an early casualty. Snowfields are shrinking, and seasonal snow patches may be disappearing earlier in the year. From caribou comfort levels to plant community compositions to water distribution, the impacts could be wide-ranging, and potentially unchill. ❯ **How to see them: Look for shady spots when you're hiking, and see if any snow has stuck around.**

Animals—like these elk in the Rocky Mountains—love to gather in snow patches.

The Disappearing Sphinx

In Scotland, mountaineers and other snow enthusiasts have tracked the persistence and recurrence of a number of snow patches for decades. The best known, called the Sphinx after a nearby climbing route, is found in the Cairngorms, on a mountain called Braeriach. At its most sprawling and differentiated, the Sphinx is visible from nearby ridges, as though someone scrubbed briefly at the landscape with an eraser.

The Sphinx survives most summers, dwindling slowly until it is replenished by winter's first snow. In October 1933, it melted completely for the first time on record, shocking the Scottish Mountaineering Club and earning a mention in the *Times of London*. It disappeared again in 1959—and then in 1996, 2003, 2006, 2017, 2018, 2021, and 2022.

The new feebleness of the once-mighty Sphinx is likely a symptom of climate change, which has warmed average temperatures and reduced snow cover across the Cairngorms. Its decline has saddened Scotland's small community of snow patch watchers, who chronicle it as it shrinks.

American Pikas

Adorable, chemically savvy stockpilers

RANGE: American mountain ranges west of and including the Rockies
SPECIES: American pika (*Ochotona princeps*)

◆ High above the tree line in the Rocky Mountains, ringing clear through the cold alpine air, comes a call like a broken squeaky toy. This is the survival cry of the American pika, who is telling his peers: "I'm alive! Don't you dare steal my hay piles!"

Bright-eyed, egg-shaped, and very furry, pikas—lagomorphs, in the rabbit family—inhabit the windswept talus slopes of the mountains west of the Rockies. Here, temperatures are low, winters unforgiving, and plants—the pikas' preferred meal—sparse, especially in winter.

Pikas don't hibernate, so they need a food source that can sustain them through the lean months. During spring and summer, they'll gorge themselves on some plants, while secreting stashes of others in caches all over the rocky talus. According to some research, pikas can make as many as 14,000 food-gathering missions in July and August, scrambling over the scree with full bouquets in their mouths.

These savvy foragers aren't just tucking away any old shoots and stems, though. They preferentially stockpile plants high in phenolic acids, organic compounds with various protective properties. Phenolic acids are toxic to insects and animals that might otherwise eat a freshly harvested stack. They're also not good for pikas; however, the compounds break down over time. As they do, they act as a natural preservative, keeping the store from spoiling and leaving pikas with ample hay to consume as winter drags on. Pikas, it turns out, can tell the difference between plant species with low and high levels of phenols, and even between individual plants of the same species that happen to have different phenol concentrations.

Pikas pick only the hardiest hay for their bouquets.

Pikas are relatively territorial and live in separate holes on the talus, like neighbors on the same street. "They all know each other on the slope," says Andrew Smith, a biologist who has been studying them for more than 50 years.

A pika follows each harvest with a screaming session, climbing atop a nearby rock and calling loudly to let nearby pikas know he's still alive and occupying his territory. If he doesn't, his neighbors may assume he has died and try to take over his food caches. (In some populations, pikas will steal from one another's hay piles regardless—a phenomenon called kleptoparasitism—although Smith says this is not common.)

Pikas' determination and flexibility are helping them adapt to climate change, at least for now. Although they are not physiologically suited to warming temperatures, they will change their behavior to deal with them. Smith observed a population of pikas living on a south-facing slope in Bodie, California, where daytime temperatures climbed to more than 78°F (25°C)—the temperature at which alpine pikas are thought to die. The pikas simply stayed in their cool caves during the day, venturing out to forage at night. When they finished, they didn't fail to announce their success, squeaking proudly in the moonlight. ❯ **How to see them:** It's not unusual to come across American pikas on mountain hikes. Park websites and trail forums have good advice about exactly where they tend to be.

Bleeding Tooth Fungi

Nicer than they look

◆ Find yourself toe-to-toe with *Hydnellum peckii* in a mountain forest, and you may think you've stumbled into a fungal crime scene. This mushroom's underside is coated in rows of toothy spines, lined up in a perpetual grimace. Meanwhile, its white cap oozes blood-colored goo from dozens of pores.

But there's no need to pull out the first aid kit: Those stab wounds are natural. Through an osmotic process called guttation, young *H. peckii* mushrooms absorb water from wet soil and excrete a thick, sap-like liquid, which is reddened by a pigment within the fungus.

This is an adolescent enterprise. Adults grow less flamboyant as they age, turning a dull beige and showing only the faintest scars from their pustulant puberty. The mushroom's "teeth"—which produce spores along their edges—stick around, although they also gray over time.

If you can get past its frightening exterior, *H. peckii* is actually quite charming. It smells sweet, like hickory nuts, and it isn't toxic, although its peppery taste is so bitter it's deemed inedible. Squint and cock your head to the side, and you can convince yourself that the red goo on its cap looks like raspberry jam on an English muffin, or perhaps a bedazzled head of cauliflower.

Plus, like other forest fungi, this species bleeds generosity. Through symbiotic underground mycorrhizal networks—which can stretch up to 11 feet (3.4 m) away from where the fruit of the mushroom appears—bleeding tooth fungi share enzymatic meals of minerals and nutrients with their tree hosts and receive photosynthesized carbon in return.

And although scientists still have not decided exactly what that red oozing liquid is, samples of it have been found to have anticoagulant and antibacterial properties. Maybe someday you'll open that first aid kit and find a little bottle of mushroom blood. ❯ **How to see them:** Look for these striking shrooms in mature or old-growth coniferous forests, in the mosses and litter around trees like hemlocks and Douglas firs. You'll find them most easily in the fall after a rain.

RANGE: Widespread in North America and Europe and occasionally found elsewhere
SPECIES: Bleeding tooth fungus (*Hydnellum peckii*), also known as devil's tooth fungus or strawberries and cream fungus

Hang on—you've got a little something right there.

Wolf Birds

Ravens make dubiously helpful wingmen.

RANGE: Most of the Northern Hemisphere, including parts of the northern US, Canada, and Russia.
SPECIES: Common raven (*Corvus corax*) and gray wolf (*Canis lupus*)

◆ When a wolf pack takes down prey, it's a gory, audacious event. The wolves rip apart their kill, scattering blood and bits everywhere. As the commotion draws nearby animals, one mob of ambulance-chasing scavengers is already poised to swoop in: ravens.

Canny and patient, ravens will manipulate everything from inanimate objects to each other in order to get what they want. Because their beaks are too small to pry apart a carcass, a wolf pack is just another tool in their toolbox. Their habit of following packs around, waiting for a free meal, has earned them the nickname "wolf birds."

"You read a lot about how ravens lead wolves to wounded animals to kill, and how they have this symbiotic relationship," says John Marzluff, a professor at the University of Washington who has studied ravens for more than 35 years. "It's really much more parasitic." While researchers have documented ravens traveling as far as 100 miles (160 km) patrolling for kills, more than 90 percent of the time, the birds are already present when a hunt is over, waiting for the wolves to fill up so they can scrounge the leftovers.

After one Michigan wolf hunt, ravens were found to stash away half of a 650-pound (295 kg) moose carcass. Some scientists even think that wolves live in packs in order to mitigate such theft.

Why do wolves—who could dispatch a raven in a few bites—put up with these moochers at all? It's possible the birds pull their weight in other ways, like by warning packs about incoming threats, says Brad Bulin, a wildlife biologist and Yellowstone guide.

Ravens have been seen playing with wolf pups, pulling on their tails and swooping in with sticks to start games of tug-of-war. This could be a trust-building tactic, so that when the pups grow up and start hunting, they're accustomed to having the birds around, Bulin says.

Ravens flock to a wolf kill in the Bieszczady Mountains in Poland.

However they do it, the ravens have successfully ingratiated themselves with their canine compatriots. In nearly two decades at the park, Bulin has never seen a wolf kill a raven—although they do sometimes snap at them, he says. Someone has to keep these birds in line. ❯ **How to see them:** Ravens and wolves can be spotted together anywhere their ranges overlap. They are regularly seen interacting in Yellowstone National Park.

More Raven Tricks

It's not just wolves who find themselves entangled in ravens' projects. Throughout history, people have noticed this bird's propensity for cleverness.

For a number of Indigenous groups in northwestern North America, Raven is a mythological trickster. One popular story, told differently by different groups, involves Raven rescuing the world from darkness by sneaking into the home of an old man and releasing the sun, moon, and stars, which had been hidden away in boxes. In Norse mythology, the god Odin has two ravens—Huginn, "thought," and Munnin, "memory"—who fly all over the world and report back what they find.

Contemporary researchers are attempting to find out how ravens use thought and memory. Over the years, in different experiments, scientists have shown that ravens know how to use tools, plan ahead, and barter for food with tokens. They also hold grudges when warranted: In one experiment, trainers made deals with captive ravens, trading one crust of bread for one nubbin of cheese. Another set of trainers then cheated the ravens, eating the cheese instead of completing the trade. Even weeks after that incident, most ravens refused to trade with these "unfair" trainers. If you make a pact with a raven, it's best to honor it.

Mountain Goats

The gravity-defying goats of western North America make themselves at home where predators fear to tread.

RANGE: Mountainous areas of Canada and the western United States, from Alaska to Colorado

SPECIES: Mountain goat (*Oreamnos americanus*)

◆ Mountain goats drop right into the vertical lifestyle. To give their offspring a leg up against predators like grizzly bears and wolves, mother goats give birth in places too steep for clumsier mammals. Within minutes, the newborns are able to walk; over the next couple of weeks, they carefully learn to climb. Step by step, they grow into their birthright: a ridiculous-looking physiology that grants them incredible mountaineering prowess.

On flat ground, mountain goats look incorrectly assembled—their legs a bit knock-kneed, their rumps nearly as high as their horns. But each piece has a purpose. Compared with other ungulates, mountain goats have short, stocky legs and compact torsos, giving them low centers of gravity. Supremely muscular shoulders help them control their bodies as they maneuver up and down slopes. Their chunky hooves are flexible, with large toes that can spread apart to give the foot more gripping surface, and bendable yet tough underpads, which can conform themselves to provide traction even on wet or snowy rock.

To turn around on a narrow ledge, a goat might stand on his back legs, press his front hooves against the rock wall, and walk his forelegs over his head in a death-defying cartwheel. He might climb into a tree growing horizontally from a cliff to munch on lichen, or wedge himself into a bottomless crevice to lick a particularly salty rock. Observers have seen the 200-pound (90 kg) animals perch with all four hooves on an area no bigger than a playing card.

Mountaineering is not without risks, and goats are occasionally injured or killed in falls. But the trade-off is worth the protection they gain by being able to outscale predators like grizzly bears, wolves, and mountain lions. Their incredible climbing prowess even helped them evade the nineteenth-century hunting boom that decimated most large North American mammals.

Some populations have been so successful, in fact, that they've caused problems for people. In 2018, officials opted to remove a group of nonnative mountain goats from Olympic National Park, where a lack of predators and habituation to hikers had made them overconfident and occasionally aggressive. Several hundred goats were sedated, suspended in slings from helicopters, and flown across Washington State to their native range in the Cascade Mountains—a journey that, had they been awake, may have struck them as the culmination of their skills. **〉 How to see them:** Take a hike above the tree line in the Cascades, the northern Rockies, or the mountains of Alaska, and you may well encounter wild mountain goats in their natural habitat. National parks with native mountain goat populations include Glacier, Mount Rainier, and Kenai Fjords in the United States, and Banff and Kootenay in Canada.

Flexible hooves, muscular shoulders, and a low center of gravity make mountain goats— even kids—comfortable traversing seemingly impossible slopes.

Potentially Immortal Bristlecone Pines

These scrappy and squat high-elevation trees can live for thousands of years without seeming to age.

RANGE: High elevations across the Great Basin region of the western United States, including the White Mountains of eastern California and western Nevada

SPECIES: Great Basin bristlecone pine (*Pinus longaeva*)

◆ The world's oldest known trees aren't outwardly impressive. The most famous, nicknamed Methuselah, has lived quietly in the White Mountains of California for an estimated 4,850 years, ignoring the rise and fall of civilizations and growing very, very slowly. From the outside, "it's a disappointing tree, to be honest," says Brian Smithers, an ecologist at Montana State University, who describes the ancient organism's form as "somewhere between a shrub and a tree."

Inside, however, marvels are occurring. Methuselah and other Great Basin bristlecone pines have found ways to handle pretty much all of life's ravages—and maybe even time itself.

Methuselah's underwhelming appearance is the result of a successful life strategy. Great Basin bristlecones root in thin limestone soils at elevations up to about 10,000 feet (3,048 m), where they face temperature extremes, drought, and raging winds. To cope, they conserve energy. Unlike big, hunky trees like sequoias, which in their youth can pack on an inch of trunk diameter per year, Great Basin bristlecones often add less than a millimeter. (In dry years, they might not grow at all.) This slow growth results in dense wood that can withstand wind and insects. Their gnarled, squat forms help them weather storms, and they can even sacrifice parts of their body when times are hard, letting one section of roots and shoots die while the rest of the tree lives on.

Bristlecones' endurance is encoded deep within. Individuals of most species on Earth decline physiologically over time, as our cells accumulate damage and eventually die in a process called senescence.

But bristlecones—along with a handful of other trees, including species of juniper, ginkgo, and redwood—might not experience senescence. Instead, their cells continue to perform as though they're young and spry, even after thousands of years. For instance, while most tree types photosynthesize more slowly in old age, a bristlecone sapling and a 4,000-year-old elder are equally efficient at making food from sunlight. Even the oldest bristlecones make healthy inner bark cells that transport water and nutrients, produce viable seeds, and don't have shortening chromosome tips—a common marker of biological aging.

So far, bristlecone immortality is hypothetical. Some researchers argue that very old trees do actually age—we just have yet to pin down what processes define their senescence. And despite their toughness, many ancient bristlecones still die from lightning strikes, drought, or insect attacks, all threats exacerbated by climate change.

They're also not immune to twists of fate. In 1964, a geographer got a tool stuck in a Great Basin bristlecone and ended up asking a park ranger to fell it. That tree turned out to have been nearly 5,000 years old—killed, in the end, by its own humble appearance. ❯ **How to see them:** Hike the trails near the Ancient Bristlecone Pine Visitor Center outside Bishop, California. The specific location of Methuselah is kept private to protect the tree, but the paths wind past numerous bristlecones 4,000 or more years old.

Two bristlecones in Inyo National Park

Mexican Jumping Beans

Is it magic, or just bugs?

RANGE: Northwestern Mexico, primarily in the state of Sonora
SPECIES: Jumping bean (seed of *Sebastiania pavoniana*) and jumping bean moth (*Cydia saltitans*)

◆ In the 1930s, a rift developed in the French surrealist movement over Mexican jumping beans. Some of these so-called beans—seedpods, really—had made their way to France, where people observed that the beans twitched and moved of their own accord when held in the palm of the hand.

Literary critic and sociologist Roger Caillois wanted to dissect the beans to investigate the phenomenon and confirm his hunch that there were worms or larvae living inside. Writer André Breton decried Caillois's desire to peek behind the curtain. The two quarreled over the nature of mystery, beauty, and reason, and the relationship between the two leaders of this intellectual movement was fractured, never to be repaired.

Nearly a century later, the jury is still out on mystery, beauty, and reason. But as for jumping beans, Caillois was correct. Living inside each twitching seedpod, which generally comes from the shrubby spurge *Sebastiania pavoniana*, is the larva of a moth, *Cydia saltitans*, whose species name derives from the Latin for "to jump."

The moth lays eggs on this plant, and when a larva hatches, it bores its way inside the seedpod, attaching itself to the internal structure with a web of silky threads. Over time, the larva will metamorphose, going through a pupal stage and eventually emerging from its seedpod nursery as a fully developed moth.

It is the larva that performs the apparent magic. When a larva experiences a spike in temperature—say, from sitting in the palm of a human hand—it moves, tugging the threads that attach it to the seedpod like a puppeteer. This forces the pod to "jump" around, and is likely an attempt to cool off or reach shade.

Many of them end up moving much farther than intended. Mexican jumping beans, or brincadores, have long been sold as novelty souvenirs—most famously in Sonora,

Sinaloa, and Chihuahua, but also roadside around the southwestern United States and, now, online. "There's a lot of interest from older people that grew up with them," says Mark Harzdorf, an importer who buys jumping beans from harvesters in Mexico and sells them, sometimes by the sack, through his Colorado-based company Amazing Beans.

Other jumping bean fans eschew nostalgia, preferring to chase practical applications. "I had a guy who was interested in using them to make a fishing lure that would move around on its own," says Harzdorf. Scientists from Georgia Tech studied the jerky locomotion of the beans and determined that their movement patterns could serve as the basis of robotic navigation and search systems—a thought that would likely displease some French surrealists. **› How to see them:** If you'd like to get close to the action, the town of Alamos, Mexico, is considered the world jumping bean capital, although climate change has been making harvests less reliable. You can also buy jumping beans online and, in some places, by the side of the road.

Monarch Overwintering Sites

Where migrating royalty gathers in the trees, by the hundreds of millions

◆ A single monarch butterfly can stop you in your tracks—her size, the fragile drape of her wings, her orange glow as the sun shines through.

Now imagine that times half a billion. Every fall, most of the world's monarchs converge in Mexico's Sierra Nevada range to spend the winter together. Starting in November, the oyamel firs here drip with so many butterflies that their limbs appear abstract and melted, like a Dali painting. The small miracle of a single insect is refracted into something truly sublime.

Monarchs' summering grounds can be as far north as southern Canada. Scientists are still unsure how these pollinators find their way thousands of miles back to Mexico year after year. Research suggests they may orient themselves via magnetic fields or an internal sun-based compass.

The trip's logistics are complicated by the fact that, like many insect migrations, the journey is much longer than any one life span—the monarch who arrives in the Mexican mountains is probably not the same one who flitted over your New England window box. By the time butterflies return north, a year after the last ones left, four generations have passed. That's like your great-grandfather starting a road trip that you have to finish.

However they pull it off, the monarchs end up clustered in a handful of colonies in west-central Mexico, coating trees at elevations as high as 10,800 feet (3,292 m). There, they sip dew from leaves and live off their fat reserves for months. The largest kaleidoscope settles inside the Monarch Butterfly Biosphere Reserve, a UNESCO World Heritage Site in Michoacán, about two hours west of Mexico City. In winter, they cluster for warmth, their combined weight dragging down—and occasionally breaking—the oyamel branches. When temperatures rise as spring begins, they spiral through the forest like confetti, soaking up the sun and occasionally returning to the trees to mate for hours.

LOCATION: The vast majority of monarchs overwinter in a small swath of the Sierra Nevada mountains. Smaller groups go to Florida, southern California, and Baja.
SPECIES: Monarch butterfly (*Danaus plexippus*) and oyamel fir (*Abies religiosa*)

Monarchs travel to Mexico to mate for hours on oyamel trees.

Though a Canadian zoologist first reported these overwintering sites to the world in 1976, Indigenous Purépecha and Mazahua people have been tracking the monarchs' return for centuries. The lepidopteran descent coincides with the corn harvest and Día de los Muertos (Day of the Dead). Many locals consider monarchs, or las parákatas in Purépecha, to be the spirits of ancestors visiting during the holiday that celebrates them.

In July 2022, the International Union for Conservation of Nature added monarchs to their Red List of Threatened Species. In the past, conservationists thought that logging in Mexico was the main threat to the raucous orange congregations. But while that risk has lessened thanks to efforts by local people, NGOs, and the government, the butterfly population continues to shrink.

Tackling problems elsewhere on the monarch migratory route is urgent. In the United States, milkweed plants—the monarch's main sustenance and the caterpillar's sole host plant—have severely declined, mostly due to agricultural pesticide use. Unlike the tree hosts at the wintering sites, these widespread but beleaguered plants are not so easily set aside in reserves—but, luckily for anyone who wants to help these iconic travelers on their journey, they are quite easily planted. ❯ **How to see them:** Parts of Michoacán's Monarch Butterfly Biosphere Reserve are open to the public and packed with monarchs from November through March. You can also visit the much smaller western overwintering population on California's central coast. Individual monarchs can be found on milkweed flowers throughout the United States and Canada in the summer.

Welcome to the bug sublime.

Five Steps to a Perfect Monarch Rest Stop

Milkweed (*Asclepias* spp.) plays a huge role in the monarch migration—monarch caterpillars hatch, grow, and metamorphose in the leafy embrace of this plant. As milkweed populations shrink across North America, monarchs are vanishing, too. Luckily, it's easy to grow this plant yourself. Just follow these steps:

1. Which weeds? There are more than 70 milkweed species native to the United States. Many are rare or endangered, while others are not cultivated. Regional milkweed guides from the Xerces Society can help point you to the ideal species for your location and provide information on where to source seeds and plants.

2. Seeds and starts: While it's ecologically ideal to plant milkweeds native to your region, monarchs will develop on any milkweed. Swamp milkweed (*Asclepias incarnata*) and butterfly weed (*Asclepias tuberosa*) are widespread and commonly available at nurseries. Avoid tropical milkweeds like blood flower (*Asclepias curassavica*), whose longer bloom times may encourage monarchs to lay eggs out of season.

3. Get growing: Plant your milkweed in a weed-free zone—almost any sunny spot that doesn't get mowed

will do. Never use insecticides or herbicides on or near milkweed.

4. Milk the experience: Congratulations, you're now a backyard butterfly hotelier! Look for monarch caterpillars, banded with yellow, black, and white, as well as their green chrysalises and the fully fledged orange-and-black butterflies sipping nectar.

5. Share the love: If you don't have space to grow milkweed yourself, encourage local garden clubs or your city parks department to plant it.

TIP: A lepidopteran cannot live on leaves alone. Once they take to the air, migrating monarchs need nectar to power their journeys. If planting milkweed gives you the gardening bug, the Xerces Society has a map showing other flowers you can grow to supplement nectar supplies for migrating monarchs and other pollinators.

Totora Reeds

In the world's highest lake, a humble marsh reed supports life at many scales.

RANGE: Lake Titicaca and nearby waters, straddling the border of Peru and Bolivia

SPECIES: Totora reed (*Schoenoplectus californicus tatora*)

◆ Lake Titicaca, which spans 120 miles (193 km) of the border between Peru and Bolivia, is the highest navigable lake in the world, as well as one of the oldest. For 3 million years, its frigid waters have lapped at rocky shores 2 miles (3.2 km) above sea level, reflecting surrounding Andean peaks.

Protecting its shoreline are wide belts of marshland grass up to 20 feet (6 m) tall, each blade green as it rises from the water and brown at its tufty tip. The plant's wispy appearance belies its superpowers: It is the stuff of life in Titicaca. Pretty much every resident of the lake, from snails to birds to people, builds their home in, around, atop, or with the totora reed.

In totoras' calm underwater stands, giant gray-green Titicaca water frogs guard their eggs until they hatch. Their young remain tadpoles for up to a year, gathering the strength to survive the lake's icy temperatures. Then they grow into the largest aquatic frogs on the planet, the length of a house cat when outstretched.

The water frogs feast on several snail species endemic to the lake. Over millennia, as the lake's salinity levels rose and fell, these resilient gastropods—most no taller than a child's fingernail—thrived on microorganisms teeming in the totora, outlasting any salt-sensitive snail cousins.

Totora reeds are foundational for everyone in Lake Titicaca.

Atop the water, flocks of flightless Titicaca grebes boast bright orange beaks and spiked mohawks. They build their nests in the safety of the totora reeds and dive for the 20-odd varieties of pupfish that evolved in the lake and still swim in its shallows.

And several miles off the coast of the Peruvian city of Puno, 50-square-foot (4.6 sq m) clumps of totora roots, which rise to the surface when unearthed, form the spongy foundation of about a hundred floating islands constructed by the Uros people. Although no one knows precisely when or why they moved onto the lake, Uros ancestors likely arrived in the region before the Inca. Their islands require ongoing fortification and periodic rebuilding, and they are carpeted with dried totora reeds, which the Uros use to build homes, buildings, handicrafts, and boats sturdy enough to survive days-long journeys to the lake's far shores.

Edmundo Moreno, a biology professor at Universidad Nacional del Altiplano de Puno, has studied Lake Titicaca's ecology for more than 40 years and looks out over its ancient waters each day. So vital is the totora that just the sight of the reeds brings with it a sense of security. "Maybe you can't see the small snails or crustaceans or the birds," he says, "but you feel the presence of life." **❯ How to see them: Along much of Titicaca's marsh shoreline, totora reeds are impossible to miss. To visit the floating islands constructed from totora by the Indigenous Uros people, go first to the Peruvian city of Puno. Day trips and overnight stays begin from Puno's port.**

ANDES MOUNTAINS

- The world's longest above-water mountain range, the Andes form a kind of spine along the western coast of South America, reaching all the way from the Caribbean to the southern tip of the continent.

- The Andes are filled with endemic species—organisms found nowhere else. Roughly 7 percent of the world's vascular plant species grow wild only in the Andes, including top-heavy monkey puzzle trees—climbing, twining plants with voluminous clusters of up to a hundred long-tubed flowers—and golden hawthorn, whose blooms resemble giant pieces of cheddar popcorn.

- The highest point of the Andes, Mount Aconcagua, sits 22,831 feet (6,959 m) above sea level in Argentina. It was sacred to the Incas—archaeologists have found the mummified remains of a human sacrifice more than three quarters of the way up the mountain, provisioned with beans and sandals for the afterlife.

KEEP AN EYE OUT FOR The blindingly white, cracked expanse of the Salar de Uyuni salt flats. This favorite flamingo hangout covers more than 4,050 square miles (10,500 sq km) of Bolivia's Altiplano.

KEEP AN EAR OUT FOR The sheeplike bleats of guanacos, the hardy wild descendants of llamas that range throughout the Andes, grazing on grasses, lichens, and even cacti.

KEEP A NOSE OUT FOR The rotten-egg scent of sulfur emanating from some of the highest-altitude geothermal fields in the world. The bubbling mud flats of Sol de Mañana in Bolivia and the sprawling geyser fields of El Tatio in Chile are simmering reminders that many of this range's mountains are volcanic.

Climbing, Armored Catfish

The missing link between two strange fish families

RANGE: Mountains east of
the Orinoco River
SPECIES: *Lithogenes wahari*

◆ Members of *Lithogenes wahari* are 3 inches (12.7 cm) long, bristling with body armor, and fond of dragging themselves up the sides of boulders using their fins and sucker mouths. Thick-bodied and marbled with brown and black, these very special catfish combine attributes of two groups of ichthy-icons: the climbing catfish of the family Astroblepidae and the armored catfish of the family Loricariidae. The species is an exemplar of mountain fish skills—and the potential missing link in the tale of how all these weird fish got this way.

To the scientists who began studying it in the 1990s, *L. wahari* was initially a puzzle. (It didn't help that their first sample was delivered in rough shape, as it had been collected by people who planned to eat it—one scientist said it looked like it had been run over by a truck.) The fish had bony armor protecting its head and tail, like an armored catfish. These rigid plates, called scutes, are much like the interlocking pieces of a turtle's shell.

But it also had pelvic fins that looked like those of climbing catfish, which live only in the steep Andes Mountains. These incredible fins can move backward and forward independently, each wired to its own muscle, an adaptation seen in climbing catfish but not in armored ones. Combined with a mouth like a strong suction cup and toothlike protrusions that help fins get traction on surfaces, they give climbing catfish the ability to leave water and lurch up and over rocky walls, like giant, fishy inchworms. This skill may help them escape fast-moving mountain streams swollen by melting snow.

You're looking at a fish triathlete.

If *L. wahari* sported all this equipment at once, which family did it belong to? To answer that question, scientists would need more specimens. After decades spent trying to figure out where the species lived, biologists headed down to the Río Cuao, an Orinoco River tributary, and plucked 84 *L. wahari* fish from where they were hanging off the sides of boulders.

These living and unsquashed specimens clearly had traits that bridged the two families. But those extraordinary climbing fins were key: It seemed unlikely that such specific tools would have developed twice. The team believes the new fish is the "missing link" of the two families—that both armored and climbing catfish evolved from a common ancestor much like *L. wahari*, losing the attributes they didn't need and gaining new ones.

Single specimens of two other *Lithogenes* species have since been found, each hundreds of miles away from the *L. wahari* collection site. While that sparsity makes it tough to perform comparative DNA tests on the family, it also suggests something amazing: that the ancestor of all these little fish was able to colonize an astonishingly large area, birthing medleys of armored, sucking, and climbing descendants as it did. ❯ **How to see them:** If you're trekking along the small tributaries of the Orinoco River, look for these tiny fish clinging to rocks in clear, fast-moving streams.

Five Fish That Can Beat Your Bouldering Personal Record

Fish across the world are on the up and up. Here are some more species that could give Spider-Man a few lessons.

1. 'O'opu nopili (*Sicyopterus stimpsoni*): Also known as Nopili rock-climbing gobies, these fish are found only in Hawai'i. They can scale waterfalls so high that an equivalent task for a human would be climbing Mount Everest three times in a row.

2. Andean climbing catfish (*Astroblepus ubidiai*): Found only in Ecuador's Imbakucha watershed, this climbing catfish's local name is preñadilla—Spanish for "pregnant"—for its alleged fertility effects when eaten.

3. *Chaetostoma microps*: These Ecuadorian members of the armored catfish family were known for clinging to river-washed boulders with their sucker mouths. But in 2015, biologists filmed one climbing a cave wall.

4. *Garra barreimiae*: One of very few native freshwater fish species left in the United Arab Emirates—where drought, water extraction, and construction have destroyed most freshwater habitats—these survivors have a suction cup on their lower jaws that they use to scale rocks and waterfalls.

5. Climbing perch (*Anabas testudineus*): Capable of crawling across dry land—including slopes of up to 30 degrees—and surviving for up to six days out of water, these Southeast Asian fishes, which swell up to suffocate anything that tries to eat them, are currently freaking out ecologists in Indonesia and Papua New Guinea, where they are invasive.

Vicuñas

Life in the world's most coveted fur

RANGE: Ecuador, Bolivia, Peru, Chile, and Argentina
SPECIES: Vicuña (*Lama vicugna*)

◆ Vicuñas look a lot like their domesticated camelid cousins, llamas and alpacas. They have the same stilt-like legs, long eyelashes, and ability to run straight up even the steepest mountainsides.

But they're much, much softer. Vicuña fur is exceptionally fluffy and warm, thanks to each strand's diameter—which is only about 13 microns on average—and hollow structure, which makes for effective insulation. That's crucial for animals living in the cold, high reaches of the Andes, 17,000 feet (5,182 m) above sea level.

Vicuñas move in family herds, each composed of a male, five to ten females, and their young. Every morning, the herd will climb down from a rocky sleeping area to their favorite grassy meadow, where they graze and ruminate while the youngsters leap and play. The group works together to mark their territory with dung heaps, while males defend the space from other vicuña groups, as well as from predators like pumas and foxes.

Vicuñas are well adapted to the high life. Soft pads on their feet help them pick their way through rough terrain, while their small teeth allow them to nibble dwarfed high-altitude plants. They have two incisors that grow throughout their lives, like the

Vicuñas are big softies.

front teeth of rats or beavers. At night, when a vicuña lies down to rest, a patch of extra-long, cream-colored chest fur acts like a built-in pillow, offering protection from the cold ground.

Vicuñas and their snuggly, cinnamon-colored fur have impressed people for centuries. In the time of the Incan empire, only the royal family had the privilege of wearing clothes made from vicuña fur. Because vicuñas cannot be domesticated, their fur was harvested annually in a ritual roundup called chaccu, during which herders carefully surrounded the wary animals, sheared them, and then let them go.

When European colonizers arrived in the early sixteenth century, they hunted vicuñas with guns, seeking to undercut Andean culture by going after a beloved Incan symbol. (They also exported the pelts to Europe for people like Spain's King Phillip II, who had his bedcovers made with them.) Despite intermittent national bans on hunting, rampant vicuña slaughter continued until the 1960s, when conservation agreements between Peru, Bolivia, Argentina, and Chile established full legal protection for the animals.

Today, Andean communities safeguard the well-being of their local vicuñas. To sate the demand for their fur—still the most expensive wool in the world—they have brought back chaccu. Now, vicuñas can be sheared once every two years. The rest of the time, they are left to wear their luxury coats in peace. ❯ **How to see them:** Each September, the community of Huachocolpa, Peru, welcomes visitors to observe chaccu.

THE WILD LIFE OF A Vicuña Veterinarian

■ Óscar Aragón Merma is a veterinarian specializing in South American camelids. His family is from Sicuani, Peru, and has raised alpacas for more than six generations. As part of the Peruvian government's program to protect vicuñas, veterinarians participate in chaccu.

• **What is chaccu?**
Chaccu is a traditional way to harvest vicuña fur that goes back hundreds of years to pre-Inca Andean civilizations. Between May and October, every community chooses their date to hold chaccu and registers the date with the Ministry of Agriculture. Rural communities that care for the vicuña and its habitat go out into the mountains to search for vicuña herds.

When they find a herd, they surround it from a great distance, then slowly close in. Vicuñas are very shy, so they bunch together in the center until they are surrounded by people holding hands. One by one, the vicuñas are caught, held down, examined, and sheared.

• **What is your role as veterinarian during chaccu?**

I check the health of every vicuña, and if any of them are sick, I treat them before we release them. The first step is a clinical exam and drawing blood samples for analysis. Then, another team does a physical exam to see if each vicuña is big enough to shear and if the fur is long enough.

• **What happens to the fur that's sheared during chaccu?**
The community can sell it to whomever they want. Most sell to international companies that export to Europe and use it to make clothing. Since the vicuña is a protected animal, any garment made with vicuña fur must have a certificate that shows it was harvested legally and ethically.

• **Why should people continue this tradition?**
Chaccu should be continued because it's a sustainable activity and an important connection to our Inca and pre-Inca ancestors. Also, chaccu creates an incentive for the community to protect the vicuña. By law, it's the communities that are responsible for the conservation of the vicuñas that live in their territory.

• **What are the biggest threats to the vicuña's survival?**
Loss of habitat due to grazing domestic animals like cows and sheep, degradation of the quality of food and water supply because of climate change, illegal hunting, and diseases like mange. The effect of climate change on rainfall is reducing their water supply. Unlike most camelids, the vicuña needs to drink water every day. As climate change reduces the quality of the plants that the vicuña eats at higher altitude, the animals descend to lower altitudes, where they come in contact with domestic animals and can contract diseases.

• **What is the best way to protect vicuña?**
Protect their ecosystem. If we can guarantee their food and water supply, then we can improve their survival rate. We need scientists with research budgets to put GPS devices on vicuñas to see where they are and what they do. There is so much we need to learn about them to protect them more effectively. ■

Camera Traps

Let's say that you want to observe wild animals doing whatever it is they normally do. But because you're around, watching, the animals aren't going to do that at all. Instead, they're going to do what they do when a strange person is nearby—up to and including never coming out of the bushes. Your thirst for knowledge has kept you from acquiring any.

Enter the camera trap. This simple contraption has helped us Big Brother our way into a better understanding of reclusive animals' behaviors, populations, and interactions—as well as, sometimes, their very existence. Its guiding principle—that we don't have to hang out somewhere in order to see what's going on there—has allowed us to expand our knowledge without doing too much high-impact stomping around.

The invention of the camera trap is generally credited to George Shiras III, a pioneering wildlife photographer bent on encouraging his fellow outdoorsmen to come out of the woods with, as he wrote, "wild-life pictures instead of antlers or rugs." Beginning in the 1890s, Shiras developed a number of strategies to get animals to "photograph themselves," including baiting strings and tying them to camera shutters as well as running trip wires over birds' nests or between trees.

His nighttime technique, which he called "flashlight trapping," involved elaborate setups of wires, tasty bait, and hermetically sealed boxes of magnesium powder, the detonation of which provided the necessary flash. (While today's camera traps privilege stealthiness, Shiras's nocturnal

snapshots came with explosions that could be heard up to 3 miles [5 km] away and often sent their subjects "fleeing in needless terror," making for some dramatic photographs.)

In 1927, the ornithologist Frank M. Chapman borrowed Shiras's methods to survey animals at his field site on Barro Colorado Island in Panama, initiating the first scientific use of camera traps. He ended up with evidence of tapirs, ocelots, and coatis—as well as a sense of the unique emotional tenor of photography that is removed in space and time from the photographer, which he described as filled with "joys of anticipation" and "pleasures of realization."

Other scientists soon caught on. In addition to species surveys, trappers began to be able to identify individual animals and document their activity patterns. These devotees also improved the technology, replacing magnesium powder with flashbulbs, getting cameras to run on portable batteries, or swapping out trip wires for beams of light that, when interrupted, caused the shutter to click.

Filmstrip-style photo series soon allowed for the elucidation of particular behaviors, like nest building and highway crossing. In the 1990s, a group of researchers in Nagarahole National Park, India, led by K. Ullas Karanth, performed the first statistically rigorous population study using camera traps, establishing through repeated photographs of individuals that about 11 tigers lived in the park.

Today, thanks to improved portability, battery life, image quality, and storage capacity, camera traps are some of the most popular tools available for wildlife study. The footage they capture has taught us about animals common and rare, gregarious and elusive.

Researchers use camera traps to ask serious questions, such as whether a certain species still exists in a particular habitat, as well as sillier ones, like what different animals do when confronted with a mirror. (Elephants inspect their reflected trunks and legs, while tapirs become startled.) And as the technology becomes more and more accessible, laypeople have been able to ask personal questions as well, such as "Who is coming by at night and eating my vegetable garden?" All, at this point, without any explosions.

THE WILD LIFE OF A Cat Camera-Trapping Team

■ The Andean cat is one of the most elusive mammals on Earth. Cintia Tellaeche and Juan Reppucci, researchers with the Andean Cat Alliance, have rarely encountered them even with years of study. Creative use of camera traps helps them learn more about these high-living felines.

● **What sort of knowledge do we have—and not have—about the Andean cats?**

CINTIA: Twenty years ago, almost nothing was known about the species. A couple of pictures proved the cat exists, and a few skulls in museums. But nothing was known about the biology and ecology. In 2004, the Andean Cat Alliance was formed by a few countries where the Andean cats are distributed.

JUAN: At the beginning, even the distribution was unknown. It was very evasive. Now we know more about habitat use, space use, activity patterns, and we have an abundance estimate for our area. We also now know that the Andean cat shares its whole distribution with another species, the Pampas cat.

● **Have you ever seen an Andean cat in real life?**

CINTIA: I've never seen one in the wild.

JUAN: It took me nine years. That day was crazy, because I saw one Andean cat in the afternoon, and in the evening, I saw a Pampas cat. In nine years, not a single cat—and then in one day, I saw both.

● **What role do camera traps play in your work?**

JUAN: Camera traps are very important. At the beginning, when the project was started, they'd find, in a month, maybe one Andean cat feces [deposit]. So all this work—camping at the site, doing nothing but looking for the cat—for one single data point. With a camera trap in a really good place, we might have, on average, one cat every 10 days.

● **How do you decide where to put the cameras?**

JUAN: The Andean cat uses latrines—small caves where they leave feces. So we look for a general area that has latrines and then we look in that area for a nice spot. With time, you start to get an eye—like, a sense. Sometimes we look for a place and say, "That looks good." You're not sure why, but you know.

● **Is it possible to ask more in-depth questions with camera traps?**

CINTIA: We have some videos of the cats making calls in Chile. And we also can study with pictures how they interact, with each other and with the Pampas cat. We can learn about the cubs, because we have some pictures of cats with kittens.

The elusive Andean cat.

● **How do you stay patient when your study subject is so elusive?**

JUAN: When you get an image of it in a new place, it's always super exciting. To see that they're walking the same places you are walking, even when you didn't ever see them. It's rewarding to see—well, they are still there. ■

Flashpoints in Animal Photography

1826/1827: Joseph Nicéphore Niépce, the inventor of photography, practices by taking pictures of the dovecote next to his office. His earliest surviving photo, from 1827, shows the dovecote—but not any of the doves, who were moving too fast to be captured.

1864: Frank Haes begins his popular series of stereoscopic photos of animals in the London Zoo. These include two now-extinct species, the thylacine (Tasmanian tiger) and the quagga.

1878: Eadweard Muybridge takes his first successful photographs of a horse running, proving that all four of a horse's feet do leave the ground and setting the stage for moviemaking.

1882: Physiologist Étienne-Jules Marey builds a "chronophotographic gun," which shoots 12 frames per second and allows him (in 1894) to demonstrate how cats nearly always manage to land on their feet.

1906: *National Geographic* publishes a full issue about wildlife photography, complete with 74 images by George Shiras III. Legend has it that multiple board members resigned in protest over the magazine becoming a "picture book." But readers—now viewers, too—went wild.

1926: Photographer-biologist team Charles Martin and William Longley take the first underwater color photograph, capturing an image of a hogfish near the Florida Keys.

1986: Marine biologist Greg Marshall begins developing the "Crittercam"—a wearable camera for animals that also captures audio and environmental data. The first prototype is worn by a loggerhead turtle.

2015: The Snapshot Serengeti project recruits tens of thousands of volunteers to help researchers identify animals in three years' worth of footage from 225 camera traps in Serengeti National Park.

Marsupial Frogs

Dozens of frog species pamper their young in special parental pockets.

RANGE: Tropical forests of Central and South America
SPECIES: Dozens of species in the genera *Gastrotheca* and *Flectonotus*, including the Andean marsupial tree frog (*G. riobambae*) and the horned marsupial frog (*G. cornuta*)

◆ If you're walking in the tropical mountain forests of Central or South America, and you spot what looks like a fractalized frog, don't panic. This is not a rainforest glitch. It's just a marsupial frog mom, sending her young into the world the best way she knows how.

There are more than 75 known species of marsupial frogs, which belong to the genera *Gastrotheca* and *Flectonotus*. By amphibian standards, they are helicopter parents. While most frogs deposit masses of eggs in fresh water and leave the resulting tadpoles to fend for themselves, moms of this group stay involved for much of the process.

Just like the mammals they're named after, female marsupial frogs have pouches where they raise their young. But unlike a kangaroo or opossum mom, who carries her babies in front of her, a marsupial frog's pouch is on her back, with a horseshoe-shaped opening at the base for entry and exit.

The female of a species like the Andean marsupial tree frog stays on land to lay her eggs. From his perch on top of her back, her mate fertilizes the eggs as they emerge and pedals each one up into the female's pouch using his back feet. Depending on the species, marsupial frogs will stow between 10 and 120 fertilized eggs in these pockets, which end up stuffed fat like a hamster's cheek. In at least one species, this special skin backpack is crisscrossed with blood vessels that deliver nutrients to the growing froggies through their gills.

A giant marsupial frog, with babies on board

Andean marsupial frog moms carry their eggs around with them as they develop into wee tadpoles. Eventually, these females find a watery oasis and "give birth," helping pull their wriggly offspring out of their back pockets with their rear feet.

But most marsupial frogs skip the tadpole stage entirely, with females toting around their broods as they transform from eggs into froglets. "They complete the entire metamorphosis in their back," says Mauricio Akmentins, an Argentinian researcher who studies marsupial frogs. "It's a trade-off [to] ensure the offspring's survival." In other words, mom doesn't mind a little extra back-breaking if it means predators won't gobble up her little ones.

When their transformation is complete, the mini frogs pop out from the base of their marsupial mom's pouch, ready to take on the world.

Unfortunately, that world is tough right now. Chytridiomycosis, a fungal disease that threatens amphibians worldwide, has not spared the marsupial frogs, and habitats in much of their range are threatened with development, wildfires, and climate change. One species from northwest Argentina's Yungas Andean cloud forests, the Calilegua's marsupial frog, has not been seen since 1996. In circumstances this difficult, a head start helps only so much. ❯ **How to see them: Many marsupial frog species are imperiled and shouldn't be bothered in the wild. El Valle Amphibian Conservation Center in El Valle de Anton, Panama, raises insurance populations of amphibians, including the horned marsupial frog.**

A pygmy marsupial frog in Venezuela

Frailejones

These Andean flowers harvest water for their neighbors.

RANGE: Colombia, Ecuador, and Venezuela
SPECIES: Frailejón (*Espeletia* spp.)

◆ Standing tall among the gentle waving grasses of the Andean páramos, the sturdy frailejón wears a brown cape of dead leaves, like the robes of its namesake, the Franciscan friar.

This dense covering makes the frailejón, a relative of daisies and dandelions, impervious to cold—an important survival skill in this sky-scraping environment, where harshly sunny days lead to nights of near-freezing fog. Adapting to life here has also granted this plant its most generous gift: the ability to collect, save, and share water.

While most plants practice transpiration, taking in water from the soil and releasing up to 90 percent of it into the air, the frailejón does the opposite. Its succulent sage-green leaves prevent water loss by maintaining a warm microclimate that discourages evaporation. Downy hairs on these leaves also sip vapor from passing clouds and low-lying fog. As temperatures drop at night and rise again the following day, each hair moves with the plant's circadian rhythm, pumping droplets toward the rosette of leaves at the frailejón's center. The plant stockpiles this water in its fleshy trunk, like a kind of living well.

Frailejones, in the ecosystems that depend on them

The frailejón uses the water it needs. But it eventually releases up to 90 percent of its cache into the surrounding soil, sharing clean water with neighboring plants and nearby streams. Water from the frailejón even reaches people: The Andean páramos are the largest source of water for many communities in Colombia, Ecuador, and Venezuela. During their flowering seasons, frailejones share their colors as well, as different varieties cover the mountainsides with deep yellow, intense magenta, or violet maroon.

People don't always return the consideration. The frailejones of the Andes—including 30-foot-tall (9 m) specimens in Colombia's Chingaza National Nature Park, some

of which have played their role for centuries—are frequent victims of "fires, tractors, 4WD rallies, construction, mining, and agriculture," says naturalist and photographer Peter Rockstroh, who has successfully grown these plants in his home garden in Bogotá.

Recently, public television station Señal Colombia has been giving these strong but silent plants a voice—and making a plug for environmental stewardship—through the character of Ernesto Pérez, an Instagram and TikTok sensation who also happens to be a cartoon frailejón. "I am your friend, and caring for water is my profession," the cartoon plant tells a growing set of followers. Pérez and his living fellows need our friendship in turn. ❭ **How to see them:** You'll find this shrubby plant in páramos (alpine grasslands) ranging from Lara, Venezuela, to Llanganates, Ecuador. Some of the tallest "big friars" live in Chingaza National Nature Park in Colombia.

White Bellbirds

The world's loudest birds like to get real close.

RANGE: Northeastern South America
SPECIES: White bellbird (*Procnias albus*)

◆ Have you ever sat down next to a guy you thought was attractive, only to have him turn away from you, sing one very loud note, swivel back toward you, and sing an even louder note directly into your face?

If the answer is "yes, and it was great," you might be a female white bellbird. Males of this species have the loudest birdcall ever measured, clocked by scientists at 125 decibels—somewhere between a chain saw and a military jet takeoff. They maximize its effect by singing as close as they can to the female, an experience that may be the closest anyone has come to being hit on by a pile driver.

Neotropical bellbirds are known for their unusual metallic-sounding songs, which stand out even in the cacophony of a rainforest. Listeners compare them to squeaky swing-set chains or the ring of a hammer striking an anvil. White bellbirds, who live in the mountains, have two song types: a "ridiculous ringing sound you can hear from over a mile away," and their clipped, sonic-blast mating call, says Mario Cohn-Haft, one of the ornithologists who measured their volume.

That mating call is the record-setter. Like other sexually selected characteristics— an elk's antlers, a pop star's eyeliner—evolution has pushed it to a comical extreme. Researchers think that over time, the call has grown both shorter and more intense, trading any tone or flourish for a pure blast of noise. Up close, it sounds like "if you asked a trumpeter to play a note as loud they could," says Jeffrey Podos, another member of the measuring team.

LOVE ME!!!!!!

Anatomically, white bellbirds achieve this ear-blasting volume through extremely strong stomach muscles. When they're ready to call, they puff up with air and then flex, forcing the sound out as hard and quickly as they can. Even through their fluffy feathers, you can see their washboard abs.

Their social strategy is less clear. The call is accompanied by a brief dance that culminates with the male spinning toward the female, shrieking the loudest note right into her ear as he whips his voluptuous chin wattle. The females often jump backward to avoid being hit full-on by the call, which (to humans, at least) exceeds the threshold for ear pain.

"There's other birds that when a female is close to them, they sing more softly— like whispering sweet nothings rather than turning up the heat," says Podos. "The bellbirds insist on singing their loudest song." If you've got it, flaunt it.

❭ **How to see them:** Within their range, it's hard to miss their famous calls—listen for loud sounds that resemble metal on metal. To see them, hike into mountains like Brazil's Serra do Apiaú, where the birds' tree perches can put them at eye level.

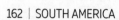

Orchid Bees

The cologne makers of the insect world

RANGE: South and Central America
SPECIES: Orchid bees (tribe Euglossini)

◆ Orchid bees are amazing to catch sight of—familiar forms gussied up in metallic green, blue, and copper.

But if you really want to be impressed by one, give him a sniff. Male orchid bees are the cologne makers (and wearers) of the insect world, carefully composing scents out of local ingredients in order to get a nose up on the romantic competition.

The bee tribe Euglossini comprises 250-odd types of orchid bee, so named for their special relationships with the flowers. Orchids draw the bees in with heady compounds, which echo the scents of everything from vanilla to eucalyptus to carrion. The bees glean inspiration from other sources, too: Different species may visit patches of fungi on rotting wood, dung piles, or wounded trees dripping with resin. In Brazil, one type has been seen scraping the insecticide DDT off the sides of houses with no apparent ill effects, perhaps drawn to the scent of danger.

Once an orchid bee reaches what he's after, he mixes up a sample, adding oil from a gland in his head and sweeping up the concoction using his bristled front legs. He then bottles it in special back leg pouches. Over time, different ingredients—such as a whiff of cinnamon-y orchid, a dollop of resin, a whisper of excrement—gel into each bee's signature scent. One study found that fragrances by *E. tridentata*, a glittering green species from Panama, contained an average of 27 different ingredients. (Chanel No. 5 has 80, but it, after all, is not made by bees.)

After weeks or months of collecting, orchid bees meet up at special spots on tree trunks to show off their creations. By this point, each bee's scents have mingled and matured, preserved by his fatty head oil like a rose petal in an enfleurage pomade. The bees buzz out from the tree and spritz their special colognes, which the discerning females then use to judge their attractiveness.

Orchid bees scour the local environment for perfume ingredients.

Over the course of his lifetime, an orchid bee may debut multiple versions of his scent, tweaking its composition between mating attempts. Some researchers think that while the basic ingredients of each species' scent are fixed, proportions may be learned through trial and error—as when a teenager puts on too much Axe before the first date, but not the second. The right stuff, we can only assume, balances elegance, personality, and flair—or maybe just doesn't overdo it on the dung. ⟩ **How to see them: You can attract orchid bees by hanging baits drenched in scents they like—wintergreen and clove are popular.**

THE WILD LIFE OF An Interspecies Perfumer

■ Taiwan– and New York–based artist Hsurae learned about orchid bees by accident while searching for a comic strip about a different organism, the bee orchid. Captivated even from afar, they made a piece called "Euglossini Cologne"—a tribute to the bees' perfume, composed through research and imagination.

● **Why did you start working with scent in your art?**

If you've been to any bio-art shows, you'll see they're full of scientific instruments. Everything is contained in glass and petri dishes. There's something about being a specimen—to be observed as a thing that lacks agency, that is waiting for science to define it.

I started doing fermentation because I felt like it was more of an embodied relationship with the subject. Their smell really starts to become like pre-linguistic communication. It's not really understood, but it's always there. It's a relationship where you're not in control.

● **How did you go about making art inspired by an organism you've never encountered?**

I was looking at examples from other artworks. In one [a group of synthetic biologists and artists] went through an archive of extinct plant matter, extracted DNA from the plants, and computationally determined the scent. I was interested in how the narrative was presented—of this scent being revived or being resurrected. If you have a little more knowledge into DNA, and how it's just a combination of different possibilities that could have been, it seems absolutely absurd to say, so determinedly, "That's the scent of this extinct plant."

I've never seen the bees, I've never smelled their perfume. And so it's like pure imagination. I was approaching it in more of a speculative way—50 years into the future, if the bees have died off, what would scientists imagine that their scent smelled like?

● **Can you describe how it turned out?**

It's very striking, the scent. The owner of the gallery had to dilute it, because people were put off. It's a very prickly smell, but then you also get base notes of really warm tones—stuff like cinnamon, cloves, nutmeg, eucalyptus, vanilla, some floral scents. I also put a little bit of fish sauce in there, the closest I could find to rotting meat.

I had already been working with skatole in my previous works. It's a microbial metabolite that gives mammalian feces its particular smell, but it's also used in perfumery as a stabilizer. Under 1 percent, it smells floral, almost like orange blossom, but over 2 percent it starts smelling animalistic. That little gap between 1 percent and 2 percent is this wonder to me, so I had it precisely at 2 percent. It was presented in a hydrothermal vessel for high-pressure and high-temperature chemical reactions— this steel piece with a little Teflon tube in it.

● **Do you think an orchid bee would like your perfume?**

I find [that gap] so interesting: What is this [perfume] exactly to the orchid bee, and what is it to us? [And I think about] the gap between what science deems as known, through instruments, and what is uncertain and completely unknown. There's so much poetry in that space. I was hoping it was something I could get people to think about a little more.

And also to consider that not knowing is a really ethical approach for positioning yourself within this interspecies relationship. I've been thinking a lot about science being a way of hunting for specimens within nature—to bring something into a laboratory in order to dictate what it is. To set what's known and unknown, when in reality, that boundary is so dynamic and porous. I think artwork can be a profound medium to think about these things. ■

AFRICA

Ethiopian Wolves

The last shot—literally—for the world's rarest canids

RANGE: Ethiopian highlands
SPECIES: Ethiopian wolf
(*Canis simensis*)

◆ In the highlands of Ethiopia, a small population of foxlike wolves has forged a home in unforgiving conditions. At the elevations where they live, up above 10,000 feet (3,048 m), temperatures are often below freezing. Winds howl. When the rain shuts off for the dry season, it often doesn't come back for many months.

But Ethiopian wolves are made from sturdy stuff. Some 100,000 years ago, their ancestors—relatives of the archetypal gray wolf—walked here from Eurasia. Finding themselves in a habitat mostly populated by little burrowing animals, these wolves evolved. They developed slim frames and narrow snouts that can snatch a mole rat out from within a tunnel. Their fur blushed reddish gold to blend into the dry grass of a summer hillside.

Fifteen thousand years ago, as the last Ice Age was ending, they were forced to adapt again. With the African continent warming around them, Ethiopian wolves pushed upward into the coolest reaches of the highlands.

Today, these hardy rust-colored predators face their greatest challenge yet: humans. Habitat loss and diseases caught from herding dogs, like rabies and canine distemper, have reduced the wolves' numbers to less than 500, making them the rarest canids in the world.

Researchers with the Ethiopian Wolf Conservation Programme, founded out of the University of Oxford's Wildlife Conservation Research Unit, have been working to vaccinate the wolves for rabies and canine distemper. Rather than capture or tranquilize the wary canids, they use an oral vaccine—developed in the United States to fight rabies in coyotes and raccoons—hidden within an irresistible meat snack.

In the first vaccination campaign, the wolves snapped up 88 percent of their baits over just two nights. The researchers are also vaccinating the thousands of semi-feral dogs in the area, which are used by shepherds to warn off leopards and hyenas and come in contact with the wolves while hunting the same rodent prey.

In a test site in the Bale Mountains, the team is slowly seeing their work pay off. There have been fewer disease outbreaks among local dogs and, accordingly, fewer in their wild counterparts. In February 2022, researchers returned to the mountains to find the best sort of surprise: puppies born to two of the three local packs, stretching their legs in the sun as happy yips and howls echoed through their mountain home. ❯ **How to see them:** Today, these wolves exist in only six small segments of their historical highlands territory in Ethiopia. Your best bet is to hike with a guide into the Sanetti Plateau, the Guassa Plateau, or the Simien Mountains.

Ethiopian wolves blend in with the hills they call home.

Kihansi Spray Toads

These tiny toads were discovered, driven extinct, and brought back to life—all within two decades.

LOCATION: **Kihansi Gorge, Tanzania**
SPECIES: **Kihansi spray toad**
(*Nectophrynoides asperginis*)

◆ For the first 10 million or so years of their existence, Kihansi spray toads didn't need much. Every single one of these tiny yellow toads lived in a 5-acre (2 ha) mini wetland in Tanzania's Kihansi Gorge, under the spray of a giant waterfall that tumbles from the southern Udzungwa Mountains. That's an entire species hopping, chomping on bugs, and raising toadlets in an area about one-third the size of Yankee Stadium—one of the smallest ranges of any vertebrate. People didn't even know they existed.

In the most recent quarter century—roughly since their discovery by humans—the toads have needed a whole lot: transoceanic plane rides, multinational collaborations, intensive scientific investigation and monitoring, and the construction of two dedicated husbandry facilities, as well as a massive sprinkler system. As the toads continue to hang on, their story serves as a reminder of the dual hope and folly involved in trying to reengineer a wild ecosystem.

A spray toad at Kihansi Falls

The toads' problems started in 1994. That's when construction began on a dam that would divert 90 percent of their waterfall to a hydropower setup, providing a large percentage of Tanzania's electricity. It wasn't until two years later that biologists even discovered the spray toads and their hidden grotto and began to keep an eye on them.

In 2000, the project switched on. The wetland was left high and dry, and the spray toads sprayless. Their soft mosses crumbled, replaced by herbaceous plants. Frogs, chameleons, and safari ants moved in. Pesticides trickled down from the dam, and amphibian-killing chytrid fungus appeared for the first time.

The toads just couldn't hack it. By 2009, they were extinct in the wild.

In the meantime, conservationists were working to mitigate the damage. Hundreds of the wild spray toads were spirited off to zoos in the United States. The Tanzania Electric Supply Company installed several huge sprinkler systems in the gorge to mimic the waterfall's spray. And biologists began frantically looking into some very basic questions—what the toads eat; what eats them—in order to properly care for them in captivity and make the gorge safe for their return.

Things are looking slightly better. After some hiccups—at one point, the toad's total world population dropped to 37—scientists have figured out how to successfully raise them. Labs have been built in Tanzania so that this can be done closer to home.

In 2012, the first captive-bred toads were brought back to the gorge to try their luck. Although the species is not yet flourishing, it is stable. Managers think it might eventually thrive again under the sprinklers—living symbols of the persistence of toads and people, as well as how many dollars and hours it takes for us to do the work of a single waterfall. ❯ **How to see them:** Captive populations can be found at the Bronx Zoo, the Toledo Zoo, or at facilities in Dar es Salaam and Kihansi. Probably best to leave the wild ones alone.

THE WILD LIFE OF **A Toad Reintroduction Coordinator**

■ Cuthbert Nahonyo is a conservation expert at the University of Dar es Salaam in Tanzania. As a project manager for Kihansi spray toad reintroduction efforts, he coordinates the contributions of dozens of people from varying areas of expertise who are trying to keep this species alive.

• **How did the discovery of spray toads come about?**
The history goes back to sometime in the 1980s, when Tanzania and the World Bank agreed to construct a hydropower dam along the Kihansi River. After the agreement between Tanzania and the World Bank, there was an environmental impact assessment, because the World Bank does not fund projects that have negative impacts to the

environment. Eventually, they found out that it was okay for the project to go on.

The project was about three quarters done. Ecological monitoring was going on in the gorge. And during that process, sometime in 1996, they discovered the toad. By 1998, they confirmed that it was a new species endemic to Kihansi.

That's where the problems started, because the World Bank now thought that they were funding a project that was going to threaten the survival of a species. One of my colleagues told me that it was so serious that the World Bank president was going to close the project, but then he was advised otherwise—don't close the project, but look for ways to save the species.

● **What is the current status of the toad in the wild?**
The guidelines say that if you want to reintroduce a species in a place where it was extinct, you must make sure that the factors that caused its extinction are not there. All this time, there's been monitoring going on in the gorge on water quality, temperature, vegetation, and water flow. In the end, there was a general consensus that the conditions have improved.

Now the toads are surviving, but at a very low rate. They reproduce—you can see gravid females, you can see young, you can see juveniles. But they are not actually increasing in number.

● **Can you talk more about the work that it takes to keep all of this going?**
Reintroducing a toad is a very difficult undertaking. We have colleagues who are looking at the toad's population, who are looking at the vegetation, people who are looking at the limnology. We have people who are looking at the invertebrates, people looking at water flow, people looking at pesticides, people looking at lead use. We have many people looking at diseases.

Thousands of Tanzanians are asking: Why are we spending so much money for a small toad? But the toad is just a small portion of the project, which is to protect the catchment. When you're protecting a catchment, it means you're maintaining a good environment— you get water, you get good climate, you get biodiversity protected. The water used for power generation is also used for fishing downstream, and for irrigation and other things. So, if you look at that context, then you understand. But if you just look at the toad, then you won't understand.

● **Have any positive things come out of this endeavor?**
We now have captive facilities in Tanzania—one at the University of Dar es Salaam, and then another one in Kihansi. The people who are taking care of the toads in the facilities are Tanzanian, the people doing the disease monitoring are Tanzanian, and the people doing the research at the gulch are Tanzanian. Most of the activities are being funded by the government of Tanzania. Everything now is done by Tanzania.

From what I understand, and the information we get from amphibian experts, the Kihansi spray toad is the most difficult toad ever to maintain in captivity. So the fact that we've managed— and we've managed to take it back into the wild, and it's surviving— I think we have learned a big lesson. I think people from other countries can come and learn from us. ∎

Nowhere to Go

Because they need both water and land to live—and because their porous skin makes them uniquely sensitive— amphibian species often end up confined to small ranges. Here are some more without a lot of wiggle room.

AUSTIN BLIND SALAMANDER (Eurycea waterlooensis): One of several secretive salamander species paddling in the Barton Springs system of Austin, Texas, these tiny purple swimmers never develop lungs. One of the largest known populations of them is found in Eliza Spring—a former swimming hole, now fenced off to protect the species.

ACHOQUE (Ambystoma dumerilii): These foot-long (30.5 cm), spade-headed salamanders are found only in Lake Pátzcuaro, in Michoacán, Mexico, and are at risk from pollution and invasive carp. A thriving captive population is maintained by a group of nuns, who raise the salamanders in bathtubs and aquariums in their lakeside convent and sell medicine made from their skins.

BLACK TOAD (Anaxyrus exsul): Black toads have the smallest range of any American frog or toad—they live only in Deep Springs Valley, California, a desert sandwiched between two mountain ranges. They rely on springs that crisscross the dry landscape and sometimes mate in puddles formed in the hoofprints of cows grazing on the mountains.

PERSIAN MOUNTAIN SALAMANDER (Paradactylodon persicus): Found only in the rainforests and caves around the southern tip of Iran, these mottled salamanders nonetheless make the best of it—they're the only salamanders known to eat bats.

AXOLOTL (Ambystoma mexicanum): Incredibly talented and incredibly cute, these smiling, swimming critters are able to regrow lost limbs. But while lab specimens gain fame and attention, the wild population—different from the domestic ones in some key respects—is disappearing from the last vestige of its home range: a grid of canals in Xochimilco, just south of Mexico City.

SKY ISLANDS

Islands, hemmed in by water, are known for their one-of-a-kind ecosystems, made singular over many years of isolated evolution. Mountaintops around the world double as "sky islands," hosting high-altitude arrays of life just as funky as those found in the middle of the ocean.

Separated by seas of low-lying terrain, these hotspots are distinct from the ecosystems below, and often from one another: Two mountain peaks less than a mile apart can sport totally different suites of species, many of which are just now being found by human trekkers. Here are a few of the world's most fascinating sky islands.

Kukenan and Roraima, two tepuis in
Venezuela's Canaima National Park

MADREAN ARCHIPELAGO · Stretching across a rugged expanse of Arizona and northwestern Mexico are more than 50 mountain peaks collectively known as the Madrean Archipelago. As you climb these mountains, the surrounding desert gives way to dense thickets of oak and pine trees, and eventually groves of prickly conifers. A herpetologist surveying these mountaintops compared them to "islands" in 1940—the first scientific description of this phenomenon.

More than 7,000 species have been observed in this range, which serves as an ecological crossroads between the Sierra Madre Occidental and the Rocky Mountains. Here, tropical South and Central American species like the metallic-green elegant trogon and the raccoon-like coati mingle with hardy desert creatures like jackrabbits and alligator lizards. Even jaguars prowl these mountains—one large male nicknamed El Jefe stalked Arizona's sky islands for years before returning to Mexico to breed in 2015.

VENEZUELAN TEPUIS · Rising thousands of feet above the northern Amazon rainforests and fringed by swirling mist, Venezuela's tabletop mountains are called tepuis, from the Pemon word meaning "house of the gods." Older than the nearby Andes, they are the remnants of an ancient seafloor that was uplifted and eroded until only columns of towering rock remained.

Early accounts of these immense, waterfall-gashed monoliths inspired Arthur Conan Doyle's *The Lost World*. While a tepui's forested highlands are devoid of dinosaurs, each is home to a set of species whose ancestors got stuck there when the land splintered around 70 million years ago. Residents include frogs that curl up into tiny balls to roll away from danger, a slew of venomous snakes and scorpions, and a rich assortment of carnivorous plants.

The Chiricahua National Monument in southern Arizona,
part of the Madrean Archipelago

SOLOMON ISLANDS-WITHIN-ISLANDS •

The Solomon Islands, a chain of volcanic islands rising out of the southwestern Pacific, themselves host a set of forested mountains. Their far-flung location and steep topography make these peaks some of the most isolated habitats in the world.

One island, the cloud-shrouded Guadalcanal, hosts a variety of understudied creatures including giant rats, gaudy parrots, and barking tree frogs. The island's most mysterious resident may be the mustached kingfisher, with a face streaked with bright blue feathers. Though the species was first described in the 1920s, a male mustached kingfisher was not discovered until 2015, and only a handful of sightings have ever been recorded.

PHILIPPINE SKY ISLANDS •

The higher you go up Philippine peaks like Mount Mantalingahan, the more the forests seem to stoop. Many trees at the tops of these sky islands are only waist-high, and spongy mosses and liverworts dominate the dank soil.

These waterlogged forests house leeches, geckos, and endemic insectivores, including moss shrews and soft-furred rats. The peaks are also studded with giant pitcher plants: One recently discovered vase-shaped species has an opening nearly a foot wide—more than enough space to gobble up and digest the local rodents.

Tokay gecko

EASTERN ARC MOUNTAINS •

Thirty million years ago, East Africa was covered with rainforest rather than sprawling savannas. Pockets of this cooler, wetter habitat persist in the Eastern Arc Mountains of Kenya and Tanzania, which harbor species from warty frogs and horned chameleons to wide-eyed bush babies, glowing mushrooms, and forest elephants.

Like many sky islands, hot spots in the Eastern Arcs are threatened by deforestation and illegal hunting. In Tanzania's Udzungwa Mountains, fragmentation threatens little-known species like the Udzungwa red colobus, a monkey with an orange cap of tufted hair found only in these forests. Surrounded by seas of savannas, these monkeys and other tropical species have nowhere to go if their mountain refuge disappears.

Mustached kingfisher

Udzuwunga red colobuses

OCEANIA

Kea

These birds are tireless pranksters.

RANGE: Throughout the mountains of New Zealand's South Island
SPECIES: Kea (*Nestor notabilis*)

◆ In the 1860s, while collecting plants high in New Zealand's Southern Alps, botanist Julius von Haast paused for a well-earned break, leaving a bundle of specimens resting on a mountain crag. This brief moment of distraction was all it took. Soon after he set the bundle down, a chunky green parrot hopped over to his collection and pushed it off the crag, straight into an inaccessible ravine. With this, von Haast joined a singular but growing club: people who have been punked by kea.

Kea are the world's only alpine parrots, living near or above the tree line throughout New Zealand's mountains. To survive in this harsh environment, they rely on their sharp beaks, claws, and wits, which they apply wherever necessary. Sheep farmers, hikers, and traffic cops regularly find themselves on the wrong end of kea-mediated pranks (or worse).

Kea take their name from their distinctive, raucous cry—*ke-aa*—which carries for miles through the scrub and tussock. As the word

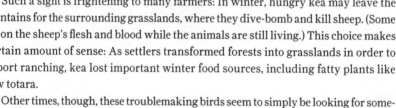

Kea, directing traffic

comes from Maori, the language of New Zealand's Indigenous people, the plural is also kea. While most of their feathers are dull olive green, the undersides of their wings are a riot of dazzling oranges, visible from below as they soar through the air.

Such a sight is frightening to many farmers: In winter, hungry kea may leave the mountains for the surrounding grasslands, where they dive-bomb and kill sheep. (Some feed on the sheep's flesh and blood while the animals are still living.) This choice makes a certain amount of sense: As settlers transformed forests into grasslands in order to support ranching, kea lost important winter food sources, including fatty plants like snow totara.

Other times, though, these troublemaking birds seem to simply be looking for something to do. When bored, kea will strip the rubber from car windshield wipers and meticulously remove the insulation from power lines. In one particularly dangerous incident, a group of kea redirected traffic by repositioning traffic cones around the entrance to a local tunnel on South Island. (To distract them, local authorities built a bird-sized gym nearby, with swings and climbing bars.)

Ski resorts in New Zealand "kea-proof" vital equipment, including chair lifts, with metal fortifications to stop the birds from chewing through wiring or opening up rubbish bins and scattering trash through the snow. And hikers beware: They will steal almost anything that catches their eye—socks, cigarettes, and even cameras.

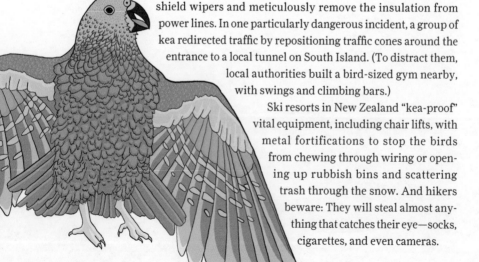

Despite their growing troves of loot, times are tough for kea. Although they are now a protected species, their sheep-killing led to decades of them being shot, poisoned, and otherwise exterminated by farmers, and their native forests and food sources have steadily been destroyed. Fewer than 7,000 of these mountain parrots now remain in the wild, entertaining themselves at all costs. ❯ **How to see them:** You can see kea in the wild on New Zealand's South Island or in bird sanctuaries across the country, including at Zealandia in Wellington.

THE WILD LIFE OF A Kea Playmate

■ Ximena Nelson knows more than almost anyone about what makes kea tick. A professor at the University of Canterbury in New Zealand, she studies how kea communicate, think, and play. She has also worked with New Zealand's Department of Conservation to build "kea gyms," meant to keep the birds entertained and out of trouble—a difficult prospect.

● **A lot of news coverage of kea in New Zealand focuses on the damage they can do. Why do they have such a reputation?**
Because kea often feed on tubers, which are not visible, they have to explore and dig, or rip open rotting logs with their sharp beaks. They look for things as part of their natural behavior, so that makes them primed for potentially being destructive.

Also, kea are unusually neophilic—they're interested in novel objects. Most animals aren't. Humans would be one exception, although even human babies aren't always interested in trying new foods for the first time.

● **Why do you think they like playing so much?**
Unlike almost every animal on the planet, kea evolved pretty much in the absence of predators. They aren't particularly risk averse, and they haven't had to be vigilant, giving them more time to be engaged in something as frivolous as play, which consumes energy and concentration.

That's my suspicion—that kea are unusual in that they had some spare time and the cognitive architecture to be able to facilitate the evolution of play—but it is unprovable. Kea adults will spontaneously play with each other. They don't need to have the young around to do so. They just like playing.

● **Does playing filter into a superior ability to problem-solve?**
In nature, kea don't use tools, but they can. [Captive] kea in Fiordland, for example, have learned how to trigger a trap by poking a stick into it so they can then take the bait. If you give them a tool in a captive scenario, they can use it.

Does play facilitate problem-solving? Potentially. Play is a way of exploring the world theoretically without hurting yourself. It's almost hypothesis-testing—testing different ways of doing things at low risk.

● **Is it difficult to keep kea entertained?**
The hardest thing about keeping kea in captivity is keeping them motivated enough to participate in experiments, because you have to provide constant reinforcement. They've got a half-life of interest of about 15 minutes before they need new toys.

We tried putting in things that would be fairly indestructible, like fenders from boats, as well as things that are easily destroyed— harakeke, or New Zealand flax, for example—but biodegradable.

We had some webcams on the gyms, and we found that, actually, it was going to be really difficult to maintain something that was going to be interesting enough. Once the kea played with anything and knew what it does, they'd decide it was boring. ■

Mountain Pygmy Possums

These living fossils hide in the rocks on the roof of Australia—but for how long?

◆ Until 1966, the mountain pygmy possum was thought to be extinct, known only from a few fossil fragments of skull and teeth. But then people noticed some strange mouselike creatures running about a Mount Hotham ski lodge, stealing bacon from the stove.

When a biologist realized these were marsupials, not mice, there was great excitement, says Linda Broome, an ecologist from the New

RANGE: The boulder fields of Australia's Snowy Mountains, with three distinct populations— one in Kosciuszko National Park (in New South Wales), one in the Bogong High Plains, and one on Mount Buller (both in Victoria)
SPECIES: Mountain pygmy possum (*Burramys parvus*)

South Wales Department of Planning and Environment who has spent three decades researching this charismatic species. "Here was this fossil that had come to life."

Because other pygmy possums live in trees, at first it was assumed this group had hitchhiked to the lodge in a load of firewood. But researchers eventually discovered that these particular miniature possums are restricted to boulder fields above the winter snow line and live a very different life than their lowland cousins.

Adults hibernate in rock crevices for seven months of the year, lowering their body temperature to just above freezing and sleeping under the snow. They wake up hungry in spring—just in time to gorge themselves on bogong moths, which migrate to the mountains in their billions to hide from the summer heat.

The possums eat seeds, invertebrates, and fruits as well, but the high-fat, high-protein moths help them reach mating weight quickly and then bulk up for hibernation. "In the autumn they're like little butterballs with legs," says Broome. "Very cuddly."

But climate change is affecting this delicate balance. Warming winters allow predatory feral cats to thrive in the possums' habitats. Without an insulating layer of snow, possums' burrows become too cold, and they may wake too early and burn too much fat. When severe droughts in the late 2010s decimated the bogong moth population by an estimated 99 percent, baby possums in Victoria starved in their mothers' pouches.

Then, the 2020 bushfires incinerated vast areas of the possums' home, and though most survived the fires by hiding in the rocks, not much else did. Broome and her colleagues had to supplement their diet with "bogong biscuits"—fortified macadamia nut cookies made to mimic the nutritional content of the moths.

An even more ambitious plan to save the critically endangered species draws inspiration from paleontology. Fossil evidence suggests the animals' ancestors thrived in lowland rainforests and that the species was stranded up in the snow only (relatively) recently. A breeding program begun in 2022 in the Blue Mountains aims to test whether these pygmy possums can once again adapt to lower elevations, where life might be a bit easier. **› How to see them: There are around 3,000 well-hidden, nocturnal mountain pygmy possums left in the wild. That means there's only a tiny chance you might spot a hungry one in an Australian ski lodge or in the surrounding boulder fields on a summer night—but a tiny chance is still a chance.**

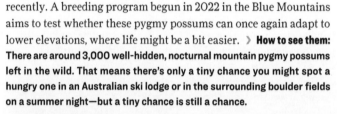

Mountain pygmy possums hibernate for more than half the year.

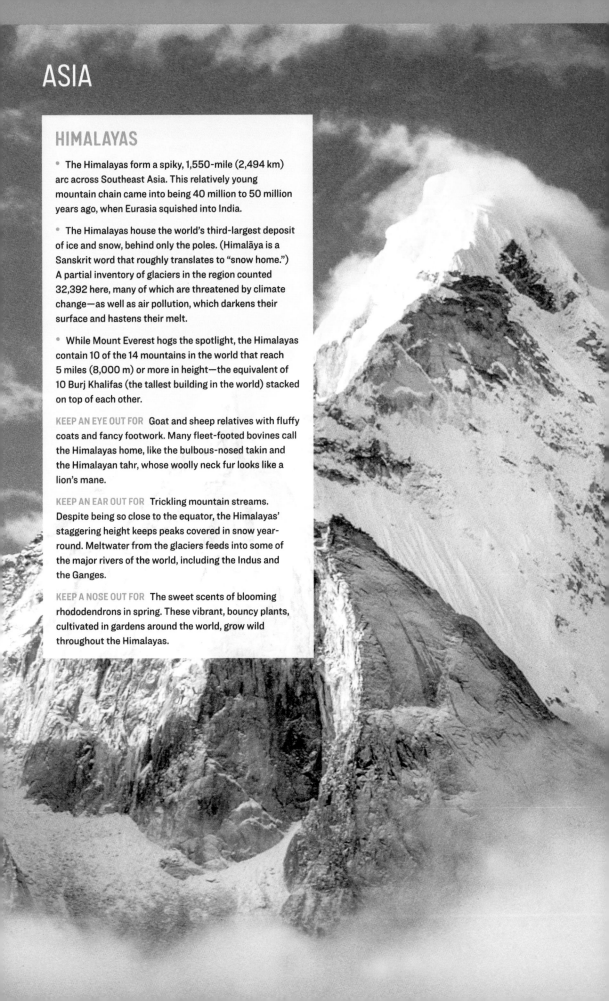

HIMALAYAS

- The Himalayas form a spiky, 1,550-mile (2,494 km) arc across Southeast Asia. This relatively young mountain chain came into being 40 million to 50 million years ago, when Eurasia squished into India.

- The Himalayas house the world's third-largest deposit of ice and snow, behind only the poles. (Himalāya is a Sanskrit word that roughly translates to "snow home.") A partial inventory of glaciers in the region counted 32,392 here, many of which are threatened by climate change—as well as air pollution, which darkens their surface and hastens their melt.

- While Mount Everest hogs the spotlight, the Himalayas contain 10 of the 14 mountains in the world that reach 5 miles (8,000 m) or more in height—the equivalent of 10 Burj Khalifas (the tallest building in the world) stacked on top of each other.

KEEP AN EYE OUT FOR Goat and sheep relatives with fluffy coats and fancy footwork. Many fleet-footed bovines call the Himalayas home, like the bulbous-nosed takin and the Himalayan tahr, whose woolly neck fur looks like a lion's mane.

KEEP AN EAR OUT FOR Trickling mountain streams. Despite being so close to the equator, the Himalayas' staggering height keeps peaks covered in snow year-round. Meltwater from the glaciers feeds into some of the major rivers of the world, including the Indus and the Ganges.

KEEP A NOSE OUT FOR The sweet scents of blooming rhododendrons in spring. These vibrant, bouncy plants, cultivated in gardens around the world, grow wild throughout the Himalayas.

Noble Rhubarbs

Extreme altitude loses its bite when plants build their own greenhouses.

RANGE: The Himalayas and Hengduan Mountains, from about 12,400 to 16,400 feet (3,800–5,000 m) above sea level

SPECIES: Noble or sikkim rhubarb (*Rheum nobile*)

◆ Hike high enough in the mountains and most plant life seems to have given up. Winds whip relentlessly, the rocky terrain offers meager sustenance, and the thin ozone layer is a feeble screen against sizzling ultraviolet rays. Chilly temperatures provide a growing season barely three months long, and even most bugs take a pass, limiting available pollinators.

So imagine, on a trek 3 miles (5 km) above sea level, coming across a noble rhubarb. This plant looks a bit like a rocket ship made out of cabbage—"a lightship in a desolate scree," says Bo Song, an associate professor at China's Kunming Institute of Botany. It has evolved to support its own kind of moonshot: a delicate flowering that happens just once in its lifetime.

Noble rhubarb's innovations start with its bizarre shape. At its base sits a dark green foliage skirt, from which grows an overlapping tower of large, translucent cream-colored bracts—leaves designed to protect budding flowers. Inside is a scaffold of hollow stalks, which provides enough support for some plants to stand 6 feet (1.8 m) tall.

It takes about 33 years for a noble rhubarb to flower. When it's time, tiny pink blossoms emerge within the bracts, which then fully reveal their protective genius: Their overlapping-umbrella structure keeps out harsh wind and driving rain, while their UV-blocking chemical makeup provides an impenetrable sunscreen.

As harmful rays are rebuffed, visible and infrared rays filter into the bracts, which then trap the heat for the tender flowers. On a 60°F (15°C) day, the temperature inside a noble rhubarb plant can reach a balmy 77°F (25°C). This warmth allows for faster fertilization and the growth of more and larger seeds, optimizing the plant's odds of sprouting a new generation.

Inside their comfortable, bespoke towers, the flowers undergo their own much shorter life cycle, becoming fruits and then seeds. But they are not lonely Rapunzels. The noble rhubarb flowers produce 2-methylbutyric acid methyl ester—a compound

Noble rhubarbs look like vegetable spaceships.

that is irresistibly aromatic to a local species of fungus gnat, one of the few insects hardy enough to live nearby. The female gnats are drawn in droves to pollinate the flowers and lay their eggs in the warm bracts. When the larvae hatch, they feed on the seeds (but leave plenty to sprout anew).

The formation of a personalized, multispecies greenhouse is a sort of "go big or go home" strategy for the noble rhubarb, says Jacob Landis, who has studied the plant alongside Song. Most of its neighbors adapted to the mountains over millions of years by hugging the ground, not rocketing away from it. But the noble rhubarb's adaptations, while unconventional, serve the same core purpose: ensuring that one more generation lives to do it all over again. **〉 How to see them:** From June through August, head to the Himalayas or the Hengduan Mountains and hike uphill. Researchers have used the Tibetan village of Wengshui, in China's Yunnan province, as a base. Others have traveled to Kathmandu, Nepal, and trekked to villages higher in the mountains, like Topke Gola.

Sequencing the Yeti

One of the Himalayas' most famous creatures doesn't quite belong in this book. The yeti—generally described as a hairy, fanged behemoth who lumbers through the mountains on two legs—does not actually seem to exist, despite its presence in Nepalese and Tibetan folklore and its cryptozoological fame.

But that hasn't stopped people from trying to find it—some using all the tools modern science has to offer. In the early 2010s, a film production company and an evolutionary geneticist teamed up to test supposed yeti samples from across the Himalayas. This included a thigh bone found in a cave, skin from a mummified "yeti" held in a monastery, and a tooth from a museum specimen.

Besides the tooth, which was from a dog, almost all of the biological samples actually came from various local bear species, including the Asian black bear and the Tibetan brown bear. Similar studies have identified supposed yeti parts as actually coming from raccoons or humans. Of course, it's very hard to prove something *isn't* out there—even with DNA.

Everest Moss

Plants and fungi form their most extreme alliance yet.

LOCATION: **Mount Everest, just above Camp 2**
SPECIES: **Tufted rock beardless moss (*Gymnostomum aeruginosum*) and several microscopic fungal species**

◆ In 2010, mountaineering brothers Damian and Willie Benegas were resting at Camp 2 Station about 21,200 feet (6,462 m) up Mount Everest when a strange rock caught their attention. That high up in the mountain, "everything is sedimentary limestone," Damian says. "But here was a little granite protrusion."

Heading over to check it out, the brothers found something even stranger: Tufts of green and orange moss were growing in a crack in the granite. "It was the last place I expected moss," says Damian, who thought he had left all the green stuff behind him at the snow line, several thousand feet before.

Experts from the group Adventure Scientists, which matches scientists with explorers, soon confirmed their hunch: This was the highest-altitude plant ever found. And it really had no business being up there, where temperatures never climb above freezing and water is quickly whipped away or turned into ice.

When the Benegases returned to Everest the next year, they brought gloves and plastic bags. Samples of the sky-high moss made their way to Rusty Rodriguez, an expert in symbiosis then working with the US Geological Survey. Analysis uncovered the moss's identity—it was a fairly common species, *Gymnostomum aeruginosum*. It also revealed its likely superpower: "Every blade, every root, every stem we looked at" was full of microscopic fungi, Rodriguez says.

Everest Base Camp 2, just below where the moss was found

Across the world, fungi and plants forge close partnerships, from the algae-fungi mutualisms that make up high Arctic lichens to the webs of underground mycorrhizae that network with tree roots. Rodriguez studies long, filamentous fungi that live inside plants and confer new capacities for endurance. Together, he has found, these plant-fungi alliances can survive in conditions much hotter, saltier, drier, or more toxic than either species can handle alone.

Although the exact mechanism for this phenomenon is not yet known, plants with these fungi seem to react less strongly to difficult situations. "They just sort of chill out and wait for the stress to go away," Rodriguez says. He suspects the fungi-moss collaboration on Everest is working in a similar way: The moss by itself couldn't grow on a freezing mountain face, and the microscopic fungi would be toast as well. But together, somehow, they make it possible.

This discovery has raised many questions, Rodriguez says. For instance, how did the moss and the fungi meet? How did they get up there? Were they separate or together? Was the moss reproducing?

Unfortunately, it's going to be difficult to answer them. When Rodriguez left his government job, he lost track of the samples. (He is now applying his methods to agriculture, adding certain superfungi to food plants to help them better tolerate stress.) And the last time the Benegases climbed Everest, in 2019, the record-setting moss-and-fungus team was nowhere to be seen. ❯ **How to see them:** Unfortunately, the moss seems to have disappeared from its perch on Everest—but you probably weren't going to make it up there anyway. If you're an experienced mountaineer interested in collecting high-altitude plants, consider getting in touch with Adventure Scientists.

THE WILD LIFE OF **A Moss-Gathering Mountaineer**

■ Damian Benegas is a professional mountaineer and climbing guide who has summited peaks around the world, including six trips up Everest. He and his twin brother, Willie, have discovered many things on their adventures, from the world's highest-living plant to a fossil of a previously unknown ancient sea lion.

● **How did you become interested in the outdoors?**
My mom is from the United States, and my dad is from Argentina. In the 1970s, my family decided to move from Buenos Aires to the middle of Patagonia. All of a sudden we were a set of twins completely in the wild. The wildlife is so rich—you've got southern right whales, penguins, guanacos, armadillos. And the Patagonian cliffs, where you can see all the fossils.

Because we grew up in Patagonia, I think we have a sixth sense—you know there are fossils, so when

you're walking, you're always aware of what you're stepping on. You gain this experience of always being on the lookout. When I see something that doesn't belong or is unusual, my eyes right away see it.

● **What was it like to find moss so high up on Everest?**
I always associate moss with the Pacific Northwest—with warm weather, a lot of humidity, water. The last place I expected moss was on the side of Mount Everest. I can expect it at the base of the mountain, on the trail, but not up there!

● **Do you think it will be found again?**
There are a lot of commercial companies out there doing trips on every single peak in the Himalayas, all the way from Pakistan to Nepal. It could be a nice project to network all these guides. With the right network, you can say, hey, could you be on the lookout for this?

● **Have you changed your approach to discovery over the years?**

We used to collect arrowheads and all kinds of stuff. I feel bad that because of human pressure, a lot of these places are losing a lot of things. Now I don't collect anymore—when I find something in Patagonia or anywhere, I hide it again.

● **Do you have any advice for people who would also like to be more attentive to the world around them?**
Right now, we're filming in Chile. Every time I go to the mountain, on the trail, I keep finding the poop of a fox. I can assure you that 99.9 percent of people would not even notice that. But me, I go, "Oh, we have a little friend walking around here."

You have to have wandering eyes—I think that's the most important thing. You can be an adventurer, mountain biker, whatever sport you do. If you don't have the essence of wandering eyes, the rock that you step on, the plant you step on—it's just another rock, another plant. What counts is the process and not the summit. ■

Other Notably High Plants

SPACE PLANTS The first plant to successfully flower in space was rock cress (*Arabidopsis* spp.), which was grown on the Soviet Salyut 7 space station in 1982. Since then, astronauts from many countries have grown everything from sunflowers to Thai basil (*Ocimum basilicum*) to romaine lettuce (*Lactuca sativa*), for research and for food.

TWISTY FORESTS The world's highest-elevation forests grow up to 16,400 feet (5,000 m) above sea level in the high plateaus of the Andes. They're comprised of moss-covered, papery-barked Polylepis trees (*Polylepis* spp.), which grow very slowly, and in twisting shapes. Current efforts to restore these forests, which have been whittled down by lumber harvesting, involve llamas who cart seedlings up the mountainside.

HIGH-UP HANGERS-ON Tall trees are often hosts to squadrons of epiphytes—plants that grow on other plants

and get their nutrients and water from runoff, decomposing leaves caught in branches, or the air. High up in the famously tall California redwoods, for example, you may find leather-leaf ferns (*Polypodium scoulerii*), blueberries (*Vaccinium* spp.), or even small sitka spruce trees (*Picea sitchensis*), which can grow big enough to hold epiphytes of their own.

TRIPPING PLANTS In 1962, a group of scientists in Canada cut dandelion flower stems (*Taraxacum officinale*) and placed them into test tubes containing solutions of psychotropic drugs, including LSD and dextroamphetamine. They observed them for several days to track when the flowers opened and closed. Flowers that had absorbed LSD closed sooner than would have been expected, while those that absorbed dextroamphetamine—a stimulant—stayed open for longer.

Bar-Headed Geese

Twice a year, these extreme goose athletes fly over the Himalayas.

RANGE: Southern and central Asia
SPECIES: Bar-headed goose
(*Anser indicus*)

◆ One night in April 1954, naturalist Lawrence W. Swan was standing on a glacier high in the Himalayas when he heard a familiar sound: the kazoo-like calls of bar-headed geese.

Tracking the birds with his ears, he swore he heard the flock clear the summit of nearby Makalu, the fifth-highest mountain in the world. "At 16,000 feet [4,877 m], where I breathed heavily with every exertion . . . I had witnessed birds flying more than 2 miles [3.2 km] above me," he later wrote. And they were gabbing the whole time.

Bar-headed geese fly over the globe's tallest mountain range once every spring and once every autumn, traveling between winter habitat in India and breeding grounds in China and Mongolia. It's one of the most arduous migrations known to science.

The trip spans more than 1,800 miles (2,896 km) and requires ascending at least 15,000 feet (4,572 m) over the imposing crest of the Himalayan mountains. Most geese complete that peak climb in a single day, flying roughly 40 miles per hour (64 kph) in a layer of the atmosphere that contains only half as much oxygen as air at sea level. As Swan understood, this is like running a marathon at elevations where most humans can barely put one foot in front of the other—only harder, because flying is the most energetically demanding way to move.

Traveling as the goose flies

How do bar-headed geese do it? Scientists have sought answers by tracking wild birds' elevations and vitals during migration and by training captive birds to fly in wind tunnels. They have learned that, like all birds, the geese are superb endurance athletes with brain cells that function well in low-oxygen conditions. They also have larger lungs than their relatives and the ability to slow their metabolism during flight.

The birds strategize, too: They maximize efficiency by flying in calm winds, and most prefer to cross the mountains over low passes rather than whooshing above the crests. (Some, perhaps including the flock Swan heard, do opt for hard mode: George Lowe, a member of the team that made the first successful summit of Everest, reported seeing bar-headed geese buzzing the world's highest peak.)

After their daring flight, the birds head to a smattering of emerald-blue lakes and lush wetlands strewn across central Asia. They usually mate with the same partner and raise a few fuzzy goslings in nests tucked away on isolated islands or cliffs. Then the well-rested flocks head south again, honking their way over the top of the world.

> **How to see them:** Visit lakes and wetlands across India in winter, or travel to Qinghai Lake in China during the breeding season. And if you're climbing a Himalayan peak and hear a noise, look up!

Ballooning

The air is filled with idealistic spiders.

RANGE: Worldwide
SPECIES: Ground crab spiders (*Xysticus* spp.), Himalayan jumping spiders (*Euophrys omnisuperstes*), and many others

◆ At the end of *Charlotte's Web*, Wilbur the pig is excited to befriend the offspring of his recently deceased spider friend. But before he really gets the chance, the just-hatched spiderlings climb up a fence post, stick their butts in the air, spin balloons out of silk, and float away.

Unlike, say, pro-pig messages written in webs, this plot point is pretty realistic. Around the world, spiders of varying species and sizes take to the skies when opportunity calls, held aloft by aircraft they secrete themselves.

Plentiful legs notwithstanding, spiders can't walk everywhere they need to go. Those looking for safety, territory, or food—or maybe just a new scene—may find it more efficient and safe to take their chances in the air. The strong, flexible silk with which spiders spin their webs is also useful for flying, capable of carrying a tiny passenger for long distances and great heights.

Bug fans have long been fascinated by this phenomenon. On Halloween in 1832, Charles Darwin described how "aeronaut spiders which must have come at least 60 miles" landed on the H.M.S. *Beagle* and decorated its rigging with webs. In the 1930s, the plane used for a

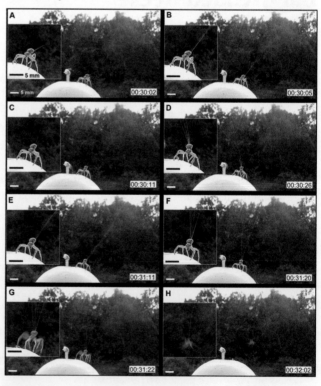

A crab spider (genus *Xysticus*) prepares for liftoff.

pioneering survey of midair insects kept running into so many arachnid ballooners that its struts ended up wrapped in silk, prompting the study's author to conclude that "the young of most spiders are more or less addicted to this mode of transportation." The same survey found a lone spider cruising at 15,000 feet (4,572 m), the maximum altitude of a Cessna.

More recently, scientists have begun to take a closer look at the behavior. Some are learning about particular spiders' aviation techniques. (Ground crab spiders, for example, tend to raise one or two legs before spinning their balloons, perhaps to test the wind.) Others are investigating how the spiders get good liftoff—different studies have focused on updrafts, electric fields, and the nanophysical forces that allow very thin threads to practically stick to the air.

Although it's hard to know for sure, ballooning has been credited with helping spiders colonize habitats both broad and narrow. Himalayan jumping spiders—the highest-living animals on the planet, who scuttle around the slopes of Everest nearly 4 miles (6 km) above the tree line—may have gotten up there via silk parachute.

And species expanding their ranges, from brown widows to joro spiders, occasionally drift into their new homes this way. This can prompt some over-the-top news reports warning of hordes of foreign arachnids about to drop from the sky. But the reality is less horror movie and more *Charlotte's Web*. If you see a few little spiders drift past, remember: They're just brave youths, seeking their fortune the best way they know how.

〉 **How to see them:** It's difficult, but not impossible, to spot a ballooning spider in action—you may just have to squint. Perhaps the best evidence of this behavior can be seen after floods or storms, when whole fields may shimmer with silk produced during airborne escapes.

Snow Leopards

Big cats so elusive and solitary they're mistaken for ghosts

RANGE: Mountains and high plateaus of central and southern Asia, China, Russia, and Mongolia's Gobi Desert
SPECIES: Snow leopard *(Panthera uncia)*

Snow leopards make their homes at elevations over 10,000 feet (3,050 m) in the mountains, plateaus, and cold deserts of heartland Asia. Individual males claim home ranges of up to 80 square miles (207 sq km), meaning there may not be more than one snow leopard in an area the size of Baltimore. Even from close by, the thick, spotted fur that insulates them also makes these leopards practically invisible in the rocky environments where they dwell. Plus, sometimes they'll use their tails as blankets, hiding their faces.

So it makes sense that it's quite difficult to find them. Researchers have struggled to pin down basic facts about these handsome animals, such as how long they can live, how many of them still roam in the wild, and why they prefer to be alone. Even the humans whose homes overlap with snow leopard habitats—from the Tuvan people, who share space with them in the Altai Mountains, to the Nepali people, who do the same in the Himalayas—tend to call these cats "ghosts of the mountains."

Much that is known about snow leopards today is arguably thanks to the borderline obsessive fascination of an American writer, the novelist and Zen Buddhist Peter Matthiessen. In 1973, after having chased the animals in the rugged Dolpo region of Nepal for three months without success, Matthiessen hung up his boots and went home. (His companion, the naturalist George Schaller—who had organized that expedition to study the Himalayan blue sheep—chanced upon the coveted leopard only a couple of days after Matthiessen had left.)

Snow leopards prefer to prowl along rocky terrain.

The Snow Leopard—the book Matthiessen wrote to document his inner and outward journey—not only helped sear the mountain cat's elusiveness and symbolism into Western minds but also sparked outsiders' desire to know more about a creature that spends pretty much his whole lifetime roaming alone across a huge, seemingly inhospitable territory.

It was another American, the biologist Rodney Jackson, who first managed to radio-collar a snow leopard in Nepal in 1981, and four more leopards in later years. By tracking their movements and habits, he gathered the first scientific data on this elusive species. He went on to found the California-based Snow Leopard Conservancy.

Forty-plus years after that first surge of foreign interest, snow leopards are somewhat easier to find—which is not necessarily good news. Climate change and overgrazing in highland Asia have drastically reduced the population of wild sheep the leopards prey upon. This has forced these formerly ethereal cats to manifest closer to human settlements and rely on domestic livestock, which brings them into conflict with local herders. Of the estimated 4,000 to 6,000 snow leopards left in the wild today, between 200 and 500 are killed every year, often by people avenging their slain livestock. The snow leopard is now considered threatened by the International Union for the Conservation of Nature.

As a result, conservationists from around the world are working with local communities to reduce livestock depredation and take advantage of the ghosts of the mountains as livelihood opportunities—encouraging leopard-spotting tourism, for example. Getting the snow leopards' neighbors on board with these efforts will be "far more impactful than intensified research into how many snow leopards may exist in any area," Jackson says. Preserving this creature's survival requires balancing the snow leopard's mystique with travelers' deep desire to see one. ❯ **How to see them:** Hemis National Park in Ladakh, India, holds the highest concentration of snow leopards. If you want any chance of seeing one, hire an eagle-eyed ranger and bring a telescope.

THE WILD LIFE OF A Snow Leopard Conservationist

■ Protecting snow leopards across the 12 nations they inhabit is no walk in the park. We asked Charudutt Mishra, executive director of the Seattle-based Snow Leopard Trust and one of the world's leading experts on this species, about his work conserving snow leopards and why we should care about these big cats.

• **Tell us about the first time you encountered a snow leopard.**
My first snow leopard sighting came after 10 years of trying. I had been on a long hike in the Spiti Valley in the Indian Himalayas and had just survived a fall into an ice-cold river. Bruised and wet, I trudged up a steep gorge while scanning the opposite slope periodically, and then what I thought was a rock in the field of vision of my binoculars moved suddenly. It was my first snow leopard.

• **What is a regular day like out in the field for a snow leopard conservationist or ranger?**
Long hikes looking for signs of life; mostly lively but sometimes tense community meetings and interactions; field data collection; data exploration and analysis; braving or seeking shelter from the elements—it's never dull.

• **What is the most surprising thing you have learned about snow leopards?**
That they don't seem to be as fond of snow as their name suggests.

• **Can you tell us a bit more about them?**
The snow leopard is nature at its perfection. The cat is tied—and, indeed, supremely adapted—to the steep mountainous terrain. Snow leopards are able to hunt on near-vertical cliffs. They can survive under immensely cold conditions, though summers can also get rather warm in the mountains they inhabit. They cover large areas that form their home ranges and occur at very low densities. It appears that an adult female can give birth only once every two years, which, along with the small population size, can make their populations especially vulnerable.

• **Why is it important to keep trying to protect snow leopards?**
Because of what they are— marvels of nature that have evolved over more than 3 billion years—but also because of what they represent. High Asia forms the water tower of the continent,

and snow leopard habitats thus feed more than a third of humanity. Snow leopards are apex predators of their ecosystems and represent a unique and specialized diversity of life. The prey of snow leopards— the wild mountain sheep and goats—gave rise to livestock, whose domestication changed the trajectory of human societies. We, therefore, have a strong historical and cultural connection with them. We will have failed our future generations if we allow these magnificent animals to go extinct.

• **What about the relationship between snow leopards and the people who live close to them?**
Local people have nuanced, multidimensional relationships with snow leopards. On the one hand, snow leopards inspire and draw admiration from people, while on the other, they are viewed as pests and are feared because of their livestock predation behavior. One of the threats snow leopards face is retaliatory persecution in response to livestock predation. Partnering effectively with local communities enables us to cooperatively transform a negative and tense attitude into one of care and stewardship. ■

Snow leopards can jump as far as 30 feet (9 m).

Himalayan Birches

These trees have helped record sacred texts for millennia.

RANGE: The Western Himalayas in India, Nepal, Bhutan, China, and Pakistan
SPECIES: Himalayan birch (*Betula utilis*)

◆ For thousands of years, people of the Indian subcontinent have used the bark of the Himalayan birch to store ideas and knowledge. Sacred Hindu and Buddhist scriptures, great Sanskrit epics, and mathematical, astronomical, and grammatical treatises have all been written on the bark of this tree, which local people call bhojpatra.

Paper became widely available in India only after the sixteenth century. Before that, if you wanted to write something down, birch bark was one of your best options. It remained in use, especially for religious writing, even after paper hit the scene, cherished for its sturdiness, longevity, and connection to tradition. A number of centuries-old birch bark manuscripts are held in historical libraries today, their writing still clearly visible.

The Himalayan birch is a tree of knowledge.

While this tradition has waned over time, you can still find it practiced in places like Sural Bhatori, a Buddhist monastery in the Indian state of Himachal Pradesh, more than 2 miles (3 km) above sea level. (The area is so remote, medieval criminals were exiled there from neighboring kingdoms.) Monks at Sural Bhatori care for a grove of Himalayan birch trees and occasionally harvest the bark to practice writing sacred texts or for other ceremonial uses.

To remove the bark, monks make a small incision in the tree and peel off an inner layer, which "looks like a sheet of thick paper," says Bir Singh Khangserpa, a trekking guide and village council member who helps manage the grove. "The tree remains and regenerates the bark, and we can do it again after a year or so."

Elsewhere in the Himalayas, these birches are subject to deforestation and the pressures of development; maintaining a protected grove ensures a safe place for these giving trees. The National Biodiversity Authority of India recently chose Sural Bhatori as a Biodiversity Heritage Site, recognizing the importance of the grove of birch trees as well as the area's other flora and fauna. The monastery "is older than recorded history," says Mr. Khangserpa. But recording will continue to happen there, with the birches' help. ❯ **How to see them: To view a sacred grove of these trees, visit the monastery of Sural Bhatori, an eight-hour bus ride over the mountain roads from the Himalayan towns of Manali or Chamba in northern India.**

Western Ghats Purple Frogs

Live, for one night only!

RANGE: The Western Ghats in India

SPECIES: Western Ghats purple frog (*Nasikabatrachus sahyadrensis*), also known as the Mahabali frog

◆ Each spring, right at the beginning of monsoon season, an underground concert series starts up in India's Western Ghats mountain range. Near steadily growing streams, from beneath the soil, calls begin to ring out: sets of double and triple chirps reminiscent of the clucks of chickens.

After about two weeks of nightly serenades, the singers appear. Thick-limbed, ruddy-skinned, and about the size of clementines, they are male Western Ghats purple frogs, all sung out and ready to mate. Clambering out of their dirt burrows, the males search for females, who are about three times the size of the males and the color of ripe eggplants.

When a male frog finds a female frog, he shimmies up on top of her and shoves his spade-like forelegs into the skin on either side of her backbone. The female then piggybacks him closer to a stream. After she has found a suitably calm place, the male uses his feet to squish thousands of eggs out of her body, fertilizing them before they fall. Then they both burrow themselves back underground to wait for next year.

It's thought that Western Ghats purple frogs have undertaken this one-day emergence annually for 120 million years, as continents formed and lineages rose and fell. The timing of the journey is critical, as the eggs take a week to hatch—if the rains come earlier, the eggs may get washed away; late, and they may dry up. Because of this, the frogs are "directly affected by the changing climate," says Sandeep Das, an expert on the species. "Early and delayed rains are causing severe loss in their clutch in recent years." The frogs also fall victim to habitat loss, pollution, and even, during their very brief open-air sojourns, passing cars.

You may not like it, but this is what peak performance looks like.

To raise awareness of these singular creatures, Das and other experts have given the species a nickname: the Mahabali frog, after the legendary king Mahabali, who also emerges from the underworld for just one day per year. ❯ **How to see them:** These frogs leave their underground burrows for only a few hours every year. If you really want to see one, follow their calls starting two weeks ahead of that time, and be ready when they emerge.

Saolas

On the trail of "Asian unicorns"

RANGE: Annamite Mountains, a tropical forest mountain range bordering Laos and Vietnam

SPECIES: Saola (*Pseudoryx nghetinhensis*)

◆ Saolas might be the world's best hide-and-seek players. Though 200-pound (91 kg) bovines should be hard to miss, these antelope-like creatures have been tiptoeing around Southeast Asia's Annamite Mountains for more than 7 million years largely undetected.

Most of the world didn't know they existed until 1992, when a hunter showed a team of forest surveyors a skull with long, straight horns. The team realized it was from a creature they had never seen before—the first large mammal new to science in more than 50 years. Stunned, the international community began calling the saola the "Asian unicorn."

The excitement of that initial find spurred three decades of attempts to learn more. Over the years, a few saolas were captured, but they died soon after, falling victim to the stress of captivity and a lack of knowledge of how to care for them. Today, we have only a handful of camera trap photos and the stories of those who have run into them to teach us about these enigmatic animals. Scientists have still never encountered one in the wild. They don't even know what saola dung or tracks look like. They want to protect these rare creatures, but this is difficult to do without knowing more about their natural habitat and behavior.

But how do you find a unicorn in the Annamites, a landscape the size of New Jersey?

The saola's elusiveness is a "weird, unique, wonderful problem," says Lorraine Scotson, CEO of the Saola Foundation. The foundation is now putting together a team of wildlife trackers in preparation for a two-year search.

To increase their chances of spotting saolas, the team plans to combine new technology with the long-held expertise of seven local Indigenous groups: the Pong, Lao Kang, Lao Loum, Toum, Hmong, Muey, and Man people. They'll use fast-acting DNA tests, developed in partnership with the New York–based Wildlife Conservation Society, to identify dung samples found in the forest, which can help them pinpoint saola territory. Another group, Working Dogs for Conservation, plans to train a dog team to help sniff out saolas, using a small breed, like spaniels, that can easily navigate the mountains' dense forests.

If these strategies can help researchers locate the stealthy saolas, they can then start working to ensure the species' survival. "Luck cannot be a part of finding saolas," says Scotson. Instead, it will take our best group efforts at hide-and-seek. ❯ **How to see them:** Good luck! You may need to camp out in the Annamite Mountains for a few years to have a shot.

Hot Springs Snow Monkeys

These primates know how to unwind.

LOCATION: Jigokudani Monkey Park in Nagano Prefecture
SPECIES: Japanese macaque (*Macaca fuscata*), also known as snow monkey

◆ After a long day of hunting spiders and munching on beech bark, there's no better way to unwind than a dip in a hot tub. At the Jigokudani Monkey Park in Nagano, Japan, a troop of Japanese macaque monkeys has become famous for soaking in man-made pools fed by natural hot springs.

The troop is about 200 strong, mostly females, and roams freely between the park and the surrounding mountains. Every day in winter, some of the monkeys take advantage of the park's onsen, a traditional Japanese bathing facility, which was originally built for humans. One study estimated that one-third of the females in the troop are "habitual bathers," spending at least 30 seconds in the hot water during at least 10 percent of field observations.

The monkeys did not come to this relaxation technique entirely by themselves. Although origin stories vary slightly, they were initially coaxed either near or into the hot springs by humans with food. But once one or a few individuals discovered the joys of kicking back in a steaming pool, the behavior spread to the rest of the troop.

It's now an entrenched group activity, to the extent that a separate bathing facility has been constructed for the macaques. Photos captured by tourists—who now come for the monkey watching as much as for the baths—show individuals and groups displaying aspirationally blissed-out faces and postures while soaking.

While macaque hot tubbing has not been observed in other wild populations, it fits well with the ecology and biology of the species. Japanese macaques live farther north and in colder climes than any other nonhuman primates—hence their nickname, "snow monkeys." They have developed physiological adaptations to the cold, including the seasonal accumulation of body fat and thickening of fur, but low temperatures still stress the monkeys out.

By measuring hormone concentrations in the feces of Japanese macaques, scientists have determined that hot spring bathing reduces this stress. The individuals who seem to spend the most time in the hot water—females high in the troop's social hierarchy—tend to have the highest baseline stress hormone concentration, meaning they are most in need of a soak. Due to their high social rank, they can demand space in the pool, a limited resource.

In other words, thanks in part to these relaxed macaques, scientists have validated that submersion in hot water is a good way to decompress. Of course, any (snow) monkey could have told you that. ❯ **How to see them:** At the Jigokudani Monkey Park in Nagano Prefecture, it's easy to observe the monkeys bathing in the hot springs.

Japanese macaques enjoy a day at the spa.

Staying Warm

Cold can be a killer, especially at high elevations, and not everyone has a hot tub nearby to take the edge off. Fortunately, many species have mastered techniques and developed adaptations to tolerate the freezing temperatures that often come with high altitudes.

FRIENDSHIP • In cedar forests high in Morocco's Atlas Mountains, **Barbary macaques** (*Macaca sylvanus*) live in small but complex social groups. These primates have dense fur and short, stubby tails, which help prevent heat loss. But their relationships are just as important: When winter temperatures roll in, Barbary macaques with more friends actually have a higher survival rate.

With a buddy to groom and fluff its coat, a macaque's dense fur achieves optimum insulating ability. And as snow blankets their mountain habitat, popular Barbary macaques huddle together, keeping each monkey's internal temperature at a more consistent level through the freezing night. Loners and outcasts are left to fend for themselves. ❶

LYING DOWN • A perfect day for a **rock hyrax** (*Procavia capensis*) in the mountains of South Africa is all about doing less. First up is a good lie-down on a sunny rock to fend off the chill from last night. The thermolabile hyraxes drop their own body temperature while they bask to cut down on metabolic energy use.

Once the sun dips down, it's time to pile up the entire family, a behavior called "heaping." Up to four generations stack themselves on top of each other in rows of outward-facing noses and inward-facing rumps, like a game of hyrax Jenga. Everyone sleeps in until high noon, and the lazy cycle starts again. ❷

PARASITISM • On the Himalayan plateau, the **caterpillar fungus** (*Ophiocordyceps sinensis*) creeps threadlike fingers called mycelium through the soil in search of a living sleeping bag. Before winter sets in, the fungus finds the larva of a ghost moth underground. It enters the caterpillar's mouth and begins feeding on the juicy entrails, snug as a bug in a rug inside its dying host's exoskeleton.

Well-fed and warmed, the growing fungus breaks through the soil in early spring as the snow begins to melt. The resulting mushroom is considered a tasty treat and natural remedy for all sorts of ailments, and it sells for more than the price of gold. ❸

SHIVERING • In winter, **mountain chickadees** (*Poecile gambeli*) feed aggressively during the warmer daylight hours, building up energy reserves. At night, they switch over to a hypothermic mode, lowering their own body temperature to conserve energy and twitching muscle groups rhythmically in a constant state of shivering that drains the reserves again. A chickadee's body temperature can drop up to 15 degrees during this nightly ritual. ❹

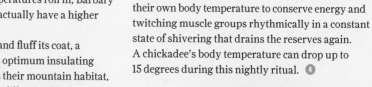

ANATOMICAL ANTIFREEZE • **Red flat bark beetles** (*Cucujus clavipes*), who live at high elevations in places like Alaska, are among the few insects who spend the winter in the open air, rather than burrowed under snow, dirt, or leaf litter. These beetles have an enzyme that works as a natural antifreeze, protecting their internal structures at chilling temperatures. The antifreeze enzyme keeps the water inside the beetle's body from freezing and slicing through delicate cell structures. Heat them up again and they spring back to life. ❺

HOT STONES · Reptiles cannot create their own body heat. To survive subzero temperatures up on the Himalayan plateau, **hot-spring snakes** (*Thermophis baileyi*) exploit their environment, which is full of steamy geothermal pools. They spend their days resting on hot stones to maintain their core body functions, and they hunt small fish and frogs in the warm water. A super-strong heart and extra-efficient red blood cells help these snakes tolerate the lack of oxygen up at their live-in spa. **6**

HAIR · Pocket-size and extremely cute, **chinchillas** (*Chinchilla* spp.) have the densest fur of any land animal. While an individual human follicle might produce two or three strands of hair, each follicle on this Andean rodent can grow up to 80 hairs. The resulting thick coat traps heat close to the chinchilla's body and even provides protection from predatory bites and tumbles. **7**

PICKINESS · **Ice worms** (*Mesenchytraeus solifugus*) are the Goldilocks of the Pacific Northwest, surviving in the just-right zone between too hot and too cold. The worms, which look like inch-long (2.5 cm) black squiggles, live beneath the clear ice of high-elevation glaciers, with billions taking up residence on a single mountain. They feed on algae and bacteria that grow within the frozen water and are often gobbled up by visiting birds. **8**

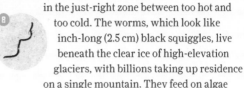

EATING · Before the long Arctic winter, **brown bears** (*Ursus arctos*) chow down on up to 30 pounds (13.6 kg) of food per day, building up insulating layers of fat like you'd throw on extra blankets.

As temperatures start to plunge, brown bears dig a sheltering hole and waddle in for a season-long nap, relying on their built-up fat reserves to keep them alive while they sleep. **9**

STAYING AWAKE · Many tree species go dormant in winter, entering a kind of power-saving mode until spring. But **quaking aspens** (*Populus tremuloides*) stay awake after they lose their golden leaves. Their bark is thin and light, and as they bask in the winter sunlight, their internal temperatures rise, which allows them to photosynthesize even without leaves and sustain themselves through the bitter mountain winters. **10**

Fritillaria delavayi

How a plucky plant remains unplucked

RANGE: The Hengduan Mountains in China
SPECIES: *Fritillaria delavayi*

◆ The mountain herb *Fritillaria delavayi* comes in many colors. On certain slopes in the Hengduan Mountains, the plants grow bright yellow flowers that dangle over green leaves, as visible as tennis balls in a gravel driveway. On other slopes, though, *F. delavayi*'s flowers and leaves are tan, gray, or brown—whatever hue best matches the surrounding scree.

Most plants that sport camouflage evolved in this way because it helps them avoid detection by hungry herbivores, like yaks or caterpillars. In this case, though, the unwelcome plant snatcher appears to be us. Botanists think humans have driven these plants to drabness over thousands of years simply by harvesting them.

The bulbs of *F. delavayi* are an important medicinal ingredient in the Hengduan area, used to treat coughs, says Yang Niu, a researcher at the Kunming Institute of Botany who studies the plant. For at least two millennia, people have been climbing the slopes and digging up the bulbs, which they then sell to herb dealers.

Some digging spots are more popular than others. By comparing transaction records from local dealers, Niu and his colleagues estimated the harvest pressure on *F. delavayi* populations at eight different sites. They then tested how well camouflaged each population is by comparing the colors of the plants and their backgrounds—and by asking volunteers to find them in "Spot the Plant," an I Spy–style online game created for the purpose.

The researchers found that populations of plants usually left alone—high up in the mountains near the Yulong range, for example—are still vivid. Meanwhile, those growing in areas frequented by human harvesters are gray or brown. Over the years, by picking the most visible specimens, people have inadvertently selected for duller colorations, until whole populations have come to match the surrounding rocks.

The next step is to figure out "how this plant balances between pollinator attraction and enemy avoidance," because bright flowers help attract necessary insects, says Niu. (So far, it appears that flies have learned to pollinate the camouflaged flowers, while the bright ones are handled by bumblebees.)

People have become so good at artificial selection, breeding everything from fancily adorned pigeons to buggy-sized pumpkins, that it's easy to forget we still participate in natural selection, too. *F. delavayi* is a reminder that our actions can have consequences we haven't planned on—and which, in some cases, we can barely even see. **》 How to see them:** If you find yourself trekking high in the Hengduan Mountains, look carefully for a drooping flower surrounded by three to five leaves. Different color morphs are found on different slopes within the range: for instance, tan near Hongshan Scenic Area, brown near Puyong Pass, and reddish brown near Pujin Pass.

Parthenogenetic Lizards

Sisters are doing it for themselves.

RANGE: The Caucasus Mountains in Armenia, eastern Turkey, and Georgia

SPECIES: Seven lizard species in the genus *Darevskia*, including *D. dahli*, *D. sapphirina*, and *D. unisexualis*

◆ Even for lizards, sex is complicated. Reptilian mating culture can involve everything from hours-long head-biting rituals to twice-daily push-up contests. It's enough to make you blink slowly and flick your tongue.

But some have found a way around it. Females of 39 lizard species—including seven in the genus *Darevskia*, which live scattered around the Caucasus Mountains—can reproduce all on their own, without acrobatics, feats of strength, or even sperm. During their spring or summer breeding seasons, these *Darevskia* lizards simply lay eggs, which then hatch into tiny versions of themselves—genetically identical clones that then grow up and do the same thing. There are "no males involved," says Susana Freitas, an expert in this form of reproduction, which is called parthenogenesis.

Researchers believe these lizards developed this ability sometime around the last Ice Age. Abrupt changes in temperature forced the *Darevskia* lizards up and down the mountains, where different species—which normally kept to themselves—encountered one another and mated. This led to a hybrid lizard baby boom, with different genetic combinations resulting in different outcomes. Some hybrids persisted into new, sexual species. Some lost the ability to reproduce at all and died out. Seven of the combos found a middle path, where females became able to birth their own duplicates. Eventually, the males of these species all died out.

Parthenogenesis affords a number of advantages to its practitioners, Freitas says. The *Darevskia* females don't need to put time or energy into finding a mate or getting jiggy. They don't have to change locations, make choices, or risk being eaten during the

A Darevskia lizard basks in the sun, no males in sight.

distracting mating process. They also can have a lot more offspring than sexual species—when Freitas goes to study *Darevskia* lizards in the field, she might see half a dozen parthenogenetic ones hanging out on the same rock, because there are so many.

Indeed, "the mother of all questions is why sex is so common when it's so disadvantaged," she says. (By *Darevskia* logic, the child of all questions is exactly the same.)

But there are downsides as well. Genetic recombination through sex helps species hedge bets—if all your offspring are identical, a disease or a change in the environment might wipe them all out. Also, harmful mutations can persist or accumulate over time, rather than being pushed out

of a population through sexual selection. This—combined with the low likelihood of evolving parthenogenetic ability in the first place—may help explain why the reproductive strategy is so rare.

Currently, the seven all-female *Darevskia* species are consolidating their power. They are still able to mate with male lizards from the species that originally hybridized in order to produce them—in fact, the males find the parthenogenetic females more attractive because they are so big. But when these asexual females mate with the sexual males, they produce infertile offspring, so instead of continuing the male's genetic line, they've just wasted his time and energy (reproductively speaking). Eventually, this may end up "decreasing the sexual population until it goes extinct," Freitas says. Girls just wanna have fun. ❯ **How to see them:** Because parthenogenetic lizards are so good at reproducing, there may be many to spot even in a small territory. Look for big crowds sunbathing on the rocks in sites around the Caucasus range.

Backbones? Yes. Sex? Not Necessarily.

Many of the world's squishier creatures, from sea stars to aphids, reproduce asexually. But this form of duplication is much rarer in vertebrates—fewer than 100 species can do it, most of them fish or lizards. Here are a few of these rare, backboned nonbreeders.

AMAZON MOLLIES (*Poecilia formosa*): Named after the mythical Amazon warriors, Amazon mollies, found in Mexico and Texas, were the first parthenogenetic vertebrates to have their secrets discovered. These small female fish "mate" with males from closely related species before reproducing but don't actually incorporate any of the males' genetic material into their offspring, producing clones instead.	**WHIPTAIL LIZARDS** (*Aspidoscelis uniparens*): Unlike almost all parthenogenetic species, the offspring of whiptail lizards are genetically different from their parents. This is because whiptail moms start the reproductive process with double the chromosomes of your average sexually reproducing lizard— although it's not clear exactly how. Instead of mixing their chromosomes with a male lizard's in order to achieve genetic variety, they just reshuffle their own.	**ZEBRA SHARKS** (*Stegostoma tigrinum*): While zebra sharks can reproduce sexually, females who never encounter males—for instance, those living in aquariums—may choose to go it alone, to their keepers' great surprise. Reticulated pythons and Komodo dragons are known to do this as well.	**CALIFORNIA CONDORS** (*Gymnogyps californianus*): Recently, two California condors from the San Diego Zoo were found to have no fathers, meaning they were products of parthenogenesis. This was especially unusual because their moms were housed with males.

Giant Hogweed

This huge relative of the everyday carrot can blind you with its toxic sap.

RANGE: Native to the Caucasus Mountains, and invasive in 11 US states and Canada, as well as other parts of Europe

SPECIES: Giant hogweed (*Heracleum mantegazzianum*)

◆ On the outside, giant hogweed doesn't seem too scary. Its stem, thick and stately, is green with purple accents. The leaves look almost like snowflakes, and the plant is topped with an umbrella of small white flowers. The overall effect is that of an enormous sprig of Queen Anne's lace, plucked from the bouquet of a giant. It's easy to see why so many plant lovers brought giant hogweed from its native range in the Caucasus Mountains to ornament their gardens in England and North America.

Unfortunately, that was a mistake. These plants are now invasive in both Canada and the United States, where they outcompete other species by producing up to 100,000 seeds at once and outshade them by growing up to 14 feet (4 m) tall. What's more, they are extremely dangerous, filled with phototoxic sap that can cause second-degree burns, years of persistent sun sensitivity, and—if it gets in your eyes—temporary or permanent blindness.

A 1971 song from the English rock band Genesis, titled "The Return of the Giant Hogweed," may have been based on an earlier incident in which London children ended up with blistered hands after touching giant hogweeds that spread from Kew Gardens. Even some scientists who study it have scars.

Throughout the giant hogweed's introduced range, plant experts stay vigilant for its appearance. In the summertime, botanical gardens and government departments make signs and reach out to media, warning the public to call if they see a looming, white-crowned plant.

If a hogweed is found, crews may put on hazmat suits and safety goggles and head into the woods with garbage bags and shovels—a confusing scene for anyone who happens to be watching. But at least they'll still be able to see when they're done. ❯ **How to see them:** If you really want to see one, annual warnings from state and local agencies about where giant hogweed grows may clue you in on where to go—just don't get too close. Those who do come into contact with the sap are advised to wash it off with soap and water and seek medical attention.

Lichenometry

Reading lichen as old as mountains

RANGE: Worldwide in cold, mountainous areas with exposed rock, and prevalent in the Cascades, Sierra Nevada, Scottish Highlands, and Swiss Alps

SPECIES: Map lichen (*Rhizocarpon geographicum*), bullseye lichen (*Placopsis* spp.), sunken disk lichen (*Aspicilia* spp.), and other rock lichens

◆ Map lichen is named for its appearance—a patch of it looks like a satellite view of Earth. In shades of yellow and green, separated by deep black spore lines, these lichen grow like continents across an ocean of rock. It's easy to imagine a spread of map lichen doubling as a chart that leads to ancient treasure.

Map lichen does hold secret information—but it's about time rather than space. Through a process called lichenometry, experts use this species and others like it to uncover the hidden ages of glaciers, rocks, statues, and other difficult-to-date objects.

Lichenometry was first thought up by the botanist Roland Beschel. Studying in Austria in the 1950s, Beschel broke up his research trips to the Innsbruck city cemetery, where he was deducing the growth rates of different lichen species with help from the dates on tombstones, with many invigorating treks into the Alps.

Even during these head-clearing hikes, Beschel continued to observe his favorite organisms, especially around moraines: the piles of rock and debris deposited by glaciers as they move through a landscape. He noticed that lichen patches were smaller near the glaciers' edges and bigger on the older moraines farther down the valley.

These "lichens may be just as old as the rock surface itself," he wrote. If you assume that they are, and you know how quickly a lichen species grows, you can turn the size of a given lichen patch into an estimate of the age of the surface it's on. Thus, lichenometry was born.

Map lichen may be able to live for up to 10,000 years, giving this method a long reach into the past. Today, experts primarily use it to reconstruct glacial movements by figuring out how long particular rock faces have been exposed. But other uses have been found. In the 1960s, a lichenologist at the University of Chile determined the age of the moai of Easter Island by clocking the growth of three types of lichen on the head-shaped statues.

Researchers have also used lichen to investigate the ages of Indigenous American pit houses atop modern-day California's White Mountains, stone labyrinths on the coast of Finland, and prehistoric tool quarrying sites in the Rockies.

Lichenometry has its limitations. For one, it's difficult to determine the exact growth rate for a given lichen patch, as lichen spreads at nonlinear speeds highly dependent on environmental conditions. To nail down these rates, lichenologists have come up with creative sleuthing methods similar to Beschel's use of tombstones—measuring the size of lichen on artifacts of known age, like zeppelin anchors or whale blubber ovens, and extrapolating from there.

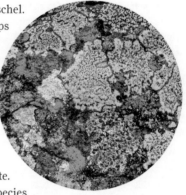

Lichens like Rhizocarpon geographicum *(left, on a stone wall in the UK)* help experts find the hidden age of rocks.

In this way, bit by bit, map lichen and similar species are helping us piece together the history of their habitats—providing a legend to some of the oldest landscapes on Earth. ⟩ **How to see them:** Look for exposed rock along mountain trails, away from city air pollution. If you see flat, green patches bordered with black lines, you've just discovered map lichen. But stick to your trail map to find your way home.

Olms

The world's largest cave dwellers don't seem to age.

RANGE: The underground waters of the Dinaric Karst, from the mouth of the Soča River in Italy across Slovenia, Croatia, Bosnia, and Herzegovina and into Montenegro
SPECIES: Olm (*Proteus anguinus*)

◆ Graced with the evocative presence of an olm, people have thought of many other creatures. In the seventeenth century, those who pulled the wiggling swimmers up out of Balkan streams or drinking wells thought they had found helpless baby dragons. Later, local people began calling them "human fish," because the animal's coloration reminded them of their own.

Olms are not fish, mammals, or mythical reptiles. They are cave-dwelling salamanders, in possession of many impressive qualities and records all their own, including "largest cave-dwelling animal." Even such disparate species as humans have much to learn from them.

All of the world's olms live in the Dinaric Karst, in sprawling limestone caves that can reach 750 feet (228 m) underground. Like dragons in stories, they are masters of their domains, gobbling up crabs, insects, and snails and fiercely defending their territory and eggs. They can also heal or even regenerate their own injured body parts at will, an ability granted not by magic, but by a physiological process not yet understood.

Living as they do in complete darkness, olms lack both pigmentation and eyesight. Sharp senses of smell and taste help olms navigate their underground world, as do other specialized senses that allow them to detect vibrations in water and changes in magnetic and electric fields.

Like humans, olms can live up to a hundred years (four times longer than other amphibians). Unlike us, however, they do this without the adverse effects that come with aging. Olms can reproduce even when they're 80, although they are not invincible: Their position at the top of the underground food chain means that, like tuna or birds of prey, they accumulate pollutants built up in their food and are especially vulnerable to pollution.

Olms thrive in their subterranean underwater world.

Olms' longevity and exceptional regenerative capacity—along with their ability to survive years of fasting followed by periods of aggressive overfeeding—have been keeping scientists very busy considering exactly what makes us different from them.

Rok Kostanjšek, a biotechnical expert at the University of Ljubljana, and colleagues are working on decoding the olm's genome—which is 15 times larger than ours—in the hope of understanding "the mechanisms behind some of the most important health burdens of modern humankind," he says. In the meantime, olms will go on being themselves, however they do it. ⟩ **How to see them:** Searching for olms in the wild is not recommended. Postojna Cave Park in Slovenia has a breeding colony with olms, including babies, on display, and SOS Info Centre Proteus, located in tunnels under the old town of Kranj, displays rescued olms brought to the surface by groundwater floods.

Cavernicolous Critters

The underground world is surprisingly crowded. Caves around the globe are home to all sorts of life forms who thrive in the damp and dark. Some are troglobites, meaning they spend their whole lives in caves, while others come and go depending on the season or time of day. Here are seven species that live in caves, surfaced so you can meet them.

CAVE ANGELFISH (*Cryptotora thamicola*) · Who needs swimming? These denizens of Thai caves have pink bodies, two sets of feathery fins, and a special talent: They can clamber up walls, even while being pummeled by tumbling water. Throughout, they move with impressive swagger, wiggling their pelvises like salamanders. ❶

GUÁCHAROS (*Steatornis caripensis*) · Guácharos, also known as oilbirds, look like owl-falcon mash-ups. They live in caves in the northern and western regions of South America, where they roost in groups of hundreds. Like bats, these birds echolocate, squeezing their syrinxes to produce low-frequency clicks and using the speed of the sounds' return to judge their surroundings. At night, they venture out to feast on fruit, then return to spatter their droppings all over the cave: helpful gifts for their invertebrate neighbors. ❷

CELLAR GLASS SNAILS (*Oxychilus cellarius*) · These mollusks slime their way around a number of caves, including Porth yr Ogof in Wales. Their blue-gray bodies loop inside amber shells that whorl like blown glass. They're not the only subterranean snails in town: Wales's Ogof y Ci cave is also home to garlic snails (*Oxychilus alliarius*), who reek like their namesake when disturbed. ❸

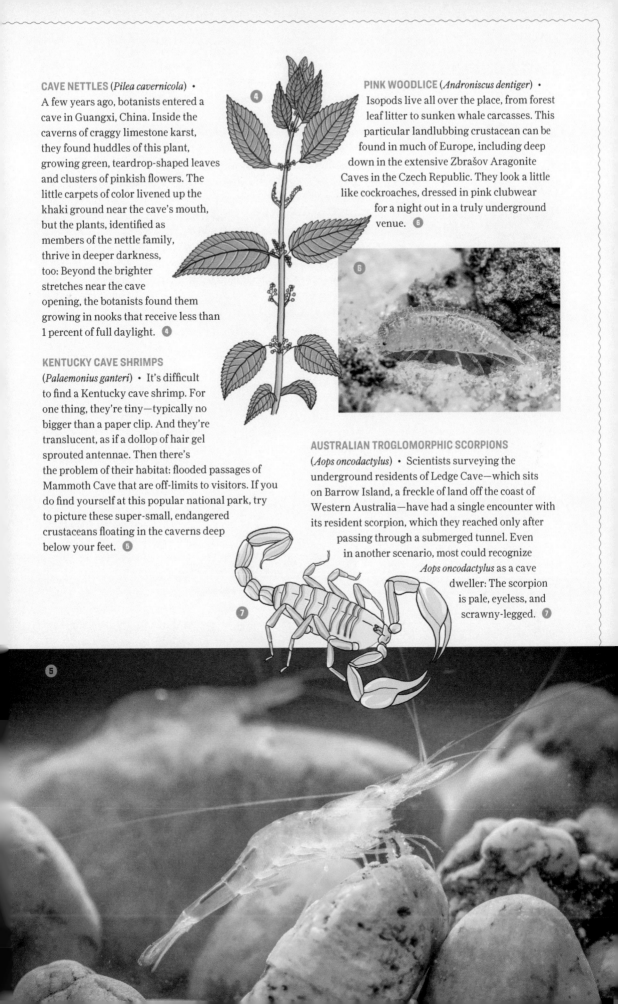

CAVE NETTLES (*Pilea cavernicola*) •

A few years ago, botanists entered a cave in Guangxi, China. Inside the caverns of craggy limestone karst, they found huddles of this plant, growing green, teardrop-shaped leaves and clusters of pinkish flowers. The little carpets of color livened up the khaki ground near the cave's mouth, but the plants, identified as members of the nettle family, thrive in deeper darkness, too: Beyond the brighter stretches near the cave opening, the botanists found them growing in nooks that receive less than 1 percent of full daylight. ❹

KENTUCKY CAVE SHRIMPS

(*Palaemonius ganteri*) • It's difficult to find a Kentucky cave shrimp. For one thing, they're tiny—typically no bigger than a paper clip. And they're translucent, as if a dollop of hair gel sprouted antennae. Then there's the problem of their habitat: flooded passages of Mammoth Cave that are off-limits to visitors. If you do find yourself at this popular national park, try to picture these super-small, endangered crustaceans floating in the caverns deep below your feet. ❺

PINK WOODLICE (*Androniscus dentiger*) •

Isopods live all over the place, from forest leaf litter to sunken whale carcasses. This particular landlubbing crustacean can be found in much of Europe, including deep down in the extensive Zbrašov Aragonite Caves in the Czech Republic. They look a little like cockroaches, dressed in pink clubwear for a night out in a truly underground venue. ❻

AUSTRALIAN TROGLOMORPHIC SCORPIONS

(*Aops oncodactylus*) • Scientists surveying the underground residents of Ledge Cave—which sits on Barrow Island, a freckle of land off the coast of Western Australia—have had a single encounter with its resident scorpion, which they reached only after passing through a submerged tunnel. Even in another scenario, most could recognize *Aops oncodactylus* as a cave dweller: The scorpion is pale, eyeless, and scrawny-legged. ❼

Lammergeiers

These skeleton-eating birds dye themselves the color of blood.

RANGE: Mountain ranges in Europe, Asia, and Africa, generally above 6,500 feet (2,000 m)
SPECIES: Bearded vultures (*Gypaetus barbatus*), also known as lammergeiers

◆ Vultures are not always the most visually appealing birds. But bearded vultures, or lammergeiers, are beautifully done up, with glossy dark wings, long thin goatees, and KISS-worthy eye masks. Their chests, heads, and legs are especially impressive, colored the rich red brown of polished mahogany.

They deserve much of the credit for their fashion sense. These vultures turn their feathers red on purpose, covering themselves in iron oxide by bathing in rusty water or rubbing themselves with damp red soil. They are the only birds known to intentionally color themselves, and exactly why they do is still not entirely settled.

Lammergeiers eat almost exclusively bones—the last remnants of the meals of other scavengers. Bones from anything smaller than a sheep they can eat whole. They'll fly larger ones high into the air and drop them onto rocks over and over again until they break up into swallowable pieces.

Bones are cleaner than the blood and guts preferred by other vultures. (Lammergeiers have feathery heads, instead of bald ones like some of their cousins, because they don't have to stick their faces inside gory carcasses.) But they're still covered in bacteria, which are there doing their own jobs as decomposers. One theory holds that the birds' iron oxide dye kills harmful microbes, keeping vulture parents from slopping them all over their nests. The vultures have been seen rubbing their ruddy chest feathers on their eggs, perhaps to pass on some of this protection.

Others think the coloring is a cosmetic strategy. When two lammergeiers want the same bones, they'll square off, puffing up their feathers and swinging their heads around. A bird's redness might indicate her fitness—her knowledge of the local iron sources, and the strength and spare time to really paint herself up. A darker-red vulture may intimidate a lighter-colored one enough that he leaves, avoiding a fight.

The idea that red is a particularly impressive color to these vultures is supported by another of their adornments: bright red bands around their eyes called scleral rings. When the situation calls, they can concentrate blood in those rings to make them extra big and bright—dyeing themselves from both inside and outside. **❯ How to see them:** You might spot these scavengers cruising along the tops of mountain ridges or to and from their cliff-ledge nests. From below, look for their thick diamond-shaped tails and rust-colored underparts.

Lammergeiers see red on purpose.

CHAPTER 4

Deserts

All desert creatures are unlikely. Life needs water, and deserts are defined by their lack of it. Deserts—whether hot like the Sahara, frozen like Antarctica, or seesawing between the two—are treated to less than 10 inches (25 cm) of precipitation for every trip they take around the sun. That's like surviving all year long on two mostly full highball glasses.

When water does come, it's an amount that most of us would consider too little: a whiff of fog, a dangling dewdrop, a dusting of snow. Or it's too much: a three-day deluge that floods the land and rips up trees. Whatever the amount of water, the environment does everything in its power to get rid of it, steaming it away or locking it into ice.

And yet, on every continent and through every season, deserts are alive. Over millennia, countless species have found their niches in deserts and evolved to make do with very little.

The result is heroic feats, fortuitous collaborations, and oddball masterworks of engineering. Beetles do handstands atop dunes, letting water trickle down their hydrodynamic shells and into their mouths. Mosses grow under the tutelage of pebbles. Trees sink taproots into deep oases. Elephants follow the sounds of distant storms, travel hundreds of miles, and dig careful wells with their enormous feet.

Indeed, the skills that desert dwellers have developed to survive the harsh limitations of their living space often resonate well enough to break the even stricter bonds of convention. In Africa, hornbills and mongooses forge a truly equal partnership so both can hang on in the middle of the food chain. The great desert skinks of Australia rebel against the loner status of most lizardkind and live together in underground mansions, family-style. Microscopic tardigrades, unperturbed by a life inside Antarctica's ice, are the only animals to ever have survived unprotected in outer space.

All desert creatures are unlikely, but they're here.

Contributors: Rosy Alvarez, Ashley Belanger, Brittney G. Borowiec, Mackenzie Breneman, Ashlen Campbell, Alexi Chacon, Erin Connolly, Emily Costa, Jonathan Feakins, Karen Fischer, Rachel Fritts, Natasha Frost, Claudia Geib, Miles Griffis, Anthony Ham, Peony Hirwani, Myles Karp, Jason Keil, Kestrel Keller, Stephanie Krzywonos, Krista Langlois, Tamlin Magee, Megan McGrath, Julie Olum, Joanna Parkman, April Reese, Linda Rodriguez McRobbie, Julia Rosen, Ethan Shaw, Elisa Shoenberger, Britta Shoot, Julia Sizek, Jack Tamisiea, Claire Turrell, Theresa van Baalen

NORTH AMERICA

Devils Hole Pupfish

In one of the hottest places on Earth, a rare fish hangs on.

LOCATION: Devils Hole, Nevada
SPECIES: Devils Hole pupfish
(*Cyprinodon diabolis*)

◆ Death Valley—scalding, parched, literally named for death—is a difficult place for living things. One Death Valley denizen, the Devils Hole pupfish, has been dealt a particular challenge. This species is found in just one place in the entire world: a cubicle-sized portion of a pool called Devils Hole, which heats up to more than 90°F (32°C) and is attached to a cavern system so deep and vast that it ripples when there's an earthquake in China. It's kind of a rough hand for an inch-long fish.

There are arguments about how these pupfish ended up in such a tight spot. The vast underground cavern system that contains Devils Hole first cracked open to the sky about 60,000 years ago, when a cave roof collapsed. It's possible that about 50,000 years after that, during the very wet Pleistocene, a flood flushed some pupfish from a nearby spring into the hole. Or perhaps some adventurous fish wriggled through cracks deep within the caverns below and then followed the light to their new home. The fish may have been present in the cave's waters before its roof fell in, or early Indigenous Americans may have stocked Devils Hole with fish to keep them on hand for dinner.

In any case, once the pupfish found themselves in Devils Hole, they couldn't get out. Isolated from their brethren, they evolved into their very own species. They have lost the pectoral fins that allow other fish to swim quickly and developed special metabolic pathways that help them survive in the bathwater-warm pool. The females and juveniles are as silver as paper clips and the breeding males an iridescent blue. They rarely live for more than a year.

The pupfish appear resigned to their lot. They don't venture too deep into the cave, instead sticking close to the surface, where the sunlight that filters through supports a small food web with the pupfish at the top. (In addition to algae, swimming worms, and water bugs, the fish munch on limestone dust that sloughs off the cave walls, which likely contains nutritious microbes.)

The twice-a-year pupfish count combines both surface and underwater tallies.

Female 23 mm

Actual Size

Male 30 mm

Their habitat—a column of water roughly 10 feet wide, 70 feet long, and 80 feet deep (3 × 21 × 24 m)—is "the smallest geographic range of any vertebrate," according to the US Fish and Wildlife Service. Spawning happens only on one particular rock shelf, which means new generations of this entire species arise in a space the size of a single parking spot.

The pupfish were on the first list of animals deemed endangered by the United States, and they remain among the rarest North American creatures. As such, they enjoy the close attention of the federal government. Park rangers undertake a scuba census of Devils Hole twice a year, in fall and spring. In 2013, the population dropped to 35, an event that spurred more provisions for the fish. The wild population is now bolstered by a propagation laboratory, where new fish are hatched, and a huge tank that serves as a refuge in case of emergencies. In 2018, a man who had broken into Devils Hole for a drunken swim and killed a single pupfish was sentenced to more than a year in jail.

Eventually, the fish's specialness may doom it rather than protect it. Small populations are particularly vulnerable to genetic mishaps, while disease and other factors can compound into what are known as "extinction vortices." Death Valley is only getting hotter, and even faraway earthquakes can cause water disturbances in Devils Hole that trigger the fish to spawn early. Some species of desert pupfish have already been lost; the Mexican Catarina pupfish, for example, became extinct in 2014 after the only spring it lived in dried up for good.

But the Devils Hole pupfish has already beaten the odds. One recent analysis found that the species had only a 2.1 percent chance of surviving for the past 10,000 years. According to most (though not all) of the evolutionary scenarios proposed, it's already done that. Let's see what it manages next. ❯ **How to see them:** Devils Hole is in Ash Meadows National Wildlife Refuge in Nevada. Access to the hole is restricted, but there is a viewing platform nearby so that visitors can see it. If you want to glimpse a pupfish, be sure to bring binoculars or a spotting scope.

THE WILD LIFE OF A Pupfish Counter

■ As an aquatic ecologist at Death Valley National Park, Kevin Wilson is in charge of the biannual pupfish census, which takes him to one of the world's least popular dive sites.

● **How does the Devils Hole pupfish census work?**
We have two teams of two divers each. One is a science diver, counting the fish, and the other is a safety diver. These two teams will enter, descend to about 110 feet [34 m], and turn around, and the first team will start counting fish as they head back up to the surface. After that first team gets to a certain point, the second team will start.

● **What is it like being inside Devils Hole?**
It's an unknown depth. Divers have been down 436 feet [133 m] and didn't see a bottom. And the water is gin-clear. So if I'm down 75 feet—seven stories—and I look up and there's an individual standing over the dive ladder, I can say, "Oh, that's Jane up on the ladder." That's how clear it is. It's a brilliant blue—it looks like the tropics.

It's a pretty straightforward dive, but it's very specialized. You have to have really good buoyancy and trim—you don't want to kick up the sediment from the walls of the cave. There's probably been fewer people diving in Devils Hole than have been in outer space.

● **What can we learn from these fish?**
The Devils Hole pupfish is a bellwether for climate change. It's already living in an extreme environment of high temperature, low oxygen, and limited food during a portion of the year.

We can apply what we learn to other arid aquatic ecosystems that will be getting warmer in the future. How are atmospheric change and increase in temperature going to influence these systems? The pupfish is the canary in the coal mine. ■

Nurse Quartz

These rocks help plants through a difficult stage of life.

RANGE: Deserts worldwide
ASSOCIATED SPECIES: Desert mosses, including *Syntrichia caninervis, Tortula inermis,* and others

◆ Growing up in the desert is tough for a young plant. As soon as it sprouts through the dirt, it's exposed to hot days, cold nights, wind, sun, and dehydration, often without the thick skin and venturesome root systems available to older, larger plants. Botanists have noticed that seedlings that are sheltered by nearby stones tend to grow better. These stoic helpers—which shade the youngsters and protect them from wind—are known as "nurse rocks."

An especially fruitful mineral partnership has been pioneered by *Syntrichia caninervis,* one of the world's most abundant desert mosses. *S. caninervis* mosses are survivors in their own right. During the long, rainless summers in deserts like the Mojave, they lose every bit of water from their cells, going into such an intense state of suspended

MOJAVE DESERT

- The Mojave is the smallest of the North American deserts, covering under 50,000 square miles (130,000 sq km) within California, Nevada, Arizona, and Utah.

- The highest air temperature on record—130°F (54°C)—occurred in 2021 in the Mojave's Death Valley Furnace Creek region. Back in 1913, the temperature supposedly reached 134°F (57°C), although that reading has been disputed.

- The Mojave River runs 100 miles (161 km) through this desert, but you likely won't see it—it flows almost entirely underground.

KEEP AN EYE OUT FOR Twisted and densely spindled Joshua trees, whose range demarcates the boundaries of this desert.

KEEP AN EAR OUT FOR The scrabble of a cactus deermouse or a chuckwalla lizard—even small noises are amplified by the Mojave's rocky landscape.

KEEP A NOSE OUT FOR Creosote bushes, whose leaves are full of oils that fill the desert with a musky post-rain smell, especially during monsoon season.

animation that they "defy what we consider being alive," says Jenna Ekwealor, a botanist who studies them. When it rains, they spring to life again.

But even these adaptable plants can use some help. As Ekwealor and her colleagues have found, *S. caninervis* moss tends to grow particularly well underneath quartz. Like other nurse rocks, a chunk of quartz can slow the evaporation of nearby water, creating a more humid environment for the moss. The quartz can also buffer temperature extremes, cooling the moss during hot summer days and warming it through nights and winters, Ekwealor says.

Quartz's milky, crystalline structure makes it uniquely qualified for the position. In the desert, the sun can be punishing, its damaging UV rays unfiltered by moisture in the air. A quartz of the right opacity will block much—but not all—of the light, so the moss underneath gets enough sunlight to live and grow, but not enough to burn. "Having the rock provides a real guarantee that the light won't be too strong ever," Ekwealor says. "It's such a great little shelter."

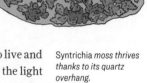

Syntrichia moss thrives thanks to its quartz overhang.

Moss spores that happen to settle underneath these quartz sunshades have a cushier life as they sprout and grow. They experience twice the humidity as those exposed directly to the sun, and temperature swings are gentled by up to 7°F (3.89°C) in either direction. These mosses can grow faster, larger, and even greener, all thanks to the care of their white-coated nurse rocks. ❯ **How to see them:** Look for rock formations veined with quartz and try to find small pieces that have broken off and rolled onto the desert floor. Lifting one of these small pieces can reveal moss underneath—but be sure to put it back!

Relocated Tortoises

As their habitats get disrupted, these ancient reptiles are being rehomed—sometimes to people's backyards.

RANGE: Alluvial fans and sandy flats in California, Nevada, and Utah
SPECIES: Desert tortoise (*Gopherus agassizii*)

◆ Desert tortoises know how to weather change. Residents of the Mojave for more than 3 million years, they've stuck around even as their ecosystem went from a dripping jungle during the Miocene to today's sunbaked desert. In recent years, the landscape has begun to shift again as new wind, solar, and housing development projects fence tortoises out of their habitat.

And so, with the help of concerned local citizens, some tortoises have taken up a new survival strategy: They live in people's backyards. Since 1998, the California Turtle and Tortoise Club has been rehoming reptiles who find themselves displaced by energy companies or housing developers. Many wild tortoises are brought to other corners of the desert, but those who might have trouble surviving there are adopted by human families. (Other rehoming candidates come from households who took them from the wild as pets decades ago, before it was illegal, but can no longer care for them.) Desert tortoises are the only species on the United States "threatened" or "endangered" lists that can be kept in this way.

The slow-paced lifestyle of these tortoises translates well to many California desert homes. Tortoise caretakers feed their charges grasses, but the reptiles are also known to nibble on garden flowers. They dig backyard burrows—private, underground spaces where some spend up to 95 percent of their time. In the wild, tortoises use burrows to hibernate during both the cold winters and the hot summers. In captivity, tortoises tend to hibernate less, but in more unusual locations; keepers often find their missing tortoises under dressers or in closets.

The tortoises are (relatively) high-maintenance in one respect: Unlike other desert creatures that can stay hydrated just by eating desert plants, they need to imbibe fresh water at least once every couple of years. A puddle on concrete, such as what you might find after a light rain, is typically enough to satisfy their thirst.

Desert tortoises help humans out, too. Companies proposing extractive projects in the desert often act as though no one lives there, ignoring not only wildlife, like the tortoise, but a number of Indigenous American groups with desert homelands. In the 1990s, a company proposed putting a nuclear waste dump in San Bernardino County's Ward Valley, part of the territory of the Chemehuevi tribe and Mojave nation—and critical desert tortoise habitat. Images of radioactive, melting tortoises adorned posters protesting the project, and in the end, the tortoise's threatened status helped stop it. ❯ **How to see them:** In the wild, wait for an overcast day when rainfall seems imminent, or try springtime when the tortoises tend to be out chomping on plants. One well-known captive tortoise, Mojave Maxine, can be found at the Living Desert Zoo and Gardens in Palm Desert, California.

THE WILD LIFE OF A Tortoise Adoption Coordinator

■ Mary Dutro has been the adoption chairman for the High Desert chapter of the California Turtle and Tortoise Club for more than 20 years. During her tenure, she has placed more than a thousand tortoises in new homes.

• **How did you first become involved with the California Turtle and Tortoise Club?**
When Charlene and Sherman walked into my backyard in 1960. They were two tortoises, a male and a female. They stayed in my backyard until they became an endangered species [in 1989]. Then Fish and Wildlife had us release them to help rebuild the wild population. So Charlene, Sherman, and their kids were released out where a high school has now been built.

• **In your role as adoption coordinator, how do you place tortoises in homes? What does someone need to do to keep a tortoise at their home?**
You have to consider the habitat—if it will be good for them. You've got to make sure that they have sun, shade, and a shallow water dish. They need dirt they can dig in. Sometimes they use doghouses to supplement their burrows.

• **Where do the tortoises that you get and rehome come from?**
The majority come from households that can no longer care for them. Either a caregiver has died or they're moving out of state, and they can't take [the tortoises]

out of state. Some of the tortoises have been in the same home for 40 or 50 years.

The other ones I've had turned in to me were living where [companies] were putting in solar fields. The ground under a solar field gets so hot that the tortoises can't stay there. So the electric company, or whoever's putting in the solar field, will rescue them and turn them in.

• **What are some of your other duties as adoption chair?**
I did get a call from one gentleman who was trying to figure out why and how his tortoise died. We went through all the things as I'm trying to diagnose her on the telephone.

Finally, I thought to ask, "How old is she?" He said, "I don't know exactly, but we've had her for over 140 years." His grandfather found her out in the desert when she was the size of his hand.

So we figured that she was probably five or ten years old when his grandfather found her—which, by the way, is against the law now; you can't pick up a wild tortoise. We figured she died of old age.

• **What do you wish people knew about tortoises?**
They are great pets. They don't bark; they don't bite! Desert tortoises don't bother anybody. They do become associated with their families; they'll recognize you when you come out. The tortoises will even knock on the patio door if you're late putting food out for them.

They make nice pets as long as you treat them right and keep them safe. And they've been around here longer than the dinosaurs. They're still here, and it would be nice if we didn't wipe them out. ■

If you see a desert tortoise in the wild, don't bother it! A tortoise might respond to being picked up by evacuating its bowels and losing precious water. If the tortoise seems to be in distress, note its location and contact the landowner or the local chapter of the California Turtle and Tortoise Club. For more information about adopting a desert tortoise, go to tortoise.org.

White Wonders

In this ecosystem, blanker is better.

LOCATION: White Sands National Park, New Mexico

SPECIES: Apache pocket mouse (*Perognathus flavescens Apachii*), bleached earless lizard (*Holbrookia maculata ruthveni*), white sand-treader cricket (*Ammobaenetes arenicolus*), and others

◆ At first glance, the sprawling dunes of White Sands National Park seem as lifeless as the moon. But look a little closer. Hidden in plain sight are 800 species of animals, from moths to foxes. Some of these creatures are found nowhere else, and many share a clever survival strategy in this harsh land: their alabaster hue.

White Sands is the world's largest swath of gypsum sands, tiny, bright crystals that glint in the sun. Layers of the sulfate mineral built up in the basin hundreds of millions of years ago, when it was still covered by the Permian Sea. Like salt, gypsum dissolves in water and recrystallizes when that water evaporates.

As the area dried up over millions of years, strong winds broke up and pushed around the exposed seabed, forming sandy dunes. Gypsum deposits still remain in the surrounding mountains, and on the rare occasion when it rains, dissolved particles ride runoff down into the basin and add to the huge, shifting mounds that stretch for hundreds of square miles.

When the brilliant white dunes began forming, the animals living here found themselves on the blank page of a new landscape. They faced a crisis: Lighten up or perish.

So while their relatives just miles away enjoy various colors and patterns, the inhabitants of White Sands look like they've been dipped in the ceiling paint section of a hardware store. The Apache pocket mouse sports ivory fur, the sand wolf spider has a pearly glow, and the bleached earless lizard looks like it's fresh out of the laundry.

Cloaked in white, they avoid detection on the dunes, where more ostentatious colors would make them easy marks for predators like the greater roadrunner and the kit fox. (There are exceptions, like the inky darkling beetle, which adequately protects itself by squirting out a kerosene-scented chemical to repel hungry bug-eaters.) The lack of pigmentation in the hardy survivors of White Sands also helps keep them cool—a necessity in a place with summer highs reaching 110°F (43°C).

If you're lucky enough to spot one of the park's white wonders, you're likely to get a good long look. "The ones that are camouflaged, they don't seem to mind people," says David Bustos, the park's resource program manager.

"It doesn't matter what animal you look at—they're all unique and strange," Bustos says. That is, if you can see them at all. ❯ **How to see them:** Try visiting the national park during MothaPalooza, an annual celebration of White Sands' unique moth species.

Camouflage experts of White Sands include the white sand treader cricket, the bleached earless lizard, and the Apache pocket mouse.

Footprints in Time

Before it became a haven for small, secretive creatures, the land that is now White Sands National Park was the stomping ground for a number of bigger animals—including us. The layers of sediment deposited in the park over time have preserved foot, hoof, and paw prints that help researchers determine who once wandered through, while seeds and other plant matter found above and below the prints allow us to figure out roughly when they were made.

10,000 YEARS AGO
A LONG TREK

About 10,000 years ago, a woman or a young man walked at least a mile across this landscape, carrying a toddler. The uneven spacing of the walker's tracks suggests the route involved slippery mud and leaping over puddles, while tiny prints occasionally appear beside the main trail, marking places where the toddler was set down. The adult traveler later retraced the route alone. Altogether, they left 400 footprints—the longest trail of this age ever found.

A woolly mammoth and a giant sloth came through the area shortly after the two travelers, leaving prints across their path. The sloth appears to have risen on two legs at one point, potentially to sniff out the pair.

12,000 YEARS AGO
TWO KINDS OF SLOTH HUNT

At the end of the Pleistocene, mammoths, giant camels, dire wolves, and saber-toothed cats all found their way to what is now White Sands—and hungry humans followed. One set of prints appears to tell the story of a giant sloth hunt. A group stalked and then rushed the sloth, rocking up onto the balls of their feet, perhaps in order to throw things. The sloth's tracks show him standing up and spinning around before his eventual defeat. Nearby, more human tracks suggest onlookers carrying kids over to watch the matchup.

Giant sloths may have been the size of modern bears. Their prints are deep and large—some about the size of snowshoes. Other trails that have been unearthed show that people purposefully stepped inside the prints—maybe while tracking the sloth, or maybe just for fun. And kids apparently enjoyed jumping in the puddles that filled them after a rain.

21,000 TO 23,000 YEARS AGO
YOUNG PIONEERS

Most recently, researchers uncovered even older tracks—those of a group of humans, mostly children and teens, who apparently frequented the area between 21,000 and 23,000 years ago. The tracks overlap and double back, suggesting that those who made them knew their way around. They may have been fetching and carrying food or other resources in order to help their communities.

These are the earliest human footprints ever recovered in the Americas. Before their discovery, many scientists thought a massive ice wall had blocked anyone from entering the area during this time. Now they are rethinking the timeline of when humans arrived on the continent. Whatever these young people were up to, it left a major impression.

Flash Flood Survival Kits

Desert flooding may seem like an oxymoron, but flash floods occur even in some of the world's driest places. In the Sonoran Desert, located in the southwestern United States and northwest Mexico, seasonal monsoons blow through roughly twice a year, in winter and late summer, bringing life-giving rain to a parched landscape and quenching the thirst of many desert creatures for months to come.

But downpours can also mean death for the unprepared. Because sandy soils don't readily absorb water, rain quickly permeates the ground and produces runoff, flooding the landscape. The force of rushing water alone can rip plants from their roots and topple trees, while puddles can drown vegetation accustomed to limited rainfall.

In response, many plants inhabiting desert ecosystems have developed unique ways to survive these brief periods of saturation—and sometimes also meet their water needs for years on end. Here are four superstar species that will show you how it's done—no floaties required.

VELVET MESQUITE (*Prosopis velutina*) • Forests of velvet mesquite are often found in floodplains, washes, and other riverine areas. Their taproots can reach as deep as 150 feet (46 m) underground, drawing from hidden water sources in times of drought and stabilizing the trees during monsoons and floods. They take advantage of flash floods for reproduction—the rushing water knocks around their seeds, which require abrasion, called scarification, in order to germinate. ❶

DESERT LILY (*Hesperocallis undulata*) • Desert lilies need heavy rains to flower, an odd strategy for a species in one of the world's most arid habitats. In fact, their striking white blooms emerge only when water penetrates nearly a foot underground. In times of extreme drought, desert lily bulbs can remain dry and dormant for several years as they await the next storm. Indigenous people, including those from the Yuba Tribe, have harvested these garlicky bulbs as a food source. ❷

BLUE PALO VERDE (*Parkinsonia florida*) • The state tree of Arizona, the blue palo verde grows in floodplains and washout areas. Like the velvet mesquite, the tree's seeds require scarification for germination, and flash floods often provide this service. Deep roots help the tree withstand the power of floodwaters that could easily knock over other species. Some blue palo verde trees live to be more than a century old—a testament to their endurance in times of drought and flood. ❸

FALSE ROSE OF JERICHO (*Selaginella lepidophylla*) • The false rose of Jericho is a real-life transformer. Known as a "resurrection" plant, this spike moss may spend years with its fronds curled into a crispy brown ball, blown to and fro by the wind. After a rainstorm, though, it dramatically returns to life— rehydrating, unfurling, and exposing its fruits, which then launch seeds away from the plant for dispersal. ❹

Amberat

Rodent urine is a window into the past.

◆ For a desert wood rat, every night is a treasure hunt. As evening falls, this efficient rodent heads out into his neighborhood to gather materials, carrying them home with the help of his large and dexterous feet. Worthwhile finds include food (like cactus pads and nuts), construction supplies (like rocks and sticks), and decorations (like bones, dead bugs, dried dung, aluminum foil scraps, and balloon strings).

Back at his multichambered nest, or midden, the wood rat goes over his haul, snacking on or storing the edibles, artfully distributing the baubles, and performing any necessary building fortifications. When he's done, he relieves himself, often right on top of everything. Another night sorted.

Wood rats have been practicing this nightly hoarding ritual for millennia, which is why many people call them "pack rats." As it turns out, their storage technique is more effective than they could possibly know.

Desert wood rat urine is sugary and concentrated. When it coats a midden and then dries out, it traps the pile of rat belongings in a resinous substance—an accidental preservative scientists call "amberat."

When tucked safely inside caves, amberat deposits can last for tens of thousands of years. Paleontologists saw out chunks of them to analyze and find cross sections of the past, each carefully curated by an ancient rat. Pollen grains, leaves, needles, and even whole mummified flowers can be stuck within the middens. All help paint a picture of the American deserts millennia ago, back when they were cooler and greener—which, as contemporary climate change accelerates, may help us predict future shifts.

For these reasons, the US Geological Survey keeps a database of amberat deposits, almost certainly the only government database devoted to pee-covered trash. So far, they've gathered intel on more than 3,000 preserved middens in the North American West, from British Columbia down to Coahuila—a collection that might impress even the rats themselves. ❯ **How to see it:** Middens, or nests, are easy to spot in the desert—look for a stylish pile of sticks. Ancient middens preserved in amberat are generally tucked away in caves, including in the Honeycomb Hills in western Utah.

RANGE: Throughout western North America, from Canada to Mexico
ASSOCIATED SPECIES: The desert wood rat (*Neotoma lepida*) and others

Amberat deposits can last for tens of thousands of years.

Salt Flat Spiders

Once thought to be extinct, these spiders were just hiding where no one wanted to look.

◆ Even by desert standards, the Mojave's salt flats are forbidding. With an otherworldly crackled crust of salt spread up to 4 feet (1 m) thick over vast dry lake beds, these flats appear to be wastelands.

But below this briny coating is a hidden kingdom of hardy invertebrates. Peel back the right chunk of salt, and life explodes from the mud below: brine flies, ant-like flower beetles, and, if you're really lucky, perhaps a salt flat spider.

These arachnids can be difficult to spot—they're so small that four of them could fit comfortably on a dime. That may be why they were presumed extinct for decades before they resurfaced at California's Soda Lake in the 1990s. As it turns out, they've been quietly thriving. Entomologist Sara Crews, who has been studying salt flat spiders

RANGE: Salt flats throughout Southern California, New Mexico, Arizona, and Texas, and near Utah's salt lakes.
SPECIES: Salt flat spider (*Saltonia incerta*)

for years, found specimens ranging from Southern California into New Mexico.

Though they live in isolated salt flats separated by hundreds of miles, Crews's genetic testing revealed that salt flat spiders represent a single species. Southern California's waterlogged past provides context: These salt flats are the desiccated remains of immense lakes that blanketed the region during the ice ages. As partially aquatic arachnids, salt flat spiders thrived here until the climate dried out and the lakes shrank. Slowly, they evolved new survival tools, including the ability to absorb moisture from mud, and possibly genes that confer salt tolerance.

While life in what amounts to the bottom of a french fry bag might sound nightmarish to most of us, it's actually a cushy existence for these spiders. The salt reflects sunlight, creating an oasis of cool, moist soil. For food, they ensnare their fellow flatmates, including each other, in webs they spin between the dirt floor and the salt ceiling. Then they feast, no seasonings required.

Salt flat spiders are so small that four could fit together on a dime.

As global temperatures continue to rise and the Mojave Desert becomes even drier, it remains to be seen how the spiders and their fellow holdouts will respond to another round of aridification. Crews spends much of her time peeling back the salt, seeking new knowledge about these rediscovered arachnids. "I think there are more of them around the world, and people just haven't really looked for them," Crews says. "Nobody wants to go out to the salt flats when it's 120°F [49°C] and look for spiders. I don't know why." ❯ **How to see them:** Head to areas like Death Valley's Badwater Basin or the Mojave National Preserve's Soda Lake, both located in California, and look for them near areas of pooling water on the salt flats. Be sure to bring a zoom lens and lots of water for yourself!

Psychedelic Toads

Join the Church of the Toad of Light.

RANGE: Sonoran Desert, particularly southern Arizona and northwestern Mexico
SPECIES: Sonoran Desert toad (*Incilius alvarius*), also known as the Colorado River toad

◆ Just one of a couple dozen amphibians native to the arid American Southwest and northwestern Mexico, the Sonoran Desert toad may have remained a relatively unremarkable species if not for the first intrepid psychonaut who decided to smoke its secretions.

To varying degrees, all toads secrete toxins through their skin and glands as a defense against potential predators. But only the Sonoran Desert toad produces 5-MeO-DMT, perhaps the most powerful psychedelic compound in the natural world. In fact, despite some unsubstantiated historical anecdotes, this toad is the only known natural source outside the plant and fungus kingdoms of a viable quantity of any hallucinogenic compound. In other words, it's the world's only psychedelic animal.

The Sonoran Desert toad is the world's only known psychedelic animal.

Despite the prominence of amphibian symbology in the art and folklore of Indigenous Americans living in its range, there was no clear evidence of the Sonoran Desert toad's use as a drug until a mysterious pamphlet appeared in underground circles in the 1980s. The author described how to milk the white liquid secretion from the glands

SONORAN DESERT

- The Sonoran Desert stretches 100,000 square miles (300,000 sq km) within California, Arizona, and Mexico. Arizona is the only state to claim a piece of all four American deserts: the Mojave, the Sonoran, the Great Basin, and the Chihuahuan.

- Thanks to intermittent but reliable rainfall clustered in the summer and winter, the Sonoran Desert is the wettest desert in the world. It's also one of the most biodiverse, home to more than 2,000 plant species.

- Nearly half the bird species in America visit the Sonoran Desert at some point during the year.

KEEP AN EYE OUT FOR Many strange cactus shapes, from the iconic and welcoming saguaro to the overwhelming organ pipe.

KEEP AN EAR OUT FOR The wall-to-wall buzz of the cicada, the only animal hardy enough to sing during the extreme heat of the day.

KEEP A NOSE OUT FOR Saguaro flowers in bloom, which smell like melons that are just going soft.

behind the toad's eyes, dry it, and smoke it. The anonymous author also proposed the creation of a religion dedicated to the toad: the Church of the Toad of Light.

Compared with other hallucinogens, like LSD and mushroom-derived psilocybin, the toad's 5-MeO-DMT–rich secretion incites a short and extremely powerful psychedelic experience. One user described it as being "shot to the beginning of time, the end of the universe, where there was nothing except a presence, sort of like a snake, neither evil nor benign, just staring at me." Beyond simple hedonism or curiosity, researchers are also investigating the use of 5-MeO-DMT in treating depression and anxiety, with preliminarily positive results.

Though milking the toad for its psychedelic secretion doesn't immediately kill it, the popularity of "smoking toad" has caused consternation among conservationists as well as psychedelic enthusiasts concerned with animal welfare. The process can disturb, disorient, and displace the toads, which are sometimes removed from their natural habitat to be milked and may eventually fail to breed or survive. Though the species is not currently classified as endangered or even threatened, an expanding interest in its psychedelic ooze may eventually imperil Sonoran Desert toad populations. For this reason, a vocal faction has emerged to advocate for the use of sustainable plant sources of 5-MeO-DMT and its relative DMT, or synthetic preparations—which, despite their less exotic origins, pretty much do the trick. ❯ **How to see them:** The toads are hard to miss in ponds and streams at night during Arizona's summer monsoon rains.

Crested Saguaros

These mutant plants are beloved by desert dwellers and poachers alike.

LOCATION: Sonoran Desert
SPECIES: Saguaro cactus
(*Carnegiea gigantea*)

◆ The silhouette of the saguaro cactus may be the American desert's defining shape. Asked to draw a cactus, almost everyone will sketch out its straight-and-true posture and beckoning arms.

But some saguaros mix it up. The crested saguaro (known more formally as the cristate saguaro) is capped not with a demure knob but with an explosion of chaotic whorls. It's as though someone took a regular saguaro and gave the top half a perm.

Saguaros grow from their tips. Normally the cells in the growing tissue form in a tight circular pattern, so that the cactus keeps a neat shape. In crested plants, the cells fan outward instead, eventually forming strange headgear.

No one is quite sure what triggers this cresting, as it's known. Some think the occasional desert freeze throws the plant out of whack. Others believe a hormone or genetic quirk causes the creases in the cactus's stem and arms, called pleats, to grow out of control. A group of scientists at Arizona State University's Biodesign Institute is currently researching how the mutations in crested saguaros might mirror those found in cancer cells in humans.

Our sense of their prevalence is also under revision. They were once thought to be extremely rare, numbering only in the hundreds. But the Crested Saguaro Society, which has been photographing and geotagging these top-heavy plants since 2005, has counted more than 3,600 so far.

No two crested saguaros are alike. Some loom like cartoon monsters, while others resemble giant gloves or landlocked corals. The society has christened some with names like "Statue of Liberty" or "I Want a Hug." "Anybody can go find them," says Joe Orman, the society's webmaster. "It's kind of cool when you find one that's never been found by anybody else."

Life can be tough for crested saguaros. Their unusual shapes make them more vulnerable to frost and strong winds—as well as to poachers, who dig them up and sell them on the cactus black market. A particularly funky-shaped specimen can fetch up to $15,000.

For this reason, the society "tries to keep their locations secret," says Orman— as much as they can with such singular plants. ❯ **How to see them:** Walk through the Sonoran Desert and look for a lumpy, looming shadow. Based on the Crested Saguaro Society's numbers, you'll have the best luck in Pinal, Arizona.

Say hello.

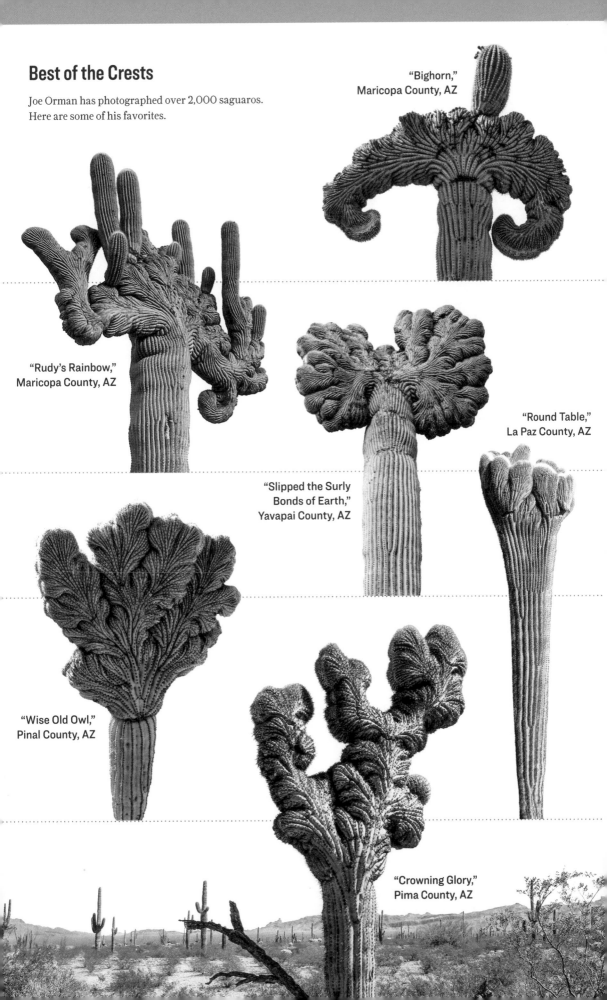

Best of the Crests

Joe Orman has photographed over 2,000 saguaros. Here are some of his favorites.

"Bighorn,"
Maricopa County, AZ

"Rudy's Rainbow,"
Maricopa County, AZ

"Round Table,"
La Paz County, AZ

"Slipped the Surly
Bonds of Earth,"
Yavapai County, AZ

"Wise Old Owl,"
Pinal County, AZ

"Crowning Glory,"
Pima County, AZ

The camouflage of this giant hairy scorpion is no match for a UV light.

Fluorescent Scorpions

An inexpensive tool lights up these sneaky desert arachnids.

RANGE: Deserts worldwide
SPECIES: In the American West, common species include the giant hairy scorpion (*Hadrurus arizonensis*), the Arizona bark scorpion (*Centruroides sculpturatus*), and the sand scorpion (*Paruroctonus utahensis*).

◆ It's hard to spot a scorpion, even if you want to. Most are the exact hues of the sand and rocks they live in. They're great at hiding in shadows and staying completely still, skills that help them ambush prey like centipedes and avoid predators like grasshopper mice.

At night, though, one simple tool erases their disguise: an ultraviolet flashlight. Sweep a UV beam over almost any scorpion, and fluorescent pigments in the arachnid's exoskeleton light up, turning the stealthy critter a bright teal color that pops against the desert floor like a glowstick on concrete.

You can take these flashlights out at night for scorpion-spotting adventures, a thrill that doesn't get old. Tracy Albrecht has been leading UV flashlight tours in California for years. Each time someone's purple beam lights up a scorpion, "it's an alarming surprise," she says. "Even though that's what you're looking for."

UV flashlights facilitate purposeful, up-close scorpion encounters that help people better understand and appreciate these feared creatures, Albrecht says.

It's unclear what the arachnids get out of the fluorescence deal. Scientists have a number of theories: By absorbing and converting harmful UV rays, the fluorescent pigments may act as a sort of sunscreen. They may enable scorpions to find mates in the dark, to evade UV-sensitive predators, or to detect moonlight so that they can stay hidden at night. (Light detection is very important for scorpions—their tails can do it as well as their eyes.) Or it might just be a coincidence—a chemical quirk.

"It's still a mystery," says Albrecht. "I think that makes it a little more fun."

❯ **How to see them:** In summer, many educational centers and groups lead scorpion spotting tours, including Friends of the Desert Mountains in Palm Springs, California. Or try it out yourself—see our tips on the next page.

Tips for Scorpion Spotting

Tracy Albrecht has led dozens of scorpion tours. Here are her tips for a successful fluorescent adventure.

1. GET YOUR GEAR. Ultraviolet flashlights are available online and at many hardware stores, usually for less than $15. It can be fun to use a variety of lights, as different ones work better depending on the conditions, Albrecht says. Make sure you have water, sturdy footwear, and regular flashlights or headlamps for navigating.

2. KNOW THE TERRAIN. Desert nights are very dark. Take a daytime walk in the area you plan to explore to familiarize yourself with obstacles and terrain changes so you don't

trip over a bush. It's also a good opportunity to look for football-shaped scorpion holes.

3. START EARLY. Just before twilight, the desert comes alive with breezes, scents, and sounds. Head out before sundown and you might encounter nighthawks, jackrabbits, or mule deer as a prelude to the main event.

4. GO LOW. Scorpions can be anywhere: outside their burrows, down in washes, or even inside fissures in the sides of canyon walls. It helps to shine your UV flashlight

low to the ground to ensure full illumination, which means that kids are often the most successful spotters.

5. OBSERVE, BUT NOT TOO CLOSELY. Once you've found a scorpion, keep your flashlight steady and observe it from a safe distance of about 4 feet (1 m). (Make sure you have open space behind you in case you have to retreat.) Most scorpions will stay put, allowing you to get a good look and a photo or two. Then switch off your beam and let everyone scuttle back into the night.

Southern Grasshopper Mice

By night, the deserts ring with the howls of venom-thirsty were-mice.

RANGE: Desert scrub, prairies, and desert grasslands across the American Southwest and northern Mexico

SPECIES: Southern grasshopper mouse (*Onychomys torridus*)

◆ For humans, the venomous sting of the Arizona bark scorpion triggers an immediate burning sensation—it's been compared to getting branded—followed by hours of intense, throbbing pain.

For southern grasshopper mice, though, the sting is no big deal. Thanks to a quirk of evolution, they barely notice it.

Grasshopper mice hunt with a ferocity that belies their pencil-length size. They spend their days tucked into burrows they've stolen from fellow rodents, and their nights on the prowl for meals of birds, lizards, arthropods, and even each other.

But scorpion slaying is where they truly shine. Grasshopper mice are naturally aggressive and boast several admirable combat moves. Their forceful jaws, needle-sharp claws, and thick digestive linings are optimized for handling exoskeletons.

Even so, grasshopper mice get stung—often—in a typical scorpion scuffle, and win by sinking their teeth straight into their opponent's venom bulb. For years, baffled scientists wondered how these little rodents could withstand such high doses of a toxin that causes humans excruciating pain.

In 2013, evolutionary neurobiologists discovered their secret weapon. Thanks to certain gene mutations, southern grasshopper mice have the opposite reaction to bark scorpion venom from other creatures: Instead of triggering intense pain, the venom actually turns off pain-sensing cells called nociceptors. In other words, in grasshopper mice, the scorpion's venom acts as a pain*killer*.

This response is likely quite surprising to the scorpion, who finds his previously heavy artillery is suddenly about as effective as a squirt gun. But

Grasshopper mice belt piercing "howls" that can be heard from more than 300 feet (91 m) away.

scorpions actually helped their foes develop this painkilling power. The adaptation likely arose through a process called reciprocal selection, wherein two organisms—often a predator and its prey—compete in a genetic arms race, each continually one-upping the other across their evolutionary histories.

Whatever chance mutation allowed a lucky grasshopper mouse to muscle through the scorpion's sting was certainly helpful for survival, and so that mutation was passed along, again and again over time, until the whole species boasted the ability. Researchers are studying this unique form of pain immunity to better understand chronic pain disorders in humans and potentially develop more precise, nonaddictive analgesics.

After a southern grasshopper mouse enjoys her meal, she's got one more surprising move. In a display of territoriality, she may perch up on her hind legs, tilt back her furry little head, and let out a piercing, high-pitched howl. She earned it. 〉 **How to see them:** Nocturnal, solitary, and widely dispersed, grasshopper mice are tough to find. But if you're wandering the Sonoran Desert after dark and a clear, high-pitched whistle cuts through the night air, you might be closer than you think.

Sonoran Pronghorns

Along the US-Mexico border in Arizona, the most watchful presence might be a fleet-footed, goat-sized creature.

RANGE: Four separate ranges cumulatively span approximately 6,660 square miles (17,000 sq km) in southwestern Arizona and Sonora, Mexico.

SPECIES: Sonoran pronghorn (*Antilocapra americana sonoriensis*)

◆ Sonoran pronghorns are always on the lookout. Each of these goat-sized creatures scans the desert with eyes the size of an elephant's, which enable nearly 360-degree vision that can spot movement up to 4 miles (6 km) away. The slightest provocation spurs a takeoff at 60 miles per hour (95 kmh)—highway cruise-control speeds, and the fastest of any North American land mammal. Those in the know call this tiny, horned speedster the "desert ghost."

While most of America's other pronghorns graze grasslands, this subspecies descended into the Sonoran Desert's driest regions about 10,000 years ago, likely in order to escape people. But recently, their home range along the US-Mexico border has brought pronghorns into conflict with another watchful entity: the United States Border Patrol.

After the post-9/11 border crackdown, the locus of unauthorized border crossings shifted from Texas to the harshest parts of the Arizona desert—and the Border Patrol followed. The influx of human activity coincided with a severe drought that caused near extinction for the Sonoran pronghorn, dropping the US population to just 21 in 2002. A binational recovery team quickly formed to respond, tracking the pronghorns and providing food and water at popular grazing spots. The team also initiated a semicaptive breeding program to support the wild population.

Over the years, human activity in the area has only increased. Border wall construction, along with roads, ranches, and encroaching development, has pushed the pronghorns from 88 percent of their range. Researchers have mapped thousands of miles of off-road tire tracks and unauthorized roads used by border agents, whose vehicles trample plants and compact the soil, destroying the pronghorns' food sources. And recent infrastructure projects at the border have drained irreplaceable water from the last permanent water source in the pronghorns' range, a spring that underpins the whole ecosystem.

Pronghorns are also so shy that the mere presence of vehicles may turn a peaceful graze into a high-alert scanfest. "There's the potential for motorized activity to result in a decrease in fitness," says Stephanie Doerries, a US Fish and Wildlife Service biologist who is the recovery coordinator for the species. Too much time watching and not enough eating, and a pronghorn could starve.

For all these reasons, researchers say that the pronghorn is likely the American animal most threatened by border activity—although they're so elusive, it's hard to determine the true impact.

After two decades of recovery efforts, the Sonoran pronghorn population in the United States and Mexico has rebounded to approximately 900 in total. But once the immediate danger of extinction passed, funding for the pronghorn dried up, even though threats are still present. The most recent record drought in pronghorn habitat stretched from August 2009 to June 2019, likely permanently altering the entire ecosystem. Without support, researchers say, one dry summer could mean another plummet in population.

And so, while the annual US Border Patrol budget climbs into the billions, the pronghorn recovery team stretches their resources, hoping to prevent the desert ghost from truly disappearing. ❯ **How to see them:** Head to Ajo, Arizona, where you can spot pronghorns along public access roads into Cabeza Prieta National Wildlife Refuge and Organ Pipe Cactus National Monument.

THE WILD LIFE OF A Borderlands Wildlife Campaigner

■ In the border region where Sonoran pronghorns roam, Laiken Jordahl is also keeping a lookout. As a borderland campaigner with the Center for Biological Diversity in Arizona, Jordahl heads into the desert every week with his phone, camera, and drones—and at least a gallon of water—to document the environmental impacts of border wall construction.

• **How does border wall construction impact biodiversity in this region?**
On a scientific level, it's very, very simple. If you destroy habitat, if you fragment migration corridors, you're going to have horrific impacts on wildlife and ecosystems. These border walls go right to the heart of the habitat of many, many species—endangered animals like Sonoran pronghorn and the jaguar, and many others. These walls cut off all north-south migration of wildlife. There are many instances where you'll see an animal that has a breeding ground on one side of the border, and their major area

to find food and water is on the other side. You've just completely isolated the areas that they need to survive.

Also there's habitat destruction. So many mountains have just been completely obliterated. All of these ancient saguaro cactuses that are homes to pygmy owls, to other birds, to bats—they are being destroyed. So not only is the habitat being fragmented, but we're also seeing a lot of habitat loss, just from the footprint of the project.

• **What does a day in the desert look like?**
Oftentimes I'll go out without being entirely sure where we'll end up. Sometimes we'll hike all day to reach an area that is miles from the nearest road. During wall construction, sometimes we would go out and find that a whole mountain had been demolished by dynamite. We'd stop there and try to document the damage.

• **As different administrations have taken charge in the United States, how have your goals changed?**

The very first day of the Biden administration [in 2020], we got word that they had issued a memo stopping all border wall construction. That was huge. In the months that followed, for the first time in years, the construction sites were quiet.

In the time since then, there has been very little meaningful action taken. We have been calling for the restoration of all these sites that have been destroyed and the removal of sections of wall that are causing the most harm. And, of course, we've been calling for community consultation and reparations to Indigenous communities who have quite literally had their sacred sites blown up to build this border wall.

• **What is important to you about the Sonoran Desert?**
In the Sonoran Desert, life finds a way to survive.

And all we have to do is leave it alone. Not mess with it. Not build walls through the center of these migration corridors. Not suck up every last drop of groundwater. ■

Borderland Jaguars

The king of American cats is making a play for the USA.

RANGE: Northern Sonora, Mexico, to southern Arizona
SPECIES: Jaguar (*Panthera onca*)

◆ In 1996, mountain lion hunters in Arizona captured the first photos ever taken of live jaguars in the United States. Historically, the mountains and deserts of the American Southwest, particularly Arizona and New Mexico, were jaguar country, but Arizona's last known resident jaguar was killed in 1965. Yet here were two of them, 30 years later, alive and well and ready for their close-up.

Since 1996, at least seven male jaguars have been seen in Arizona, presumably after crossing the border from Mexico. These "northern jaguars" are less than half the size of some of their rainforest-dwelling species-mates farther south, and they may possess unique genetic qualities that allow them to adapt to the hot, arid conditions of the borderlands.

No one is quite sure why jaguars are expanding their territory into the United States. Until very recently, experts were following the big cats' lead, allowing them to "rewild" themselves and return to their historical range on their own, as they chose, braving the difficulties of the border zone.

But early in 2021, after evaluating potential habitat in Arizona and New Mexico and finding that it could support a viable jaguar breeding population, a group of scientists officially recommended the reintroduction of these big cats to the country. Restoring jaguars to this habitat would help support the species, while adding another top predator to the region could improve its ecosystems. However, some people, including ranchers and hunters, wonder what jaguars could mean for their potential prey—both wild and domestic.

> **How to see them:** Good luck—some people spend their whole lives studying borderland jaguars and never see one! A visit to the Northern Jaguar Reserve in Sonora, Mexico, might yield a track or two, or even fresh scat. Recent camera trap photos can be found on the Northern Jaguar Project's website and Instagram page.

THE WILD LIFE OF A Jaguar-Friendly Rancher

■ José Coronado runs a cattle ranch in Sonora, Mexico. As a member of the Viviendo con Felinos (Living with Felines) program, Coronado provides local nonprofit Northern Jaguar Project (NJP) with photos of feline predators that happen to cross his land. The NJP compensates ranchers for these photos—jaguar snaps being the most valuable—to encourage peaceful coexistence with these big cats.

● **How would you describe the relationship between jaguars and ranchers in Sonora?**

Many ranchers here don't even know we have jaguars. So raising awareness that these animals are living here is important. Many ranchers dislike jaguars because they're afraid of cattle predation. Our cattle are expensive, and predators like pumas, coyotes, and jaguars all pose a threat. But if you take good care of your livestock and manage your ranch well, they will usually be safe.

Ranchers and jaguars want the same thing: a balanced ecosystem. We all need water, most importantly, because it is so hot and dry here. And we all need biodiversity—good plants for cattle to forage, and prey species like deer and javelina for jaguars to eat.

● **How has working with NJP changed the way you view jaguars?**

NJP has taught me and my neighbors a lot about jaguars and how to keep our ranches safe from them. I want jaguars to be here, and I want them to have cubs here and be safe, too. Jaguars were here first, so we are sharing the land and resources.

● **How do you feel when you see photos of jaguars on your camera traps?**

I am always excited to see pumas and jaguars, because it means we'll get money for the ranch [from the NJP]. Jaguars are extremely beautiful animals, and I'm proud of these photos and proud that they choose to come through my land. Jaguars are strong and dangerous, so we need to be careful on the property. But my family and my cattle are still safe, even when we get these photos, which is a relief. ■

The Bat Nectar Trail

A lesser long-nosed bat may travel hundreds of miles—and help out thousands of plants—in pursuit of her sugar fix.

◆ Lesser long-nosed bats love nectar. With the help of a florally attuned sense of smell and a tongue as long as her body, the lesser long-nosed spends her nights hitting up blossom after blossom. In the dry forests of southern Mexico, certain plants produce so much nectar in an attempt to attract these first-class pollinators that a strong breeze will send it dripping out of their flowers, a phenomenon known as "sweet rain."

Many bats stay in this paradise year-round, pollen perpetually on their chins. But about a quarter of the members of each colony—roughly half the females—choose instead to make a long but rewarding journey. After mating with the males in the winter, the pregnant bats set off for even sweeter pastures, along a well-timed route that experts have named the nectar trail.

The female bats head north around February. First they hit up southern Sinaloa, sipping on the blossoms of morning glories and agaves. By April, they're farther into the desert—exactly in time for Mexico's many species of columnar cacti to erupt in delicious, sticky flowers.

The plants use scent and moonlit color to attract the bats. Many iconic species, including the organ pipe cactus and the saguaro, rely on the lesser long-nosed and other bat pollinators for pollination. Without the bats, "the whole look of the desert would change," says Rodrigo Medellín, an ecologist at the University of Mexico who studies them.

Around June, the crew arrives in the Sonoran Desert, where they rejoin into flocks of thousands, forming maternity colonies in caves or abandoned mining tunnels. Each bat mom gives birth to a single pup. Their summer nights are split between grooming, childcare, and dipping in and out of flowers and, later, fruits.

When fall comes around, the pups are weaned and ready to fly. The bats head back south, this time taking a different route. The second half of the nectar trail runs along the mountainous west coast, where, starting around October, dozens of species of agave plants put up towering flower stalks.

These multitiered buffets sustain the traveling bats until they make it back to the dry forests of southern Mexico. There, they introduce the next generation to their compatriots, drink their fill of sweet rain, and rest up for next year's sugar-seeking trip. ❯ **How to see them: The lesser long-nosed bat's desert roosting spots are not well known, but a well-placed cactus or agave plant will attract many nectar-feeding bats during its blooming season. An infrared camera can help make them easier to see.**

RANGE: The best-known nectar trail leads from the western coast of Mexico up to the southwestern United States and then back down again.

SPECIES: Lesser long-nosed bat (*Leptonycteris yerbabuenae*), organ pipe (*Stenocereus thurberi*), cardon (*Pachycereus pringlei*), and other cacti, and century plant (*Agave americana*) and other agaves

This lesser long-nosed bat is about to take a sweet sip of cardon cactus.

Sexy Bat Bald Spots

Lesser long-nosed bats have an unusual mating ritual. During courtship, a male bat will smear a spot on his back with his own bodily fluids: urine, saliva, feces, and semen. As this cocktail ferments, it attracts the females, who will grab the male, sniff his dorsal patch, and then pass out, sleeping through copulation.

Researchers think the strength of a male's brew correlates with his health and fitness. With some males, the stinky smear is so potent that the hair underneath temporarily falls out, growing back only after mating season is over.

Cuatro Ciénegas

Mexico's hot tub time machines

◆ Every desert dweller loves an oasis. In the depths of Mexico's Chihuahuan Desert, miles of parched soil and craggy mountains are suddenly broken by a long string of neon green and turquoise ponds, or pozas. This is Cuatro Ciénegas, a sanctuary for birds, box turtles, 17 types of fishes, and even an oddball community of marine snails living more than 280 miles (450 km) from the ocean.

But it's their tiniest life forms that make these blue pools special. Cuatro Ciénegas marks the remains of an ancient ocean, and its pozas are full of time travelers: bacteria and archaea that resemble some of Earth's earliest life forms. Scientists use these liquid portals to learn about the small but mighty forces that shaped our modern world.

A quick history lesson: About 3 billion years ago, when Earth's atmosphere was full of methane and carbon dioxide, archaea dominated the planet. These still-mysterious single-celled organisms may be the ancestors of all complex life. Then, about 2.4 billion years ago, cyanobacteria evolved as the first organisms to turn sunlight into oxygen. They pumped this life-giving gas into Earth's ancient ocean until it was saturated,

LOCATION: Coahuila, Mexico
SPECIES: More than 5,000 species of bacteria and archaea, including *Bacillus coahuilensis* (a bacterium found only in these desert pools), *Thermococcus* spp., and *Archaeoglobus* spp. (archaea more commonly found around deep-sea hydrothermal vents)

This desert oasis is a bright blue portal to the past.

then breathed it out into the atmosphere. Eventually, oxygen levels in the air grew high enough that life was able to crawl above the waterline for the first time.

Cyanobacteria accrete with sand to form ankle-high, brain-shaped rock formations called stromatolites. While fossilized stromatolites can be found across the world, Cuatro Ciénegas is one of just a few places where we still see living ones. It's also home to hundreds of species of archaea. "It's like we have the first car and the original motor—we have all the pieces," says Valeria Souza, a scientist who studies microbial life in the pozas.

In addition to these ancient heavyweights, Cuatro Ciénegas is swimming with more bacterial families than any other place on Earth. Scientists think many of these microbes are refugees of two planetary cataclysms: the breakups of supercontinents Rodinia and Pangaea. When these ancient landmasses cracked apart, the ocean rushed into the new gaps to form shallow seas, carrying with it marine microorganisms whose ancestors remain at Cuatro Ciénegas today. Some of these stranded species still sport unusual, old-school adaptations—like the ability to build fat membranes from sulfur, instead of the phosphorus that nearly everyone else on the planet now uses.

Yet Cuatro Ciénegas's locale has put everything from its snails to its unique microscopic life at risk. Alfalfa farms in this desert area have been draining the aquifer below the pozas for decades. In 2016, one of them, El Churince, dried up. Local scientists are now racing to keep these ancient portals blue as they discover new shades of life in their depths. ❯ **How to see it:** You can tour the protected Cuatro Ciénegas area from the visitors center at Poza Azul (Blue Pool).

THE WILD LIFE OF **An Archaea Archaeologist**

■ Mexican ecologist Valeria Souza was drawn into the ancient, azure world of Cuatro Ciénegas by accident. Now, its microscopic denizens help her look billions of years into the past.

• **How did you come to study Cuatro Ciénegas?**

One of our colleagues brought me and my husband there more than 20 years ago. From then on, our lives changed. It's so beautiful and so mysterious. More diverse in stromatolites than anywhere else. Nobody understood why it's so diverse, and they needed ecologists like us.

• **What's so special about being able to study archaea?**

[In 2016] we discovered this amazing little pond that nobody had paid attention to.

This spot is different from anything else. When it's not rainy, it's just a crust of salt. In it, these creatures, archaea, are gathering salt like bees, growing

little pyramids. We call them archaean domes because they have methane—they recreate the atmosphere of the archaean world, before oxygen took over.

Even then, they're rare, because this world is not for archaea. They have to hide.

• **What about the unique bacteria found here?**

The ocean turned blue at the end of the Precambrian. A big part of that was bacteria now unique to Cuatro Ciénegas—the ones that breathe oxygen. So we have the original architect that made the blue planet. Nobody else has that.

Most of the bacteria aren't so interesting to see. They don't have many shapes—they are not pretty, like starfish or even atoms. I study them because they are fascinating—they have built it all, and they are so tiny. That story of how we become is amazing, and it is in Cuatro Ciénegas.

• **How has working with this one environment for so many years influenced how you look at the world?**

We are working on a hypothesis where the unit of [evolutionary] selection is the community. The twentieth century was dominated by the idea of survival of the fittest—the one who can step on the others better wins. It was an interpretation of Darwin in the Victorian colonial times, and we do science in a social context—you cannot take yourself out of that social context.

But I think today, more than ever, we need to cooperate and shift from that [survival of the fittest] idea. Here these communities are surviving because they cooperate. Everybody matters, even tiny archaea. It wasn't competition, it was coexistence that made life so diverse. ■

Boojum Trees

These otherworldly monsters of Mexico's succulent forests have resisted human description.

RANGE: The middle third of the Baja Peninsula and the Gulf Coast of Sonora
SPECIES: Boojum tree (*Fouquieria columnaris*), also known as cirio or cototaj

◆ As the story goes, in 1922, American botanist Godfrey Sykes paused in the middle of Mexico's Sonoran Desert, pulled out his telescope, and trained it on the nearby hills. Strange, dancer-like shapes could be seen there, many of them dozens of feet tall, with spike-covered tendrils reaching every which way. Peering through the scope at one specimen, Sykes made his diagnosis aloud. "A boojum," he said. "Definitely a boojum."

The name—a joking reference to a Lewis Carroll poem, where it is used to describe a mysterious beast who can make people disappear—fit well enough to stick.

Except for a small population on Mexico's mainland, boojum trees live only in a roughly 350-mile-long (560 km) swath of central Baja, including the Valle de los Cirios conservation area. Inside this restricted range, these trees grow by the millions alongside stands of towering cardon cacti and as many as 20 other succulents, forming dreamlike forests.

Boojum grow only a handful of inches annually but can persist in rocky soils for hundreds of years. Some have lived long enough to reach nearly six stories tall. They display surreal storybook shapes; some have many sinuous branches that seem poised to pluck up passersby into the air, while others have wild looping arms reminiscent of a portal into a "wizard's garden," as the naturalist Joseph Wood Krutch wrote. They shed the tiny leaves that bristle along their arms in the dry season, and they sprout new leaves only when it rains, a strategy known as drought deciduousness.

Sykes was not the first person moved to poetry by an encounter with these unique trees. Oral histories of the Indigenous Seri people, who call them cototaj, hold that touching or harming the trees can cause strong winds or rain. Their Spanish name, cirio ("candle"), comes from their appearance in the summer, when their spindly trunks, topped with shocks of flame-colored flowers, resemble cartoonish wax candles.

Others have been left a bit tongue-tied. Various observers have called the plant "grotesque," the "strangest of the strange," and "certainly one of the most weird-looking plants in North America, if not on Earth."

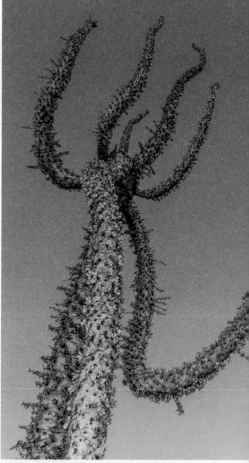

A boojum reaches for the moon in Baja California.

For a number of nonhuman species, these trees are simply home. In foggy areas, they host lichens and air plants. Raptors favor their branching crowns for nests, and Gila woodpeckers find their spongy trunks convenient for drilling out nest cavities.

If you want to try your own luck at describing the boojum, a trip to the Valle de los Cirios will give you plenty of inspiration. And if you'd like to add one of these not-so-mythical monsters to your own dwelling, start saving up: Mature boojums raised in commercial nurseries can fetch roughly $1,000 per foot. ❯ **How to see them:** Wild boojum trees lord over the Valle de los Cirios conservation area in central Baja, Mexico. The San Diego Zoo also has a collection of boojums and occasionally sells garden-raised seedlings to the public.

SOUTH AMERICA

Pink Fairy Armadillos

Whimsically colored cuties you will probably never see

RANGE: Central Argentina
SPECIES: Pink fairy armadillo
(*Chlamyphorus truncatus*)

◆ Looking at a pink fairy armadillo—his bubble-gum armor, his fuzzy white undercoat, his tiny and quizzical face—you're probably thinking, "I want to know everything about that guy."

Alas, you are about to be disappointed. The world's smallest armadillo—they average about the length of a Hershey's bar—is also our most elusive.

Pink fairy armadillos spend almost all their time beneath the dunes of the central Argentinean desert, digging with their hefty, coral-colored claws, and keeping the sand at bay with their soft yet flexible shells. They leave their burrows only at night to dine on nearby ants and shrubbery. In such a way, they have made themselves almost impossible to study in the wild. Most encounters with them happen by accident.

These armadillos don't live long in captivity or adapt well to environments outside the desert. One who was rescued from a parking lot and kept under careful watch managed to survive in an enclosure for eight months, eating bugs, milk, and ground cat food, and provided with plenty of sand to hide in. Even then, "any slight modification to its environment or diet triggered a stress response," which manifested as the armadillo running around the enclosure while screaming, observers wrote. (Despite this, the black-market pet trade is a threat to the species' survival, as are pesticides and free-roaming dogs and cats.)

We do know what's the cause of their iconic pink look. The blush of the shell, nose, and feet is the result of blood vessels close to the surface, which release excess heat during the day, lowering the armadillos' body temperature. As the desert climate downshifts into extreme cold in the evening, their fluffy underbelly keeps them warm.

Most of the pink fairy armadillos' habits remain a mystery. But this is part of the creatures' charm. In an age when most of the world's information can be accessed by a few keystrokes, it's good to remember that some things remain unknown. ❯ **How to see them: They don't really want to be seen—but if you must, keep your eyes peeled for an eraser-colored bump on the Argentinean desert floor.**

Llaretas

Lumpy, long-lived furniture of the desert

RANGE: Peru, Bolivia, northern Chile, and western Argentina
SPECIES: Llareta (*Azorella compacta*), also known as yareta or yarita

◆ Imagine: A high-altitude hike in the Atacama. The air is thin and the sun close and bright. Just as you think you can't take another step, you happen upon a love seat–sized green blob. It looks velvety and nappable, as though it's been beamed into the desert from an extraterrestrial IKEA.

Don't be fooled. This is a llareta, one of the high desert's most stoic plants. If you were to sit, lie, or even jump on it—which you certainly should not—you would find it surprisingly rock-solid, withstanding your weight as surely as it does heat, cold, drought, wind, and time itself.

Llaretas are by far the largest of the plants that grow above the tree line in the Atacama. They look out of place up there; even guidebooks sometime mistake them for moss-covered boulders, says Cath Kleier, a botanist who studies the plants.

But what seems like a soft, strokable surface is actually thousands of tiny, tightly packed leaves. The bulky substrate they appear to be growing on is part of the plant—branches that have grown out from a central axis and squished together over time, compressing into a sturdy core.

Overall, the texture is not plush but "carroty," says Kleier. "You need a saw to actually get into the center of the plant."

The llareta is related to the carrot, as well as to celery, fennel, and dill. While it shares with these plants certain life strategies—like a long taproot, a pithy center, and herbaceous leaves—it has used them to become not tasty, but nearly indestructible.

The plant's lumpy shape limits wind resistance, important in environments where airflow can steal scarce water away from plant tissue. The leafy rosettes that lie flat on the surface can soak up lots of sun without risking wind damage. As for the taproots, no one is sure how long and deep they might get. Kleier once followed the root of a backpack-sized llareta for 30 feet (9 m) before giving up.

While people sometimes use the llareta's resin-filled tissue as fuel—it was heavily harvested during railroad construction in the desert in the early 1900s—the plant appears to have no nonhuman predators. Flies pollinate its flowers, and long-eared viscachas will build nests in its shade, but Kleier has never seen any animals give a llareta so much as a nibble.

This may help explain the plant's most mysterious attribute: its extreme longevity. While it's hard to precisely age a llareta, some smaller ones have been clocked at 200 to 300 years old. The largest plants, which can be the size of a car, may be much, much older—the strangest antiques in the desert showroom. **> How to see them: Llaretas crop up all over high-altitude areas of the Atacama Desert and are pretty much unmissable. The tourist town of San Pedro de Atacama, Chile, is a good place to start.**

Llaretas can live for hundreds of years, untouched by herbivores like these vicuñas.

ATACAMA DESERT

- Chile's Atacama Desert is the driest place on Earth, outside the polar deserts. The central region of the Atacama saw zero rain for four centuries, from 1570 through the 1970s.

- This extreme dryness makes it difficult for life to survive. NASA uses the desert as a stand-in for Mars and the moon during astronaut training.

- The soil—which is almost always dry and often salty—is home to very few plants but many well-calibrated microbes. When it does rain, these communities are devastated, experiencing up to 85 percent mortality.

KEEP AN EYE OUT FOR The rest of the universe. The Atacama's low humidity allows it to offer one of Earth's most glorious views of the stars.

KEEP AN EAR OUT FOR The thump-thump of the desert's crusty surface cracking as the temperature shifts from hot to cold and back.

KEEP A NOSE OUT FOR The plants; though few, they often have unique scents. Rica rica, a large green bush, smells like weak mint.

Desierto Florido

Every five to seven years, the Atacama shows its true colors.

LOCATION: Southwestern areas of the Atacama Desert, in Chile
SPECIES: Pata de guanaco (*Cistanthe grandiflora*), garra de león (*Bomarea ovallei*), añañuca (*Rhodophiala rhodolirion*), and many more

◆ Most of the time, Chile's Atacama Desert is gritty, cracked, and red. The desert gets less than 0.6 inch (1.5 cm) of rain per year, the equivalent of six or so hours of light drizzle. Sometimes it doesn't get any at all. Generally, the only plants living here have lucked out with real estate, growing near one of the rare streams or groundwater reserves or along the fog-ribboned coast.

Other years, though, are just a little bit damper, juiced by El Niño, a weather pattern that increases rain in the Americas. With a few drops more water, trillions of seeds sleeping just under the sand begin to stir. They send up shoots, which grow leaves and buds. Eventually, whole swaths of the desert let loose, unfolding in yellow, pink, orange and purple, the colors sweeping across the desert like watercolors, and the petals more numerous than the stars above.

Chileans call this phenomenon desierto florido, or "blooming desert." The "unusual and explosive" onrush of vegetation, as scientist Andres Moreira-Muñoz and his colleagues have described it, begets a whole accelerated ecosystem, with insects and small rodents rushing to take advantage of the sudden and colorful feast. Botanists, ecologists, and camera-toting tourists aren't far behind.

In 2019, Moreira-Muñoz and his team reviewed satellite imagery of the region to make a timeline of blooms in the Atacama and get a sense of their extension, duration, and intensity. They counted 13 desiertos floridos between 1981 and 2015, with an average duration of nearly six months. The largest, in 2011, stretched 4,300 square miles (11,000 sq km)—roughly the size of Hawai'i's Big Island.

They also found that sites are shifting to where they haven't been before, likely due to regional changes in climate. Climate change overall looms as a threat to wildflowers across the world, with other stressors like development, agriculture, land clearing, invasive species, and mining also contributing to habitat loss.

For this reason, many groups "have wanted to declare a 'blooming desert' protected area" in the Atacama, says Moreira-Muñoz, "but it's like trying to put a fence around a phantom." At the end of a desierto florido, the flower seeds drop back into the underground bank and return to their slumber, until the next marginally muggy year draws them back out. ❯ **How to see them:** The Atacama's desierto florido tends to occur between September and November in years when rainfall has been (relatively) high. One popular vantage point is near the small city of Copiapó in northern Chile.

Damp years bring trillions of flowers to the Atacama.

Superbloom Road Trips

The Atacama isn't the only desert that occasionally dresses up. Desert superblooms happen across the globe whenever flowering plants accumulate enough water to show off. Some places offer well-placed routes that let you wind your way among these fanciful landscapes, like a thread through a Technicolor dreamcoat. (Just stay on the path and be respectful as you walk, bike, or drive—no selfie is worth destroying a plant's rare chance at reproduction.)

CALIFORNIA'S POPPY PARK • In superbloom years in Southern California, explosions of California poppies (*Eschscholzia californica*) turn hillsides into rippling seas of orange. The diverting Day-Glo flowers cause traffic jams, road closures, and even landscape destruction as visitors trample plants while vying for a closer look.

At Antelope Valley California Poppy Reserve in Lancaster, the poppies—California's official state flower—are officially protected from this type of overzealousness. Eight miles (13 km) of trails allow careful visitors to wander among the blooms, which are as bright as traffic cones. ❶

NAMAQUALAND'S FLOWER ROUTE • In South Africa, a vibrant flower season takes place in the region of Namaqualand, located on the western side of the Northern Cape province and extending into the southern tail of Namibia. This special ecosystem, known as the Succulent Karoo, hosts more than 6,000 species of flora, including the famous Namaqualand daisies (*Dimorphotheca sinuata*) that blanket the area in a tapestry of tangerine.

Many tourists take the N7 highway, also known as the Namaqualand Flower Route, to see the flowery show. As the road ascends over the region, it passes by bloom sites, towns, and parks like Namaqua National Park and Goegap Nature Reserve. Petal-peepers might also spot animals like oryx, springboks, and caracals living in the kaleidoscope. ❷

WESTERN AUSTRALIA'S EVERLASTINGS TRAIL • Western Australia is hatched with wildflower routes that cross over what some naturalists say are the most extensive bloom fields in the world. The state's tourism board lists 13 multiday drives where flowers can be seen from June to November across the region's "Golden Outback."

One of the most popular, the Everlastings Wildflower Trail, is a loop route north of Perth. This trail cuts through a carpet of multicolored blooms, its cheerful tone set by white and pink everlastings (*Rhodanthe chlorocephala*). ❸

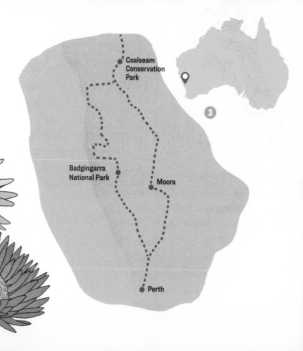

Coalseam Conservation Park

Badgingarra National Park

Moora

Perth

Magellanic Penguins

Penguins where you least expect them

RANGE: Pacific and Atlantic coasts of Argentina and Chile, and the Falkland Islands
SPECIES: Magellanic penguin (*Spheniscus magellanicus*)

◆ If, while making your way through a desert, you saw a penguin pop out of a hole in the ground, you would be forgiven for suspecting you had suffered a thirst-induced hallucination.

But the Magellanic penguins of the Patagonian Desert are no monochromatic mirage. These birds spend about half of each year perfectly at home in this sandy expanse along the coast of Argentina, which is shaded from rain by the Andes Mountains. The dry habitat makes life safer for newly hatched penguin chicks, who can die of hypothermia if they get rained on before their waterproof feathers come in.

Male Magellanic penguins leave their more northerly feeding grounds for the desert in September, often returning to the same place where they were born. There, each scopes out a home for his prospective mate, which can be a hole in the ground or a nest in the bushes. They dig their own holes or reuse ones from prior years, pushing out any current occupant if they can.

When the females arrive shortly afterward, males compete for their attention by sprucing up their nests, braying, and nibbling and patting at their romantic prospects. After mating, female penguins will usually lay two eggs, four days apart. The pair take turns incubating the eggs, caring for the hatched chicks, and braving predators like sea lions to gather sardines, krill, and other marine morsels from the ocean.

Because most of their time is spent at sea, the penguins' bodies are optimized with thick, oily feathers that keep them warm in the water. To deal with the desert, they lose face feathers to help their bodies cool down. They will also "lie prone on the ground with their flippers and feet extended, which helps them regulate their temperature," says Eric Wagner, a writer and researcher with the Center for Ecosystem Sentinels at the University of Washington.

Punta Tombo, a nature reserve in Argentina, used to be the seasonal home of more than a million Magellanics. While pollution, oil spills, fishing net entanglements, worsening storms (due to climate change), and other penguin perils have reduced those numbers by half, the colony remains the largest penguin assemblage in the world outside of Antarctica.

Researchers live in the area for much of the year, keeping tabs on the birds. "Human cares kind of melt away and you start living on penguin time—up early, out all day, back late," Wagner says. "You feel a little like a monk among the penguins."

Besides their predilection for the desert, Magellanic penguins are distinguished by black collars around their necks and a braying call that has led some fans, including Charles Darwin, to call them "jackass penguins." If another animal bothers them or their chicks, they'll shake their heads in apparent exasperation—as if to say, "I'm a penguin who summers in the desert. Why would you mess with me?" ❭ **How to see them:** The Punta Tombo nature reserve, in Argentina, is home to one of the biggest colonies and is open to tourists.

AFRICA

Golden Moles

These tiny, blind fluff balls swim through sand and shimmer with mysterious iridescence.

RANGE: Select areas in Namibia and South Africa
SPECIES: Grant's golden mole (*Eremitalpa granti*)

◆ Who has paddles for feet, uses his head as an amplifier, lives underground, and shines?

It sounds like the setup for a riddle you'd give up on. But it's all biological reality for the Grant's golden mole, an iridescent insectivore that "swims" through the sand of the Namib desert with oar-like limbs, locates food by detecting vibrations among the grains, and gleams in the sun for seemingly no reason at all.

Grant's golden moles—one of 21 known golden mole species—are only about 3½ inches (9 cm) long, the size of a large fingerling potato. Rather than taking up a permanent home, they pass the day wherever they happen to be, buried roughly a foot beneath the sand's surface and enjoying the stable thermal environment there.

When night falls, the moles get busy. They have no optic nerves, and their vestigial eyes are covered in a thin film of skin. To hunt, they instead rely on an extremely sensitive middle ear bone—the largest relative to body size of any mammal.

Plunging their heads into the sandy expanse, they feel for delicate vibrations that indicate nearby meals, like termites or the occasional skink. When they catch a signal, they use all four feet to push themselves toward it, scooting along beneath the ground as the sand collapses behind them.

It's when the moles come up to the surface that their strangest trait reveals itself. Of all mammals, only golden moles—and their unrelated but, thanks to evolutionary convergence, uncannily similar Australian doppelgängers known as kakarratul or marsupial moles—have fur that appears iridescent.

The fine hairs on a golden mole's body are arranged in layers, alternating between light and dark pigments. These act as reflectors that create color through thin-film interference, the same phenomenon that puts rainbows in soap bubbles.

Grant's golden moles hunt with their ears, snagging prey like this locust.

The animal's paddle-like shape offers a flat reflective area for light to bounce off, and the compressed cuticles of the hair keep this surface smooth. The result is a gleaming, pocket-sized mole that reflects the desert sun into twinkling greens, blues, and violets. Its shimmer resembles that of "the dark feathers on a magpie," says Robert Asher, curator of vertebrates at the University of Cambridge Museum of Zoology.

The golden mole's gleam is a bit of an evolutionary riddle. The world's many iridescent bugs and birds generally use their flashy colors to attract mates. But because golden moles are blind, they probably don't care whether their partners are glowed up. Instead, researchers speculate, their glittering coats may be an accidental consequence of the arrangement of their fur, which is optimized for a life of incessant burrowing.

This mole family remains a mystery, and the task of studying them isn't helped by the fact that they're so difficult to observe in the wild. Ten of our known golden mole species are under threat, meaning there's little time left to locate these elusive creatures—let alone understand exactly why they shine. ❯ **How to see them:** Grant's golden moles are quite difficult to observe in the wild and are generally not kept in zoos. But a couple of their relatives, including the Cape golden mole, occasionally show up in South African suburban gardens.

NAMIB DESERT

- The Namib, whose name means "vast place" in the Khoekhoe language, runs from South Africa along the whole coast of Namibia and into Angola.

- The 62,000-square-mile (160,000 sq km) desert contains a patchwork of terrains, from sunset-colored sand dunes to the gray, rocky Moon Valley to the wave-carved Skeleton Coast.

- Considered to be the world's oldest desert, it may have been dry since the Cretaceous period 80 million years ago.

KEEP AN EYE OUT FOR The spectacular fog that shrouds the Namib for about 80 days out of the year. It's created when a cold wind blows in from the Atlantic and meets the warm air over the dunes.

KEEP A NOSE OUT FOR *Boscia foetida*, also known as the smelly shepherd's bush, which has hairy berries and a sewage-like smell.

KEEP AN EAR OUT FOR The very occasional rainstorm, which, as the drops hit the ground, may bring to mind melodic percussion.

Fairy Circles

The desert's strangest geometry problem

◆ The Namib desert is covered in mysterious circles. Fly low over certain parts of the landscape and you'll see them sprinkled across the ground like ecosystem chicken pox. At the edges of the rings, grass grows extra tufty, as if to delineate a boundary. Inside the rings, nothing grows at all.

As you head north, the circles' diameters get wider—they go from 5 feet (1.5 m) across in northern South Africa to 130 feet (40 m) in southern Angola. Individual circles also expand and contract. Oh, and the soil within them tends to be slightly more magnetic than the soil outside.

Overall, they seem to be trying to tell us something. But what?

For decades, scientists have argued over this question. Some have blamed radiation, large termites, or the toxic residue of a specific bush. Most of these possibilities have been debunked.

Many now think the rings inscribe competitive sagas: scrappy plays for survival that happen to leave orderly footprints. As desert plants scrounge for water, this theory goes, they end up clumped together, with their collective shade encouraging growth in certain spots, while their collective roots slurp nearby patches dry. Eventually, a neat, loopy grid emerges.

Still others think the rings are engineered by savvy insects. In this hypothesis, the tiny sand termites are making the circles by chewing away plant roots, forming bare spots where water can sink more deeply into the soil. This leaves the termites with an underground reservoir for dry times, one that living grasses can tap into when they need to.

RANGE: Throughout a band spanning the length of the Namib desert about 100 miles (160 km) inland, and in the Pilbara region of Western Australia

SPECIES: Most rings occur in *Stipagrostis* grasses. Although the culprit remains unclear, chief suspects over the years have included melkbos or milkbush (*Euphorbia damarana*) and two species of termite (the larger *Hodotermes mossambicus* and the smaller *Psammotermes allocerus*).

Fairy circles in Namib-Naukluft National Park, Namibia

Increasingly, researchers believe that a combination of these factors may be at play. (It could also, of course, be fairies.) ❯ **How to see them:** Fairy circles tend to be in remote parts of the Namib desert. But if you do get out there, they're difficult to miss—just look for, well, the fairy circles. Several tour companies, including Namibia Eco Tours, lead trips to see them.

Desert Elephants

Wandering hot and hostile terrain in search of an oasis

◆ The life of desert elephants is first and foremost a search for water. These are the marathoners of the elephant world, carried by long legs and supported by pancake-like feet, big even by elephant standards, that spread their weight on the soft sand. In Mali, they tour a 12,000-square-mile (31,000 sq km) circuit—the longest elephant migration we know of—in search of this precious resource, guided by the sounds of distant rainstorms and the memories of senior herd members. In Namibia, they

RANGE: There are two distinct ranges: a 12,000-square-mile (31,000 sq km) semiarid region in central Mali and a 44,000-square-mile (114,000 sq km) region of desert, mountains, and gravel plains in northwestern Namibia.

SPECIES: African bush elephant (*Loxodonta africana*)

follow water over generations and in the past few decades have moved in and out of different mountain ranges and valleys.

When the elephants finally do reach a watering hole, you'd expect them to rush in, splashing and trumpeting in joy. But that's not the case. Instead, they dig wells into the sand with their trunks and feet.

This preference is a matter of safety. Wildlife researchers have determined that Namibian desert elephants avoid surface water because it has higher levels of bacterial contamination. By digging their own wells, the elephants can access the water while avoiding the bacteria. If you're going to binge-drink more than 40 gallons (151 L) of water, best to make sure it won't make you sick.

When water isn't available, the elephants have other tricks for keeping cool: They store water in a pouch hidden under their tongues, and they'll suck up gallons of it to squirt over their backs. Sometimes they'll even pee on the ground, then slather themselves in the mixture of urine and sand. Not the most appealing method, perhaps, but it beats the heat. 〉 **How to see them: The area near the village of Boni, Mali, is an elephant hot spot during the rainy season.**

A herd of elephants marches into the desert in Damaraland, Namibia.

Fog-Harvesting Beetles

These bugs wring water from the very air using engineering and acrobatics.

RANGE: The Namib desert, especially the Skeleton Coast
SPECIES: Tenebrionid beetles, including the head-stander beetle (*Onymacris unguicularis*) and the trench-digging beetle (*Lepidochora discoidalis*)

◆ Some deserts have rivers, oases, or reliable rainstorms. The Namib has fog. In some areas, about a quarter of the days of the year feature thick ribbons of mist winding over the dunes—water, water everywhere, and not a drop to drink.

In response, many animals and plants of the Namib have developed fog-drinking hacks. Spiders trap condensation in their webs, then scurry around gathering the droplets. Adders and chameleons drink the water that collects on their own bodies, and jackals and steenbok antelopes have both been seen licking fog-soaked plants.

But only a few enterprising beetles have figured out how to sip from the air. The most acrobatic of the Namib's vapor drinkers, head-stander beetles—a very small subset of the tenebrionid beetle group—live near the Skeleton Coast, where the fog typically descends around midnight. Though normally diurnal, they drag themselves out of their sand beds on foggy nights and scrabble to the tops of dunes. There, they lift themselves into headstands, their butts pointing away from the wind.

If the wind is too strong or the fog too weak, the beetles abandon their posts. But if it's just right, they'll stay there in their upside-down pose for as long as it takes—they are "obsessive about their fog basking," as one group of researchers put it. As the fog rolls over, droplets slowly condense on their shells. When the droplets get big enough, they run down special grooves into the beetles' mouths, quenching their thirst and making it all worth it.

Other beetles eschew gymnastics in favor of engineering. Several members of the genus *Lepidochora* prepare for foggy nights by carefully excavating long trenches. The ridges that line these trenches trap the water vapor, concentrating it into a more easily accessible form. On a particularly active evening, a whole dune might be covered with digging beetles, trundling across the surface like bite-sized bulldozers. In both cases, it's unclear how the beetles know the right weather is coming, as they spend most of their time deep underground.

Onymacris unguicularis beetles atop a dune. Members of this species gather fog by standing on their heads.

Human engineers and product designers have sought to copy these efficient insects, designing everything from water-harvesting bottles to hydrophobic surfaces after their bumpy carapaces. (Researchers argue about the efficacy of these attempts, some of which appear to have been based on the wrong species of beetle.) In any case, it will be a while before we can drink from the air via our butts, let alone while standing on our heads. Compared with the Namib's experts, we haven't the foggiest. ❯ **How to see them:** Head out to the dunes on a foggy night. Bring a flashlight.

Welwitschia

Get shredded with one of the world's longest-lived plants.

RANGE: **The Namib desert of northern Namibia and southern Angola**
SPECIES: **Welwitschia (*Welwitschia mirabilis*)**

◆ Experts agree: Welwitschia is not terribly hard to grow. Put one of its pine nut–like seeds in a pot and water it regularly.

Or not. It doesn't really care. Its two leathery leaves will keep stretching out for years—until they are longer than crocodiles, until you're old and gray and your children's children are, too, and on after that, perhaps until modern civilization has collapsed or transformed beyond recognition. In its native habitat, the Namib desert, many welwitschia plants have lived for more than five centuries, and some likely as long as 3,000 years.

Welwitschia is a dwarf tree that rarely rises above waist height. The plant has a thick woody stem from which its pink-tinged green leaves grow "like a conveyor belt," as one team of scientists put it. These leaves store moisture and can serve as a source of water during times of drought for desert animals like rhinos, springbok, and oryx. The plants also provide oases for birds, beetles, and fungi, and the Herero and Damara people harvest and eat the seed cones.

Over a welwitschia's considerable lifetime, the leaves could theoretically grow hundreds of

Welwitschia has changed very little since the time of dinosaurs.

meters long. In reality, they usually shrivel and shred into curled ribbons, leading many to compare the plant to a giant dehydrated octopus. Upon seeing a specimen for the first time, the director of London's Kew Gardens remarked that it was "out of the question the most wonderful plant ever brought to this country and one of the ugliest." Public greenhouses occasionally have to label their specimens with signs that say "I'm not dead."

Charmed despite its looks, scientists continue trying to unravel the plant's secrets, including basic questions like how it survives in the often-parched Namib. Researchers have proposed that welwitschia uses a long taproot to access groundwater, or that it subsists on sips of coastal fog. Efforts to relocate plants because of a recent mine expansion revealed that they can also develop wide networks of surface roots. "My best guess is that the plants are capable of doing it all," says Kathryn Jacobson, a biologist and welwitschia expert at Grinnell College.

Today, populations remain healthy across the plant's modern range in northern Namibia and southern Angola. In Namibia especially, welwitschias draw tourists eager to see a living fossil that has changed little since it first evolved more than 100 million years ago, when it shared the Earth with dinosaurs. To some devotees, this history gives the plant's longevity a whole new meaning. "That's what really grabs me," Jacobson says. "It's so humbling when I'm around it." ❭ **How to see them: Take a self-guided driving tour through the Welwitschia Plains near Swakopmund, Namibia.**

Halfmens

These iconic succulents always face north.

◆ It's easy to feel alone in the desert. That is, unless there's a halfmens in sight. These 6-foot-tall (2 m), mop-topped plants lend an anthropomorphic bounce to the landscape, a trait that has inspired names and stories. From a distance, especially, they resemble people frozen in action, leaning their leafy "heads" a little toward the north.

Like the boojum trees of the Baja Peninsula and the saguaros of the Sonoran Desert, these upstanding succulents are icons of their ecosystem—in this case, South Africa's Richtersveld, a mountainous desert in the northwest of the country. They tend to grow on barren, exposed slopes, unconcerned with the extreme wind, dryness, or summer heat, which can reach 118°F (48°C).

Halfmens trees are iconic in the Richtersveld.

The Afrikaans word *halfmens* means "half-human" or "human-like." (The plant's other common name, elephant's trunk tree, is similarly evocative but less social.) Their growing season is brief, occurring only during the winter months, when there is a greater chance of rain.

By curving north toward the sun, the halfmens ensure that their short-lived leaves and developing flowers get as much of the winter light as possible. The sunshine also makes their flowers more visible to pollinators, increasing their chance of producing seeds. When spring comes, halfmens drop their leaves to prevent scorching.

Another, more melancholy explanation for why the halfmens face north is found in the stories of the Nama people, nomadic herders who live in and help manage the Richtersveld. According to their oral histories, they once lived in more verdant parts of Namibia, to the north, but were driven out by conflicts with other groups. Upon crossing into this new and difficult desert, some paused to look back. The pitying gods transformed them into halfmens—looking north to their old homeland, rooted in their new one. ❯ **How to see them:** Well-known populations are found in |Ai-|Ais/Richtersveld Transfrontier Park, as well as the greater Richtersveld area on the Atlantic Coast in South Africa.

RANGE: The arid northwestern mountains of South Africa and the southern mountains of Namibia
SPECIES: Halfmens or elephant's trunk tree (*Pachypodium namaquanum*)

Succulents

You've probably run into some succulents. Smaller and more sculptural than your typical potted plant, these lumpy trendsetters have lately charmed their way into boardrooms, bathrooms, and magazine spreads, winning us over with their low-maintenance lifestyles and diversity of shapes and hues. Maybe you're sharing space with a few right now.

They look great in pots,but they're built for a wilder life. Succulents—which, rather than making up their own group, hail from almost every branch of the plant kingdom—are perfectly suited for dry environments like deserts. An example of convergent evolution, they have developed a suite of traits that help them survive the harsh conditions found there.

Each succulent plant has at least one body part that's plump and juicy, perfect for storing excess water. The leaves of *Aloe vera*, for example, are full of thick sap, something you'll know if you've ever snapped one in half. Many cactus species famously store their water in fattened stems—but plants from other families are also stem succulents and often look quite similar, needles and all. Other cactuses, like the bottom-heavy *Pterocactus tuberosus*, keep their water reserves in their roots.

In addition to their built-in water tanks, many succulent plants have evolved a water-saving form of photosynthesis, called Crassulacean acid metabolism, that allows them to photosynthesize during the day but do most of their "breathing" (gas exchange) in the cool dark of night, when the air is less dehydrating.

If you haven't seen these plants in their natural habitat, it can be difficult to appreciate their innovations. Your best bet is the Succulent Karoo, a low-rainfall semi-desert in South Africa. The landscape here is covered in a rainbow of succulents, many of them found nowhere else on Earth.

Some are tiny, like pebble-sized "living stones" (*Lithops* spp.). Each of these succulents has just two leaves that swell to the point of being nearly spherical—an adaptation that reduces their surface area and therefore their water loss.

Some are enormous. Quiver trees or kokerbooms (*Aloidendron* spp.), distant cousins of the familiar aloe plant, store water in their fleshy trunks and can grow nearly 30 feet (9 m) tall.

Others are just plain weird. Ice plants (*Mesembryanthemum* spp.) are covered in millions of translucent, water-containing "bladder cells," which make them look as though the morning dew formed upon them and froze in place.

All are beautiful. And when you're in their world, it's hard to imagine any of them in pots.

Lithops, *or living stones, swell up when filled with water.*

Hornbill-Mongoose Alliances

Some of the world's most extraordinary mutually supportive interspecies relationships

RANGE: Central and eastern Tanzania, Kenya, and most of Ethiopia

SPECIES: Von der Decken's hornbill (*Tockus deckeni*), eastern yellow-billed hornbill (*Tockus flavirostris*), and dwarf mongoose (*Helogale parvula*)

◆ The dwarf mongoose is Africa's smallest carnivore. Weighing in at just over 11 ounces (326 g)—less than a can of soup—these weasel-like fuzz balls have their work cut out for them: They must snap up termites, beetles, and other treats while avoiding becoming wriggly snacks themselves.

Luckily, they've got friends in high places. Local birds forage alongside the mongooses while helping to warn them about overhead predators. Their very best buds are two species of hornbill: the Von der Decken's and the eastern yellow-billed.

These hornbills and mongooses have a lot in common—especially considering how far apart their perches are on the tree of life. They like the same foods and have many of the same enemies, mostly large raptors. They all spend much of the day foraging in and around massive termite mounds that loom large across the desert landscape—mongooses with their dexterous paws, and hornbills with their precisely curved bills.

Neither wants to start without the other. In the mornings, hornbills will sometimes sound a wake-up call for mongooses, urging their sleepy mammalian sidekicks to emerge by yelling *wok wok wok* into their burrows' ventilation shafts. If the mongooses are up first, they'll patiently sunbathe—one of their favorite activities—until their hornbill pals swoop in. When everyone is ready, they move in tandem through the surrounding grass, the mongooses sniffing out and snatching up insects and the hornbills pecking at the leftovers they flush out.

They've got personal protection locked down, too. Mongooses send guards to stand sentinel while everyone else hunts. If a guard spots a hungry raptor, he'll cry out, sending everyone scampering or flying for cover.

Meanwhile, both types of hornbills cluck loudly to signal approaching danger—even when the approaching predator eats only mongooses, and not hornbills. This takes the pressure off the mongooses, who have fewer guards on duty when the birds are around.

Relationships of this type, where individuals from different species help each other out, are known as mutualisms. This particular fur-feather alliance starts early in life: Baby hornbills and young mongooses both accompany their parents on foraging trips. Guides in South Africa once filmed a mongoose pup flopping on his back in front of a hornbill, as though trying to goad his winged friend into a wrestling match. Who knows what they do when we're not watching? ❭ **How to see them:** These hornbill and mongoose species overlap most frequently in the Nyiri Desert, north of Mount Kilimanjaro in southern Kenya.

Date Palm Oases

Carefully engineered desert respites

RANGE: Throughout the Middle East and North Africa
SPECIES: Date palm (*Phoenix dactylifera*)

◆ Oases, those improbable, lushly vegetated rest spots amid seemingly endless sand dunes, come in many forms across continents. No kind is more closely associated with human settlement than the date palm oases amid the deserts of the Middle East and North Africa.

Traditional date palm oases reflect at least 7,000 years of human engineering and horticulture. So long have people propagated this stout, handsome palm that its wild origin isn't clear, though many believe its ancestral region to be somewhere in ancient Mesopotamia, where date palm groves are described in millennia-old cuneiform texts. (Rules regarding their cultivation even appear in Hammurabi's Code c. 1780 BCE.) By 400 BCE, date culture had already spread widely across Arabia and North Africa, including to the Nile Valley and deep into the Sahara.

The lush stands of trees typically owe their existence to groundwater, which despite appearances can be significant in deserts. Though some oases are fed directly by springs, humans irrigated many via wells, dams, underground tunnels, and other aquifer- and drainage-tapping constructions.

Date palms are the perfect plants to provide respite from the harsh desert climes. They grow up to 75 feet (23 m) tall and provide shade, fruit, and windbreaks. Bacteria associated with date palm roots boost plant growth and promote drought resistance. Through the fruits, fronds, fibers, oil, and other products the trees provide, and the associated crops and animals raised in their shade, these oases have long allowed for larger human populations in hyperarid zones.

Oases and their settlements fueled the great trading caravans that once crossed these sandy expanses and became coveted prizes for those seeking geopolitical power. Resilient as they've been, Saharan oases are also under threat from salinization, desertification, urbanization, pathogens, and simple neglect. ❯ **How to see them:** If you've seen enough desert films, you know what to expect—right when you think you're about to keel over, one will appear in the distance (hopefully).

Date palms growing in Garmeh, Iran

Desert Lakes

If water is life, then water in a desert is the center of a small universe. Around the world, desert lakes host fascinating and diverse ecosystems and bring relief to travelers crossing these unforgiving environments.

Lake Turkana

LAKE TURKANA
TURKANA, KENYA

Lake Turkana, which straddles southern Ethiopia and northwestern Kenya, sits in the Great Lakes region of the Rift Valley. The world's largest permanent desert lake and the largest alkaline lake in the world, its impressive size and striking green color have earned it the nickname "The Jade Sea."

The lake and surrounding areas have landed themselves yet another nickname: "The Cradle of Mankind." The oldest recorded hominoid remains, including the incredibly complete *Homo ergaster* skeleton known as Turkana Boy and the famous *Australopithecus afarensis* known as Lucy, were found to the east of this very lake. So were the oldest known stone tools— knives, hammers, and anvils dated to more than 3 million years ago.

Scattered whale and stingray skeletons suggest that millions of years ago, the land was linked up to the Indian Ocean, now more than 600 miles (965 km) to the east. One of Turkana's islands is home to Nile crocodiles, evidence that the lake also spent some time as part of the Nile River basin. Another island provides a resting spot for thousands of migrating flamingos. And the most frequently visited island, Central Island, is a dormant volcano with three crater lakes— lakes within lakes within a desert.

Dune Lakes

DUNE LAKES
BADAIN JARAN DESERT, CHINA

Some of the world's highest stationary sand dunes form part of the Badain Jaran Desert in northwest China. At nearly 1,500 feet (457 m), the tallest dune outstrips the Empire State Building.

Dozens of shimmering lakes dot this undulant landscape, like mercury from a broken thermometer.

The lakes, found mainly at the southern end of the desert, are believed to glean their water from groundwater and mountain runoff, though they have not been extensively studied. Some are fed by freshwater springs; Yinderitu Lake, for example, contains more than 100 bubbling springs—yet the lake itself is saline, as are roughly half of the other dune lakes here. A few intrepid travelers make the trip to Yinderitu to drink its sweet spring water every year.

LAKES OF OUNIANGA
OUNIANGA, CHAD

Perched at the center of the Sahara Desert, northern Chad's Ounianga lakes are the perfect desert oasis, offering up mirage-worthy shrubbery, palm trees, and fresh water—all in a region that receives less than 0.1 inch (.25 cm) of rain per year.

Despite the region's low rainfall and frenzied rate of evaporation, this basin manages to hold the world's largest permanent desert lake system, topped up from beneath by fossil water. The largest of the 18 lakes, Lake Yoa, is also the deepest in the Sahara, plunging to 85 feet (26 m).

Lakes of Ounianga

Various fish, reptile, and amphibian species call these lakes home. Centuries of sand-bound isolation have given some of them new forms. For instance, cichlid fish of the Ounianga have larger teeth and longer bodies than related species in West and North African river basins. Camels, watch your noses.

Salar de Uyuni

SALAR DE UYUNI
POTOSÍ, BOLIVIA

More than 40,000 years ago, a prehistoric lake stretched out in the Bolivian Andes. When the lake receded, it left behind an estimated 11 billion tons of salt spread over 4,000 square miles (10,400 sq km)—the planet's largest salt flat—as well as massive amounts of lithium.

When it rains, the ghost of the lake returns: Just a few millimeters of water covering Salar de Uyuni switches on what some call "the largest mirror in the world." The level landscape and reflective white salt make it almost impossible to determine where the land ends and the sky begins. Each November, this visual drama is enhanced by three flamingo species, who congregate on the flat to breed.

Lake Van

LAKE VAN
VAN, TURKEY

On its surface, Turkey's largest lake may seem like your average blue-watered tourist attraction. But those who dare to look a little deeper come back with tales of teeming life—and plenty of intrigue, too.

Lake Van sits in southeastern Turkey, close to Iran. It lacks outlet streams, leaving evaporation the only escape for the carbonated, alkaline water that fills the lake. The world's largest microbialites (coral-like pillars of hardened mud, built by microbes) are found in these swirly, calcium-rich waters.

For decades, stories have told of a long, dark monster in the lake, known simply as Van Gölü Canavari (Lake Van Monster). While searching for him in 2017, a group of divers instead found the ruins of a castle under the lake's surface, bringing to mind local tales of submerged ancient cities. Currently the jury is still out on exactly when the ruins come from—the Urartian empire of 3,000 years ago, the more recent Middle Ages, or both.

Saharan Silver Ants

The fastest ants in the world are in a lifelong race against the sun.

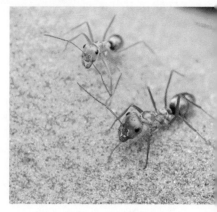

RANGE: Deserts of North Africa and the Arabian Peninsula
SPECIES: Saharan silver ant (*Cataglyphis bombycina*)

◆ Saharan silver ants live in one of the most punishing deserts on Earth. To avoid hungry lizards, they forage at midday, when the sun is high and the sand is 140°F (60°C)—as blistering as a beach parking lot during a heat wave. With each journey out of the nest, they expose themselves to temperatures that should, by all rights, denature their proteins like an egg in a pan.

Instead, on every grocery trip, these little hellions outrun, outstep, and outwit death. The fastest known ants, Saharan silvers can blaze across 3 feet (1 m) of desert—more than 100 times their own body lengths—every second, a rate comparable to a cheetah keeping pace with a Boeing 747. To stay this quick on shifting sands, they momentarily gear into what's called an "aerial phase," in which not a single one of their half-dozen legs touches the ground.

As these ants motor along, they make efficient navigational decisions, ensuring they don't spend a second more out in the open than is absolutely required. They do this by combining three tactics: counting every step, remembering every landmark, and wayfinding using the sun's ultraviolet light, which appears to them as recognizably patterned arcs across the desert sky. No matter how far and wide they may travel—some journeys take them hundreds of meandering feet—they can rocket back to their nest with barely an inch of error.

Their anatomical equipment helps, too. The shiny, prism-shaped hairs that cover most of their bodies form a heat shield, reflecting visible and near-infrared light. These hairs also absorb mid-infrared heat energy from the ants' bodies and release it into the air. To avoid the absorption of similar heat energy that radiates from the scorching sand, the ants' undersides are actually bald.

These adaptations shave precious degrees from their internal thermometers. There's also innovation under the hood: The ants' hemolymph (that is, bug blood) is packed with heat-shock proteins that protect their cells, countering the sun's murderous efforts.

What would happen if any of these fail-safes faltered? The answer lies in the silver ants' dinner. As they sprint across the sand, they're gathering and eating sun-dried arthropods—all the desert bugs that were less skilled, less lucky, and less well built.

> **How to see them:** Look for freakishly fast ants dashing across the North African desert in the midday sun.

Silver ants beat the heat with extreme speed.

Painted Lady Butterflies

One of the world's longest known insect migrations includes a 3,000-mile (4,800 km) dash across the desert.

RANGE: This butterfly's migration circuit goes from subtropical Africa and the Sahel, across the Sahara and the Mediterranean, and into Europe.
SPECIES: Painted lady butterfly (*Vanessa cardui*)

◆ You're planning a trip from Europe to Africa. The journey will start during the British summer and reach Chad at the tail end of the rainy season. You'll spend a number of days over the Mediterranean Sea and yet more crossing the Sahara Desert. How will you even begin to pack?

If you were a painted lady butterfly, you'd manage it with just the wings on your thorax. These delicately spotted orange-and-gray athletes spend their lives in flight, completing one of a number of migration circuits, depending on where they're born.

One recently discovered route takes them from subtropical Africa to Europe and then all the way back again. At about 7,000 miles (11,000 km)—including a double set of desert flyovers and ocean transits—it's one of the lengthiest insect migrations yet known.

How these painted ladies cross the desert is a mystery.

Because each individual painted lady spends only about a month in its winged form, they treat the trip like a generation-spanning relay race. In late summer, large groups of adults leave Europe. Their grandkids and great-grandkids arrive in sub-Saharan Africa by late September and October. In February, their own descendants start heading north again, and their offspring are in central Europe by June.

On either end of the trip, the butterflies are plentiful and well known. In Chad, Ethiopia, and Benin, they're often seen flitting around by the dozens, sipping nectar and fighting over hilltop territory. Good rain years in that region mean huge population booms across the circuit; in 2019, there were tens of millions of painted ladies in the United Kingdom alone.

But they're rarely seen crossing the desert. Researchers modeling potential trajectories have found a few routes that could work, assuming the butterflies fly for four days straight at 13 miles (20 km) per hour—the equivalent of a moderate cycling pace—resting at night but not stopping to eat. In order to achieve this, they likely take advantage of high-altitude tailwinds, thousands of feet above the ground.

So if you do end up crossing the Sahara in the fall, you're probably not alone. Thousands of determined butterflies are flapping high above you. **〉 How to see them: Few people will have seen this species migrating across the desert, as they likely fly high and fast. But it's easy to appreciate the butterflies themselves—they're found everywhere in the world except South America and Antarctica.**

A Dusty Care Package

Butterflies aren't the only thing the Sahara ships out. Each year, the vast desert gives up a bit of itself in the form of millions of tons of dust. These gritty offerings are whipped up by strong storms and carried thousands of miles, their direction dependent on the prevailing winds.

In summer, the dust payload might get sprinkled over North America—where it causes asthma and orange sunsets—or dumped into the Pacific. But in spring and winter, it's shipped directly to a place that really needs it: the Amazon Rainforest.

In order to support its multistory panoply of life, the Amazon needs a lot of nutrients. It's especially hungry for phosphorus, which, given the abundant rainfall there, quickly washes out of its soil. Without phosphorus, plants could no longer photosynthesize and the rainforest would grind to a halt.

Thanks to its lush past and low-biota present, the Sahara has phosphorus in spades. Much of it is concentrated in the Bodélé Depression, a sunken bit of Chad that was once a teeming lake. Wind shrieks through the nearby mountains, picks up the phosphorus-laden dust, and trucks it 3,000 miles (4,800 km) to Brazil, a particulate love letter between two of the world's most famous ecosystems.

ASIA & THE MIDDLE EAST

Last Remaining Wild Camels

They've survived in the desert, resisted domestication, and taken over a former nuclear testing site.

RANGE: Most of these camels are found in the Lop Nur Wild Camel National Nature Reserve in China and the Great Gobi Strictly Protected Area in Mongolia.
SPECIES: Wild camel (*Camelus ferus*)

In the Lop Nur region of the Gobi Desert, wild camels thrive. They bat their long eyelashes through punishing sandstorms and use their hooves to dig for salty water. They mate only in the dead of winter, when it's –30°F (–34°C). They were unfazed, for decades, by the Chinese nuclear tests that were conducted nearby. Just don't try to put a saddle on them.

There are only about a thousand wild camels in the world, all in small sections of China and Mongolia. For many years, these brave and stubborn holdouts were thought to be feral descendants of Bactrian camels, the two-humped species that was domesticated in Afghanistan around 2500 BCE and then ferried traders along the Silk Road. (The one-humped dromedary camel native to the Arabian peninsula—the so-called "ship of the desert"—was likely tamed before that.)

But recent genetic testing has shown that the Gobi camels are actually a species all their own. They've likely been wild forever, using their desert talents for their own ends. The entire continent of Asia was probably once filled with wild camels—stately and long-necked, toting double humps and shaggy coats, chewing cud and carrying no one.

These free-ranging camels have more widely spaced humps and hairier kneecaps than their domestic cousins. According to John Hare, founder of the Wild Camel Protection Foundation, they also have extra abilities: He's seen them drink extremely salty water that Bactrian camels won't touch, and those nuclear tests—stopped for good in 1996—don't seem to have affected them in the least.

Despite their undeniable toughness, the camels' low numbers put the species at extreme risk. With the help of donors, volunteers, and the governments of China and Mongolia, the Wild Camel Protection Foundation has begun to raise awareness about these dromedaries' unique history and abilities. They've also set up a camel reserve and a captive breeding site in an attempt to increase the population. Although it's slow going—a camel's gestation period is 13 months, and they never have twins—the foundation has successfully released nearly a dozen camels back into the Gobi, with satellite collars so we can learn more about their lives. ❯ **How to see them:** You'll have your work cut out for you—most camel habitats are off-limits to visitors, as they have been set aside to protect camels. Your best bet is to get in touch with the Wild Camel Protection Foundation.

Gobi Desert camels have always been wild.

GOBI DESERT

- The Gobi Desert arcs along the border of China and Mongolia, covering about half a million square miles (1.2 million sq km).

- Like the Atacama Desert, the Gobi is a "rain shadow" desert, meaning that precipitation is blocked from the area by another land formation, in this case the Tibetan Plateau.

- Different rainfall patterns and elevations make for varied temperature and land types, from the ravine-sliced Junggar Basin to the pink sandstone Flaming Cliffs, known for their stash of dinosaur eggs.

KEEP AN EYE OUT FOR The winter frosts, when powdery snow falls on the dunes and bare rock.

KEEP AN EAR OUT FOR The squawky brays of kulans, the Gobi's species of wild ass. Fenced out of half their natural range for decades by a railroad, they're beginning to reclaim their original homelands.

KEEP A NOSE OUT FOR Wild onions, or taana, which carpet the ground in some places and taste like hazelnuts.

Why Do Camels Have Humps?

It's tempting to assume that camel humps are water reservoirs, but those humps actually store fat for times when food is scarce—and metabolizing that fat into usable calories uses precious water and dehydrates camels even further.

Like many bodily functions, fat metabolism requires oxygen, which requires breathing. Every time a camel breathes, though, he loses a torrent of water vapor to the arid desert air. Studies indicate that camels give up half a gram of water for every gram of hump fat that they use. If a camel had an internal water ledger, going through his fat store would put him deeper in the red.

So how do camels survive in deserts? It turns out that they are very dehydrated a lot of the time—they're just good at weathering it. A camel can lose up to a quarter of the water in his body before he even begins to show signs of dehydration. For comparison, a human who has lost 5 percent of his total body water may feel parched, weak, and dizzy—and one who has lost 25 percent will almost certainly be dead.

The secret to the camel's ability lies not in his hump but in his blood. His red blood cells are oval-shaped, allowing them to flow through blood vessels easily even when the blood is thick from lack of water. The cells are also extremely elastic, and when the camel does finally get a drink, they plump up with enormous amounts of fluid. The camel then continues his journey with the equivalent of millions of tiny waterskins in his blood—a more effective strategy than carrying one or two big ones on his back.

Long-Eared Jerboas

These patchwork-looking critters have talents all their own.

◆ The long-eared jerboa is pretty silly looking. With jackrabbit-esque legs, a piggy snout, and satellite-dish ears, this desert dweller resembles a kindergartner's drawing come to life.

But don't underestimate this tiny Frankenmammal. A long-eared jerboa can run a four-minute mile, leap about 10 feet (3 m) in a single bound, and spend all day underground without breaking a sweat. Good luck keeping eyes on one long enough to laugh at him.

RANGE: Desert regions of China and Mongolia, including the Taklamakan and Gobi Deserts
SPECIES: Long-eared jerboa (*Euchoreutes naso*)

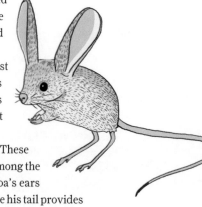

This jerboa appreciates his alone time, remaining solitary for most of the day in a cool yet cozy sand burrow. Once the sun goes down, this cautious rodent emerges to hunt and find mates. He'll stick to areas with limited vegetation to avoid going toe-to-fuzzy-toe with his closest rival: the gregarious, brutal Mongolian gerbil.

Out in the open, the rodent's massive ears quickly come into play. These spectacular organs—30 percent bigger than the rest of his head—are among the largest ears of any animal, proportionately speaking. When the jerboa's ears pinpoint an insect in midair, his long legs propel him up to catch it, while his tail provides balance. If a predator nears, the jerboa escapes into the night in great leaping bounds. (While this species' jump height hasn't been measured, other jerboas have been seen getting 6 feet (2 m) of air, meaning they could hurdle a man of average height.)

Beyond providing contrast to his large ears, long tail, and legs for days, the jerboa's small body allows him to travel long distances without expending much energy—a helpful strategy in the challenging environment of the desert. He doesn't even have to drink water, relying on his diet to provide him with the hydration he needs.

It all works out pretty well for this furtive creature. While some other members of the world's 33 jerboa species are much easier to find, our long-eared friend was not captured on video until 2007, when a group from the Zoological Society of London led an expedition to the Gobi Desert. They managed to record jerboas hunting, hopping, and attempting to snuggle down into a scientist's sandal.

Since then, more sightings, as well as targeted research, have been helping to establish the long-eared jerboa's range and to pinpoint and address current threats to the species' survival, which include motorbikes and artifact digging. Even if we don't see much of them, it's better if they're there. ❯ **How to find them:** These mammals are difficult to spot in the Gobi Desert due to their nocturnal nature, small size, and speed. If you can find a video of them, consider yourself lucky—even that is a recent development.

Leopards of Bera

In Bera, the largest concentration of leopards on the planet live alongside the Rabari people.

RANGE: India, Nepal, Bhutan, and Pakistan
SPECIES: Indian leopard (*Panthera pardus fusca*)

◆ Across the world, from Wyoming to Western Australia, ranchers and wild predators come into conflict. Wolves, dingoes, and lions eat goats, sheep, and cows. Ranchers, fearing for their livelihoods, may respond with violence. It can be one of the most difficult aspects of sharing land.

But not in Bera. In this small town in the south of India's Rajasthan district, people walk the same tracks as leopards—the largest concentration of them in the world. For over a century, these predators have lived side by side with humans without much conflict, in one of the only places in the world to enjoy this kind of harmony.

This alliance is dependent on the Rabari people, who came to Rajasthan from Iran around a thousand years ago, by way of Afghanistan. Because much of the nearby land is privately owned, the Rabari graze their livestock in the Aravalli hills, where dozens of leopards live. They do their best to warn the big cats of their presence, shouting and throwing stones as they walk with their goats and cows.

When leopards do eat the Rabari's animals, the ranchers don't hold it against them. Hindu deities worshipped by members of the Rabari community include the goddess Chamunda Mata Ji, who is often depicted riding on a leopard, and Shiva, who wears a leopard skin. Ranchers like Sohan Rabari consider any loss to a leopard a contribution to Chamunda, whom they trust will make it up to them twofold.

"A couple of leopards have killed some of my goats in Bera," Sohan Rabari says. "Every time that has happened, I've had an amazing monetary year." The state forestry department helps by compensating for slain animals, although some ranchers don't claim their losses. Poaching and retaliatory killing, a problem elsewhere in the country, is nonexistent in Bera.

For their part, the leopards rarely escalate. In the rest of India, attacks on humans are a problem—the government counts hundreds of leopard-related injuries and dozens of deaths every year. Despite the extremely high density of cats in Bera—there are about 50 living in the small area—there has been only one such occurrence: in 1999, when a leopard grabbed a one-year-old girl in a village called Vellar. When her family screamed, the leopard dropped the infant and fled. The girl, who survived with toothmark scars, now goes by the nickname Setri, the local word for a female leopard.

The Rabari protect this rare and delicate balance from outside threats as well. Recently, they joined with Bera's royal family to campaign against mining in the region, which would have destroyed their grazing lands as well as the leopards' habitat. The land was instead converted to a conservation reserve.

Visitors now come from far and wide to spot the leopards, who can be found resting on rocky slopes or wandering around the Chamunda Devi temples, basking in their unique coalition. **❯ How to see them: Your best bet is to hire an experienced Rabari villager or another local from Bera to guide you into the hills.**

Three leopards in Bera

THE WILD LIFE OF A Leopard Prince

■ Yaduveer Singh Bera is a wildlife photographer, a leopard advocate, and the prince of the Bera royal family. His family settled in the region over 350 years ago and began leading leopard-spotting tours in the early 1990s, a practice Yaduveer continues today.

● **How did you become interested in the leopards in your region?**
[My relatives] were the first ones to start leopard safaris in Bera, in 1993. The ground was initially a hunting area for the royals of Rajasthan and other states. So I spent my childhood with leopards, as my father took me out every day to spot these magnificent cats. He gifted me a camera—that's how I got addicted to wildlife.

● **More leopards live in your area than anywhere else in the world. How do you maintain good relations with the species?**
In Bera, leopards and humans have coexisted for generations without any conflict. We have worked very hard to protect the big cats. There was a time when the mining lobby had infiltrated Bera and there were 110 mines allotted in the area, which would have destroyed the entire habitat of the leopards. But our family along with the locals fought against the lobby and had the land converted into a leopard conservation reserve.

The Rabari community is the reason the leopards live and survive, as livestock is their main prey base. The only reason they don't attack humans is because of the Rabari. Whenever a leopard takes a livestock, the Rabari consider it a sacrifice to their deities. Today, we locals are protecting the big cats, as we have guards in the jungle who keep a watch out for poachers. It's a very unusual relationship.

● **Have you ever had a scary encounter with a big cat?**
Yes, I have had many scary encounters. I have been mock-charged many times—sometimes we don't realize if the leopard is hiding in a bush nearby.

I also have a vintage German caravan gifted to me by my great-granddad. I take the caravan into the jungle, where I have private land next to a leopard cave. I like to camp there, and I have had instances where leopards and sloth bears have visited, and have come very close to the caravan while I was peeping through the window. Also, on foot, I have been very close to a wild leopard, almost 30 feet [9 m].

● **Are there any misconceptions about the leopards of Bera that you'd like to correct?**
They will never attack humans. They live close to the temples, and you can spot them sitting on the stairs. ■

Great Indian Bustards

This huge bird's chance to shine was cut off by one tiny letter.

◆ Everyone graced by its presence is impressed by the great Indian bustard. At up to 4 feet tall (1 m) and 33 pounds (15 kg), this avian big shot—known to fans as the GIB—is one of the heaviest flying animals on Earth. It's not just stats: Any human who has seen this bird overhead will attest to its ability to inspire a primal mammalian fear, perhaps dredging up an ancient memory of flying dinosaurs.

But such encounters are now few and far between. Once spread across the Indian subcontinent, the birds' population is now estimated to number fewer than 100, restricted to swaths of desert and dry grasslands in the northwest of India and the southwest of Pakistan.

If these bustards weren't so large, they might look a bit goofy. They have long, squat bodies, black caps, and unfeathered legs a bit like an ostrich's. They're known for their mating displays, during which the male will stick up his tail feathers, march in place, and make a loud, deep *ooooooooom* sound. Once his overtures have been accepted, he'll nibble the female's head and neck while waggling his enormous air-engorged neck pouch.

Combined with the birds' endemicity—they've always been found only on the Indian subcontinent—all of this so impressed celebrated Indian ornithologist Salim Ali that in the 1960s, he fought for the GIB to be named the country's national bird. As the story goes, the huge creature was felled by a single letter: Officials nervous that people might mispronounce "bustard" as "bastard" ended up giving the honor to the Indian peacock.

Without the honor and resources afforded by that title, the GIB has fallen into a bit of trouble. Although it is protected by law, after years of land loss and degradation, the species' only remaining habitat now overlaps with one of the world's most militarized borders. Parts of this land have also been used for nuclear missile testing, and more recently for large wind farms and other renewable energy setups.

RANGE: Most of these bustards live either in the Thar Desert or the Rann of Kutch, both of which span the northwest border of India and Pakistan.
SPECIES: Great Indian bustard (*Ardeotis nigriceps*)

The shift toward greener energy actually represents the greatest current threat to the bustard. The Wildlife Institute of India estimates that about 16 great Indian bustards die each year after colliding with the high-tension power lines used to ferry windmill-generated electricity. Even though the courts have banned such overhead lines, renewable energy companies have yet to re-lay all their cables underground.

But all is not lost. Some local communities have given up parts of their land to conserve and protect the bustards, and a conservation breeding program is underway in Rajasthan. If the energy companies follow the court's decree, the bustards' remaining habitat will be relatively free for flying, roaming, and pouch waggling. ❯ **How to see them:** Your best bet is to visit the Desert National Park in Rajasthan, where the Indian Forest Service has set up wire fences to protect the birds' habitat.

Spider-Tailed Horned Vipers

It's a spider! No, it's a snake!

RANGE: Western Iran
SPECIES: Spider-tailed horned viper (*Pseudocerastes urarachnoides*)

◆ Over the mountains near the western Iranian desert, a peckish migrating lark spots a welcome sight: a big, juicy spider, out in the open like a pie on a windowsill. The lark descends upon the naive arachnid, little claws outstretched. And then: WHAP.

The meal-seeker has become the meal, trapped in the jaws of an enormous snake. The lark's would-be snack was not a real bug but an anatomical forgery: the incredible appendage of the spider-tailed horned viper.

Lots of predators use their own body parts to attract prey: Anglerfish grow their own glowing lures, horned toads wiggle their worm-like toes, and alligator snapping turtles make their tongues squirm.

But the bait used by the spider-tailed horned viper has a special panache. Millennia of evolution have sculpted the end of its tail into a near-perfect replica of a spider. For a while, this snake's jewelry was difficult for even researchers to believe: A team examining specimens in 1970 thought at first that their snake had been preserved with a small spider clinging to her tail, or that she had a tumor or parasite.

This snake's special lure fools birds and researchers.

But further encounters and careful observation have revealed the ornament's development and use. Baby snakes are born with normal tails; as they grow, an abdomen-like knob develops at the tail's end, while the nearby scales splay outward until they resemble legs. To hunt, a viper coils up on a limestone rock and twitches her tail slightly, sending the "spider" marching around on her well-camouflaged body until a bird or lizard falls for it.

The capture rate is not 100 percent. Researchers have seen wizened birds successfully resist the temptation of the twitching lure, as well as snakes whose spiders have lost limbs. But when it works, it's one of the natural world's freakiest and most impressive bait-and-switches— a snake in spider's clothing. ❯ **How to see them:** Look for a tempting spider— and then check to see if that spider is attached to anything.

ARABIAN DESERT

- At more than 700,000 square miles (2 million sq km), the Arabian Desert covers almost the entire Arabian peninsula, including most of Saudi Arabia and Kuwait and parts of Jordan, Iraq, Qatar, the United Arab Emirates, Oman, and Yemen.

- Its southern section, known as the Rub'al-Khali or "Empty Quarter," is one of the world's largest expanses of sand, roughly the size of Texas.

- The desert's warm red-orange color comes from iron oxide that coats the sand.

KEEP AN EYE OUT FOR Sabkha salt flats, where hard crusts cover custard-thick mud. Errant travelers can get trapped in the sabkha, the closest thing to quicksand that exists outside an action movie.

KEEP AN EAR OUT FOR Saw-scaled vipers, who hiss by rubbing their serrated scales together. Definitely pay attention—saw-scaled vipers are venomous and quick to bite.

KEEP A NOSE OUT FOR Frankincense, the potent, gummy resin of *Boswellia* trees that traders carried across the desert and the Red Sea thousands of years ago.

Singing Sand Dunes

On a still day, a sand desert is one of the world's quietest places. There's nothing there to rustle, ripple, or rasp. Noise made by you or any other visitor is muffled by the dunes.

But then the wind blows. As it rushes by, the landscape itself rings with low, rumbling tones. You're being serenaded by a singing sand dune.

There are about 30 places around the world where the sand sings. Though the dunes get the credit, wind is the real maestro. First, it meticulously accumulates sand, building the dunes into an appropriate height and shape: at least 120 feet (35 m), with a 30° slope. Then the wind blows away the finer grains, until those that remain in the dune's top layer are all of a similar size.

Then a big-enough gust of wind sends the sand at the top tumbling down. As the grains rub against each other, the friction produces sound waves—a dune boom. The hotter and drier the sand, the louder the sound. (If you're visiting a desert concert hall and the wind isn't cooperating, you can start up a song yourself: Just climb to the top of a dune and slide.)

Each locale has its own unique dune tune. The Kelso Dunes, in the Mojave, are said to be cello-like, while the Gobi Desert's singing dunes are so eerie that Marco Polo blamed their sounds on evil spirits. Dunes in Chile's Mar de Dunas croon a midrange F, while Nevada's Sand Mountain belts a low C. The dunes of Al-Ashkharah in Oman are widely considered to have the most beautiful sound—a sonorous, whalelike hum.

A Glossary of Dune Types

A stretch of desert dunes gives the impression of endless sameness. But dunes take many different shapes, each the result of a specific collaboration between wind, gravity, and sand. The prevalence of particular shapes helps give a desert its visual character. Here are five of the most common.

1. Crescentic. Crescentic dunes are formed when wind blows from one direction, pushing the sand into a C shape. (The surface of the dune the wind blows over is called a slipface—in this case, it's the gently sloped outside edge of the C.) Crescentic dunes are common in Central Asia, on Mars, and underwater, where currents play the role of wind. They are also the world's fastest dunes, able to sweep across the desert at a rate of more than 60 miles (95 km) per year.

2. Linear. Linear dunes occur when equally strong winds blow in opposing directions, leaving long ridges bordered by two slipfaces. They're also called seif dunes, after the Arabic word for sword. You can find extensive ones in the Sahara and the Empty Quarter—some of them snake for hundreds of miles.

3. Parabolic. Although parabolic dunes look like crescentic dunes, they form in the opposite way. The arms of these dunes are stabilized by wet sand or vegetation. When wind blows, it excavates the loose sand inside of the C shape, leaving the fortified rim intact. For this reason, they're also sometimes called blowouts. Parabolic dunes are often found in coastal deserts.

4. Dome. The only dunes that lack a slipface, dome dunes have a rounded top, and sand can be blown onto them from any direction. They can be circular or elliptical and are rare—they mostly form far upwind in dune fields, including in China's Taklamakan Desert and Antarctica's Lower Victoria Valley.

5. Star. Wind blowing in many directions can form star dunes: radially symmetrical mounds that look a bit like starfish-shaped pyramids. The wind piles the sand higher over time, rather than wider or longer. Some star dunes in China's Badain Jaran Desert have been mounded a mile high and are likely the tallest dunes on Earth.

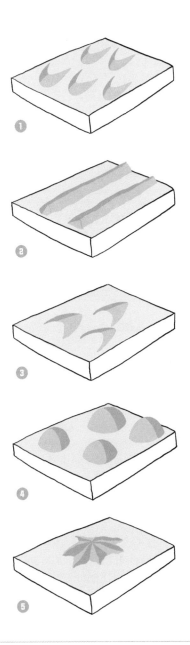

Ghaf Trees

These evergreen desert trees defy droughts.

RANGE: Western Asia, Arabian Peninsula, and the Indian subcontinent
SPECIES: Ghaf tree (*Prosopis cineraria*)

◆ There is an Arabic saying: "Death will not visit a man if he has a ghaf, a goat, and a camel." The ghaf, a gnarled evergreen, is the national tree of the United Arab Emirates. From a distance, it resembles a willow tree, with long branches that may hang low enough to sweep the sand.

But no willow could do what the ghaf does. Irrigation studies show that this tree survives on about 11 gallons (42 L) of water a day—a mere sip compared with a weeping willow, which can guzzle a hundred gallons (378 L) daily in the summer. Even the date palm tree, a common oasis plant, needs nearly eight times the ghaf's ration.

Unmissably vertical, ghafs provide homes for insects, reptiles, and birds, as well as nutrition for oryx, camels, and goats, which nibble their leaves and bark. Bedouin people take shelter under ghaf branches to protect themselves from the harsh sun and sandstorms and eat the protein-rich pea-like pods the tree offers. In a way, ghafs hold the whole landscape together—their 115-foot (35 m) roots, which allow them to access deep pockets of water, help stabilize sand dunes.

These ghafs don't look thirsty at all.

When it's young, a ghaf's branches are protected by small thorns, but these fall away as it matures. After that, this special tree is instead protected by law—in 2008, the United Arab Emirates made it a crime to uproot or cut down a ghaf—and its reputation. Although the ghaf has suffered from urbanization, overgrazing, reduced groundwater, and competition from the introduced mesquite tree, which strangles its roots, it continues to persevere and inspire.

"The ghaf tree not only symbolizes the harsh life in the desert, but also survival," says Tatiana Antonelli Abella of Goumbook, a Dubai nonprofit that runs a tree-planting campaign called Give a Ghaf. Properly respected, a ghaf can live for a long time—about 120 years, although Bahrain's famous Tree of Life, or Shajarat-al-Hayat, is said to be 400 years old. ❯ **How to see them: You can view them at the Dubai Desert Conservation Reserve, the first national park in the United Arab Emirates, or scattered throughout the desert. The famous Tree of Life, in Bahrain, is a ghaf tree and a popular tourist destination.**

Cryptobiotic Soil Crusts

The desert's living skin

RANGE: Deserts worldwide
SPECIES: Biocrusts are composed of mosses, lichens, fungi, cyanobacteria, and other microorganisms. There are generally dozens of species involved, and the exact composition differs from one location to the next.

◆ Searching for life in the desert, it's tempting to focus on what catches the eye: lizards scuttling across the dunes, birds of prey revolving overhead, plants in profile on the horizon.

If you want to see what really holds things together, look down—but don't move. Arid ecosystems around the world depend on a surface layer of microorganisms just a few inches thick. Known as cryptobiotic soil, biological soil crusts, or simply biocrusts, this living skin of mosses, lichens, cyanobacteria, and other tiny critters can be hundreds of years old. If you quilted all of Earth's biocrust patches together, they'd cover an area the size of South America.

Biocrusts play a vital role in desert ecology. To begin, they secrete a polysaccharide-based matrix—a sticky, sugary gel—that glues particles of dirt together, keeping loose desert sands from blowing away. They also store carbon, water, and nutrients that help plants survive harsh environmental conditions. Without them, many deserts would be barren dunes; with them, shifting soils stay stable enough for plants to take root, making it possible for a diversity of animals and insects to move in.

While mighty, biocrusts are fragile. Human activities, from hiking to livestock grazing to housing development, imperil their integrity. (Desert visitors will be familiar with signs that warn "Don't bust the crust!")

Where crusts crumble, the ecosystems they underlie can, too. And unlike human skin, the desert's is slow to heal—one study in the Mojave Desert compared tank tracks made by General George Patton with undisturbed soil nearby and estimated that based on the rate of recovery, the biocrusts Patton tore up would take 2,000 years to regrow.

Rupturing crusts also causes erosion, freeing dust and sand that would otherwise be trapped beneath. While wind-borne desert sand brings needed nutrients to other ecosystems, too much of it can have far-reaching consequences, ruining air quality in cities and melting snowcaps on distant mountaintops. Dust found on the snowy peaks of the Colorado Rockies comes not only from nearby New Mexico and Utah but also from as far away as China's Gobi and Taklamakan Deserts.

Because cryptobiotic soils can take so long to form, scientists are trying to speed up the recovery of degraded deserts by cultivating the crusts in labs and greenhouses and then transplanting them to the wild. With controlled temperatures, water, and light, biocrusts that usually take decades to grow can sprout in as little as four months indoors.

Getting those same crusts to survive outdoors is trickier, but we're getting there. In Inner Mongolia, for instance, scientists are growing cyanobacteria in ponds and trucking it to places where the Kubuqi Desert is

(top) Useful and beautiful

(bottom) A closer look

encroaching into nearby grasslands. Eight years after they inoculated the desert soil with cyanobacteria, the researchers found that a whopping 27 plant species had recolonized the area, while a nearby control plot stayed practically barren. Not bad for an early try at a desert skin graft. ❯ **How to see them: Because many biocrusts have been torn up by grazing and development, your best bet is in a remote area, like China's Gurbantünggüt Desert (almost 30 percent of its surface is covered by biocrusts), or a protected one, like Utah's Canyonlands National Park. When you come across a biocrust, make sure not to bust it.**

A Desert Magic Trick

Next time you're in the desert, try this biological magic trick: Dribble a little bit of water onto some cryptobiotic soil. The dry crust will transform into a plush green carpet before your eyes.

Because water in the desert is fickle, the organisms that make up biocrusts must be able to survive lengthy dry spells and then act quickly to take advantage of

rainfall or runoff. Scientists have found that cyanobacteria accomplish this by burrowing deeper into the soil during droughts, then surging to the surface at the slightest hint of moisture. The researchers who documented the behavior say it's the first time a microorganism has been shown to actively follow water to improve its chance of survival.

AUSTRALIA

Thorny Devils

They're not mean—just thirsty.

RANGE: **Throughout Australia's central and western deserts, including in Western Australia, the southern half of the Northern Territory, South Australia, and western Queensland**
SPECIES: **Thorny devil (*Moloch horridus*)**

◆ Thorny devils look like they mean business. Covered in scaly, complicated armor—their spikes have spikes—these banana-sized dragons of the Australian outback are easily mistaken for kitted-out fighters. The zoologist who first officially described the species called their appearance "the most ferocious of any [lizard] that I know" and named them after Moloch, a biblical god with a fondness for child sacrifice. They even have fleshy knobs on the backs of their necks meant to look like extra heads. (Those have spikes, too.)

But beneath their prickly exteriors, these lizards are utterly harmless—a threat only to small black ants, which they consume by the thousands every day. In fact, the thorny devil's mouth is so well adapted to vacuuming up ants, it can't lap at water.

That's where those spiky scales come in handy. The thorny devil's armor contains a network of microscopic channels that are etched into the overlaps between the scales. When basically any part of the lizard's body comes in contact with moisture, it is pulled into the channels by capillary action—the same force that draws a spilled drink up into a paper towel.

Water collects in the scaly piping system and is routed to its ultimate destination: the lizard's mouth. When she comes across a puddle in the parched Australian outback, a thorny devil can simply stand in it to drink, gulping contentedly as her body acts like a giant straw.

If there's not enough water to get her feet wet, the lizard will shovel damp sand onto her body, and her scales will draw the moisture out of it. If it happens to rain—rare, but welcome—her spikes help collect the raindrops and usher them into the channels. Even brushing her spiny belly over dewy vegetation may allow a thorny devil to quench her thirst.

The spikes have one other main purpose—keeping predators away. When troubled by a snake or a buzzard, the lizard will puff up like a barbed balloon. If that doesn't work, she'll tuck in her head and expose her back-of-the-neck knob in an effort to redirect that hungry mouth away from her real skull. If it works, the lizard will live to drink another day. ❯ **How to see them:** Though thorny devils are far from endangered, it is difficult to see them without visiting the Australian outback. You can visit some at the Alice Springs Desert Park in Alice Springs.

All spike and no bite

Bloody Shocking

Texas horned lizards (*Phrynosoma cornutum*), found in western North America and known to some as horny toads, have a water-collecting strategy similar to that of the thorny devil. They can also stand in puddles and drink, pulling water up into the channels in their scales, against the force of gravity, by capillary action. When it rains, they strike a particular pose—legs splayed, head and tail lowered, abdomen bowed—to maximize their harvest.

Once they've filled up, these lizards use the moisture in a surprising way. When a Texas horned lizard feels threatened, he can constrict special muscles near his eyes, redirecting blood from his heart into his head. The extra blood flows into his ocular sinuses (cavities near the eyes), building up pressure. Another squeeze, and a jet of blood shoots out of the lizard's eyes, thoroughly freaking out his agitator and buying him some time.

A number of horned lizard species can do this "auto-hemorrhaging" trick, as it's called. Some can squirt blood 4 feet (1 m) away!

Skink Mansions

These outback skinks survive with the help of unlikely allies—each other.

RANGE: Arid regions of the Northern Territory and Western Australia
SPECIES: Great desert skink or tjakura (*Liopholis kintorei*)

◆ The scorched heart of the world's driest continent, Australia's central outback is brutal. Most of the dozens of lizard species that scuttle over its red dunes and salt lakes have a fittingly Mad Max look, armed with whiplike tails or encased in prickly spines.

Not great desert skinks. Sporting smooth, rust-colored scales, these large skinks are plump and unmenacing (unless you're a termite). Another attribute has allowed them to survive in the harsh desert for millennia: a sense of family unique among lizards.

While most lizards are loners, great desert skinks are nurturing parents and often monogamous. These skinks also work together to construct elaborate burrows for their families, a trait undocumented in the more than 5,000 other known types of lizards. (Modern genetic research recently verified that the individual skinks living in each burrow are closely related, confirming centuries of observations by the Aboriginal Anangu people, for whom this lizard is a celebrated part of traditional lore.)

The foot-long skinks' burrow systems—which researchers compare to mansions—can stretch the length of a school bus and may contain 20 different entrances. They're often located near termite mounds for easy snacking, and they even contain designated latrine areas for snacking's aftermath. Adults fastidiously maintain the tunnels, and juveniles pitch in, digging small "pop" holes used for quick exits.

This great desert skink would prefer to be underground.

Life is blissful when the skinks are snug in their burrows. But the rest of the world can be cruel. Venturing outside to eat exposes them to feral predators like cats and foxes—a threat exacerbated by wildfires, which scorch the spinifex grass that otherwise provides them cover. To a cat, an unarmed skink is basically a sausage, says Natasha Cadenhead, a researcher at the University of Queensland: "a fat little tasty treat."

So, another unusually social animal—the human—has stepped up to help. At northern Australia's Newhaven Wildlife Sanctuary, which houses one of Australia's largest great desert skink populations, conservationists working with the Australian Wildlife Conservancy are attempting to exterminate cats and foxes from a huge area of lizard habitat. They have also begun implementing controlled burns in the cooler months to clear brush and regenerate vegetation, mirroring how Aboriginal people maintained the outback for tens of thousands of years, before the arrival of cats and climate change–fueled fires endangered prime skink real estate. ⟩ **How to see them:** Your best bet is at northern Australia's Newhaven Wildlife Sanctuary or Uluru–Kata Tjuta National Park. Keep a lookout around dusk, when the skinks exit their burrows and head toward the nearest termite mound.

Come Outside! It's Raining!

Australia's deserts are subject to the whims of a very fickle weather system. Unlike in places like central Africa or the American Southwest, where rainfall is scant but reliable, Australia's precipitation doesn't follow a plan. Droughts of up to eight years may be followed by a full-on monsoon. It's a landscape of "utter unpredictability" and the most variable rainfall regime in the world, says botanist Angela Moles.

When the clouds finally do open up, it's time to party. Here are some outback residents who love getting soaked.

SHIELD SHRIMPS (*Triops australiensis*) • Look twice before splashing: Any given puddle in the Australian desert is probably teeming with big-headed, wriggly shield shrimp. The eggs of these hardy crustaceans can hang out dormant in dry soil for up to seven years, awaiting their cue. When rain finally comes, they hatch, sometimes by the millions.

Each shrimp then lives life as though on fast-forward, eating, metamorphosing, mating, and (for females) laying eggs as quickly as she can before the world dries out again. Then the shrimp dies, and the eggs of the next generation begin their long wait. ❶

DESERT SHAGGY MANES (*Podaxis pistillaris*) • Most fungi prefer damp habitats. But some, like the desert shaggy mane, try their luck in the desert. These fungi spend most of their lives as large bundles of hyphae, or tendrils, growing slowly underground and sucking up any water that comes their way. About two weeks after a rainstorm, they send up "fruiting bodies"—what we might call mushrooms. (Theirs look a bit like papier-mâché cattails.) The fruiting bodies release spores, which are carried by the wind to take root elsewhere. This cycle occurs in deserts across the world—the quieter cousin of the more colorful superblooms. ❷

TRILLING FROGS (*Neobatrachus sudellae* and others) • Trilling frogs of various species hunker down underground during dry spells and are summoned to the surface by the sound of rain. When they come out, they add to the cacophony, singing for dear life so as to pair off while their ponds still exist. Tadpoles develop quickly and start the cycle over. ❸

ULURU WATERFALLS • Uluru, one of the most recognizable rocks in the world, is impressive any day of the year. When it rains, though, things get really special. The sacred formation is ribboned with waterfalls, which change the color of the sandstone from dusky pink to a rich clay red and usher in a brief moment of plenty for those who call the monolith home.

Visitors with lucky timing might see or hear frogs calling en masse, galahs bathing upside down in the falls, and shaggy manes popping up near water holes. Shield shrimp have even been found on top of Uluru, potentially blown up there by wind when they were still eggs. ❹

GALAHS (*Eolophus roseicapilla*) • Galahs, some of Australia's most common and widespread cockatoos, are notoriously open with their opinions, squawking at the slightest provocation or sometimes none at all. Their take on rain tends to be unequivocally positive. Many greet showers with an acrobatics show: hanging upside down on branches or power lines, spreading their wings, and swinging back and forth. ❺

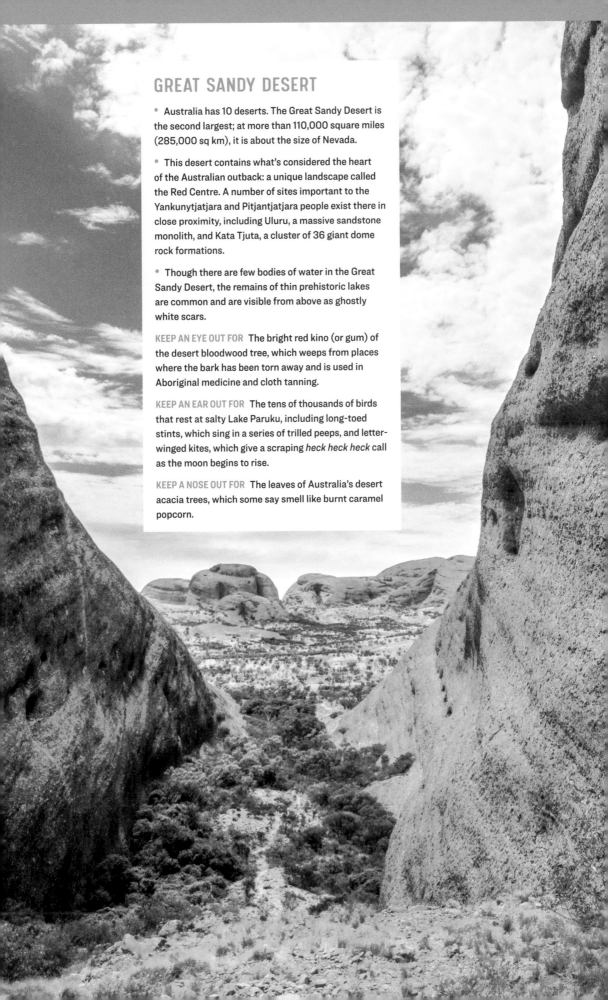

GREAT SANDY DESERT

- Australia has 10 deserts. The Great Sandy Desert is the second largest; at more than 110,000 square miles (285,000 sq km), it is about the size of Nevada.

- This desert contains what's considered the heart of the Australian outback: a unique landscape called the Red Centre. A number of sites important to the Yankunytjatjara and Pitjantjatjara people exist there in close proximity, including Uluru, a massive sandstone monolith, and Kata Tjuta, a cluster of 36 giant dome rock formations.

- Though there are few bodies of water in the Great Sandy Desert, the remains of thin prehistoric lakes are common and are visible from above as ghostly white scars.

KEEP AN EYE OUT FOR The bright red kino (or gum) of the desert bloodwood tree, which weeps from places where the bark has been torn away and is used in Aboriginal medicine and cloth tanning.

KEEP AN EAR OUT FOR The tens of thousands of birds that rest at salty Lake Paruku, including long-toed stints, which sing in a series of trilled peeps, and letter-winged kites, which give a scraping *heck heck heck* call as the moon begins to rise.

KEEP A NOSE OUT FOR The leaves of Australia's desert acacia trees, which some say smell like burnt caramel popcorn.

Spinifex

The unlikely, spiky base of the Australian desert food chain

◆ As deserts go, Australia's look rather gentle. Instead of bare rock or spiny cacti, you'll find hummock after hummock of lush, waving grass. These plants, called spinifex, are so common that some estimates have them covering 20 percent of the continent's surface. If llaretas (page 221) can be mistaken for the desert biome's cushy love seat, spinifex could be its high-pile carpet.

RANGE: Across the Australian outback
SPECIES: Spinifex or tjanpi (*Triodia* spp.)

That is—surprise!—until you get too close. Spinifex may look "soft and lovely," says Australian botanist Angela Moles. But "you go to touch it, and it's the spikiest thing."

Like many desert plants, spinifex has adapted to its lot in life by toughening up. Each blade of grass rolls into a tight, finger-pricking cylinder at the first sign of drought. In some species, the blades are armored with small shards of silica, better known as the main ingredient of sand. In others, the whole plant is filled with gluey resin.

These defenses protect the plant from hungry animals. The only creatures able to regularly eat spinifex are termites—microbes in their stomachs dissolve the tough grass into a nutritious vinegar. Without termites, spinifex would take over the outback, crowding out other vegetation.

With their intervention, though, the plant forms the foundation of life here, allowing scores of other species to eat, make homes, and reproduce. Spinifex-fed termites build towering mounds out of desert dirt, aerating the soil and allowing other plants to grow. Skinks, dunnarts, and other creatures eat the termites. Larger animals, like sand goannas and black-shouldered kites, eat those in turn.

Spinifex hummocks, which are rigidly anchored to the ground by 9-foot (3 m) water-seeking taproots, serve as shelters for many other animals, including night parrots and hopping mice.

Even the resin can be helpful under the right circumstances. For thousands of years, Aboriginal people have harvested the sticky stuff and used it as an adhesive to build and repair tools and houses.

The resin also makes spinifex extremely flammable—enough for each hummock to burn as hot as a bonfire for about two minutes. Fire-based management by the Martu and other Aboriginal people, along with natural lightning-based blazes, help regenerate the spinifex landscape by making room for new growth.

Might it be nice to have a cushier grass? Sure. But in the desert, you take what you can get. ❯ **How to see it:** Go to the outback and look around—you've got a very good chance of spotting some. Approach carefully.

MYSTERIOUS MICROBES · Old spinifex tussocks often die off in the middle, leaving a ring of grass around a patch of bare ground. Recent research suggests the older grass in the middle falls prey to soil microbes, which outcompete the plants and make it impossible for seedlings to grow. The spinifex responds by moving outward, like a ripple in a pond, continuing its quest for desert domination. ❺

IN THE SPINIFEX

CATHEDRAL TERMITES · Some of the most architecturally talented bugs in the world, cathedral termites (*Nasutitermes triodiae*) construct mounds that can reach 26 feet (8 m) high. That's more than 2,600 times the height of a single worker termite—the equivalent of humans building a 1,400-story tower out of mud, grass, spit, and feces. **❶**

WESTERN PEBBLE-MOUND MICE · If you come across an arrangement of similarly sized stones in the middle of the desert, you have probably stumbled upon the home of a western pebble-mound mouse (*Pseudomys chapmani*). These mice spend their nights gathering stones and dragging them over to their burrows, where they may help disguise the entrance from predators. Overnight, the pebbles collect dew, providing the mice with fresh water in the morning. **❸**

GOLD-DIGGING BUGS · Spinifex grasslands hide deep deposits of gold, zinc, and other precious metals. Several tunneling insects, including certain ants (*Rhytidoponera mayri*) and termites (*Schedorhinotermes actuosus*), accumulate these minerals in their nests—and even their bodies—as they dig. Prospecting companies are considering using these species to find new promising mining areas. **❹**

COMB-EARED SKINKS · Thanks partly to spinifex, Australia supports more species of lizards than anywhere else in the world. One subtype, the comb-eared skink (*Ctenotus* spp.), is so diverse that scientists find it confusing—there might be as many as 11 species of comb-eared skink coexisting in a single small area of the desert. Researchers still aren't sure how the skinks manage this, although they likely partition resources by focusing on different hunting times and termite species. **❷**

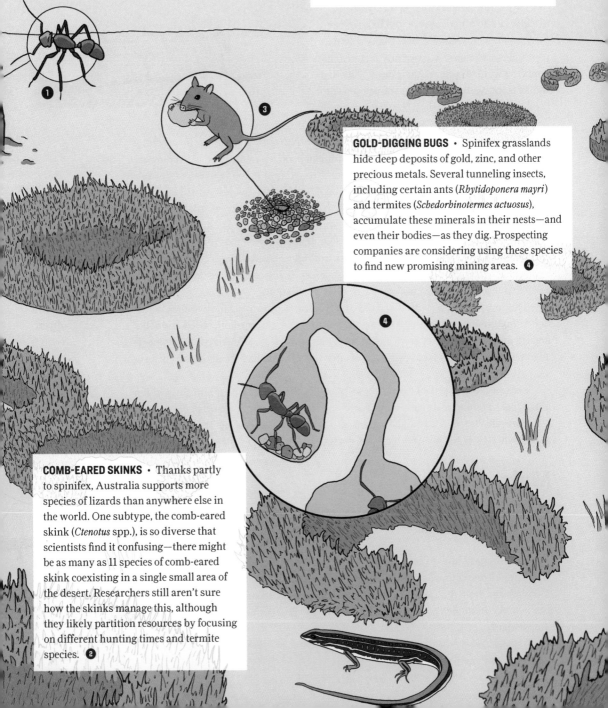

The Dingo Fence

One of the longest structures in the world was built to keep desert dogs away from sheep.

◆ No one is quite sure how dingoes got to Australia. These tawny, sad-faced canines arrived on the continent between 5,000 and 10,000 years ago, either brought here by seafarers from Asia or making their way via a onetime land bridge from Papua New Guinea. Once they arrived, they quickly took their place at the top of the food chain, developing a taste for kangaroos, emus, and other large herbivores. Aboriginal people formed close relationships with the dogs and may even have domesticated them.

When Europeans reached the continent in the 1800s, the dingoes were given a different role: public enemy number one. Many colonists were sheep ranchers, wary of any large carnivore who wanted to share their land. "The Red Riding Hood/wolf scenario was transposed onto the dingoes," says ecologist Thomas Newsome.

LOCATION: The fence runs from the town of Jandowae, in east Queensland, over and down to Nundroo, in the southern crook of the continent.

SPECIES: Dingo (*Canis lupus dingo* or *Canis dingo*)

So, they built a fence. At just under 3,500 miles (5,600 km), Australia's Dingo Fence is one of the largest structures in the world, longer than the China-Mongolia border. It lops off the entire southeast corner of the continent. And it's pretty good at keeping out dingoes—for better or for worse.

The fence has been successful enough that it "essentially divides two different ecological universes," says Newsome. On the northern side, where dingoes still roam, there is a reasonably balanced ecosystem. On the southern side, kangaroos, emus, and other large herbivores have run amok. They eat so much vegetation that researchers have clocked the difference between the two zones from space. And without dingoes to keep them in check, cats, red foxes, and other more recently introduced predators tear into small marsupials and rodents, decimating their populations.

This imbalance is so stark that it has come back around to affect the livestock industry. Although they may sleep easier without fear of being carried off, sheep and other grazers now have to compete with wild herbivores for pasture. In fact, some economic analyses have suggested that ripping down the fence would have "a net economic benefit," says Newsome.

For now, dingo vigilance continues: The Australian government puts $10 million (AUD) per year into maintaining the fence and is considering proposals to expand it.

❯ **How to see it:** Visit the northern end of the fence, in Jandowae, Queensland. There you can find plaques and statues related to the fence and see it stretching into the distance.

Mala

Three decades after near-extinction, these tiny marsupials have returned to the wild.

LOCATION: Newhaven Wildlife Sanctuary, central Australia

SPECIES: Mala or rufous hare-wallaby (*Lagorchestes hirsutus*)

◆ Australia has suffered more extinctions than any other country. According to one count, 34 mammals have disappeared since European colonization 230 years ago, from the Tasmanian tiger—which hopeful diehards still search for in the bush—to the Bramble Cay melomys, considered the first mammal to go extinct due to climate change.

The mala could have been a statistic—one more bad news story in this grim catalog. In 1991, it disappeared from the wild. Instead, thanks to the perseverance of those who care about it, the species is making a comeback.

Although the mala looks like a foot-tall kangaroo, it's actually the mainland Australian subspecies of the rufous hare-wallaby. Each mala has a distinguished white mustache, shaggy red fur with silver highlights, and a tail the color of sand. Primarily solitary and nocturnal, they seek refuge from the sun in shallow burrows, emerging after dark to feed on leaves and desert grasses. When startled, they explode from their hiding places and bound away in frenetic zigzags.

Historically, the mala's home range was vast, extending across the arid zones of South Australia, Western Australia, and the Northern Territory. For the Aboriginal people who inhabit these deserts—the Warlpiri, Pintupi, Luritja, and Pitjantjatjara—the mala plays a vital role in the stories from what is known as Jukurrpa, or the Dreaming, a period when Earth was created and marking the beginning of its creatures, natural features, and laws. The mala Jukurrpa begins in the dry spinifex country of the Great Sandy Desert. From there, the mala's ancestors spread out across the land, creating landmarks as they went.

As recently as the 1950s, these marsupials remained abundant. But as feral foxes and cats expanded into desert regions, mala numbers plummeted. By the early 1990s, only a small, disparate, and fast-disappearing population held out in the remote Tanami Desert. With time running out, scientists took the planet's last wild mala into captivity.

For nearly three decades, there were no naturally occurring wild populations. Scientists began a captive breeding program at different sites across Central Australia, and numbers rose rapidly. The first efforts failed—in 1997, a single fox wiped out more than 50 mala. Finally, in 2019, Australian Wildlife Conservancy scientists and Indigenous Warlpiri rangers released 100 mala into an enclosed 40-square-mile (104 sq km) area at Newhaven Wildlife Sanctuary in the Great Sandy Desert, from which feral cats had been eradicated.

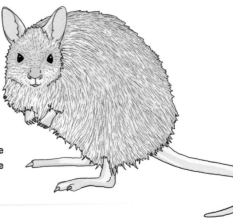

It was a homecoming: Not only does Newhaven lie within the mala's former range, but the most sacred site of the Mala Dreaming story is near the enclosure. For the first time in a generation, the mala were back where they belong. ❯ **How to see them:** In the wild, they're found only in the Australian Wildlife Conservancy's Newhaven Wildlife Sanctuary. To see them in captivity, try Alice Springs Desert Park.

THE WILD LIFE OF **A Warlpiri Ranger**

■ Alice Ellis, a member of the Warlpiri people, has lived her whole life in the Great Sandy Desert. She is a ranger with the Australian Wildlife Conservancy and played a leading role in tracking and eradicating feral cats from the enclosure where mala were reintroduced in 2019.

• **When and where were you born?**
I was born in the desert, out in the bush, a long time ago, in 1951. Back then, many Warlpiri and Pintupi people still lived in the desert.

• **What was the best thing about growing up in the desert?**

Spending time with my family out in the bush, going hunting, and getting bush tucker [traditional Indigenous foods], like bush tomatoes, bush onions, and bush potatoes. Good food, not sugar and flour.

• **Did you go to school?**
No school. There are no schools out there. Only bush school.

My mother and my father taught me to track the animals. They took us out as soon as we could walk. We learned by listening, by walking through country, and by watching how the elders did it. In Warlpiri language we call it yitakimani, which

means "reading the country." We tracked pussycats, goannas, mala. When we see a track on top of the other tracks, we know it's fresh and we follow it. We learned things like that. Some people hunt now in cars, but we follow the tracks by walking.

• **When you were growing up, did you see mala?**
There were lots of mala out in the bush. We used to hunt them. They live down burrows. We'd follow the tracks to their burrows and pull them out. Sometimes people burned the country, then

hunted them with spears. For a long time, we didn't see any mala. Too many pussycats. Now the mala are all gone. They're only here at Newhaven. We're rangers now. We bring back the animals.

• **Can you tell me about the Mala Dreaming story?**

The mala started not far from here. One old man mala went to Uluru, the other went that way, to the north, into the Tanami Desert. We know all the sites where old man mala camped on his journey. Our elders told us.

• **What are the most important lessons and traditional knowledge for young people to learn?**

This knowledge is very important. If we don't pass it on, it might get lost when there are no elders. Most important is to take the young people out [to the] bush so they can learn about the animals and bush tucker and bush medicine. It's better for the young people out here, not like in the towns. I don't like going to town. Much better here in the desert. ■

Night Parrots

The world's elusive birds

RANGE: The Australian outback, including southwestern Queensland and inland regions of Western Australia
SPECIES: Night parrot (*Pezoporus occidentalis*)

◆ The night parrot gets its name from a simple fact: It is one of two known nocturnal parrot species. (The other, the kākāpō, is from nearby New Zealand—see page 402.)

Night parrots were once widespread, documented by early natural historians across Australia's deserts until 1912. At that point, they seemingly vanished from existence. Bird-watchers, biologists, and state surveyors combed the deserts—where these parrots had been known to forage and nest among the spinifex—and came up with nary a feather.

As the decades passed, many believed the night parrot had been lost to extinction. But in 1990, hope was renewed: A dead night parrot was found on a roadside.

So began the frantic search for a living specimen. But the Australian outback is a vast expanse, with plenty of room for a shy parrot to hide. Another wasn't found until 2006, and it too was dead.

Then, in 2013, a breakthrough: Naturalist John Young captured the first evidence of a living night parrot in modern history when he snapped images of one in Western Queensland. Two years later, researchers Steve Murphy and Rachel Barr became the first people to capture and tag a live night parrot, with the hope of using the data to help protect the species.

As time goes on, more is being learned about the birds who evaded sight for a century, including their interesting nesting habits, which involve concealing their eggs at the end of a tunnel that they create by chewing and shaping spinifex grass. Some recent discoveries provide hope that other populations are hiding across Australia's arid expanse; the species' high-pitched piping and soft croaks have been recorded in the Great Sandy Desert by Ngururrpa and Kiwirrkurra rangers and in the Pilbara region by Martu rangers.

For a long time, most knowledge of the night parrot came from records made before the 1900s.

There's one thing we know for sure: A bird this hard to find must be rare. Experts estimate there are fewer than 500 night parrots left, each in danger of being caught by a feral cat or a poacher or rotisseried by a bushfire. When the Pullen Pullen Reserve was established to protect this fragile population, researchers decided not to share its location with the public, figuring this is one night parrot secret that is best kept. ❯ **How to see them:** The exact location of the night parrot conservation area is kept secret, but if you find yourself out at dusk among the grass tussocks of the outback, you may just strike bird-watching gold and catch a glimpse of one.

ANTARCTICA

Antarctic Midges

This continent's largest endemic land animal is a small insect.

RANGE: Antarctica's northwest peninsula and surrounding islands
SPECIES: Antarctic midge (*Belgica antarctica*)

◆ In most places, midges don't command much respect, inspiring annoyance and vague shooing motions and disappearing by the billions into the mouths of larger creatures.

At the bottom of the world, though, everything is topsy-turvy. The Antarctic midge is the largest land animal endemic to the continent. In other words, Africa and Asia have elephants, North America has bison, and Antarctica has the midge.

Antarctic midges are flightless, long-limbed, and about the size of sugar ants. They live in ice-free areas near colonies of seals and penguins, who bring nutrients to Antarctica's otherwise low-cal soil by going out to sea, eating lots of fish, and coming back on land to poop. Mosses and other plants grow in this soil, and the midges eat these plants as they decay. Because nothing eats them in turn, they are, in a way, at the top of their little food chain—another strange place for a midge.

The species has endured a lot to take this high position. About 40 million years ago, when Antarctica first split off from South America and began to drift, "there were probably thousands of insects living down there," says Nicholas Teets, an entomologist at the University of Kentucky and an expert on the midge. As the continent became colder and drier, the rest of them died off. Somehow, these midges persisted, even through long periods when their entire home was layered thickly with ice. They may have found tiny thawed pockets or hunkered down underneath the glaciers, Teets says.

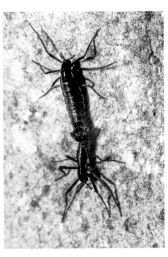

A couple of the biggest land animals endemic to Antarctica

In the process, the midges evolved an arsenal of strategies that allow them to live relatively comfortably. They got rid of their wings—likely to reduce heat loss, along with their chances of getting blown away—and a lot of extra DNA in their genome, giving them one of the smallest known genomes of any insect. Their streamlined genetic toolkit is focused on metabolic control and environmental responses and underlies a mysterious Popsicle-ification process that allows the midges to dehydrate themselves and literally freeze. Unlike their northern cousins, who can be born and die in a single season, Antarctic midges take two years to go from egg to adult, emerging to feed only in the relatively balmy summers (which last from December through February) and spending the rest of their time frozen underground.

These midges do have something in common with others, though: They form their own kind of swarm. When hunting for study subjects, Teets and his colleagues sometimes find up to 40,000 larvae in a single desk-sized patch of dirt—a gathering of future kings. ❯ **How to see them:** Look for a wet, iceless area with some moss and grass, and start flipping over rocks.

Southerly Bouquets

A two-bloom posy in an icy desert

◆ Red roses mean passion. Zinnias are for steadfastness. But if you're trying to send a message of true devotion, consider a more unusual bouquet: pearlwort and hairgrass, the only two flowering plants that can hack it in Antarctica.

Even among deserts, Antarctica is a tough sell for plants thanks to its heady mix of cold, darkness, drought, and wind. Most of the species that make it here are mosses, lichens, and liverworts, which are able to (figuratively) keep their heads down, passing nutrients quietly from cell to cell and growing slowly outward as opportunities arise.

Pearlwort and hair grass stick their necks out instead. As vascular or flowering plants, they must maintain different body parts—roots, leaves, shoots, and flowers—and transport water and nutrients between them.

RANGE: The South Orkney Islands, the South Shetland Islands, and along the western Antarctic Peninsula

SPECIES: Antarctic pearlwort (*Colobanthus quitensis*) and Antarctic hair grass (*Deschampsia antarctica*)

Pearlwort stands only 2 inches (5 cm) high. In the summer, it blooms with tiny buttercup-like flowers, which nestle into the rest of its mossy greenery like pins in a cushion. Hair grass has slender green blades and grows in roughly foot-wide tufts, often among rocks. It's anchored by very strong roots that draw water from deep underground, where it isn't locked in by ice. While hair grass plants on the coasts can be several inches tall, those in the coldest and most wind-exposed sites grow only about the height of a thimble and have folded blades.

For nutrients, both plant species rely mostly on penguin and seal manure, which is produced in quantities that occasionally smother them. They respond to the long cold winters by going dormant, and to the harsh light of summer by producing protective chemicals that shield them from UV rays. They are pollinated by the wind, as there are no flying insects to help them out. They can also self-pollinate, just in case. As the Antarctic warms, the plants, especially the hair grass, have been taking advantage and are being found in new places.

If you want to gather your own flower-and-grass Antarctic bouquet, you too will have to endure wind, cold, and penguin poop. You will also have to travel to and from the continent, dodge the plant-trafficking authorities, and explain exactly what these strange small blossoms are and why they're cool. Honestly, it might be easier to grab some roses. ❭ **How to see them: Visit during the summer, when these plants come out of dormancy and are hard to miss. Both are most common in rocky coastal areas.**

Hair grass (left) and pearlwort manage to bloom despite the icy, dark conditions.

You Snooze, You Lose

The best time to pick flowers in Antarctica was about 90 million years ago, during the Cretaceous period. At that point, the continent was not a frozen expanse but a dense temperate rainforest, similar to those currently found in New Zealand. When researchers pull up sediment cores from the continent, the layer corresponding to the Cretaceous period is so stuffed with pollen, fossilized roots, and bits of dead flowers that it is a different color from the layers above and below it, forming a kind of stripe of life.

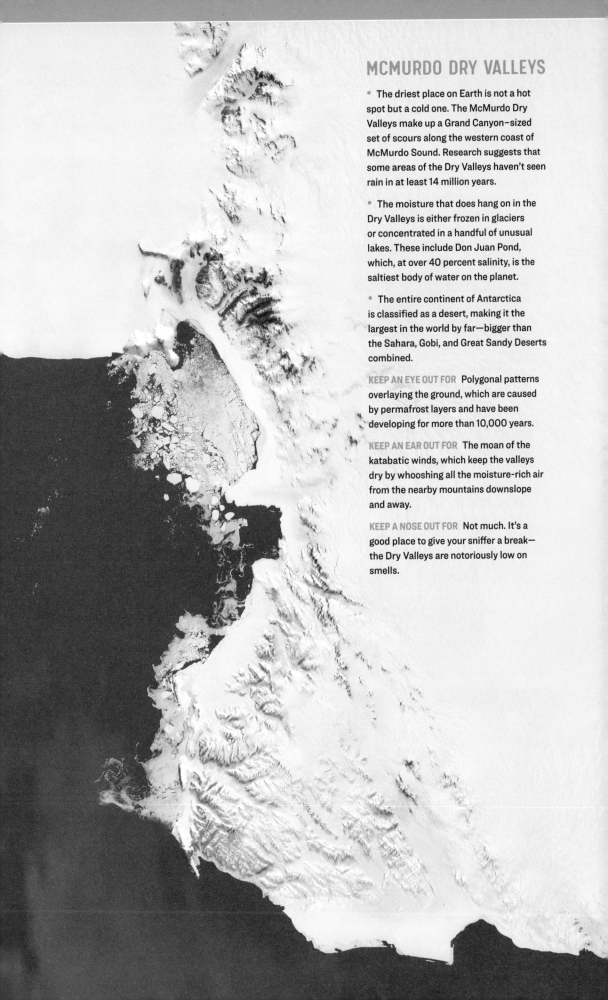

MCMURDO DRY VALLEYS

- The driest place on Earth is not a hot spot but a cold one. The McMurdo Dry Valleys make up a Grand Canyon–sized set of scours along the western coast of McMurdo Sound. Research suggests that some areas of the Dry Valleys haven't seen rain in at least 14 million years.

- The moisture that does hang on in the Dry Valleys is either frozen in glaciers or concentrated in a handful of unusual lakes. These include Don Juan Pond, which, at over 40 percent salinity, is the saltiest body of water on the planet.

- The entire continent of Antarctica is classified as a desert, making it the largest in the world by far—bigger than the Sahara, Gobi, and Great Sandy Deserts combined.

KEEP AN EYE OUT FOR Polygonal patterns overlaying the ground, which are caused by permafrost layers and have been developing for more than 10,000 years.

KEEP AN EAR OUT FOR The moan of the katabatic winds, which keep the valleys dry by whooshing all the moisture-rich air from the nearby mountains downslope and away.

KEEP A NOSE OUT FOR Not much. It's a good place to give your sniffer a break— the Dry Valleys are notoriously low on smells.

Tiny Yet Tough

Y ou might not want to live in the McMurdo Dry Valleys, but a number of microscopic creatures manage it just fine. Here are a few.

NEMATODES · Antarctic nematodes (*Scottnema lindsayae*) are the hardiest and most prolific worms in the Dry Valleys. Like other southerly bugs, they spend their summers enjoying feasts of bacteria and yeast, as well as sexual reproduction, and their winters in cryptobiosis, a deathlike state of suspended animation.

To survive the extreme cold, these tiny Houdinis lower their freezing point and produce packing peanut–like proteins in order to protect themselves from shards of ice. If it's both cold *and* dry where they are, they freeze-dry themselves into little Cheetos, halting their metabolism. Like deep-space astronauts in hibernation, they sleep while getting blown around by Antarctic storms, sometimes on grains of sand or pebbles, until they encounter water, rehydrate, and reanimate themselves. Just how long they can snooze is a mystery. ❶

TARDIGRADES · Under a microscope, a tardigrade (*Tardigrada* spp.) looks like a cross between a gummy bear and a pug. These chubby eight-legged creatures are aquatic but can't swim. Instead, they wiggle and paw through liquid like puppies walking on ice, adorable and bumbling.

But don't let their cuteness fool you: Tardigrades are just about the toughest animals on the planet. Of the 1,300 tardie species roaming Earth, eight are able to live in the Dry Valleys—in glaciers, on lake shores, and in super-dry, wind-scoured soils.

Like nematodes, tardigrades survive extreme Antarctic temperatures and lack of water through

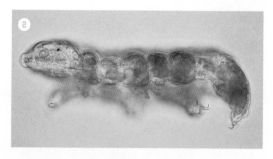

cryptobiosis. When dormant tardigrades encounter liquid water, they reanimate into their wriggly selves once more.

They are so good at weathering extreme environments that some tardigrades have actual astronaut experience—researchers from several countries have taken them into orbit to see whether they could withstand the temperature, vacuum, and cosmic radiation of outer space. They seemed unperturbed. (Some even found it a fitting situation in which to reproduce.)

This makes them the only animal that has survived unprotected outside of our atmosphere. Tardigrades may be a bit clumsy-looking, but with a resume like that, the Dry Valleys are a cakewalk. ❷

BLOOD FALLS · In the largest snow-free patch of its desert, Antarctica has a nosebleed. To be specific, the snout of the Taylor Glacier oozes blood-red liquid into Lake Bonney.

Although early Antarctic visitors assumed that algae created the hue, the "blood" in Blood Falls is the result of the iron in this saltwater oxidizing—the same process that rusts metal. The water, which is three times brinier than most seawater and does not freeze, is a remnant of an ancient ocean that has been trapped under the glacier for more than 1.5 million years. It holds the descendants of prehistoric bacteria, like a liquid time capsule.

The bacteria, cut off from light and oxygen for generations, have adapted to feed on the plentiful sulfur and iron compounds in the water. Their survival in these extreme conditions may offer clues to the early days of life on Earth, before the planet had an oxygenated atmosphere, and hint at how primordial life might exist under ice on moons or other planets. Indeed, Blood Falls is considered to be the place on Earth most similar to Mars, thanks to its climate and geology. (The red color helps, too.) ❸

THE WILD LIFE OF **A Microbe Moviemaker**

■ In 2018, Ariel Waldman spent five weeks in Antarctica, including the McMurdo Dry Valleys, filming life at a microbial scale. Her final project, *Life Under the Ice* (sponsored by the National Science Foundation and the National Geographic Society), is a virtual microscope showcasing the many tiny creatures who inhabit this polar oasis and are usually overlooked.

● **How and why did you become a microbial wildlife filmmaker?**
My degree is in graphic design. In 2008, I unexpectedly got a job at NASA, which completely changed my perspective on how I could participate in science. While there, I heard about amazing Antarctic research with analogs to Mars and other places in our solar system. Becoming a microscopist and going to Antarctica was my version of becoming an astronaut.

Many biologists study creatures in Antarctica in great detail but may only take one or two photos of them, which often get hidden behind scientific publications' paywalls. Filming microscopic creatures reveals them to people all over the globe and helps researchers understand microbial behaviors.

It's the difference between flipping through a book of wildlife photos versus seeing a documentary where you watch animals go about their day.

● **Why film microbes in Antarctica specifically?**
A lot of people think Antarctica is barren and lifeless, that there's just penguins there and nothing else. Antarctic microbes show the continent is full of life. It would be sad not to have these really unique ecosystems captured on film now so we can compare them to how they might look in 20 years.

● **How do Antarctic extremophiles inform our search for life in outer space?**
We know from studying Earth that once life takes off on a planet, it clings to that planet everywhere it can. If another planet or a moon has life, it's not going to be a single microbe hanging on for dear life. It might be closer to a binary—someplace either has life or it doesn't.

What form that life takes is a different matter. When looking in extreme environments like the Dry Valleys for microbial life—which is what we suspect life would be like

on moons in our solar system—we learn what type of equipment and knowledge we need to be able to detect life as we *don't* know it.

Certain types of imaging or chemical analysis might miss life because we're looking for the wrong things or searching in the wrong way. Some propose detecting motility as a way of discovering life on other planets, which ties into microscopic wildlife filmmaking because the vast majority of life moves. Some life moves at an extremely slow pace, maybe even over decades, but all of it moves either itself or at the cellular level.

● **Was there anything that surprised you about microbes on the ice or about Antarctica?**
Even though my expedition proposal was about Antarctica being full of life, I didn't know just how rich in life it is until I got there. I expected it might take a while to find certain microbes, but once I got samples from the sea floor and inside glaciers it took seconds to find life. It's grounding to see just how full of life Antarctica is. ■

Ariel Waldman's work can be seen at lifeundertheice.org.

3

Algae Blooms

A new paintbrush comes to Antarctica.

◆ Traditionally, Antarctica viewed from above has been one of Earth's most minimalist sights—a foreboding blot of ice white, gray, and blue.

But in recent years, some color has crept in. As climate change warms Antarctica and its surrounding ocean, algae have been taking advantage, parking themselves in melting snow and turning huge swaths of the coast red, green, and orange.

Like many of Antarctica's living things, algae are powered by sunlight and excrement. Blooms tend to occur along the coast, where summer temperatures rise just above freezing, turning snow into slushy water and allowing the algae to reproduce. As the tiny plantlike organisms sate themselves with nitrates from seal and seabird poop, they multiply wildly, spreading their color—which may be green from chloroplasts or red or orange from sun-protective pigments—across the snow.

The same phenomenon has been occurring in snowy climates across the world, with algae causing blooms from the French Alps (where locals call the red snow sang de glacier, "glacier blood") to Greenland's ice sheets, which become bruised in the summers with purple and brown. In Antarctica, blooms have been growing more dense and prevalent: A satellite study from 2020 found 1,679 separate lime-green splotches covering a combined area of about .73 square miles (2 sq km), roughly the size of Monaco.

Researchers are unsure of the long-term effects of algae blooms. On the one hand, changing the color of snow tends to lower its melting point, hastening the demise of glaciers and snowpacks. On the other, the algae themselves gobble up so much CO_2 that, in Antarctica at least, they actually serve as carbon sinks.

Don't eat the green snow.

If the continent continues warming as predicted, snow will likely disappear from Antarctica's islands and low coastal fields altogether, taking the algae with it. But melting will continue on higher ground, allowing the colors to seep closer to the continent's icy heart. **❯ How to see them:** Aerial imagery—or a summer helicopter ride over the Antarctic continent—gives the best views of this phenomenon.

RANGE: Along the Antarctic Peninsula and its islands
SPECIES: Many types of algae, including *Sanguina* spp. and *Hydrurus* spp.

Mummified Seals

No one is quite sure why these seals came here . . . but we know why they stayed.

◆ On Antarctica's Lake Bonney, plunked on top of a layer of ice, there lies a long-dead seal. This seal is many miles from the coast, where his living relatives are diving, hunting, and sliding around. His yellowing body is on its back, flippers in the air, as if to say, "Why did I come here again?"

Most nonmicroscopic creatures don't enter the McMurdo Dry Valleys—after all, there isn't much for them there. But since the early twentieth century, human visitors to the valleys have repeatedly stumbled across the mummified carcasses of seals, often very far from the shores they're meant to frequent.

LOCATION: Across the McMurdo Dry Valleys
SPECIES: Crabeater seals (*Lobodon carcinophaga*), Weddell seals (*Leptonychotes weddellii*), leopard seals (*Hydrurga leptonyx*), and others

It's unclear where these lonely pinnipeds were scooting off to, or why. One member of Robert Scott's 1901 *Discovery* expedition, Edward Wilson, reported the remains of "old seals" on the tops of high glaciers and wrote that they must be retiring there to die in peace.

Newer observations suggest that most of the mummified seals are young. Currently, the leading theory is that they got disoriented during snowstorms and wandered into the desert instead of back to shore. A straight line of tracks found behind one mummy suggests a seal hell-bent on wherever she thought she was going—an idea bolstered by stories of two Antarctic teams who have seen seals headed into the McMurdo Dry Valleys and tried in vain to point them back in the right direction.

A mummified seal can weather the centuries.

After the seals die, the dry climate preserves their bodies until the wind disintegrates them. During a recent study, researchers found and examined hundreds of mummified seals in the Dry Valleys and found that some had been there for centuries—monuments to their own mistakes. ❯ **How to see them: There is a mummified seal outside Discovery Hut in McMurdo Sound. For others, find someone who has seen one and ask them where to go.**

Antarctic Animal Explorers

An international treaty passed in 1994 bans the introduction of nonnative animals to Antarctica. Before that, though, explorers loved nothing more than bringing unsuspecting pets, working animals, and stowaways on their journeys south. Here is a timeline of some notable animal visitors.

1899

The *Southern Cross* expedition, from Britain, included dozens of Samoyed sled dogs. When the ship first landed at Cape Adare, the human and canine explorers were greeted by several hundred curious Adélie penguins, who quickly waddled up to them. The dogs went on to kill a "heartbreaking" number of the birds, wrote expedition cartographer William Colbeck. From then on, the explorers chained the dogs up when they were in penguin territory.

1903

After the Swedish ship *Antarctic* foundered in the Weddell Sea, the crew ran across an ice floe to nearby Paulet Island, managing to bring along the ship's cat and her newborn kitten. While the cat eventually died, the kitten lived with the stranded crew, ate seal and penguin, and was rescued along with her human companions the following summer.

1910

Crew member Tom Crean snuck a pregnant rabbit onto Captain Robert Scott's disastrous *Terra Nova* expedition, hiding her among hay bales meant for the group's ponies. She had 17 kits on Christmas Day, which Crean distributed among his shipmates.

1933

To sate his crew's thirst for milk—and his own for publicity—Admiral Richard E. Byrd brought three Guernsey cows to Antarctica on the SS *Jacob Ruppert*, along with 10 tons of feed, various farm equipment, and a milking machine. When one gave birth on the ship, the crew named the calf Iceberg.

1960

Hoping to determine whether animals' circadian rhythms are affected by their sense of Earth's rotation, scientist Karl Hamner brought hamsters, cockroaches, fruit flies, cocklebur plants, bean plants, and a *Neurospora* fungus down to the South Pole. Hamner's experiments didn't show any correlation, but some of his guests caught on. Fellow scientists cultivated the bean plants and oversaw several generations of hamsters, even hosting hamster obstacle races during one winter celebration.

Inanimate Zones

Even life has its limits (maybe).

LOCATION: Dry, high-elevation soils in the Transantarctic Mountains (84–85°S, 174–177°W)

SPECIES: None!

◆ Life can hack it almost anywhere. Microscopic bacteria, archaea, and fungi live in the boiling mouths of geysers, hop onto lava as soon as it cools, and swim happily inside high-pressure deep-sea vents.

But there are some places they haven't yet conquered. Researchers recently sampled dirt from hundreds of areas in the Transantarctic Mountains and looked for any signs of genetic material or metabolic activity. Most of the dirt was full of microorganisms or their traces. But in a few cases, they found something that shocked them: absolutely nothing.

Antarctic soil is unlike your average spadeful. Without much organic matter to round it out, it's basically a broken-down version of the geological formations all around it. "It looks like a bunch of small rocks," says Nicholas Dragone, one member of the team at the University of Colorado in Boulder who has been sifting through the dirt.

The soil in the peaks and valleys of the Transantarctic Mountains, which slice down the continent from the Weddell to the Ross Sea, is particularly inhospitable—dry, salty, cold, and sunstruck. Some of it has probably lingered in one place, exposed to the elements and essentially unchanged, for millions of years. Still, most of the samples the team collected were home to small communities, averaging 205 bacteria species and five types of fungus.

As the soil samples came from higher up and farther inland, though, diversity dropped. And in several of them—those from the tallest, driest, saltiest, and most exposed spots—the researchers didn't find any signs of life at all, not even a proverbial microbial nail clipping. To the team's knowledge, this was the first time such a discovery (or non-discovery, as it were) had been made.

Roberts Massif is one of the least lively places this planet has to offer.

Just because we haven't found life in these soils doesn't mean it's not there, Dragone says. There are always more tests to be run. And as Antarctica gets warmer and wetter, life may find a way in its most difficult places as well.

For now, though, he and his colleagues are excited to look deeper. These inanimate zones could help us refine the ways we check for biological material, provide analogs for other planets, and let us narrow down what, of all the extreme conditions on offer in Antarctica, made microbes draw the line. Plus, sometimes you just want to be alone. ❯ **How to see them:** There aren't a lot of good reasons to go up into the Transantarctic Mountains, but if you do find yourself there, the most lifeless areas studied so far are Roberts Massif and Schroeder Hill.

Last Fungus Standing

Of all the types of life, bacteria and archaea are widely considered to be the best at tolerating extreme environments. But when researchers were testing samples of Antarctic dirt for signs of life, they often found fungi were the last holdouts, present in samples that appeared to have no bacteria at all.

One species, a slow-growing black fungus, was especially tenacious, and often the only living thing found at very high elevations. The researchers found it was fairly closely related to fungi of the genus *Cladophialophora*—which are known for growing in very challenging conditions, including inside of dishwashers.

CHAPTER 5

◆

Shallows & Deeps

Some experts think life began in the deep sea, about 3.5 billion years ago. Miles below sea level, in a pocket of chemical soup spat out by a hydrothermal vent, molecules crashed and combined until they formed something discrete and self-replicating.

That tiny pioneer's descendants now live on all continents—high in trees or on mountains, deep in caves or buried in desert sand. But many stayed in (or returned to) the ocean, which remains a cauldron of instantiations.

In the shallows, where land and sea entwine, beings of all shapes and sizes move between realms. Orcas beach themselves to chase down seals, while trees bend to the will of offshore winds. Fish walk and rays fly.

In open waters, where resources we land dwellers see as indispensable are nowhere to be found, organisms make their own way. At the surface, the world's only oceanic insects skate, living out their whole lives thousands of miles from shore. Heading down, as colors of the rainbow blink out one by one until no light is left, swimmers find new ways to see. At the bottom, in the cold, blackness, and crushing pressure, crews of industrious microbes support dancing crabs, red-tipped tubeworms, and snails who forge shells from volcanic iron.

Connections and cycles are vivid in the ocean, where water churns everything into contact. Corals send gametes to mingle by the light of the moon. Sea slugs borrow attributes from sponges and algae, gaining special powers. Blue whales subsist on krill, transforming tiny animals into the world's largest. When the whales die, they sink to the bottom, where whole communities are brought to life by their flesh and bones.

The ocean is most of our planet. It wraps islands and embraces continents, concocts weather and, through its currents and pumps, runs many of Earth's essential functions. But humans learn about the ocean very slowly: One estimate suggests that 91 percent of marine species remain undescribed. Their home, familiar and mysterious, is all around us. Let's sink in.

Contributor list: *Richard Constantine Arghiris, Chris Baraniuk, Sita Bates, Ashley Braun, Christina Couch, Elyse DeFranco, Jenny Elliott, Kate Evans, Leah Fabel, Rosie Flanagan, Rachel Fritts, Claudia Geib, Kate Golembiewski, Mara Grunbaum, Alice Harman, Michael Hunt, Myles Karp, Alexandra Keeler, JoAnna Klein, Bill Kte'pi, Krista Langlois, Matt Lilley, Matt Malinowski, T. J. Olwig, Amir Sadiq, Keegan Sentner, Melissa Scott Sinclair, Cassidy Ward, Patricia Kelly Yeo, Lauren J. Young*

OCEANIA

Sponge Crabs
Leaders in crustacean fashion

◆ The seafloor is full of inspiring costuming materials. Some crustaceans looking to craft a disguise pluck up colorful shells to hide inside or use their dexterous claws to scrap together seaweed capes.

It's the world's sponge crabs, though, who are on the cutting edge of sustainable fashion. These marine milliners don living garments made of some obliging neighbors: sea sponges.

The sponge "caps," as marine biologists call them, are true fascinators. The sheer variety of sponges used, along with the crabs' deft shaping, makes for an array of forms worthy of a royal garden party. Some hats are fluffy and velvety; others are spiny and bulky. Western Australian Museum curator Andrew Hosie once saw a sponge crab strutting across the seafloor underneath a branching, log-like sponge about three times its own width—truly daring. And some crabs instead wear sea squirts, which tend to yield a more avant-garde look.

Crabs and their hats bond for life. Wielding her front two pincers, a young crab will snip pieces of a nearby sponge and place the clippings snugly on her body, like a series of small berets. The sponge—which can regenerate a full body from fragments—survives the process and grows over the crab, molding to her shape. When a crab sheds her exoskeleton, she holds onto her sponge, which provides safety as her new shell hardens.

Hat pins are required: To secure the sponge in place, the crab uses two of her smaller hind legs to hold on to the sponge throughout her life. "I would like to know how they actually do it without getting cramps," says Hosie. Perhaps, as the French say, il faut souffrir pour être belle: Beauty is pain.

The work is worth it for the crabs. A well-made sponge cap provides both camouflage and active defense, as many sponge species produce toxic or bad-tasting chemicals that drive away predators. (Imagine a bonnet that also sprays mace.) Others conceal skeletal frameworks that can be sharp and tough to munch on within deceptively soft, furry-looking bodies.

It's unclear, though, whether the sponges get anything out of the relationship. Hosie says traveling around on crabs may slightly expand the otherwise sedentary sponges' range—but the crabs aren't known to move incredibly great distances. Perhaps they simply enjoy taking part in an ongoing fashion movement. ❯ **How to see them:** Sponge crabs are difficult to see—in addition to their effective hats, many are nocturnal and deep-dwelling. A few species can be found in the shallows; seek them out in the evening, showing off their looks as they scavenge for dead marine creatures and plants.

RANGE: Throughout the Mediterranean and the Atlantic and Pacific Oceans. Species are more diverse and abundant in the Indo-Pacific regions and around the Philippines, Malaysia, and Indonesia.

SPECIES: Crabs in the family Dromiidae. Notable members of the 130 or so species include the sleepy crab (*Dromia personata*) and the furred sponge crab (*Pseudodromia latens*).

A sponge crab shows off a well-maintained living sponge hat.

GREAT BARRIER REEF

- The world's largest living structure, the Great Barrier Reef underpins 133,000 square miles (21,000 sq km) of the Coral Sea, off the coast of northeastern Australia. If the area housing the reef were a country, it would be the world's 65th largest.

- The Great Barrier Reef is home to one of the world's smallest vertebrate species, the stout infantfish—adults are as long as a pencil is wide—as well as the world's largest bivalve species, the giant clam, which can weigh as much as a baby grand piano.

- Visitors can send mail postmarked from the Great Barrier Reef, using a special post office box located on the Agincourt Reef.

KEEP AN EYE OUT FOR Colorful fish! Ten percent of the world's fish species live in the Great Barrier Reef, and many are quite flashy, from parrotfish, who look glowstick-painted, to clownfish, who stick out like traffic cones. Coral reefs are great homes for colorful fish— the clear water lets them show off, while the many nooks and crannies give even the most visible a place to hide when necessary.

KEEP AN EAR OUT FOR The fizzy crackle of snapping shrimp, who stun their prey by snapping their large claws. Animals may use this sound as a beacon to locate the reef.

KEEP A NOSE OUT FOR The smell of stressed-out corals. As climate change warms the Coral Sea, the Great Barrier Reef is suffering from increasingly frequent and severe bleaching events, during which the algae that help support the coral flee. Recent research suggests that before they bleach, the coral smell different—and worse—somewhere between low-tide seaweed and rotting cabbage.

Synchronized Coral Spawning

The world's largest living structure renews itself in nights of moonlit passion.

RANGE: 1,400 miles (2,250 km) of reef in the Coral Sea, off the coast of Queensland

SPECIES: The Great Barrier Reef is made up of hundreds of species of coral, many of which participate in full-moon spawning events.

◆ Once a year, the corals of Australia's Great Barrier Reef pull off an orgy so massive it can be seen from space. Warmed by the water, tugged by the tides, and sparked by the full moon, coral polyps release eggs and sperm in a vast cloud. The buoyant bundles of gametes rise to the surface, forming vast slicks shaped by ocean currents.

As adults, the tiny animals that build and make up coral reefs are immobile, stuck in their own magnificent skeletons. They reproduce asexually throughout the year, cloning themselves into expanding colonies.

But because they cannot swim to find each other, they must achieve the genetic reshuffling that comes from sexual reproduction in a different way. Most use a signal that is both reliable and romantic: the full moon.

Polyps detect the moon's state with cryptochromes, a type of receptor that can sense blue light. Different species wait different lengths of time after the full moon to let loose, generally between three and five days. "They're very synchronized," says Muhammad Abdul Wahab, a benthic ecologist at the Australian Institute of Marine Science. Some species patiently hold their gametes until the right time and then let them go. Others spew without warning, like volcanoes. Mushroom corals—which are solitary, enormous polyps—become visibly plump and then, about 30 minutes before sunset, eject their eggs. If you're diving around the reef at the right time, you'll see and feel a flurry of coral reproductive packets in hues of red, orange, and yellow.

Once the bundles reach the surface, wave action breaks them apart and fertilization occurs. Within 24 hours, tiny coral embryos develop. The resulting larvae, most no bigger than sesame seeds, drift here and there.

After four or five days of mobility—the only time these animals will experience movement—the larvae sink to the seabed and decide where to settle. They must find a place populated by the symbiotic algae upon which they depend while avoiding being eaten by a grazing fish or bulldozed by a snail. Wherever they end up, Wahab explains, "they have to be content for the rest of their lives."

As the coral polyps begin constructing their calcium carbonate skeletons, they're rebuilding the Great Barrier Reef, which has been severely damaged by the warming and acidification of ocean waters. If they survive and grow, they too will get the chance to participate in the moonlit rite that regenerates this living structure. ❯ **How to see it:** Scuba diving is the best way to experience this event for yourself. Check with local dive shops to coordinate your visit, because timing is everything. Great Barrier Reef coral typically spawn during the first week of the full moon in October or November.

When the moon hits your polyps...

Common Reef Cuttlefish

Rainbows hiding in plain sight

LOCATION: Eastern Pacific waters from southern Japan to northern Australia, and along shallow Indian Ocean coasts

SPECIES: Common reef cuttlefish (*Sepia latimanus*), also known as broadclub cuttlefish

◆ The turquoise-blue waters of the South Pacific are home to masters of disguise so versatile they can practically become invisible: common reef cuttlefish.

Cuttlefish are cephalopods, like octopuses and squid, and look a bit like a cross between them. A small torpedo-shaped mantle rests atop eight short, grasping arms and two long tentacles. In common reef cuttlefish, one of more than 120 cuttlefish species, the arms on either side of that mantle have evolved into thicker, crescent-shaped limbs, inspiring their other nickname, the broadclub cuttlefish.

All cuttlefish species share a skin-deep knack for disguise. At will, a cuttlefish can change individual sections of her skin to nearly any color, from the mottled sandy brown of the seafloor to the fiery flame red of a coral.

This artistry is achieved through the cuttlefish's precise orchestration of millions of special skin cells called chromatophores. Contracting the muscles around these cells reveals the different red, brown, black, or yellow colors stored in pigment sacs within them. Relaxing the muscles reverts the skin to its original color—usually a sandy tan or light brown.

Common reef cuttlefish can change their skin colors and patterns at will.

A cuttlefish controls these colors with her brain, choosing when and how to flex the specific muscles that reveal different pigments. In labs, scientists sometimes use these flickering hues as a measure of neural activity—essentially, watching cuttlefish think with their skin.

Cuttlefish can flex another set of muscles, called papillae, to raise their skin into bumps and spikes. By adopting different shapes and patterns, the cuttlefish can take on the appearance of rocks, coral, barnacles, algae, and even other ocean species. They use these disguises to ambush smaller prey and to hide from their own predators.

To catch more difficult prey, they have a special strategy. As a common cuttlefish approaches a crab, for instance, she extends those broad outer limbs like a swooping ghost while animating her skin with scrolls of black and white stripes. These moving patterns seem to hypnotize her target. In an instant, the cuttlefish strikes with long tentacles, drawing in her stupefied prey.

Mealtime over, the cuttlefish shifts color and texture again. Is that a rock? A spiky bit of reef? Too late to tell: This polychromatic patroller has already disappeared.

> **How to see them:** You'll need lots of patience and a bit of luck to spot these shifty cephalopods. Try strapping on scuba gear and swimming through the coral reefs of the South Pacific, particularly around Indonesia, Papua New Guinea, and Australia's Great Barrier Reef.

Handfish

Swimming is overrated.

◆ Asked to describe how fish get around, many would say "they swim." While not a bad answer, it's not quite comprehensive. In the shallow coastal waters of southern Australia and the island of Tasmania live some fish who much prefer to walk.

Handfish lack swim bladders, the gas-filled organ that controls buoyancy in most other fish. If startled or threatened, they can do something that resembles swimming, but only in short bursts. As bottom-dwelling (or benthic) species, they're happiest just sitting in the sand, waiting for excitement to come to them.

Of course, sometimes travel is absolutely necessary. In these cases, they propel themselves across the ocean floor with a set of uncanny appendages—webbed, many-fingered pectoral and pelvic fins that extend from what look like stubby arms. In other words: fish hands.

Between their hands and their faces—which, with bulging eyes and downturned smiles, lend them a sad clown aspect—handfish look a little like they're making fun of humans. In reality, their strange form predates our own. At least one prehistoric handfish species, *Histionotophorus bassani*, was strolling the seafloor around what is now Italy some 50 million years ago, during the Eocene epoch. Today's handfish, which live more than 10,000 miles away, look very much like their ancient relatives.

Scientists speculate that, like the dinosaurs, many handfish species succumbed to mass extinction events during the Tertiary period. While this was happening, Australia's unique oceanography provided a haven for those species that survived—leading us to today, when all species of handfish are found in the southern waters of this island nation.

In the centuries since Australia's colonization, handfish numbers have plummeted. Climate change, sediment runoff from industry, salmon factory farming, and invasive species all threaten these once abundant evolutionary wonders. Conservationists are trying to stave off extinction through captive breeding and habitat protection. But half of the 14 remaining species are endangered—a state of affairs that deserves as many thumbs-down as fish and humans can collectively muster. ❯ **How to see them:** It's rare to come across handfish, which hang out along the bottom of a few shallow estuaries and bays in southeastern Australia and Tasmania and are often both critically endangered and chronically shy. If you do find one, resist the impulse to attempt a high five.

RANGE: Southern and southeastern Australia and Tasmania

SPECIES: There are 14 known handfish species in the family Brachionichthyidae. These include the red handfish (*Thymichthys politus*), Ziebell's handfish (*Brachiopsilus ziebelli*), and spotted handfish (*Brachionichthys hirsutus*).

A red handfish self-propels along the ocean floor.

Who's Who in Sea Slugs

Sea slugs' bright colors and eye-catching looks have earned them the nickname "butterflies of the sea." But these gorgeous ocean dwellers also boast secret powers, many of which they borrow from other creatures. Here are just a few of the most notable.

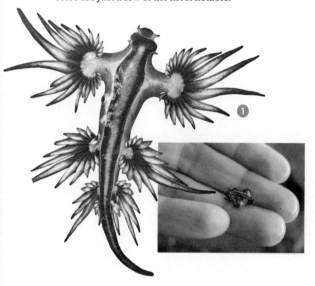

BLUE DRAGON (*Glaucus atlanticus*) • This rare and beautiful nudibranch (a variety of sea slug) lives out in the open ocean and floats upside down on the water's surface, letting winds and ocean currents carry it along. The tiny, frilly, quietly drifting creature preys on the famously venomous Portuguese man-of-war, apparently able to remain unharmed thanks to various layers of skin protection. As it eats, it absorbs the man-of-war's stinging cells, storing them to use itself against any predator who gets too close. **❶**

LOCH'S CHROMODORIS (*Chromodoris lochi*) • Scientists think that this striking sea slug could help us develop new treatments for cancer. It feeds on a sponge that contains a powerfully toxic compound called latrunculin A, storing this compound in its own body to poison predators without any internal damage. Ongoing research suggests that latrunculin A could be used to kill cancer cells, among other things. This stripy sea slug already has a significant legacy in the human world: It is said to be the inspiration for the Pokémon Shellos and Gastrodon. **❷**

SEA ANGEL (suborder Gymnosomata) • A sea angel propels its ghostly, translucent form gracefully through the ocean with a pair of winglike fins. But don't be fooled: This elegant sea slug is a merciless killer. Sea angels like to prey on their close relatives, known as sea butterflies, using deadly hook-covered appendages to pull them out of their shells. Some species of sea angel prefer to ambush their unfortunate victims, while others chase them down and attack.

Their beautiful mating rituals can make it easy to forget their murderous impulses. Marine biologists have captured videos of sea angels joined side by side, their four "wings" beating together, as they swirl and sway like dancers for hours on end. Like many sea slugs, sea angels are hermaphroditic, with both male and female reproductive organs, but they start out male and turn female over the course of their life cycle. **❸**

SPANISH SHAWL (*Flabellinopsis iodinea*) • This impressive-looking nudibranch is a color thief! It gets its brilliant purple, orange, and red pigments from a toxin called astaxanthin, which it absorbs from its prey. It swims by twisting and thrashing its body back and forth, earning its name from its resemblance to the swishing fringed shawl of a Spanish flamenco dancer. **4**

LEAF SHEEP (*Costasiella kuroshimae*) • These tiny sea slugs spend their whole lives on one species of algae. Divers have even spotted flocks of these mini "sheep," each only a third of an inch long, grazing on the same patch.

Despite their resemblance to sheep, these slugs have a power that sets them apart from almost every other animal on Earth: They can photosynthesize. The "leaves" on a sea sheep's back function similarly to the leaves of a plant, using chlorophyll to capture the sun's energy. They're filled with chloroplasts absorbed from the algae, which can keep working

in the slug's leaf-like tissues for up to 10 days. This means the slug can supplement its algal diet with the sunlight shining down on it through the water above. **5**

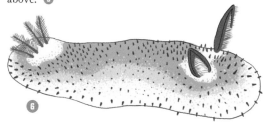

SEA BUNNY (*Jorunna parva*) • This adorable sea slug became internet-famous back in 2015, when people discovered its uncanny resemblance to a fluffy white rabbit. Its speckled "fur" is actually made up of tiny rods, called caryophyllidia, clustered around little knobs. Its long "ears," called rhinophores, sense chemicals rather than sounds and help the slug track down food and mating partners. And that slightly raggedy suggestion of a puffball tail? Those are its gills. **6**

False Depths of Piopiotahi

Thanks to misplaced pigments, deep-sea creatures thrive in these shallows.

LOCATION: Piopiotahi, also known as Milford Sound, on the west coast of New Zealand's South Island
SPECIES: Unique inhabitants include the black coral *Antipathella fiordensis* and the snake star *Astrobrachion constrictum*.

◆ Milford Sound, or Piopiotahi, in the Māori language, is a sliver of the Tasman Sea tucked between steep, glacier-carved mountainsides. Thanks to a climatic quirk, the waters 30 feet (9 m) below the surface here are as dark as the waters 230 feet (70 m) below the surface elsewhere in the ocean.

Each year, Piopiotahi is deluged with an average of 22 feet (6.7 m) of rain. As water streams down the near-vertical grades, it picks up tannins—the same compounds found in red wine and black tea—from the roots of mountainside trees. Upon reaching the sound, the tannin-stained rain floats on the surface of the denser ocean water, forming a dark liquid layer that filters out sunlight. A number of unique life forms make a life in these dim shallows.

The planet's 280 or so black coral species typically live in the deep ocean, down as far as 20,000 feet (6,000 m). Unlike their shallow-living brethren, black corals don't depend on photosynthetic algae for energy. Instead, they grow in inky waters beyond sunlight's reach and feed on plankton in the dark. But here in Piopiotahi, a black coral, *Antipathella fiordensis*, "thrives just 20 feet (6 m) below the surface—barely deeper than an Olympic dive pool.

Antipathella fiordensis's symbiotic partner, the wormlike snake star, *Astrobrachion constrictum*, is often found cleaning off silt and debris that might otherwise smother the coral. In exchange for these services, the coral provides the snake star with some of the plankton it snags in its tentacles.

Above the water, too, many species benefit from the rain and remoteness that have helped protect Piopiotahi from development. The last natural mainland population of kākāpō, a flightless, nocturnal parrot, was found hiding in Piopiotahi's dense, foggy forests. Not far away was a jewel-colored, rotund rail called a takahē that had been previously presumed extinct. These rare birds make their home near Fiordland crested penguins, which nest among mossy tree roots; glacier-hopping kea; and a panoply of other weird, wonderful—and very wet—creatures. **❯ How to see them:** The Milford Sound Underwater Observatory features an underwater viewing room 30 feet (9 m) below the ocean's surface. Inside, you can sneak a peek at black corals and other wildlife in their natural habitat. Book a boat tour to the observatory or a scuba-diving trip in the sound.

Black corals don't look black—their name comes from their black skeletons lurking beneath the whitish-gray living tissue and polyps.

Bar-Tailed Godwits

These ultra-endurance athletes make the longest nonstop migration of any land bird.

◆ *Kua kite te kohunga kuaka?* "Who has seen the nest of the kuaka?" According to some Māori oral traditions, godwits guided their Polynesian ancestors to Aotearoa/New Zealand, and they were a symbol of mystery. Every spring, they showed up on tidal mudflats around the country, probing the sand with their long, upturned bills and moving in shuffling flocks with the tide. But as the summer died, most of them left again. No one knew where they went, and no one had ever seen their eggs.

It was only when satellite trackers were miniaturized enough to be implanted in godwits that these tiny birds' epic migrations were fully revealed. In 2007, a female kuaka, designated E7, carried a transmitter for a year, starting in February. She fattened up near the mouth of the Piako River in the Firth of Thames, doubling her weight, bulking up her pectoral muscles, and restructuring her internal organs in preparation for flight. In mid-March, she left, flying more than 6,000 miles (9,656 km) northwest past Papua New Guinea and the Korean Peninsula before landing, one week later, at a coastal wetland nature reserve established at China's Yalu River estuary, near the border with North Korea.

After five weeks spent refueling, she then flew to the Yukon-Kuskokwim Delta in western Alaska to breed. But it was her return journey to New Zealand that astounded bird experts and the public alike. In late August, E7 flew south over Hawai'i, crossed the international date line near Fiji, and landed back at the Piako—just before the transmitter battery blinked out. She had traveled 7,257 miles (11,679 km) in eight days, a world record for nonstop flight by a non-seabird. (Unlike seabirds, godwits cannot land on the water to rest—if they do, they will die.)

Bar-tailed godwits flying with red knots over the UK

"With each new discovery you think, surely we've got to the limit of what this bird is capable of—and then it throws another surprise at you," says Keith Woodley, who manages New Zealand's Pūkorokoro Miranda Shorebird Centre and has been watching the godwits arrive and depart for almost three decades.

RANGE: Godwits' flight paths give them an enormous range. Birds of this subspecies migrate each autumn from New Zealand and eastern Australia via the mudflats of the Yellow Sea to breed on Alaska's Yukon-Kuskokwim Delta, then return in the spring, crossing the entire Pacific Ocean in just over a week.
SPECIES: Nunivak bar-tailed godwit (*Limosa lapponica baueri*), also known as the kuaka

"Their first ever outing is a nonstop crossing of the Pacific!" he says. "These birds are in the middle of the ocean without any landmarks, and yet they know exactly where they are, where they're going, and how to get there." (Well, mostly—the most recent godwit record was set by a juvenile who, thanks to a wrong turn that took him to Tasmania, ended up flying a total of 8,435 miles [13,560 km] at the age of five months.)

New Zealanders eagerly follow the tracked birds' journeys on social media and welcome their arrival with the ringing of cathedral bells. While godwits remain mysterious, they now symbolize endurance, resilience, and interconnection. **》 How to see them:** In New Zealand, godwits can be seen feeding on tidal flats during the spring and summer in almost any of the country's harbors or estuaries. They are particularly easy to spot at the North Island's Parengarenga, Kaipara, and Manukau harbors, at the Miranda shoreline in the Firth of Thames, and at Farewell Spit at the top of the South Island.

THE WILD LIFE OF A Shallow and Deep Fish Guy

■ Yi-Kai Tea—known online as Kai the Fish Guy—is a biodiversity fellow in the ichthyology division at Sydney's Australian Museum. In 2022, Tea was part of the first team of scientists to map terrain and collect specimens in the depths of the Indian Ocean surrounding Christmas Island and Cocos (Keeling) Islands, on a research vessel that uses imaging sensors to remotely trawl the seafloor. The researchers estimate that a third of the deep-sea fish discovered there are new to science.

● **Can you describe a typical day on a deep-sea voyage?**
We work a 12-hour shift. My shift starts at 2 a.m., so it typically involves me waking up at around 1:30 a.m. and then starting my day with a coffee. After that, it really depends on what the plan is for the particular day. Aside from the sampling and organization of organisms (in my case, fishes), I was also involved in environmental DNA sampling and hydrochemistry. The former is a technique used to identify organisms living in an area by detecting trace amounts of DNA left behind, instead of actually detecting the organism itself.

Fish sampling is more straightforward. The nets are deployed, sampled along the bottom of the seafloor, then pulled up on deck. Once it hits the deck, it's a mad rush to try and bring everything in on ice as fast as possible. Then the fun begins.

● **What was your favorite deep-sea fish to observe and handle up close?**
There were so many amazing fishes, but a personal favorite of mine was getting to see and hold a specimen of the grideye (*Ipnops* spp.). Grideyes are members of the tripod fish family, but unlike other tripod fishes—which stand high above the seafloor on long sturdy stilts, or modified fin rays—grideyes rest directly on the bottom of the seafloor. They don't have eyes. Instead they have a depressed, concave skull that is highly flattened. In this concavity are two neon yellow plaques, which are not true eyes but rather are thin light-sensitive tissues. We have no idea if they're able to see anything, but we think that they're able to detect changes in light and possibly motion.

● **What anatomical features among deep-sea fish boggle your mind the most?**
There are so many, but one of the more bizarre features are those that belong to the viperfish. They have enormously long teeth that go beyond their mouths, but these teeth, despite being so fearsome, are also highly transparent, making them hard to see. They also have poorly ossified vertebrae behind their heads, which allows them to flex and expand their mouths backward in incredibly high gapes.

● **Which was the most surprising finding from this recent expedition?**
My answer may not be something you'd like to hear. All the amazing fishes—and even a graveyard of shark teeth—were gorgeous and exciting. But perhaps the most surprising [thing] is that we found so much trash in almost every single one of our trawls. Even more surprising were masks, no doubt from the pandemic. We were finding used masks in our sampling nets down to nearly 5,000 meters [16,400 feet] deep!

● **How do deep-sea expeditions like these further science beyond the discovery of new species and terrain mapping?**
These sampling efforts also act like time capsules, offering a glimpse into what's living here at this exact moment in time. These specimens will then be stored in museums for as long as time permits, and scientists in the future may return to these sites and compare what they find to what we found. It lets us know how species diversity changes over time.

Expeditions like this also help us understand the natural distribution of animals. We have no idea how wide-ranging some of these are, so finding them in new locations helps us better understand their geographical boundaries and how to better manage and protect them in the future. ■

ASIA

Heikegani Crabs

Where did those samurai come from?

RANGE: The waters of East Asia, from Japan to Vietnam
SPECIES: Heikegani crabs (*Heikeopsis japonica*), also known as samurai crabs

◆ For hundreds of years in imperial Japan, the Heike clan wielded immense political and military power. In the twelfth century, after they were defeated in a seminal naval battle, some Heike warriors died by suicide, jumping into the sea. Legends, echoed in centuries-old works of art, hold that the warriors live on in the form of seafloor-dwelling crabs.

Confronted with a Heikegani crab, it's easy to see why. These crabs, named for the clan, have ridges on their exoskeletons that incontrovertibly resemble classic depictions of Japanese samurai warriors. How their carapaces got that way is a matter of mythology, evolutionary biology, or perhaps something in between the two.

In a 1952 article in *Life* magazine, an evolutionary biologist posited an origin story that seems consistent with both science and myth: Due to the association of crabs with Heike warriors, fishermen superstitiously or reverentially threw back any crabs that resembled samurai, while keeping ones that did not. Over the course of centuries, this altered the composition of the surviving crabs' gene pool and placed evolutionary pressure on crabs to look as much as possible like samurai—an example of artificial selection, or evolution via human intervention. Carl Sagan later summarized this potential mechanism: "The more you look like a samurai, the better your chances of survival. Eventually, there are a lot of crabs that look like samurai warriors."

Other scholars have been skeptical of this account. Marine biologist Joel W. Martin contends that the shape is a simple result of crab morphology: Places where muscles attach internally to the exoskeleton are indented, and the muscles happen to attach in a pattern that resembles a scowling face.

After all, other crabs who live outside the sphere of influence of Japanese mythology have similar face-like structures on their backs. Some of them have even been named for this feature, such as the North Atlantic's masked crab and various species in China referred to as ghost crabs or demon crabs.

This fact of muscle morphology does not necessarily contradict the artificial selection hypothesis: The naturally occurring feature could have been a starting point, with evolution honing it into a more detailed depiction of a face. But because tiny Heikegani crabs are not, and have not been, a significant part of the Japanese diet, it seems unlikely that fishers managed to hunt the animals into the shape of samurai warriors.

Depending on individual perspectives on mythology and science, it may be more or less impressive that the crabs resemble samurai simply due to their inherent biology, rather than some complex interplay between human superstition and crustacean evolution.

The real evocative power of this crab's exoskeleton may come from a different force: the human mind's tendency to see samurai where there are none. Pareidolia,

Ridges on this crab's exoskeleton resemble artistic depictions of Japanese samurai warriors.

the phenomenon whereby humans perceive faces in or on inanimate objects, may itself be the result of evolution—an instinct honed to allow the quick detection of potential threats, such as angry warriors. ❯ **How to see them:** Your best bet is scuba diving in the Sea of Japan, which is easiest to do via the Oki Islands. Consider catching a kabuki show featuring samurai characters on the mainland before your expedition, to have a point of comparison.

Pacific Footballfish

How can we learn about creatures from the literal twilight zone?

RANGE: Depths of 656 to 3,280 feet (200–1,000 m) in the Pacific Ocean, from northern Japan to the shores of California and south to Ecuador
SPECIES: Pacific footballfish (*Himantolophus sagamius*), one of 22 known species of footballfish

◆ Far below the ocean's surface, where light has waned and pressure has multiplied beyond human experience, a speck of brightness shimmers like a lonely star in the night sky. It comes from an orb full of bioluminescent bacteria, dangled from the head of an unseen predator. Curious swimmers are drawn to its glow—and end up in the mouth of a female Pacific footballfish, whose razor-sharp teeth and spike-ridden black skin remain cloaked in darkness.

At least, this is what we assume. Despite recent advances in deep-sea navigation technology, no one has ever observed one of these famously deceptive hunters in her natural habitat.

The Pacific footballfish is the largest member of the family Himantolophidae, or globose deep-sea anglerfishes. Much of what scientists know about the football fish they've inferred from knowledge of similar species, or from an extremely small number of specimens that have been pulled up in research trawls or washed up on the beach, says biological oceanographer Anela Choy. In this way, researchers have managed to learn some basics about these inaccessible fish, which are named for the soccer-ball shape of the females.

Fewer than three dozen Pacific footballfish specimens have ever been collected.

While males are much smaller than their mates and lack their distinctive shape and glowing lure, their anatomy also provides scientists with clues about their lifestyle. Male Pacific footballfish don't hunt as adults—they must subsist off food they ate during their larval stage, which is stored as energy in their livers, and attempt reproduction as quickly as possible before dying. Their unusually large nostrils and the tooth-like hooks they have in lieu of a jawbone suggest that the males track down females by their scent before latching onto them and releasing sperm.

In 2021, Choy and her colleagues at the Scripps Institution of Oceanography got to meet some (dead) Pacific footballfish in the flesh after three were found in Southern California. They felt "prickly—kind of weird and soft," Choy says.

Only once have researchers managed to spend time with a living specimen. In the 1960s, a group of Japanese scientists found and captured a Pacific footballfish floating in the ocean, says Ben Frabel, a collections manager at Scripps. The fish survived in a tank for a week; whenever it was disturbed or poked, it would dart away, ejecting bioluminescent goo from its body. Whether the fish act like this in the privacy of their own homes, we may never know. ❯ **How to see them:** If you see one in the deep-sea wild, you will be the first. If you're lucky or persistent, you could score a private collections tour at Los Angeles County's Natural History Museum, the Scripps Institution of Oceanography (La Jolla), or the California Academy of Sciences (San Francisco).

The Mysterious World of Deep-Sea Fishes

The deep sea is the single largest ecosystem on the planet, and the world's largest carbon sink. It is also threatened by climate change, ocean acidification, and mining operations that strip the seafloor for metals.

Despite the importance of the deep sea and our eagerness to exploit it, humans still know very little about how it functions—or even what lives there. Oceanographers estimate that more than 90 percent of life in the deep has yet to be discovered.

The deep sea officially begins at 656 feet (200 m) below the ocean's surface, where sunlight dwindles in a region known as the twilight zone. Journey deeper, below 3,280 feet (1,000 m), and the all-encompassing darkness brings with it temperatures just above freezing and crushing pressures that would reduce your body to the consistency of butter. Go deeper: You'll reach the abyss, and eventually the ocean's trenches—including the Mariana Trench, the deepest of all, which is about 7 miles (11 km) down.

In the world we know, sunlight equals life. But in the sunless world below, fantastical-looking marine creatures still find ways to thrive. And though most of us will never be lucky enough to hop in a submersible and visit Earth's mysterious depths in person, we can still get to know some of our deep-sea neighbors from afar.

Anglerfish

CUT THE LIGHTS: In the absence of light, the bright coloration of fishes seen in shallow waters disappears, and most species are translucent or black, says Anela Choy of the Scripps Institution of Oceanography.

Some, like the **anglerfishes** (order Lophiiformes) and the **gossamer worms** (*Tomopteris* spp.), make their own light to attract prey or avoid predators. In the twilight zone, **bristlemouths** (family Gonostomatidae, the planet's most abundant vertebrates), and **lanternfishes** (family Myctophidae) can even change shade to match the light intensity of their immediate surroundings. This helps them avoid any nearby predators.

Spotted lanternfish

NO NEED FOR MUSCLE: The **Mariana snailfish** (*Pseudoliparis swirei*) looks like a tadpole's ghost, which fits: No tadpole you know could survive where the Mariana snailfish does. At home in the ocean's deepest trench, this snailfish can withstand 800 times the atmospheric pressure.

Many deep-sea dwellers have also evolved lower muscle densities to survive high-pressure depths. Fish with these watery muscles, like the **smooth-head blobfish** (*Psychrolutes marcidus*) and **deep-sea batfishes** (family Ogcocephalidae), deflate like week-old party balloons if brought to the surface in a research trawl or a predator's mouth.

Black swallower

LIMITED MENU: Opportunities to feed in the deep sea are relatively scarce. Deep-sea creatures tend to be more creative about how they eat than what they eat.

The deep-sea fish known simply as **swallowers** (family Chiasmodontidae) have enlarged mouths and hooked teeth that allow them to swallow fish larger than their own bodies. Their teeth retract to take in oversized prey and then lock together, trapping their unlucky victim.

This tendency to bite off more than they can chew is what clued researchers in to the swallowers' existence. No one has ever observed one of these fishes up close in the wild. But if a swallowed carcass decays faster than a swallower can digest it, the gas released from decomposition can cause both fishes to bubble up to the surface, where there's a greater chance of discovery.

STILL LIFE: Some deep-sea dwellers don't move much. Energy-saving locomotion strategies and a sluggish metabolism help make their food last. Many anglerfishes, for example, spend their lives floating through the water, lures dangling, waiting for dinner to bite. Batfishes appear to sit along the seafloor until food comes to them, or "walk" slowly with their muscular pectoral fins in search of prey. After all, in the darkness, you don't need to get very far away from predators, says Choy. You just need to disappear.

Bluntnose sixgill shark

ENDLESS MYSTERIES: During a 2006 submarine dive off the northeast coast of Moloka'i, Hawai'i, an 18-foot (5.5 m) **bluntnose sixgill shark** (*Hexanchus griseus*) lurking about half a mile below the surface jostled the research vessel. The filmed encounter racked up millions of hits on YouTube, revealing to the world that this apex predator of the deep indeed exists.

But more than a decade later, scientists still don't know exactly what it eats. They don't know what it was doing there. (Was it migrating?) They don't even know how it reproduces.

University of Hawai'i scientist Jeffrey Drazen, who was in the submarine during the encounter, has embarked on dozens of deep-sea expeditions. "Every time you bring up a trawl or you're driving around via remotely operated vehicle, you see something fascinating," he says. "Often something very few people have ever seen."

An Unusual Annelid

A worm with 1,000 anuses

◆ Segmented worms, or annelids, are among the world's most common animals. They exist in just about every ecosystem, from atop city sidewalks after rainstorms to within the bones of Antarctic whales. Wherever and whoever they might be, they tend to follow a specific body plan: tube-shaped, with a mouth on one end, an anus on the other, and a digestive system in between.

But in the shallow waters around Japan's Sado Island, there's a worm who didn't get the memo. There, unknown to science until very recently, lives an annelid with one head and a seemingly infinite number of anuses.

RANGE: The Sea of Japan, near Sado Island
SPECIES: *Ramisyllis kingghidorahi*. So far, two other similarly branching worms are known to exist: *Ramisyllis multicaudata* and *Syllis ramosa*.

Researchers first found this special worm in 2019 while investigating the area's *Petrosia* sponges. Inside each sponge, taking advantage of its nooks and caverns, was an individual worm with a body that branched out like the roots of a tree. The team named the species *Ramisyllis kingghidorahi*, after one of Godzilla's nemeses, the three-headed dragon King Ghidorah.

Some views of the many-anused worm

All annelids are able to grow new segments in order to asexually reproduce or heal from injury. But while most grow linearly and can conjure up new segments only from certain spots on their bodies, *R. kingghidorahi* can branch out just about anywhere, including from already developed segments. The result is a freewheeling, asymmetric worm with essentially unlimited butt-generating abilities—the same principle as its namesake, but the opposite execution, and taken to a true extreme.

Having that many rear ends can come with benefits. Sometimes, instead of building another anus at the end of a segment, a worm builds a tiny copy of itself, complete with a brain, eyes, and reproductive materials. These tiny clone segments, known as stolons, then break loose from the worm and drift away to mate.

But sustaining all this branching must be difficult. Scientists estimate that the average *R. kingghidorahi* body could measure dozens of feet in length if all the segments were laid out in a line. It's still unclear how these worms find enough food to sustain themselves with only one mouth. ❯ **How to see them:** If you find yourself near Sado Island, Japan, look for small caves or steep rock walls and then a *Petrosia* sponge. If you're lucky, you may spot a worm butt or 12 poking out.

Artificial Reefs

Coengineered biodiversity hubs

◆ When it comes to coral reefs, nature isn't too fussy about her canvas. Ships, planes, tanks, and thousands of New York subway cars have all been successfully transformed into teeming aquatic wonderlands, thanks to conservationists and the generative power of the seas.

RANGE: Global
SPECIES: Artificial reefs support species from tiny phytoplankton to enormous whale sharks (*Rhincodon typus*).

Since ancient times, so-called artificial reefs have been built to enhance harbor defenses and fisheries. Persians, for example, constructed them to block the mouth of the Tigris River and stymie raids by Indian pirates. Today, these underwater structures' primary purpose is to restore ecologically damaged seabeds. Reefs, whether natural or artificial, stimulate the formation of complex food chains that convert inert physical structures into lively marine oases.

The process begins when drifting, nutrient-dense plankton accumulate on a structure's outer surfaces. Over time, diminutive fish arrive to take shelter among the reef's warren of enclaves, drawing a succession of ever larger predators. As the ecosystem matures, the reef acquires a living skin of crusted barnacles, sponges, algae—and, of course, corals.

The corals, like the plankton, drift by and cling on. In tropical or subtropical latitudes, for instance, stony coral polyps—tiny, tentacled, venomous organisms usually no larger than a pinhead—attach themselves to the reef structure and self-replicate. As the polyps extrude calcium carbonate, forming exoskeletons, they merge with the reef. Over time, the structure becomes more and more elaborate, until the artificial substrate is essentially subsumed.

A diver inspects corals growing on the USS Spiegel Grove, which was sunk as an artificial reef in 2002.

Although artificial reefs are often wildly successful at attracting and boosting marine life, some biologists have criticized them as mere "fish-aggregating devices" that siphon their inhabitants from other ecosystems. Scientists will have to conduct more long-term studies on these reefs to determine their costs and benefits.

Nonetheless, many researchers and conservationists are staunch supporters of artificial reefs. Some have even suggested them as the right afterlife for the planet's growing array of defunct oil and gas rigs. ❭ **How to see them: Many artificial reefs can be observed with a snorkel or from the safety of a glass-bottom boat. An advanced course in wreck diving will enable you to get up close.**

Artificial Reefs You Can Visit

"THE GREAT CARRIER REEF," PENSACOLA, FLORIDA, US: In 2006, the USS *Oriskany*, a 911-foot-long (277 m) aircraft carrier, was dispatched to a watery grave 22 miles (35 km) off the coast of Pensacola. The retired vet is now a placid, cavernous shipwreck, hosting angelfish, whale sharks, manta rays, and more.

UNDERWATER MILITARY MUSEUM, AQABA, JORDAN: In 2019, a small battalion of decommissioned military vehicles was stripped of hazardous materials and sunk near the shores of Aqaba. The equipment, which includes tanks, a troop carrier, an ambulance, and a helicopter, now has a second life hosting both corals and tourists.

MUSEO SUBACUÁTICO DE ARTE, CANCÚN, MEXICO: This underwater art museum features more than 500 life-size sculptures by Jason deCaires Taylor, wildly embellished with thousands of kaleidoscopic corals. Among them are dozens of human figures modeled on real-life members of a local fishing village, an angel with outstretched wings of Gorgonian sea fans, and an assembly of besuited bankers with their heads buried in the sand.

KENYALANG WRECK, MIRI, MALAYSIA: The oil rig Baram-8 collapsed in 1975. Nearly 30 years later, using lessons from other "rigs to reefs" efforts around the world, the rig was cut in two and dropped into the shallows off the Malaysian coast. Today, divers here see soft corals, moray eels, and giant groupers.

JUNKYARD REEF, KOH TAO, THAILAND: One of Koh Tao's many dive sites, Junkyard Reef is a carefully considered hodgepodge. Stuff people didn't want on land—including toilets, old cars, bicycles, and gym equipment—has been interspersed with purposefully built structures and is now enjoyed by lionfish, leaf sheep, and many others.

THE WILD LIFE OF **An Artificial Reef Architect**

■ Kirsty Magson has been restoring coral reefs since 2015. As the program manager of the New Heaven Reef Conservation Program, she works closely with the government to design, deploy, and monitor artificial reefs off the island of Koh Tao, Thailand.

● **How did you get interested in marine biology?**

For as long as I remember, marine biology was something I wanted to do. Some of my earliest memories are sitting with my granddad in a big wingback armchair watching the Discovery Channel and Animal Planet. And then as I was growing up, my sister was like, "I want a Barbie doll," and I'd be like, "I want a book on dolphins."

● **How do you select a site for an artificial reef?**

It really depends on what the purpose of your artificial reef is—what's going to be used as restoration and conservation versus something that's used more for artistic appeal or to pull divers to that area.

The first thing we want to address is, is there a need for a reef where you're trying to put one? What kind of wave action happens throughout the year? Because if you're trying to put one somewhere that gets heavily affected by monsoon weather and strong waves, it's not going to survive. Do you have a viable feedstock of corals that you can collect from? Because if you don't have fragments, and you're having to move them from one place to restock that area, it's also not the best option.

● **What are the best materials for artificial reefs?**

Metal works very well for restoration purposes. It's easy to attach corals to. It's easy to deploy. It's cheap. It's easy to bend and adjust to the shapes you need. But it rusts very easily, and you're not expecting corals to land there naturally. You're pretty much just attaching corals to it yourself, so whatever work you're doing has to be based on your interaction with the reef.

We know that concrete has very good natural recruitment. The downside is, it's very heavy. If you have a 3D printer that can extrude concrete, you can do immense things, but most people need to hire a crane and other equipment.

Recently we've been trying out a combination of both metal and concrete. We also use mineral accretion technology, where an electrical current passed through the structure starts to secrete out a calcium carbonate skeleton. The reef that we've been working on with that has had incredible growth rates. We've seen a reduction in the level of damage to the structure itself because we're now reinforcing it with calcium carbonate, and we've seen better success rates with giant clams.

● **What are the indicators of a successful and resilient artificial reef?**

First and foremost, a strong genetic pool of corals. This includes everything from your fast-growing to your slow-growing corals—your least resilient to your most resilient, designed in a way that provides a lot of habitat for different marine life. Having fragments that are going to grow in unique shapes and sizes is going to be very, very important for that.

● **What is the biggest challenge when creating an artificial reef?**

Knowing when to stop.

● **What amazes you most about creating artificial reefs?**

I think it's being able to see the impact that you're having—being able to watch and monitor and understand how the reef is interacting, the interactions with different marine life, with fish, with different corals, and seeing which fragments work best on different types of structures. It's kind of like you have your own little babies that you're watching grow. Because every time I go out there, even now, after eight years, there are still coral that I know I transplanted. And seeing them thrive is just incredible. ■

EUROPE

Saimaa Ringed Seals

These rare jewels are found in just one Finnish lake.

LOCATION: Lake Saimaa, in southeastern Finland
SPECIES: Saimaa ringed seal (*Pusa hispida saimensis*)

◆ About 10,000 years ago, during the last Ice Age, Finland's Lake Saimaa was cut off from the Baltic Sea. The rising landmass trapped some saltwater ringed seals in the lake. It's thought that these stranded mammals eventually evolved into one of the few freshwater seal species in the world: the Saimaa ringed seal.

These seals, cloaked in furry coats that resemble sunlight-dappled water, exist only in Lake Saimaa. The largest of Finland's 188,000 lakes, and the fourth-largest lake in Europe, Saimaa's serpentine shoreline runs 8,500 miles (13,679 km) near the Russian border. Its namesake seals, after adapting to their freshwater environment, thrived for millennia. But in the early twentieth century, commercial fishermen—who saw them as competition—hunted the seals nearly to extinction.

While conservation measures have led to a population rebound, Saimaa seals remain threatened. The biggest dangers today are climate change and fishing nets, which drown entangled seals. Warmer winters also interfere with their life cycle: During the relatively warm winter of 2019, conservationists fabricated dens to help sustain the population.

Like their saltwater cousins, Saimaa ringed seals are great divers, able to hold their breath for up to 15 minutes. They use their whiskers to track down and hunt small schooling fish. Pups are born in February and spend their first months in mother-built snowbank dens along the lake's edge. Adult Saimaa seals are 3–5 feet long (1–1.5 m) and weigh up to 200 pounds (90 kg).

As their numbers increase, the seals have become more accustomed to humans. Some surface yards away from tourists without apparent fear. ❯ **How to see them: The best time to spot the seals is in May, when they climb on lakeshore rocks to molt in the sun. Seal-focused boat tours are available.**

THE WILD LIFE OF **Norppa**

■ Retired author, photographer, and documentarian Juha Taskinen is one of Finland's leading authorities on the Saimaa ringed seal. Over more than 40 years working to raise public awareness of the endangered species, Taskinen has seen the seal population grow from 100 to about 430 individuals. Known throughout the country as Norppa, the Finnish word for the animal, Taskinen has helped elevate the rare freshwater seal to a beloved national icon.

● **How did you first become involved with Saimaa ringed seals?**
I was a 22-year-old dairy farmer in 1979 when a friend took me fishing on Lake Saimaa in [the town of] Savonlinna. He told me he had recently spotted one of the seals sunning on the nearby rocks. That was unusual back then because few people had ever seen one of the seals. I returned to the same spot a year later with my camera, hoping to photograph it, and there it was. It took the young

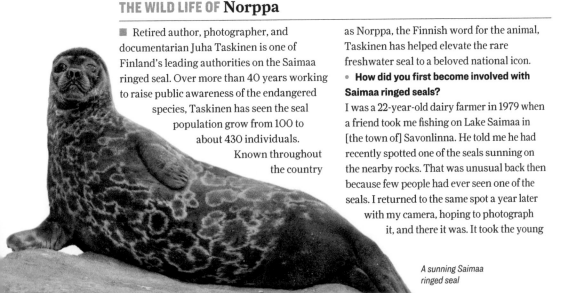

A sunning Saimaa ringed seal

man away [a Finnish phrase for love at first sight]. It was a key turning point in my life.

- **How does it make you feel that your grandfather was one of the seal hunters who nearly drove the species to extinction?**

I have a photograph of him standing on the rocks with a shotgun. That gave me the inspiration to begin photographing and documenting their lives.

- **The seals were once reclusive. But now that their numbers are rising, they are easier to spot in the lake or while molting on the rocks in the spring, and people want to see them. Is the rise of Saimaa tourism and seal-watching tours good or bad?**

It is a positive that the seals have returned to the places they were driven away from by hunting. You can see their transformation from the very timid, once-hunted seal to something that is more trusting and comfortable with the human presence.

- **The biggest current threats to the seals are climate change and fishing, but many Finns are avid fishermen. How do they feel about the seals' preservation?**

The general public is overwhelmingly for protection of the seal. People here are very protective and very proud of it. It is our national animal.

- **You've retired from photographing, filming, and writing about the seals. What do you do now?**

I am a commercial fisherman. I make and sell fish traps that are safe for the seals. I want to show that the seals and responsible fishing can coexist.

- **You did so much for the preservation of the seals. Do you feel like you have left them in good hands?**

For so many years I raged and fought those wars. Over the years I've had the responsibility for the seal, but now I'm tired of fighting. I've done what I could. Somehow, it's good to leave this to let things work out for themselves. It's easier to be when you no longer have to carry the life of the seal on your shoulders. Its life is now in the care of the whole nation. ∎

Immortal Jellyfish

These tiny jellies can age in reverse.

♦ The promise of eternal life—and youth—has held an undying fascination for the human species, from alchemists of yore searching for the philosopher's stone to today's shelves of skin creams that claim to reverse aging. But if the jellyfish *Turritopsis dohrnii* were to learn about all the time and money we spend trying to cheat death, they wouldn't get what all the fuss is about. To them, reverse aging is simply a part of life.

T. dohrnii, also called the "immortal jellyfish," is a tiny and unpretentious jellyfish—as an adult, his translucent, bell-shaped body is about the size of a pencil eraser—whose life cycle initially mirrors that of other jellyfish species. He starts out as a free-swimming larva before settling down on a rock or other hard surface and forming an immobile polyp. This polyp grows and buds a medusa, which is the floating, tentacled adult phase that we typically associate with jellyfish.

For the immortal jellyfish, though, the story doesn't end there. In this species, a medusa who grows old or gets hurt can collapse back into himself, sink to the seafloor, and return to his polyp phase. From there, he can start the developmental process over again.

This remarkable ability—akin to an injured butterfly turning back into a caterpillar—was discovered by accident in a lab in Italy in the 1980s, when a student noticed that a jar holding *T. dohrnii* medusas suddenly had several polyps on the bottom. Subsequent observation revealed that the medusas weren't reproducing but instead were turning back into polyps themselves. Researchers in Japan later found that the

RANGE: Originally from the Mediterranean and Adriatic Seas, this jellyfish has been introduced to many other locations, including waters off of the southern coast of California, the Caribbean, and coastal Japan.

SPECIES: Immortal jellyfish (*Turritopsis dohrnii*)

immortal jellyfish can repeat this process multiple times, meaning if an individual doesn't get eaten or damaged beyond repair before he gets a chance to do his party trick, he could theoretically carry on indefinitely.

Forty years on, there is a lot left to learn. Researchers now know that this transformation is made possible through a cellular process called transdifferentiation—in this case, all the jellyfish's adult cells transdifferentiate into cells that make up a polyp body plan. Exactly how they do this is still a mystery, but researchers are looking for answers in the jellies' DNA.

Even when scientists untangle how this process works in immortal jellyfish, its lessons are unlikely to apply to humans, for whom aging remains frustratingly monodirectional. But perhaps we should look on the bright side—at least we don't have to relive our awkward teenage years on an endless loop. ❯ **How to see them: These teeny jellyfish are common in warm coastal waters around the world, but they are tricky to spot in the wild given their size.**

Seagrass

A blooming marvel

◆ Wisp-like fronds may give seagrasses an unassuming appearance. But don't underestimate their collective power. Together, the fronds form rippling underwater meadows—a mighty ecosystem crucial to the lives of millions of animals and humans.

All life on land is believed to have come from the ocean around 500 million years ago. But after undertaking the long evolutionary slog from marine algae to land plant, seagrasses returned to the water. They first crept back into the coastal margins around 100 million years ago, when dinosaurs like *T. rex* were still crashing around on land, but retained their roots, stems, and seeds. They are now the only flowering plants able to live in the sea.

RANGE: Seagrass thrives near coastlines in 163 countries, on every continent except Antarctica.
SPECIES: There are more than 50 known seagrass species. Many of their common names, such as eelgrass (*Zostera marina*), ribbon weed (*Posidonia australis*), and spoon grass (*Halophila ovalis*), suggest the plants' assorted shapes and sizes.

Like all flowering plants, seagrasses reproduce through pollination. This isn't easy underwater, where pollen produced in male flowers must make it to female ones through swirling sea currents. To up the odds, seagrasses make thread-like pollen grains, rather than the yellow dust we're used to seeing on land flowers. Eelgrass releases the world's gangliest pollen, with grains up to 5 millimeters long. The rice-sized pollen floats well, upping the chances of successful fertilization.

At least one seagrass species, turtle grass, receives assistance: Worms, small crustaceans, and other creatures who feast on this grass's gooey pollen masses accumulate it on their bodies and shuttle it from flower to flower like little sea bees.

Like terrestrial grasses and some trees, these lithe plants also reproduce by cloning, sending out horizontal roots called rhizomes that sprout into genetically identical copies of their parent. This asexual growth has resulted in both the world's oldest and the world's largest known plants. A Mediterranean tape weed in waters off the Spanish island of Formentera is estimated to date back to the dawn of humanity. Meanwhile, a ribbon weed discovered off the coast of Australia covers an area bigger than Washington, DC.

This knack for procreation has resulted in dense seagrass beds that provide food and shelter for thousands of species of invertebrates, fish, and marine mammals. These meadows supply 20 percent of the world's fisheries, in turn providing nutrition and livelihoods for millions of people. They also improve water quality, quell storm waves, limit coastal erosion, and—square foot for square foot—capture and store more carbon than tropical rainforests.

Still, people have overlooked and destroyed these slender plants for years: The world has lost an estimated third of its seagrass meadows since the late nineteenth century. Today, seagrass patches as big as soccer fields disappear every half hour, mostly due to coastal development, certain fishing practices, pollution, and climate change. Seagrass restoration projects are helping us recognize the underwater flower power packed within these ancient plants. ❯ **How to see them:** Head to sheltered shallow bays and estuaries. SeagrassSpotter.org is a global tool for identifying and mapping seagrass species.

Seagrass reproduces by cloning.

THE WILD LIFE OF A Seagrass Meadow Restoration Officer

■ Andy Jayes is the native oyster and seagrass restoration officer for Yorkshire Wildlife Trust in the United Kingdom, a job that involves reestablishing dwarf eelgrass meadows at Spurn National Nature Reserve. This sandy, shifting peninsula, popular with walkers, bird-watchers, and fossil hunters, swoops out between the North Sea and the Humber Estuary on the east coast of England.

• Why is it necessary to restore the seagrass at Spurn?
We used to have 480 to 500 hectares [roughly 1,200 acres] of seagrass meadow here. This dwindled to a few scattered patches. We've now got around 20 hectares [50 acres], although some of that is still very sparse. Seagrass is fairly resilient, but a combination of habitat loss from coastal development, pollution, and a wasting disease triggered by stressors led to its decline.

Water from once heavily industrialized areas such as Leeds and Sheffield drains through the Humber. There was a lot of pollution coming through here. But over the past 40 years, the water quality has improved massively. We're now in a position where we can attempt restoration.

• How do you harvest seagrass seeds?
We start seeing seagrass flowers at the end of May, and that's our cue to keep a close eye on the beds. If we see flowers have dropped off and the seeds transform, we know we've probably got 10 to 14 days to harvest that seed.

The collection is really simple. We operate on the edges of the meadow to minimize damage. Usually around August and September, we go out with bodyboards. We then use the boards to walk across and sit on while plucking the seedpods from the plants by hand.

• What do you do next?
Once the pods are picked, we put them in [large containers of] temperature-controlled water and throw some air bubbles at them. Eventually the dense seeds drop to the bottom for collection.

We then make biodegradable seed bags and plant them directly into the ground. The bags protect the seeds and allow us to introduce plants into new areas. Or we grow the seeds in our aquaculture system. Once we've got any growth, we know we can plant them back out. As soon as there's growth, there's a rhizome, and when there's a rhizome, the mortality rate

decreases massively. Around 95 percent of seagrass seeds don't germinate into a plant. So, if we can cut the mortality rate, we can positively affect their survival.

• Are you seeing the benefits of the project?
It's still in the early stages, but it's really cool to monitor the finfish assemblage at the seagrass. You can see young bass swimming through it and periwinkles grazing on the algae that grows on it. When the tide drops, it looks like it's fizzing with all the shrimp jumping and panicking at being exposed. So, you've got a lot of life in there. The seagrass is operating as an excellent fish nursery, as well as a feeding station for sea and bird life. But when we look at the control sites away from the meadows, we don't see that at all.

Seagrass also helps with sediment stabilization. Behind our seagrass, we've typically got salt marsh. Seagrass, of course, is exceptional at carbon storage, but salt marsh areas are absolutely fantastic at storing carbon too. Restoring the seagrass here has a larger benefit: It's allowing the salt marsh to stabilize and pull in more carbon from the atmosphere. ■

European Eels

They cross the globe to mate, but after that, things get hazy.

◆ We know where baby eels come from. Every year, crowds of the translucent wormlike creatures, each about the length of two small paper clips, arrive in the coastal waterways of Europe, Russia, and North Africa, having drifted up to 6,000 miles (9,600 km) or more from their birthplace in the Sargasso Sea, east of Bermuda.

RANGE: Coasts and inland rivers in western and southern Europe, Russia, and North Africa, and through the North Atlantic Ocean to the Sargasso Sea
SPECIES: European eel (*Anguilla anguilla*)

But we don't really know where they *come from*. Despite centuries of curiosity and decades of study, it's still unclear how—or even specifically where—European eels reproduce in the wild.

European eels appear to defy many of nature's laws. After anywhere from 6 to over 20 years spent maturing in inland freshwaters, they swim thousands of miles back across the Atlantic to their birthplace in the Sargasso Sea. To survive this epic migration—a journey that takes them comparable distances to whales, which are orders of magnitude larger—these fish go up to 15 months without eating, dissolving their own fat stores along the way. In wet conditions, they can even move on land, and are occasionally caught slithering their legless bodies up dams to reach the other side.

But the biggest mystery about this species is what they need to multiply and thrive. Questions about where eels come from and how they reproduce have captivated great minds for centuries. Aristotle believed that these animals simply appear, no mating required, while Sigmund Freud dissected 400 of them in a bloody quest to find their sex organs.

European eels are private about their reproductive habits. They stay sexless for most of their lives—their genitals appear only in their last life stage as they migrate toward the Sargasso, which is apparently the only spot on Earth where they spawn.

An adult European eel, with secrets

Despite intensive efforts, though, no one has ever seen them doing so at sea. Scientists still don't know what makes the Sargasso a watery sex den for eels, where exactly in this vast sea reproduction happens, or what social and environmental factors drive successful spawning. (Captive breeding efforts have largely failed.)

They do know that as these eels struggle to rebound—populations in Europe's inland waters have dropped by more than 95 percent since the 1980s, mostly due to habitat loss and fishing—any details that can improve eel health, sexual or otherwise, could help prevent this secretive species from vanishing for good. **› How to see them: European eels can be spotted in inland rivers and coastlines throughout their range. If you find one, try asking about its dating life.**

Phronima

Tiny pirates of the deep sea

◆ Life in the deep sea is dark, cold, and unforgiving. To survive here, it helps to be cunning and invisible. *Phronima sedentaria* is both.

With an elongated, bulbous head, several claw-tipped legs, and an extended tail, a *Phronima* is a tiny crustacean with a haunting presence. Four blood-red pupils stand out from her translucent body—the only indication that her entire head is composed of eyes, giving the *Phronima* nearly 360-degree vision. In the dark of the ocean's depths, this tiny parasite uses this gift to locate her victims.

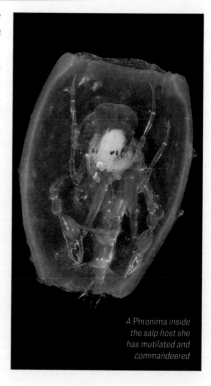

First, the *Phronima* mutilates the clear, gelatinous body of a salp, a type of zooplankton, carving the salp into an open-ended tube and consuming its flesh and organs as she goes. Next, the *Phronima* crawls inside and commandeers her host's body, using it to float effortlessly around the deep sea during the day and propelling her toward the more nutrient-rich surface waters by night.

The glassy walls of the salp evoke an eerie and reluctant womb, helping protect the *Phronima* from predators and serving as a floating nursery for any young. Female *Phronima* will raise as many as 600 eggs inside. If the young venture too close to the edges, she spins the salp like a dreidel to align them inside by centrifugal force.

A Phronima inside the salp host she has mutilated and commandeered

Phronima don't rely entirely on cocooning themselves inside salps for survival. To evade the bioluminescent searchlights of predators, they're covered in a living invisibility cloak that makes light pass directly through their bodies. This mysterious anti-glare coating appears to move and replicate and may be made up of bacteria or nanoplankton hitching a ride in exchange for camouflage. But—as with many mysteries of the deep sea—scientists are still trying to figure out exactly how it works.

> **How to see them:** *Phronima* occasionally wash ashore inside their floating homes, where they can survive for several hours before drying out. They may also be seen while scuba diving.

RANGE: Temperate and tropical seas worldwide

SPECIES: *Phronima sedentaria* and their host species, gelatinous zooplankton like salps, siphonophores, and pyrosomes

THE WILD LIFE OF A Deep-Sea Live Stream Superfan

■ After a childhood spent just half an hour from the Gulf of Mexico, Lisa Price was diagnosed with a progressive and debilitating spinal disease that interrupted her dream of becoming a veterinarian. Under the moniker The Unknown Explorer, she has now become a leading figure in a small but dedicated online community that watches and discusses live streams of deep-sea dives. These viewers help scientists track and ID what appears on the cameras while spreading the word about deep-sea research.

• **What's the best part of live streaming a deep-sea dive versus watching highlights afterward?**
It's the interaction you get with the scientists, the people in the chat room, or the people on Twitter [X]. When you find something really cool or something nobody's seen, and you send out a picture. And then all of a sudden you watch as the numbers—the people watching—go up.

On Twitter [X], we send each other GIFs. And I send postcards to some friends I met in Australia through the chat. It's fun. They're good people.

• **Do you have a favorite research group to follow?**
The [Schmidt Ocean Institute's research ship] *Falkor* and [the replacement ship] *Falkor (too)*. They're absolutely my favorite because of the interaction they have with regular, everyday people like me. It makes you feel like you're a part of it.

All the scientists that I've met—different experts in their

fields—they're all so nice. No matter the bazillions of questions I send them, they answer every single one of them. I might have to see the same fish 18 different times, and I still will not remember the name of it. And every time I'm like, *What was this again?* they remind me, knowing full well I'm going to ask again.

• **What are some of the most memorable things you've seen during dives?**
I was there when they got the very first image of a ram's horn squid in situ on the *Falkor*, in one of their expeditions off the coast of Australia. Nobody had ever gotten video of one alive before. They also saw a giant siphonophore—I think the biggest one ever filmed.

[During a March 2020 expedition], the pilots, J-Rod and Cody, were the only ones on the ship while everybody was being quarantined. They went down with just a little hand fishing net and that robot's arm—14,000 feet [4,267 m] down—and caught a faceless cusk eel. How did he catch this fish, that far down, with a net, in a robot arm? It's just absolutely amazing.

• **These expeditions are happening all over the world, in all different time zones. Will you stay up all night or wake up super early to watch a dive?**
I try. When [Schmidt Ocean was] in Australia, everything was so flip-flopped because it's in the middle of the night. I was up all night and sleeping half the day. My sleep schedule is whatever their dive schedule is, pretty much.

• **Has your relationship with the ocean or the planet changed since you started watching these streams?**
Definitely. I'm way more aware of all the wastefulness—of all the crap that we buy and how all of that eventually finds its way there in one form or another. I don't put chemicals in my yard anymore. I used to spray for bugs—I just completely stopped doing all that. I have a creek right behind my house that dumps right into the bay that dumps right into the ocean, and you can follow it in the dang kayak. I'm very aware of that kind of stuff.

We're absolutely oblivious. We live up here, and we just don't think about it. And it's not anybody's fault—technology is just catching up to be able to show everybody. But that's a great thing, because now maybe more people will become more aware. It isn't just about saving the things that are alive down there. It's about saving us.

• **How can others get involved streaming live dives?**
Go to Nautilus Live on YouTube. The *Okeanos Explorer*, Schmidt Ocean Institute, Woods Hole—just start there. If you want to meet people, go into Schmidt Ocean Institute dives when they're live, and chat and start asking questions. Follow them on their social media—Twitter [X], Instagram, Facebook. Just check it out. You're either going to love it or it's just not going to be for you. ■

A DEEP DIVE
ON DEEP DIVES

It's a long way to the bottom. On the way are many ocean species who stay at one depth for much of their lives. But others—from fish and birds to mammals and even insects—are capable of impressive vertical journeys. Here are some top athletes of the water column.

SEA OTTER (*Enhydra lutris*) • [318 feet (97 m), Pacific Ocean] In 1975, workers on a fishing vessel discovered the decayed remains of a sea otter in a crab pot placed this far down on a seabed, granting this mammal the provisional title of deepest-diving four-legged animal on Earth. ❶

HUMAN (*Homo sapiens*) unassisted • [335 feet (102 m), Atlantic Ocean] The deepest known free dive without any equipment was completed in 2016 by William Trubridge in the Bahamas. ❷

SEA SNAKE (*Hydrophis* spp.) • [804 feet (245 m), Timor Sea] A sea snake was filmed wriggling underwater at this depth by researchers in 2014, off the coast of northwestern Australia. Although they're not sure what species the snake belonged to, they narrowed it down to the venomous *Hydrophis* genus. ❸

HUMAN (*Homo sapiens*) assisted • [830 feet (253 m), Aegean Sea] In 2012, expert diver Herbert Nitsch reached this depth in a single breath, with the help of a line, weight, and streamlining

equipment that turned him into a sort of human torpedo. He suffered severe decompression sickness and nearly lost his life. ❹

EMPEROR PENGUIN (*Aptenodytes forsteri*) • [1,850 feet (564 m), Southern Ocean] A 2006 study described two separate dives by two different emperor penguins, both reaching 1,850 feet (564 m) and lasting for more than 20 minutes each. They bested their royal peers, king penguins, who are known to dive to 1,125 feet (343 m). ❺

NAUTILUS (*Nautilus pompilius*) • [1,870 feet (570 m), Pacific Ocean] According to the fossil record, nautiluses have remained largely unchanged for 500 million years. By controlling the volume of water and air inside the compartments of their swirled shells, they can move from the relative shallows of about 425 feet (120 m) down to nearly 2,300 feet (700 m), a 2011 study found. ❻

LEATHERBACK TURTLE (*Dermochelys coriacea*) • [4,200 feet (1,280 m), Atlantic Ocean] The deepest dive ever recorded for a reptile was achieved by a leatherback turtle

in 2006, southwest of the Cape Verde islands. Leatherbacks are also among the fastest reptiles, clocking speeds of up to 22 miles (35.4 km) per hour (6.7 kph) in the water. ❼

WHALE SHARK (*Rhincodon typus*) • [6,325 feet (1,928 m), Atlantic Ocean] Whale sharks are the largest fish on Earth. In 2010, one satellite-tagged individual was recorded more than a mile (1.6 km) deep off the coast of Florida. ❽

SPERM WHALE (*Physeter macrocephalus*) • [7,382 feet (2,388 m), oceans worldwide] These majestic whales, who sleep in a vertical position in shallow water, can spend more than an hour underwater. Their prey of choice is the formidable giant squid. ❾

SOUTHERN ELEPHANT SEAL (*Mirounga leonina*) • [7,835 feet (2,388 m), Southern Ocean] Whales aside, no mammal can dive with quite the gusto of a southern elephant seal. By tracking these seals on their subsea journeys, researchers have even discovered new features of the seafloor—troughs that carry currents of warm water into the Antarctic. ❿

SOUTHERN ELEPHANT SEAL LOUSE (*Lepidophthirus macrorhini*) • [7,835 feet (2,388 m), Southern Ocean] The lice that attach themselves to the flippers of southern elephant seals sneak their way to astonishing depths by proxy—so they might as well sneak onto this page too.

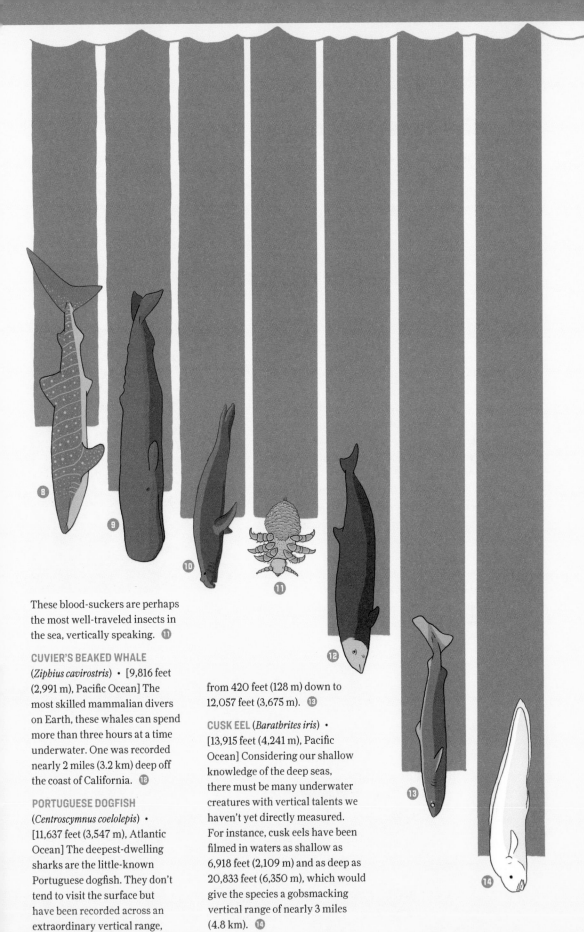

These blood-suckers are perhaps the most well-traveled insects in the sea, vertically speaking. ⑪

CUVIER'S BEAKED WHALE
(*Ziphius cavirostris*) • [9,816 feet (2,991 m), Pacific Ocean] The most skilled mammalian divers on Earth, these whales can spend more than three hours at a time underwater. One was recorded nearly 2 miles (3.2 km) deep off the coast of California. ⑫

PORTUGUESE DOGFISH
(*Centroscymnus coelolepis*) • [11,637 feet (3,547 m), Atlantic Ocean] The deepest-dwelling sharks are the little-known Portuguese dogfish. They don't tend to visit the surface but have been recorded across an extraordinary vertical range,

from 420 feet (128 m) down to 12,057 feet (3,675 m). ⑬

CUSK EEL (*Barathrites iris*) • [13,915 feet (4,241 m), Pacific Ocean] Considering our shallow knowledge of the deep seas, there must be many underwater creatures with vertical talents we haven't yet directly measured. For instance, cusk eels have been filmed in waters as shallow as 6,918 feet (2,109 m) and as deep as 20,833 feet (6,350 m), which would give the species a gobsmacking vertical range of nearly 3 miles (4.8 km). ⑭

AFRICA

Atlantic Mudskippers

Land-loving fish hint at our own past.

RANGE: Along the Atlantic coast of Africa, from Morocco to Angola
SPECIES: Atlantic mudskipper (*Periophthalmus barbarus*)

◆ With protruding eyes and downturned grins, mudskippers look as if they are perpetually pondering the nature of their existence.

They're not the only ones. The world's roughly two dozen mudskipper species, some of which spend up to 90 percent of their time on land, have both prompted and answered a number of questions about what exactly they're doing there.

Mudskippers get around on land by "crutching," moving their right and left forelimbs together to propel their bodies forward. During courtship, males up the ante, using their tails to hurl their bodies out of the mud to attract potential mates and getting up to 2 feet (60 cm) of air.

Mudskippers show off their adaptations: climbing forelimbs (above) and blinkable eyes (below).

Videos of these behaviors inspired Daniel Goldman, a physicist who studies animal locomotion at Georgia Tech, to build a robot that could provide clues to an enduring question: How did Earth's early creatures move from water to land? The mudskipper's rudimentary appendages are likely akin to those of the first terrestrial explorers, and the muddy, sometimes sloped environment they crutch around in is similar to what these pioneers would have faced in the Devonian period, when they first climbed out of the sea.

Goldman built a robot—"MuddyBot"—that mimicked the mudskipper's body and movements and tested it out on sandy surfaces. Sand, like Devonian mud, flows according to the pressure applied. A little push, and it stays stable; a harder push, and it moves. By observing MuddyBot's movements, Goldman and his colleagues modeled how a well-coordinated tail push, combined with the thrust of a forelimb push-up, propels the mudskipper up slippery slopes. MuddyBot's insights, published in 2016, helped solve a mystery about how life may have transitioned to land that static fossils couldn't explain.

Mudskippers have other adaptations for land life. They can extract and absorb oxygen through their skin, gills, and gill chamber. Compared with other fish, their eyes can detect more colors, are less sensitive to UV light, and are less likely to suffer from nearsightedness in air. Their top-mounted eyes rotate, retract, and move independently, providing a peripheral view for detecting land-dwelling predators.

More recently, scientists uncovered another clue about the evolution of landlubbers hiding in the mudskipper: Unlike most fish, they blink. Each eye retracts within a dermal cup that works like a socket and lid combined. Although they evolved this trait separately from humans, mudskippers blink for about as long as we do, and for the same reasons: Blinking helps them protect, clean, and moisturize their eyes.

While land life comes naturally to us humans, the mudskipper reminds us that getting here required some work. ❯ **How to see them:** From Lagos, book a day trip to Epe, a small fishing village where you can visit the mangroves where mudskippers live. When there's an ebb tide, look for leaping males, who will appear larger and are more colorful than females.

Killer Algae

The world's largest single-celled organism is a ruthless, pepper-flavored sea lettuce.

RANGE: Native to tropical waters in the Pacific and Indian Oceans and the Caribbean Sea; invasive in the Mediterranean and coastal waters off Australia and California
SPECIES: *Caulerpa taxifolia*

◆ At first glance, *Caulerpa taxifolia*, a member of the sea lettuce family, looks like normal seaweed. But looks can be deceiving: Each individual plant is made up of a single, massive cell.

In multicellular animals, different types of cells specialize to fulfill different roles—for instance, skin cells protect, blood cells transport, and muscle cells push and pull. Plant cells, however, tend to be more jack-of-all-trades; that's how new roots can grow from a plant cutting's stem.

About a hundred species of algae in the genus *Caulerpa* take this plant characteristic to the extreme. A *Caulerpa*—waving fronds, rootlike rhizoids, and everything in between—is one big cell. Multiple nuclei are scattered throughout, unseparated by cell walls. This is all the more impressive considering that some stems have been reported

From waving fronds to rooted rhizoids, a Caulerpa is just one giant cell.

to reach lengths of more than 9 feet (2.7 m). By certain measures, *Caulerpa taxifolia* is the world's largest single-celled organism.

Its supersized cells carpet the seafloor in its native habitat: tropical waters in the Pacific and Indian Oceans and the Caribbean Sea. However, since a cold-tolerant strain became popular in aquariums, it has been cropping up in places like the Mediterranean Sea and the California coast. Scientists suspect the culprit is dumped aquarium water.

C. taxifolia grows quickly, and specialized bacteria living in its tissues help it take up nutrients. These traits may have helped the alga thrive and become an invasive species—it often decimates native reef and coastal communities where it is introduced. Plus, the seaweed produces a noxious peppery chemical. Some animals in its native habitat have adapted to tolerate the toxin, but for uninitiated species, it's chemical warfare.

Conservationists have spent decades attempting to fight back against the algae. For instance, *Caulerpa*-eating sea slugs were deployed in the Mediterranean, but the "crumbs" of algae the slugs left behind were able to propagate and spread, making the problem worse. Other interventions have had better luck: When *C. taxifolia* reared its feathery fronds off the coast of San Diego in 2003, isolation of affected areas and treatment with chlorine bleach helped eradicate these giant killer cells. ❯ **How to see them:** Try snorkeling and diving in shallow coastal lagoons in one of the many areas where they've spread.

Really Big Cells

Caulerpa taxifolia is not the only shockingly large cell in the world. Here are some others:

GIRAFFE NEURONS: Big animals have big nerve cells. Giraffes' sciatic neurons, which run from the spinal cord down the leg, can be 15 feet (4.6 m) long.

OSTRICH EGG YOLKS: In general, eggs are some of a body's largest cells—in humans, they're one of the only cells visible to the naked eye. They're especially big in animals whose embryos are nourished by yolk rather than through a placenta. Ostrich egg yolks are among the heaviest, densest cells out there.

BUBBLE ALGAE: These singled-celled marine plants, nicknamed "sailor's eyeballs," take the form of shiny globes the size of Ping-Pong balls. They can be found growing on submerged tree roots in mangrove forests.

STENTOR ROESELII: At ¾ inch (2 cm) long, these single-celled, trumpet-shaped ciliates are bigger than many multicellular organisms. In experiments, they've been seen to contort away from and bat at irritants, demonstrating decision-making skills despite lacking brain cells—or any specialized cells at all.

Peacock Mantis Shrimp

These crustaceans punch hard, wield energy balls, and see colors we can't imagine.

RANGE: Shallow reefs in the Indian Ocean and southwestern Pacific Ocean
SPECIES: Peacock mantis shrimp (*Odontodactylus scyllarus*)

◆ With a curved crustacean body, bright polka-dot legs, and a shell that shimmers in all the colors of the rainbow, a mantis shrimp looks a bit like a jumbo prawn crossed with a birthday cake.

But that description doesn't give this impressive creature quite enough credit. A mantis shrimp—neither a shrimp nor a mantis, but a type of crustacean called a stomatopod—can regrow lost limbs, perceive light outside the visible color spectrum, and punch hard enough to break open a sealed clam shell or a double-paned aquarium tank.

Stomatopods have stalked eyes, thirteen pairs of limbs, and thick, articulated abdomens that come in a wide range of vivid colors. "I tend to call them alien lobsters," says Ilse Daly, a biophysicist who studied mantis shrimp at the University of Bristol.

Appearance aside, the peacock mantis shrimp's greatest claim to fame might be that extraordinary punch. Its muscular front arms, called raptorial appendages, strike with such speed and precision that a single out-and-back jab can take as little as 2 milliseconds, making it one of the fastest known movements in the animal kingdom.

The motion is so fast that it vaporizes the water molecules around it, creating a bubble of energy that slams into the mantis shrimp's target and nearly doubles the force of the original strike. Mantis shrimp use this superior smashing ability to bust apart clams, snails, and other hard-shelled invertebrates to eat. (They also use it to defend themselves, earning them the nickname "thumb-splitters" among fishermen.)

Equally excessive—but less well understood—are the mantis shrimp's eyes, which contain 12 kinds of color receptors (compare that to a human's measly three). Theoretically, this means that a mantis shrimp could perceive up to 100,000 colors, from infrared to ultraviolet. But experiments at the University of California at Berkeley have found they are unable to distinguish between many hues that are roughly similar to each other.

In fact, because the color receptors are found only in a narrow band across the center of each eye, the mantis shrimp's overall vision is probably extremely blurry. "I wouldn't want to see one behind the wheel of a car," says Daly. She has found that mantis shrimp do prefer some colors over others: "Yellow is quite a favorite," she says. Scientists' best guess is that mantis shrimp use color in a way that people don't yet understand. ❯ **How to see them:** Scuba diving off the coast of Tanzania, Indonesia, or another coastal Indo-Pacific nation is the best way to spot one of these colorful crustaceans—but watch your thumbs.

Mantis shrimp can theoretically perceive up to 100,000 colors, but only out of a narrow band in the center of each eye.

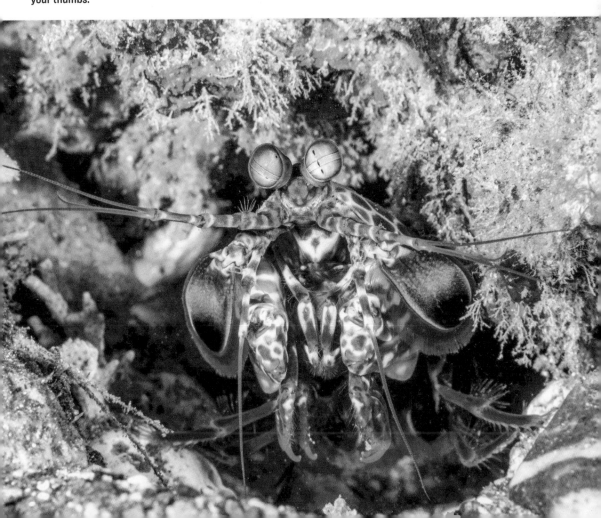

Seeing Beneath the Waves

Light works differently in the ocean, whether it's absorbed and bent by water, emitted by glowing bacteria, or snuffed out by sheer depth. Many ocean dwellers have complex ocular adaptations that allow them to look around anyway. Grab a set of goggles and dive in to learn more.

WINGHEAD SHARKS (*Eusphyra blochii*) • The sporty, elongated head extensions that give hammerhead sharks their name is known as a cephalofoils. Winghead sharks have the largest cephalofoils, which separate their eyes by up to 3 feet (1 m)—nearly half the length of their bodies. These spread-apart eyes take in sweeping views of the environment, enhance the binocular overlap of the shark's field of vision, and improve depth perception.

SCALLOPS (*Pecten* spp.) • Astronomers of the ocean realm, scallops gaze up from the seafloor out of up to 200 eyes. Unlike human eyes, which use lenses to focus incoming light onto the sensitive retina, scallop eyes are backed by curved mirrors. The mirrors are made of tiny stacked crystals that reflect light back up to two retinas with different sensing properties. A scallop's brain may be able to process the hundreds of simultaneous images produced by these mirrored eyes into a coherent view of the world.

BLUE SEA STARS (*Linckia laevigata*) • When the lights go out, humans fumble around with extended arms to avoid unseen obstacles. A navigating blue sea star not only feels with its outstretched arms—it can also see. These starfish traverse tide pools and stony reefs using visual information collected from a single compound eye on the tip of each arm, which they'll angle upward for a better vantage. Although their eyes lack the lenses they'd need to properly focus, scientists have found that blue sea stars plucked from reefs and placed a short distance away can find their way back home.

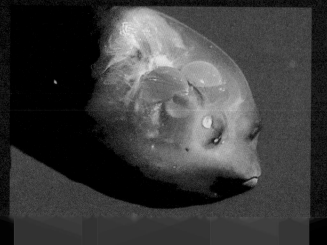

BARRELEYE FISH (*Macropinna microstoma*) • The glowing green eyes of the barreleye fish look like two aliens in the cockpit of a fish-shaped submersible. These tubular eyes gaze up toward the surface, watching for predators and prey from within a clear, jellylike head dome. The eyes rotate forward when hunting and are protected within the translucent barrier from the painful stings of the barreleye's favorite food, siphonophores. The two eyelike spots on this fish's gelatinous cranium are actually olfactory sensors, used for smelling.

LITTLE BLUE PENGUINS (*Eudyptula minor*) • Many animals, including most birds and reptiles, are equipped with transparent third eyelids called nictitating membranes. Researchers studying little blue penguins have found their membranes work like built-in goggles, preventing their eyes from drying out in harsh salt water. They also shield against dirt and debris and help the petite penguins focus their vision while they're hunting underwater. Other ocean dwellers with nictitating membranes include some sharks and seals.

CALIFORNIA HALIBUT (*Paralichthys californicus*) • Not long after a California halibut hatches, one of his bulging eyeballs starts to travel toward the other. Eventually both peepers are on the same side of his body, allowing the fish to rest on the muddy seabed and look up for predators and prey. The fish's eyes are able to detect patterns on the seafloor around it—and once the fish's brain receives that information, it signals specialized skin cells called chromatophores to change color as needed to provide the fish with appropriate camouflage.

BLOODY-BELLY COMB JELLIES

(*Lampocteis cruentiventer*) • The bloody-belly comb jelly pulses through the deep sea like a beating heart. These creatures have no eyes; instead, they use light-detecting proteins called opsins to perceive flashes of bioluminescence emitted by other organisms. The glowing red color on the jelly's belly masks any bioluminescent bits of prey already consumed—and itself is not visible in the depths, where low-wavelength red light fails to reach.

FIDDLER CRABS (family Ocypodidae) • Fiddler crabs have compound eyes that rest atop elevated structures called stalks. By controlling blood flow within the stalks, the crabs can raise and lower their eyes like periscopes, peeping up from sandy burrows or tidal flats. Their eyestalks are slightly curved to allow them to watch for bird attacks from the skies, while their mobility grants them panoramic views of the rest of their environment. Specialized corneas make for an easy visual

COCKEYED SQUID (*Histioteuthis heteropsis*) • Like a photographer with cameras set up for different shots, the cockeyed squid is an optical specialist. As this squid cruises the ocean's twilight zone, one bulging yellow eye searches for threats from predators above. On the opposite side of its body, a second, smaller eye squints into the depths to spot flashes of light from bioluminescent prey. Between the two,

Mangrove Babies

Plants that deliver live offspring

◆ You're familiar with how most plants reproduce: They make a seed, then drop it, or release it to the wind, or put it in fruit that some other creature carries off. In one way or another, that seed makes its way into soil, where it germinates and begins to grow into a new plant. But many mangroves—coastal trees that thrive in an environment where most trees can't—deliver live babies.

Through a process called vivipary, the mangrove fertilizes and germinates a seed while it's still on the tree, nourishing it either with nutrients from the tissues of the parent tree or through photosynthesis. By the time it leaves the parent tree, the little one is a fully independent plant called a propagule, as much as a foot and a half (45 cm) long.

Exactly what happens when the propagule strikes out on its own varies by species. Some just drop to the ground and take root. But many of them float on the surrounding water and may not settle down until they've traveled a great distance; they can even grow leaves while at sea, which act as sails to help ensure that they find land eventually.

You can find mangrove forests along coasts in the intertidal zone, above water during low tide but submerged during high tide. The mangrove isn't a family of plants so much as it's a name for a set of strategies trees use to live in these conditions, which alternate between hot and dry and salty and sodden.

Live birth is just one of their many extraordinary adaptations. To breathe while standing in water, many have adapted special roots that remain aboveground, like snorkels for trees. To get rid of excess salt, some species may secrete sodium crystals through glands on their leaves. ❭ **How to see them:** Mangrove forests are found throughout the world's tropical and subtropical coastal regions and in some river deltas. The Malindi and Watamu Marine National Parks and Reserves in Kenya include mangrove forests and are popular tourist destinations.

RANGE: Brackish coastal regions of Africa, Asia, the Americas, and the Middle East. In Africa, the greatest diversity of species is found in Mozambique, Tanzania, Kenya, and Somalia.

SPECIES: Major species in East Africa include tulip mangrove (*Heritiera littoralis*), white-flowered black mangrove (*Lumnitzera racemosa*), and loop-root mangrove (*Rhizophora mucronata*)

Salt crystals on a mangrove leaf

Scaly-Foot Gastropods

These battle-ready snails construct armor from volcanic metals.

RANGE: Hydrothermal vent sites, about 1½ miles (2.4 km) deep in the Indian Ocean, off the coast of Madagascar
SPECIES: Scaly-foot gastropod (*Chrysomallon squamiferum*)

◆ Scaly-foot gastropods don't need to eat—they're nutritionally supported by chemosynthetic bacteria that live in enormous pouches in the snail's esophagus and juice them up like portable power packs. They're also hermaphroditic, so they don't have to mate. Instead, much of their life's work appears to lie in creating unique and impenetrable armor.

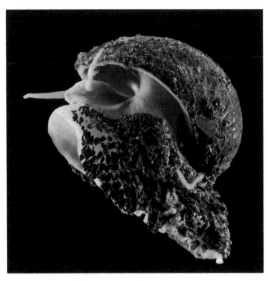

These snails, about the size of billiard balls, reside in high-pressure hydrothermal vents situated around submarine volcanoes deep in the Indian Ocean. The hydrothermal fissures, also known as "black smokers," exude acidic, magma-heated water and carry along metals and chemicals from beneath Earth's crust. In 2001, researchers investigating the Kairei hydrothermal field deep in the Indian Ocean discovered how these mollusks—also known as armored snails or sea pangolins—elegantly build the most difficult aspects of their environments into their own protective gear.

The snails incorporate iron sulfide minerals, including pyrite (fool's gold) and greigite, into their shells, as well as the plated sclerites that cover their feet. This form of biomineralization hasn't been seen in any other living animal. Scientists believe it could be an adaptation against the snail's major predators—crabs and venomous cone snails—or a mechanism to dispose of toxins picked up from the smokers.

The scaly-foot gastropod's shell is triple-layered: An aragonite-based innermost layer that closely resembles the shells of other mollusks is covered by a squishy, force-absorbing organic layer and topped by the volcanic minerals. This armor's strength and endurance are so impressive that governments and scientists are attempting to replicate it for defense materials.

As effective and inspiring as this protection is, it likely won't be enough to protect these very rare snails from humans—our own thirst for deep-sea minerals has led us to develop underwater mining technology that won't spare the unique communities around hydrothermal vents. ❯ **How to see them:** Scaly-foot gastropods are found only in the Kairei, Longqi, and Solitaire submarine hydrothermal fields along the ridges of the Indian Ocean.

The foot of this tough snail is covered in hard, iron-coated tabs called sclerites.

Self-Stranding Orcas

Orcas go to extraordinary lengths to capture their favorite meals.

RANGE: Punta Norte's orcas are most frequently spotted off the north end of Peninsula Valdés, along Argentina's remote Patagonian coast.

SPECIES: Orca (*Orcinus orca*)

◆ If you see a whale on land, it usually means something is wrong. But along the remote central coast of Argentina, where Peninsula Valdés juts into the South Atlantic like a Rhode Island–sized fist, members of a small band of orcas beach themselves day after day.

Punta Norte orcas—named for the northernmost point on the peninsula, where this population sometimes gathers—have developed a mysterious yet ingenious style of hunting. They intentionally strand themselves on the beach, where sea lions take refuge, and then lunge to capture them, often with the assistance of an incoming wave.

The strategy is extremely risky. Stranded for too long, orcas face mortal threats like dehydration and the collapse of vital organs under their own massive weight.

Such an unlikely practice doesn't come naturally, so they teach it. When the tide is low, a female orca will swim parallel to the beach with a young calf between her and the gravelly shore. The little one will then strand him- or herself on the beach and "capture" washed-up kelp.

The calf doesn't eat the kelp—that would be like a lion hunting a carrot. It's just a prop, standing in for the eventual real prey. The kelp lessons also may educate the young orcas about hydrodynamics, says Jorge Cazenave, a researcher for the nonprofit group Punta Norte Orca Research. The pupils watch the kelp as it washes toward the beach and is carried out again, similar to the movement of a floating sea lion pup. "They know the tides," Cazenave says, and the orcas don't practice when the tide is going out, because it's too risky.

Observers at Punta Norte first recorded the self-stranding technique in the late 1970s. Some think these orca-run hunting classes may be a response to a dwindling sea lion population, brought down by decades of human hunting and unregulated fishing. The number of orcas who practice intentional stranding here has grown from a few to more than half of the group of about 25 orcas most frequently spotted here, as it's passed down to offspring and to unrelated newcomers.

It's "a culture that's taught, learned, and practiced," says Cazenave. "There's no doubt about it." ⟩ **How to see them:** Between February and May, which coincides with sea lion pupping season, fly into Buenos Aires and take a connecting flight to the city of Trelew. From there, rent a car or join an excursion to Punta Norte, a three-hour drive along rocky roads to the north and east. Once you arrive, head to a designated overlook (most of the beaches are off-limits to tourists), cross your fingers, and wait.

Orca Cultures

Orcas live, hunt, and play in tight family groups. Over time, these groups may develop special behaviors and interests—some passing fads, some longer lasting.

THE SALMON HAT TREND: In 1987, a female orca in Puget Sound started festooning her snout with a dead salmon, starting a craze that swept the area for six weeks before it petered out.

PEBBLE MASSAGES: In the summers, orcas living off the coast of British Columbia like to visit shallow areas lined with smooth rocks. They exhale through their blowholes, sink to the bottom, and rub their backs and bellies on the pebbles. Family groups return to the same "rubbing beaches" year after year.

THE LAW OF THE TONGUE: Into the early 1900s, Aboriginal Yuin and European whalers in Eden, Australia, had a special arrangement with the local orcas: The animals helped the hunters take down large whales in exchange for their favorite part of the kill, the lips and tongue. This agreement, known as "the law of the tongue," appears to have lasted until a beached orca was stabbed, at which point things began to fall apart.

BOAT RAMMING: Since 2020, members of an orca pod near the Iberian Peninsula have been roughing up boats, slamming into them with their heads and even snapping the rudders with their teeth. No one is quite sure why.

THE WILD LIFE OF A Self-Stranding Orca Photographer

■ Jorge Cazenave is a wildlife photographer and a principal researcher for Punta Norte Orca Research, based on Peninsula Valdés in his native Argentina. Formerly a lawyer, he has used his legal expertise to help found two NGOs, Punta Norte Orca Research, and We Are Wildlife, which provides funding to small wildlife conservation projects in Argentina, Brazil, and Chile.

● **How did you get started in wildlife photography?**
As a kid, I lived for a couple of years in Potomac, Maryland, while my dad was an attaché for the Argentine embassy in Washington, DC. He loved watching squirrels—we don't have them in Argentina. He bought a nice Nikon camera and was crazy enough to let me use it, so I learned photography by taking pictures of squirrels.

● **How would you describe your scientific contribution to research on Punta Norte orcas?**
A lot of it is taking the photographs that are used to identify individual orcas and their behaviors. I also process some of the data used by our scientists, who can't be in the field all the time. Right now we're working on a paper about orcas' social networking. A lot of that data comes from interpreting what's going on with the orcas out in the water.

● **What do you learn about an orca's personality through the practice of photography?**
I use a lens that allows me to be 20 times closer than the human eye. When you do that, you can see when the orca is looking at you or paying attention to you. You're seeing them as they're vocalizing and communicating. It's a weird connection: They don't understand us; we don't understand them. But because the camera allows you to get closer to them, you see more clearly their social structure, their intelligence, their playfulness.

● **Have the orcas taught you anything about yourself?**
One of the things about photographing orcas is that you spend a very long time sitting and waiting for them to show up. I've spent 30 days on the beach by myself, like a monk, looking at the ocean, and nothing has happened.

So they've taught me to be patient— to lower my expectations, but not to lose hope.

● **When you're talking to friends about your work, is there a story that stands out?**
There's an orca called Maga who is one of the oldest matriarchs— she leads a group of about 10 to 12. Once, I saw Maga strand herself for 35 minutes. But she showed no nervousness, no frantic movements. She was completely calm.

The little ones in the water were starting to get nervous for her, but she just got into position, turning herself with her pectoral fins to face headfirst into the water, and waited. Her knowledge of tides, of hydrodynamics—she knew she'd be okay.

● **For every good shot you take, how many are bad?**
Thousands! For the orca, almost any shot where we can see the animal is good because it's used for identifying each individual and understanding its details. But for the most beautiful shots, where everything goes right at the same time? Those are once every 20 years. ■

Wind-Sculpted Trees

Hanging on at the end of the world

◆ To visit Ushuaia, a remote outpost perched along a sliver of land in Argentina's Tierra del Fuego, is to witness one of the world's slowest dramas. Here, relentless, battering winds wrench trees sideways over the course of years or decades.

These trees—most of which belong to three species of southern beech native to the area—cling to the earth in twisted surrender, their branches reaching out as though for help. Sometimes called "flag trees," they take on "the most exquisitely distorted, twisted shapes," says ecologist and nature photographer Alan Watson Featherstone.

The westerly winds that blow through Ushuaia can exceed 60 knots—not quite powerful enough to break the trees, but ruthless enough to blow them into submission. While inland trees of the same species grow tall and straight, draping themselves with lichens, mosses, and edible fungi, the side-lying wind-ravaged coastal trees are smaller and support less wildlife.

But they are very much alive. For those who live near them, the coastal beeches are symbols of strength and character, bearing the story of life-long struggle and resilience in Earth's southernmost forest. **> How to see them: Journey to Ushuaia by flight, bus, ferry, or cruise. A challenging hike snaking around the Dientes de Navarino mountain range will lead you to the most severely contorted trees.**

LOCATION: Ushuaia, in Tierra del Fuego, Argentina
SPECIES: Southern beeches of the genus *Nothofagus*, including Magellan's beech or guindo (*N. betuloides*), lenga tree (*N. pumilio*), and Antarctic beech (*N. antarctica*)

The wind-shaped trees of Ushuaia, in Tierra del Fuego. These lopsided trees are called "flag trees" because they blow like flags, reflecting the direction of the strong winds that created them.

NORTH AMERICA

Gulf Corvinas

The loudest fish in the sea

RANGE: **Northern Gulf of California, Mexico**
SPECIES: **Gulf corvina**
(Cynoscion othonopterus)

◆ During a few months in spring, 2-foot-long (60 cm) silvery fish gather along the northernmost edge of the Gulf of California. They arrive around full or new moons, when the tide is highest. Although there are millions, the chocolate-milk waters of the Colorado River Delta hide them from view.

But a low roar gives them away. Above the surface, it's louder than a boat engine. Below, it could deafen a sea lion. This is the rumble of romance—the Gulf corvina's mating song.

"It's kind of like a machine gun going off," says Timothy Rowell, who used underwater microphones to record the calls of hot-and-bothered male corvinas for a study published in 2017. Individual fish registered volumes louder than any other marine fish—and even humpback whales, who are more than three thousand times their size. The chorus of millions of corvinas tops 202 decibels, as loud as a rocket launch.

These croakers turned crooners do not sing using vocal cords. Instead, a calling corvina repeatedly squeezes special "sonic muscles" around his swim bladder, a gas-filled organ that helps buoy the fish in place. The effect is like a drumstick hitting a drum, with the pulses of sound reverberating from the bladder out into the murky waves and beyond.

Like singles in a packed bar, the male corvinas may have to shout to attract attention—particularly in the gulf's sediment-filled waters, says Rowell. Or perhaps the calls help synchronize the fishes' spawning behavior, an event exquisitely timed to occur at this one site. Over the course of three months, roughly between March and May, what researchers assume to be the entire adult Gulf corvina population swarms into the narrow channel of the Colorado River Delta. Once there, males and females release sperm and eggs in unison. Shortly after, researchers speculate, moon-powered tidal currents whisk fertilized future offspring off to sea.

The corvinas' loud lunar rendezvous isn't exactly subtle. The sheer volume of their calls makes them easy to find, and Gulf corvinas are vulnerable to overfishing. In just a few minutes, fishers in small boats called pangas can land 2 tons of corvinas with a single net. The local fleet of some 500 boats can swoop up as many as 1.8 million fish over a spawning season.

Regulations are in place to prevent overfishing, but enforcement is "minimal," says researcher Catalina López-Sagástegui. Recently, economically troubled local fishers have raised alarms that the corvinas they catch are getting smaller, suggesting fewer fish are escaping the nets to grow large and old as well as loud. ❭ **How to see them:** Visiting is not recommended, but you can hear Gulf corvina calls online.

Dead Zones

Sneak peeks at the ocean's future

◆ Each year, spring rains across the American Midwest funnel massive amounts of agricultural runoff, sewage, and industrial pollution into the Mississippi River. When this flood of nutrients reaches the sea, it sparks massive algal blooms, resulting in an alarming but fascinating phenomenon: the Gulf of Mexico Dead Zone, named for the fact that almost no life can survive within its bounds.

This swath of water, which has been known to spread to 8,500 square miles (22,015 sq km), is hypoxic, meaning its oxygen content is extremely low. In these conditions, larger oxygen-dependent species like fishes and cetaceans are forced to flee. The phytoplankton and cyanobacteria that make up algal blooms eventually die and sink to the seabed, where they are consumed by benthic bacteria. Like us, these bacteria take in oxygen and release carbon dioxide when they respire. More phytoplankton means more bacteria, which in turn means surrounding oxygen is depleted faster.

Dead zones are not new—they've been around for at least 1.2 million years. However, they are growing in size and number as a result of human activities, notably climate change.

In general, the world's oceans are slowly running out of oxygen—levels have declined by 2 percent since the 1960s. Under stable conditions, the upper layers of the ocean are heated by the sun and eventually sink as they cool down and become denser. This mixing process helps oxygen reach even the deepest waters. However, global warming is disrupting this cycle, causing the ocean to become ever more stratified and oxygen-deficient.

Most species, especially immobile species like reef-building coral, will struggle to adapt to this changing environment, but a select few seem poised to thrive. Massive swarms of jellyfish have been recorded in hypoxic waters around the world; their lack of brains and blood means they have very little need for oxygen. With no predators left to keep the jellyfish in check, dead zones' rich supply of plankton are theirs for the taking, which has worrying knock-on effects for the ecosystem. Scientists have also discovered diverse communities of nematode worms flourishing in the fully oxygen-free, or anoxic, waters of the Baltic Sea. **How to see them:** By definition, dead zones don't offer a lot of wildlife sightings; however, satellite imaging can show us the algal blooms that often mark them out.

RANGE: Globally, more than 400 low-oxygen areas have already been recorded across oceans and coastal waters, notably in the Gulf of Mexico, in the Baltic Sea, and off the coast of Northern California.
SPECIES: Dead zones are characterized by algae, jellyfish, nematodes, and plankton.

Some dead zones, like this one in the Baltic Sea in 2005, are large enough to be viewed from space.

Munk's Pygmy Devil Rays

A mysterious marine circus act in the shallows of the eastern Pacific

LOCATION: Gulf of California off the coast of La Ventana, Baja California Sur, Mexico

SPECIES: Munk's pygmy devil ray (*Mobula munkiana*)

◆ The sound of thunder cracks the silence of the open ocean. It emerges from the water, not the sky, as hundreds of floppy marine animals launch themselves out of the sea. In near unison, these Munk's pygmy devil rays flip and somersault through the air before belly-flopping back, flat on the water's surface.

The Munk's pygmy devil ray can be found throughout the eastern Pacific, from the coast of Baja California Sur to Peru. These rays are most often spotted between April and July, congregating in large underwater masses or jumping out of the shallow waters of the Gulf of California. The massive groups they form are called fevers. And their shows are hot.

Munk's pygmy devil rays are the most acrobatic members of the *Mobula* genus, which also includes devil rays and manta rays. They can leap up to 10 feet (3 m) into the air, and often do so in concert, with hundreds leaping synchronously.

Below the surface, the show continues with more impressive stunts. Thousands-strong fevers move together in coordinated chaos, forming giant, swirling masses. The entire display can last hours. Then the rays stop jumping, the swirling slows, and silence retakes the ocean.

The reason for this mysterious marine circus act is unknown. Scientists think the aerial movements may remove parasites, attract mates, or send messages to other fevers. And observance of nearby ray pups and juveniles suggests the submarine cyclones of rays may be mating aggregations. (The younger rays' proximity also hints at the potential location of elusive nursery grounds.)

Understanding and protecting nursery grounds is particularly important for this species, whose slow-to-mature young may get caught in nets before they reach their reproductive years. Pregnant rays face another test—caring for an internal egg until it hatches, then giving live birth. Mothers birth just one pup per litter, every one to three years.

Munk's pygmy devil rays can leap 10 feet (3 m) into the air.

Researchers, conservationists, and community fisheries are increasingly working together in the eastern Pacific to promote ray conservation. And in Baja California Sur, local fishers like Guillermo Lucero Leon are starting to see the benefits of protecting the raucous rays in the area's budding ecotourism industry. "I started working in tourism, and I really liked the change," he says. Fishers can make money guiding tours instead of fishing, and "the tourists get benefits because they have a good time."

Now visitors can hop on a boat and, a short sail later, witness one of the greatest acrobatic shows on Earth. ❯ **How to see them:** From April to July, these creatures congregate in the tens of thousands a few miles off the eastern coast of Baja California Sur in the Gulf of California. Book a tour with one of several ecotourism companies based in La Paz, Cabo San Lucas, or La Ventana, Mexico, and spend a day swimming near the underwater swirling masses. Or join a weeklong expedition and scuba dive alongside the animals.

Sea Skaters

The ocean's only full-time insects

◆ Land is buzzing with over a million known insect species. But the open ocean has very few—five, to be exact. Called sea skaters, these bugs—all members of the genus *Halobates*—spend their lives entirely at sea, poised atop the water's surface. They are the only insects to never set foot on land.

Sea skaters resemble, and are related to, the water striders common in freshwater ponds. But they're wingless and much smaller—each is about the size of a peppercorn, says Lanna Cheng, a *Halobates* expert with the Scripps Institution of Oceanography. Being tiny and exposed makes them alert, hardy, and dexterous: They can leap in the air, dodge fish and birds, flee passing nets, and grab prey.

Sea skaters are covered in nano-hairs, which they groom almost constantly, adding a waxy secretion. This gives them water repellence, buoyancy, and the ability to survive surprise dunks, as the waxed hairs trap air bubbles like a built-in scuba tank. Despite constant daylight exposure on the open sea, they also appear resistant to heat and UV damage—even during their early developmental stages, which can last for two months.

RANGE: Collectively widespread across most of the world's oceans, from 40° north to 40° south
SPECIES: Five species in the genus *Halobates*: *H. germanus*, *H. micans*, *H. sericeus*, *H. sobrinus*, and *H. splendens*

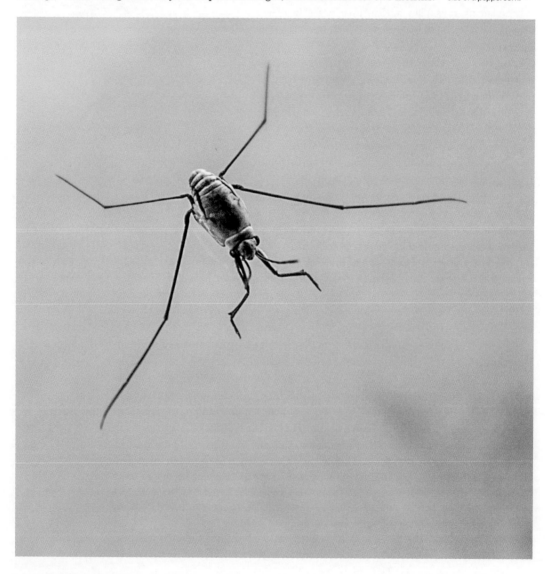

A sea skater is the size of a peppercorn.

When they're ready to mate, they somehow manage to find each other in their vast, ever-changing, and undifferentiated environment, potentially with the help of waterborne pheromones, Cheng says.

If this nautical meet-cute is successful, mother sea skaters glue the resulting eggs to feathers, floating shells, or even trash. (Good vessels are in demand—one milk jug pulled up off the coast of Costa Rica had 70,000 *H. sobrinus* eggs stuck to it—and sea skaters are thriving in the ocean's many garbage patches.) Nymphhood is another mystery: It's not known what newborns eat, although the answer may be "each other."

Sea skaters are hard to spot, let alone study. The first records of them come from the 1820s, when a Russian ship picked some up while circumnavigating the globe. Even now, researchers have trouble directly observing them in the wild—although the distribution of collected specimens suggests they're found all around the world. Interested parties are left to piece things together from the behavior of related, easier-to-find coastal *Halobates* and wait for the occasional lucky encounter with this bug of the high seas. **〉 How to see them:** When the ocean is calm, watch the surface for tiny, shiny dots skidding around. If you're on a research vessel, check the plankton nets for spiderlike creatures.

THE WILD LIFE OF An Oceanic Entomologist

■ Lanna Cheng is a research scientist at the Scripps Institution of Oceanography at the University of California, San Diego. A world expert on *Halobates*, she has to work hard to get support to study these elusive bugs—and to find them in the first place.

• **What was known about sea skaters when you started researching them?**
Nobody had done any biology on the oceanic species. Adults are about 5 millimeters in body length, totally wingless, with long legs. Can you see something like that from your cruise ship? No. How do you catch them? Nobody knows.

• **What was it like learning how to catch them at sea?**
I had the opportunity to sail from Honolulu to San Diego. Before I went, I worked with a technician and we designed a net, called a neuston net [after the word for organisms that dwell on the ocean's surface or high in the water column]. It's rectangular rather than round, and it has two floats at each end—it will float on the surface, but the lower part is below.

We would tow the net for 30 minutes or an hour—but when it came out, we'd have insects mixing with gluey [plankton]. I couldn't get any live ones to study.

There was a little cage for the crew to clean the side of the ship, or to paint it. My husband went with a little tiny aquarium net. When the ship tilted, if there was an insect around, he'd try. But he couldn't catch any. Then I said, "Let's do very, very short tows with the net." We'd do a 5-minute or 10-minute tow, and then finally I was able to get some live insects to study.

• **Are there other ways to get hold of sea skaters?**
If you're a marine biologist, when you collect plankton samples, you'll get a bag full of things. Some are [*Halobates*]—little black things, like spiders with long legs. So almost all the major marine research institutions around the world have people picking out these things from their plankton samples. I began to get inquiries from these institutions: "Please, can you help us analyze them?"

• **What have you been able to observe about them?**
They are oceanic animals—they have no idea what a physical barrier is. As soon as you put

them into a small aquarium, they hit themselves on the wall. Fortunately, we had a huge, big aquarium on the deck, so I was able to keep some alive for about 10 days. After that, they died—they're just not happy to be enclosed.

Also, they have wonderful eyesight. When a bird flies over and there's a shadow, they get really agitated. For fish to feed on them is almost impossible. I tried to go underwater and [photograph] them above me, but if there's a fish making movement, they will escape, no problem.

• **What else makes it hard to study these animals?**
There's almost no money to support marine insect research. They are of no economic value in marine science, and for entomologists, there's millions of land insects—they don't care about [ocean] insects. I have very little chance of getting support. But if you think of how they can avoid drowning, UV, and heat ... the implications down the line are unimaginable, right? ■

COSTA RICAN MARGIN

• The Costa Rican margin is located about 30 miles off the western shore of Costa Rica, along a subduction zone. There, underwater mountains on the Cocos Plate are sliding under the Caribbean Plate, squeezing heat and natural gas up through the seafloor and forming the base for productive undersea ecosystems, hydrothermal seeps—relatively warm environments that can host communities accustomed to cooler methane seeps as well as those that prefer explosive, hot hydrothermal vents.

• It was once assumed that high-pressure, light-free undersea environs like these were largely lifeless. But we now know these ecosystems can be as dense with life as tropical rainforests, thanks largely to bacteria that break down methane and hydrogen sulfide from the vent for food-making fuel, in lieu of the sunshine land plants would use. The Costa Rican margin hosts life forms ranging from finger-sized purple eelpouts to hyptonic yeti crabs that wear bacteria like fleece coats.

• These bacteria, and other creatures that use methane as an energy source, keep this potent greenhouse gas from dissolving out of the ocean and into our atmosphere. Researchers are racing to learn more about these delicate ecosystems before deep-sea mining projects disturb them.

KEEP A NOSE OUT FOR The classic submarine smell, which is musty and—as you descend and the cabin pressurizes—brings to mind a dentist's office. Once you get back to the surface, you can sniff what you've collected: Some xenophyophores smell earthy, like a forest, while most of the creatures give off whiffs of rotten eggs due to hydrogen sulfide in the muddy sediments.

KEEP AN EAR OUT FOR Loud and fast bubbling sounds from highly active seeps. Listen for them over the submarine pilot's special playlist.

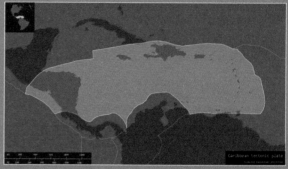

Carribbean Plate

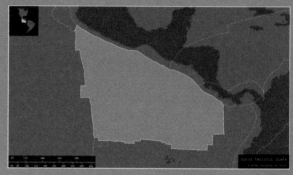

Cocos Plate

KEEP AN EYE OUT FOR "Yetisburg"—a yeti crab hot spot, "Mussel Beach"—full of bivalves, and "VW"—a tubeworm bush the size of a Volkswagen bus. At a hydrothermal seep called Jaco Scar, watch for an iridescent shimmer rising from the craggy seafloor like heat from a car hood. That's a hydrothermal methane seep, and it's slightly warmer than the surrounding water.

Xenophyophores

Acing the test without a single brain cell

◆ Everyone knows about the ocean's flashier builders—the corals that sculpt reefs, the mollusks that spin up perfect pearls.

But thousands of feet down, underappreciated creatures called xenophyophores work hard to build themselves some of the most fascinating homes on the seafloor, from studio apartments to elaborate, multichambered compounds that resemble morel mushrooms or chunks of honeycomb.

Xenophyophores—xenos for short—are some of the deep sea's most abundant organisms. Able to grow their single-celled bodies as large as a cantaloupe in some cases, they live on seabed rocks or in sediment, often in places where a current can bring by construction materials.

RANGE: Common near continental margins and seamounts in the deep sea, below 1,300 feet (396 m). They're even found in the Mariana Trench, which dips some 7 miles (11 km) below the surface.
SPECIES: While xenophyophores are poorly studied and their taxonomy is not well agreed upon, there are dozens of known species—counts range from around 40 to more than 80.

To shelter their huge, blobby bodies, many xenos stick bits of stuff together to form self-built abodes called "tests." Lacking more solid appendages, xenos use extended threads of protoplasm to collect sediment or other drifting particles and glue them together grain by grain. A few "naked" xenos do things differently, secreting a transparent casing and building tests from their own fecal pellets. "They're incredible bricklayers," says Lisa Levin, one of a handful of deep-sea ecologists who has studied them in their natural habitat.

Xenos make good neighbors. Like trees or reefs, they are diversity hot spots, providing other creatures places to perch, feed, and hide. They're also sediment stabilizers and particle traps on the seafloor. Some researchers have even proposed that xenos may be master gardeners, growing and harvesting microbes down on their sunless, submarine farms.

In some regions, these exceptional community members are now considered indicator taxa for vulnerable marine ecosystems—an honor usually reserved for corals or sponges. If observed or harvested as bycatch, these indicators tell observers that where they are is fragile, special, and worthy of protection.

A xenophyophore built this squiggly "test," or home, grain by grain.

As the xenos gains fame, conservation groups are taking note of their stomping grounds around the world. Just west of Costa Rica's fishery-threatened seamounts, for example, the Clarion-Clipperton Zone has been targeted for deep-sea mining. But it's also a xeno hot spot, researchers have found—and perhaps it's time to protect, rather than knock down, the Dali-esque test of the giant amoeboid architect in the neighborhood. ⟩ **How to see them:** Unless you're lucky enough to snag a spot on a deep-sea research cruise, your best bet is to seek them out in videos. If you see a structure sticking out on the seafloor, there's a good chance it's a xeno.

Pacific Lampreys

These ancient, toothy fishes keep on giving.

RANGE: The Pacific Rim of
North America and Asia
SPECIES: Pacific lamprey
(*Entosphenus tridentatus*)

◆ Jawless and vertebrae-less, the Pacific lamprey is a single muscle, up to 30 inches (76 cm) long. Its most infamous attribute, however, is its so-called oral disk. Three cuspid teeth line the front of this sucker mouth, circling around a tiny, angular tongue. When a salmon, hake, or whale gets this parasitic fish's attention, the lamprey latches on, tongue-puncturing its prey's flesh to feed on blood and other bodily fluids.

For about half a billion years, these features have proved a winning strategy for Pacific lampreys. The wriggly sea beasts have sucked their way through three ice ages and five mass extinction events. Today, they favor coastal habitats, where they support whole ecosystems across several distinct stages of life and death.

Following the March-through-July spawning season, Pacific lampreys hatch in freshwater streams in the form of small, wormlike larvae. Eyeless and toothless, these youngsters clean up muddy river bottoms, filter feeding on plants, algae, and the excrement of fish and insects.

Sometime between the ages of three and seven, the lampreys metamorphose into juveniles, developing eyes as well as that trademark sucking mouth and pointy teeth. Ready to parasitize, they make their way out to sea, often traveling more than

100 miles (161 km) before reaching the open ocean. There, the adult fish spend their time dining and hitchhiking on whales, salmon, and other marine life.

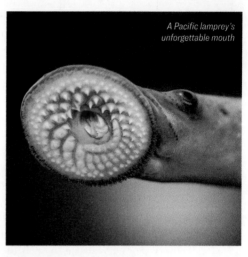

A Pacific lamprey's unforgettable mouth

After one to three years away, lampreys migrate back to their freshwater hatching grounds en masse in the fall. They quit eating, spawn in the spring, and die.

But their legacies live on. Spawn-spent lamprey carcasses, packed with micronutrients from years eating at sea, fall to riverbeds, boosting plant life and food biodiversity for the whole freshwater ecosystem, as well as nearby forests. Scientists have even found evidence of the lamprey and other ocean life in giant evergreens of the Pacific Northwest, in the form of phosphorus from the sea. ❭ **How to see them:** Adults can be seen entering the mouths of the Klamath and Columbia Rivers during the fall. Upriver, throw on some snorkeling gear: You may find adults suctioned to a rock, resting between bursts of swimming. To see Pacific lampreys in their larval stage, dig up a shovel full of sand from almost any West Coast river; the larvae look much like worms.

THE WILD LIFE OF A Yurok Fisheries Biologist

■ For centuries, Indigenous American tribes of the Pacific Northwest and California have considered lampreys sacred sustenance, celebrating them in feasts and with ceremonial songs. As a Yurok tribal member and senior fisheries biologist for the Yurok Fisheries Department, Keith Parker monitors fish harvests, collects tissue for genetic evaluation, and analyzes water quality and salmon-run size from the mouth of California's Klamath River. In 2018, he discovered two new subspecies of Pacific lamprey.

● **Lampreys and their fatty oils have been dubbed a "superfood." Can you describe some of the health benefits of these age-old fish?**
Eels provide Tribal people with high lipid content during winter months when the salmon are not running. It is not by default but by design that the Creator gave our people this rich, fatty food when our people need to put on body fat to weather the cold. When Coho salmon stop running in December, the lampreys show up.

● **What fishing methods snag Pacific lampreys?**
Lampreys are slow anguilliform swimmers that avoid the main current and travel on the river's edge. Yurok men use an eel hook with a carved wooden handle, usually a hardwood like Pacific yew, that's connected to a metal shank with a 180-degree bend, which creates the hook. Eel baskets are also used to gather lamprey swimming upriver.

● **How do they taste compared with other seafood?**
Similar, but even better than unagi served in Japanese restaurants. They are usually smoked over madrone or alder wood and require long smoking times due to their high lipid content. I only half-smoke them before pressure-cooking them in sealed jars.

● **How have you honored Yurok culture in your research?**
When I discovered two new genotypes of Pacific lamprey, in recognition of their importance as a native fish to Pacific Northwest fishing tribes, we adopted the names *key'ween* (lamprey "eel") and *tewol* (ocean) for the river-maturing and ocean-maturing ecotypes, respectively, using terms from the Yurok language, which I'm proud of.

● **Why is this ancient fish so crucial to the Yurok way of life?**
We are river people, and the river is our grocery store. The mass destruction of the Klamath River Basin and its ecosystems has significantly impacted our food security and food sovereignty. At the core of Tribal sovereignty is food sovereignty. Our traditional foods provided by the Creator could be wiped out. Traditional foods feed much more than our physical bodies. They feed our spirits too.

● **What needs to be done to ensure a healthy future for lampreys and their habitat?**
Dam removal, which has blocked hundreds of miles of historical spawning grounds in rivers. Halting water diversions for agriculture, which caused the largest adult salmon kill-off in US history in 2002, when an estimated 68,000 returning adult salmon died because of low water flows and high water temperature. Lastly, stopping deforestation. Poor logging practices cause erosion issues, which fill spawning sites with sediment and destroy riparian plants that cool streams and provide bank stability. There is more carbon locked up in the world's trees than in all the fossil fuels remaining in the ground. ■

Hermit Crab Housing Swaps

**Home-seeking hermit crabs model some familiar
market forces.**

RANGE: Worldwide, except
Antarctica
SPECIES: Hermit crabs
(superfamily Paguroidea)

◆ Unlike most crabs, whose full-body exoskeletons help shield them
from hungry predators, the world's 800-some species of hermit crabs
have small, soft, and eminently edible abdomens. To cover their butts (and bellies), members of most species move into discarded snail shells, which they choose, upgrade, and
swap according to the rules of a surprisingly hot hermit crab real estate market.

When choosing a new shell, size is key: Too small, and the shell won't provide
enough protection. Too large, and carrying it around takes more energy than the crab
can spare. This Goldilocks problem crops up regularly throughout a hermit crab's life
as he outgrows old shells and seeks out new ones.

The constant need for upgrades leads to ruthless house-hunting. When a predator attacks a snail, the snail releases chemicals that the hermit crabs can detect. They'll
mob the crime scene, waiting for the snail to die, says Ivan Chase, a sociologist who has
studied hermit crabs' shell-swapping behavior since the 1980s.

Early on, Chase realized that groups of hermit crabs share the wealth of a newly
available snail shell using what had previously been understood only as a human phenomenon: the vacancy chain. A vacancy chain allows more than one individual to benefit from what could otherwise be a zero-sum competition for resources. If more than
one hermit crab wants the shell of a newly departed snail, the bigger and stronger one
will likely win the scuffle to move in. But the winning crab's old shell might still be an
upgrade for the next-smallest crab in the tide pool—and *that* crab's discarded shell opens
the game for an even smaller compatriot to move on up.

In his experiments, Chase watched as hermit crabs of varying sizes gathered around
a new shell and made deals. After a series of swaps, at least three or four of them had
moved into a roomier space. The process is similar to how humans trade habitation
spots, or how a high-ranking employee's retirement can trigger a chain of promotions.

That isn't to say the process is always orderly among hermit crabs, because each one
has his own picky selection process. Before leaving his old shell, a hermit crab inspects
a new shell carefully, turning it in his claws to assess the surface and sticking his front
legs in the opening to feel around on the inside. If the shell passes muster, the crab tries

*Hermit crabs across the
world engage in shell
swapping. This group is
in Mozambique.*

it on, quickly sliding his soft backside out of the old shell and into the new candidate. "If there are other [hermit crabs] around, you might run off in your new shell while holding your old shell so you can make your decision in a more leisurely fashion," says Chase.

Only after confirming that the new shell is a better fit does the crab release his grip on the old shell and abandon it on the seafloor—where, in all likelihood, the next occupant is already waiting to move in. **⟩ How to see them:** Most rocky shorelines around the world are home to some species of hermit crab. When the tide goes out, check the crevices under rocks for snail shells moving in suspiciously un-snaillike ways.

Giant Acorn Barnacles

Big muscle in a small package

◆ The Arnold Schwarzenegger of the animal kingdom has never hit the gym in its life. In fact, it spends most of its time in one place. This immobile meathead is the giant acorn barnacle, the largest barnacle in the world, capable of growing up to 6 inches (15 cm) wide and a foot (30 cm) tall.

RANGE: Low intertidal and subtidal zones along Pacific North American coasts, from Baja California to southern Alaska
SPECIES: Giant acorn barnacle (*Balanus nubilus*)

The giant acorn barnacle is best known for its bulked-out muscles, which boast the world's widest muscle fibers. In adults, a single fiber can reach up to 3 millimeters wide, roughly equivalent to two strands of spaghetti side by side. (For comparison, human muscle fibers are usually between 100 and 20 *micro*meters wide, about the width of a human hair.)

Do its tubby tubules make the giant acorn barnacle the world's strongest animal? Not exactly. A 1963 study describing these "fibers of giant dimensions" noted that while bigger nerve fibers allow information to travel faster, the same doesn't hold true for bigger muscle fibers, whose benefit—if there even is one—remains unknown.

While other of the giant acorn barnacle's characteristics are even stranger, at least they seem to serve a purpose. For instance, this barnacle secretes a special brown glue from behind its eyes, which helps it affix its own head to a firm surface among its brethren. This glue can't be dissolved by either acids or bases, and it will hold even after the barnacle dies.

And like all barnacles—which have the largest penis-to-body ratio of all animals, at about eight to one—giant acorns are spectacularly endowed. This hermaphroditic crustacean uses its extraordinarily long penis to reach over and fertilize a neighbor's egg sac. In a sign of true strength, the barnacle then discards what it doesn't need: At the end of mating season, the penis dissolves, to be regrown the next year. **⟩ How to see them:** Look for giant acorn barnacles growing on rocks or dock pilings just below the low tide line, primarily in places with strong waves or currents. They'll look like shells until the tide rolls in, when their pink appendages begin fanning through the water for food.

Other Noteworthy Barnacles

Balanus glandula: Barnacles may be renowned for the size of their penises, but *B. glandula* demonstrates that these organs can be as adaptive as they are impressive. Individuals of this species living in more intense, wave-crashed shores grow shorter and stronger penises than those in protected bays. Experiments have shown that barnacles transplanted from quieter to wilder environments are able to adapt their penis size and shape to their new environments.

Dosima fascicularis: Known as "buoy barnacles," these goose barnacles create their own life preservers. They secrete a material from their peduncle, the muscular stalk growing off their shell, that's similar to Styrofoam and filled with carbon dioxide bubbles—allowing them to float at the water's surface. The barnacles hang down from this float, often in groups, happily filtering food from the water as they sail ocean winds and currents.

Xenobalanus globicipitis: These barnacles live life in the fast lane, exclusively surviving on the skin of fast-moving whales and dolphins—often on the outer edges of the flukes and flippers used to swim. Scientists theorize that hitching a ride in this location allows the riders to take advantage of fast-moving water currents, which bring more food for them to filter out.

Dulse

**A sturdy seaweed offers sustenance
to humans and animals alike.**

RANGE: Intertidal waters along North Atlantic coasts up into the Arctic, from Portugal to northernmost Norway on the east side and from Long Island up to Arctic Canada on the west side
SPECIES: Dulse (*Palmaria palmata*)

◆ Canada's massive Bay of Fundy is shaped like the forked tongue of a snake, reaching northeast, beyond the coast of Maine, into the deep and rocky gap between New Brunswick and Nova Scotia. Its tides, the highest in the world, swell up to 53 feet (16 m), with enough force to reverse the flow of incoming rivers.

At the tide's midpoint, a shiny band of reddish-purple seaweed called dulse grows in thick patches that stand about a foot and a half (45 cm) tall underwater. When the tide flows out, the dulse flops on the now-exposed rocky terrain and much of it dries in the sun and wind. When the tide crashes back in, it reabsorbs the bay's nutrient-rich waters, concentrating vitamins and minerals in its rubbery, ribbonlike fronds.

Happiest in the wild, dulse supports much life in the rough and wet terrain. Fish and crustaceans rely on dulse for food, reproduction, and protection from the harbor seals and seabirds that eat them. Scores of periwinkles (small snails also known as penny-winkles or winklers) munch on dulse, too, particularly when it's decaying in the sun, indulging most along the seaweed's bits of decay. After the winklers come the microbes. Bacteria break down the decaying dulse further, releasing raw nutrients into the roiling waters and helping to ensure filter-feeders like mussels and clams have healthy meals.

For thousands of years, humans like John Banks have also depended on dulse. Banks lives on the Canadian island of Grand Manan, where he carries on an ancient practice of harvesting seaweed for human consumption. Nearly every day between April and October, about an hour and a half before low tide, Banks descends a ladder to his 16-foot (5 m) inflatable boat, which is loaded with buckets, rope, and a grappling hook. He seeks out dulse protected from the bleaching effects of the midday sun and picks it in clumps by the fistful.

Wild dulse drying along the shores of the Bay of Fundy

Back on shore, Banks lays the dulse to dry on nets spread atop rocks. Within several hours, about 80 percent of the moisture has evaporated, leaving the slightly chewy, slightly salty, slightly bitter taste of the sea ready to pack and eat.

Like all marine algae, dulse does not put down roots like a plant but sprouts from a holdfast—a sort of life-giving suction cup no wider than an eighth of an inch (3 mm)—attached to rock or mussel beds. "Even if you tried, you couldn't detach the holdfast," Banks says. Once the dulse is plucked, a new supply grows from the remaining holdfast within weeks.

While dulse is hearty in the wild, it can't be cultivated commercially, due to complex reproductive cycles too tricky to replicate. "It is a nightmare for the aquaculturist," says Thierry Chopin, an algae specialist at the University of New Brunswick.

But off the coast of Grand Manan, where Banks spots humpback whales leaping and crashing into the water, energized by the bay's rich nutrients, the abundant dulse grows like a dream. ❯ **How to see it:** Dulse is easy to find along the rocky shores of the North Atlantic. At low tide, look for a thick band of reddish-purple fronds, flopped along the shore and dancing with tiny sea critters.

ANTARCTICA

Antarctic Krill

From stubby blob to esteemed member of the community

RANGE: Southern Ocean
(the waters around Antarctica,
south of the circumpolar
Antarctic Convergence)
SPECIES: Antarctic krill
(*Euphausia superba*)

◆ By collective weight, Antarctic krill are likely the most abundant form of life on Earth. But before they're subsumed into their blue-whale-feeding, ecosystem-supporting, visible-from-space superswarms, each krill must undergo a transformative adolescence.

A krill begins life as a half-millimeter egg floating near the ocean's surface. As the egg's cells divide, the capsule sinks. About a mile down into the ocean, he hatches into a faceless, poppy-seed-sized larva with six stubby appendages, which he wriggles to propel himself back up out of the depths.

On his journey upward, the krill undergoes more changes. He metamorphoses, forming and then shedding new shells as he grows. He takes about two weeks to reach the surface. Despite never having eaten, the baby krill is now three times the length he was when he emerged from the egg. His six stubs have elongated to form limbs. He now has an abdomen, a thorax, and a face, complete with little black eyes.

*A rare sight—
a krill alone*

Crucially, he also has a mouth: He must eat soon or die. Luckily, by the time he reaches the top layer of water, autumn has arrived, bringing thickening sea ice. Rich communities of algae grow on the underside of the ice layer, like a soft ceiling. They create a hanging garden for the krill, who spends winter grazing, growing, and metamorphosing some more.

Spring arrives, and the ice breaks up. Our young krill, now a juvenile, has begun to resemble an adult. Six little limbs have become 26 feathery legs for swimming or feeding. Long antennae have sprouted from a small head, garnished with large, tapioca-pearl eyes. The krill has a stomach for holding and digesting plankton—which, after big meals, is visible through his translucent abdomen—and a tail, which he can flip like a lobster's to make a quick escape. He has even grown organs to make his own light: bioluminescent photophores on his underside, which help him blend in with the water's dappled sunlight and potentially hide his shadow from predators below.

Our 6-centimeter crustacean is now all grown up, the former faceless dot now bigger than a peach pit. And he's made friends. There are krill (the individuals), and then there are *krill* (the swarm). Krill aggregations can get so massive that they're visible from outside Earth's atmosphere.

Having reached adulthood, our hero is often sacrificed for the greater good. Krill are the primary food source for most larger animals in the Southern Ocean, downed like cocktail snacks by Adélie penguins and crabeater seals and gulped up by larger animals like baleen whales. Blue whales, the planet's largest animals, feed almost exclusively on Antarctic krill. A single whale can gobble up around 6 tons (5.4 metric tons) of them every single day—each krill forever part of something bigger. ❯ **How to see them:** Different species of krill inhabit oceans around the world, but if you want to see Antarctic krill, you'll have to take a trip to the Southern Ocean, which surrounds Antarctica. Most ships to Antarctica leave from ports in Argentina, Australia, or New Zealand.

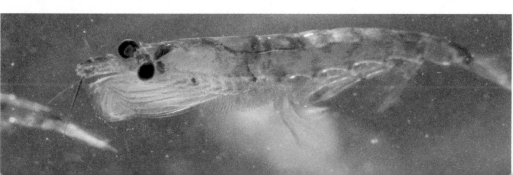

Welcome to the Chemosynthesis Buffet

In 1977, geographers studying oceanic crusts in the Galápagos stumbled on hydrothermal vents for the first time. These underwater hot springs hosted a level of deep-sea life formerly thought impossible, on par with that of tropical rainforests. Critters large and small were thriving in a high-pressure soup of hydrogen sulfide, methane, and iron, compounds that are largely toxic to us and other landlubbers. How could this be?

On land and in shallow waters, life runs on photosynthesis, a process through which plants and algae transform sunlight into energy. But deep underwater, where no light reaches, chemosynthesis powers the day. In chemical-rich areas like hydrothermal vents, cold seeps, and whale carcasses, chemosynthetic bacteria turn chemicals into fuel, forming the basis of incredible food webs as they feed or team up with an array of mind-bending larger organisms. Here are just a few.

Microbial mats

GIANT TUBE WORMS (*Riftia pachyptila*) • This tall glass of muscle—actually a bivalve mollusk—is a regular at hydrothermal vent sites across the Pacific Ocean. It has no mouth or gut, but boy can it eat, bulking up to 9 feet (2.7 m) tall in some cases. Tube worms inspired microbiologist Colleen Cavanaugh's pioneering work on chemosymbiosis—the process through which deep-sea organisms work with bacteria to fuel themselves—when she found hydrogen sulfide–oxidizing bacteria living inside a tube worm's tissue.

Using hemoglobin-red plumes extending from the top of its tube, this mollusk takes in oxygen and hydrogen sulfide from the water and directs them down to a spongy tissue called the trophosome, where billions of diverse bacteria live. Bacteria use the hydrogen sulfide as fuel and give their host what they make. Sulfur crystals sprinkled about the trophosome might serve as energy reserves.

MICROBIAL MATS • Bacterial mats are the oldest form of life on Earth. They began around hydrothermal vents and eventually made their way to the surface, establishing the oxygen-rich world we know today. In the deep sea, they consume and store about 80 percent of the ocean's methane, a powerful greenhouse gas.

These mats are made of sulfide-oxidizing bacteria that get their energy from the waste of other microbes. Beneath the mats, their power partners—methane-oxidizing archaea and sulfate-reducing bacteria—share nutrients, metabolically cooperating to get by on the chemical-rich seafloor and fueling the spreading carpets in the process. The bonds are both inspiring and aesthetically arresting: Different mats may resemble olive-green scum crusts, marigold meshes, snow-dusted cobwebs, or purple velvet lattice.

Giant tube worms

YETI CRABS (*Kiwa puravida* and others) • These fuzzy white crabs dance for their life in chemical-rich methane seeps. Each yeti crab holds her claws in front of her body as if giving a ghost a hug, then waves them slowly in a kind of rotation from side to side. In some places, they congregate by the hundreds and move leisurely in near unison.

This dance is top-of-the-line farming technology. Chemical-munching bacteria cling to the crabs' hairs, and the motion mixes up the water column while dragging these bacteria through a bath of nutrients, preventing stagnancy and maximizing their access to essentials like oxygen from the water and methane from the seep or vent. When they need a snack, the crabs eat the bacteria directly from their arms, and wait for a new crop to plant itself along their hairs.

DEEP-SEA GIANT MUSSELS (*Bathymodiolus* spp.) • Found around hydrothermal vents and methane seeps, giant mussels—who host microbes that convert inorganic chemicals like hydrogen sulfide into sugars—are helping us figure out how chemosymbiosis may have gotten started in some animal lineages. These deep-sea mussels are closely related to wood-eating species, and likely evolved from some as well.

Wood also releases hydrogen sulfide as it decays. Over the course of evolutionary history, wood may have been a stepping stone between habitats—as well as a bridge from "eating" hydrogen sulfide from decaying material to producing it in-house via chemosynthetic symbiosis. This hypothesis, which microbiologist Dan Distel calls "wooden steps," might also be relevant to other hydrogen sulfide–enjoying species like giant shipworms, who spend their lives buried in mud in lagoons.

WHALE FALL COMMUNITIES • Scientists estimate that some 70,000 great whales die each year, leaving behind perhaps one carcass every 3 to 10 miles (4.8–16 km) along the seafloor of North America's Pacific coast. As the massive bodies drop inch by inch to the seafloor, slowly decomposing, they attract and nourish an ever-changing and sometimes overlapping cascade of ecosystems. A single one can provide as much material as several thousand years' worth of marine snow, the tiny particles of organic matter that fall like flaky fish food from the water's surface.

A dead whale is devoured in stages that can last years. First come the mobile scavengers, like hagfish and sleeper sharks, who nibble flesh and blubber. Next come the enrichment opportunists, mostly polychaete worms and crustaceans, who colonize the bones and surrounding sediment and strip off any remaining soft tissue. This makes way for the final stage, driven by bacteria that can break down lipids in the whale bones. Their waste, hydrogen sulfide, forms the base for a self-contained food web made up of hundreds of macroscopic species. Scientists think whale carcasses are deep-sea way stations, serving as fueling stations for animals traveling between other chemosynthetic oases on the otherwise energy-scarce ocean floor.

Osedax

These whale-bone-eating mistresses of the deep are attended to by millions of dwarf males.

RANGE: Osedax appear to have a worldwide distribution—different species have been identified off the coasts of Sweden, the Mediterranean, Papua New Guinea, Australia, New Zealand, South and Central America, and Antarctica.

SPECIES: Osedax (*Osedax* spp.), with around 30 species and counting, including *O. rubiplumus* ("red feather"), *O. mucofloris* ("snot flower"), and *O. fenrisi* (named after the Norse god Loki's son, Fenris the wolf)

◆ When a large animal dies and sinks to the seafloor, osedax are there waiting. These worms live in huge groups in the blackness of the benthic sea. Their name is Latin for the role they perform: "bone devourer."

Osedax were discovered by accident in 2002 on the carcass of a fallen whale, nearly 2 miles (3 km) down at the bottom of California's enormous submarine Monterey Canyon. Researchers were there to study communities living around cold seeps, habitats characterized by chemicals, fluids, and gases escaping from cracks in the seafloor. When the scientists came across the skeleton of a juvenile gray whale covered in what looked like red shag carpeting, they were flummoxed. They collected the rib bones to see what this was.

The shag turned out to be the red plumes of hundreds of female osedax. These worms, each no longer than a toothpick, have no mouths or guts; their trunks, which contract like human colons, are mostly muscle and ducts. A bulbous sac of eggs is sheathed in chartreuse tissue, and this ovisac branches out into a root system that invades the bone. To eat, they secrete an acidic, bone-dissolving mucus and metabolize the collagen inside with the help of symbiotic bacteria.

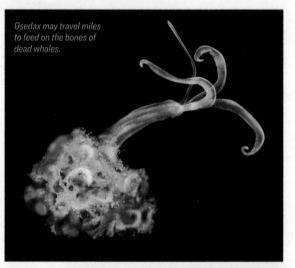

Osedax may travel miles to feed on the bones of dead whales.

Osedax larvae wait, suspended in the water column, to cue into a dead whale. When scientists sink whale carcasses to the seafloor, "they come from miles," says Shana Goffredi, who coauthored the first description of the *Osedax* genus.

Nearly identical species found in Monterey and Japan must have traveled more than 7,000 miles (11,000 km), presumably hopping from one massive carcass to the next like stepping stones. Because these worms were around millions of years before today's whales, they likely once broke down the bones of protocetaceans like *Basilosaurus*.

Wherever the larvae land, scientists suspect, determines their sex: Those who land on bone become females, and those who land on females become males.

As with many deep-sea species, osedax sex is multitudinous and, for the guys, all-consuming. Each female worm manages a harem of microscopic males who cluster around her oviduct. These "dwarf males" outnumber females 17 to 1, and larger females may maintain a collection of more than 100 at once.

Male osedax are basically tiny sperm sacs, filled with developing sperm and yolk droplets. They cling to their female with curved teeth and chiton hooks. After fertilizing the female, they die, having served their mistress and the greater good of seafloor maintenance. ❯ **How to see them:** It's unlikely you'll encounter an osedax in its wild habitat at the bottom of the sea. But there's a doom metal band called The Osedax that might bring you close.

CHAPTER 6

Cities

Humans prefer cities to any other habitat. Worldwide, more than half of us live in one; by 2050, that share is predicted to rise to 70 percent. We build them according to our priorities, disrupting the systems and structures that already existed in a place to create new ones we think will suit us better—digging up existing roots in order to put down our own.

Fortunately, our efforts at displacement are never completely effective. Marsican brown bears and Sri Lankan fishing cats do not understand, or follow, our laws about trespassing and theft. Parrots and peregrines do better in cities than in the dwindling habitats outside of them. Clovers are not only pushing up through cracks in most of the world's sidewalks, they're evolving to suit their new homes.

As we cross paths, we learn about each other. Researchers can solve old mysteries about alligator lizards because they mate in people's courtyards, and snowy owls because they make stopovers at city airports. Patience and care turn cicadas from screaming annoyances into celebrated time capsules, and crows from aliens into beloved neighbors. And—as it always goes with city culture—the observant are granted entry to a dense and hidden world, where rare orchids grow next to highways, spiders dance in backyards, and unassuming trees have been to the moon.

Sharing space, we also change each other deeply—emotionally and politically, anatomically and genetically. Librarians and bats take up common cause. Mussels watch our water supply, while we build tunnels to ease the commutes of amorous toads. People glean hope from fungi and architectural inspiration from termites. Moths shift from white to black to white again, tracking a country's commitment to clean air, a utility produced for free by street trees.

This is the network that brings cities to life, reminding us that we never do anything—even the things that seem most human—by ourselves.

Contributors: *Maria Adelmann, Nuna Kim Jones Arakaki, M Bhatia, Ashlen Campbell, Amanda De George, Cecil Dzwowa, Jenny Elliott, Jonathan Feakins, Rachel Fritts, Ben Goldfarb, Miles Griffis, Jessica Leigh Hester, Grace Hunter, Laurie Jackson, Lilia Kilburn, Patrick Kuklinski, Casey Langton, Anna Lebedeva, Maryanne Macharia, Ada McVean, Leonie Mercedes, Sofia Quaglia, Carla Rhodes, Becki Robins, Linda Rodriguez McRobbie, Melissa Scott Sinclair, Sarah Sloat, Joshua Sokol, Thayer Taft, India-Jayne Trainor*

EUROPE

Water-Quality Mussels

Polish cities trust their water supplies to elite shellfish teams.

LOCATION: About 50 water treatment plants in different Polish cities, including Warsaw and Poznan
SPECIES: Swan mussel (*Anodonta cygnea*) and other freshwater mussels

◆ Gruba Kaśka is one of Warsaw's largest water filtration plants. Every day, it pumps tens of millions of gallons out of the Vistula River and through taps across Poland's capital. Each drop is guaranteed by the plant's unusual quality-control team: freshwater mussels hooked up to a computer.

The concept is simple. All kinds of pollutants can sneak into drinking water: Heavy metals seep up from industrial waste sites; pesticides and fertilizers trickle in after big rainstorms. Because chemical tests are contaminant-specific, it's impossible to check the water for every possible problem before it's piped out to the populace.

Mussels, however, aren't picky. If something is wrong, they clam up. Their broad sensitivity and predictable response have allowed engineers to build them into a straightforward quality control system, which runs alongside other mollusk-free monitoring schemes.

Worker mussels are recruited from nearby lakes and rivers. They're deployed in teams of eight, each equipped with a magnetic sensor that connects them to a computer system that can register whether they are open or shut. When four or more mussels close off, so does the water supply.

These selfless shellfish have been employed in at least 50 of Poland's water treatment plants. (Similar monitoring systems, using bluegill fish, have been employed in several American cities.) Those who work closely with the mollusks appreciate the risks they (inadvertently) take. After all, a toxic event could kill them.

Each worker mussel spends three months on duty—after that, they become too accustomed to their new surroundings and are no longer sensitive enough to properly monitor the water. For retirement, they are gently tossed back where they came from. ❯ **How to see them:** Ask for a tour of a water treatment plant—as they are secure facilities, calling ahead is recommended.

Gruba Kaśka filters water from the Vistula River with help from mussels.

LONDON, UNITED KINGDOM

- Despite its rainy reputation, London receives less precipitation than New York or Paris. What it does get are low-hanging clouds, which arrive via the North Atlantic jet stream and can settle over the city for long periods. The high humidity from the Atlantic helps support parks and private gardens, which in total cover nearly half the city.

- London's Natural History Museum, with a world-spanning collection of scientific specimens, doubles as a series of object lessons in British colonial history. Curators here are making new efforts to bring to light this aspect of the collections and the stories of those typically left out— like John Edmonstone, the formerly enslaved taxidermist who mentored a teenaged Charles Darwin.

- Since the twelfth century, all of the mute swans on the River Thames have been censused in an annual ceremony called "swan upping." The ritual was once meant to properly apportion the city's supply of swan meat, traditionally split between the British Crown and two livery companies. Eating swans is now illegal, so in present iterations of the census, swans receive a health check and a band.

KEEP AN EYE OUT FOR Swaggering stag beetles, the largest of London's 2,000 or so beetle species. Stop by in early summer for a chance to catch a glimpse of the males' mating duels.

KEEP AN EAR OUT FOR The thunderclap of clashing antlers during the autumn deer and stag rut. London's Richmond and Bushy Parks hold more than a thousand red and fallow deer. Originally stocked to be hunted by kings like Henry VIII and Charles I, they now are kept as tourist attractions—and natural lawn mowers for the city's grassy parks.

KEEP A NOSE OUT FOR A strong, coffee-like odor spread through the city by London's sizable red fox population. These resourceful canids hunt in urban gardens and rummage through rubbish. While they are most active at dawn and dusk, they can also be seen—and smelled—during the day.

London Underground Mosquitos

A bite at the end of the tunnel

RANGE: All continents, except Antarctica
SPECIES: London Underground mosquito (*Culex pipiens molestus*)

Every commute has its special annoyances. Those who take the London Tube may have to contend with a particularly bloodthirsty one: *Culex pipiens molestus*, the London Underground mosquito.

C. molestus, a form of the common house mosquito *Culex pipiens*, has adapted beautifully to subterranean life. While its aboveground brethren, *Culex pipiens pipiens*, feeds mainly on birds and prefers to power down in the winter, *C. molestus* is active all year round and—much to the irritation of today's subway maintenance workers—loves to bite humans. These sunken skeeters can mate in tighter spaces than other mosquitos and lay eggs without a blood meal. Females chase down rats and people, while males live off trash, sludge, and the shed hair and skin flakes of commuters. Scientists have found genetic differences between populations of these mosquitoes on different underground lines, and suggest that trains thundering down the tunnels move them from breeding site to breeding site.

Subterranean homesick alien

C. molestus is often held up as a classic example of an animal quickly adapting to city life, and the idea that they evolved in the Tube system has caught fire. However, it's more likely that this particular biter has been menacing people for centuries, since long before the era of the subway, with one hypothesis proposing that the species arose with early farming groups in the Middle East before winging it north.

Underground networks, with their stagnant water and stable year-round temperatures, provided an ideal niche in this new climate. As subway systems sprang up in metropolises around the world, the mosquito found more places to settle, and new humans to feast on.

Although widely associated with the Tube—thanks largely to the itchy impression they made on people sheltering underground during the Blitz of World War II—these insects are found in underground structures all over the world. In 2011, they rose from the sewers of New York's Upper West Side, making themselves a nuisance to their new neighbors. ❯ **How to see them:** These mosquitoes have been spotted in cellars, sewers, and subway tunnels across the globe. Keep an ear out for someone whining during your commute.

Roadside Verges

Bustling ecosystems right on the highway

RANGE: Worldwide
SPECIES: Verges support a diversity of plants and animals. Around London, look for common poppies (*Papaver rhoeas*), oxeye daisies (*Leucanthemum vulgare*), and pyramidal orchids (*Anacamptis pyramidalis*), all locally important species.

◆ A few hundred years ago, the UK was mostly meadows. Grazing and hay-cutting left much of the country covered in huge swaths of what is called "unimproved grassland"—a seminatural landscape that, in some places, can host 10 plant species per square foot. For many, the image of soft grass stippled with wildflowers is essentially British.

Over the past century, though, people have dug up or paved over all but 3 percent of the country's meadows. Important and beloved flowers that once had starring panoramic roles in the UK landscape have been demoted to bit players, popping up occasionally in fragmented spots. Concerned ecologists and gardeners looking to supplement these flowers' habitat have turned their attention to promising scraps of urban infrastructure: roadside verges.

Verges—the narrow strips of land that line roads and highways—are literally meant to be overlooked. For drivers' safety, they must provide unoccluded views and emergency pull-off space. Because there's no reason to disturb them, many of the verges that lie alongside older roads have been left largely to themselves, sometimes for centuries. The occasional mowing required for maintenance actually imitates historic grazing practices and encourages wildflower growth.

Under these conditions, even a small verge can support a bustling ecosystem—flowers draw pollinators, which bring birds, lizards, and small mammals. Roadside surveys regularly count dozens of rare butterfly and orchid species, including hybrid orchids never before seen. Conservationists estimate that, collectively, the country's verges cover as much area as England's largest national park and could support billions of individual plants. Animals and seeds use them as their own parallel highway system, traveling from verge to verge to find the right place to settle.

In counties like Suffolk, Norfolk, and Kent, rich stretches of verge are designated roadside nature reserves, marked out by wooden posts and traditionally managed by highway employees and volunteers. Meanwhile, those in charge of beautifying verges are increasingly choosing to fill them with locally important plants.

As with most civic issues, people don't always see eye to eye on verge management. Native plant ecologists balk at seed mixes that prioritize flashy flowers rather than creating the right mix for ecosystem support. And some true curmudgeons argue that this is all just a big excuse not to cut the grass.

But when things go well, verges can provide a posy's worth of good things: history, beauty, and interspecies coexistence, all right by the side of the road. ❯ **How to see them:** In spring and summer, keep an eye out while driving—odds are you will encounter many patches of colorful blooms. Dorset's A354 Weymouth Relief Road and Devon's A38 are both intentionally managed verges with many species present.

The bright side of stop-and-go traffic

ALAN: The Dark Side of Light

Artificial light has changed our relationship with darkness, making it possible for humans to work night shifts, hang out in bars, and stay up later than we should. But we're not the only species profoundly affected by artificial light at night—or ALAN, as experts call it.

We are only beginning to discover what happens when plants and animals encounter light in new places and at unnatural times. Here's a look at some of what we've found.

SMALL ERMINE MOTHS BUCK THE STEREOTYPE.
Moths are well-known victims of ALAN, famous for flying mindlessly into porch lights. But at least one urban subset may be learning to cope: In 2016, researchers found that city-dwelling small ermine moths (*Yponomeuta evonymella*) were less likely to meet an untimely end on a hot light bulb than their rural counterparts.

While this seems like good news for the moths, this evolutionary step may have created larger problems. Scientists speculate that urban moths might not be as good at processing visual information as rural moths. Alternatively, they might be less mobile, and therefore less productive pollinators (and less available as food sources for their own predators, like bats and spiders). Gaining a fighting chance against the malevolent porch light may have interrupted their important role in the ecological web.

CYANOBACTERIA BECOME MORE PROLIFIC.
Cyanobacteria love climate change. The EPA predicts that blooms of these toxic microorganisms will become more common as average temperatures increase. Worse, in 2015, scientists found that cyanobacteria can use ALAN as an energy source, becoming even more abundant in its presence. This is also true for other phototrophs, including diatoms and green algae.

There is a potential bright side: ALAN might be able to turn bodies of fresh water into carbon sinks—places that absorb more carbon than they release—which could potentially help to slow climate change. But the overall costs of such a significant ecosystem shift are unclear.

FIREFLIES LOSE THEIR SPARK. Female fireflies (family Lampyridae) appear to be most attracted to males with brighter, faster flash rates. But in a 2016 study, scientists found that fireflies reduce their flash frequency in the presence of ALAN. This could make it more difficult for them to find each other and decrease attraction when they do. Another study found that *Aquatica ficta* fireflies exposed to short-wavelength light, such as blue light, flashed less often but more intensely—perhaps their way of compensating for this reduced visibility.

LAMPENFLORA GO DEEPER. *Lampenflora* is an umbrella term for a broad group of organisms: mosses, ferns, lichens, and algae that live near artificial lights installed underground. Before humans brought electricity into the depths, these creatures eked out a meager existence in the mouths of caves. Now, thanks to human curiosity, many of the world's most splendid caves have been fitted with artificial lights, giving lampenflora an opportunity to proliferate underground. While these species are benefiting, there are also unintended effects: Many lampenflora produce acids that can degrade the very cave formations people come to see.

MOSQUITOES CHANGE THEIR SCHEDULES. Mosquitoes are already the most unwelcome guests at summer barbecues, but ALAN might be making it possible for them to crash your Halloween parties too. This is because artificial light messes up the female mosquito's internal clock. Under normal circumstances, shorter days cause female northern house mosquitos (*Culex pipiens*) to enter a period of dormancy in which they don't reproduce, take blood meals, or buzz around annoyingly in people's ears. When those shorter days are lengthened by artificial light, mosquitoes skip the break and keep on biting.

Peregrine Falcons

These feathered wanderers are finding success in our cities.

◆ In 2004, a macabre mystery baffled the residents of Derby, England. The grounds of the city cathedral were, suddenly, regularly scattered with bird corpses: a smattering of songbirds; a headless ruddy duck dropped unceremoniously at the west entrance. Speculation was rife, with the *Derby Telegraph* even suggesting Satanists might be pelting the holy building with animal remains.

By 2005, however, the real culprits had been spotted on the cathedral tower: a pair of peregrine falcons. This discovery was met with elation, and by the following year a wooden nesting platform was in place. The couple gained thousands of fans worldwide, who watched through webcams and from the cathedral's green as the raptors found a regular date spot atop the sign of a nearby hotel and raised brood after brood of ungainly

RANGE: Peregrine falcons are present on every continent except for Antarctica, but are particularly widespread in Europe, Asia, Africa, and Oceania.
SPECIES: Peregrine falcon (*Falco peregrinus*)

A peregrine enjoys the city of Bristol.

chicks. When this pair of falcons disappeared after more than a decade of towertop living, new ones nested on the platform, continuing their legacy.

The name *peregrine* stems from the Latin *peregrinus*, meaning "pilgrim" or "wanderer." In recent decades, more and more of these birds have strayed from their traditional habitats, managing to knock together fulfilling lives for themselves in cities all over the world.

Many find stone churches a fitting substitute for cliffs and bluffs: Peregrines have been seen swooping outside the UK's Salisbury Cathedral since at least 1864. Others make their homes, called aeries (or eyries), in skyscrapers or even tall chimneys. A recent study determined that the peregrines of London prefer the city's parks, gardens, and built areas to its fields, farms, and woodlands.

In addition to high vantage points for nesting, cities offer peregrines an abundance of delicious prey. Pigeons are plentiful and easy pickings. The raptors are also fond of ducks, and have even learned to hunt London's feral flock of ring-necked parakeets. With a stooping (diving) rate of around 200 miles per hour (322 kph)—faster than the takeoff speed of a passenger jet—a peregrine can easily break another bird's spine.

There is even evidence these birds have adapted further to city life by using urban streetlights to hunt nocturnally. Though the behavior had been anecdotally reported by observant fans for decades, Derby Cathedral's webcams provided the first publicly available footage of a peregrine making a kill by night.

Their penchant for city life has helped peregrines in the UK recover from a decades-long population crisis. During World War II, the birds were culled to protect the homing pigeons used in the war effort; later, DDT and other pesticides had a catastrophic effect on the thickness of the birds' eggshells. Their numbers, which fell by 80 percent, have now greatly recovered, and the global population is currently estimated to be in the hundreds of thousands. In many places, humans now make for helpful neighbors: During one unusually frosty March, concerned Derbians cleared snow and ice from the falcons' roosting platform by lowering a hot water bottle off of the cathedral roof on a string. ❯ **How to see them: Seek them out in big cities, particularly those with tall buildings like cathedrals or skyscrapers. New York and London are the two urban places with the most peregrine pairs.**

Industrial Melanism

England's Industrial Revolution killed off local lichen and coated tree bark with windblown soot. In response, in the mid-1800s, the country's population of peppered moths (*Biston betularia*) began to transform: Dark morphs of the insects, which camouflaged well against the blackened trees, started outnumbering the lighter morphs, which better matched lichen and bare bark. When the air got cleaner again, the trend reversed.

While the peppered moth is the most famous, a number of species have adapted to urban environments by developing darker colors and markings. This effect, called industrial melanism, can help with more than just camouflage, as these examples demonstrate.

TURTLE-HEADED SEA SNAKES (*EMYDOCEPHALUS ANNULATUS*): These egg-eating underwater serpents, which are typically striped with dark and light bands, can turn entirely black when living in polluted waters. This color change may help the snakes camouflage in dingy water. It also indicates the increased presence of melanin, which can bind toxic metals like arsenic and zinc—allowing the snakes to excrete these harmful elements when they shed.

PIGEONS (*COLUMBA LIVIA*): Urban pigeons may also use the melanin in their feathers to sequester toxic metals. Experiments in Paris have suggested that dark-colored pigeons can store more zinc in their feathers (thereby removing it from their bloodstreams) than lighter-colored ones can, and that their immune systems are stronger too.

TWO-SPOTTED LADYBUGS (*ADALIA BIPUNCTATA*): In highly polluted areas, these beetles tend to be black with red spots rather than red with black spots. Sporting more black may allow them to better absorb heat from sunlight, giving them a thermal advantage in places with less sunshine.

Starling Murmurations

Little birds create overwhelming spectacles.

◆ One European starling doesn't tend to garner much interest. These small, sharp-beaked birds are common enough that even their iridescent plumage often fails to catch the eye.

But it's a different story when they're all together. In winter, huge groups of starlings—sometimes numbering up to a million—move in coordinated swooping patterns, treating city commuters to documentary-worthy nature spectacles. These kinetic displays, which can happen at a moment's notice, are known as murmurations.

Murmurations generally occur at dusk. Subgroups of the small brown birds expand and contract, scatter and converge, like iron filaments chasing unseen magnets. The flock shape-shifts over the horizon; a smoke plume might break up into a set of fingerprints. The largest murmurations verge on apparitional—as hard to track and comprehend as the aurora borealis or the inside of a lava lamp.

RANGE: Murmurations can occur wherever starlings are found. This includes much of the northern hemisphere, as well as South Africa, southwestern Australia, New Zealand, Argentina, and Venezuela.
SPECIES: European starling (*Sturnus vulgaris*)

According to research teasing out the math of murmurations, these complexities arise from relatively simple behavior. Within the billowing collective, each bird mimics the direction and speed of his or her six or seven nearest flockmates. In this way, small decisions ripple through the whole, enabling group-wide sensitivity and responsiveness. Similar behavior has been observed in midges and in schooling fish.

It's not certain what drives this choreography in the first place. Many scientists think flying en masse makes it harder for predators like falcons and hawks to pick off individual starlings, while others suggest that keeping a large group together helps them stay warm. While most murmurations are short in duration, a flock may swirl in the sky for up to 45 minutes before the birds decant back into their local roost.

Once grounded, starlings generally lose their sway. Introduced in much of its current range, the species—like many that have found themselves out of place—is often treated as a pest, charged with crimes that range from spreading weeds across Australia to, in 1949, stopping time in London by landing en masse on Big Ben's minute hand. But all is forgiven, for a little while, when they rise again. **❯ How to see them:** Murmurations occur anywhere starlings congregate. Particularly spectacular ones happen in Friesland, Denmark, and in Gretna Green, Dumfries, and Galloway, Scotland.

Pseudoscorpions

Tiny clawed hunters are ride-sharing their way onto your bookshelf.

RANGE: Global, except Antarctica
SPECIES: Thousands of members of the order Pseudoscorpionida

◆ Look at this page carefully. Are any of the letters moving? Does what looked like a bulky-stemmed Y have, on closer inspection, eight little jointed legs in addition to two outstretched claws?

If so, count yourself lucky—your book may be hosting a pseudoscorpion. Discreet yet omnipresent, these tiny arachnids have been making cameos both in and on texts since at least the fourth century BCE, when Aristotle, in his *History of Animals*, wrote of "the little scorpion-like creature found in books."

As it turns out, pseudoscorpions are found almost everywhere. Like their close relatives, the spiders, pseudoscorpions are hunters, with venom glands in their claws for subduing prey. (Unlike spiders, most pseudoscorpions are only about 4 millimeters long, and all are completely harmless to humans.) Individuals travel via phoresy, a transportation strategy in which one animal grabs onto another and hitches a ride. They often hop onto beetles and flies, treating their mounts gently enough that scientists have determined they must be riding them intentionally.

(Not actual size)

Bug-based ride-sharing has helped pseudoscorpions spread out and, over time, specialize for different habitats. Indoors, house pseudoscorpions go after human-associated microcritters, like book lice and dust mites. The great outdoors is home to thousands of types: A recent survey in Vienna's city center found 17 pseudoscorpion species thriving in various pockets, from damp tree hollows and compost heaps to leaf litter and the spaces beneath tree bark, where insects and springtails make for plentiful prey.

Pseudoscorpions are threatened by monocultures and vigorous landscaping—clear every fallen leaf from the park lawn, and they have nowhere left to go. Cities could "allow a little more untidiness," says Christian Hörweg, the curator of the arachnid collection at the Vienna Museum of Natural History and the survey's author, and thus help diverse pseudoscorpion populations thrive. ❯ **How to see them:** Bring a magnifying glass to a park, a streetside tree, or even your own bookshelf.

Marsican Brown Bears

Sweet bears with a sweet tooth

RANGE: In and around the Abruzzo, Lazio and Molise National Park in southern Italy. There have also been sightings in the Gran Sasso and Laga Mountains National Park in central Italy, and in the Sirente, Velino, Simbruini, and Sibillini Mountains.
SPECIES: Marsican brown bear (*Ursus arctos arctos*, or possibly *Ursus arctos marsicanus*)

◆ Marsican brown bears live wild in the mountains and valleys of Abruzzo, just a hundred miles (160 km) from the ruins of the Colosseum. They are behaviorally and morphologically distinct from Europe's other brown bears—some scientists consider them to be their own species entirely—and although their population numbers fewer than 60, their home range is small enough that Abruzzo, Lazio and Molise National Park, created in 1923 to protect the animals, boasts one of the highest bear densities on Earth.

The region of Abruzzo is also dense with people. Over the course of thousands of years living alongside the bears, farmers and shepherds killed any that got too close. As a result, while few of the world's brown bears are overtly aggressive, Marsican ones are unusually shy and gentle. There are no records or stories describing bear attacks on humans in Abruzzo. Even moms with cubs will only feint at rushing a disruptive person before fleeing.

The majority of Marsican bears take care not to overlap with humans. But some, drawn in by the promise of rubbish bins and chicken coops, lose their fear of people and become a frequent sight in towns and villages. In Abruzzo, social media is filled with videos of Marsican brown bears climbing garden fruit trees, drinking from street fountains, and peeking over fences. Fitted with radio collars, these cheeky bears (scientists call them "confident") are well known to park rangers and locals and are given affectionate names, like Gemma, Bambina, and Amarena.

Most Marsican bears stay far from people.

One young and intrepid bear named Juan Carrito reached celebrity status, making at least 676 appearances across 13 different villages in 2021 and 2022. Local and national media ran regular stories about his exploits: breaking into a local bakery to devour trayfuls of pastries, strolling along the pistes of a ski resort, spending the night in someone's garden, and attempting to play with village dogs.

His audacious behavior put a lot of pressure on park rangers, conservationists, and police. They clocked hundreds of eight-person shifts tracking his movements, trying to keep him away with loud sirens and shouts, and even transferring him to a more isolated area of the park, from which he quickly returned. However, Juan Carrito could not be deterred from visiting the village, and in 2023, he was hit and killed by a car, a fate these teams had hoped to help him avoid. ⟩ **How to see them:** In late summer, Marsican bears come out of the forests at sunset to gorge on juicy alpine buckthorn berries and can be observed from a safe distance through binoculars. Several tour companies in the town of Pescasseroli also offer organized bear hikes.

Library Bats

In one of the world's most beautiful libraries, pest control is left to the true experts.

LOCATION: Joanine Library at the University of Coimbra in Coimbra, Portugal
SPECIES: European free-tailed bat (*Tadarida teniotis*) and soprano pipistrelle (*Pipistrellus pygmaeus*)

◆ The 60,000 books in the Joanine Library are all hundreds of years old. Keeping texts readable for that long, safe from mold and moisture and nibbling bugs, requires dedication. The library's original architects designed 6-foot (1.8 m) stone walls to keep out the elements. Employees dust all day, every day.

And then there are the bats. For centuries, small colonies of these helpful creatures have lent their considerable pest control expertise to the library. In the daytime—as scholars lean over historic works and visitors admire the architecture—the bats roost quietly behind the two-story bookshelves. At night, they swoop around the darkened building, eating the beetles and moths that would otherwise do a number on all that old paper and binding glue.

The library dates the bats' entry to the late eighteenth century. That's when records indicate the purchase of large leather sheets from Russia, presumably to protect the hall's desks and tables from the nightly rain of guano. Employees use the same system today, while the books themselves are behind wire mesh, says the library's deputy director, António Eugénio Maia do Amaral. (The bats' tendency to pee next to a portrait of the library's namesake, King John V, is harder to address.)

Although visitors tend to be very curious about the bats, library employees mostly leave them in peace to do their jobs. As such, less is known about them than you might expect, given that they live in a knowledge repository. Two types have been identified: European free-tailed bats and soprano pipistrelles, both small and nimble species. Although no one sees them hunt, it's easy to imagine them free diving from the painted ceilings and slaloming between the gilded balusters.

Their skill and discretion—rarely do you have to hush a bat—make them valuable members of the community. Maia do Amaral calls them "honorary librarians." When the Joanine's enormous wooden doors were replaced in 2015, carpenters preserved the gaps the bats use when they leave each night to drink from the river. Some speculate that previous caretakers introduced them to the building on purpose.

The Joanine Library is majestic and filled with bats.

But those who work with them now think it's more likely the bats, who value peaceful homes, found their way in on their own. After all, says Maia do Amaral, "What can you think of quieter than a library by night?" ❯ **How to see them: The Joanine Library offers regular guided tours, during which you may hear a bat squeak. If you want to see one in action, your best bet is to attend one of the library's evening concerts, which occur right at the start of their dinnertime. Try to feign interest in the books, out of politeness.**

Bats in the Everything

Many bat species love to roost communally, often in dark, cool spaces. As their natural habitats are lost to development, some colonies who choose city life end up in unexpected places.

MORE LIBRARY BATS: The world's other best-known library bats work at the Mafra Palace Library, also in Portugal. Grey long-eared bats (*Plecotus austriacus*) and serotine bats (*Eptesicus serotinus*) come into the library every night to feast and spend the winter hibernating there.

BRIDGE BATS: Driven out of their caves by land-use changes, millions of Mexican free-tailed bats (*Tadarida brasiliensis*) have moved underneath the Congress Avenue Bridge in Austin, Texas. On summer evenings, huge crowds gather on the bridge at sunset to watch them swoop over the river.

SCHOOL BATS: A survey of public buildings in the Madagascar city of Moramanga found that about one-

third of them housed colonies of Peters's wrinkle-lipped bats (*Mormopterus jugularis*) and little free-tailed bats (*Chaerephon pumilus*). Ninety percent of the high schools surveyed had bats.

STADIUM BATS: A number of bat species roost in the tunnels beneath the University of Georgia's Sanford Stadium. These include tricolored bats (*Perimyotis subflavus*) and gray bats (*Myotis grisescens*)—rare in the state.

(ERSTWHILE) BOTANIC GARDEN BATS: The Royal Botanic Gardens in Sydney were once home to more than 20,000 grey-headed flying foxes (*Pteropus poliocephalus*), which roosted in—and occasionally defoliated—the garden's collection of important trees. After their defenders lost a federal court case, the bats were driven to a nearby park using loud percussion.

NORTH AMERICA

Potomac Dolphins

A special population of bottlenoses congregates downstream from Washington, DC.

RANGE: Tropical and temperate waters around the world
SPECIES: Tamanend's bottlenose dolphin (*Tursiops erebennus*)

◆ The bottlenose dolphin is a saltwater creature, frequenting open ocean and coastal waters. Why, then, do so many spend their summers in the lower Potomac River, near Washington, DC? In one incident recorded in 1884, dolphins swam all the way past Chester A. Arthur's White House and upriver to Aqueduct Bridge, pursued by a boat full of armed men.

Since 2015, the Potomac-Chesapeake Dolphin Project (PCDP) has cataloged close to 2,000 dolphins that come to the Potomac—a tributary of the Chesapeake Bay—seasonally from other waters. Dolphins can be identified by the unique patterns of notches and scars on their dorsal fins. The Potomac regulars, who return year after year, are given names from American political history: presidents, vice presidents, Supreme Court judges, first ladies, activists, and senators. George Washington's fin is craggy and crosshatched, while Betsy Ross's is notched in a way that looks a bit flaglike. People have strong feelings about these names, and so researchers are careful to keep them politically balanced: There's a Melania Trump dolphin as well as a Jill Biden.

Researchers were originally spurred to study the ecology and activities of these wayward dolphins by a mass mortality event. From 2013 to 2015, a respiratory virus caused some 1,600 dolphins to beach themselves on the East Coast, many in Virginia. Investigating how the disease had spread among populations led project researchers to some curious findings. One is a foraging strategy in which groups of five to ten dolphins move in coordinated circles in shallow water. Ann-Marie Jacoby, associate director of the PCDP, believes they're working together to corral fish, disorienting their prey with clouds of sediment so they can more easily chase them down.

Onlookers watch a dolphin leap out of the Chesapeake Bay.

Researchers have witnessed the birth of a dolphin calf and seen many mother-calf pairs in the Potomac. This has lent support to the hypothesis that the river is an optimal dolphin nursery, full of food and with few predatory sharks. However, they have also observed mysterious incidents of aggression toward newborn calves, in which adult dolphins will toss babies out of the water or try to hold them down and drown them.

Currently, Jacoby and her colleagues are focusing on demographics: Is the presence of dolphins in the Potomac changing over time? If so, what is driving that change? Conditions fluctuate dramatically in the bay from year to year, and so trends are difficult to quantify—a problem familiar to many of the dolphins' political namesakes. ❯ **How to see them:** July and August are the best months for dolphin activity in the Potomac. Take a boat out in higher-salinity waters, such as the river's mouth. By law, you must remain 50 yards (46 m) from wild dolphins. You can help researchers by reporting dolphin sightings through the PCDP website.

Airport Snowy Owls

Our journey is their destination.

◆ Snowy owl migrations are hard to understand. We aren't sure why each fall, some but not all of these iconic birds leave their breeding grounds in the Arctic Circle and head south, occasionally as far as Texas. It's difficult to imagine their solitary flights, powered by sets of wings the size of love seats and hushed by noise-reducing feathers.

But snowy owls do have one thing in common with human travelers: They often end up at the airport. It turns out that airfields and runways—which provide flat, tundra-like expanses, even in the middle of built-up places—make these raptors feel at home.

Owl expert Norman Smith has been finding and catching snowies at Boston's Logan Airport since 1980. More of these birds are found at Logan than anywhere else in the northeastern United States, and Smith has seen them there "in every imaginable weather condition, every imaginable hour of the day," he says. He watches takeoffs and landings, departures and arrivals, and, often, in-flight meals.

Smith's airport stakeouts—and his work tracking the owls, which over the years has involved banding, color marking, and now outfitting them with radio transmitters—have helped overturn some misconceptions. Researchers once thought that snowy owls left the Arctic Circle due to a lack of lemmings and that they became starved and weak during their winters away.

RANGE: Arctic North America, Europe, and Asia. In winter, snowies can be found throughout Canada and the northern United States, and occasionally as far south as Texas.
SPECIES: Snowy owl (*Bubo scandiacus*)

This owl has touched down at Logan Airport.

But the hundreds of owls Smith and colleagues in other states have caught have all been healthy. It now appears that, at least sometimes, it's an abundance of food that causes more competition up north, sending some owls down south to try their luck.

Years of city observations have also led to a much clearer picture of who these venturesome birds are and how they make it in their borrowed ecosystems. While snowy owls are diurnal in the Arctic Circle, where the sun doesn't set for part of the year, those at Logan are perfectly capable of hunting at night.

They're also happy to branch out from their typical lemming diet to take advantage of Boston's local food scene. Smith has watched owls take down Canada geese and great blue herons and pluck small, nimble snow buntings out of a flock. Boston's animals often underestimate them, he says—he once saw a peregrine falcon bop a napping snowy on the head, which turned out to be a fatal mistake.

Of course, they can't tangle effectively with airplanes. Like all birds, snowy owls can get sucked into engines (not great for the plane either) or harmed by jet blasts. Smith now traps and relocates as many as he can each year, using baited nets. Other airports, including New York's JFK, have since adopted this practice.

It's good not to let our journeys interrupt theirs. One snowy owl Smith caught and tagged at Logan came back nine months later, having traveled 7,426 miles (11,951 km)—the equivalent of three cross-country trips. "It's just amazing what they do," he says. **❯ How to see them:** Generally, it's illegal to visit airport land without a permit. You can keep track of birds Smith has banded online via Project SNOWstorm.

Have a safe flight!

Unexpected Havens

Infrastructure humans build for one reason is often repurposed by other species. Here are some urban and suburban spots where animals like to hang out.

GOLF COURSES—Large, interconnected grassy areas with low foot traffic that are quiet at night—what's not to love? A study in Melbourne, Australia, found that the city's links housed more beetle, bee, bird, and bat species than its parks or backyards. Animals especially prefer the areas that golfers try to avoid: the oases of water features and the dense vegetation of the roughs.

CEMETERIES—Our willingness to leave the dead in peace, even in dense cities, pays off for wildlife. Surveys of cemeteries in London have found thousands of species, including orchids seen nowhere else in the city, mosses and lichens growing on the gravestones, and cave spiders in the crypts.

SEWERS—Some animals find their niche in sewers, enjoying their easy conveyance and—sometimes—nutrient supply. Some of the best-suited species include Norway rats (*Rattus norvegicus*), who make nests with those things you're not supposed to flush, and blobby

colonies of tubifex worms. Mientien tree frogs (*Kurixalus idiootocus*), found in Taiwan, have learned to use Taipei's storm drains to amplify their mating calls.

CHIMNEYS—Many animals that once lived in tall, hollow trees, including bats and raccoons, have found chimneys to be suitable substitutes. Chimney swifts (*Chaetura pelagica*)—birds that build sticky nests with their own spit and are unable to stand up, instead using batlike feet to cling to vertical surfaces—are even named for the practice. Concerned homeowners should invest in netting or other nest excluders, because moving active nests is illegal.

LANDFILLS—Landfills, with their endlessly regenerating heaps of food and nesting material, are incredibly appealing to many birds (as well as many birders, who flock to them to see their favorites). Some studies have even found rare species at landfills, at higher densities than in the surrounding areas. There are downsides: Landfills can spread diseases, and at least one population of white storks (*Ciconia ciconia*) in Portugal appears to have given up their annual migration, content to live on trash year-round.

Gynandromorphs

Beautiful individuals combine male and female characteristics.

◆ In the winter of 2019, a bird went viral. "This non-binary cardinal is flipping gender the bird," announced the queer news site Logo TV, showing a bird with distinct half-red and half-tawny plumage, as though split down the middle.

The cardinal (or their doppelgänger) reentered the limelight in 2021, having been spotted in the same region of the northeast United States. As similar headlines followed, the large songbird became one of the best-known recent gynandromorphs—organisms that exhibit both male and female physical characteristics at the same time.

These characteristics can be displayed bilaterally, as with the cardinal, zebra finches, or a rose-breasted grosbeak found in Pennsylvania in 2020 with two different colored inner wings, yellow on the left and pink on the right. Bilateral gynandromorphs are sometimes called "halfsiders" or "chimeras." Halfsiders are particularly striking when the species is sexually dimorphic, meaning males and females have different physical characteristics.

The second-largest butterfly in the world, the Goliath birdwing of New Guinea, can also appear as a halfsider. Goliath birdwing gynandromorphs have different sized and colored wings, making them look like patchwork creatures. Many butterfly and moth chimeras have become important symbols in intersex and nonbinary human communities.

While it isn't something you see every day, gynandromorphism does happen in a variety of animals besides birds and butterflies, including other insects, reptiles, crustaceans, and even some mammals, like rats. But because many species are not sexually dimorphic, it isn't always immediately noticeable.

RANGE: Worldwide
SPECIES: Some of the most striking gynandromorphs commonly seen include northern cardinals (*Cardinalis cardinalis*), Goliath birdwings (*Ornithoptera goliath*), and jumping spiders (*Myrmarachne formicaria*).

Scientists believe that gynandromorphism is mainly attributable to genetic mutations associated with cell division. As these mutations occur at different stages of development, they produce different types of gynandromorphs. While many are bilateral, some present as mosaics, meaning male and female characteristics are splashed across the organism's body like tie-dye—as with some gynandromorphic Pamela and blue morpho butterflies. Others are polar, meaning the dividing line occurs elsewhere on the animal's body.

This phenomenon challenges assumptions about the natural world. For instance, in some types of ants, gynandromorph queen-males have been found, with one black, winged male side and one red queen side. Even in species that tend toward rigid sex roles, individuals have a way of surprising us. ❯ **How to see them:** Finding a gynandromorph in the wild takes patience and regular observation—either that or a ton of luck. Many examples can be seen online and in museums.

This Kentish glory moth has a "female"-colored left wing and a "male"-colored right wing.

17-Year Cicadas

These bugs share the prime of their lives with us.

◆ When American humans turn 17, they can donate blood, get a pilot's license, and (often) participate in fulfilling coming-of-age ceremonies that pertain to their specific cultures.

When American cicadas turn 17, they can come out of the dirt for the first time ever, scream for several weeks, mate, and then die. Such is the magic life of the three *Magicicada* species native to the eastern and central United States.

Like all periodical cicadas, the 17-year varieties enjoy an extensive underground adolescence before a brief adulthood of packed, sunlit ecstasy. Different groups of cicadas, called broods, emerge together at high densities—more than a million cicadas per acre in some places.

Coming up all at once has its perks. Individually, periodical cicadas are big, loud, and unwieldy and make easy targets for predators, which include birds, snakes, rodents, larger bugs, and dogs. Emerging en masse means that no matter how many individuals get snarfed, some will survive. The 17-year waiting period helps ensure that predators with shorter life cycles will not be able to time their own boom years to match the cicadas'. (Other cicada species use different prime numbers, presumably also as a time-based evasive maneuver.)

Magicicada nymphs are cued to emerge by changing soil temperatures. After scaling trees and molting—leaving behind perfect hollow replicas of their former selves—they take a little less than a week to reharden, then begin to seek out mates.

Male cicadas form choruses, which climb high up into branches and join together in their special song, a quavering drone. (Amplified by hollow chambers within the bugs' own bodies, the sound can surpass 85 decibels, which is the recommended workplace exposure limit in the US.) Females are drawn by the music and flock up there to join them and mate.

Cicada fans come too. Broods with large and broad emergences—such as Brood X, which holds territory from Georgia and Illinois all the way up through New York and Michigan—inspire celebrations, community science surveys, and

RANGE: Large patches of the eastern and central United States, from Oklahoma up through Massachusetts. Different broods emerge in different places and at different times.

SPECIES: *Magicicada septendecim, M. cassini,* and *M. septendecula*

What did I miss?

endless news coverage. New York's Onondaga Nation credits Brood VII cicadas with saving them from hunger in 1779, when a military campaign led by George Washington drove them out of their villages and into the forest.

After their raucous open-air orgy, the female cicadas saw nest holes into twigs and stack their eggs inside. They and the males die soon after, totally spent from all that living. About two months later, a new generation of nymphs will hatch, drop to the ground, dig themselves in, and find some roots to suck on while they wait. The party is over . . . for now. 〉 **How to see them:** Because cicadas emerge at relatively predictable times and locations, it's possible to plan a cicada-scouting trip or to prepare for your local brood. (If you do, use the Cicada Safari app to report your findings!) The Cicada Mania website is a great resource for tracking emergences as they occur.

Moon Trees

These trees went to space—and then we spaced on them.

◆ In 1971, just before he blasted off with Apollo 14, astronaut Stuart Roosa—a former smoke jumper for the US Forest Service—stashed several hundred tree seeds in his personal kit, the small tube in which crew members can stow items unrelated to the mission. The seeds spent a total of nine days in space before splashing back to Earth with the crew.

RANGE: Throughout the United States, with a few in other countries
SPECIES: Coast redwood (*Sequoia sempervirens*), loblolly pine (*Pinus taeda*), American sweetgum (*Liquidambar styraciflua*), American sycamore (*Platanus occidentalis*), and Douglas fir (*Pseudotsuga menziesii*)

The Forest Service watched over the seeds until they sprouted. Once they had grown hardy enough, the seedlings, known as moon trees, were fanned out across the country. In 1975 and 1976, local papers from Las Vegas, Nevada, to Huntsville, Alabama, reported on astronauts, politicians, and other public figures dropping by to help place the 18-inch (45 cm) sycamores or foot-tall (30 cm) pines into their new homes in parks and squares, in honor of America's bicentennial. A few were sent to allies in Brazil, Switzerland, and Japan. There was something heroic about trees grown from seeds that had traveled so far from home—fragile things that Americans had successfully shepherded through a cold, dark trip.

Unfortunately, after this first burst of publicity, we largely lost track of the trees. No one is quite sure how many there were to begin with; of the roughly 100 currently accounted for, about a third are already dead, including the White House Rose Garden's loblolly pine and the Kennedy Space Center's sycamore. Some have been replaced by stand-ins or their own clones.

Their fate has little to do with their jaunt in space—which, biologically speaking, did not change them—but with the tough lot that can come with being a tree among people. Many likely died in the first year or two, given that freshly transplanted trees are especially vulnerable to getting parched, infested, or toppled. Others were uprooted during construction or injured by weather events.

Today, what we know about moon trees is thanks to one devoted

This loblolly pine, which once went to the moon, now lives outside the Sebastian County Courthouse in Arkansas.

NASA employee, Dave Williams, who has taken it upon himself to sleuth out their locations and statuses. Meanwhile, America is working on the next moon tree generation: In 2022, NASA sent up one thousand seeds with the Artemis I mission. They are currently under the care of the Forest Service and will be distributed to worthy parties as soon as they are ready to give things a shot on this planet. 〉 **How to see them:** A list of known moon trees can be found on NASA's website. Anyone with information about potential lost moon trees should contact Dave Williams at dave.williams@nasa.gov.

Animal Math

Mathematics may seem like a human invention. But numerical competency comes in handy for lots of everyday animal tasks: everything from mating and decision-making to hiding and hunting. As we investigate animals' numerical skills, we uncover abilities in almost every group, from insects and arachnids to fish, amphibians, birds, and mammals.

DESERT ANTS (*Cataglyphis fortis*) · Faced with vast, undifferentiated landscapes, desert ants measure distances with an internal pedometer. Researchers trained ants to find food exactly 30 feet (9 m) away. When they outfitted the ants with makeshift stilts that elongated their strides, the insects overshot the target, suggesting they had been internally counting their own steps. **❶**

PSEUDOSCORPIONS (*Cordylochernes scorpioides*) · Several male harlequin beetle-riding pseudoscorpions mate with a single female, but the first partner usually has a higher chance of succeeding in fertilization. To avoid wasting a lot of their sperm on a mate who is less likely to bear their children, male pseudoscorpions count the number of competitors who've copulated with her before them through a series of olfactory tells and decrease their ejaculation accordingly, in a progressive and proportionate fashion. **❷**

BANDED ARCHERFISH (*Toxotes jaculatrix*) · Many fish live in groups and are able to gauge how many members are on their team. Rainbowfish can distinguish between groups of eight and ten companions, while three-spined sticklebacks can discriminate between six and seven fish friends. Banded archerfish, who can tell groups of two from groups of three, have a skill particularly helpful to scientists: They can be trained to spit out jets of water at groups of dots on a screen to communicate their responses to counting exercises. **❸**

TÚNGARA FROGS (*Engystomops pustulosus*) · To flirt with their female counterparts, male túngara frogs engage in back-and-forth sing-offs. Each performs a call that ends with a repeated *chuck*. A frog will add one extra chuck for every chuck added by competitors—until he reaches his limit, usually four to six chucks. The male who chucks the most wins. Specialized cells in the frogs' brains are thought to allow them to keep track of the sounds, as long as they're emitted at appropriate intervals. **❹**

CARRION CROWS (*Corvus corone*) · The concept of the numerical quantity zero—which is a little bit different from the concept of nothing—is challenging even for humans to fully grasp. But crows seem to get it. In experiments, crows were found to more frequently confuse images with zero dots and images with a single dot, compared with images with two, three, or four dots—suggesting they consider the quantities of zero and one to be close together. And cerebral activity scans show that crows' brains react to zero the same way they do to other numbers. **❺**

RHESUS MACAQUES (*Macaca mulatta*) · Not only can macaques reliably count to six, they can understand the concept of "the middle." Taught to identify the middle dot within a line of three dots, the monkeys were also able to spot the middle dot of a five- or seven-dot sequence. Macaques can also be trained to match a numerical symbol with a numerical quantity—for instance, associating six balls with the symbol "6." **❻**

Georgia's South River

Bringing a waterway back to the people

LOCATION: The South River runs 60 miles (96 km) aboveground, beginning in the city of East Point and eventually draining into the Jackson Lake reservoir.

SPECIES: River otter (*Lontra canadensis*), white-tailed deer (*Odocoileus virginianus*), great blue heron (*Ardea herodias*), and many more

◆ Each morning, the sun sparkles on Georgia's South River. Fish nab insects from the surface, songbirds warble from overhanging branches, and deer stop to drink. Along its 60-mile (96 km) length, the river hosts calm scene after calm scene, often separated from busy neighborhoods by a scant curtain of trees.

Generally, though, few people are there to enjoy the natural beauty. Although the river runs through several major cities and its first boat launching point is just 20 minutes from downtown Atlanta, decades of intermittent pollution have meant that people stay away, says Jacqueline Echols, board president of the South River Watershed Alliance (SRWA), a group dedicated to restoring the river's health and reputation.

The river, which runs through predominantly Black neighborhoods, "has struggled," Echols says. Part of Atlanta's sewer system is combined (meaning sewage and stormwater flow through the same pipes), and even a modest amount of rain can overwhelm its capacity, sending contaminated water into the river and surrounding communities.

Although pressure by Echols and others has led to infrastructure improvements, storms still cause problems, as do occasional leakages and overflows. Court-mandated overhauls have been ignored or delayed for decades. The river's plight is an environmental justice issue—one of many instances in which underserved demographics are denied equal access to green spaces, clean air, and clean water. "The environment is the community—it's the center of it," says Echols.

Most of Georgia's South River—40 of its 60 miles (64 out of 96 km)—is navigable and could be used for recreation.

This neglect mars a river that, most of the time, is clean, beautiful, and "really still very wild," says Echols. The land around the river is undeveloped, and much of it is publicly owned. The first time Echols traveled there, she was accompanied by a Panola Mountain State Park ranger who, she says, identified 46 bird species during a 6.5-mile mile (10.5 km) river paddle.

Unlike many urban waterways, which are forced into underground pipes in some places to allow for development, the South River is also fully daylighted—out in the sun from beginning to end. Thanks to this open-air run, river otters can be spotted rolling around in Intrenchment Creek, not far from the center of Atlanta: "They just follow the river upstream," Echols says.

People, meanwhile, can follow it downstream, along 40 miles (64 km) of navigable waterway. In addition to organizing public advocacy campaigns, hosting trash cleanups, and performing water testing, the SRWA holds community paddling events. The group is also threading together what it calls the South River Water Trail, a linked set of boat launches that provide safe river access and that Echols hopes will eventually draw the interest of an outfitter who can rent boats to the public.

In 2021, for the first time, the Georgia Environmental Protection Division (EPD) designated 13 miles (20.9 km) of the South River as "recreational"—a status that comes with stricter water quality standards and more protection. The SRWA is working to get the remaining 27 miles (43.5 km) to this point. The more people visit the river when conditions are good, the more incentivized the state is to make it that way all the time. **❭ How to see it:** Popular South River launch sites are found at Panola Shoals Trailhead and Lorraine Park.

THE WILD LIFE OF A South River Advocate

■ As board president of the South River Watershed Alliance (SRWA), Jacqueline Echols has spent decades working to improve the river's water quality—and to help people who live nearby access a wild place they didn't know they could enjoy.

• **What do you want people to know about the South River?**

Folks who go down the river, the first thing they notice and are totally in awe of is just how intact the natural infrastructure is—the trees and the quality of the water. The river is really very pretty with all of the greenery. It's not intimidating, because it's an urban river, so it runs shallow. Good flow, but folks can see the bottom.

It's 20 minutes from downtown Atlanta, and people are just amazed at this community resource that's been there forever that folks didn't know about and really didn't take advantage of.

• **What role does a group like the South River Watershed Alliance play in changing things?**

Through our canoe paddles we run in the summer, we've introduced thousands of people to the river—the folks in the community, the predominantly

Black population that lives there. Over the years, neglect has perpetuated a culture of avoidance, all centered around pollution issues that were tolerated by the Georgia EPD and the US Environmental Protection Agency. That's what has caused South River so many issues—it's been polluted so long, people didn't bother.

Over the last 10 or 12 years, through the work that we have done, I've seen that people are really interested and there is a lot of support out there for the river. When we have the need for public comment sessions, folks do it. It puts more pressure on Georgia EPD and the municipalities to do what they are supposed to do, and uphold water quality standards and protect communities. It takes a community advocating on its own behalf, but it does require a group to lead that effort.

• **What is the SRWA working on now?**

The river has 40 miles [64 km] that can float a canoe or a kayak. That's the South River Water Trail. There are water trails all over this state, but this is the first one for an urban river serving a predominantly Black constituency. We have five

launch sites in three counties that are being redeveloped, with several others planned.

The next goal is to extend the water trail upstream [into urban Atlanta, connecting communities to the river through existing green spaces]. Folks upstream have just as much right to benefit from the river as folks downstream. There's no reason why people who live in the city of Atlanta should not enjoy the river from a passive standpoint.

The City of Atlanta and DeKalb County aren't very supportive of recreational use or contact with the river. They want to keep pollution, because it's actually the easiest and cheapest thing to do! Then they don't have to fix anything. But they are going to have to deal with pollution issues while I'm around.

• **How can interested people help with this project?**

All you need to do is go to southriverga.org. Folks can get our newsletters so they can learn about our paddles, and they can learn about our cleanups that we have three or four times a year to help deal with the trash. A healthy river, healthy environment, definitely requires that the community get out and support it. ■

P-22

How one "Hollywood cat" pushed the boundaries of coexistence

RANGE: Mountain lions are found as far north as Canada and as far south as Chile.
SPECIES: Mountain lion (*Puma concolor*)

◆ Mountain lions have the greatest range of any mammal in the Americas, inhabiting mountains, forests, deserts, and wetlands. But it's where the mountain lion designated P-22 made his home that earned him the fame most Hollywood transplants only dream of.

For a decade, P-22—who received his name through a National Park Service study—lived in Griffith Park, a slice of nature in Los Angeles, California. To get there from the Santa Monica Mountains, he had to make the dangerous journey across the 405 and 101 freeways.

P-22 soon became an unofficial city mascot, known to some as the "Brad Pitt of mountain lions." (He was a nepo baby: His father was P-1, the first mountain lion collared by the National Park Service.) He made appearances in backyards, on surveillance camera footage, and on the front page of the *Los Angeles Times*. His likability even survived

Fighting Traffic

Roads connect people, but they divide wildlife. Crossing them—to explore new habitats, migrate, seek food, and find mates—is fraught with danger. In America alone, more than a million vertebrates get hit by cars every day; worldwide, traffic threatens species from the Iberian lynx to the maned wolf with extinction.

Happily, there's a solution to this vehicular crisis: wildlife crossing structures, bridges and tunnels that permit wide-ranging creatures to traverse highways unharmed. (Roadside fences typically guide animals to the passages.)

Here are five common types of crossing, and the animals they serve.

THE UNDERPASS • In 1970, the US Federal Highway Administration faced a quandary. Interstate 70, one of the massive new highways springing up around the country, would soon block many of Colorado's migratory mule deer from reaching important habitat. So the feds installed a concrete tunnel, 10 feet (3 m) wide and 100 feet (30 m) long, to allow deer to cross the interstate safely—among America's first wildlife underpasses.

By now, it's nearly impossible to name a mammal that *hasn't* moved through one of the several thousand underpasses beneath North American roads, from elk herds that stroll through Arizona underpasses to Florida panthers that have been spotted using them to tote their cubs between swaths of protected land. Because animal crashes cost the country more than $8 billion a year in hospital bills, car repairs, and other expenses, these passageways and their fences often pay for themselves.

THE OVERPASS • Farsighted and skittish creatures like the pronghorn tend to avoid cramped undercrossings, and some wide freeways don't lend themselves to tunnels. In those situations, ecologists favor bridges, whose long sightlines appeal to even the wariest animals, and which can be covered with shrubs, trees, and rock piles to mimic natural habitat.

Overpasses aren't cheap—$5 million is a standard price tag, and Los Angeles's mountain lion crossing will run $90 million by the time it's completed in 2025—but there's no doubt they work. Today grizzly bears lumber across overpasses in Canada's Banff National Park, wolves use "green bridges"

to disperse through Germany, and pangolins and civets traipse over the Eco-Link, an overpass that connects two patches of forest cleaved by a highway in Singapore.

THE TOAD TUNNEL • Many of the world's most road-imperiled creatures are amphibians. Frogs, toads, and salamanders cross busy streets as they flock to their breeding ponds each spring and get crushed en masse on the way. Since the 1960s, when "toad tunnels" first popped up in Europe, conservationists have been outfitting roadkill hot spots with miniature underpasses, anywhere from 12 inches (30 cm) to 5 feet (1.5 m) wide.

Well-built tunnels usually have open grates that allow water and moist air to penetrate the passages, fostering the damp conditions that these tiny migrants favor. And they're made to last: America's first amphibian passage, built in 1987 in Amherst, Massachusetts, is still funneling spotted salamanders across Henry Street.

THE MAMMAL SHELF • Not all wildlife crossings are expressly designed for animals. Roads are underlaid by millions of culverts, concrete or corrugated metal pipes that convey rivers, streams, and runoff. Animals regularly slink through these inadvertent crossings, but there's a problem: When water levels rise, terrestrial critters can't use them.

To get around this issue, biologists outfit culverts with "critter shelves," metal catwalks that allow animals to pass through flooded culverts without soaking their paws. In Montana, where critter shelves debuted in the early 2000s, they're used by weasels, raccoons, striped skunks, and some enterprising house cats.

THE CANOPY BRIDGE • Many arboreal creatures spend their entire lives among the treetops—so when roads fragment their forests, standard wildlife underpasses won't help them. These animals require rope canopy bridges that stretch across highways and connect forest patches.

Some of the first canopy bridges were built in the late 1990s in Kenya, where scientists documented hundreds of daily crossings by Sykes' monkeys, colobus monkeys, and vervets. Tropical conservationists have since built ladders for creatures from sugar gliders to gibbons, which happily scamper—or, in the case of sloths, creep—along the ropes. And while big overpasses cost millions, canopy bridges can be installed and maintained for just $160 or so per year.

A black bear underpass in Florida (above) and a wildlife overpass in Banff National Park (below)

his own Hollywood scandal: In 2016, he was suspected of scaling the wall of the LA Zoo and mauling a sleeping koala.

"P-22 was a full-on celebrity," says Ed Pert, a regional manager with the California Department of Fish and Wildlife. "He reminded people that even a city like Los Angeles could be a wild space."

But living in the smallest home range ever recorded for an adult mountain lion came with hardships. His isolation made him unable to find a mate; a car struck him. An uncharacteristic attack on dogs—he typically ate mule deer, coyotes, and raccoons—prompted a health inspection, which revealed a host of critical conditions. In December 2022, P-22 was humanely euthanized. He was 12 years old, a senior citizen among wild cats. Governor Gavin Newsom eulogized him, and his home city gave him a send-off befitting a leading man: a sold-out memorial at the Greek Theatre.

P-22 is now "a symbol of conservation and what's possible," Pert says. His story inspired interest in and funding for the Annenberg Wildlife Crossing, an overpass that will be the largest wildlife corridor in the world when it is completed in 2025. It will allow mountain lions living in the Santa Monica Mountains to safely cross the 101 freeway. While P-22 miraculously completed the same journey without help, the remaining Santa Monica population is trapped and suffers from inbreeding—unable to make their own Hollywood dreams come true. ❯ **How to see them:** You probably won't see a mountain lion—even those who live in urban areas tend to stay out of the spotlight. But if you do, try to make yourself look bigger.

Southern Alligator Lizards

Getting it on out in the open

RANGE: Along the Pacific Coast of North America, from southern Washington to northern Baja California
SPECIES: Southern alligator lizard (*Elgaria multicarinata*)

◆ A certain neighborly etiquette is required in cities, where people live shoulder to shoulder and privacy can be hard to come by. When you encounter someone who has failed to properly secure it, it's often best to simply look away.

These rules do not apply to southern alligator lizards. If you see these reptiles getting it on—which they will do on the sidewalk, in yards and courtyards, and occasionally in the middle of the street—you are encouraged to watch closely, and even snap a photo.

Someone throw them a sheet.

Southern alligator lizards are the most widespread reptile in a number of California cities, happy to hunt insects and skulk around in bushes almost anywhere in Los Angeles, San Diego, and San Francisco. While they're normally shy, their courtships are dramatic. Male lizards bite females on the neck or head and hang on for hours—sometimes days— using special, high-stamina muscles similar to those found in human vocal cords. Sometimes two males will bite the same female at the same time.

LOS ANGELES

- More than 4,000 different plant and animal species live in Los Angeles County. These include 52 endangered species, from marcescent dudleya—a tiny star-shaped succulent that stretches out its golden blooms in spring and early summer—to North Pacific right whales, which number less than 100 worldwide.

- Located between the Pacific Ocean and the San Gabriel Mountains, Los Angeles has a dry subtropical climate, with humidity that can drop to desert levels and frequent droughts exacerbated by climate change. Through its turf replacement rebate program, the city offers residents money to replace grass lawns with native and drought-tolerant plants.

- The La Brea Tar Pits, a set of bubbling asphalt seeps located in what is now Hancock Park, have been trapping insects, hapless animals, and plant bits for about 40,000 years. Paleontological study of these remains helps paint a picture of Ice Age California, where saber-toothed cats hunted ground sloths and oaks and junipers responded to a changing climate. Later on, Indigenous Chumash and Tongva people used the tar to seal their redwood canoes.

KEEP AN EYE OUT FOR The ethereal blue glow of bioluminescent algae swirling in the waves. While the appearance of this oceanic aurora borealis can be tricky to predict, your best chance of catching it is to head to a dark beach in the spring and summer months.

KEEP AN EAR OUT FOR The high-pitched buzz of hummingbird wings. These tiny jewels of the bird world have the personalities of miniature fighter jets. Several species migrate to California in the spring, where they wage epic, zippy battles over the best flowers and hummingbird feeders.

KEEP A NOSE OUT FOR The minty, medicinal smell of the area's eucalyptus trees, originally introduced as seeds from Australia in the 1800s. Californians have a love-them-or-hate-them relationship with these tall, fast-growing trees, which were planted as windbreaks and timber into the twentieth century.

A passerby who comes across such a scene may not know whether they're witnessing "mating, fighting, or cannibalism," says Greg Pauly, the herpetology curator at the Natural History Museum of Los Angeles County. Pauly and his colleagues have harnessed the curiosity that results for a community science project that collects evidence of this behavior, whose motivations remain mysterious—even for lizards, there are a lot of downsides to being in such a vulnerable position out in the open.

The project, ongoing at the museum, has gathered hundreds of observations over nearly a decade and is helping researchers learn about everything from how weather affects alligator lizard mating habits—wetter years mean higher reproduction rates—to how the COVID-19 pandemic changed Angelenos' relationship to nature. (Since the lockdowns, "many have finally learned something that has always been true—nature is all around us at all times," Pauly says.)

It has also sidestepped what can be a difficult aspect of city science: In Los Angeles, "almost everything is on someone's private property," which makes it hard to survey in more traditional ways, says Pauly.

So the next time you surprise some mating lizards, take a picture. Send it to your friends or even your local museum. These neighbors won't mind. ❯ **How to see them:** Keep an eye out for mating southern alligator lizards from February through April. If you see some, send your photos and observational notes to nature@nhm.org, or upload them to the iNaturalist app.

Crow Problem-Solving

How clever corvids make the most of city life.

◆ Imagine you're a crow with an unshelled walnut. You'd really like to get at what's inside. But you don't have a nutcracker (or, for that matter, hands). What's your move?

Across the world, crows faced with this and similar dilemmas have come up with a number of ingenious methods. In Sendai, Japan, carrion crows crack nuts by placing them in the paths of vehicles. (They stake out spots where cars stop or go slowly, like traffic lights and driving schools.) In Davis, California, American crows drop them from great heights onto roads, calibrating the perfect release altitude based on the hardness of both nut and surface.

Crows have been famed for their problem-solving skills since at least Aesop's time—see his fable about the crow and the water jug. But the advent of large cities has provided new opportunities for them to showcase, and benefit from, their flexibility and cleverness.

Crows can learn from each other, work together, and consciously consider problems before attacking them, abilities that allow them to figure out tricky human inventions like water fountains and garbage bags. A recent survey of scientific literature found that in 72 percent of cases studied, urbanization of a particular area actually improved things for corvids, a group that includes crows, ravens, magpies, and blue jays.

RANGE: Most of the world
SPECIES: Common city species include the American crow (*Corvus brachyrhynchos*) in North America, the carrion crow (*Corvus corone*) in Europe, the large-billed crow (*Corvus macrorhynchos*) in eastern Asia, and the pied crow (*Corvus albus*) in Africa.

Crows like this one learn to take advantage of city infrastructure.

Crows' success in cities occasionally brings them into conflict with another street-smart species: us. And unlike our disagreements with most other animals, who will readily anger us by dumpster diving but not hold a grudge when we install a lock, conflict with crows can cut two ways. Crows remember faces and can recall when someone has wronged them—or, on the other hand, done well by them. If crows live near you, consider building up a reputation as a good neighbor. You might even learn some new tricks. **› How to see them:** Pay attention to your local crows, and odds are you'll catch them doing something impressive. To see Japan's famous walnut-cracking crows, try spending time near the Kadan driving school in Sendai.

THE WILD LIFE OF A Crow-Human Conflict Mediator

■ Yvette Buigues is an artist, wildlife rehabilitator, and animal craniosacral therapist in Oakland, California. Her fluency in animal communication—particularly her relationship with Carl, a crow fledgling she healed and raised—has led her neighbors to call on her to resolve their disputes with the area's crows.

• **When did you first become interested in crows?**
Crows have been special to me my whole entire life. They're so black and so big—as a kid, I found them pretty impressive. And for a young punk rocker, what's cooler than a crow, right?

• **How did you start getting to know the crows in your neighborhood in Oakland?**
That was through Carl the crow. My husband, Chuck, brought him home. He was tiny. The other crows would fly above me in a circle, and he would run over and hide underneath me. He was afraid of them at first.

Over time, it became a routine where I would be out in the yard with Carl for my first cup of coffee in the morning, and the crows would all come and circle. We had him for about a year, and every day, they would check up on him a couple of times a day that way.

• **Can you talk about the first crow-human conflict you helped out with—when the crows in a family's yard had grown very aggressive, and they didn't know why?**

I was a little bit nervous going in. I had my hood on, because I didn't want [the crows] to recognize me and then bring the trouble on myself.

As I walked in, I started saying under my breath, "I'm here to help." And then I took it inward and I got quiet. I didn't notice it, but according to [one of the family members], the crows got quiet too.

They were all sitting up in the tree. They watched my every move. I found a little baby bird. It was tragic—its wing was literally hanging on by a thread. It came over and jumped into my hand. I told the family they should give the fledgling a comfortable place to die. Once they had done that, the crows calmed down and their problems stopped.

It was kind of surreal for me. It was the first time I had done something like that, where I just went to help.

• **What are some other situations you've helped out with since then?**
There's a fancy restaurant in Berkeley called Chez Panisse. They called me because they had a family of crows in the trees out in front of their place. And the baby, when it was learning to fly, would jump out of the tree and land in their patio, and they didn't want to have to close the patio down.

So they called me I think for three days straight. I went over there. I'd pick up the chick, and I'd take it back onto the roof of the restaurant, and the parents would be there waiting.

Our neighbor Dan has a tree with crows in his yard that we believe are Carl and his partner. Last year he called me up. He was really upset. His cat got a fledgling and killed it. And he went out in the backyard and the crows were in his tree yelling at him.

I said, "Bring the cats inside. Take the body outside and sit with it. And apologize. And then if you guys have peanuts or cat kibble, leave it next to the bird's body as an offering. The crows will eventually come down to check it out and have a snack. And they'll hopefully forgive you."

American crow

Dan was sitting next to this little fledgling's body, feeling how sad he felt. Feeling "Sorry—it happened on my watch. I'll do better next time." He was feeling it, and, of course, the crows did too. Dan said it worked like a charm. ■

Get To Know Your Neighbors

Certain species are so ubiquitous in cities that most of us don't take the time to properly appreciate them. Here are some fun facts about a few of America's most common city-dwelling creatures.

NORWAY RATS (*Rattus norvegicus*)

› In New York City, there are uptown rats and downtown rats, and the two don't mix. In 2017, researchers discovered that the city has two genetically distinct rat communities that each keep to their own territories.

› Rats are incredibly playful and social—researchers have even taught them to play hide-and-seek with humans.

› Rats are abundant across the inhabited continents of the world, with a notable exception: The province of Alberta, in the middle of Canada, is entirely rat-free, due to a strict control policy that goes back decades. ❶

COMMON DANDELIONS (*Taraxacum officinale*)

› Dandelions are native to Europe and Asia but have taken root in lawns all over the world, including the Americas, Africa, Australia, and New Zealand.

› Dandelions have been used for medicinal purposes by a variety of cultures for hundreds of years. A sixteenth-century physician named William Langham, for instance, directed patients to rub dandelion juice on their heads as a cure for baldness. While dandelions likely won't help you get your hair back, there is evidence that these vitamin-packed plants might have antioxidant properties and aid digestion—all parts of the plant can be safely eaten, though city foragers should be careful of plants exposed to pesticides or heavy metals.

› These bright yellow flowers might be interlopers in many parts of the world, but they typically aren't harmful to the ecosystems in their adopted countries. In fact, they can often benefit native pollinators. ❷

ROCK PIGEONS (*Columba livia*)

› What we think of as city pigeons today are actually feral rock doves, a species of pigeon first domesticated by humans for meat thousands of years ago in Mesopotamia. (They may be the first birds humans ever domesticated.) Over time, escaped pet pigeons made homes for themselves in cities worldwide.

› Pigeons are romantics, forming deep pair bonds and mating for life, with both parents taking part in nest site selection and chick-rearing.

› Pigeons are also dedicated parents, even making something called "pigeon milk" that sustains their chicks in the days after they hatch. This "milk" is produced by both parents from sloughed-off fluid-filled cells lining their crop (a pouch in their neck).

› Like many animals who adapt well to urban life, pigeons are quite intelligent—they can be trained to pass the famous self-recognition "mirror test" and are capable of distinguishing written words from random strings of letters. ❸

GERMAN COCKROACHES (*Blattella germanica*)

› Cockroaches have earned their reputation for being difficult to kill. They can go without food for a month, and even live on for weeks after being decapitated.

› Female cockroaches will mate with males when they're around, but they don't actually need them to reproduce. Cockroaches are capable of

parthenogenesis, or "virgin" births, whereby females produce viable offspring from unfertilized eggs. Groups of female roaches will even synchronize their fatherless reproduction to increase the chances that their offspring will survive.

〉 While they might like hanging out in our trash, cockroaches are actually quite fastidious when it comes to personal hygiene. They meticulously groom themselves, paying special care to their antennae, which they need to keep clear of residue in order to detect smells in the air. ❹

HOUSEFLIES (*Musca domestica*)

〉 Flies can taste food just like humans do, experiencing flavors like sweetness and bitterness. But there's a key difference—flies taste with delicate hairs on their bodies, while our taste receptors are confined to our tongues. For flies, this intermingling of touch and taste fast-tracks the process of looking for food, telling them exactly where they should stick their proboscis to start slurping up the good stuff.

〉 Houseflies are capable of bursts of speed of up to 15 miles per hour (24 kph)—pretty fast for an insect the size of a small black bean.

〉 Flies' compound eyes allow them to see motion so quickly that they would see a typical 24-frames-per-second movie as a series of static images. No wonder they're so hard to swat. ❺

HERRING GULLS (*Larus argentatus*)

〉 The herring gull has a built-in desalination system. These seabirds can gulp water straight from the ocean, thanks to a gland above their eyes that removes the salt and flushes it out through their nostrils.

〉 Herring gulls are often seen performing a tap dance–like motion with their feet, sometimes called a "rain dance." Many believe that this motion imitates rain, tricking worms into wriggling to the surface and scoring the gulls an easy meal.

〉 Like many children, young herring gulls like to play with their food. They favor an activity known as "drop-catching," in which they will drop something, like a crab, from a great height and attempt to catch it before it falls to the ground. ❻

Eastern Gray Squirrels

Your yard is full of furry geniuses.

RANGE: Throughout the eastern United States. Gray squirrels have also been introduced (and, to the detriment of other squirrels, are thriving) in British Columbia, the United Kingdom, Italy, South Africa, and elsewhere.

SPECIES: Eastern gray squirrel (*Sciurus carolinensis*)

◆ Which creature could both plausibly bring on and survive an apocalypse? Smart money is on the squirrel.

The world boasts more than 270 different species of squirrels, found almost everywhere on the planet and falling into three broad categories: tree, ground, and flying. But of all of these, the most successful—and the one you might be picturing now—is the eastern gray.

The ubiquity of these bushy-tailed park acrobats is a testament to their problem-solving skills and adaptability. To witness the first, look no further than the thousands of videos of resourceful squirrels defeating obstacle courses and breaking into allegedly squirrel-proof bird feeders. (According to one study, up to 44 percent of visits to bird feeders are made by gray squirrels.)

Even in the lab, the eastern gray squirrel performs better at problem-solving tasks than other species of squirrel do, displaying greater behavioral flexibility—a willingness to try different approaches until one works—and a higher degree of tenacity. "Eastern gray squirrels are just really good at doing what they do," says squirrel expert John Koprowski, dean of the University of Wyoming's Haub School of Environment and Natural Resources.

Such skills underlie—and come from—the squirrel's main pastime: "exploring and identifying new sources of foods," Koprowski says. Building up a diverse portfolio means that if certain trees have a bad seed year, other options are available to the squirrels. These days, some of their go-to alternatives are not even trees: Urban squirrels have been known to scamper into bodegas to make off with chocolate bars, and porch pirate squirrels have been caught on doorbell cams stealing packages.

Squirrels are committed to exploring new food sources.

Because squirrels don't hibernate, eastern grays store caches of food to consume through the leaner seasons. They consider perishability when deciding which items to keep, dropping those that smell rotten or show cracks, and preferentially storing nuts and seeds that have higher levels of preservative tannins rather than eating them immediately. As scatter-hoarders, they spread their caches over large areas: A single squirrel can stash 10,000 nuts each year, over a range up to 7 acres (2.8 ha).

To keep track of their loot, research shows that squirrels use what scientists call "spatial chunking," organizing the locations of their caches by type—acorns in this area, hazelnuts here, stolen chocolate bars there—and creating mental maps to recall the general locations. Once in the vicinity, they deploy their sense of smell to narrow down the search. Squirrels are able to retrieve up to 95 percent of their buried nuts, although success rates vary considerably.

Squirrels also exhibit what scientists call "social learning"—they pay attention to what other animals are doing and use that information to their

benefit. Squirrels dig false holes if they believe they're being watched by other creatures who might want their caches, and they eavesdrop on birds to gauge whether a predator is near.

These higher-level cognitive processes are part of what makes squirrels so adaptable and help explain why squirrels are equally comfortable in urban, suburban, and rural spaces. Even though squirrels enjoy a better reputation than that other super-successful rodent who lives alongside humans—the rat—our proximity to them, combined with their curiosity, sometimes causes problems. Any hole a squirrel can get its head through, the rest of its body can follow, and they're more than happy to make those holes with their ever-growing teeth. In 1987, a squirrel shut down the NASDAQ for 82 minutes after it chewed through power cables; the same thing happened again in 1994. According to some sources, more electrical and internet outages are attributable to squirrels than to damage from any other animals—including humans. All part of their devious plan. ❯ **How to see them:** In cities, visit your nearest park and wait patiently next to the garbage bins, or perhaps check out the local bodega.

Myxomycete Slime Molds

These roving, single-celled blobs solve problems better than you do.

RANGE: Worldwide

SPECIES: There are hundreds of known species of myxomycete slime mold. Notable ones include *Fuligo septica* and *Physarum polycephalum*.

◆ In 1973, a mysterious and foamy substance oozed across a lawn in the suburbs of Dallas. With each attempt to destroy it—hacking it up, poisoning it, spraying it with a fireman's hose—the "Texas Blob" seemed to rise from the dead, returning the following day bigger and blobbier. Then it started multiplying. Locals wondered if the tenacious substance was extraterrestrial.

As usual, though, Earth didn't need help being weird. For perhaps billions of years, slime capable of learning, remembering, and even solving labyrinths has been roaming our planet. Moving between amorphous plasmodial stages and visually distinct reproductive ones, the world's many species of myxomycetes—also called slime molds—impress those who encounter them with their striking looks as well as their smarts.

Like most living things, a slime mold has two main jobs: eat and reproduce. In its initial nutrition-seeking stage, a slime mold takes the form of roving mucus, sucking up bacterial meals in forests, cities, or suburbs.

Although most slime molds consist of just a single multinucleated cell, they are pretty smart. In lab experiments, slime molds like *Physarum polycephalum* have demonstrated the ability to anticipate repetitive

Two notable slime molds, "Scrambled eggs" *(top)* and "dog vomit" *(bottom)*

actions (like puffs of cold air), avoid unpleasantness (like salt), and acclimate to said unpleasantness in the name of getting something nice (for instance, by braving salt to get to food). When one slime mold joins up with another, it can "teach" its new blobmate to habituate too.

Slime molds also demonstrate extreme efficiency in their quests for food, quickly pruning large webs of exploratory ooze into high-speed transmission networks. Placed in a labyrinth with a tasty oat flake at the center, *P. polycephalum* solves the maze. And placed on a map of Tokyo with 36 tasty oat flakes in the position of nearby population centers, *P. polycephalum* creates an impressive facsimile of the actual Tokyo railway system.

In the right conditions, a wild slime mold could ooze around forever. But when the bacterial buffet runs out, it transforms, often overnight, into a more ostentatious form: the fruiting body. Depending on the species, these may take any number of evocative shapes, from "glass-head pin" to "pile of tapioca pudding."

While most slime mold fruiting bodies measure just a few millimeters, a few, like the aforementioned Texas Blob, can easily grow Frisbee-sized or larger. That particular species, *Fuligo septica*, has earned a number of other nicknames over the years, including "dog vomit slime mold," "scrambled egg slime," and "demon droppings." **❭ How to see them:** Slime mold fruiting bodies frequently form on fresh, moist hardwood mulch and decaying matter, such as dead leaves and logs. In cities, keep a special eye out for *Fuligo septica*, the "dog vomit slime mold," which does indeed look like bright yellow dog barf.

High Park Controlled Burns

A welcome fire in the middle of the city

LOCATION: High Park in Toronto
SPECIES: Black oak (*Quercus velutina*)

◆ In the heart of Canada's largest city sits one of the last surviving fragments of an ecosystem that once stretched across nearly 5 million acres (2,000,000 ha) of land: This rare ecosystem is called black oak savannah, and it is made up of prairie grasses, wildflowers, and towering black oak trees.

Toronto's High Park, a mere 400 acres (162 ha) of green space surrounded by a city of almost 3 million people, protects about 60 acres (24 ha) of black oak savannah. But for this ecosystem to survive, an event must take place that is at odds with city life: The black oak savannah in High Park must burn.

A prescribed burn in High Park in 2016

The black oak savannah ecosystem is rejuvenated through fire. Flames clear out invasive species, create space for germinating seeds, and release nutrients into the soil. Before the arrival of European settlers, fire regularly shaped the ecosystem. Indigenous people in the High Park area managed the land with controlled burns, and lightning strikes would naturally start fires.

But when High Park opened in 1876, the landscape drastically changed to meet a growing demand for recreational space. Sports fields, toboggan runs, and other facilities clashed with an environment that needed fire to thrive. "The biggest reason oaks weren't regenerating is that High Park was a typical urban park with trees and manicured lawns," says Jason Sickel, a prescribed burn specialist. "There was no ideal seed bed for acorns to set and germinate in. Any acorns that did fall, the squirrels were all over them."

Recognizing that a change was needed to save what remained of the black oak savannah, the City of Toronto reintroduced fire to High Park. Sickel has been the burn boss for High Park since 2010, and he leads a team that carefully and deliberately uses fire to regenerate the park's rare ecosystem.

With prescribed burns bringing the heat, oak trees are on the rebound. "We now see an abundance of germination of all oak species in High Park," Sickel says. That's good news for High Park's wildlife, and for city residents seeking a shady picnic spot.

> **How to see it:** The city of Toronto announces plans for prescribed burns on social media and on its website, but areas of the park near burn sites are closed to visitors.

THE WILD LIFE OF A City Park Burn Boss

■ Jason Sickel, a prescribed burn specialist, has been the burn boss for Toronto's High Park since 2010. He makes sure burns go safely and according to plan, from ignition to extinguishment.

• **What is your role as a burn boss?**
I plan and orchestrate prescribed burns. In a nutshell, our intent is to safely ignite and manipulate a fire that will self-extinguish once available fuel is consumed. I need to produce a fire that's hot enough to meet our objectives, but not so hot that it starts negatively impacting the site and becomes unsafe. All of that has to be calculated.

There are a million variables that go into it. I can burn a site every year for 10 years in a row and it will be different every time.

• **Can you describe one method for igniting a prescribed burn?**
Typically we start with a backburn ignition. All ignition is started off a fuel break, where there's no dried vegetation for the fire to consume. In High Park, that could be a walking path, a sidewalk, a roadway, or a break that staff have created with rakes and a leaf blower.

We start the ignition off this line, and we allow the fire to burn back into the wind. That extends and widens the fuel break and acts as a control. Fire can't burn stuff that's already been burned.

• **What are some ways to protect wild animals during a burn?**
We can time it so the burn is when insects are in a dormant state, or it's outside their migratory schedule. A slow-moving burn allows burrowing species to burrow down into cool, deep soil where the heat doesn't penetrate. We do wildlife flushes of our sites prior to ignition so we can push out larger animals.

In High Park, there are many old or dead trees with cavities that are used by animals. They're called wildlife trees. All the debris is raked and cleaned out from around those trees so there isn't any fire at the base of them.

• **How do you make sure the fire goes out?**
We conduct a mop-up after all the flame fronts have self-extinguished. Fine fuels like grasses, leaves, and twigs will readily ignite and burn down to ash. Coarse fuels like stumps, large branches, and hollow trees can smolder.

In a mop-up, you're doing a final extinguishment of all these hot spots. We do a patrol and put them out with water and hand tools.

• **What is it like being on-site during a burn?**
Because I'm orchestrating the whole burn, I take it very seriously. It has to be conducted safely. I feel 100 percent dialed in to the present moment. I'm one with the fire, and nothing else matters in the world other than what's in front of me. I really enjoy that feeling. ■

Axolotls

These beloved amphibians can be seen almost anywhere—except in the wild.

RANGE: Xochimilco, outside Mexico City
SPECIES: Axolotl (*Ambystoma mexicanum*)

◆ Long before the internet came to love their goofy faces and lacy gills, axolotls were more famous than your average amphibian. The Aztecs named the large salamanders living in the canals of their capital city after Xolotl, a deity associated with monsters and the underworld.

Some of their traits do seem supernatural. If they lose an arm, axolotls can sprout a new one. They can even grow new organ tissue. And while most salamanders are born in the water with gills and then later transition into air-breathing, land-crawling adults, adult axolotls dwell underwater their whole lives without transforming, like amphibian Peter Pans suspended in a never-ending childhood.

(top) Wild axolotls are brown, not white like their cousins in captivity.

(bottom) A group of axoltls being released into a preserve in Mexico.

Axolotls thrived in precolonial Mexico City, where an expanse of waterways and floating gardens called chinampas kept the waters clean. They were still paddling around in the mid-1800s, when France briefly invaded Mexico and its soldiers carted a few axolotls back to Paris. Wild traits were bred out of their descendants, who by this point are milky white instead of brown, and more like pets or lab animals than monstrous gods. "They'll just instantly make eye contact, come to the edge of the tank, and start begging for food," says Randall Voss, a biologist at the University of Kentucky who works with them.

These captive axolotls, now bred in tanks around the world, have led to a string of remarkable discoveries. In 2018, scientists sequenced the entire axolotl genome. Many medical researchers hope to somehow copy an axolotl's regenerative abilities in humans who have lost limbs.

Axolotls' undeniable cuteness and charisma have also gained them cultural fame: Argentinean author Julio Cortázar wrote a short story about transforming into one, Mexican sociologist Roger Bartra used them as a metaphor for his country's national identity, and Mexico City chose the axolotl as its official emoji. It's never been easier to buy one as a pet or stumble onto one in a university lab.

But so far, the popularity of their cousins in captivity hasn't done the wild axolotls much good. Recent surveys have struggled to find any at all in their last remaining habi-

tat, a tourist-filled neighborhood of canals and floating farms called Xochimilco. Although this area most closely resembles the Mexico City that existed in precolonial times, local researchers believe pollution, loss of wetlands, and invasive species are the culprits behind this decline.

Today, though, scientists and farmers are working together to eventually reintroduce captive-bred axolotls to Xochimilco and to bring back traditional agricultural traditions like the chinampas—the ones that helped axolotls thrive for millennia, and may well do so again. 〉 **How to see them:** Captive axolotls are both visible and charismatic. In the wild, try your luck in the waterways of Xochimilco, Mexico, but finding one will be tricky.

AFRICA

Nairobi National Park

The only national park within a capital city

◆ On the outskirts of Nairobi, in an area called Langata, an unassuming jungle-green gate marks the entrance to Nairobi National Park. The small portal opens into a unique treasure—a tranquil oasis within sight of Nairobi's bustling offices and business complexes. As you make your way inside, a sign cautions: "Warthogs and children have right of way." A few of those warthogs will likely welcome you in the parking lot.

Established in 1946, Nairobi National Park was Kenya's first national park. Sitting on just 45 square miles (116 sq km) of land—only about one-sixth the size of the city itself—the park still manages to support more than 100 different mammal species and more than 400 types of birds, more than in the whole of the UK. Visitors regularly encounter cheetahs, hyenas, and giraffes, as well as ostriches, cranes, martial eagles, and many more.

The park remains unfenced along its southern border, allowing zebras and antelopes to migrate in and out. Lions have occasionally been spotted outside the park, too, causing traffic snarl-ups when they make their way onto the city roads and highways.

The uniquely situated park must balance the needs of many. Visitors can embark on safari drives, take in city skylines and sweeping savanna views from one of the well-situated picnic sites, or visit the Nairobi Animal Orphanage, which houses abandoned and injured wildlife. Meanwhile, researchers study how the rapidly growing city affects the park's wild residents—human development is encroaching on buffer zones where grazers once ranged, and an access road that now slices through the park was built in 2020. And those interested in the fraught history of conservation in Kenya can find a microcosm of it here: The British colonial government originally took the park's land from Maasai pastoralists, who today continue to fight to have their perspectives included in management plans. ❯ **How to see it:** Go for a morning drive, before the sun gets too high for lions.

LOCATION: Nairobi, Kenya
SPECIES: Many of East Africa's iconic wildlife species live in the park, including four of the "Big Five"—African lions (*Panthera leo*), leopards (*Panthera pardus*), African buffalo (*Syncerus caffer*), and black rhinoceroses (*Diceros bicornis*).

Animals backed by the Nairobi skyline

HARARE, ZIMBABWE

- Nicknamed the Sunshine City, Harare averages eight hours of sunlight per day—six in the rainy season. Its location on a high plateau gives it a cool climate despite its tropical latitude.

- Many say that the name "Harare" comes from the area's first Shona residents and their chief Neharawe, who lived in the area before its invasion by the British South Africa Company. Others riff that "Harare" comes from the Shona word *haarari*, meaning "someone who doesn't sleep"—an appropriate moniker for this bustling city of more than 1.5 million people.

- Harare and its surrounds are scattered with many nature parks and sanctuaries, where visitors can see native wildlife including giraffes, elephants, and impala. One popular spot, the Mukuvisi Woodlands, is located in the heart of the city.

KEEP AN EYE OUT FOR The enormous, dome-shaped nests of hamerkop birds. These impressive constructions look like hay piles perched in trees and may be studded with bones and trash. They are so large that smaller birds, like weavers, sometimes build their own nests on top of them.

KEEP AN EAR OUT FOR The barks and cries of vervet monkeys. These curious primates can be seen on rooftops and in trees all around town.

KEEP A NOSE OUT FOR The subtle, sweet scent of blue jacaranda trees in flower. These trees, originally native to South America, have become iconic in Harare—even though they are classified as invasive and no new planting of them is permitted. Their bloom-laden branches form vibrant purple tunnels throughout the city in October and November.

Termite Mound Architecture

Learning from some of the world's best architects, again and again

RANGE: Termite mounds built by different species can be found throughout South America, Australia, and Africa.
SPECIES: Fungus-growing termites, including *Macrotermes natalensis* and *Macrotermes michaelseni*

◆ The Eastgate Centre in Harare, Zimbabwe, is one of the city's most recognizable structures. Aesthetically unique, with vine-hung outer ledges and a large inner atrium, it is also considered a feat of engineering. Its creators—architect Mick Pearce and firm Ove Arup & Partners—have earned awards and international recognition for their work on the building, which houses shops and offices.

But they can't claim all the credit. Commissioned to create a large space that could maintain a stable climate without pricey air-conditioning. Pearce drew inspiration from some other builders whose work he saw all over the city: termites.

From the outside, termite mounds, or termitaria, look a bit lumpy and haphazard. Inside, though, each mound has been carefully calibrated to support the termite colony's various projects, from fungus farming to reproduction. The edifice, made of sunbaked dirt, is riddled with tunnels that allow for worker transit as well as gas exchange, surrounding a hollow middle that serves as a vertical chimney. (The termites themselves live in an underground nest, beneath the base of the mound.) It takes workers an entire year to complete a mound, and the largest ones can reach nearly three stories tall.

When Pearce was designing the Eastgate Centre, it was thought that a termitarium's tunnels and chimney work together to stabilize the temperature inside the mound, and therefore in the nest. Pearce planned his building accordingly: Dozens of brick chimneys on the roof vent hot air out, while banks of ground-level fans draw in cooler

Baboons enjoy their own version of a termite mound office building.

CHIMNEYS VENT
HOT AIR OUT

PLANTS HELP ABSORB HEAT

FANS DRAW IN AND COOL AIR

The inner workings of the Eastgate building (left) and a termite mound (below). Red arrows show CO_2 and heat exiting, and blue arrows show cool, oxygenated air coming in.

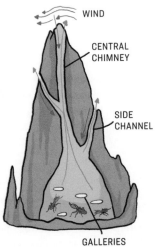

WIND

CENTRAL
CHIMNEY

SIDE
CHANNEL

GALLERIES

The Sincerest Form of Flattery

The tools and strategies different species use to survive have been honed over millennia by evolution. Human designers, who must work on much shorter timescales, often imitate or pay homage to them—a practice called biomimicry.

BURDOCK (*Arctium* spp.) • The seeds of burdock plants are covered in hook-tipped spines. In the 1940s, engineer George de Mestral came home from a hunting trip and found his pants—and his Irish pointer—covered in the burrs. De Mestral copied their sticking mechanism in inventing what would become Velcro fasteners. **❶**

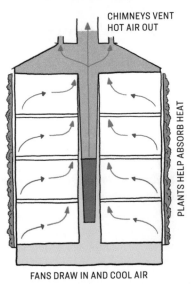

MAPLE (*Acer* spp.) • Maple seeds disperse with the help of samaras—aerodynamic wings that help the seeds spin themselves far from their parent tree. Researchers have developed artificial samaras that work in a similar way. They may someday help distribute tiny sensors over a broad area to gather information about decentralized events, like weather or wildfires. **❸**

KINGFISHER (family Alcedinidae) • Looking to make their bullet trains quieter, engineers at the West Japan Railway Company turned to kingfishers, who can dive beak-first into water with barely a splash. They redesigned the trains with noses that resemble the birds' bills, and today those trains achieve speeds of 170 miles per hour (274 kph) without excessive noise. **❷**

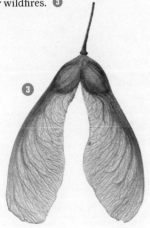

air to replace it. This has gone very well, and the temperature in the Eastgate building sits comfortably around 70°F (20°C), even when it is much cooler or hotter outside. Pearce has since implemented similar designs for buildings in Melbourne and Shenzhen.

In the meantime, our understanding of termite architecture has deepened. More involved studies of different mound designs suggest that the nest's placement beneath the soil is enough to keep the temperature fairly stable. Instead, it's now thought, the structure's main purpose is gas exchange: As the wind blows, fresh air percolates gently through the tunnels like water soaking into a sponge. To make things more or less airy, worker termites actively adjust the chimney's height.

J. Scott Turner and Rupert C. Soar, authors of a paper on these discoveries, predict they will be harnessed for "a veritable universe of new termite-inspired building designs." Look out for one coming to a city near you. **❭ How to see them: Eastgate Centre is located on Robert Mugabe Road in Harare. It is easy to find termite mounds in unpaved places nearby, including the city's gardens and golf courses.**

ORB WEAVER SPIDER (family Araneidae) • Orb weaver spiders decorate their webs with UV-reflective silk—potentially to deter birds that otherwise might collide with and destroy them. Inspired by this, German company Arnold Glas has designed glass panels coated with a UV-reflective design that resembles a web. It is hoped that the panels will prevent some of the millions of window-collision bird deaths that occur each year. **❹**

MORPHO BUTTERFLY (*Morpho* spp.) • Morpho butterflies display what is called structural color: special hues that come not from pigments but from physical structures that block and reflect different wavelengths of light. In the morphos' case, tiny scales on their wings create the impression that they are changing color, from dull brown to dizzying blue, as they flit about. Companies are working on applying similar light-diffracting techniques to everything from paint to anticounterfeit badges on currency. **❻**

LOTUS (*Nelumbo nucifera*) • Lotus leaves are riddled with microscopic crevices that trap air, leading raindrops to slip off them as easily as a puck slides across an air hockey table. Legend has it that this water-repellent quality originally inspired the invention of the umbrella in China thousands of years ago. Today, engineers are working on fabrics, glass, and paint that mimic this structure, hoping to design surfaces that can clean and dry themselves. **❺**

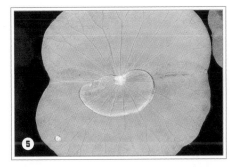

House Sparrows

The world's most widely distributed bird loves to hang out with people.

RANGE: House sparrows are found on every continent except Antarctica.
SPECIES: House sparrow (*Passer domesticus*)

◆ It's a story that has repeated all over the world: House sparrows arrive somewhere, adapt, and get comfortable. Soon after being introduced in South Africa around 1900, these hardy brown birds began expanding their range by 50 miles per year, often with the help of railway lines. By 1958, they were in Zimbabwe. Now firmly established in cities and towns there, "they are among the first birds to arrive in the morning and the last to leave," says frequent observer Walter Moyo of Chiredzi. They nest around people's houses on roofs and in tree crevices, which makes for a quick trip.

Native to Europe, the Mediterranean Basin, and some parts of Asia, house sparrows have become the world's most widespread wild birds, found on every continent but Antarctica. They have achieved an outsized presence in cities and towns, building enormous nests and often outcompeting shyer native species.

Across the world, local house sparrow populations have micro-evolved in response to their adopted environments. For instance, birds in northern cities tend to be larger and darker-colored than those in southern ones, which helps them handle cold temperatures. All urban populations share a special enzyme that allows them to digest starchy foods, a key adaptation for life near humans. Zimbabwe's house sparrows tend to enjoy sadza, a local staple made from ground and boiled corn, squabbling for crumbs outside homes or at restaurant dump sites. In some areas, they even enter houses through doors or windows to find food or sip water from a dripping tap.

House sparrows can make themselves at home just about anywhere.

In their small way, these social birds repay their human hosts for their hospitality. By munching bugs like flies, mosquitoes, and roaches, they provide a free and natural pest control service. The loud morning cheeps that signal their arrival at most homes double as a reliable wake-up alarm for those getting up for school or work. Large swarms of house sparrows also gang up on snakes, chirping aggressively to fend them off—a warning people find useful.

While other birds may be bigger and more colorful, house sparrows "deserve our respect," says Andrew Mathema, an avid birder. "House sparrows spend more time around us than any other wild animal—even more than our so-called loved ones in some cases." ❯ **How to see them:** House sparrows are easy to see (and hear) in most places humans are. Take a moment to give your local population a second look.

THE WILD LIFE OF A City Snake Catcher

■ When people in Harare come across snakes in places they don't want them, they call Chawatama Marimo. A snake catcher since he was 17, Marimo has dedicated himself to fostering harmony between people and reptiles in his home city.

● **How did you get started in this unusual job?**
Since I was a young boy, I was always fascinated with wildlife—especially those small creepy creatures like frogs, lizards, and snakes. When our family moved to Concession, a mining town, in the early 1990s, I used to encounter different types of snakes in the mine shafts. It is there where I began capturing snakes.

● **How common are snakes in cities?**
There are more snakes in the cities than most people think. As long as they can find something

to eat or somewhere to hide, snakes can show up anywhere, including inside our homes. Here in Zimbabwe, cobras are the most common snakes in most towns and cities. I have also captured two mambas in Harare—they can be found in cities and towns in trees, drainage pipes, or even your garden.

• **What attracts snakes to urban homes and yards?**

Food, of course. As long as there are rats, frogs, bird nestlings, or any other creature that snakes can feed on, do not rule out the possible presence of snakes.

The best way to keep snakes from your yard is to maintain it. Always cut the grass, lawn, or hedge. Always fill up the holes in walls and make sure there are no hollow objects in the yard that can provide refuge for them.

• **Have you had any unforgettable close encounters?**

Catching any dangerous snake is always a risky and unforgettable encounter. I can't forget an incident in Harare where a spitting cobra scratched me with its fangs just to scare me away. Considering the nature of my job and some of the snake species I handle, every time I go back home alive it's a lucky day for me. ■

African Penguins

These beach penguins have a taste for city life.

◆ On Boulders Beach in Simon's Town, South Africa, beautiful houses are up for grabs. Rangers have set dozens of ceramic and fiberglass boxes in the sand, framed by blue skies and glimmering seas. They are hoping to attract some special residents: African penguins.

This continent's only penguins have black belly speckles, pink eyebrow stripes, and distinctive donkey-like calls that have earned them the good-natured nickname "jackass penguins." For most of their history, they all lived on rocky islands off the southern coast of Africa, where they were safe from land carnivores like leopards.

As the growth of Cape Town and other coastal cities pushed those predators farther inland, ambitious penguin couples began moving to mainland beaches. At least three colonies now thrive on the south coasts of South Africa and Namibia. Mainlanders and tourists have fallen in love: Half a million people come to Boulders Beach every year to watch them sunbathe, frolic in the waves, and kick up sand with their little black feet.

But there is a small problem: The penguins have grown quite comfortable with city life. During breeding season, many wander into developed areas, looking for safe, cool places to lay their eggs. They toddle through gardens and houses and take shade breaks underneath cars. Some years, more than half of the Simon's Town colony's breeding birds end up trying to start families outside the bounds of the protected area on the beach.

From February through May, rangers sweep the city for misplaced penguins three times per week, relocating those who have chosen dangerous locations, like storm drains. In an attempt to keep the penguins safe, they also tempt them with the aforementioned nest boxes, well-ventilated shelters designed to mimic the conditions of the guano burrows the birds once dug on their island homes. (Unfortunately, harvesting for fertilizer has decimated that resource, so conservation groups are building similar boxes for island birds as well.)

Keeping the Boulders Beach population safe and healthy is vital for the overall survival of the species, which is severely endangered from overfishing and oil spills. It's also good for us humans, who love seeing penguins live that luxe beachfront life. ❯ **How to see them: Boulders Beach, in the Cape Town suburb of Simon's Town, is the best place to see these penguins. Take a tour or just hang out—they will show you how to make the most of this choice location.**

RANGE: The southern coast of Africa, encompassing Namibia and South Africa, as well as Namibia's offshore islands
SPECIES: African penguin (*Spheniscus demersus*)

This penguin couple has chosen a difficult place to live.

Small-Town Hippos

A South African suburb is the country's only remaining hippotopia.

RANGE: Scattered areas across Africa, south of the Sahara
SPECIES: Hippopotamus (*Hippopotamus amphibius*)

◆ In February 2020, cars at a gas station in St. Lucia, South Africa, were joined by another large commuter seeking to fuel up: a hippopotamus. Video on the local news showed onlookers tickled, but not necessarily surprised. Pretty much every night, these two-ton mammals emerge from the wetlands near the small town to graze on inhabitants' lawns and gardens.

St. Lucia is right next to the iSimangaliso Wetland Park. This large protected area contains the continent's largest estuarine lake, Lake St. Lucia, which funnels into a roughly 12-mile (19 km) channel to the ocean known as the Narrows. It's a perfect spot for hippos, who spend about 16 hours each day relaxing in the water. After centuries of hunting and poaching, these wetlands are the only place in South Africa that supports a sustainable hippo population, which currently numbers about 800.

The dynamics of St. Lucian ecology—in particular, the carefully maintained lawns of residential housing tracts—give the neighborhood a unique appeal. Around dusk, the hungry hippos take to their network of "hippo paths"—well-worn grass walkways that resemble monorail tracks, carved into the town's outskirts. (Locals avoid these seemingly ideal footpaths, as hippos who feel threatened use them to barrel toward the water at terrifying speeds.)

They then get to munching, keen to hit their quota of roughly 100 pounds (45 kg) of vegetable matter per day. Especially in times of drought, when more untamed foraging areas become limited, these man-made lawns can serve as a welcome smorgasbord. The hippos bring their bounty back to the estuary, where their poop provides an influx of nutrients and organic matter for the rest of the aquatic food web.

Hippos might not seem well tailored for suburbia. Generally considered one of the world's most dangerous mammals, they are thought to be responsible for hundreds of human deaths each year. In St. Lucia—where the hippos are a huge tourist draw—public signs and hotel proprietors educate guests on how to maintain a carefully calibrated atmosphere of mutual respect. ❯ **How to see them:** In St. Lucia, take one of the town's famed estuary boat tours, where guides will give you details about each hippo family. Then, at night, wait and see if any of your new friends come into town.

A hippo takes a stroll in St. Lucia.

ASIA

Sika Deer

Deer structure the year in Japan's Nara Park.

RANGE: Worldwide, including throughout Europe, South Asia, and China. Japan has the highest concentration.
SPECIES: Sika deer (*Cervus nippon*)

◆ In Japan, legend holds that during the eighth-century Nara period, thunder god Takemikazuchi rode to Mount Wakakusa on the back of a white deer in order to protect Heijō-kyō, then the capital. Ever since, Nara Prefecture's many sika deer have been considered national treasures. Until 1637, killing one of the sacred deer was punishable by death.

Today, about 1,200 deer live peacefully within Nara Park, in the center of Nara, Japan. Friendly, inquisitive, and extremely numerous, the park's deer have become a popular tourist attraction. While touching the animals is prohibited in the park, tourists often find themselves being nudged by curious deer eyeing a handful of deer biscuits (shika senbei), sold at local food stands.

Throughout the year, deer-centric events draw even more visitors. In July is the Presentation of the Fawns, during which people watch newborn deer following their mothers on unstable legs around the park. Each autumn breeding season, when bucks become most aggressive, there is an antler cutting ceremony in which deer herders (seko)

A Sika deer greets a photographer in Nara Park.

carefully saw off the deer's antlers—to protect tourists from being gored—and present them as an offering to the gods. And the start of winter is marked by the Deer Calling: A musician loudly blows a French horn, summoning hundreds of deer, who are then fed while they enjoy a program of classical music.

Although the deer are heavily protected, they face the dangers of living in a city, such as road accidents. However, the biggest threat to the population is lack of food, says Yoshiko Asahiro, president of the Sika Deer Supporters Club, an organization made up of concerned locals. The club works closely with the Nara Deer Preservation Foundation to protect the deer and facilitate their continued coexistence with humans.

The shika senbei are little more than nutritious snacks, and the deer's major food source comes from plants like Noshiba grass and acorns, which grow wild in the park. But with an increasing deer population, grass and acorns become scarcer by the year, despite generous donations from visitors, Asahiro says. As a result, the deer end up nibbling young shoots, preventing them from growing, and disrupting the park's ecosystem. Some experts worry that, unchecked by the natural predators that once balanced out their population, a growing herd of hungry deer could lead to biodiversity loss in Kasugayama Primeval Forest and other nearby protected areas.

Social media has had a huge impact on the deer's popularity, but erroneous information is widespread. The foundation continues to educate people from across the world about how to safely and respectfully visit these animals, especially during June and November, which have been designated official Nara Deer Protection months.

> **How to see them:** Visit the Nara Deer Park in Nara Prefecture, Japan, where the deer readily interact with people. You may also spot them crossing roads in the city.

White Clover

How a world traveler gets used to city life

RANGE: White clover is native to Europe and Asia but can be found today on every continent.
SPECIES: White clover (*Trifolium repens*)

◆ White clover looks about the same everywhere in the world: three oval-shaped leaflets and a long stem, topped by a firework of white petals. It looks like this in pastures, where it's a forage plant for livestock and wildlife; on farms, where it's a primo cover crop; and in suburban backyards, where it has become a trendy and bee-friendly replacement for Kentucky bluegrass. It even looks like this in cities, where it pokes up opportunistically in parks, along roadsides, and even through sidewalk cracks.

But a closer inspection reveals key differences. Like the city mouse and the country mouse, urban and rural white clovers are adapting different lifestyles to suit their differing environments. They're doing it quickly enough that in many ways, white clovers in Toronto and Tokyo are now more similar to each other than they are to their rural counterparts. "It's a small, unassuming plant that's helping us tackle large scientific questions," says James Santangelo, a postdoctoral fellow at the University of California, Berkeley, who studies white clover evolution.

White clover produces hydrogen cyanide, which protects it from hungry herbivores and increases its tolerance to drought. However, city life is changing that. In metropolises around the world, white clover is producing less of the toxin. Santangelo and colleagues analyzed more than 110,00 samples of white clover collected from 160 cities across 26 countries, ultimately finding an association between lower toxin levels and distances from city centers.

That white clover is so widespread is part of why scientists view it as an ideal specimen. "White clover has a really long history of being moved around by humans—wherever we have gone, it's come with," says Santangelo. "Our main interest was trying to understand how cities are influencing evolution, so it's really helpful to have this plant that you can find almost everywhere."

Researchers are still figuring out why this is happening, but it may have to do with city clovers' reduced risk of being eaten. In some cases, drier habitats outside of cities may also be driving hydrogen cyanide production. The study team claims this is, so far, the largest-scale study on parallel evolution and urban adaption. The findings suggest that "a suite of environmental changes do seem to be happening in the same way across different cities," says Santangelo.

With the number of people living in cities expected to double by 2050, white clover's biological split hints at the ways in which urbanization is already influencing the evolutionary direction of the natural world. If we're lucky—or would like to be—we can already rely on clover for a smaller-scale biological surprise: On rare occasions, it grows four leaflets instead of three. ❯ **How to see them:** You can find white clover in many biomes, from grassy fields to city sidewalks. All you have to do is look down.

Fishing Cats

Anglers with webbed paws slink through Colombo.

◆ In 2015, Eshan Witana set up security cameras outside his family's home in a residential neighborhood of Colombo, Sri Lanka's capital. He was keen to catch whoever kept scaling his backyard wall to pilfer his expensive butterfly koi. The culprit surprised everyone: Caught on video, paws in the pond, was one of the country's rarely seen wild fishing cats.

Researchers spurred to action by the thief were further startled to discover that a number of these nocturnal felines were hanging around Colombo, spending time in suburban gardens, sleeping in attics, and dashing across busy roads, well away from their presumed homes in the city's wetlands.

The fishing cats' closest relatives include the famously fluffy Pallas's cats and the tiny rusty-spotted cats of India and Sri Lanka. They have evolved to fit their realm, with a call reminiscent of a duck's quack and a full kit of fishing equipment. Drooping whiskers help them sense fish flitting below the surface during nighttime hunts, while partially webbed front paws and semi-retractable claws net the slippery meals. All the while, their dense, layered fur acts like a waterproof wetsuit, keeping their muscular bodies—about twice the size of a house cat's—warm and dry.

Some accounts describe fishing cats as adept swimmers. But often, they'll wait at the water's edge for passing prey before "cannonballing, headfirst, with their butts in the air," says Anya Ratnayaka, founder of the Urban Fishing Cat Conservation Project. It's goofy but effective: The pond-robbing cat gobbled down seven prized koi within 10 minutes. Fishing cats are also happy to devour small mammals, rodents, birds, snakes, and frogs.

RANGE: Fishing cats are found in South and Southeast Asia, usually in dense wetlands and mangroves. The only known urban population lives in Sri Lanka's capital city, Colombo.

SPECIES: Fishing cat (*Prionailurus viverrinus*)

Who said cats don't like water?

Despite their versatility and hunting skills, fishing cats are listed as vulnerable across their range, largely due to habitat destruction. In Sri Lanka, their situation is especially precarious: Colombo's fishing cats are considered endangered, and the city has lost an estimated 40 percent of its wetlands over the past 30 years. This rapid urbanization not only threatens the city's biodiversity but increases the risk of floods and soaring heat waves.

Ratnayaka hopes that these beguiling felines will now act as an ambassador species, galvanizing policymakers, politicians, and locals to work together to protect the city's vital wetlands network. After all, she says, "the wetlands and the fishing cats are interconnected. One is needed for the survival of the other." The koi will be thankful too. ❯ **How to see them:** Fishing cats are quite elusive, but visiting Thalangama Lake, Diyasaru Park, or Beddagana Wetland Park in Colombo may result in a chance encounter. During the dry season, keep your eyes peeled for striped blurs stealing in and out of the city's storm drains.

THE WILD LIFE OF A City Fishing Cat Researcher

■ As the founder of the Urban Fishing Cat Conservation Project, biologist Anya Ratnayaka has spent much of the past decade studying these stealthy felines in her home city of Colombo. In 2015, her research established their presence in high-density urban neighborhoods.

• **Why did you decide to work with fishing cats?**

I'd actually started writing a research proposal about leopards when a colleague asked if I wanted to see an orphaned fishing cat kitten who was being looked after by a local vet. I'd never heard of fishing cats, but as a procrastinator, I said, "Yeah—anything to put off writing this proposal."

It was such an incredible experience, and I wanted to

start working on these small guys because so little was known about them. When I started in 2013, fishing cat conservation was less than five years old, whereas research on tigers had been going on for around 100 years. When it comes to small cats, everything we learn about them is so important.

- **How did you begin collecting data on these mysterious cats?**
We use camera traps and GPS collars to find out what habitats they use, what affects their movements, and where they cross roads. We also study their diets by analyzing their scat. We just published a paper on fishing cats having plastic in their scat, which has transferred through their prey. So that's cause for concern for the food chain.

- **Why are fishing cats successfully living in Colombo when they can't be found in other cities?**
That's what we're trying to find out. What is it about Colombo that is allowing the fishing cats not just to live at the city borders, but to hang out here 24/7? Is it all the gardens? Is it the windowless attics? Is it that this used to be a wetland city, and these are the areas where the cats have been living for generations? That's what we're trying to understand.

- **In your experience, how do fishing cats react to people?**
Perhaps it's because these urban cats are more used to people, but they don't run off if they see you. They'll stop, watch, and gauge how close you're going to get. If you do start walking toward them, they'll look for an escape route.

We've spoken to people who say they've been sitting in their gardens when a fishing cat walked by a few feet away, grabbed one of their chickens, and hightailed it out of there. So they're risk-takers. But they wouldn't attack you—not unless you threaten them. Even then, they'd just want to stun you so they can escape.

- **How do people react to finding out they're living close to these predators?**
It's a mixed reaction. Some people freak out. Some people are very excited. I've learned that in low-income communities, when they've lost poultry or something of value to them due to a fishing cat, they just want somebody to empathize and ask, "How can we help?" Interacting with humans is a big part of this job.

- **Do you know how many fishing cats live in Colombo?**
We have absolutely no idea. They're so elusive. Also, between September and December, all our cats disappear from all our study sites. This happens every year, and we have no idea yet why this happens. We assume it's due to the breeding season. I have one collared male cat who has gone missing right now. I'm just waiting for him to come back so I can download his data and see where he went. ■

Greater Adjutants

One person's trash bird is another person's treasure.

RANGE: More than 80 percent of the world's greater adjutants live in Assam, India. The rest are found in Cambodia and Bihar, India.
SPECIES: Greater adjutant (*Leptoptilos dubius*), or hargila

◆ Like most dump sites, the Boragaon landfill in Guwahati, Assam, is an overwhelming place, made up of ever-shifting piles of colorful trash.

Unlike most dump sites, the Boragaon is overseen by a platoon of enormous, Muppet-like endangered storks known as greater adjutants.

Nearly 5 feet (1.5 m) tall, with striking ice-blue eyes and large wedge-like bills, any greater adjutant could easily star in a punk rock version of *Sesame Street*. The skin of their bare Technicolor necks ranges from yellow to red orange, depending on the individual and breeding season. Each has a crinkly, inflatable pouch hanging at the base of the neck, the purpose of which remains unknown.

In Assamese, greater adjutants are called hargilas, or "bone swallowers," after their greatest skill—horking down large chunks of food. Though they primarily scavenge

Adjutants survey their territory.

on carrion, they will gladly eat vertebrates such as fish and can even swallow ducks in one gulp. At the landfill, they strut around on top of the trash, plucking morsels from the piles and occasionally stretching out their 8-foot (2.4 m) wings to soar upward on thermals. If they get too hot, they defecate on their own legs, a strategy called urohidrosis.

Greater adjutants are some of the world's rarest storks—an estimated 800 to 1,200 individuals remain worldwide. For a long time, their habits and appearance gave the birds a reputation as "a bad omen and a carrier of diseases," says biologist

Purnima Devi Barman. Persecution and habitat destruction, including draining of wetlands and loss of nesting trees, brought down their numbers.

In 2007, Barman founded a grassroots greater adjutant conservation group, the Hargila Army, that operates in villages in Assam. Through community conservation efforts—from incorporating hargila motifs into traditional Assamese textiles to educating people about the storks' role as vital links in the ecosystem—the Hargila Army has managed to more than double the local population of greater adjutants. Barman even does impromptu educational events at the landfill, helping people better appreciate the power of the birds who spend their time there. ❭ **How to see them:** Look for greater adjutants scavenging at the Boragaon landfill in Guwahati. A short distance away, you can spot them high up in their nesting trees in the villages of Dadara, Pachiria, and Singimari, in the Kamrup District. The two sites have the highest concentrations of these storks in the world.

THE WILD LIFE OF A Hargila Baideo/Stork Sister

■ Purnima Devi Barman is a wildlife biologist and the founder of the Hargila Army, an all-female conservation team in Assam, India. Her innovative community-led approach has successfully involved rural homemakers in conservation and has vastly increased the number of local storks and stork nests.

• **What inspired you to help greater adjutants?**

My bond with nature was fostered early on by my grandmother, who always pointed out storks and vultures to me. One day, when my children were two and a half years old, I witnessed a man cutting down a nesting tree, causing baby greater adjutants to fall.

The sight of these helpless baby birds resonated, and I felt a deep connection, viewing them akin to my own children. Seeing them in distress and being referred to as bad omens was heart-wrenching. Holding my children that night, I realized my PhD wouldn't mean much if these birds continued to be mistreated.

• **How does the Hargila Army work?**
The Hargila Army is a rural, all-women grassroots movement. When I began, I didn't have a detailed plan. But once I befriended the local women and heard how the hargila is considered a bad omen, I felt it needed to be part of our tradition and culture.

When a woman pledges to be a part of the Hargila Army, her role extends to educating her husband

about it. So, while it's a women-led initiative, we work with everyone. Through the Hargila Army, rural women get a voice. They show the world and our society that a so-called "bad omen" can become a cultural symbol.

• **How does the community help to directly support greater adjutants?**
Greater adjutants are colonial nesting birds that prefer certain trees for breeding, often returning to the same ones year after year. Our motto is to protect the trees to save the birds—protect the backyard, protect the biodiversity. If you come, you'll see the coexistence: greater adjutants nesting in trees and people working and living nearby. We've put nets under nesting trees to catch greater adjutant fledglings that fall.

Our communities, especially our women, also throw baby showers for greater adjutants, similar to how we celebrate for expecting mothers. Once we initiated this, it became a massive movement. This and other events, like integrating the birds into our folk songs and traditions, show our connection and commitment.

• **How else have the greater adjutants been integrated into your culture?**
Women are vital carriers of our culture. While many viewed the hargila as a bad omen or even ugly, based on various perceptions, I always believed the opposite. I felt the hargila should be seen as beautiful and fashionable. To change these perceptions, we

thought of celebrating its beauty through our traditions—weaving the hargila into fabrics.

The turning point was when we incorporated the hargila into the gamosa, an integral part of our Assamese tradition. It's a cloth we hold in high regard, used in rituals, to welcome guests, and during prayers. Weaving the hargila into the gamosa made people appreciate the bird more.

Additionally, we began weaving hargila motifs into our traditional mekhela chadors. It became a fashion statement, merging our passion with fashion. Now, we even sell these weavings. People love creativity, and when they saw the hargila woven into our traditional attire, it resonated with many.

• **What do you wish the world knew about the hargila and other lesser-known species?**
These birds, often viewed as bad omens, play a vital role as cleaners. They scavenge, purifying our environment. They are working so much for us. What I've learned from hargila is they are swallowing all the pains and negativity, but they are ultimately spreading positivity.

Every species, big or small, deserves respect. Our perceptions of beauty and ugliness are just mental constructs. Coexistence is fundamental. We are all interconnected threads in the tapestry of life. ■

Split-Gill Fungi

These metropolitan mushrooms offer valuable lessons in resilience.

RANGE: Found on all continents except Antarctica
SPECIES: Split-gill fungus (*Schizophyllum commune*)

◆ In New Delhi, India, air quality monitors regularly read "999," meaning the air is too polluted to measure. Eucalyptus and mesquite trees struggle to breathe as dust and soot settle over the city, dulling even the brightest greens to a muddy gray.

But in shadowed crooks and hollows within tree trunks, a microclimate forms. The humidity is slightly higher, and the temperature slightly lower. Within this cloistered, miniature realm, small, fuzzy, pinkish-white mushrooms grow, spreading out over the bark. These are the fruiting bodies of *Schizophyllum commune*, the split-gill fungus.

Evoking shells or hand fans, the bracket-shaped mushrooms are slightly hairy, with scalloped edges and folded brown gills underneath. This fungus exhibits immense environmental defiance—it refuses to be restricted by lack of rainfall or limited to specific species of wood, thriving equally in dense, untouched forests and woody pockets of concrete-filled urban spaces. During dry spells, its mushrooms simply shrivel up and wait; when it finally rains again, they quench their thirst and revive themselves.

However, weather is not all the split-gill fungus defies. This species has tens of thousands of distinct "mating types," each with the ability to reproduce with almost all the others, rendering our binary understanding of sex redundant. The breadth of being encompassed in this single species of fungus serves as an educational model for the vastness of gender expression in the natural world—including humankind.

Known as kanglayen (to the Mizo people), pa si (to the Manipuri), and hubsi (to the Galo), the split-gill fungus is an essential foraged food for Indigenous Indian communities. Cooked into pancakes or stewed alongside meats, the fungus is a

useful source of protein in lean times. Not only is it found during the dry season, when edible mushrooms are scarce, but it can withstand the high humidity in which other fresh mushrooms quickly rot.

While many large animals have been driven out of cities by human settlement, and native plants replaced by introduced ones, small wild kingdoms continue to exist within our metropolises. Once our eyes attune to its existence, it's possible to see the split-gill fungus everywhere—from fallen trees to wooden beams, abandoned chairs left out in the garden, or even ornaments made of treated wood. In the grayest parts of our cities, this small, pale pink mushroom reminds us that we are a part of a greater ecology that sustains us, and keeps us living in color. ❯ **How to see them:** In urban green spaces, look for decomposing wood in patches of shade. Pay special attention to the nooks and crannies where sunlight doesn't reach.

THE WILD LIFE OF A Queer Mushroom Tour Guide

■ On M Bhatia's first mushroom foraging trip, they almost got poisoned by a chanterelle look-alike. They've learned a lot since then and now lead fungus-focused walking tours in their home city of Delhi.

• **How did you become interested in fungi in the first place?**
In college, someone that I had a crush on was very interested in mushrooms. And so—"Oh yes, so am I, for sure!" I bought a field guide.

I dropped out of college after a couple of years and moved back to India. Delhi is a really concrete city, very built up. Still, I started noticing mushrooms around more, even on the sidewalks outside my house or in a window-ledge herb garden. That's when I really started thinking about them from the perspective of an ecosystem. I started studying and learning and realizing—it's not an inhospitable environment at all, actually, for them.

• **How did you start doing mushroom tours?**
I was doing them with friends and acquaintances at first. In 2020, during the [COVID-19] lockdown and monsoon season, I started doing them every weekend, open to all. It was the

only thing I could do outside the house, and the only thing I wanted to do. That same kind of shock I had when I first realized that there are so many mushrooms in my own surroundings—seeing that shock on other people's faces was just magical.

• **What do you think people can learn from mushrooms?**
More recently, I've been doing queer mycology workshops. We use mushrooms as a lens into how we see the world in binaries. And mushrooms are kind of perfect for that—they're not just plants or just animals. They're not just in the wild, and they're not just cultivated. They're not just food, because they can be poisonous. They just play a lot of different roles in our world.

We also talk about mycophobia, that revulsion we can have around mushrooms, the fear of seeing something that you're not used to. It's felt very similar to me in my own life journey with understanding not just queerness, but specifically queer culture in India. It's been amazing to work through this stuff with other queer people and environmental enthusiasts here.

• **Can you describe one of your favorite recent mushroom-finding experiences?**

India is so diverse, and I love learning about the presence of mushrooms in our different cultures here. Up in the Himalayan foothills, there is a mushroom that grows near pine trees. A friend and I were out foraging—it was the wrong season, it was too dry, and we hadn't found anything, but we came upon it. It shouldn't have been there, but it was, and it should have been way more dried out, but it wasn't.

We took a piece of it. But then I was like, "What have I done?" We were staying in a hostel, we didn't have a kitchen—we had nothing we could do with it.

As we were walking, this lady stopped us. She was selling cherries with her husband by the side of the road. She asked us about the mushroom, where we found it, and she was telling us about how she cooks it. We asked her, "Why don't you take this?" She said, "Absolutely not. The mushroom chooses who it was found by. You can't give it to me."

We ended up finding another guy at the side of the road who was selling boiled eggs. He cooked it for us, and then she agreed we could all eat it together. That was a really beautiful encounter. ■

Singapore Street Trees

The city's real skyscrapers

RANGE: Lining roads across Singapore
SPECIES: Common street tree species include the rain tree (*Samanea saman*), tembusu (*Fagraea fragrans*), and angsana (*Pterocarpus indicus*).

◆ Over the past few decades, the people of Singapore have dedicated money, innovation, and legislative power to a specific goal: to become the world's greenest city. They have much to show for it, including affordable and environmentally friendly public housing, a network of linked parks, and a cluster of 15-story, solar-energy-collecting "Supertrees" festooned with vertical gardens.

But certain residents have been doing their quiet best at this for even longer. Singapore has about 3 million roadside trees—nearly 800 trees per street mile—planted over the years by the National Parks Board and local councils. In addition to supporting wildlife species in a dense urban area, these trees are valued community members, treasured for their beauty and the role they've played as witnesses to history.

Up until the late 1970s, street trees were chosen to maximize shade and maintained in a way that prioritized neatness. Now, though, a team of hundreds of arborists supports the trees' ecological potential, as well as their structural integrity. Singapore's street trees currently comprise at least 600 species, from bushy native sea gutta trees to imported rain trees, which have crowns that can spread as wide as three school buses put end to end. Biologists point out that this is only about 100 fewer species than are found in the area's dedicated rainforest nature reserves.

Their presence scaffolds life for thousands more: Thanks to street trees, you can find honey buzzards perching above lines for the post office, pied hornbills flapping over road junctions, and fruit bats occasionally entering apartments through windows. Epiphytic plants like bird's nest ferns and pigeon orchids piggyback on the trees, offering color, fruit, and nectar, as well as support for further species.

While trees work together to harbor this second metropolis, some individuals have earned a special status. In 2001, the city's National Parks Board announced a "Heritage Trees" program, dedicating protection and resources to select leafy denizens. Eligible trees have a circumference of more than 16.4 feet (5 m)—a sign of their long lives—along with special historical, botanical, or cultural importance.

So far, more than 250 trees have been recognized in this way. They include a set of 22 rain trees along Connaught Drive, each more than 150 years old—which, in the words of the Parks Board, "witnessed historic events in the Civic District including the declaration of independence for Singapore" in 1963. Those trees currently form a shady tunnel over the pedestrian-only street, doing their part to support all kinds of civic life. ❯ **How to see them: It's easy to find impressive street trees anywhere and everywhere in Singapore—pay special attention to the life within. Heritage Trees are found across the city and noted by small plaques.**

Street Tree Heroics

While they may not all be as impressive as Singapore's giants, street trees in general don't get enough credit. Over and over, studies show the benefits they bring to cities across the world. Here are just a few of the things they can do.

PROTECT STREETS: Trees can improve road safety by helping drivers calibrate and reduce their speed. Studies have shown that trees slow motorists down by up to 15 miles per hour (24 kph) and are as effective as speed cameras. They also appear to reduce incidents of road rage.

REDUCE FLOODING: Trees absorb water through their leaves and roots, greatly reducing the impact of storms and runoff.

CLEAN AIR: Trees take up harmful gases like carbon monoxide and ozone and release them as oxygen. They also buffer against traffic noise.

COOL TEMPERATURES: By providing shade and giving off water vapor, street trees can reduce the average felt temperature by up to 20 degrees. Some researchers have measured the cooling effect of one street tree as equivalent to that of 10 room-sized air conditioners. Shading also greatly increases the longevity of asphalt,

which is otherwise prone to cracking as it expands and contracts.

REDRESS WRONGS: In the United States, the legacy of segregationist housing policies affects street tree distribution to this day. According to one study, neighborhoods that were redlined in the 1930s have, on average, only half the trees of those that weren't. Tree-planting efforts across the country are currently attempting to close this gap.

Raccoon Dogs

We're all from the same hill now.

RANGE: Native to East Asia, and introduced in much of Europe
SPECIES: Common raccoon dog (*Nyctereutes procyonoides*)

◆ The Mandarin expression "raccoon dogs of the same hill" is similar to the English phrase "birds of a feather." Currently, it has something of a negative connotation, having been coined by an imperial courtier who used it to disparage his superiors during the Han Dynasty.

That may have to change. More and more raccoon dogs now hail from the same hill as many people: the suburbs of Shanghai, China's biggest city. In recent years, they've

been greatly expanding their numbers and territory—apparently attempting to establish themselves as the area's resident cute mammal, like foxes in London or wombats in Sydney.

Raccoon dogs also enjoy city life elsewhere—the above are in a culvert in Tokyo, Japan.

Stealthy and sharp-nosed, raccoon dogs are neither raccoon nor dog. (In fact, they are most closely related to foxes.) As with many urban wildlife situations, they got to Shanghai first. They once lived in fields on the banks of the Yangtze River, eating frogs, insects, and plants and sharing space with leopard cats, badgers, and river deer. As the city's suburbs sprang up and human homes started replacing the fields, other animals fled, but raccoon dogs adapted. They've since learned to make their homes in culverts and the bases of walls, to dumpster dive at night, and to steal kibble left out for stray cats.

In the past half decade, they have really gotten comfortable, and researchers are tracking their progress. A community science survey in Songjiang District found that raccoon dogs appeared in 22 of 50 residential areas—sometimes alone, sometimes with dozens of friends. They are now thought to be spotted more often than any other wild mammal in Shanghai.

They are not always welcome. Large groups of raccoon dogs can rove noisily at night, and reports of attacks on people and dogs, though largely unsubstantiated, have caused some controversy. Meanwhile, the raccoon dogs can get parasites from stray cats and dogs, be poisoned by pesticides, or be hit by cars, but the easy food and shelter they find here in the city seem to counterbalance these threats. One recent analysis of the Shanghai area calculated that raccoon dogs are currently inhabiting only 4 percent of their potential range there, suggesting that everyone had better learn to get along. ❯ **How to see them:** Watch for raccoon dogs at night, near dumpsters or bodies of water. If you see one (or more!), be sure to let them have their space.

OCEANIA

Peacock Spiders

What happens when you dance like no one is watching?

RANGE: All over Australia, especially the southern half
SPECIES: Peacock spider (*Maratus* spp.)

◆ Spring has come to Australia. Acacia trees explode with fluffy golden blossoms; kookaburra laughter greets the dawn. And across the continent, in almost every habitat you can imagine, male peacock spiders shake their groove things.

Peacock spiders are very tiny—even the largest species top out at the size of a grain of rice. For much of the year, males resemble gray or brown specks, preoccupied with catching insects and leaping out of danger. In spring, though, they molt into their breeding finery. Newly daubed in metallic colors, their bodies delicately plumed and fringed, they are ready to woo.

The females, dressed down in mottled browns, are not easy to impress. A bit of sparkle alone won't be enough to win one over.

And so the male spider performs an intricate courtship dance. Choreography varies by species: He may wave his elongated third legs to get the female's attention, or flip his abdomen upward to highlight its vibrant patterns. Individuals of many species

Male peacock spiders have incredible moves. Pictured here are Maratus pavonis *(left),* M. volans *(bottom), and* M. jactatus *(next page).*

unfurl posterior flaps usually hidden under the body, then perform shimmies worthy of a burlesque bar. The female waits and "listens" for the vibrations the arachnid artist makes with his body. This dance is not only meant to be seen—it's supposed to be felt.

M. jactatus

As with many of the world's tiny, multisensory spectacles, humans were not clued in to the extent and specifics of these spider discos until quite recently. While the first two peacock spiders were officially described back in 1874, the vast majority of species—which currently number more than 90—weren't known to science until the last decade.

Thanks to macrophotography (which enables close-up appreciation of the arachnids' moves and outfits) and social media (which always rewards good dancing), more people than ever are now paying attention. Recent discoveries include *Maratus nemo*, whose spring costume is striped orange and white like a clownfish; *Maratus felinus*, whose abdomen looks like that of a tabby cat; and *Maratus constellatus*, whose purple body, adorned with golden flecks, resembles the night sky. Spider scouts have found these new types everywhere from bush tracks to sand dunes to urban backyards—each one more than ready for his close-up. **>** **How to see them:** Cast your gaze downward, and keep your glasses on! These tiny spiders are generally found in the leaf litter or jumping along on small twigs and branches below waist height. Lane Cove National Park in downtown Sydney is known to be a good spot for finding peacock spiders.

Superb Fairywrens

Polyamorous songbirds keep it drama-free.

RANGE: Throughout eastern Australia
SPECIES: Superb fairywren (*Malurus cyaneus*)

◆ Peer into the dense shrubs of Melbourne's Royal Park, and a flash of turquoise feathers may catch your attention. You've spotted a superb fairywren in his resplendent breeding plumage. Drawn in by his glamour—he's so different from other city birds!—you might be tempted to follow him home.

You wouldn't be the only one. The amount of intrigue contained in the life of your average superb fairywren could fill a (human) celebrity memoir: hangers-on, sitcom-style intergenerational living, parallel affairs. For the birds, of course, it's just how things are done.

Male fairywrens are very handsome...

A male wren starts things off by displaying for a female, flaring his cheek feathers and executing an intricate airborne dance full of tilts and dips. Sometimes he even uses props, holding a yellow petal in his beak to highlight his contrasting colors. If the female is impressed, the two form a pair. They often bond for life, defending a territory, foraging for insects, and raising chicks together.

They're assisted by a group of subordinate wrens—mostly males waiting to climb the social ladder when the top male leaves or dies, or when a female becomes available in a nearby territory. Until that happens, they prefer to stay where they were born, which means wren groups can contain sons from the current and previous dominant female. Many beaks make light work: In a single breeding season, the group may raise three clutches.

Often, the chicks that the dominant male helps raise are not actually his own offspring. Sometimes the female mates with one

of the unrelated subordinate males—but more frequently, the chicks are the result of her predawn forays, during which she sneaks into other territories under cover of darkness to mate with neighboring males. And, of course, while this is happening, the dominant male meets with females sneaking in to mate with him.

This way of living suits the wrens just fine. For them, social monogamy provides a coordinated approach to group leadership, ensuring that multiple adults are focused on rearing chicks and defending a territory, while sleeping around increases the distribution and genetic diversity of their offspring. Even the female's predawn escapades are designed to reduce conflict—by sneaking into adjacent territories in the dark, they avoid being detected and confronted by other dominant females.

Unfortunately, even this depth of intimate collaboration can't safeguard the wrens from outside pressures. Sightings have declined in recent years, and the species' range in the city has become restricted to small patches of bush. The Superb City Wrens project, based in Melbourne, calls for members of the public to record wren sightings on the iNaturalist app to help scientists better understand the wrens' habitat preferences and guide restoration projects. With enough paparazzi, these wrens could once again take center stage as some of the city's most creative socialites. ❯ **How to see them:** While walking in the urban parks and gardens of eastern Australia, be sure to check dense shrubs. It's there you'll most likely see the wrens flitting about.

… and so are females, in their own way.

THE WILD LIFE OF A Bird-Loving Community Scientist

■ Peter Petinatos rediscovered his love for wildlife photography after retiring from his career in product development. Now, he uses his photography to help conserve the superb fairywren and other wildlife in Melbourne, Australia.

• **What is the process for a community science survey?**
There's my normal process, where once a week I do a walk through the park and I take photos [of plants and animals]. My camera captures the coordinates as well. Then I upload them into iNaturalist when I get home, and we identify them, and they get tagged automatically to the project.

And there's another process with Friends of Royal Park. There's normally a group of people and we all walk into four designated areas together. We've got 20 minutes in each area, and we record the species we see and I'll try to take a photo. That information ends up in

iNaturalist and gets uploaded into another database, the Atlas of Living Australia, after a few months.

• **Are you more familiar with the superb fairywrens now than you were when you began?**
I know them much better, and I know where to go to find them. Being able to predict that is a highlight. Especially one female—she's famous because she's so old that her testosterone levels are higher than those of a normal female, and that has caused her to have male coloring.

I had a lot of trouble finding her to start with. It was actually on my birthday, just as I was leaving the park, that this wren popped up on a branch and a bit of light came in and she shined up beautifully. She was there for a split second and I just took a photo. I didn't realize it was her until I came home.

Every time I go there I can tell who it is now—I know the area

she lives in. So I stay there for about five minutes and she'll just show up. She changes through the seasons, so in the winter, she looks like a normal female, and in summer she's got blue coloring.

• **What are your hopes for the future of community science in the city?**
I'm hoping more and more people start doing it. You don't notice things unless you really look. I'm hoping that, by looking, people will start caring a lot more about the environment and then take some action somehow, even just when they vote.

One of the goals for me is not just to capture information on the wrens, but to capture information on all the wildlife and insects. You never know what you're going to see and how it might help someone do the work that they're doing to protect a species. ■

Useful Poop

There are many creative uses for poop. Here are some other animals who refuse to waste waste—their own and others'.

GREEN LACEWING LARVAE (family Chrysopidae) • Lacewings are voracious predators even in youth. To mingle freely among aphids—their favorite food—the larvae of some species cloak themselves in camouflaging debris, including fragments of leaves and the husks of past meals. Their frass (insect poop) provides the perfect glue to secure these trash backpacks, which conceal an unforgiving set of jaws. The disguise ensures that the larvae look and even smell like their prey, allowing them to mingle freely among aphids even as they devour them, and reducing the risk of attacks from ants guarding their aphid livestock. ❶

ELEPHANTS (family Elephantidae) • Dung is a nutrient-rich resource, and coprophagy—a fancy word for poop eating—is practiced by many species. Elephant calves seed their digestive tract with a diverse microbial community by eating the dung of family members, a choice which helps them tackle a long future of fibrous meals. This behavior may have been in use for hundreds of thousands of years: Fossilized evidence from Siberia suggests woolly mammoth calves did the same. ❷

BUTTERFLIES (order Lepidoptera) • During courtship, many male butterflies demonstrate their resourcefulness through the provision of an ejaculated "nuptial gift." This package, crammed full of sodium, amino acids, and other nutrients, is passed to the female during mating and is believed to increase longevity and boost fertility. Males source this tempting cocktail by "puddling"—congregating, often in large numbers, to probe mud, carrion, and dung with their long proboscises. ❸

PIKA (*Ochotona* spp.) • Pika, too, are coprophagous—but when not ingesting their own poop, they put it to an equally important use. A day in the life of a pika involves amassing hay piles to see them through the winter months. To defend these hard-won resources against raiding neighbors, pika delineate their territories with latrines, attaching their round scat to rocks with urine. Well-built poop piles look like fortress walls. ❹

HIPPOPOTAMUSES (*Hippopotamus amphibius*) •
Hippopotamuses also use dung to mark their territory, as well as to entice nearby females. Males broadcast their message far and wide, wagging their tails as they defecate to increase its range. The sight, sound, or whiff of an unfamiliar hippo can provoke a frenzied spraying episode, covering a considerable area. One unexpected side effect of these excretory battles is the overloading of watercourses with nutrients—although hippo poop is an important resource for the environment, fish caught in the crossfire can suffocate to death. **5**

MARABOU STORKS
(*Leptoptilos crumenifer*) •
A number of long-legged bird species have found an easy way to stay cool: They poop on their own legs. This process, referred to as urohidrosis, has been observed in vultures, condors, and storks. For birds living in especially hot climates, like the sub-Saharan marabou stork, the droppings often evaporate before they even reach the ground, leaving behind a fashionable white residue. **6**

BLACK LARKS (*Melanocorypha yeltoniensis*) • On the steppe grasslands of Kazakhstan, black larks give dung an architectural flair. The ground-nesting females use the droppings of local grazers to build patios around their nests.

By constructing these fecal fortifications, the shrewd birds take advantage of the unwillingness of animals to graze near their own dung piles, thus protecting their nests from clumsy hooves. The dung may also provide a heat source for the growing chicks. **7**

HYMENOPTERA LARVAE (order Hymenoptera) •
The larvae of many social insects, including bees, ants, and wasps, don't poop at all—they have a "blind gut" with no anus, an adaptation that keeps the hive or nest from filling up with excrement. The larvae finally get some relief when they pupate, at which point they expel a whole childhood's worth of waste as one big pellet. **8**

SOUTH AMERICA

Red-Rumped Agoutis

These rodents are helping bring the world's largest urban forest back to life.

LOCATION: Rainforests in northern South America
SPECIES: Red-rumped agouti (*Dasyprocta leporina*)

◆ Tijuca National Park in Rio de Janeiro is most famous for housing *Christ the Redeemer*, a 98-foot (30 m) statue of Jesus with his arms spread wide. But if they're lucky, some of the park's millions of annual visitors might also come across a more recently resurrected inhabitant—a sleek, long-legged rodent called the red-rumped agouti.

In 2010, after decades of absence, agoutis were brought back to Tijuca National Park to rejuvenate what is by some measures the world's largest urban forest. Cat-sized and with singular habits—males court by spraying potential mates with urine, and all communicate through screams—these industrious rodents plant trees like squirrels do: by burying seeds to eat later, and then forgetting to dig them back up. Without them, the fruits of native trees like the agouti palm simply rot on the ground.

Tijuca National Park is part of Tijuca Forest, which was established in the nineteenth century to safeguard the rivers that provide Rio's water supply. Unlike most other protected areas, this forest was primarily planted by hand, rather than preserved from existing stock, because the land here had been clear-cut for coffee plantations. A mix of native and introduced trees were painstakingly rooted, one by one, and as the forest grew, the city grew around it. Meanwhile, habitat fragmentation, vehicle collisions, and hunting eliminated two-thirds of the large vertebrates who were once found here.

Red-rumped agoutis help trees spread.

The forest became "a Frankenstein ecosystem . . . a puzzle where several pieces are missing," says Marcelo Rheingantz, a biologist with Project Refauna, a group working to replace those pieces. The agoutis came first, taken from a nearby plaza—where they're so abundant that they're considered pests—and brought into the national park in pairs.

After a careful reintroduction process, the rodent gardeners have successfully folded themselves back into the park's ecosystem—with benefits for all. "In areas where there are agoutis, two species of native plants have returned," Rheingantz says.

Project Refauna is following up on this successful agoutization by slowly introducing more species—recently yellow-footed tortoises and howler monkeys. (Both of these species are also excellent at dispersing seeds, an act they generally perform by pooping.) Future candidates include blue-and-yellow macaws, green iguanas, and ocelots. "A forest without animals is similar to a stage without actors," says Rheingantz. "We need to put them back." ❯ **How to see them:** Red-rumped agoutis can be found across Tijuca National Park. Look for a scampering, glossy-furred critter, potentially carrying a nut.

Blue-and-Yellow Macaws

Bright and beloved birds in Campo Grande

RANGE: Northern South America through central Brazil, as well as parts of Panama
SPECIES: Blue-and-yellow macaw (*Ara ararauna*)

◆ Located in the bull's-eye middle of the South American continent, Campo Grande, Brazil, is a diverse and growing city, home to thriving communities of immigrants from as far away as Japan and the Middle East. But some of the most recent arrivals are from right next door: blue-and-yellow macaws.

A few dozen of these jewel-bright parrots first arrived in Campo Grande in the late 1990s, driven out of the nearby Cerrado by fire and deforestation, says avian biologist Neiva Guedes, who heads up a local research initiative called the Urban Birds Project. The newcomers quickly adapted to city life. They shop around in the city's many trees, eating dozens of different kinds of fruits and nuts. They've learned to nest in cavities in imperial palms—imported ornamentals that are taller and larger than the native palms the birds would otherwise inhabit, providing them with spacious apartments and great views.

Their new home has welcomed them too. According to surveys by the Urban Birds Project, more than 90 percent of Campo Grandeans say they are proud the birds chose their city. Blue-and-yellow macaw pairs mate for life and raise chicks in backyards,

gardens, and parks, bringing them into close contact with people. Scientists like Guedes get a lot of help from residents, who monitor nests and report injured birds or new behaviors.

Of course, it's not all easy fruit, big houses, and good neighbors. Macaws get electrocuted and hit by cars, and choice penthouse palms are chopped down for development. Even so, it seems to be a better bet than living elsewhere—about 80 percent of chicks in Campo Grande survive their youth, a much higher rate than they'd experience outside the city. "They do very well here," says Guedes. There are now around 700 blue-and-yellow macaws in residence, brightening commutes and treetops from east to west.

❯ **How to see them:** In Campo Grande, take a tour with Urban Birds Project (Projeto Aves Urbanas), or look for the unmistakably hued parrots peeking out of cavities or flying overhead. They can also be spotted in nearby cities, including Sinop and Rondonópolis.

City Parrots

Parrots, like people, are adaptive and social—traits that allow them to thrive in cities, even when they're very far from home. Here are some to watch out for.

Although they come from Indonesia and Timor-Leste, about 10 percent of the world's **yellow-crested cockatoos** (*Cacatua sulphurea*) now live in Hong Kong. Like many out-of-place parrots, they're thought to be the descendants of released or escaped pets. They can be seen showing off their flowery headgear near Hong Kong University and in Hong Kong Park.

Bright green **monk parakeets** (*Myiopsitta monachus*), native to South America, live in groups in big, shaggy stick nests. Listen for their screeches across the United States, including at the entrance to New York's Green-Wood Cemetery and in Chicago's Hyde Park neighborhood.

Rose-ringed parakeets (*Psittacula krameri*), kept as exotic pets since ancient times, have spread across the world from their native ranges in Africa and India. Imperious green birds with bright red beaks, they can be found from Istanbul to Kauai, and they tend to cause trouble by killing or displacing local birds.

A small population of **rosy-faced lovebirds** (*Agapornis roseicollis*), a species from southwestern Africa, has made a home in Phoenix, Arizona, where they have learned to nest in cacti and to perch on air-conditioning units when it gets too warm.

CHAPTER 7

Islands

slands are up to something. That shimmering blob across the sunlit water, that dot on the map engulfed by blue—they have been left to their own devices. Far from the mainland's prying eyes and normalizing influences, ordinary processes are accelerated, with wonderful results.

Living things that arrive on islands often do so by accident: pushed by wind, yanked by tides, or downed by storms. Some of these species shapeshift. In Hawai'i and the Galápagos (among other places), a few wayward birds have radiated into a set of unique descendant species, each with a different, finely honed beak.

Others grow or shrink: Fossils reveal that dog-sized rabbits once hopped around islands in the Mediterranean, while Madagascar features a chameleon that could perch on your finger. And some adapt their behavior. Off the coast of Brazil, former ground vipers have begun to climb; in the Pacific Northwest, a special set of island-hopping gray wolves has learned to swim; and off the coast of Australia, ferns are forging new methods of plant collaboration.

Like all evolution, this change happens slowly, over generations—but it's speedier on islands than anywhere else. Because a relatively small number of species end up finding their way to any given island, those that do are able to change and diversify more quickly, filling empty roles rather than fighting for resources.

The topsy-turvy assemblages that result have inspired generations of people: researchers tracking the ins and outs of evolution, extreme birdwatchers seeking new finds, and islanders working to protect the creatures they share their homes with—creatures who are not anomalies, but perfect examples.

Contributors: J. Besl, Ashlen Campbell, Katie Dancey-Downs, Christina Ayele Djossa, Maggie Downs, Claire Eamer, Kelly Eden, Leah Fabel, Jonathan Feakins, Lobato Felizola, Rachel Fritts, Lindsey Galloway, Alice Harman, Michael Haslam, Annika Hipple, Mara Johnson-Groh, Johanna Juntunen, Kestrel Keller, Lilia Kilburn, Mari Kramer, Krista Langlois, Jimena Ledgard, Julian Nowogrodzki, Oriana Pauli, Becki Robins, Amir Sadiq, Isaac Schultz, Joshua Sokol, Jack Tamisiea, Kamala Thiagarajan, Joanna Thompson, Christian Thorsberg, Tiare Tuuhia, Mary Vorsino, Fehmida Zakeer

MADAGASCAR

- Madagascar is the world's second-largest island country, behind Indonesia. And although the two countries are 3,500 miles (5,633 km) apart, Madagascar's population and its Malagasy language are most closely related to Indonesia's. Recent genetic research suggests that Madagascar's earliest settlers included a group of 28 women from Indonesia, who may have landed there after a shipwreck or navigational accident.

- A law passed in the mid-1990s encourages community conservation in Madagascar, providing a framework for the government to transfer control of forests, lakes, and other natural resources to local people.

- The name "Madagascar" is said to have come from thirteenth-century Venetian explorer Marco Polo, who called the island "Madageiscar"—his version of the name of the Somali city Mogadishu, which is where he thought he was. Today, Madagascar's residents often call their country simply "Mada."

KEEP AN EYE OUT FOR Madagascar's leaf-tailed geckos. If you manage to spot one of these mottled masters of disguise, give yourself a pat on the back— their bodies are patterned to look like tree bark or leaf litter, while their tails mimic dried-up leaves.

KEEP AN EAR OUT FOR The shrieks, grunts, and rumbles of Madagascar's social lemurs—noises with surprisingly complex meanings that researchers are beginning to decode.

KEEP A NOSE OUT FOR The rich bouquet of scents on offer on Nosy Be, a volcanic island off the northwest coast of Madagascar that is often referred to as the "perfume island" or "scented island" due to crops like vanilla, cinnamon, and the bright yellow ylang-ylang flower.

Treetop Lemur Gardens

Through strategic pooping, mouse lemurs keep their favorite plants close to home.

RANGE: Western Madagascar
SPECIES: Reddish-gray mouse lemur
(*Microcebus griseorufus*)

◆ Reddish-gray mouse lemurs are fist-sized primates with long, limber tails and eyes like cartoon space aliens. They like to hunt insects and lap up tree gum, but their absolute favorite food is fruit. On their nightly foraging trips around the dry forests of Berenty, Madagascar, they frequent fruit-bearing plants, gobbling whatever they can find: the red drupes of the elephant tree, the bumpy green fruits of the solety bush, or waxy berries from a mistletoe known as hovala.

A mouse lemur in her garden

When morning comes, they retreat to family nests in the branches or trunks of trees. They settle down to sleep. Eventually, like many of us, they wake up and poop. And this is when the magic begins.

By relieving themselves near their nest, the mouse lemurs are essentially seeding their backyard with their favorite plants—creating "inadvertent gardens," says biologist Fabien Génin. The more fruit they eat, the more fruit-producing trees and shrubs they happen to cultivate, turning their immediate surroundings into little lemur Edens.

The matriarchs of lemur families share the fruits growing around their nests with relatives and protect them from would-be plunderers like roving males and members of rival clans. They also mark the gardens with urine, creating playpens for their babies, who stay home when the adults go out foraging and know not to venture beyond the familiar scent. When they grow up, these young lemurs will inherit the whole estate and add to it just as their forebears did. "They will continue to construct this garden for generations and generations," says Génin.

Génin and his colleague Hajarimanitra Rambeloarivony discovered this correlation between fruit plants and lemur nests by following foraging mouse lemurs for hundreds of nights and carefully surveying the plants near their homes. They also showed that the seeds of some fruits, including those of the solety bush and hovala, germinate better after taking a trip through a lemur gut, suggesting that both primate and plant benefit from this relationship.

Different species of mouse lemurs living in other parts of Madagascar also create gastrically mediated gardens, with whatever plants happen to be on hand. Over time, their strategic defecations reorganize the forest. Génin and Rambeloarivony can now recognize a mouse lemur homestead even when its occupants are out "because they have lots of typical mouse lemur plants," Génin says. If only gardening were so easy for the rest of us. ❯ **How to see them:** Take a night hike in the Berenty Reserve, a private reserve on the south end of Madagascar. The lemurs' large eyes will catch the light of your headlamp like bicycle reflectors.

How Did Lemurs Get to Madagascar?

The question of how animals originally arrived on islands is sometimes easy to answer: Birds fly, insects ride the wind, marine mammals swim.

Other times it's more difficult. Researchers frequently argue over how lemurs—Madagascar's most iconic residents—ended up there in the first place.

Madagascar has been more than 250 miles (400 km) away from the rest of Africa for at least 120 million years. Meanwhile, mammals have been around for only about 90 million years. All of Madagascar's land mammals, including lemur ancestors, must have gotten to the island after it split off from the mainland. But how?

Some scientists argue that the primates forged across the Mozambique Channel on a huge plant raft. According to this theory, a group of accidentally adventurous lemurs were hanging out in trees when a storm came up and broke off a large, buoyant mat of vegetation, sending it down a river and into the sea. Trapped on this floating chunk, the lemurs voyaged for about eight weeks, sustained by food plants within the raft. They may have even hibernated, saving energy.

Others contend that ocean currents and lemur physiology make this scenario impossible. Instead, they assert, prehistoric seismic activity pushed a land bridge up and out of the water tens of millions of years ago, connecting Madagascar to the mainland for several million years before retreating again. Models suggest such land bridges may have arisen three different times, allowing many animals, including lemurs, to mosey across.

Nanochameleons

Small almost everywhere

RANGE: **Northern Madagascar**
SPECIES: **Nanochameleon**
(***Brookesia nana***)

◆ There are many means by which a species might elude human discovery. Maybe it's well camouflaged, or rare, or shy. Maybe it lives in a difficult-to-access place. Or maybe it's just really, really, *really* tiny.

The nanochameleon is the smallest reptile on the planet. Called *Brookesia nana*—or *B. nana* for short—this taupe-colored chameleon mottled with brown splotches does look a bit like a rotten banana, though it would take eight nanochams lined up nose to tail to equal a banana's length. The males, which span less than 22 millimeters, can stand comfortably on a thumb tip. The slightly larger females are the size of mini Tootsie Rolls. The species was first found just a few years ago, for reasons that are hopefully now clear.

Nanochameleons make their home in the cloud forests of northern Madagascar, as do a number of other types of miniature chameleons, which range in size from "petite" to "where are my glasses?" All have opposable thumbs on their hands and feet—good for gripping twigs—and the wizened gaze of an animal that has been around since the time of the dinosaurs.

While color change is often considered a classic trait of chameleons, most of the smaller lizards in the family have no need for it; like *B. nana*, they are easily enough concealed in the leafy underbrush of the jungle. Only a few local guides have the expertise to spot the animals, which have a very limited range and can easily be overlooked in a place full of lemurs and fossas.

So far, little else is known about *B. nana* specifically—their role in the environment, what they like to eat, or what likes to eat them. Fortunately, we may yet find out: Their region of origin was recently given legal protection, sparing it from the deforestation that threatens many wooded parts of Madagascar.

Male nanochameleons are less than 22 millimeters long.

B. nana does have one other notable trait: The genitals—called hemipenes—of a male nanochameleon are quite outsized, stretching nearly 19 percent of his body's total length. For scientists, the shape and relative size of this chameleon's hemipenes have been crucial in distinguishing it from its minuscule neighbors. But they are also likely crucial for the species' continued existence, due to the size difference between sexes. To properly match with the larger females, the males need to be big in this one particular way.

❯ **How to see them:** Careful examination of plants at night may reveal a roosting nanochameleon or two, but your best bet is to ask a guide for help.

Common Russet Grass

Not as cuddly as a lemur, but every bit as fundamental to Madagascar

◆ There's a story about Madagascar that goes like this: For millions of years, the giant island existed as a tropical forest wonderland where lemurs trapezed from tree to tree.

Then, sometime between 2,000 and 10,000 years ago, humans arrived and torched the place, gradually turning much of the forest to grassland in order to feed their cattle.

RANGE: Madagascar's Central Highlands, including Isalo National Park

SPECIES: Common russet grass (*Loudetia simplex*)

Within this framing—which first took root in the colonial era, perpetuated by scientists and their lumber-hungry benefactors—Madagascar's modern-day grasslands are little more than ecological catastrophes in need of reforestation, stat. This is the take taught in many Malagasy schools, and it serves ambitious contemporary tree-planting efforts for uses ranging from local fuel to international carbon offsets.

But it's only partially true. In fact, recent research suggests grasslands covered wide swaths of the island well before humans arrived, playing host to magnificent, now-extinct wildlife. Giant tortoises trudged across them; when they stretched their leathery necks, they spotted pygmy hippopotamuses grazing and soaking up the sunshine.

A number of Madagascar's grass species have outlasted these huge herbivores. Most visible among them is the steadfast common russet grass, which has thrived here for a million years. Tall, dry, and tufted at the tips, the grass "plays a clever game with fire"—its brushy ends burn quickly, while its shallow roots store enough nutrients to resprout as soon as a blaze subsides, says Maria Vorontsova, a botanist with Britain's Royal Botanic Gardens at Kew.

As the new grasses grow, the charred remains of the grass decompose—forming "the biotic infrastructure" of the central island surface, Vorontsova says, and nourishing termites, other insects, fungi, and microorganisms essential to the health of Malagasy soil.

For years, European botanists derided *Loudetia simplex* as a weedy import that arrived in Madagascar with the same humans who allegedly sabotaged the forests. But genetic testing has revealed it to be a completely unique grass compared with the species of the same name found in southern Africa. (Current research into its genetic history and diversity may result in a new classification in the future.) "The differences are so big, they could not have happened in the last 10,000 years," Vorontsova says.

More likely, a million years ago, a bird carried a seed from mainland Africa across the ocean to Madagascar. There, it sprouted and spread and evolved and burned and grew again and again. Its challenge today is to hold its ground, along-side dozens of its native grassy neighbors, against the unchecked advance of trees.

❭ **How to see it:** Between January and April, drive south from Madagascar's capital, Antananarivo, along the country's main thoroughfare, Route Nationale 1. Look for humble clumps of grasses, wispy and brownish at the tips, along the road on either side.

THE WILD LIFE OF **A Botanical Illustrator**

◼ Nantenaina Herizo Rakotomalala is a Malagasy botanist specializing in grasslands. An accomplished artist, she illustrates Madagascar's long-misunderstood native grass species, capturing their diversity so that future generations can protect them.

• **What inspired your interest in grasses?**

Early in my studies, I was like everybody else—not paying attention to grasses because they're not attractive like orchids

or other flowering plants. They're seen as weeds in Madagascar. But the more I studied them, the more I appreciated their diversity and the beautiful shapes and particularities that make them different from flowering plants. I grew to love them.

• **Do botanical illustrations require special equipment?**

At the sketching stage, we need only drawing materials and a good understanding of the structure of the plant. Because grasses have

very small details, we also use microscopes and hand lenses. At Kew (in London), there are microscopes that can project onto a screen for the drawing, and a special tool that can reflect the shading of the plant. We don't have such equipment yet at the Madagascar office, so I typically look at the specimen under the microscope and draw at the same time.

• **How does drawing the grasses enhance your understanding of them as a scientist?**

386 | AFRICA

As I look at the collected grasses through the microscope, I'll sketch them to show off the details and the very small differences between species of the same genus. The memories of what I observed through the microscope come back quickly when I look at the drawings. It's like taking notes, but instead of words, I draw.

• **What do you hope your research and illustrations are able to do for future generations?**

I hope my work can inspire more Malagasy students and scientists who will defend grasses. Right now, people privilege the lemurs, amphibians, reptiles, and orchids. But I want Malagasy scientists to highlight our grass species, too, so that people know they are natural in Madagascar and play an amazing role in our history and ecosystem.

When I talk to children and they ask why we're interested in such nonsense as grasses, I give them my hand lens. And they're amazed! It's very interesting to me—relaxing in a way—when children are amazed by what they see. ■

World's Ugliest Orchids

Then again, they don't care what we think.

◆ Orchids are prized around the world for their elegant beauty, glorious colors, and delicately patterned petals.

Well, most orchids are. The charms of *Gastrodia agnicellus* are less immediately obvious. While other orchids mimic beautiful butterflies and bees, this one's flower looks disconcertingly like the inside of a human mouth. Add pimply petals and a knobbed stem into the mix, and it's not difficult to see why this species is widely known, even to botanists, as "the ugliest orchid in the world."

Those who manage to clap their eyes on one, though, should consider themselves lucky. *G. agnicellus* spends most of its life underground, unfurling its fleshy-looking flower for only a month or so per year, in August and September. While the vast majority of plants get their energy from the sun, this orchid lacks chlorophyll and can't process sunlight. It lives instead by nicking nutrients from fungi, which in turn get them from green plants. This strategy, called mycotrophy, is shared by most orchids and some other wildflowers, including North America's bloodless-looking ghost plants.

RANGE: **A few hectares of humid evergreen forest in southeast Madagascar**
SPECIES: *Gastrodia agnicellus*

When it does push above ground level, *G. agnicellus* smells a lot better than it looks. Plants with a similar "decayed" aesthetic often stink like rotting flesh, to attract the carrion-loving insects that pollinate them. But this one gives off a roselike fragrance, which intensifies as the temperature rises.

It's unclear who, if anyone, responds positively to this particular combination of cues: Scientists aren't sure how this species is pollinated. Their best guess is flies, based on the activity of a similar *Gastrodia* orchid on Réunion Island. What smells roselike to our noses might remind the flies of rotting fruit, the theory goes. To its intended audience, this orchid could be utterly irresistible—so why should it care what we humans say about it? ⟩ **How to see them: In late summer, travel to Ranomafana National Park in southeast Madagascar, where these orchids are known to grow. Then scour the dark forest floor, gently lifting the leaf litter and humus, until you spot a tiny brown flower.**

Missing Seal Island Sharks

The world's most acrobatic great whites have left town.

LOCATION: **False Bay, South Africa**
SPECIES: **Great white shark**
(*Carcharodon carcharias*)

◆ One spring morning in 1996, naturalist and photographer Chris Fallows and a colleague were motoring through the South African inlet of False Bay, towing a yellow life jacket behind a tiny inflatable boat. As they passed Seal Island— an outpost for basking Cape fur seals and their pups—something stirred in the depths.

Moments later, "a great white comes flying out of the water," Fallows recalls. The shark grabbed the life jacket, then spit it out. Then he jumped again, and again.

South Africa once had more great white sharks in its waters than any other country. As Fallows learned that day, the ones around Seal Island were special—prone to flinging themselves after their blubbery targets in spray-laden aerial displays. "There was no other location on the planet where they breached as regularly and as spectacularly," says Fallows, who sometimes counted 45 seal snatches in a single morning. His action shots of the sharks—

Jaws who?

clearing the water's surface by multiple feet, toting baby pinnipeds like they were chew toys—helped propel them to global fame.

Fallows and his wife, Monique, spent thousands of days among the sharks, taking pictures, leading tours, and getting to know them personally. They also gathered data, eventually publishing dozens of papers on their own and with other researchers.

Great whites, observers at False Bay have learned, hunt most easily just after dawn, tracking seal silhouettes from below before hurling themselves up for an attempted kill. If they miss, they open and close their mouths silently above the surface, possibly to express frustration. The sharks keep to a strict social hierarchy—another group of researchers has seen them size each other up through swim-bys and games of chicken.

In the early 2010s, the impressive and educational great whites of False Bay began to disappear. Many pin the great whites' exodus on a pair of even fiercer predators: two orcas, nicknamed Port and Starboard, who first appeared in 2014 and developed a taste for shark liver. Famous sharks with their organs ripped out were found on beaches in nearby Gansbaai. Some researchers say that seeing or smelling their mutilated peers may have impelled the sharks to safer waters.

But Fallows says the blame falls more squarely on overfishing—particularly by a shark longline fishery that opened in South Africa before the orcas arrived. Outside the winter sealing season, the great whites lived off the same smaller species of sharks targeted by the fishery. As people snapped up their prey, the great whites either starved or left for bluer pastures. Fallows and others have called for better regulation of the fishery, but to no avail.

Fallows misses the sharks and their spectacular leaps. More important, though, he sees this loss as indicative of a worse one, like a fin breaking the surface of the water, with something more frightening beneath.

"It's a sad indictment of what we're capable of as a species," he says. "If we can lose the most famous of sharks, how many other things are we losing?" **⟩ How to see them:** Great whites haven't been common in False Bay since 2014, and breaching is rarely observed in other locations. It is possible to responsibly view these sharks elsewhere by cage diving.

Pisonias

When trees and birds don't get along

RANGE: Tropical islands in the Indo-Pacific region

SPECIES: Pisonia tree (*Pisonia grandis*)

◆ At certain times of the year, walking into a pisonia forest can feel a little like entering a nightmare. The forest floor is carpeted with hundreds of dead and dying seabirds. Above, hundreds more birds call back and forth from their perches in the pisonias—the same trees that killed their brethren.

For island-dwelling seabirds in the Indo-Pacific tropics, pisonias must seem like a godsend. These bright green, sprawling trees provide much-needed shelter and breeding habitat in places where not much else will grow. Black noddies make nests with their leaves, white terns lay eggs in the crooks of their branches, and shearwaters dig burrows around their roots.

The trees get a lot from the birds too: They're one of a few plant species able to thrive in soils made acidic by large amounts of guano. Stoked by nutrients from the droppings, the trees flourish on rocky cays, abandoned coconut plantations, and other generally inhospitable sites.

But one thing these trees can't do on their own is spread their seeds across the ocean to other islands. So they evolved seeds sticky enough to cling to birds' feathers, through saltwater baths and long-distance flights, relying on their winged friends to carry them to new lands.

That's where the relationship took a turn. At some point, pisonias started developing seeds that are perhaps *too* sticky. While some birds might pick up one or two seeds on their way off an island, others find themselves so entangled in seeds that they can't fly. Trapped and debilitated, they either starve to death or are eaten by predators. Piles of bird bones occasionally amass underneath the trees.

Some people believe that the bird carcasses provide nutrients for the pisonia, a myth perpetuated by popular nicknames like "bird-eating tree." However, research has found that the birds are worth more to the trees alive than dead, because of the nutritional value of their droppings and fallen eggs—and because dead birds can't transport seeds. Pisonias' dispersal strategy is accidentally sadistic.

(top) The deadly, sticky seeds of the pisonia tree

(bottom) A seabird tangled in pisonia seeds

But Lisianski Island, a thousand miles northwest of Hawai'i, is proof it works. Thirty years ago, there were only grasses and small shrubs on the island. Now a tiny pisonia forest is beginning to take root. Apparently the birds on the island already love it. ❯ **How to see them:** Cousin Island, in the Seychelles, and Heron Island, off the coast of Australia, are two relatively accessible islands with pisonia forests. If (for some reason) you want to see the trees packed with nesting seabirds, research ahead of time so that you come during their breeding season.

More Potential Bird Prisons

Another type of spooky avian entrapment appears to have arisen on Morocco's Mogador Islands—this one bird-on-bird.

Eleonora's falcons (*Falco eleonorae*) are small raptors that, for most of the year, live off insects caught on the wing. During the nesting season, though, adults and newborn chicks bulk up on migrating songbirds, swifts, and hoopoes that pass over their breeding colonies. The bird supply is so plentiful that the falcons often store their kills in stone larders.

In 2014, while counting falcons on the islands, researchers discovered small birds, with their wing and tail feathers ripped off, imprisoned in rock crevices near where the falcons nest. A fisherman familiar with the area told them that he had seen Eleonora's falcons attacking the birds and sticking them into holes, as if to save them alive until later—a behavior that, if confirmed, would make the falcons uniquely skilled (and twisted) among birds.

ASIA

Tool-Using Long-Tailed Macaques

To enjoy a tropical seafood buffet, these monkeys have entered their own Stone Age.

RANGE: Islands near the west coast of Myanmar and Thailand in the Andaman Sea, plus Kho Ram, off Thailand's east coast
SPECIES: Burmese long-tailed macaque (*Macaca fascicularis aurea*)

◆ In 1887, British naval officer Alfred Carpenter sent a frustrated note to the scientific journal *Nature*. While sailing through the islands of the Mergui Archipelago, he wrote, he often spotted monkeys engaged in unusual behavior: They would "[prowl] about the shore when the tide is low, opening the rock-oysters with a stone."

He saw these monkeys "constantly," he claimed, but people rarely believed him. It took until the early 2000s for biologists to officially confirm: This particular archipelago is indeed crawling with tool-using, oyster-busting macaques.

In Carpenter's day, and through the mid-twentieth century, the idea of handy wild animals seemed fanciful. Tools, most thought, were a solely human invention, something that set us apart from other species. This view turned out to be wrong—species of insects, birds, cephalopods, crustaceans, and mammals have all been observed using tools, from boxer crabs (who wield stinging anemones for hunting and defense) to palm cockatoos (who drum on trees with sticks). And now that our minds have been opened to the possibility, more examples are regularly noted.

Taking a crack at it

But what leads a given animal to implement an implement is still debated. The monkeys first reported by Carpenter were Burmese long-tailed macaques. Although monkeys of this species live in large groups across mainland tropical Southeast Asia, so far only those on islands are known to use stone tools.

Researchers studying these primates think they were driven to them by the unique potential—and difficulties—of seaside dining. Island macaques spend most of their time sleeping and hanging out in the forested interior, eating fruit, plants, and small animals. They emerge daily as the tide falls and exposes the rocky, mangrove-lined shore. Food here is super abundant and full of nutrients, but often trapped inside very sturdy packaging.

In response, the macaques evolved cutlery. They use small, pointed stones to precisely crack oysters for their salty meat. When faced with tougher marine snails or sea almond nuts, they'll place them on a convenient flat-stone anvil and bust them open with a heavier rock. The monkeys don't shape their tools, but they are picky, selecting just the right weight and material from the thousands of possibilities scattered on the beach. Youngsters take years to hone their skills in choosing and using the best ones.

Long-tailed macaques are one of very few species living in their own Stone Age. Archaeological excavations of their feeding areas show that they've been there for a long time. However, just as is the case for humans, monkey technology comes at a price: Their clever tools have led some groups to overharvest shellfish, degrading and depleting the food that inspired their innovation, and that they now depend on. ❯ **How to see them: Look for macaques using tools at low tide on the island of Kho Ram in Khao Sam Roi Yot National Park, Thailand, about 155 miles (250 km) south of Bangkok.**

Dragon's Blood Trees

Rooted in a magic greater than myth

LOCATION: Socotra, Yemen
SPECIES: Dragon's blood tree
(*Dracaena cinnabari*)

◆ From the outside, a dragon's blood tree boggles the eyes. Broad, root-like branches form an umbrella, capped with a bristled layer of slender green leaves. This uncommon structure, which helps the tree trap the moisture it needs to survive on the dry island of Socotra, makes it look positively upside down.

Inside, things look even stranger. Cut open a dragon's blood tree and it oozes crimson-colored resin. This sticky fluid—colored intensely by a number of flavonoids, the same chemicals responsible for the fall colors of New England's deciduous forests—carries nutrients and water from the roots to the twig tips and back again.

For hundreds of years—perhaps dating back to the first century BCE—powdered "dragon's blood" was a major commodity for Arab, Italian, Greek, and African traders, making its way into clay, dye, lipstick, nail polish, toothpaste, and various medicines. Rumor has it that the resin lends its deep, mellow hue to Stradivarius violins.

According to local legend, the first of these trees grew when a dragon was injured fighting an elephant and dripped some blood onto the ground. Their true origin draws from other magic—that of geography and time. Socotra split off from mainland Africa some 18 million years ago, giving this tree and other flora and fauna plenty of time to become both strange and specific. Of about 825 species of plants on the island, 307, including *Dracaena cinnabari*, are endemic, meaning they grow here and nowhere else.

And their real animal enemy is much smaller than an elephant. In addition to cyclones and droughts, introduced goats are overnibbling dragon's blood tree saplings—bad news for a number of other Socotran species, including humans, who benefit from the adult plants' fruits, shade, and general aura. ❯ **How to see them:** Dragon's blood trees are found only on the island of Socotra, where they grow in scattered fashion across plateaus and hilltops. They are unmistakable.

Uses of Stones

Macaques aren't the only animals who know how to have a smashing time with a rock. Here are a few ways other species use them.

SHOVELS: In Brazil, bearded capuchin monkeys (*Sapajus libidinosus*) dig with rocks to unearth tasty underground treats, like louro roots and tarantulas.

SINKERS: Tadpoles of several frog species, including green-eyed tree frogs (*Litoria genimaculata*), purposefully swallow sand and gravel in order to better control their buoyancy.

LOOFAHS: In 2011, an Alaskan brown bear (*Ursus arctos*) was observed exfoliating his or her face with a series of barnacle-encrusted rocks, in between bouts of play-fighting with a friend and snacking on a dead whale.

ANVILS: Members of a number of tuskfish species (*Choerodon* spp.) bring mollusks, young turtles, and other

catches over to stone anvils, where they proceed to bash them open. Favored anvils are often surrounded by shell fragments.

TRAP EXTENSIONS: In the Namib desert, corolla spiders (*Ariadna* spp.) encircle their den entrances with rings of seven or eight quartz stones, attaching one stone to each leg with a strand of silk. If a smaller bug brushes a stone, the spider feels the vibration and pounces.

EGG SPOONS: Egyptian vultures (*Neophron percnopterus*) use rocks to smash open the thick-shelled eggs of other large birds like ostriches and emus, either hammering directly or throwing the rocks with their beaks. In Israel, ravens hang back and watch the vultures do this, then steal the eggs—using the tool-using vultures as tools in turn.

Money Cowries

A snail's slow journey into currency

RANGE: Indian and Pacific Oceans
SPECIES: Cowries (family Cypraeidae)

◆ Across tropical seas in the Indian and Pacific Oceans, members of a family of marine snails known as Cypraeidae trail along the sandy, shallow bottoms, using minerals from seawater to build curved shells that protect their soft bodies from predators. Some species grow as big as a clenched fist; others stay as small as a thumbprint. No two shells are exactly alike. And when the snails die, the shells—known as cowries—often wash up on shore.

Cowries build their shells for protection, but humans have found other uses for them.

That's where their strange afterlife begins. Since ancient times, curious people have picked up the sensuously shaped, intricately patterned cowrie shells and carried them far, far away. Archaeologists have found cowries as far afield as Egypt, Japan, Ghana, and the southeastern United States, transported by people who saw the shells' labia-like opening as a symbol of fertility, or as suffused with healing or prophetic powers. In West Africa, people were especially enamored with cowries: Priestesses used them in fortune-telling, midwives ground them into herbal drinks, rulers wore them as jewelry, and mourners placed them in the graves of loved ones.

People's tendency to place value in cowries—combined with their durability, ease of transport, and resistance to counterfeiting—made these shells one of the world's earliest forms of currency. Before coins became widespread, cowries were used as money throughout parts of Asia, the Pacific, Africa, and Europe. As early as the eleventh century, traders strung them on fibers in multiples of 10 for easy counting and carried them via camel caravan across the Sahara Desert.

By the 1600s, British ships were importing 200,000 pounds of cowries a year from the Maldives to West Africa, partially for use in the transatlantic slave trade. Many of the 12 million

people sold into slavery between the sixteenth and nineteenth centuries had their lives traded for the shells. In his 1789 autobiography, Olaudah Equiano, who was kidnapped in Benin, recounts being sold from one merchant to another for 172 cowries.

Despite the horrifying conditions that enslaved people faced on their journey across the Atlantic, some managed to smuggle with them important objects from home, including cowries. In the Americas, practitioners of Santeria and voodoo integrated cowrie shells into their religious traditions, while archaeologists have excavated them from former plantations, including Thomas Jefferson's Monticello.

Scattered across the planet, far from the tropical seas that birthed them, cowrie shells remain symbolic—only here, they stand for the persistence of the beliefs, traditions, and humanity of people whose lives were once considered only as valuable as shells. ❯ **How to see them:** You can see money cowries on display at the Smithsonian's National Museum of American History, in the Value of Money exhibit. Or try your luck beachcombing in the Maldives, in Hawai'i, or along the Sea of Cortez, where cowrie shells often wash up on shore.

Globe Skimmer Dragonflies

Bugs hitch a ride on a high-altitude speedway.

◆ When marine biologist R. Charles Anderson noticed globe skimmer dragonfly flocks appearing in the Maldives in October every year, he was intrigued. These insects lay their eggs only in freshwater pools, and the Maldives are about as salty as can be—a matrix of seawater-suffused cays, where even rainfall quickly becomes brackish. As an origin point, they were impossible; as a destination, they seemed like a dead end.

And yet the dragonflies kept showing up. Everyone knew to look out for the swarms, which clotted the sky with iridescence. They peaked in number in November and December before disappearing again. Where exactly were they coming from? And where did they go?

In 1996, Anderson and other researchers started keeping track of the arrival and departure dates of the ephemeral travelers, hoping to unravel their itinerary. They cross-referenced their logs with radar readings, weather models, and stable isotope analysis, a method that can help determine where migrating animals come from.

RANGE: Most of Africa, Australia, and South America, as well as the southern parts of Asia and North America
SPECIES: Globe skimmer dragonfly (*Pantala flavescens*)

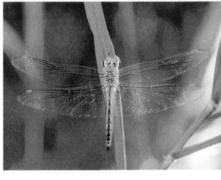

Globe skimmer dragonflies travel thousands of miles to follow the monsoon season.

Over years, a potential route emerged: The dragonflies, they thought, were coming over the ocean from southern India and pit-stopping in the Maldives before they took off again for East Africa. Later, in spring, the swarm would return to India, starting the cycle over.

This was a surprise. When the globe skimmer dragonflies arrive in the Maldives, surface winds are blowing toward India. A trip from the mainland to the islands at low altitudes would be like climbing up a descending escalator for 500 miles (800 km).

A few thousand feet higher, though, it's a whole different squall game. Up here, in what's called the Intertropical Convergence Zone, winds move from India toward the Maldives and East Africa. The globe skimmers are likely hitching a ride on this high-altitude speedway, where their rapidity "is dependent not on their own strength, but on the monsoon winds," says Vivek Chandran, an entomologist based in Kerala, India.

Way up here, the dragonflies may travel alongside Amur falcons, pied cuckoos, Eurasian rollers, and other wind-surfing birds. Some of them likely end up eaten by their avian fellows. The globe skimmers themselves probably feed on plankton and other tiny beings that are blown into the air from the ocean, snapping them up midflight.

As of now, only this leg of the dragonflies' proposed journey—from India to the Maldives—has been confirmed. If the full route from India to East Africa and back is verified, this group of globe skimmers may claim the record for longest migration relative to body size: a 9,000-mile (15,500 km) cycle that takes them four generations to complete.

They do it, it's thought, for their offspring. By following monsoon season from India to East Africa, each generation manages to lay their eggs in tropical puddles. There, their nymphs can grow up quickly (since the water is so warm) and safe from predators—since the pools, like the insects they house, quickly disappear. **〉 How to see them:** In much of the world, globe skimmers are easy to spot—look for them around bodies of water. In the Maldives, they can be seen most easily from September through December, as indicated by their Maldivian name, hei nakaiy dhooni ("October flyer").

Sulawesi Warty Pigs

Some of humankind's earliest muses

RANGE: Rainforests in central, east, and southeast Sulawesi, as well as on some neighboring islands
SPECIES: Sulawesi warty pig (*Sus celebensis*)

◆ Wilbur, Porky, Peppa Pig—across cultures and through generations, pigs have inspired humans to great heights in art and storytelling.

This started earlier than you might think. Archaeologists recently discovered a painting of a pig in a cave in Sulawesi, Indonesia, that dates back at least 45,500 years, making it the oldest piece of nonabstract art ever found.

The species in the painting is thought to be a Sulawesi warty pig. These creatures, who are about the size of potbellied pigs, live high in the hills of Sulawesi, an island near eastern Borneo. As their name suggests, they are adorned with three pairs of facial warts on their snouts, along with white or yellow side whiskers and bushy mustaches that would make Rutherford B. Hayes jealous.

Sulawesi warty pigs' daily life is equally envy-inducing: They forage in groups in the morning, roll in mud baths in the afternoon, and at night sleep off the fallen fruit they ate for lunch. Researchers debate how humans related to these pigs tens of thousands of years ago, with some hypothesizing that they may have been domesticated quite early, for food or even as pets.

In any case, they were muses. In December 2017, Indonesian archaeologist Basran Burhan and his team entered a previously unexamined cave called Leang Tedongnge, in South Sulawesi. Sketched in red ocher on a limestone wall was a drawing of two pigs brawling as a third looked on. Radiometric dating of mineral deposits on the painting determined that it was painted at least 45,500 years ago. Similar pig images, nearly as old, have been found decorating other caves in Sulawesi and Indonesia—upending previous conceptions that placed Europe at the center of ancient art-making.

Paint me like one of your cave pigs.

Most aspects of the porcine portraits, down to the warts, are realistic. But the artists seem to have taken one creative liberty: Although Sulawesi warty pigs are relatively small and lean in real life, the ones in the paintings tend to be quite big. Contemporary admirers of the art debate whether this reflects the painters' dreams of a good hunt, the cultural importance of the pigs, or something else entirely. Tens of thousands of years after these larger-than-life swine were first painted, the descendants of their creators puzzle over them, while the descendants of their inspiration run around outside.

> **How to see them:** Warty pigs are common in Sulawesi's forests, where they tend to roam in small groups. Cave art of the pigs can be seen in the Leang-Leang Prehistoric Park, near Bantimurung Bulusaraung National Park.

Animal Rock Art Through the Ages

Ancient rock art portraying animals has been found in more than 100 countries. While large mammals are the form's best-known subjects, birds, insects, reptiles, and fish also make appearances, hinting at the rich relationships we have always shared with our fellow creatures.

COSQUER CAVE, FRANCE, C. 17,000 BCE. This huge limestone chamber is covered in engravings and paintings. Alongside horses and other quadrupeds, artists here illustrated an unusual amount of marine life, including seals, fish, jellyfish, and now-extinct great auks. Rising seas have immersed much of the cave, which can be reached only by scuba diving.

KIMBERLEY, AUSTRALIA, C. 15,300 BCE. Some of the oldest cave art found in Australia is of kangaroos, monitor lizards, and snakes. Archaeologists determined the age of particular paintings thanks to the work of another species, mud wasps, whose nests both underlying and overlying the rock art can be reliably dated.

SERRANÍA DE LA LINDOSA, COLOMBIA, C. 10,000 BCE. Eight miles (13 km) of rock art in the Colombian Amazon include what appear to be now-extinct Ice Age megafauna: a giant sloth, an elephant-like gomphothere, and a long-nosed ungulate of the order Litopterna. Researchers still argue over how old the art is and whether it represents these species or more recent analogues.

TAJO DE LAS FIGURAS CAVES, SPAIN, C. 8,000 BCE. Two caves within this complex contain as many as 208 different images of birds, including flamingos, ducks, and an avocet. The sloped floor and landscape views provided by one cave suggest it was not lived in but instead used to scope out hunts and for bird-watching..

TASSILI N'AJJER, ALGERIA, C. 8,000 BCE. Rock art in these caves showcases the changing Sahara ecosystem, from annual migrations of birds and antelopes to the former presence of animals like hippopotamuses and rhinoceroses, who lived here when it was much wetter. One famous section, the "Tassili Mushroom Figure," is perhaps more imaginative—it appears to show a man with a bee for a head completely covered in small toadstools.

ASTUVANSALMI SITE, FINLAND, C. 4,000 BCE. On cliffs overlooking Lake Saimaa, artists painted elk, humans, and watercraft in red ocher mixed with fat or blood. The position of the artworks means they must have done so while boating or standing on the ice. The elk are often painted with dots over their hearts.

19TH UNNAMED CAVE, ALABAMA, UNITED STATES, C. 1,000 CE. Some of the largest cave art images yet found in North America were made here by Indigenous Americans, who engraved them into the ceiling of a completely dark chamber. One depicts a 10-foot (3 m) snake, patterned much like a modern diamondback rattlesnake, and crafted to look as if emerging from a crack in the cave ceiling.

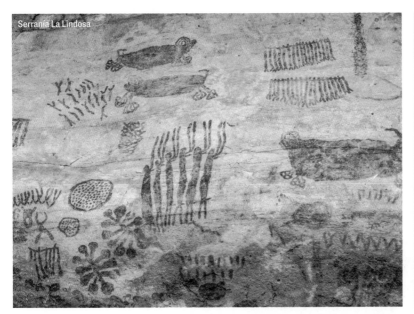
Serranía La Lindosa

Cosquer Cave

Olive Ridley Sea Turtles

Moms on the beach, nesting en masse

RANGE: Tropical expanses of the Atlantic, Pacific, and Indian Oceans
SPECIES: Olive ridley sea turtle (*Lepidochelys olivacea*)

◆ The most numerous of the world's seven sea turtle species, olive ridleys spend most of their lives on their own, in the open ocean. It's hard to know what they get up to out there.

On shore, though, their behavior is too dramatic to miss. The olive ridley is one of just two turtle species that nest en masse. (The other is the Kemp's ridley, found along the US Atlantic coast and the Gulf of Mexico.) When the time is right, female turtles surf currents and tides to their beach of choice—often the same one where they themselves hatched. They gather offshore and then, upon some as-yet-unknown signal, clamber all together onto the beach, where they dig out nests for clutches of about a hundred eggs, each the size of a billiard ball. Then they scoot back into the water.

In India, the ridleys lay eggs along the coast of the eastern state of Odisha. From there, some of them migrate more than a thousand miles to the southeast coast of the country, along the Gulf of Mannar, says evolutionary ecologist Kartik Shankar. In 2023, a beach in Odisha hosted a record 600,000 turtle moms in a single week. (Other olive ridley mass nestings happen in Mexico, Costa Rica, and Gabon.)

Habitat loss and egg poaching are seen as major threats to India's sea turtles. But warming caused by climate change also poses a specific problem: The sex of sea turtles is dependent on the temperature of the sand where they incubate, with warmer sand leading to higher ratios of female turtles. "Our models show that the olive ridley offspring in [Odisha] a hundred years from now would be mostly female," Shankar says.

While turtles can be incubated in temperature-controlled hatcheries, doing so on the scale of the hundreds of thousands of olive ridleys that are born every year would be challenging to the point of impossibility.

But it is possible, and advisable, to help individual turtles when you can. On Pamban Island, off India's southeastern coast, Kadal Osai (Sound of the Sea), the local radio station for the fishing community, champions the olive ridley. Radio jockeys run a "Protect the Seas" challenge, giving a certificate and a cash prize to any fishers who release snagged turtles from their nets. Dozens have already taken part, meaning that many more turtles are free to live their mysterious ocean lives. ❯ **How to see them:** Odisha is the largest mass nesting site for olive ridleys in the world. Nesting occurs from November through March. Visit the Rushikulya River in Odisha's Ganjam district, or travel to Bhitarkanika National Park, which houses the state's turtle sanctuary, part of Gahirmatha Beach.

Climate change threatens to skew the sex ratios of olive ridley sea turtles, which develop as male or female depending on the sand temperature.

THE WILD LIFE OF A Sound of the Sea Radio DJ

■ In 2016, Lenin Raj quit his corporate job, left the city, and returned to Pamban Island, where he grew up. There, he became one of the first radio jockeys for Kadal Osai (Sound of the Sea), a station dedicated to informing India's fishing community about marine life, climate change, and proactive solutions.

• **What made you give up your engineering career to become an environmental DJ?**

My parents are fishers, and they always wanted me to do well in school so I could escape the upheavals of a fisher's life. After graduating in automobile engineering, I worked at a bicycle manufacturing company in Chennai for two years. I liked the work, but honestly, my life felt empty. I'm used to a rural islander's life—I relish the open skies, the churning sea, the salty breeze. City life seemed drab and impersonal. But I'm the first graduate in my family and I didn't have the luxury to explore a career in the arts, which is where my inclinations lay.

Eventually I did quit. I wandered without work in the city for an entire month, trying to pick up the courage to go to a radio station to apply for a job. But I would hesitate at the door. At that time, as luck would have it, I went back to Pamban for a visit. That's when I heard that a community radio station would be opening up in my own hometown.

• **When did your first environment-related show go live?**

In 2019, I was asked to host a show called *Samudhram Palagu* ("Learn about the Oceans"). I grew up with the sea all around me, and yet I was stumped. What could I possibly say?

For the first time, I realized that what I didn't know was as vast as the ocean. I didn't know, for instance, that some fish have a fixed territorial range while others

were rovers and would swim all over, and that deep-sea fish had specialized features that helped them adapt to high-pressure conditions, like the darkness and cold. As I started digging into trivia about the ocean, it was inextricably related to the environment and science.

I started to share what I saw and experienced within our fishing community. I gathered my information at the local boatyard, where I would see all kinds of people—the grandmothers who were salting and drying fish, fishers who sell the fresh produce from their boats, the many women who would buy from them and hawk it in the marketplace. People of different kinds—tourists and fishers alike.

• **What did you learn from these meetings that opened up conversations on your show?**

I learned that the group of people feeling the most severe impacts of climate change is the fishing community. It directly affects our livelihoods. Warming waters are causing fish to migrate and affecting marine life, but it's more than that. For instance, the homes that I knew that were built along the shoreline when I was younger are now all gone. We're experiencing widespread erosion, stronger winds, and inundation caused by frequent storms and cyclones. We talk about how climate change affects us directly a lot on our show.

• **How did you get involved with the cause of freeing the seas of plastic waste?**

We are advocating proactive solutions. The major causes we've taken up are reducing plastic and saving sea turtles. In 2019, on the occasion of World Radio Day, I'd invited three fishermen onto the show for a freewheeling chat. I asked one of them what they did with all the snack packaging they took out to sea.

Usually, all the provisions fishers take in their boats—sugars, salt, curry powders—are wrapped in plastic. So what happens to it? He said they dumped it into the ocean. So we did the math. There are 4,000 boats on our island, and if everyone dumped about five plastic covers out to sea, wouldn't we be catching more plastic in our nets than fish?

• **Did this conversation have an impact on your listeners?**

It can seem that words on the radio dissipate into thin air. I've seen that for a message to have an impact, you need to keep repeating it. So that's what we did. I spoke about the microplastics that scientists are finding in our blood and breast milk. Over the years, a lot of people reached out to me about it, saying they were stunned by the sheer amount of plastic waste.

The fisher I spoke to for World Radio Day said he no longer dumps plastic into the ocean anymore. He avoids plastic as much as he can and rolls up the rest to recycle on shore. It's important for people to understand that every road on Pamban leads you to the ocean. We depend on it to live and it should never be a personal garbage dump! ■

This interview has been translated from Tamil by Kamala Thiagarajan.

Hainan Gibbon Rope Bridge

A simple intervention helps the world's rarest primates stay connected.

RANGE: Six square miles (15 sq km) of rainforest in the Bawangling National Nature Reserve on Hainan Island in China
SPECIES: Hainan gibbon (*Nomascus hainanus*)

◆ Hainan gibbons never touch the ground. After warming up with a morning sing-along, gibbon families—which consist of two clementine-colored adult females, a black-furred adult male, and their children—set off through the trees. They leap and dance as they gather fruit, leaves, and insects and rest by hanging their bodies like hammocks.

These ropy-limbed primates may be the world's rarest mammals. Though they were once common in the rainforests of China's Hainan Island—the only place they live—poaching and deforestation has devastated the species, cutting them off from each other and their resources. In the 1970s, there were fewer than 10 Hainan gibbons in the world, in just two family groups. It took decades of concerted work by researchers, the Chinese government, and local communities to prevent their extinction.

Hainan gibbons spend their entire lives up in the trees.

So when three juvenile gibbons started a new family in 2011, everyone was thrilled. They settled down in an area of forest at the edge of the Bawangling National Nature Reserve and soon had several acrobatic children.

Then, in 2014, Super Typhoon Rammasun slammed into the island. Landslides crushed a lot of the family's infrastructure and swept away one of their favorite treetop paths—what researchers call an "arboreal highway." Now, instead of swinging easily from branch to branch, the gibbons had to fling themselves across a gap that averaged the length of a large school bus.

Although the gibbons found ways to traverse the gap, researchers saw females and juveniles hesitate before they began the new maneuvers, which often involved taking off from flimsy branches or dropping several stories from high limbs into sections of lower canopy. (Imagine doing an Evel Knievel–style motorcycle jump just to get from your house to the supermarket.)

To help them, in 2015, a team at the Kadoorie Farm and Botanic Garden decided to install a simple intervention: a two-pronged canopy rope bridge. Professional climbers affixed a pair of mountaineering ropes to two trees on either side of the gap. They also put up camera traps so they could see whether the gibbons would use the new system.

According to the footage, it took the gibbons half a year to attempt their first rope crossing. After that, the canopy bridge became a popular route for the family, especially the females and small juveniles. They scoot across, with their hands on the top rope and their feet on the bottom one, or hang down from all four limbs, sloth-style, to pull themselves hand over foot. Occasionally they strut along the rope like tightrope walkers or swing hand over hand, often with a baby in tow. (The adult males and larger juveniles mostly skip the bridge, apparently preferring to hurl themselves through space.)

Everyone is pleased that a relatively simple approach has helped keep this family's home range connected. But the bridge is the equivalent of a bandage over a much larger wound. The team has been planting native trees in the forest, so they can fill in the gaps and give the gibbons more choices. In the meantime, they've successfully thrown these rare, high-living primates a line. ❯ **How to see them:** Visit Kadoorie Farm and Botanic Garden to learn more about efforts to protect and support Hainan gibbons, including the rope bridge. Listen for their birdlike song, a whooping *hooooooo-weep!* intercut with babbles.

OCEANIA

Lord Howe Island Stick Insects

Thought to be extinct, these huge insects were just hiding out.

LOCATION: Ball's Pyramid, a sea stack 14.3 miles (23 km) from Lord Howe Island, Australia
SPECIES: Lord Howe Island stick insect (*Dryococelus australis*)

◆ In most situations, Lord Howe Island stick insects are hard to miss. These arthropods' long, crenulated bodies, which might barely fit on a human palm, have earned them the nickname "tree lobsters." At night, they climb nearby shrubs in search of leaves and punctuate the darkness with steady crunching. During the day, they form conspicuous clusters in tree hollows near the ground.

When black rats snuck onto the Australian island via a run-aground European ship in 1918, they also found the stick insects easy to spot—as well as good to eat. The wingless, slow-moving phasmids had no defense against the rats, and their numbers plummeted. People stopped seeing the big bugs around the island in 1930 and figured they were gone forever.

But the sea around the island held a secret. Rising out of the water less than 15 miles (24 km) away from Lord Howe Island is the tallest volcanic rock stack in the world, Ball's Pyramid. Decades after the supposed extinction of the species, climbers here reported finding dead stick insects as they traversed the rock.

In 2001, a team of scientists and rangers mounted an expedition to see if they could find live ones. After a 200-foot (60 m) climb up a near-vertical slope in darkness, they came upon two dozen Lord Howe Island stick insects, clinging to existence on a lone melaleuca shrub. When scientists compared their massive genomes, about 25 percent larger than our own, with those of old museum specimens, they confirmed that the Ball's Pyramid stick insects were the very same species that had vanished from Lord Howe Island decades before. While it's unclear how they got there, females likely helped keep the population going through parthenogenesis—the ability to reproduce without males.

Although this is a useful talent, when possible, Lord Howe Island stick insects prefer to form bonded pairs. In 2003, scientists successfully captured a male, named Adam, and a female, named Eve, and sent them to the Melbourne Zoo to start a breeding program. This couple beget a lineage that now numbers in the thousands. Scientists have been given the chance to study the captive population, observing as females bury their pale eggs in soil and watching each new generation of bright green nymphs hatch and darken as they grow.

It's a tree...lobster!

As the species recovers, so too does Lord Howe Island: The recent success of a rat eradication program means that the goal of returning these beloved tree lobsters to their ancestral home is closer than ever. ❭ **How to see them:** The wild population of these stick insects is currently restricted to Ball's Pyramid, a jagged rock stack in the Pacific Ocean. Climbing it is permitted only for scientific purposes. A few captive tree lobsters are on display at the Lord Howe Island Museum, and many more live at the Melbourne Zoo.

Staghorn Fern Colonies

Surprisingly social plants

RANGE: Lord Howe Island, Australia
SPECIES: Staghorn fern (*Platycerium bifurcatum*)

◆ Staghorn ferns living on Australia's Lord Howe Island have a tough job. These plants grow as epiphytes, hanging in clumps off rainforest trees. High above the soil, they must find a way to gather the water and nutrients they need to survive.

While epiphytes elsewhere have developed strategies of self-reliance—Spanish moss soaks up fog; bromeliads have solo cups—these staghorn ferns instead work together. A research team thinks these ferns may be the first known plants to demonstrate eusociality, the colony-based lifestyle best known from bees, ants, and termites.

Eusocial animals can be thought of as superorganisms; rather than focus on their own needs, individuals play roles that serve the whole. Their behavior and physiology reflect this, with, for instance, sterile worker bees gathering food for the hive while the much larger queen handles reproduction.

In Lord Howe Island's staghorn ferns, individuals also seem built for different tasks. Plants near the bottom of a clump grow many fan-shaped, absorbent fronds that can hold more water and nutrients while providing structural stability. Meanwhile, those at the top of the tree grow a higher proportion of long, waxy fronds that direct water like downspouts and produce spores for reproduction.

Nearly half of the individual plants studied didn't reproduce at all, instead dedicating all their fronds to water storage—creating a spongy center for the group that everyone can sip from through their roots. The team looking into this, led by K. C. Burns of Te Kura Mātauranga Koiora School of Biological Sciences in Wellington, calls these interconnected clusters "colonies."

Eusociality is considered a major step in evolution, akin to how single cells came together to form multicellular organisms. Despite our knack for collaboration, even humans don't count as eusocial—we'll have to leave that to these fast fronds. ❯ **How to see them: Staghorn fern colonies on Lord Howe Island can be seen along rainforest paths, hanging on to trees at eye level. If you spot one, look for the varying frond shapes that indicate individuals with different roles.**

To survive, members of staghorn fern colonies divvy up the labor.

Christmas Island Crab March

An entire island makes way for the annual migration of 43 million red crabs.

RANGE: Christmas Island National Park, Australia

SPECIES: Christmas Island red crab (*Gecarcoidea natalis*)

◆ Every year around September, park rangers on Australia's Christmas Island begin rearranging infrastructure in the island's small town. They clear vegetation and debris from dozens of underpasses. They close roads and put up 12 miles (20 km) of temporary barriers, as though preparing for a marathon.

At the first sign of rain, rangers and residents start looking for the athletes: more than 43 million red crabs, who travel each year from the island's interior to the coast. The males give themselves a head start, to leave enough time to dig burrows on the beach. The females follow. When they meet on the sand, they will mate, and the females will spawn—always at the turning high tide during the last quarter moon, the best conditions for their tiny offspring.

But first, they must make an arduous six- to eight-week journey. While they always hit their lunar date, the crabs will slow their pace if it's too rainy or too hot—to avoid being washed away or cooked in the sun—and speed up again when needed. That leaves everyone else working around them for the duration of their trek.

Twenty years ago, "you wouldn't even be able to walk, let alone drive," during the migration, says Azmi Yon, senior ranger at Christmas Island National Park, who was born and raised on the island. Now it is more like a torrent than a tidal wave. The crabs have faced introduced threats, like the invasive yellow crazy ant, estimated to have wiped out at least 10 million crabs in recent years with their relentless acid attacks on migrating crabs who enter ant-colonized territory. Human impact—including climate change and the introduction of more vehicles—also takes a steep toll.

So Yon and his colleagues work hard to minimize disruption—moving with the crabs to redirect traffic and close roads, and maintaining a 15-foot-tall (5 m) crab bridge over a busy highway. They also educate and assist new visitors to the island, reminding them they might have to walk instead of drive to their destination during high-activity hours. "I do this so that the younger generations can see what the crab migration is all about," Yon says.

At the start of the wet season, Christmas Island's red crabs take over the town.

Meanwhile, the next crustacean generation has its own journey to complete. Of the 10,000 eggs each female red crab releases into the ocean, the vast majority are eaten by fish, manta rays, and whale sharks that visit the coast for the bounty. When the still-tiny survivors are finally seen on land, rangers breathe a sigh of relief. "When you have a good migration, a perfect tide, a perfect moon, you get a good return," says Yon. "You see a whole beach or road covered with red carpet. This is success." ❯ **How to see them:** The migration is dictated by the first major rainfall of the wet season, which typically occurs in November or December but can be as early as October or as late as January. The Christmas Island Parks Department puts out live alerts on its blog and Facebook page for possible sighting dates.

Kākāpō

These special parrots are hanging on by a techno-mediated feather.

RANGE: Five islands off the coast of New Zealand, as well as a small area of the country's North Island

SPECIES: Kākāpō (*Strigops habroptila*)

◆ On a handful of isolated islands off the coast of New Zealand, an adorable clan of flightless parrots lives a life that seems ripped from a science fiction anthology.

On the one hand, kākāpō don't have to worry about much. Rats, stoats, cats, and other introduced predators with a taste for these Pomeranian-sized birds have been eradicated from their islands by conservationists. Trackers and remote activity monitors—kākāpō Fitbits—allow scientists to intervene if they get very sick.

On the other hand: the "spermcopter."

Kākāpō once thrived in the forests of mainland New Zealand. Years of relatively isolated evolution shaped them into a collection of unusual traits—they are nocturnal, can live for up to 90 years, and (uniquely for parrots) cannot fly, instead using their claws to climb trees and their wings to finesse things when they fall out. They also have elaborate courtship rituals, which involve all-night male calling competitions and large quantities of a specific fruit, the vitamin-rich rimu berry. The aforementioned introduced mammals made short work of most of the kākāpō by the 1980s.

Alarmed, conservationists turned to the last surviving outpost of birds, on Stewart Island (Rakiura). The population numbered only a few dozen, and inbreeding had become rampant. This spurred concern about a fitness-reducing genetic bottleneck, even after the birds were moved to a wildlife refuge on nearby Codfish Island (Whenua Hou). Luckily, the surprise discovery of a kākāpō on the mainland—given the name Richard Henry, after an Irish ex-hunter who tried and failed to create his own kākāpō island refuge in the 1890s—provided an injection of desperately needed genetic novelty.

Over the years, through chick-monitoring and matchmaking, researchers with what's known as the Kākāpō Recovery Programme have brought the total number of kākāpō to more than 200. Now spread over five islands and a mainland reserve, the parrot population lives surveilled by scientists, who balance their desire for the birds to live a relatively natural life with the mandate to intervene when a need (or an opportunity) presents itself.

New Zealand's historic lack of large mammals led to the evolution of many unusual birds, including the kākāpō.

In spring and summer, they give special food to ensure healthy breeding. Annual checkups ensure they can catch and treat the occasional case of cloacitis, aka "crusty bum." And when it's time to make more kākāpō, they may at times call in the afore-mentioned spermcopter—a delivery drone that whisks a viable sample away to a (rela-tively) distant first cousin in 10 minutes flat. ❯ **How to see them: The Kākāpō Recovery Programme hosts up to 200 volunteers per breeding season, which doesn't happen every year. If you can't make it, try checking out the New Zealand Department of Conservation's online Kākāpō Cam.**

Kākāpō Matchmaking Interventions

Scientists attempting to square the inflexibility of the kākāpō's natural mating instincts with the need to guarantee their continued existence have hit upon some interesting ideas.

One early attempt to obtain sperm took the form of "Chloe." Named as a pun on the all-purpose cloacal orifice, this "female" kākāpō puppet roamed the islands on the back of a remote-controlled toy car. Although meant to seduce male parrots, the uncanny valley honeypot attracted precisely zero suitors.

Another was the "ejaculation helmet," a pragmatic albeit undignified crown of condoms. A male kākāpō in a certain mood will attempt to mate fairly indiscriminately, including, occasionally, with a researcher's head. The helmet seemed like a good way to use this tendency to everyone's advantage. It was discarded after the realization that the kākāpō coupling style—notoriously intense and long-lasting—might also come with risk of head trauma.

Researchers now obtain kākāpō sperm manually, via skilled massage, before flying it off in the spermcopter. Artificial insemination in general has successfully produced at least four chicks, impressive for a technique that rarely works in free-living wild birds. And despite their lackluster performances, both Chloe and the ejaculation helmet now hold places of honor in New Zealand's national museum.

THE WILD LIFE OF A Predator-Removal Conservationist

■ As the operations and research lead for Predator Free Rakiura, Kevin Carter is helping to attempt the world's largest predator removal project on Rakiura (also called Stewart Island). While the project is still in its very early stages, the goal is to eradicate and keep out four introduced predators—rats, European hedgehogs, possums, and feral cats—in hope of eventually reintroducing native species, including kākāpō.

● **What's it like up in the alpine tops of Rakiura?**

Being in the middle of the national park, you do a 360-degree look around and you just can't tell that humans have been present.

It's everything from these beautiful alpine turfs, down through subalpine scrub vegetation, then forests and the river valley. Then you've got a wetland sequence, a dune habitat, and then you're down to the coast. You get this real sense of wilderness and untouched landscapes.

I find those kinds of moments really motivating. You go, "Okay, this is why I work in conservation, because I want to do everything I can to protect places like this."

● **What's one of your favorite memories with the wildlife on Rakiura?**

I was doing some New Zealand sea lion pup tagging. As I was going through the bush looking for some, I heard pup calls. I popped out and there was this amazing backdrop of huge granite domes on the landscape.

There were these two little sea lion pups hanging out on a rock. They were looking out at the view. Then one little guy put his flipper up and over the other one's back. And I was imagining a conversation they might have been having, like, "Hey, bro, isn't this the greatest thing you've ever seen?" That's one of those really cool moments.

● **If the project is successful, what would that mean on a bigger scale?**

We're trying to redefine what's possible. Ten years ago there was a feasibility assessment on the project and it said, "You can't achieve it for these reasons." But in that time, technology has moved forward. We've got new science and new tools.

When we're able to deliver and make Rakiura predator-free, it's going to redefine what's possible. Then hopefully the mainland [of New Zealand] and other places are going to say, "If you could do it, we can do it too."

● **Why does this project matter so much?**

One of the things about Rakiura is that we've got a whole bunch of endemic species that are found only here. We've got highly endemic invertebrates, reptiles, birds, and plants.

So in terms of global biodiversity, those species will be safe, whereas if we lost them, they wouldn't be lost only from New Zealand, they'd be lost from the whole world. So those are the stakes. ■

Bramble Cay Melomyses

These rats were the first mammalian victims of human-caused climate change.

RANGE: Previously, Bramble Cay (Maizab Kaur) in Australia
SPECIES: Bramble Cay melomys (*Melomys rubicola*)

◆ Since 1900, the world's oceans have risen somewhere between 5 and 8 inches (12–20 cm). This doesn't necessarily seem like a lot. Researchers think the impending rise, which will bring with it coastal inundations and enormous human displacement, will be larger—between 12 and 40 more inches (30–100 cm) before 2100.

But it was enough to wipe out the Bramble Cay melomys. These reef rats once lived on a tiny blip of coral within the Torres Strait, between northeast Australia and Papua New Guinea. As the sea encroached and storms became more frequent, their home shrank rapidly: Between 1998 and 2014, the area of the island accessible at high tide dwindled from 10 acres to about 6, leaving its inhabitants a living space about the size of a big-box store.

There's a lot we don't know about Bramble Cay melomyses and how they lived. Recorded human interactions with them are few and standard: In 1845, bored European sailors shot at them with bows and arrows; in 1924, the first specimen was described and named. Physically, they looked like most rats, each about as long as a butter knife, with limpid eyes and a mosaic-like scaling pattern on their tails. They were nocturnal, skittish, and quick, given to hurdling vegetation as they ran from disturbances.

Last seen in 2009, the Bramble Cay melomys is officially extinct.

People started counting them in the late twentieth century. In 1978, there were a few hundred. In 1998, there were 93; in 2004, 12. In 2008, alarmed experts proposed a recovery plan for the species.

In 2014, researchers did a very thorough sweep, involving daytime surveys, camera traps, and cages baited with oats, peanut butter, and syrup. None turned up at all. One of the island's few regular visitors—a fisherman named Egon Stewart—told them he had last seen a couple of melomyses in 2009, hiding under a heap of sticks and canoe debris.

An official report declared the melomys likely extinct. It blamed inundation, which cut off the plants the rats needed for food and shelter, crowded them, and possibly drowned some. "This probably represents the first recorded mammalian extinction due to anthropogenic climate change," the authors wrote.

In 2019, the country of Australia agreed, officially recognizing the extinction. At this point, the rats made global headlines, slightly too late. ❭ **How to see them:** You can't.

Endlings

Before a species goes extinct, there is always a final representative—the last of its kind on Earth. In recent years, people have begun calling these individuals "endlings." Most, like the last Bramble Cay melomys, remain anonymous to us, but a few end up with names and stories.

MARTHA, THE PASSENGER PIGEON (*Ectopistes migratorius*): Passenger pigeons were once the most numerous bird in North America, with flocks said to block out the sun

as effectively as an eclipse. Over the course of a few decades, they were completely extirpated. Martha, who spent her whole life in captivity, died in 1914 in the Cincinnati Zoo, after years of receiving visitors moved by her plight.

ORANGE BAND, THE DUSKY SEASIDE SPARROW (*Ammodramus maritimus nigrescens*): Dusky seaside sparrows, once found only along a small stretch of Florida coastal marshes, fell victim to development associated with the Cape Canaveral space program. The last one, Orange Band, named for his colored foot tag, died in 1987. He was eulogized briefly by the Associated Press.

TURGI, THE POLYNESIAN TREE SNAIL *(Partula arguta):* Turgi, who was the size of a peanut, died in 1996 in the London Zoo, where it had been hoped he would reproduce. His wild brethren, who move less than 2 feet (60 cm) per year, had been driven to extinction by two other snails—the giant African snail (introduced as a food species) and the rosy wolf snail (introduced to control the giant African snail, with unexpected and tragic results).

LAÑA OR CELIA, THE BUCARDO *(Capra pyrenaica pyrenaica):* Bucardos were wild goats who climbed cliffs and grazed valleys in the Pyrenees. The last one, known as Celia by outsiders and as Laña by local people, died in 2000, when a tree fell on her. Scientists tried to clone her by implanting her DNA into the eggs of other goats. One clone—perhaps the true endling—survived for 10 minutes before passing away.

淇淇 (QI QI), THE BAIJI *(Lipotes vexillifer):* Baiji, shy and toothy river dolphins, once lived in the Yangtze River. In 1980, a male was captured and brought to the Wuhan Institute of Hydrobiology in an attempt to create a breeding population for the species, which was threatened by indiscriminate fishing methods and hydrology projects. The dolphin, named Qi Qi,

died in 2002 and became an endling retrospectively in 2006, when scientists surveyed the river for wild baiji and didn't find any.

LONESOME GEORGE, THE PINTA ISLAND GIANT TORTOISE *(Chelonoidis abingdonii):* When scientists found Lonesome George on Pinta Island in the Galápagos, he was already the last of his kind, his fellow Pinta Island giant tortoises having been hunted to death. He died in 2012 after having lived for more than a century—nearly half of that time as an endling.

King's Holly

The world's oldest living thing continually remakes itself.

◆ From one perspective, there are a few hundred King's holly plants in the world. Some grow wild in a very small area of temperate rainforest in Tasmania, while others live in the state's botanical gardens, cared for by horticulturists. Each grows for up to 300 years, bearing spiky deep green leaves and blooming annually with raspberry-colored flowers.

But those flowers are a bit of a pink herring. Most plants with blooms use them as reproductive structures, to attract pollinators that bring them new genetic material. But King's holly is triploid (meaning its cells contain three sets of chromosomes instead of two) and sterile (because those chromosomes cannot divide evenly to make eggs or pollen). The plant reproduces only by dropping branches, which root and become identical clones.

For this reason, from another perspective, there is only one King's holly on Earth. All existing plants are genetically indistinguishable and thus—despite their geographic separation—can be said to constitute one individual.

King's holly gets its name from Australian naturalist and tin miner Deny King, who first encountered it in 1934 at his home in Melaleuca, a remote inlet in southwest Tasmania. It was not until three decades later that he found it again and sent a sample to botanist Winifred Curtis, who described it as a new species. In the early 1990s, King hosted paleobotanists Gregory Jordan and Raymond Carpenter on a fossil dig in Melaleuca, where they found fossilized King's holly leaves.

RANGE: A single ¾-mile (about 1 km) strip of temperate rainforest in the Tasmanian Wilderness World Heritage Area in southwest Tasmania
SPECIES: King's holly (*Lomatia tasmanica*), also called King's lomatia

Radiocarbon dating showed the leaves to be 43,600 years old—meaning that King's holly has been successfully cloning itself for at least that long, making it the oldest living thing ever discovered. (Other clonally reproduced organisms are sometimes described as the oldest living thing in the world—Pando the quaking aspen, for example, or a seagrass colony off the coast of Spain. But they are dated in less precise and more disputed ways, rather than from a specific fossil.)

The plant's life strategy, while arguably quite successful so far, has its downsides. King's holly has no genetic diversity to draw on to help it survive the unexpected. Researchers are currently worried about a fungal root rot called *Phytophthora cinnamomi*, which is known to infect the plant's closest relatives and has been found in the forest less than 100 feet (30 m) from the Melaleuca colony. And with its extremely limited native range, King's holly is also vulnerable to wildfire and climate change.

King's holly is a very sensitive plant.

The Royal Tasmanian Botanical Gardens has grown King's holly clones from cuttings since 1994. Cuttings can take a year to grow roots, and they are so sensitive that often they die when repotted. Still, the horticulturists have persisted, developing new techniques to graft the cuttings onto hardier root stocks and aiming to help the world's oldest plant continue its quiet legacy. ❯ **How to see it:** King's holly is so critically endangered that people are not allowed to visit it in the wild—and even the cuttings grown at the Royal Tasmanian Botanical Gardens are not on public display. But counting the many, many leaves it has produced across space and time is a soothing way to fall asleep.

Marshallese Stick Charts

Imagine a time before GPS, before compasses, even before paper maps. Then imagine you have to pilot a dugout canoe across a vast expanse of open ocean, navigating so deftly that you land precisely on the only speck of land for hundreds of miles in any direction.

As recently as a century ago, such feats of navigational prowess were common in the Republic of the Marshall Islands, an independent Pacific island nation that spans more than 180,000 square miles (466,198 sq km) of ocean just above the equator. Scattered across all that open ocean are 1,200 islands, arranged into constellations of 29 atolls. The average elevation is 7 feet (2 m) above sea level.

For at least two thousand years, the ancestors of modern Marshallese people found their way between these far-flung islands with a series of sophisticated systems. The canoes themselves were works of art, with outriggers for stability and sails woven from dried pandanus leaves. Men navigated using not only the winds and stars but the ocean itself; from childhood, navigators were trained to feel subtle patterns in the ways waves and currents behave when refracted off distant islands or underwater geology.

Later, far from home, they could determine their course just by the feel of the sea beneath them.

To capture and share all this information, the Marshallese created an ingenious tool known as the stick chart, or rebbelib. To the untrained eye, a stick chart looks like a loosely woven mat of sticks—often the midribs of palm fronds—punctuated by cowrie shells. To a Marshallese sailor, though, it's a map, with each cowrie representing an island or atoll, and the sticks connecting them representing major oceanic swells and currents. Modern mapmakers using satellites and computers have found that stick charts show the location of islands and atolls with uncanny accuracy. Tests done in the 2010s found that skilled navigators could detect changes in the waves so minute that even computerized buoys couldn't pick them up.

In the decades following World War II, traditional canoe building, sailing, and navigation declined in the Marshall Islands. But today, a new generation of Marshallese sailors is reviving these age-old techniques. Rather than become a relic of the past, rebbelib may instead help Marshallese people chart a path toward a future—one where even rising sea levels can't drown their cultural knowledge and identity.

Coconut Crabs

Colorful, thieving giants of the tropics

◆ Can you imagine a crab the size of a cat scuttling around your backyard, climbing up trees, and quietly sneaking away with your shiniest pots and silverware? No? Then perhaps you've never had the privilege of meeting a coconut crab.

Coconut crabs are the world's largest land-based crustaceans. These mostly gentle giants can weigh as much as a small terrier and have a leg span of up to 3 feet (1 m). But their most impressive assets are their front claws, which grip with tremendous force. They use them to drag around objects weighing more than 60 pounds (27 kg) and to crack open coconuts, a feat few other species can pull off.

These crabs are curious and unfussy. In addition to coconut flesh, fallen fruit, nuts, and seeds, they'll eat the remains of dead rats, seabirds, and even their own kind. This has led to speculation that these giants may be partly responsible for the disappearance of famed aviator Amelia Earhart, who perished in the remote Pacific. Some researchers believe that her remains were eaten by coconut crabs, who then dragged away the bones.

But don't let that put you off. While they will defend themselves if provoked, coconut crabs aren't aggressive toward people. They have, however, earned the nickname "robber crabs" for their love of human-made objects, which they often drag away to their burrows for further inspection and, when possible, degustation.

While they seem especially drawn to shiny pots and pans—probably because they smell like food—researchers and tourists have recorded the crabs carrying off everything from whisky bottles and sandals to expensive camera equipment. In one legendary example, a crab on Australia's Christmas Island stole—and crushed—a rifle that had previously belonged to a soldier making camp.

Coconut crabs live in a variety of homes over their lives, which can span many decades. Baby crabs are born in the ocean, hatched from eggs a mother crab releases directly into the water. After hatching, the tiny larvae spend about four weeks floating

RANGE: Tropical islands around the world, including in Polynesia, Micronesia, the Philippines, and Taiwan, as well as coastal areas in Japan, Mozambique, Tanzania, and Papua New Guinea

SPECIES: Coconut crab (*Birgus latro*), also known as the robber crab

Coconut crabs are very curious and very strong.

around before metamorphosing into juvenile crabs. For the next few years they live by the shore as hermit crabs, using other animals' discarded shells for shelter and protection.

As the crabs grow, their bellies turn rock hard and they ditch their borrowed shells. Adult coconut crabs' exoskeletons settle into a range of vivid colors, everything from orange, red, and brown to light violet, deep purple, or even blue.

But this beautiful and newly tough exterior comes at a price—the crabs lose their ability to breathe underwater. They move farther inland to live out the rest of their lives, taking advantage of what landlubbing life has to offer, from coconuts to the odd wristwatch. ❯ **How to see them:** Some of the world's largest individuals live on Australia's Christmas Island, where they are protected. Locals on the island nation of Niue, in the southwestern Pacific, offer coconut crab tours, where you can get up close with the crustaceans and learn about their cultural importance.

THE WILD LIFE OF A Coconut Crab Advocate

■ Ruaruhina Teariki Sholan, an Indigenous Polynesian environmentalist and coconut crab advocate, lives on the remote atoll of Rangiroa, in the Tuamotu Islands of French Polynesia. For centuries, her family has had a special connection with the coconut crab, or kaveu. Today, Ruaruhina Teariki Sholan and her family rescue kaveu and release them back into the wild.

• **How has the kaveu population changed since you were young?**
When I was little, I'd go out into the village of Tiputa and we'd see coconut crabs by the church, on the football fields, crossing the roads, on the sand. You could spot them everywhere. You'd have to wait till the evening to see them— it's true that they like to hide during the day—but we'd see the kaveu. Today, in the village, we don't see them anymore at all.

• **Why is the kaveu important in your family?**
The kaveu here in the Tuamotus and for my family in particular is a totem, a taura'a. It's one of our animal protectors, on my grandpa's side. My grandpa Meihea Tipehu is from Tiputa [a village on Rangiroa], and his ancestors communicated with the kaveu and they had a lot of connections to this totem.

For me, the kaveu represents the memories of my ancestors. This animal lived with my ancestors. It delivered news to them, whether good or bad. My ancestors lived during a time when they didn't have the modern communication tools we have today. So there's a spiritual connection with the kaveu.

• **Why is it important to save the kaveu?**
I'd like to change your question. What are we going to leave for our children and grandchildren? There are countries today that have lost

important animals in their life cycle, in their environment. There are animals that have completely disappeared from the earth. When I've left this world, I'd like my children and grandchildren to be able to see the coconut crabs again. To understand their history. I'd like them to know how to prepare and eat them in the traditional way. To perpetuate our culture and our traditions.

One last thing I'd like to add is that my memories tell me we are descendants of a people who were aware of the cycle of life, in an era where they didn't have telephones or electricity or all the things we enjoy today. But our ancestors, they had everything. All because they knew how to live with the environment that surrounded them. And that's how I live with my family today. ■

This interview has been translated from French by Tiare Tuubia.

ANTARCTICA

Southern Bull Kelp

Antarctica's oceanic shuttle bus

◆ For optimum survival on land and at sea, southern bull kelp is strong on the bottom and floaty on the top. At the bottom of the world—Antarctica, New Zealand, and Chile—this kelp grips rocky coastlines with its holdfasts: rootlike protrusions that anchor it in the relentless surf, which can reach 25 feet (7.6 m) in height.

The long, flat fronds—which resemble car-wash mitter curtains—dampen the force of these waves, providing gentler habitat for other shoreline plants and animals. Little isopods called gribbles help too, chewing holes inside the holdfasts that fellow invertebrates can move into. On the shores of Macquarie Island, nearly a hundred species of tiny animals live inside kelp holdfasts, making them the most popular habitat.

If kelp does get ripped from its berth, no matter. Hollow pockets in the fronds make this species exceptionally buoyant, able to float high in the water. Bull kelp often tangles into large rafts, which then ride currents all over the place, from island to island or even continent to continent. When they reach a new shoreline, their descendants take root.

Researchers estimate there might be as many as 70 million bull kelp rafts floating in the ocean at any one time, bringing numerous animals and plants along with them. Kelp raft censuses have found starfish, shellfish, worms, and even intertidal spiders. Some rafts have been seen toting rocks weighing 7 pounds (3 kg).

This well-traveled algae has also floated its way into human history. According to Maori narratives, the navigator Ui-te-Rangiora paddled his canoe, *Te Ivi-o-Atea*, to Antarctica many centuries before any European explorers. How do we know this? When he came back, he told of bare icebergs, arrowroot-white expanses of frozen water, and a giant woman "whose tresses wave about in the waters"—southern bull kelp.

> **How to see them:** Look for bull kelp on beaches in New Zealand, where it often washes up. You'll see thick ribbons as long as 100 feet (30 m), attached to broken-off holdfasts that look like suction cups. Be sure to check for hitchhikers!

RANGE: Coastal Chile, southern New Zealand, and Macquarie Island, Antarctica, along with associated islands

SPECIES: Southern bull kelp (*Durvillaea antarctica*), also known as rimurapa or cochayuyo

Bull kelp in Dusky Sound in New Zealand's Fiordland National Park

HAWAIIAN ISLANDS

- The Hawaiian archipelago has eight main islands: Oʻahu, Maui, Kauaʻi, Lanaʻi, Molokaʻi, Niʻihau, Kahoʻolawe, and Hawaiʻi (aka "the Big Island"). To the northwest of the archipelago's main islands lies a 1,350-mile (2,173 km) stretch of smaller formations known as the Papahānaumokuākea Marine National Monument. Covering 582,578 square miles (1,508,870 sq km), Papahānaumokuākea is bigger than all of the US mainland's national parks combined.

- Before there were cowboys in the American West, there were cowboys in Hawaiʻi. King Kamehameha III invited Mexican vaqueros to teach Hawaiians how to wrangle cattle in the early nineteenth century, and soon Hawaiian cowboys were calling themselves paniolos (a Hawaiian version of the word *español*) as a tribute to their Mexican tutors. Later, Hawaiian paniolos cleaned up at rodeos on the US mainland. Hawaiʻi still has many ranches today, especially on the Big Island.

- All beaches in Hawaiʻi are fully open to the public, making it one of just a handful of US states—and arguably the most scenic—to guarantee this right.

KEEP AN EYE OUT FOR Lots of rainbows. Hawaiʻi's mountain peaks accumulate cumulus clouds and disrupt the airflow of trade winds across the Pacific, causing isolated rainstorms quickly broken up by dazzling tropical sunshine—a perfect recipe for colorful skies.

KEEP AN EAR OUT FOR The distinctive calls of Hawaiʻi's birdlife, like the *yip-yip-yip* of the wetland-loving Hawaiian stilt (aeʻo), the judgmental-sounding sigh of the forest-dwelling ʻamakihi, or the squeaky call of the Pacific golden-plover (kōlea) from urban rooftops.

KEEP A NOSE OUT FOR Fragrant blooms of *Plumeria*, a flower frequently used in Hawaiian leis that has come to symbolize Hawaiʻi for many, though the first specimen of this tree came to the island only in the mid-1800s.

'Akikiki

Some of the last of Hawai'i's famous honeycreepers

LOCATION: Kaua'i, Hawai'i
SPECIES: 'Akikiki, or Kaua'i creeper
(*Oreomystis bairdi*)

◆ If you are lucky and a fearless hiker, you might see one of the few remaining 'akikiki in the wild. It will not be easy.

Before humans arrived, the Hawaiian Islands were quite literally for the birds. With no land mammals around, birds filled most available niches: flightless ducks the size of turkeys grazing on the ground, eagles casting shadows from the air.

The forests in between were ruled by honeycreepers, a stunningly diverse bird group with a whole toolkit's worth of beaks between them. Like the more-celebrated Galápagos finches 5,000 miles (8,000 km) southeast, honeycreeper species prolifer-

An 'akikiki, hanging on

ated through adaptive radiation, diversifying from an ancestral finch into more than 50 different types, each with a specialized bill shape that allowed it to patronize its chosen food source without competition.

The arrival of successive waves of people shook things up. European colonizers in particular were very hard on the honeycreepers, cutting down their forest homes and bringing along egg-eating invasive species like rats and mongooses. There are now only 17 honeycreeper species left.

The 'akikiki, also known as the Kaua'i creeper, is the rarest of these, and among the most unassuming. Fewer than 10 individuals remain in the wild, all living in one patch of the Alaka'i Plateau, a swampy high-elevation forest in northwestern Kaua'i.

Here, the last 'akikiki flit among giant ferns and decomposing tree trunks. Small and agile, like nuthatches, they follow the contours of twisting branches, occasionally hanging upside down. Their pink bills are shaped like tweezers, perfect for levering up bark and extracting tasty insects.

They often forage in ō'hi'a trees and may even take a sip or two of nectar from their bright, brushlike flowers. They nest there, too, building soft cups out of moss and lichen for their small broods.

The main threat to 'akikiki (and several other honeycreeper species) is avian malaria, which was brought into and around Hawai'i by invasive southern house mosquitoes. Native birds here have no natural resistance to the disease. As the climate warms, the mosquitoes have been able to reach higher and higher elevations, where they sniff out birds and bite their exposed legs, bills, or eyes. Having hemmed the 'akikiki into their patch of forest, they continue to menace them.

Researchers are working on a biological control plan for the mosquitoes, including one involving a strain of bacteria that renders the bugs unable to reproduce. In the meantime, a captive breeding program, in which 50 'akikiki are cared for by humans, acts as an insurance policy against the total extinction of these birds, some of the last remaining members of one of evolution's greatest arrays. ❯ **How to see them:** 'Akikiki may disappear from the wild by the time this book is published. If they are still around, they're most likely to be found in the Alaka'i Wilderness Preserve.

Bills, Bills, Bills

Hawai'i's many honeycreepers are thought to have descended from a small flock of rosefinches. These intrepid birds translocated from Asia to the American tropics around 5 million years ago, when the islands of Ni'ihau and Kaua'i were just starting to take shape in the middle of the Pacific Ocean. They found a home with plenty of different foods to choose from and no predators to worry about.

Over about 200,000 to 300,000 years—a pretty short time, evolutionarily speaking—the offspring of these finches spread out and relaxed into a variety of niches, with a variety of special bills. When it comes to demonstrating the sheer creative power of adaptive radiation, Hawai'i's assemblage of 54 living and extinct honeycreeper species outshines even the Galápagos finches (which, after all, number just 14). Here are some examples of their finest nosegear.

• 'Akeke'e (*Loxops caeruleirostris*) have cross-tipped bills that allow them to open the leaf buds of 'ō'hi'a—the forest's most common tree—and reach for small insects.

• Now extinct, Kona grosbeaks (*Chloridops kona*) had chunky, powerful beaks that could break open the hard seeds of naio tree fruits. The powerful cracking sound this produced once reverberated for long distances.

• Lesser 'akialoa (*Akialoa obscura*) had bills with a deep, near-90-degree curve, which they used to glean for bugs and dip into their favorite flowers. They were declared extinct in 1940.

• A very special beak can be a double-edged sword. 'I'iwi (*Vestiaria coccinea*) have a more all-purpose curved beak that can take advantage of several different flower species, which helps explain their continued success—although they, too, are losing ground.

'I'iwi

• Kiwikiu (*Pseudonestor xanthophrys*), or Maui parrotbills, use their severely hooked bills like crowbars, prying up bark and chopping into fruits to find hidden insects. Like the 'akikiki, they are threatened by encroaching mosquitoes.

Kiwikiu

THE WILD LIFE OF A Native Hawaiian Conservationist

◼ Ku'ulei Wong, a former field technician with the Kaua'i Forest Bird Recovery Project (KFBRP) and a Native Hawaiian, is currently pursuing a degree in botany, anthropology, and Hawaiian studies at the University of Hawai'i at Mānoa. She approaches conservation from the perspective that every phenomenon and living thing comes with an identity and a mo'olelo, or story.

• How do you think about your own and your culture's connection to nature?
Kānaka Maoli or Native Hawaiians view our land, 'āina, as an elder sibling: a being we respect and mālama (take care of). In return, it will protect and take care of us. Everything that is done to our land will fall back on us—if not our generation, then the next. When the land is rich with the essentials of life, we too are rich.

This connection comes from one of our origin stories with Papa and Wākea, or a Polynesian version of Mother Earth and Father Sky. Together they created the islands, other gods, and us. This made us related not only to the land but to other divine beings as well.

With the introduction of Western culture, there was a shift in how 'āina was viewed. Westerners saw it as something to conquer, own, and make money [from]—a completely foreign ideology.

- **What is the meaning and importance of ancestral guardians for Native Hawaiians?**

In Hawaiian culture, we have this significant spiritual being called an 'aumakua, or ancestral guardian. It is believed that 'aumakua are family members who have passed into the next realm to protect and take care of the family or a specific place. In some cases, these beings are kākū'ai, or transfigured, into animals, insects, stones, and plants.

The pueo, or the Hawaiian short-eared owl (*Asio flammeus sandwichensis*), is one of my 'aumakua. Seeing a pueo is a hō'ailona, or sign, that danger could be nearby, but he is watching over you and protecting you. Lives have been saved because of them.

- **How do Native Hawaiians think about birds?**

Our native birds connect us to our culture in a deeply religious and spiritual way. They are the beings that can touch the heavens and come back down. Some species of birds are considered other forms of akua, or gods.

To be in the presence of our native birds means to be in the presence of our akua. They remind me of a past when our 'āina (land) was rich and full of life, a time before Western influences, a time when Hawaiian culture was thriving. Every time I am in their presence, I am incredibly grateful.

- **Did some birds also give valuable information to people?**

Traditionally, 'elepaio (*Chasiempis sclateri*), our native flycatcher, was used as a form of quality control for canoe building. These birds primarily feast on bugs and grubs.

If an 'elepaio is present and feeding on a tree, it is assumed that the tree has many holes, so it is not appropriate for a water vessel.

- **What would losing these species mean from a cultural aspect?**

We lose us. Our origin stories tell us everything that is living is connected to us. [Our native species] are used in our art, our homes, our tools, our stories, and our food. When we lose them, a large chunk of our culture disappears. Therefore, it is important to share these mana'o (thoughts), because once a species such as the 'akikiki is lost, they are near to impossible to recover.

In recent years KFBRP has been doing more events with our keiki (children). The fire I have seen in some of these little scientists really makes me hopeful that our birds may have a fighting chance. ■

Plant-Sampling Chain-Saw Drone

A flying blade joins the war against a killer fungus.

◆ The 'ōhi'a tree is one of Hawai'i's most iconic plants and endemic to the six largest islands in the chain. Able to grow everywhere from wet bogs to rocky lava flows, these trees make up half of the native canopy on Hawai'i Island. Honeycreepers nest in them, mosses hang off them, tree snails lumber up them, and people love them.

Unfortunately, so does a fungus called *Ceratocystis lukuohia*. After sneaking in through broken branches or scraped bark, this intruder colonizes the trees' vascular systems, interrupting their ability to move water around. The resulting condition, called rapid 'ōhi'a death, has killed upward of 90 percent of the trees on some parts of Hawai'i Island.

To learn more about this disease, test treatments for it, and prevent its spread, it's necessary to diagnose infected trees as quickly as possible. The leaves of fungus-infected 'ōhi'a trees turn a dull reddish brown—from above, they stick out in the green canopy like spots on lungs. But drought and other conditions can also cause leaf reddening.

The only way to know if the fungus is present is to take a wood sample—something that's often difficult to do in Hawai'i's forests, which stretch up mountains and down ravines. So researchers are developing a new tool to help: a flying chain saw.

LOCATION: 'Ōhi'a trees are found on the six largest Hawaiian islands. The drone is currently being flown only on Hawai'i Island.

SPECIES: 'Ōhi'a (*Metrosideros polymorpha*), and *Ceratocystis lukuohia*

'Ōhi'a growing on Hawai'i's Kīlauea volcano.

Ryan Perroy, a professor of geography and environmental science at the University of Hawai'i at Hilo, came to the island in 2013. Work with camera drones gave him a sweeping view of his new home's native forests, as well as a sense of the scale and speed of the problems facing them. Keeping track of forest decline, while necessary, "gets a little depressing," he says. He wondered if there was a way to put the drones to active use.

And so—inspired by work done at ETH Zurich, a research university in Switzerland, as well as an international competition for rapid 'ōhi'a death solutions—Perroy and his students decided to outfit a camera drone with some extra gear. Their drone add-on wields a rotating saw at the end of a long pole, along with a robotic claw that can grasp samples during cutting and carry them while the drone zips them back. While previous drone sawing attachments have only been able to collect twigs, this one can handle the thicker branches necessary for diagnosis. Perroy and his team call their device Kūkūau, after a type of shore crab with a strong grip.

Kūkūau is controlled by teams of three: one licensed drone pilot, one remote saw-and-claw operator, and one observer, who watches for safety hazards like curious 'io (Hawaiian hawks). They follow current Federal Aviation Administration regulations, which require them to fly only within their own line of sight and stay out of certain airspaces.

While the tool is still in the early stages of development, Perroy hopes that using drones for certain conservation interventions will make them safer and more efficient. He and his students are working on a follow-up drone that can help with another conservation project: releasing a controlling mite onto an invasive species, strawberry guava, that is currently outcompeting native plants. "It definitely is different than taking photos," Perroy says. ❯ **How to see them:** Only licensed drone operators can fly Kūkūau, but 'ōhi'a are prevalent on the six largest Hawaiian islands.

Carnivorous Inchworms

Deadly masters of the "bend and snap"

RANGE: Throughout the Hawaiian archipelago

SPECIES: Eighteen species of the pug moth caterpillar (*Eupithecia* spp.)

◆ Chances are you're not particularly scared of inchworms. In most of the world, members of this caterpillar subset are adorably benign, scooting along branches and nibbling on vegetation until it's time for them to cocoon up and become moths. Even the most bug-squeamish can generally appreciate the tickle of an inchworm's feet on the back of their hand.

In Hawai'i, though, it's a whole different story. Of the archipelago's 20 *Eupithecia* inchworm species, 18 are carnivorous, subsisting on other creatures of their scale, which they catch and eat alive. These enfants terribles have done what their brethren never thought to: successfully weaponized the cute little inchworm body plan.

All inchworms have a set of legs on each end, and none in the middle. This causes their famous looping gait, which scrunches the worms' bodies into and out of an inverted U shape as they travel. It also allows them to stabilize themselves with their hind legs while waggling the rest of their bodies up and around to figure out their next move.

Hawai'i's carnivorous versions do all of this with their own special twist: Those normally tickly front legs have evolved into sharp-tipped appendages that, when flexed, join to form a kind of claw from hell. Meanwhile, sensitive hairs on their rears act as trip wires, alerting them to the presence of prey.

A carnivorous inchworm on the hunt will camouflage himself on a twig or leaf, holding tightly with his hind legs. When an unsuspecting passerby, like a fly or ant, bumps into his butt, the inchworm's flexible body turns into a spring trap. The inchworm snaps backward, snatches his prey with his claw vortex, then straightens back out and goes on to devour his catch alive, sometimes eyes-first.

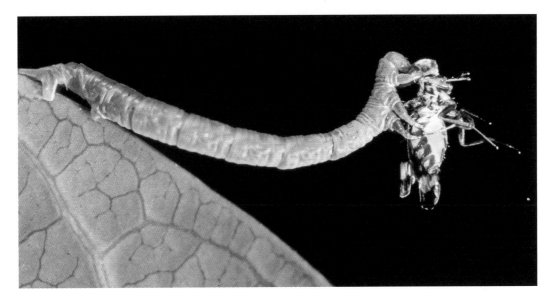

Exactly what route these inchworms took from herbivory to carnivory is still murky; their unusual diet wasn't even known to science until the 1970s. Since then, different Hawaiian species within the genus *Eupithecia* have been observed preying on everything from cockroaches and crickets to aphids and spiders. Meanwhile, an entirely different kind of Hawaiian caterpillar, *Hyposmocoma molluscivora*, has been seen catching snails in webs and eating them from the inside out. Very hungry, indeed. **> How to see them:** Notoriously well camouflaged, Hawai'i's carnivorous inchworms live in wet forests and scrublands. Look for a twig with a suspicious set of claws.

This bug never saw it coming.

Featured Bugs

The Hawaiian Islands are crawling with invertebrates found nowhere else on Earth—roughly 6,000 species of them. After millennia of evolutionary dice rolls, a number now go against the grain. They include the following.

FLIGHTLESS FLIES: Like birds, flies that find themselves on islands occasionally find that the cost of wings outweighs their benefits and end up downsizing. Hawai'i has more flightless fly species than anywhere of comparable size, including the crane fly *Dicranomyia gloria*, which stalks its prey through leaf litter on stilt-like legs, and the tiny *Campsicnemus hao*, one of the only species able to survive among introduced ants. Many flightless flies live on windy mountaintops, where airworthy wings might get them blown away.

SMILING SPIDERS: Half of Hawai'i's spiders are unique to the islands. One species, known as happy-face spiders (*Theridion grallator*), comes in a number of color and shape morphs. Their abdomens may look like colorful shields, the Eye of Sauron, or smiling yellow balloons. Researchers think this variation may help them confuse their honeycreeper predators, who don't know exactly what to look for.

LANDLUBBER DAMSELFLIES: Damselflies are usually born in water, and that's true for most of Hawai'i's species, which lay their eggs everywhere from tumbling waterfall faces to the small pools that collect in the pockets of native plants. But one species, *Megalagrion oahuense*, is entirely terrestrial: Its naiads grow up in the soft leaf litter that gathers beneath specific ferns.

SILENT CRICKETS: Hawai'i's oceanic field crickets (*Teleogryllus oceanicus*) once filled the night with sonorous chirps, just like their fellows around the globe. But in addition to females, their noise began attracting a species of parasitoid fly (*Ormia ochracea*). Now the most successful males are the quietest, and it's crickets for the crickets' song.

SINGING SNAILS: Like the honeycreepers, many of Hawai'i's candy-striped, long-lived tree snail species have fallen victim to habitat loss and invaders. According to Native Hawaiian stories, the snails, known as kāhuli, once sang in the forest—a popular hula is sung from the perspective of a snail trilling to a plover, asking for a drink of dew. People debate the source of the singing, attributing it to nearby crickets or the wind blowing over snail shells, but no one is sure.

Hawaiian Monk Seals

Hawai'i's "dogs of the sea" bark—and bite.

RANGE: The main and northwestern Hawaiian islands

SPECIES: Hawaiian monk seal (*Neomonachus schauinslandi*)

◆ Forget Hollywood stars or social media influencers. One of the most photographed sunbathers on Waikiki's crowded shores is a Hawaiian monk seal mom known as Rocky.

Monk seals get their English name from the folds of skin around their necks, which call to mind a monk's loose cowl. Their Hawaiian name is perhaps more apt: 'īlio holo i ka uaua, "dog that runs in rough water."

These playful and curious creatures have called Hawai'i's waters home for an estimated 13 million years—longer than some of the islands themselves have existed. This impressive run almost ended in the nineteenth century, as hunters seeking meat and fur drove the seals nearly to extinction. More recently, conservation efforts have brought numbers up to just under 1,600.

Most Hawaiian monk seals prefer the unpopulated shorelines of the northwestern Hawaiian islands. But some 400 call the main Hawaiian islands home, including Rocky. She has twice given birth on Waikiki, triggering a full-scale response from conservationists, who cordon off a section of Hawai'i's most famous shoreline so that mom can raise her pup in peace.

Seal motherhood is a big job. Like the dogs they're named for, nursing seal moms have been known to chase after swimmers who inadvertently approach them, or to bark menacingly at beachwalkers who venture too close. They are both fierce and self-sacrificing—for up to seven weeks while they're nursing, monk seal moms don't eat, losing about a third of their body weight as they focus on protecting and nourishing their young.

Once successfully weaned, young seals have no shortage of threats to contend with, most of them human-caused. Seals may get entangled in fishing nets, starve in overfished waters, or lose pups to rising sea levels. Biologists are also worried about their low genetic variation, a consequence of inbreeding. In rare cases, they've even been intentionally killed, incidents that bewilder and infuriate those racing to save this ancient species. ❯ **How to see them: If you're lucky, in the wild—but keep your distance. For a sure encounter, head to the Waikiki Aquarium.**

A Hawaiian monk seal hangs out on Sand Island.

Nēnē and ʻŌhelo

Linking island landscapes through flight, song, and poop

RANGE: Hawaiian islands of Oʻahu, Maui, Kauaʻi, Molokaʻi, and Hawaiʻi

SPECIES: Nēnē (*Branta sandvicensis*) and ʻŌhelo (*Vaccinium reticulatum*)

◆ In the alpine shrublands and grasslands of the Hawaiian archipelago's largest islands, the world's rarest geese roam. As they amble through low-lying vegetation in search of greens and seeds to graze, they communicate with low, gentle murmurs: *Neeeeeee, neeeeeee.*

Considered guardians of the ecosystem, the nēnē is Hawaiʻi's official state bird. The goose is said to be a favorite of Pele, the Hawaiian volcano goddess, and to spiritually connect two very different island landscapes: the coasts that ribbon the edges, and the volcanic mountains at the centers.

Despite a misconception that they are flightless, the geese regularly wing themselves thousands of feet from the shores up to the mountaintops, where their tough feet—less webbed than those of other geese—allow them to traverse the rough lava floodplains that cap the volcanoes.

These heights are where nēnēs feed on some of their favorite native fruits, including red, round ʻōhelo berries. The trailblazing ʻōhelo, a cousin of the cranberry, was one of the first plants to make a home in the high-elevation volcanic landscapes. Today, it also thrives in mid-elevation shrublands.

Humans who also enjoy ʻōhelo berries, generally in jams or tarts, have nēnēs to thank. The two species enjoy a mutualistic relationship: The geese eat the berries and then, on the waddle, poop all over, spreading ʻōhelo seeds across grasslands and rocky mountains alike and ushering forth the next generations of the tasty plant.

Nēnēs share this relationship with a few different native fruits, not just ʻōhelo. The name of one such fruit, the kūkaenēnē, gives credit where it's due: It translates from Hawaiian to mean "nēnē poop." **❯ How to see them:** Nēnē have been reintroduced in secluded areas around Hawaiʻi's national parks, though the birds frequently travel to low-elevation recreational areas, including golf courses and hotel resorts. When driving in Hawaiʻi, exercise caution, as the geese are known to wander near, and sometimes cross, roads.

Bee Hummingbirds

The world's smallest birds are larger than life.

RANGE: Cuba, including the Isla de la Juventud

SPECIES: Bee hummingbird (*Mellisuga helenae*), also known as zunzuncito

◆ A flash of shimmering color, a whirring sound, tiny wings beating too fast to track—is that an insect you've spotted, darting from flower to flower at the edge of the forest?

Maybe. But if you're in Cuba, and are very lucky, it might instead be a bee hummingbird.

If species had trophy cases, this hummingbird's would be full. Officially the world's smallest bird, each one is only about the size of an AA battery. Males weigh less than a US dime, while females tip the scales at a little more than a penny. Researchers credit these hummingbirds with the largest proportion-ate heart weight of any animal, as well as the highest body temperature.

This big heart goes incredibly fast—about 1,200 beats per minute—to power the hummingbird's busy lifestyle. These miniature flyers spend more of their life in the air than any other animal. Each individual may visit some 1,500 different flowers daily, consuming the equivalent of her body weight in nectar and insects while the sun is up and sleeping in a state of torpor to save energy during the night. (A bee hummingbird requires 10 times more calories relative to body size than a marathon runner.)

A bee hummingbird's heart beats 1,200 times per minute.

Along the way, these tiny birds rack up more achievements. They can reach speeds of up to 30 miles per hour (48 kph), stop suddenly in midair, hover in place, and fly in all directions, including straight up, backward, and upside down. Everyday wing speed reaches 80 beats per minute, about eight times as fast as the blink of a human eye.

During the late spring mating season, everything ramps up even further. Males—already garbed handsomely in iridescent greenish blue—develop brilliant red coloring on their heads and throats, including long feathers that sprout from their heads like a glorious avian version of muttonchop sideburns. A courting male's wings can beat an extraordinary 200 times per second as he performs elaborate ascents and dives while opening and closing his tail feathers like a fan.

The Island Rule

Landing on an island can be the evolutionary equivalent of stepping into Wonderland. Some species shrink, while others grow considerably larger. Scientists call these trends *insular dwarfism* and *insular gigantism*—or, more succinctly, the "island rule."

Though it wasn't officially defined until the 1970s, researchers have been aware of the island rule for well over a century. Among the concept's early champions was Welsh paleontologist Dorothea Bate, who in 1902, on the island of Cyprus, unearthed one of the first dwarf elephant skeletons known to science. The elephant—just one of a number of prehistoric mini-pachyderms whose remains have been found on islands around the Mediterranean—was about the size of a pony. Bate went on to describe the remains of a new species of mouse-goat, as well as extinct dwarf hippos and giant tortoises.

What is it about island living that makes a species get bigger or smaller? An animal's size determines how much food it needs, what it can eat, where it's able to live, and which other species pose a threat. Jumbo herbivores are harder for predators to tackle, but they need to eat a lot in order to survive; tiny scavengers can easily find food, but they make a tasty meal for many larger animals.

When a new species first arrives on an island, it might find that its current niche is already occupied. However,

a new niche might be readily available—if the species were slightly smaller or slightly larger. That's where selective pressure comes in. Dwarf elephants on Cyprus, for example, likely shrank because food was scarcer on their island home compared with mainland Europe and Africa. Conversely, some giants, like the extinct dog-sized rabbit *Nuralagus rex*, which once lived on the island of Minorca, may have evolved to be larger and bolder in the absence of predators.

Selective pressure is very strong on islands, which can lead to extreme results. "The very nature of being on an island means there's less interchanging and mixing," says Michael Benton, a paleontologist at the University of Bristol who studies island dwarfism in dinosaurs. This sends evolution into overdrive, enabling new species to arise up to three times faster than they would on the mainland. Today there are many island dwellers who seem supersized or shrink-rayed, from Komodo dragons to nanochameleons.

Unfortunately, island dwarves and giants are particularly vulnerable to ecological shifts. The dodo, a giant flightless pigeon native to Mauritius, was famously hunted to extinction after humans colonized the island in the 1600s. And the last of the dwarf elephants disappeared some 6,000 years ago, probably due to changing climates.

After mating, the female builds a nest no larger than a golf ball in which she lays two eggs, each the size of a coffee bean. Teeny-tiny nestlings pop out three weeks later, ready for their ordinary yet record-setting lives. **❯ How to see them:** Because of habitat depletion, your best chance of spotting the bee hummingbird lies in the far western and eastern provinces of Cuba, as well as in and around Zapata Swamp. Look for them in woodland, shrubs, and gardens with mature growth and plenty of flowering plants—and if you think you've seen a large bug, be sure to look twice!

Hurricane-Proof Lizards

Tough enough to outlast Category Five winds

RANGE: Islands across the Caribbean
SPECIES: Brown anole (*Anolis sagrei*), as well as other Caribbean anole species

◆ On good days, a Caribbean anole lizard lounges around, enjoying beachy vibes and a clear blue sky. All he needs to do is find insects to slurp or crunch, scram when a predator approaches, and look for mates.

Then there are the bad days. Once every few years, storms like 2017's Hurricane Irma slam Caribbean islands with screaming winds of up to 170 miles per hour (274 kph). Birds can flee, and small mammals can take cover underground. But anoles have a different strategy: Their anatomy helps the tiny lizards white-knuckle it through storms without getting blown away.

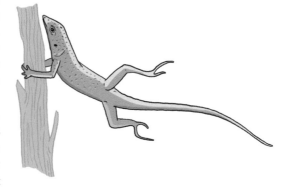

Say an anole clinging to a tree starts to feel strong gusts. First he moves to the downwind side of a branch. Then, as the wind picks up, the lizard hugs his legs and belly close to the branch, gripping as hard as it can. If his back legs blow free, the lizard will continue to cling with his strong front limbs, the back half of his body flailing like a reptilian windsock.

To understand how they manage this, researchers from Harvard University lassoed wild Caribbean anoles and brought them to a lab, where they filmed them struggling to hang on to sticks in the face of a leaf blower. They then modeled the process with the same kind of aerodynamic simulations used to design race cars and fighter jets.

Real hurricanes are a life-and-death evolutionary test: Hang on, or the storm could brain you against a tree or toss you into the ocean. The researchers found that, compared with the full pool of anoles on a given island right before a hurricane, those lizards who survive tend to have big toepads for more secure gripping, and shorter, stubbier back thighs that don't catch as much wind.

Their children inherit the big toepads, which in turn seem to come from more distant ancestors: Anoles on islands that have been hit by several big hurricanes in the last 70 years appear to have, on average, larger toepads than their relatives on other islands that haven't faced a direct hit. A Caribbean anole's feet, then, can be a local history lesson, holding the memory of a very, very bad day. **❯ How to see them:** You can find anoles throughout the Caribbean, often on branches sunning themselves—and very occasionally hanging on for dear life.

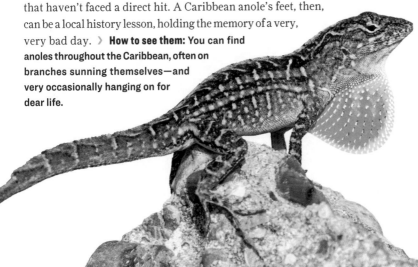

Sea Wolves

Canids or marine mammals?

RANGE: Islands and coastlines in the Pacific Northwest, between southern Alaska and southern British Columbia

SPECIES: Sea wolf (*Canis lupus*), aka coastal island wolf

◆ The creek looks like a crime scene. Decapitated salmon lie haphazardly along the banks. A raven picks at the remains. The culprit? wSea wolves.

In the fall, when the salmon return to rivers across the coastlines and islands of the Pacific Northwest, the sea wolves gorge. A single pack can eat hundreds of fish in one night. Up to 85 percent of a sea wolf's diet can be fish and other marine life—barnacles, crabs, clams, mussels, herring eggs, and whatever else washes up on shore. They'll even pounce on unsuspecting seals taking refuge on land.

Sea wolves are born to swim. Packs island-hop in search of food, sometimes swimming 8 miles (13 km) at a time to new islands. Pups as young as four months swim with their pack, dog-paddling among archipelagos.

For the Indigenous people who live on this coast, sea wolves are an important cultural icon, featured in art, stories, and architecture. To the Wolf Clans of the Tlingit, Tsimshian, Nisga'a, and other groups, sea wolves represent loyalty and strong family ties. The Tseshaht tell a story of a supernatural sea wolf named Kukuwanchis who transforms into an orca when he jumps into the water.

Western scientists are only just catching on to how special these wolves are. At the turn of the century, researchers began closely studying coastal sea wolf populations, largely by collecting samples of their poop. They've concluded that these wolves make up a distinct population of gray wolves, with their unique seafood diet, smaller stature, and thinner coats undergirded by genetic differences from their inland cousins.

As for the decapitated salmon, no one knows for sure why sea wolves eat only the heads. It could be because they've learned the bodies can be contaminated with tapeworms. Or maybe the fatty heads are simply the tastiest part. **❯ How to see them:** These wolves travel through dense coastal rainforests and can be hard to see. The best time to catch them is when they emerge along wide-open beaches in search of food. During the fall, they can be found around the rivers where salmon spawn.

A sea wolf surveys the water off of Vancouver Island, Canada.

Arctic Woolly Bears

Prolonged adolescence on tundra islands

RANGE: Primarily the islands of the Arctic Archipelago in Nunavut, Canada, and the coastal plain of Greenland. Subspecies have been found on Wrangel Island, Russia, and in the alpine tundra of the southwest Yukon, Canada.
SPECIES: Arctic woolly bear moth caterpillar (*Gynaephora groenlandica*)

◆ For most caterpillars, life is short. They eat fast, grow fast, and turn into butterflies or moths in just a few weeks.

Not Arctic woolly bears. These chunky, patient insects spend seven years developing from egg to moth in one of the harshest environments on Earth, the Arctic tundra. They do it by packing all their growth into brief, sun-drenched bacchanals—and spending the rest of their time frozen solid, like inch-long Han Solos.

One of the largest terrestrial insects in the Arctic, the Arctic woolly bear is a plush toy of a caterpillar, covered in a thick coat of long hair in rich shades of tan and reddish brown. It's most frequently found in coastal Greenland and on the islands of the Canadian Arctic Archipelago. Scientists have had trouble getting to know the species—it's hard to understand a creature that passes most of its life as a small, hairy block of ice.

Recent study of the caterpillar's instars has shed some light. An instar is the period between molts, when a caterpillar does all its eating, growing, and maturing. The Arctic woolly bear goes through approximately seven instars—one per year—to reach its adult form, the Arctic moth.

Each year's development takes place in less than a month. The Arctic woolly bear emerges from hibernation in early June, when the snow melts on the tundra. With the sun shining day and night, vegetation starts to green up. Among the earliest plants to push out new growth is this caterpillar's favorite food, the Arctic willow, a tiny, inconspicuous shrub that grows close to the ground.

An Arctic woolly bear caterpillar enjoying a rare day out

The caterpillar spends about three weeks nibbling on willow leaves and shoots and basking on the tundra's sun-warmed rocks while it digests. Around the end of June, it crawls back into clefts in the tundra rocks and spins a silken hibernaculum, a kind of double-layered sleeping bag that shields it from parasites. There it stays until the next June, its body protected by a natural antifreeze.

In the Arctic woolly bear's seventh summer, the routine changes. The newly awake caterpillar becomes a pupa, the form in which it changes from caterpillar to moth. After two weeks, a gray, hairy, and fairly nondescript moth emerges. For the next couple of weeks, the moth and its kindred generation flutter about the tundra, living off their fat, mating, and laying eggs. Then they are gone.

The eggs hatch in late July or early August. With autumn already creeping over the tundra and most plants withering, the newborn caterpillars, starting the cycle over again, retreat into cracks in the tundra rocks and vegetation and spin tiny silken hibernacula. There they settle for the first of many long winters, just as their parents did before them. **How to see them:** The only time these caterpillars can be seen is in June in the High Arctic. If you get there, look for fuzzy guys nibbling, making the most of their time in the sun.

ALEUTIAN ISLANDS

- The 69 islands and countless tiny islets of the Aleutians form an upside-down arc across the Pacific, like a jump rope held slack by southern Alaska on one side and the Kamchatka Peninsula on the other. They form the southern border of the Bering Sea.

- Like most of the world's islands, the Aleutians are almost all volcanic, composed of lava that has bubbled up from between undersea tectonic plates. Some of the chain's volcanoes are still active, including Mount Shishaldin, which last erupted in 2020.

- The Unangax̂, the Indigenous people of the Aleutians, have lived on some of these islands for at least 9,000 years. Over that time, they have developed a number of creative and cooperative fishing traditions to grapple with large animals in small boats at sea. The Unangax̂ hunt sea lions, for example, for the useful materials they provide, including bones for tools, whiskers for decorating chiefs' hats, and intestines for waterproof parkas and boat covers.

KEEP AN EYE OUT FOR Sperm whales "logging" in the waters between the islands. A group of this social species will all rest on the surface facing the same direction, like a flotilla of supersized driftwood.

KEEP AN EAR OUT FOR Raucous burbles, trills, and chitters from some of the largest seabird colonies in North America. Crested auklets with cartoonish orange grins, least auklets with startled-looking stares, and dozens of other bird species nest in huge, noisy aggregations that can reach more than a million strong.

KEEP A NOSE OUT FOR The fishy stench of seabird guano—which, as detailed elsewhere in this section, is rich in both history and nutrients. Here in the Aleutians, it transforms otherwise barren islands into riots of greenery.

Bald Eagles of Unalaska

Day-to-day life with America's national bird

LOCATION: Unalaska, Alaska
SPECIES: Bald eagle
(*Haliaeetus leucocephalus*)

◆ For most American birders, a bald eagle is a rare and thrilling sight—that broad sweep of dark wings soaring through the blue, bolstered further by the grandeur of national symbolism.

For residents of Unalaska, the population center of the Aleutian Islands, a bald eagle is in some ways more like a very large pigeon. Hundreds of them nest along the city's roads, swoop over its backyards, and dumpster-dive behind its supermarkets. "They're so ubiquitous," says Suzi Golodoff, an Unalaska resident who spent years as a naturalist guide. Taking outsiders for tours, she notes, "I'd be pointing birds out to people and I'd just drive past eagles, not really seeing them."

Bald eagles are scavengers and fishers rather than hunters. Unalaska's miles of coastline and salmon streams support a large resident population, but its eagle capacity is artificially bolstered by the fishing port of Dutch Harbor, which hosts a billion dollars' worth of seafood trade every year. Between the harbor and nearby processing plants, "there's this incredible amount of scraps for them to eat," says Golodoff.

Birders have counted as many as 800 eagles in and around the city in a single day. (This is around the same number as existed in the entire Lower 48 in 1963, before the pesticide DDT was banned.) This adds up to lots of encounters, which range from majestic to goofy to dangerous. Subsistence fishers cleaning salmon on the beach may end up with several dozen onlookers, white-feathered heads cocked in their direction. Officials put up signs under roadside nests, warning joggers to steer clear lest they get beaned by a protective eagle parent.

Eagles will perch on cars and roofs and occasionally end up inside a supermarket. People add to the confusion by feeding them—Golodoff once had a coffee cup knocked out of her hand by a bird expecting a handout. "It startled the heck out of me, but it left me grinning," she says.

For Golodoff, living among eagles hasn't lessened their grandeur. What she has learned of their day-to-day habits—their loyalty to their lifelong partners, their resilience in tough times—makes up for any lost loftiness. This is true even when they're covered in fish guts. "They spend their entire lives trying to clean things up," she says. "It's not their fault humans make a mess." **〉 How to see them: Head to Unalaska. Golodoff recommends watching bald eagles circle fishing or crabbing boats as they come into the harbor.**

A few of Unalaska's many bald eagles, passing the time

Walrus Haulouts

Very spiky cuddle puddles

◆ In 2014, 35,000 Pacific walruses gathered on the northwestern Alaska coast near the Iñupiat village of Point Lay. Never in modern times had so many of these mustachioed, car-sized marine mammals congregated in one place. The grunting, snorting herd drew international media attention and concern from environmentalists.

Haulouts like these are becoming increasingly common. As one of the ocean's most ice-dependent species, walruses use floes to display, give birth, and rest between bouts of worm and clam foraging. They do these things on land only when ice is not available.

RANGE: Coasts and islands of the Pacific Arctic in the Bering and Chukchi Seas, from Alaska to the Russian Far East

SPECIES: Pacific walrus (*Odobenus rosmarus*)

Walruses haul out on Round Island, Alaska.

Song of the Walrus

Male Pacific walruses have a little-known talent: They can sing. Tucked within a walrus's bulky neck and shoulders are a pair of air sacs called pharyngeal pouches. When a male is feeling expressive, he fills these with air—up to 13 gallons' (50 L) worth, the capacity of your average kitchen trash can—and then squeezes them, letting out a song like a low, mournful wind chime. Males can sing underwater as well as on land, with the best crooners attracting the most females. They may also blow up their pouches when they want to rest at the water's surface, using them as built-in life jackets.

Now summer sea ice in the Arctic is disappearing, forcing these highly social pinnipeds onto land earlier, more frequently, and in larger numbers. Every decade, summer sea ice shrinks by 13 percent, according to the National Snow and Ice Data Center. It could disappear by 2040.

The loss of ice means longer, more arduous swims from the new rest areas on the coast to foraging grounds, which could be especially challenging for calves. And there are risks when so many animals gather in one place on land. Walruses are sensitive to sounds and smells, for example. If they are spooked by a ship, a polar bear, or a low-flying plane, they can stampede and trample one another.

Walruses have sustained the lives and cultures of Indigenous people in Alaska and Russia for thousands of years, and continue to do so. But hunters, too, are dealing with a changing environment, with thinner and more dangerous pack ice, and they are having to venture farther afield to find walruses—with rare exceptions, they do not hunt at haulout sites. Now, facing these and other effects of climate change, Indigenous hunters and scientists are working together to learn more about walrus adaptability, resilience, and conservation. ⟩ **How to see them:** Treating haulouts as tourist spectacles could cause stampedes, plus strain resources in the remote villages stewarding the sites. Interested members of the public may view walruses in person in Bristol Bay, Alaska, or view live webcams during the summer season.

THE WILD LIFE OF **A Walrus Watcher**

■ For nearly 30 years as a government scientist, Anthony Fischbach has observed walruses from many vantage points—as a harvest monitor with Alaska Natives, as a radio tagger in collaboration with scientists from Russia, and now through satellite imagery. All methods are meant to answer one surprisingly difficult question: "How many walruses are there, and how are they doing?"

● **How did you start working with walruses?**

I started studying walruses as a harvest monitor. There are people who feel that the [walrus] harvest is wrong, and then other people who have been conducting this harvest for thousands of years, where it's central to their identity and their food security. So there's a conflict there. And then a government agency steps in and says, "We'll bring the facts"—we'll make note of how many animals are being harvested, the nature of the harvest, how many females and young versus males, and what that may mean for the sustainability of the harvest.

● **What questions are you trying to answer with your surveys?**

None of the questions we have now are really new: How many walruses are there, and how are they doing? Is the harvest sustainable? What are the challenges for maintaining a healthy population? These are the questions people have had for a long time.

● **How did you develop your latest counting methods?**

We can count walruses on the ice or on the shore, but we don't know what proportion are in the water. We worked with some whale biologists, who came up with ways to harpoon a whale with a small barb that holds on a [tracking] radio. We used a crossbow—basically a big rubber band that lets us put a radio onto a walrus without drugs. The radios we use are proportionally smaller than my wristwatch and can be carried for weeks before falling off. We put out a lot of radios using that method, and we were able to get some idea of the population size from that.

[Meanwhile], we would fly small drones over the walruses to get precise counts. We can repeat [a drone] survey a bunch of times. We can do it, our Russian colleagues can do it, we can harmonize our methods, and we can get a very

precise population estimate using that methodology.

We were ready to apply that [method] over on the Russian side to see if we can tighten up our confidence intervals. And then, well, we lost our ability to work with our Russian colleagues [in 2022]. So we're waiting for that to change.

● **What is it like to experience a walrus haulout in person?**

They look tired when they come onshore. And they're very large animals. If you can imagine the largest human you can conceive of, like a linebacker, and you take seven of these and you duct-tape them together and lay them down—that would be one female walrus. If you can get 11 of them, you'd have one male walrus adult.

We've counted, on the American side, up to 58,000 walruses at one time resting together. And it's not like they're scattered across the beach—they're almost on top of each other. It's pretty endearing to watch them. It's very clear that there's a lot of social interaction. They not only vocalize in the water for breeding displays, but they also seem to vocalize to maintain contact. ■

Life on Ice

Ice caps may seem as barren as frosted moonscapes. But these frigid floes are actually floating refuges for some of the hardiest creatures on the planet, from cold-tolerant microbes to prowling polar bears. Here are a few resilient species that call these seasonal—and shrinking—habitats home.

MICROSCOPIC COMMUNITY · When seawater freezes, salt is expelled as the ice crystals fuse together. On its way out, the extra salt carves channels and pores into the ice, creating a labyrinth of briny habitats. Here, a rugged assemblage of minuscule creatures, all capable of surviving salinity spikes and bitter temperatures, make their home. Conditions are so unforgiving that researchers use these icy chambers to think about what life could be like on extraterrestrial ice-covered moons. Some of the most common occupants are single-celled diatoms, housed in baguette-shaped silica shells. In large quantities, these photosynthesizing algae give the ice a brownish hue. Munching on the diatoms are grazers like miniature crustaceans, flatworms, and protists, alongside bacteria and a slew of viruses.

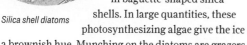
Silica shell diatoms

Ice algae

ICE ALGAE · Roughly 1,000 species of ice-living or sympagic algae grow in clumps along the bottoms of floes or inside their networks of brine channels. Just like plants growing on solid ground, algae rely on sunlight to practice photosynthesis. In this case, ice-dwelling algae make use of the faint glimmers of light that penetrate the ice, like ferns growing in the shadow of a towering tree.

Many species of ice algae are packed with fats, making them a pantry staple for this ecosystem. Everything from transparent gastropods called sea angels to planktonic crustaceans called copepods nibble on ice algae. These grazers are then picked off by larger animals like polar cod, sending the algae's fats further up the food chain. Eventually, they work their way to the very top—a 2016 analysis of fats in the tissues of polar bears concluded that 86 percent of this apex carnivore's diet could be traced to ice algae.

Along the fringes of ice floes are communities of floating algae called phytoplankton. When the ice melts each summer, the volume of phytoplankton in the water explodes in the increasing sunlight. This algal "bloom," as it's called, feeds a rising population of zooplankton, which in turn attracts fish, whales, and seabirds. But warming temperatures are shifting the timing of seasons at the poles, potentially throwing this calibrated feeding frenzy out of sync.

ANTARCTIC KRILL · (*Euphausia superba*) Antarctic krill are among the most numerous animal species on Earth. These tiny crustaceans, which look like bug-eyed prawns, are inescapable in the waters around Antarctica, sometimes amassing in such density that they give the ocean a rust-colored hue that can be seen from space. While each individual krill weighs a small fraction of an ounce, an estimated 400 million tons of krill are swimming around in the Southern Ocean.

Antarctic krill.

Krill are a key cog in the Antarctic food web. As their bright green guts attest, they have a taste for algae. In turn, krill are a seafood staple for everything from fish and squid to penguins and whales.

However, life below the sea ice is tough for krill. During the frigid winter months, when thick ice makes algal blooms scarce, Antarctic krill may go months without food. So they downsize, harvesting the proteins within their body as fuel. This causes them to shrink and molt into successively smaller shells. At the end of the grueling Antarctic winter, adult krill resemble their juvenile forms again.

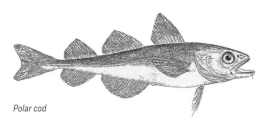

Polar cod

POLAR COD • (*Boreogadus saida*) One of the most important creatures in the Arctic is the polar cod, perhaps the world's northernmost fish. Topping out at around 16 inches (40 cm), with bulging eyes, this fish swims at the crux of the Arctic food web, acting as the connective tissue between trophic levels. As the cod snap up zooplankton and shrimp, they themselves become salty snacks for seabirds and marine mammals like narwhals and beluga whales.

Nearly the entire polar cod life cycle revolves around ice. During spawning, each female cod releases up to 21,000 eggs under the sea ice for nearby males to fertilize. After these fertilized eggs hatch, the juvenile cod retreat into crevices along the underside of the ice to avoid predators and bulk up on tiny crustaceans and algae.

Polar cod are able to live inside the Arctic pack ice thanks to a suite of specialized proteins in their blood that act as natural antifreeze agents. Similar antifreeze proteins are found in fish that make their home in the Southern Ocean, including the Antarctic silverfish. Like polar cod, these cold-tolerant fish provide important sustenance for penguins and seals.

MANDT'S BLACK GUILLEMOT • (*Cepphus grylle mandtii*) and **IVORY GULL** • (*Pagophila eburnea*) While the penguins of Antarctica are often the first birds we associate with sea ice, the Arctic is home to its own avian ice specialists. The Mandt's black guillemot, a dark bird with bright red feet, roosts along ice edges and scans the chilly water for polar cod, occasionally picking the fish directly out of cracks in the sea ice. This taste for cod is shared by the ivory gull, an all-white seabird that nests directly on the ice. But ivory gulls are not above scavenging when fish become scarce—the seabirds pick polar bear kills clean and flock to the birthing grounds of hooded seals to eat the nutritious placentas.

These creative food sources are likely becoming increasingly important for ice-bound seabirds as polar cod move even farther north to find colder water. Another downside of warming temperatures is new competition. In recent years, Mandt's black guillemots have been plagued by the arrival of horned puffins from the south. These puffins outmuscle guillemots by knocking their eggs out of the nests and killing their chicks.

Mandt's black guillemot

Ivory gull

Guano Islands

That's the good shit.

◆ Guano is an ideal fertilizer. Made almost entirely of nitrogen, phosphate, and potassium, it's basically a splat of straight-up energy for plants. Plus, thanks to the social habits of the birds that produce it, it tends to be available in huge, concentrated, perpetually regenerating heaps. Many of these are located along the coast of Peru, on rocks and small landmasses where birds rest and relieve themselves.

RANGE: Hot and dry climates worldwide. Especially common in coastal South America and the Caribbean.
SPECIES: Prolific poopers include Guanay cormorants (*Leucocarbo bougainvilliorum*), Peruvian pelicans (*Pelecanus thagus*), and Peruvian boobies (*Sula variegata*).

Humans have known the value of guano since at least "the times of the Inca kings," as Garcilaso de la Vega wrote in 1609. (*Guano* comes from the Quechua word *wanu*.) At that point, he noted, each town was assigned its own island—and each household a share of that island—according to need. Anyone who harmed a seabird or disturbed one during breeding season was subject to execution, under what some consider the world's first conservation-focused penal code. In this way, said kings took the resource out of the hands of privatizing guano lords and ensured a sustainable harvest.

Peruvians thrived on guano for hundreds of years. Seventeenth-century seacoast farmers used "no other manure but the dung of sea birds," which was available in such abundance that "from a distance the heaps of it look like the snowy crests of a range of mountains," de la Vega wrote.

Europeans and Americans got the scoop in the early 1800s. This period of what historians call "guano mania" spurred a lucrative international trade built on coerced labor, first of local Peruvians and then of indentured Chinese workers. The Guano Islands Act, signed into law by President Franklin Pierce in 1856, allows any citizen who finds an unoccupied, unassociated bird dung heap to claim it on behalf of the United States. Now considered America's first imperialist experiment, it is still on the books today.

By the twentieth century, overharvesting and the development of artificial fertilizer had ended the guano rush. Of course, seabirds continue to poop. In 2020, researchers estimated the value of their combined contributions, taking into account direct sales of guano fertilizer along with how much it would cost for humans to replace the bird-mediated phosphorus and nitrogen that fuels marine ecosystems. They came up with a figure of $470 million per year. 〉 **How to see them:** Peru's Guano Islands, Islets, and Capes National Reserve System protects a chain of seabird rest stops along the coast, including Islas Ballestas, a popular tourist destination. Guano itself is easy to find—sometimes it even drops out of the sky.

Golden Lanceheads

These special reptiles give "Snake Island" its name.

LOCATION: Ilha da Queimada Grande, about 20 miles (32 km) off the coast of Brazil in the state of São Paulo

SPECIES: Golden lancehead pit viper (*Bothrops insularis*)

◆ Ilha da Queimada Grande, off the coast of Brazil, is just over 100 acres (40 ha) in size. It is also home to about 2,500 golden lancehead pit vipers—extremely venomous butter-colored snakes that are unique to this tiny piece of the world. Do the math on this, and you'll get some impressive snake density figures. It's no wonder almost everyone now calls this bit of land "Snake Island," after the unusual reptiles who rule the roost.

The golden lancehead is thought to have evolved from the jararaca, a pit viper species found on the Atlantic coast of South America. As recently as 11,000 years ago—the end of the last Ice Age—it was possible to walk (or slither) the 20 miles (30 km) between this coast and what is now Ilha da Queimada Grande, which was then part of a mountain range. As Earth's temperature climbed, the Atlantic rose in turn, transforming the mountaintop into an island and flooding the intervening land. This trapped a group of jararaca, isolating them from their brethren and much of their usual prey.

The snakes quite literally rose to the challenge. While their mainland relatives have a diversity of ground-based meals available, golden lancehead pit vipers now specialize in catching migratory birds. Over thousands of generations, the species has gone from horizontal hunter to "an animal that moves vertically," explains Otávio Marques, a biologist at Brazil's Butantan Institute.

In Snake Island snakes, the heart is positioned unusually close to the head, to pump blood more effectively against gravity. The snakes are also smaller and thinner than their mainland counterparts, with more of their bodies dedicated to tail length. (Snakes may appear to be all tail, but the official body part starts just past their anal vent.) This shape makes it easier for them to climb and hold on to trees, where they lie in wait.

Welcome to my island.

When a passing bird, such as a yellow-legged thrush or a double-collared seedeater, stops for a breather, the golden lancehead takes the opportunity to pounce. An unusually large head and small fangs enable a snake to hold on to her victim until the venom takes effect. While other lancehead species may also hunt in trees, they are not nearly as specialized for the task, says Marques.

Golden lancehead venom is so poisonous that it has inspired legends: People tell of deadly attacks on fishermen and lighthouse keepers. But there are no official records of a golden lancehead biting a human. Still, the Brazilian Marine Corps has banned visitors from the island. Only researchers can land there, generally with a doctor in tow.

The prohibition protects these special snakes too—despite the density of their occupation, this species is rare enough to be considered critically endangered. Its population has declined by half in the past two decades, partly due to poaching for the exotic pet trade. Adaptive as they are, it goes without saying that these snakes should be left where they belong. ❭ **How to see them: Access to Ilha de Queimada Grande is forbidden without permission from the Brazilian Marine Corps. You probably don't want to go there anyway.**

Island Royalty

Islands across the globe have ended up effectively overseen by a single species. Some of these animals were brought by humans, some were born into royalty, and others are surrounded by an air of mystery. This is how they ascended to their thrones.

LAMBAY ISLAND, IRELAND • On an island far from their home, a group of red-necked wallabies (*Macropus rufogriseus*) has found new footing. The weather in Ireland might be very different from southeast Australia's, but the grassy, rugged conditions suit these marsupials perfectly.

The family who owns this private island introduced a handful of wallabies to it in the 1950s. In the 1980s, the Dublin Zoo set some of their extra wallabies free there, too. They're all getting along well enough—estimates of their numbers range from 60 to more than 100. When it's cold, they huddle for warmth. ❶

KOMODO NATIONAL PARK, INDONESIA • *Jurassic Park*'s Isla Nubar may be fictional, but there is one real-life home to giant lizards in our modern world: the collection of volcanic islands known as Komodo National Park, in Indonesia. Here, around 5,700 Komodo dragons (*Varanus komodoensis*)—the world's biggest lizards at 10 feet (3 m) long—reign supreme. These endangered reptiles hunt deer and other large prey with their venomous saliva. If their dinner-in-waiting doesn't die after the first bite, they stalk it until it does. ❷

ŌKUNOSHIMA, JAPAN • Bunny overlords have earned this island the nickname Usagi Shima, "Rabbit Island." Tourists flock to visit this colony of around 1,000 rabbits (*Oryctolagus cuniculus*), whose provenance is debated.

From 1929 to 1945, Ōkunoshima was the site of a mustard gas factory that used white rabbits as test subjects. Unverified reports claim that some rabbits were set free to monitor gas levels—the indicator being their untimely deaths. However, the current population is more likely descended from rabbits released by schoolchildren in the 1970s.

The rabbits' dense population on the small island is unsustainable, and their survival strategy centers on cuteness. Tourists bring food and water, so the rabbits have learned to be extra friendly, timing their activity around the ferry schedule rather than their natural dawn and dusk tendencies. ❸

ASSATEAGUE ISLAND, VIRGINIA, UNITED STATES ·

There haven't always been wild horses (*Equus caballus*) on this 38-mile-long (61 km) barrier island between Virginia and Maryland, but today two herds, divided by a fence, have sovereignty across beaches and forest. While some say the horses' ancestors were survivors of a shipwreck, the more likely (but less fantastical) explanation is that they were kept here by mainlanders to avoid fencing and taxation laws. Now visitors are required to keep a 40-foot (12 m) distance from the island's ruling species, or face a powerful kick.

Those on the Virginia side of the fence are known as Chincoteague ponies. Each July, cowboys round up approximately 150 of these ponies and their foals, encouraging the adult horses to swim across the water to the more bustling Chincoteague Island. The horses are checked by veterinarians and the foals are auctioned off, raising money for the volunteer fire service that manages them and keeping the wild population under control. ❹

ROTTNEST ISLAND/WADJEMUP, AUSTRALIA ·

Is it a rat? A wallaby? No, it's a quokka (*Setonix brachyurus*)! These miniature marsupials command their island kingdom from their large back feet. Around 10,000 of the native macropods live here, with only small populations found elsewhere. Conservationists keep the island free of introduced predators like foxes and feral cats.

The quokkas' habits influence pretty much everything on the island—from the vegetation types to the presence of tourists, who come to see their photogenic smiles and springy maneuvers. They even gave it one of its names: A Dutch explorer, unfamiliar with the animals, dubbed their homestead Rotte Nest (rats' nest) in the seventeenth century. For much longer, the Whadjuk Noongar people have called it Wadjemup, meaning, roughly, "land across the sea where the spirits are." ❺

CAYO SANTIAGO, PUERTO RICO ·

Although no humans live here, this island's kingpins were introduced for our purposes. In 1938, a number of rhesus macaques (*Macaca mulatta*) were captured in India and transported to Cayo Santiago to be used in tropical disease research.

Currently, the Caribbean Primate Research Center uses this spot, nicknamed "Monkey Island," to further our understanding of primate biology and behavior. Over the years, research teams here have observed more than 11,000 monkeys.

The macaques truly lord over this 38-acre (15 ha) island, which is about a quarter of the size of Disneyland. After they wreaked havoc on the native plant life, researchers began bringing them a daily buffet. An attempted gibbon introduction ended horribly, with the first gibbon baby brutally murdered by the macaques. ❻

Vampire Finches

The ones Darwin didn't tell you about

RANGE: Wolf and Darwin Islands
of the Galápagos
SPECIES: Vampire ground finch
(*Geospiza septentrionalis*)

◆ As readers of this book probably know, Galápagos finches are famous for their beaks. Years of evolution have specialized their schnozzes for different purposes—the formidable bill of the large ground finch cracks nuts, the woodpecker finch's tapered beak drills into trees, and so on.

And what of the elegantly curved, sharply pointed beak of the vampire finch? Well.

Vampire finches live way out on Wolf and Darwin Islands, the most far-flung of the Galápagos. (Darwin himself stuck to a more centralized area and never encountered them.) It can be hard to find food there, especially during the dry season, which runs from July through December.

So a finch may slake his hunger and thirst by sticking his beak into a Nazca or red-footed booby. The finch pecks the much larger bird—usually just under the wing—waits for the blood to flow, and slurps it down. Other finches often wait around to tap in, or maybe to pick up some pointers.

Many small birds peck bugs and parasites off larger animals. Researchers think the ancestors of the vampire finch may have been among this group, and that the species' thirst for blood arose when a bug-pecker dug in a little too hard.

This theory may help explain why boobies generally ignore their attackers, even as red stains bloom over their snow-white feathers. Although they may just be outnumbered—observers have noticed that a booby who tries to bat away a finch quickly gets swarmed.

In the wet season, vampire finches scratch for seeds and insects and sip nectar from cactus flowers. They'll also eat guano, seabird-regurgitated fish, and booby eggs, which they work together to roll off cliffs.

A Nazca booby snapping at a vampire finch.

But by now, blood is an entrenched part of their diet. Finch feces analysis has revealed the presence of iron-digesting gut microbes, from the same bacterial group housed by South and Central American vampire bats. And analysis suggests that their beaks are, indeed, uniquely long and sharp. ❯ **How to see them: Visitors are not allowed on Wolf or Darwin Islands—you'll have to hitch a ride with a research group (if you dare).**

"First, a little refreshment to reward my exertions."

THE WILD LIFE OF A Galápagos Ecoguide

■ Visitors to Galápagos National Park must be accompanied by a licensed guide. Sofia Darquea has been leading ecotours and expeditions on the islands for more than 30 years, from short day tours to weeks-long boat expeditions.

• **How did you end up becoming an ecoguide in the Galápagos?**
I started at a very young age, when I finished university, which I did in Spain. I studied tourist management in protected areas. I never thought about going to the islands because back then, for Ecuadorians, traveling to the Galápagos was pretty expensive.

But my sister was working there for a tour company, and she wrote to me and said, "Look, this is your place." So I decided to go. I clearly remember the first day when I landed in Baltra Airport, and I crossed the channel between Baltra and Santa Cruz. I just fell in love with the islands. The plan was to stay there for 10 days, just visiting my sister, but I never left.

• **How is guiding in the Galápagos different from elsewhere?**
The guides have become a very important tool for conservation. We represent the national park, even though we're hired by independent companies. Since the national park does not have a lot of rangers patrolling, we do a lot of reports and observations—[like] if we see garbage on one of the islands, or a boat that doesn't belong. We also report on introduced species, or if something is not common, or we haven't seen it before, or if the trails or the little docks are not in good shape—things like that.

• **What is something surprising that visitors might see?**
Many times on tours, we've seen female sea lions having their pups right there in the middle of the trail in front of everybody, less than 6 feet [1.8 m] away. You're not supposed to be that close, but because the trails are so narrow and small, sometimes you end up there. And then suddenly you have a female sea lion in the middle of the trail having a baby.

[You might see] dolphins that you didn't expect, and you can swim with them and they stay around you. Or orcas getting super close. Especially if you're with kids, it's so amazing, because of their reaction to seeing these animals so close. [It's something] between fear and joy. ■

Galápagossip Column

For centuries, the striking creatures of the Galápagos have driven humans to wonder, confusion, and understanding. Despite study and exposure, some aspects of their lives remain unexpected, mysterious, or just downright goofy.

GIANT TORTOISES—THEY'RE ON THE MOVE! Famously long-lived, slow-moving, and confined to islands, some Galápagos giant tortoises (*Chelonoidis nigra*) nonetheless migrate. Tracking studies have shown that adult males on Santa Cruz Island travel from the grassier highlands to the shrubbier lowlands during the rainy season and return when things get drier. Making the journey requires them to cover up to a thousand feet (300 m) of ground per day—20 times more than they usually would. ❶

BLUE-FOOTED BOOBIES—THEY'RE KIND OF GROSS! Rather than build a nest, blue-footed boobies (*Sula nebouxii*) lay their eggs on a scraped-off bit of ground and then surround them with a circle of their own feces, which they replenish over time. While this behavior hasn't been studied in depth, it might be a convenient way for parents to mark their territory. To keep cool, these birds also poop on their trademark blue feet. ❷

LAND SNAILS—THEY'RE HIDING! Like the islands' notorious finches, the scores of snail species (subfamily Bulimulinae) endemic to the Galápagos have diversified to take advantage of different habitats—they're just a bit more quiet about it. Research shows that these snail species display shell colors matched to the hues of their local rocks and vegetation, likely helping them avoid detection by predators like the Galápagos mockingbird. A number are endangered today, threatened by invasive

fire ants and rats, but their status is often overlooked because they are less charismatic than many of their island neighbors—as well as harder to see. ❸

MARINE IGUANAS—THEY'RE SALTY! As the world's only oceanic lizards, marine iguanas (*Amblyrhynchus cristatus*) have a lot of unique anatomical quirks, including flat, paddle-like tails for motoring through the water and death-grip claws for riding out currents. Perhaps the most startling is their method of salt excretion. As they browse marine algae, they end up swallowing a good amount of seawater. To get rid of the excess salt, the iguanas filter their blood through a gland in their noses and squirt out the brine in an expulsion that resembles a jet-propelled sneeze. The excreted salt sometimes collects on the iguana's head like a crusty face mask. ❹

RED-LIPPED BATFISH—THEY'RE NOT WEARING LIPSTICK! Unique to the Galápagos, red-lipped batfish (*Ogcocephalus darwini*) tiptoe over the seafloor with their pelvic fins and attract prey with a spiny, chemically enhanced lure that sticks out of their backs. The male fish's most notable feature—his fluorescent scarlet lips, which make him look like a toddler who got into a makeup bag—is also his most mysterious. Researchers still aren't sure whether they're for prey attraction, mate attraction, species recognition, or something else entirely. ⑤

INTRODUCED LADYBUGS—THEY'RE SAVING THE DAY! The first (and thus far only) biological control organism ever purposefully brought to the Galápagos, these spotty insects were introduced in 2002 to control an invasive sap-sucking species, the cottony cushion scale. The ladybugs (*Novius cardinalis*), who evolved with the scale bugs in Australia, have successfully brought down their numbers, reducing pressure on native plants. Scientists are contemplating a similar intervention against the fly *Philornis downsi*, which was accidentally introduced to the Galápagos and parasitizes birds. ⑥

Inaccessible Rails

The world's smallest flightless birds thrive on a remote island fortress.

LOCATION: Inaccessible Island, a small, well-named island in the Atlantic Ocean

SPECIES: Inaccessible Island rail (*Atlantisia rogersi*)

◆ Inaccessible Island earns its ominous name. Thousand-foot cliffs ring this small slab of rock in the dead center of the Atlantic. The few beaches are steep, rocky, and usually blocked by violent crashing waves.

It would make an excellent hideout for a supervillain. Instead, it's the secret lair of the world's smallest flightless bird: the Inaccessible Island rail.

Just 6 inches (15 cm) tall from head to spindly toes, these feathered recluses—each with soft brown plumage, beady red eyes, and a plump little pear-shaped body—live only here, on the 5-square-mile (13 sq km) island they're named for. Despite the limited real estate, the rails are territorial. Each bird defends his or her own tiny slice of the island, and confrontations are common. A face-off starts with loud chirping, after which opposing birds circle each other with beaks to the ground until one backs off or a quick clash occurs.

Visitors to Inaccessible Island (top) . . .

. . . may meet the world's smallest flightless bird. (Young rails, like the one pictured below, have black eyes.)

For many birders, the Inaccessible Island rail is an irresistible challenge, a tempting jewel for their life lists. But even if you do manage to land on the island, the rails are difficult to spot. "A lot of the hardest birds to see in the world are rails," says Adam Walleyn, a guide for Rockjumper Birding Tours. Inaccessible Island rails prefer to hide in dense undergrowth and to nest in domed underground tunnels.

They are much easier to hear. These birds are so chatty that in 2018, a research team censused them by sound—using a speaker and a smartphone to play the bird's call and recording how many rails chirped back. After two months, they made a conservative estimate of the global population: There are about 10,300 Inaccessible Island rails, all on the same dot in the ocean.

That may sound like a lot, but the flightless species is extremely vulnerable to introduced predators. Any rodents who reach the island will find an itty-bitty bird buffet.

For now, Inaccessible Island rails thrive on their rocky little fortress, alongside endemic finches, colonies of albatross, and beach parties of rockhopper penguins. The fact that the world's smallest flightless birds are so hard for humans to reach may be their best defense against extinction. ❯ **How to see them:** Start by taking a boat ride from Cape Town Harbor to Tristan da Cunha, the world's most remote human settlement. Inaccessible Island is another 21 miles (34 km) from there. You'll need permission to land from the government of Tristan da Cunha.

THE WILD LIFE OF **A Far-Out Birding Guide**

■ Birding guide Adam Walleyn spends up to 300 days a year taking guests to the world's most remote islands, often on board icebreakers in the Arctic and Antarctic. He has made four different attempts to land on Inaccessible Island and failed each time.

● **How many birds have you seen in your life?**

I've seen about 9,000 species of birds, which is quite a bit. There are probably about 11,000 in the world. I've been pretty lucky to see a big chunk of the world's birds.

● **Are there any special requirements before you step onto a remote island?**

There can be very strict protocols for some of the islands, down to [what to do about] little seeds in your boots. When we're going to pristine islands, we do a really heavy check and people have to dip all their stuff in a chemical that would kill anything. In some cases, we even make people bring brand-new clothing.

● **When you're approaching Inaccessible Island, how do you know if you can land?**

We set aside three days to try and do Tristan de Cunha, Nightingale Island, and Inaccessible Island. The problem with landing on Inaccessible is there are a couple of rocky beaches where you can land, but the island is a round volcano, so there's nowhere you have any lee from the ocean. The swell just pounding on a rocky beach makes it a tricky landing to try and get a hundred people ashore. Oceanwide [the tour company] reckons it's about a 1 in 10 chance that you'll get ashore at Inaccessible.

● **Why do you want to see the Inaccessible Island rail so badly?**

Partly it's just the name— "Inaccessible rail," I've got to see that. It's famous among people who go birding around the world. There's never been a dedicated Inaccessible Island trip for birders because it's so far from anywhere— it's a minimum of 10 days there and back just to get to Tristan de Cunha, which is considered the most remote inhabited island, and then you have to budget in several days to get permission to land.

It would be a very long and very expensive trip for just one or two birds, but I'm trying to get enough people interested to do it. I'm sure the people are out there. ■

You're Grounded!

Island living does a funny thing to birds. They move in, get comfortable—and get lazy.

Life on islands often leads birds down a counterintuitive evolutionary path: from flight-*ed* to flight-*less*. Worldwide, flightlessness has evolved independently in at least 150 different avian species, many of them island dwellers.

Over time, these birds' flight muscles and wings shrink and their legs get longer. They even lose the breastbone extension that attaches to their flight muscles, known as the keel. This is also happening in some island species that haven't yet lost the ability to fly. In other words, they're heading in the same direction, but at different speeds.

Proto-birds like archaeopteryx gained the ability to fly during the Jurassic. Why go to all that evolutionary trouble only to give it up millions of years later? Researchers point to a simple cost-benefit analysis—flight comes with such a high energy cost that on islands with no land predators, losing this ability is actually a gain.

Flight loss is such an effective evolutionary strategy that the Aldabra rail (*Dryolimnas cuvieri aldabranus*) has gone through it not once, but twice. This rail—a subspecies of the white-throated rail (*Dryolimnas cuvieri*), which does fly—inhabits the Aldabra Atoll in the Indian Ocean, about 600 miles (966 km) southwest of the Seychelles.

In the 1970s, scientists described a bone from a flightless Aldabran *Dryolimnas cuvieri* that lived during the Pleistocene. It was essentially identical to the bones of today's Aldabra rails, suggesting that this flightless subspecies has been in the same place for a very, very long time. But this is impossible—around 340,000 years ago (and possibly also as recently as 118,000 years ago), the atoll was completely inundated by seawater, making life there impossible for a flightless bird (and almost everything else).

Instead, researchers think the island was colonized by flighted *Dryolimnas cuvieri* at least twice. The first population evolved flightlessness and became extinct when the atoll flooded. The second population arrived much later and then evolved flightlessness in almost exactly the same way. This is one of only a few known examples of "iterative evolution"—when the same adaptation evolves at different times in two distinct populations of the same species.

But the low-stress, predator-free conditions that lead to island flightlessness are disappearing. Rats— the bane of flightless birds—have made it as far as the sub-Antarctic South Georgia Island (though a recent eradication program appears to have been successful). They and other introduced reptiles and mammals may eliminate this special island niche.

EUROPE

Glanville Fritillaries and Parasitic Wasps

An accidental experiment in parasite turduckens

RANGE: Finland's Åland Islands, particularly Sottunga and Seglinge
SPECIES: Glanville fritillary (*Melitaea cinxia*), its parasite (*Hyposoter horticola*), and its parasite's parasite (*Mesochorus stigmaticus*)

◆ In 1991, ecologist Ilkka Hanski brought 72 webs' worth of caterpillars from one Finnish island to another. Hanski wanted to track how Glanville fritillary butterflies—paper clip–sized nectar sippers with checker-spot wings—would spread across this island, called Sottunga, where they hadn't previously lived. For decades now, scientists have counted the descendants of these insects in thousands of discrete meadows across Sottunga, gaining a better understanding of how species evolve in patchy habitats.

More recently, these scientists made a different discovery: When Hanski brought the caterpillars over, they weren't alone. Inside some of them were the small larvae of parasitic wasps, called *Hyposoter horticola*. And inside some of them were the even smaller larvae of hyperparasitic wasps, of the species *Mesochorus stigmaticus*.

Across Sottunga, these freeloaders now cause gory drama in miniature. Adult *H. horticola* wasps lay their eggs inside Glanville fritillary eggs. Before the resulting caterpillars have a chance to pupate, the parasites instead erupt, *Alien*-style, from their bodies.

That is, except for cases in which an *H. horticola* has itself been parasitized by *M. stigmaticus*. If that occurs, the smaller hyperparasitic larva pulls off a rock-paper-scissors-style domination gambit, killing the larger parasite at about the same time that the larger parasite kills the caterpillar. The hyperparasite—the sole survivor—then emerges triumphant from the bodies of both hosts.

A lucky escapee

While the introduction of this freaky turducken was an accident, it has provided more opportunities for researchers. Studies of the wasps and sub-wasps have found them to be quite successful, with *H. horticola* sneaking into about one-third of Sottunga's fritillary caterpillars and riding out population dips and swells.

And unlike the butterflies themselves, who are poor flyers, the wasps appear to be expanding through the archipelago without the help of humans—they are now found bothering the natural population of Glanville fritillary butterflies on the nearby island of Seglinge, likely blown there from Sottunga on a gust of wind. ❯ **How to see them:** You can travel to Sottunga from mainland Finland via the Åland ferry line. In September, look for Glanville fritillary caterpillars living together in hammock-like, plant-engulfing webs—and imagine who else might be in there.

More Spooky Parasites

Many organisms manipulate their surroundings in order to survive. For some, those surroundings just happen to consist of another living creature. Here are some of the eeriest parasites we know about, and their unlucky hosts.

TONGUE-EATING LOUSE (*Cymothoa exigua*) • These widespread isopods make their homes inside the mouths of fish, doing a job no one asked them to. After sidling in through the gills of a snapper or grunion, a young female *Cymothoa* will latch on to the base of the fish's tongue, helping herself to whatever the fish tries to eat. The fish's new "tongue" often grows so large—from the size of a tick to the size of a cockroach—that she eventually suffocates her host.

GREEN-BANDED BROODSAC (*Leucochloridium paradoxum*) • This flatworm species completes its life cycle inside the gut of a bird. To get there, the flatworm eggs first hatch inside a snail. They then grow striped, cylindrical organs called broodsacs, which they push up into their host's eyestalks. The engorged eyestalks wave around and pulsate rhythmically, turning the hapless snail into the equivalent of an inflatable air dancer and attracting hungry birds, who mistake them for caterpillars. Infected snails are more likely to move to high, open areas with good lighting, increasing their chances of being seen.

CRAB-INVADING BARNACLE (order Rhizocephala) • Larval females of these parasitic barnacles inject themselves into crabs' bloodstreams and set up shop. When fully grown within a crab, a Rhizocephala parasite consists of two parts. The *externa*—a blister-like sack extruded through the belly of the crab host—holds the parasite's eggs and the tiny male larvae that fertilize them. The *interna*—a network of copper-colored tubules that reaches throughout the host's body—sucks nutrients from the crab's stomach and intestines and exerts control through the nervous system. The parasite destroys the crab host's ability to reproduce, instead puppeting the crab to care for the parasite's egg sac.

SPIDER-CONTROLLING WASP (*Hymenoepimecis argyraphaga*) • Like the type of wasp that bursts forth from Glanville fritillaries, these parasites lay eggs inside their hosts—in this case, orbweaver spiders. But on the night they brutally emerge, they first induce the spider to weave a modified web that can bear an unusual amount of weight. They then eat their way out of their host and spin a cocoon, which hangs suspended below the special web, safe from predators.

ZOMBIE FUNGUS (*Ophiocordyceps unilateralis*) • Perhaps the most famous of the zombifying parasites, *Ophiocordyceps* fungi penetrate the exoskeletons of their insect hosts, then stealthily take over their bodies. An infected ant goes undetected by others in the colony, even though ants usually notice and remove sick members. The fungus eventually compels its host to clamp onto the underside of a plant, hanging upside down about 10 inches (25 cm) off the ground. Once the host is in position, the fungal fruiting bodies erupt from its head and sprinkle spores down on unsuspecting victims, continuing the cycle.

Atlantic Puffins

On the island of Heimaey, young humans help out baby birds.

 Imagine an Easter egg hunt in the dark—except the eggs can run away from you.

That's what the puffling season is like on Heimaey, a volcanic island in the Vestmannaeyjar archipelago along the southern coast of Iceland. Every year in mid-September, lost and confused baby puffins wander the streets at night. "They're everywhere," says Audrey Padgett, manager of the Sea Life Trust Beluga Whale Sanctuary in Heimaey. "It feels like puffins are raining from the sky."

Heimaey is home to the world's largest puffin colony. The neon-billed birds have dug more than a million burrows along the island's steep, grassy cliffs, which rise above the town of 4,500 people. Once a source of food for islanders, they have more recently become some of Iceland's most famous residents, attracting tourists and serving as unofficial mascots for the whole country. (Stuffed toy versions of the birds have become so ubiquitous as souvenirs that stores geared toward tourists are colloquially known as "puffin shops.")

RANGE: Puffins traverse the North Atlantic from Canada to Norway and as far south as Spain. Puffling rescue occurs on Heimaey, in Iceland.

SPECIES: Atlantic puffin (*Fratercula arctica*)

While puffins spend most of the year at sea, bobbing on the water and diving for fish, they return to the same burrow every summer to breed. From mid-April to early May, puffin pairs—who mate for life—can be spotted coming ashore to get comfy, lay eggs, and raise their chicks, who are known as pufflings.

The chicks hatch around July and are cared for by their parents for roughly 45 days. Just as the midnight sun ebbs and Iceland's nights grow dark again, the young birds are ready to leave the colony. They're supposed to aim for the open sea, using moonlight as their guide. However, they often become confused by the artificial lights across the harbor and end up stranded in town instead.

It's a dangerous situation for the pufflings, who are usually too disoriented to correct their course. Instead, they wander around, swarming streetlights and making themselves vulnerable to hazards such as cars, cats, and walls.

That's where the grassroots Puffling Patrol comes in. The human residents of Heimaey scour the streets at night, chasing down the chicks and placing them gently into cardboard boxes. They then take them to the Sea Life Trust, where the young birds are weighed, measured, and tagged. "Everyone gets into the weird habit of carrying around a puffling box," says Ewa Malinowska, who runs the puffin hospital there.

Once they receive clean bills of health, the pufflings are taken to the cliffs and lobbed into the sea below, just like fluffy baseballs. They'll remain at sea for two to three years before returning to the island and making a home in a burrow of their own. ❯ **How to see them:** Look for clifftop colonies in coastal areas during the breeding season (late spring to late August or early September). Tourists who'd like to join the Puffling Patrol should check in at the Sea Life Trust first for guidance.

THE WILD LIFE OF A Puffling Patrol Family

■ Sandra Sigvardsdóttir and her children, Íris Dröfn Gudmundsdóttir (age 8), Eva Berglind Gudmundsdóttir (age 6), and Sara Björk Gudmundsdóttir (age 15 months), live on the island of Heimaey and are famously prolific members of the Puffling Patrol. Every year, they rescue between 200 and 300 chicks during the four-week-long puffling season.

● **How did your family start looking for pufflings?**

SANDRA: My first puffling ride was when I was three months old, and every year after that, so I don't remember my first years as a puffling rescuer. But when I think back to being a kid, the most memorable thing is the excitement— Are we going to find some?—and the rush—Are we going to catch it? Now I try to do the same with my kids. We are like the crazy puffin family on the island—that's how people think of us.

ÍRIS DRÖFN: I was born and raised into this. Every year, it's what we live for.

● **What's the puffling season like?**

SANDRA: We go out every night, [starting] when we hear about the first puffling until we hear about the last one. So we really participate in the rescuing. It can get kind of crazy when the first puffling arrives, because everyone goes out, and you can see cars and flashlights on almost every street. There are crowds. It's like Black Friday.

And when the season ends, we start counting down to the next one.

What does a night of puffling rescuing typically entail?

SANDRA: We start looking around midnight, which is long past bedtime, so on the nights we plan to go out, the children go to bed very early. Then I wake them up when it's time to start looking for pufflings. I do feel very lucky my children aren't afraid of running around in the dark. On a good night, we bring home about 15 to 20 pufflings.

What kind of equipment do you need?

SANDRA: During the season, we keep boxes in our car. We put grass in the bottom of the boxes, so we can use them longer. When I was a kid, we used a box for two or three nights—then [the pufflings would] poop all over, and you cannot use the box anymore. But you don't need much to get started. Since they arrive at night, you only need some reflective gear, flashlights, and patience.

ÍRIS DRÖFN: And pufflings.

What does a puffling feel like?

SANDRA: They're soft and really small. You can hold them in one hand. They have a lot of down, and it's just like the softest cotton you've ever touched. Sometimes if they are really small and they have too much down on their bottom and the wings, then we have to keep them at home for a few days before they can be released.

ÍRIS DRÖFN: They're so soft, it's like floating in the air.

Why do you enjoy helping pufflings?

ÍRIS DRÖFN: It's fun when I go to school the day after, and I can talk to my friends about how many pufflings we found. There aren't many parents who are as crazy as mine, so my friends don't always get to go out every night. So we get the high score and can brag a little bit.

SANDRA: For us, the grown-ups, the joy is the happiness in the kids' faces. There's also the rush of trying to catch the pufflings before anything happens to them. Then when we catch one, it's wonderful. And there's the happy feeling of releasing them, knowing you've done something good. ▧

Svalbard Reindeer

The world's smallest, cutest, and most relaxed reindeer

RANGE: Svalbard archipelago, Norway

SPECIES: Svalbard reindeer (*Rangifer tarandus platyrhynchus*)

◆ Svalbard reindeer are the world's smallest reindeer—each is "the size of a big sheep," says Arctic ecologist Mathilde Le Moullec. They are also, by many accounts, the cutest, with stubby little legs, rounded snouts, and thick cloud-colored fur.

Their morphology supports their lifestyle, which is almost aggressively chill. Around 6,000 years ago, this species' ancestors, who likely originated in Siberia, floated to the Svalbard archipelago on some large chunks of sea ice. When they arrived, they had no choice but to stay put. Really, really put.

While other reindeer species are out there setting migration records—one herd of barren-ground caribou in Canada treks 840 miles (1,351 km) every year—the ones on Svalbard have nowhere to go. And with no natural predators on the archipelago, they rarely find a reason to hoof it anyway. Even within Svalbard, herds maintain small territories and rarely mingle with other groups. "They don't move unless they really have to," says Le Moullec.

Instead, these fluffy ungulates focus on two important tasks: eating and resting. In summer, they tuck into moss and grasses, building up their fat stores. (By winter, they can have chub 4 inches [10 cm] thick.) Over the course of a day, they tend not to move more than the length of a city block.

Collaborators of Le Moullec once outfitted some reindeer with video cameras and ended up with footage of two things: the reindeers' own fur (filmed while munching) and—whenever a cervid cinematographer lifted its head—a view of the same mountain. "You think, 'Again?'" says Le Moullec.

Their priorities in order, these little reindeer prosper in their chilly home. Thus far, the benefits of climate change have outweighed the difficulties—the extra buffet hours provided by longer summers generally make up for the difficulty of rainier winters, which can freeze vegetation under impossibly thick ice.

While large mortality events sometimes occur, this is mostly a sign of the species' success, Le Moullec says—populations are increasing overall, and numbers in one herd occasionally swell beyond what the land can support. But those who study them worry about their adaptability, as their genetic diversity was curtailed by aggressive hunting before the species was protected in 1925.

Slow cinema aside, Le Moullec appreciates the Svalbard reindeer's persistence, saying that learning from these steady creatures helps researchers better understand the challenges facing all Arctic species. "Maybe they don't do much, but it's really extreme where they live," she says. "It's so impressive." ❯ **How to see them:** Svalbard reindeer can be found across the archipelago, including in the town of Longyearbyen, where they like to amble slowly down the road.

It's time for a rest.

ACKNOWLEDGMENTS

We've been lucky to have a great team of dedicated editors, designers, and publishers at Workman over the years who care deeply about every detail of this work and have driven us to always push for excellence. To Maisie, Lia, Janet, Rae, Kate, Barbara, Sophia, Doug, Nancy, Analucia, Rebecca, Chloe, and Moira: Thank you for being our partners. To Elyse, thank you for being the best agent anyone could possibly ask for.

To all the contributing writers, who brightened these pages with their curiosity and skill, and to the many expert sources who lent their knowledge and voices, thank you for being a part of this project. To Rachel Fritts, thank you for braving the thickets of the internet and coming back with such incredible information. To JoAnna Klein, thank you for bringing in your deep-sea experience and steady editing hand at a crucial moment. To Iris Gottlieb and Zoe Keller, thank you for bringing this book to life.

Cara

I am grateful to be a member of so many exciting ecosystems. The Atlas Obscura team, past and present, has shaped how I think about writing, the world, and how they go together. Josh, thank you for bringing me into this orbit, and for the gravitational power of your enthusiasm, which keeps me there. Reyhan, Sarah, Lex, Ella, Paula, Tao Tao, Eric, Blake, Megan, Chris, Samir, and so many others, thank you for making it fun. Ella and Cecily, this book wouldn't exist without you; you blazed the trail. Marc, it wouldn't exist without you either; you brought the trail mix. Doug and Dylan, thank you for bringing your precise and creative vision to this project. To Josh P. and Michael H., thank you for helping us wrangle communications and resource allocation for such a sprawling project; you are the vital fungus in our underground root network. My local pals—Adhy, Don, Pepper and Poppy; Adam, Evan, Jackson and Max; Hava, Martha, Lena and Lucie; Josh, Joelle, Audrey and Michael; Amulya, Margaret, Chris, Chris, and Carol—thank you for keeping me rooted and making me laugh. My farther-out friends—Caroline, Kristine, Linda, Matt, Max, and Max—thank you for always flying in at the perfect time with new kinds of pollen. My family—Deb, Mike, Tori, and Mari and now Ben, Tyler, and Mark—thank you for supporting me, and spotting me through years of tree-climbing. Lilia—you are my first, last, and best reader; I love being alive with you. My interspecies community— this is for you most of all. I'm sorry so many of you can't read it. Maybe it tastes ok?

Josh

First and foremost, thank you to Cara, whose name deserves to be at least twenty times bigger than mine on the cover of this book. I feel lucky to be hitched to your rising star, and grateful to Seth Mnookin for first connecting us so many years ago. Dylan Thuras, thank you for bringing your keen eye and wisdom to so many aspects of this book, and even more for being the best partner and cofounder a guy could ask for. Thank you to Marc Haeringer, who knows how to drive a publishing project like nobody else, and to Doug Baldinger whose impeccable taste and judgment always shine through. To Warren Webster, for shouldering every burden and turning a great brand into a great business; Megan Roberts, the magician, for making the promise of Atlas Obscura real for people; Dan Sobo, for guiding us technologically; Alex Mangum, for keeping this whole Rube Goldberg contraption running; Samir Patel, for bringing rigor, joy, and curiosity to our editorial efforts; Sara Ewell, Arie Azoff, and the BP team for empowering Atlas to do its best work; Mike Parker, for taking our community by the hand to the farthest corners of the globe and returning them home safely; and the entire Atlas Obscura team and community for being a part of this mission to bring more wonder into the world. And to Dinah, Leo, and Bea: Everything is ultimately for you.

CONTRIBUTORS

FORESTS & RAINFORESTS

"Strangler Figs" by Christina Ayele Djossa
"Flying Rivers" by Claudia Geib
"Ghost Dogs of the Amazon" by Claudia Geib
"The Wild Life of A Ghost Dogsitter"
    by Claudia Geib
"Ancient Arapaima" by Claudia Geib
"Salty Clay Licks" by Jason G. Goldman
"Gopher Tortoises" by Vanessa Gregory
"Synchronous Fireflies" by Vanessa Gregory
"Humongous Fungus" by Julian Nowogrodzki
"Spirit Bears" by Vanessa Gregory
"The Wild Life of A Spirit Bear Advocate"
    by Vanessa Gregory
"World's Largest Beaver Dams" by Ben Goldfarb
"Salmon Forests" by Krista Langlois
"The Original Social Networks" by Claudia Geib
"The Wild Life of A Tree Eavesdropper"
    by Claudia Geib
"Snowshoe Hare Cycles" by Lori Fox
"Wood Frogsicles" by Julian Nowogrodzki
"Scottish Wildcats" by Linda Rodriguez McRobbie
"Sphagnum Moss" by Krista Langlois
"Larval Couture" by Julian Nowogrodzki
"The Wild Life of A Caddis Fly Collaborator"
    by Julian Nowogrodzki
"Rainbow Eucalyptus" by Myles Karp
"Japanese Rhinoceros Beetles" by Lauren J. Young
"Marimo Balls" by Natasha Frost
"Exploding Ants" by Ashley Braun
"Bum-Breathing Turtles" by Ella Morton
"Flute Lyrebirds" by Ella Morton
"The Wild Life of A Zoomusicologist" by Ella Morton
"Giant Gippsland Earthworms" by Kim Thomson
"Bowerbird Bachelor Pads" by Myles Karp
"Swamp Kauri" by Natasha Frost
"Mad Hatterpillars" by Mara Grunbaum

GRASSLANDS & TUNDRAS

"The Wild Life of A Conservancy Game Changer"
    by Stuart Butler
"A Step-by-Step Guide to Giraffe Transport"
    by Jonathan Feakins
"Whistling Acacias and Ants" by Elyse DeFranco
"African Wild Dogs" by Oriana Pauli
"Savanna Eavesdropping" by Claudia Geib
"Grassy Glades" by Michael Parks
"The Wild Life of A Dedicated Mufudzi"
    by Cecil Dzwowa
"Sharp-Nosed Grass Frogs" by Richard Constantine
    Arghiris
"Stargazing Dung Beetles" by Joshua Sokol
"Navigating by the Stars" by Joshua Sokol
"Kangaroo Grass" by Kate Evans
"Seeds on the Move" by Austin Price
"Why Grasslands Get Overlooked" by Kate Evans
"Lemmings" by Linda Rodriguez McRobbie
"Waxcap Grasslands" by Lisa Holmes

"Wood Mouse Waypoints" by Laurie Jackson
"Ancient Zombie Pithoviruses" by Christina Couch
"Your Guide to Fashionable Horns and Antlers"
    by Matt Malinowski
"The Wild Life of A Jogi Snake Charmer"
    by Aysha Imtiaz
"Arctic Tree Line" by Stephanie Krzywonos
"Arctic Poppies" by J. Besl
"Mighty Arctic Lichens" by Alex Tesar
"Remnant Tallgrass Prairies" by Kestrel Keller
"Burrowing Owls" by T.J. Olwig
"Under the Prairie" by Kate Golembiewski
"Death Camas Symbiosis" by Holly Secon
"Sage Grouse Seduction Grounds" by Mara Grunbaum
"The Wild Life of A Prairie Photographer"
    by Annika S. Hipple
"Loggerhead Shrikes" by Jack Tamisiea
"Out-of-Place Oryx" by Sam Moore
"*Ananteris* Scorpions" by Solimary García-Hernández
"Fire-Resistant Plants" by Pierre Le Duff
"Pantanal Apple Snails" by Jacob Kuppermann
"Helpful Scavengers" by Mackenzie Breneman
"Capim Dourado" by Jamie Ditaranto
"The Wild Life of A Golden Grass Weaver"
    by Jamie Ditaranto
"Giant Anteaters" by Andrew Warner

MOUNTAINS

"Timber Rattlesnake Hibernacula" by Melissa Scott
    Sinclair
"Appalachian Mountains" with Rachel Fritts
"Hawk Mountain" by Kate Golembiewski
"The Wild Life of A Raptor Surveyor"
    by Kate Golembiewski
"Snow-Patch Havens" by Ethan Shaw
"American Pikas" by Linda Rodriguez McRobbie
"Bleeding Tooth Fungi" by Stephanie Krzywonos
"Wolf Birds" by Elizabeth Hlavinka
"Mountain Goats" by Mara Grunbaum
"Potentially Immortal Bristlecone Pines"
    by Ula Chrobak
"Mexican Jumping Beans" by Myles Karp
"Monarch Overwintering Sites" by Kestrel Keller
"Five Steps to a Perfect Monarch Rest Stop"
    by Kestrel Keller
"Totora Reeds" by Leah Fabel
"Andes Mountains" with Rachel Fritts
"Climbing, Armored Catfish" by Claudia Geib
"Five Fish That Can Beat Your Bouldering Personal
    Record" by Claudia Geib
"Vicuñas" by Heather Jasper
"The Wild Life of A Vicuña Veterinarian"
    by Heather Jasper
"Marsupial Frogs" by Ashley Braun
"Frailejones" by Angie Drake
"Ethiopian Wolves" by Claudia Geib
"Sky Islands" by Jack Tamisiea
"Kea" by Natasha Frost

PHOTO CREDITS

FORESTS

Alamy: All Canada Photos pp. 29, 29 (inset), anjahennern p. 21 (top right); Antisana p. 5; Arctic Images p. 42; Auscape International Pty Ltd p. 61; Jens Büttner/dpa p.6 (top); Pat Canova p. 24; Denis Crawford p. 70 (inset); Piter Lenk p. 6 (bottom); Nature Picture Library pp. 20 (top), 22, 58 (middle left); Gabi Wolf p. 23. **Courtesy of Atlas Obscura Contributors:** Parks Canada p. 26; Lary Reeves p. 7 (top). **Flickr:** cclborneo p. 52. **Getty Images:** John Carnemolla p. 62; Danita Delimont p. 54 (top); kurga p. 14; Justin Paget p. 44(right); Anton Petrus p. 47; Cede Prudente p. 51 (top left). **Minden Pictures:** Chien Lee p. 21 (bottom left); Mark Moffett p. 57. **Nature Picture Library:** Stephen Dalton p. 50 (bottom left); Tony Heald p. 51 (bottom right). **Science Photo Library:** ANT Photo Library p. 66; Anthony Bannister/Gallo Images p. 49; Mark Boulton p. 68; Mark Bowler p. 11; Tony Camacho p. 8 (top); Stephen Dalton p. 50 (bottom right); Hermann Eisenbeiss p. 20 (bottom right); Eye of Science p. 46 (bottom); Dante Fenolio p. 13; Fletcher & Baylis p. 21 (bottom right); Brian Gadsby p. 16; Francois Gohier p. 8 (middle left); Jan Hamrsky/NaturePL p. 46 (top); Joi Ito p. 55; Bjanka Kadic p. 4; Ted Kinsman p. 34; Jean-Michel Labat p.15; Dr. P. Marazzi p. 3; Steve & Dave Maslowski p. 9 (top); Tom McHugh p. 51 (top right); MerlinTuttle.org p. 21 (top left); NHPA/Photoshot p. 67 (bottom); Danny Radius p. 58 (bottom); Marie Read p. 17; Nicolas Reusens p. 58 (middle right); Phil Savoie p. 54 (bottom). **Science Source:** Science Source p. 59 (top); John Serrao p. 18 (bottom); Millard H. Sharp p. 19 (top); Steve Shattuck p. 58 (top); Martin Shields p. 44 (left); Inga Spence p. 20 (bottom middle); Paul D Stewart p. 67 (top); Dan Suzio p. 19 (bottom); Karl H. Switak p. 18 (top); B.G. Thomson p. 8 (bottom); Francesco Tomasinelli p. 9 (middle); T. Ulrich/ClassicStock p. 8 (middle right); M. Watson p. 10 (bottom); Terry Whittaker p. 41; Ignacio Yufera/FLPA p. 25. **Shutterstock:** Serafima Antipova p. 22 (inset); Arthur Balitskii p. 32; Ernie Cooper p. 20 (bottom left); Jim Cumming p. 33 (top); Danita Delimont on Offset p. 28 (bottom); FotoRequest p. 33 (bottom); juerginho p. 10 (top); Julia Soul Art pp. 38, 39 (top and bottom); Isabelle Ohara p. 48 (right); Rob D the Pastry Chef p. 60; YegoroV p. 28 (top). **Superstock:** Roger de la Harpe p. 37; Ragnar Th. Sigurdsson/age fotostock p. 56. **Wikimedia Commons:** The following image is used under a Creative Commons Attribution CC BY-SA 4.0 License (https://creativecommons.org/licenses/by-sa/4.0/deed.en) and belongs to the following Wikimedia Commons user: April Nobile p. 59 (middle). The following image is used under a Creative Commons Attribution CC BY-SA 3.0 License (https://creativecommons.org/licenses/by-sa/3.0/deed.en) and belongs to the following Wikimedia Commons user: Noah Elhardt p. 21 (top left). **Public Domain:** Bulletin of the American Museum of Natural History 28 p. 40; CPeeters p.59 (bottom); csirogram p. 70.

GRASSLANDS

Alamy: All Canada Photos p. 121; blickwinkel p. 131 (top); BrazilPhotos p. 132 (top); Sitthipong Chuanpo p. 77 (middle right); Delphotos p. 95; Dorling Kindersley Ltd p. 92; Bob Gibbons p. 106 (top); Ken Gillespie Photography p. 119; Martin Battilana Photography p. 90 (top left); mauritius images GmbH p. 130 (top); Florence McGinn p. 117 (bottom); Diana Meister p. 90 (top right); Nature Picture Library p. 81 (bottom); Marianne Pfeil p. 90 (bottom); Paul Pickford p. 93; Lee Rentz p. 86 (middle); Worldwide Picture Library p. 128 (bottom). **Courtesy Use:** Pleistocene Park p. 103; Ernd Schöllhorn p. 87 (middle); Daniel Szalai p. 86 (bottom right); The Wildlife Society p. 88. **Dreamstime:** Brian Sedgbeer p. 76 (middle right). **Flickr:** Ray p. 104 (bottom right). **Getty Images:** Anil p. 105 (bottom upper left); James Keith p. 115; Cormac McCreesh p. 124. **Minden Pictures:** S and D and K Maslowski p. 122; Mark Moffett p. 130 (bottom). **National Geographic:** Michael Rose p. 105 (bottom right). **Nature Picture Library:** Emanuele Biggi p. 87 (bottom left); Neil Lucas p. 91 (bottom). **Science News:** Julia Bartoli and Chantal Abergel p. 101. **Science Source:** Bryan and Cherry Alexander p. 111 (bottom); David Aubrey p. 100; Eric Baccega p. 77 (bottom); Peter Cairns/NaturePL p. 131(bottom); Nigel J. Dennis p. 81 (top); Gregory G. Dimijian, M.D. p. 78 (bottom); Eye of Science p. 131 (inset); Fletcher & Baylis p. 126; Simon Fraser p. 108; Bob Gibbons pp. 112, 120; Erlend Haarberg/NaturePL p. 98; Adam Jones p. 104 (middle); Ivan Kuzmin p. 105 (bottom); Thomas & Pat Leeson pp. 104 (top), 117 (middle); Jeffrey Lepore p. 91 (top left); Michael Male p. 110; Dr P. Marazzi p. 104 (bottom left); S. Nagendra p. 107; NHPA/Photoshot pp. 73, 74, 133; Tierbild Okapia p. 117 (top); Ron Sanford p. 109; Millard H. Sharp p. 134; James Steinberg

p. 114; Dan Suzio p. 105 (middle right); B.G. Thomson p. 105 (top left); Ignacio Yufera/FLPA p. 125 (middle). **Shutterstock:** Andrew M. Allport p. 129 (bottom); AnnstasAg p. 105 (top middle left); ArCaLu p. 75; Julian Buijzen pp. 76–77; Jordan Comley p. 89 (bottom); Darcy Rogers Images p. 125 (top); Digital_Lions p. 82; Glassmarq p. 99; Abdelrahman Hassanein p. 83; Brad Helms p. 77 (top right); ilovezion p. 105 (top right); In Art 78 (top and bottom); Incredible Arctic p. 111 (top); Eric Isselee p. 77 (top left); Kelp Grizzly Photography p. 77 (middle left); Yusif Khalilov p. 129 (top); Kletr p. 76 (middle left); Jim Lambert p. 125 (bottom); Rafael R Sandoval p. 105 (inset); Simon_g p. 76 (top left); Tropicalvision p. 128 (top). **Wikimedia Commons:** The following image is used under a Creative Commons Attribution CC BY-SA 4.0 License (https://creativecommons.org/licenses/by-sa/4.0/deed.en) and belongs to the following Wikimedia Commons user: Mark Marathon p. 89 (top). The following images are used under a Creative Commons Attribution CC BY-SA 2.0 License (https://creativecommons.org/licenses/by-sa/2.0/deed.en) and belong to the following Wikimedia Commons users: Nick Miller p. 91 (middle); VasenkaPhotography p. 91 (top right). **Public Domain:** Casa Rosada p. 87 (bottom right); Pequi p. 132 (bottom).

MOUNTAINS

Alamy: All Canada Photos p. 153 (top); Sabena Jane Blackbird p. 192 (top); blickwinkel p. 158 (top); Larry Doherty p. 195 (top); Murilo Gualda p. 163; Arto Hakola p. 196 (bottom); Robert Harding p. 175; JHVEPhoto p. 151; Sébastien Lecocq p. 153 (bottom); mauritius images GmbH p. 181; Don Mennig pp. 139 (middle), 139 (top), 140; Raquel Mogado p. 161 (top); Nature Picture Library pp. 161 (bottom), 183; Navè Orgad p. 149; Mike Read p. 143; Aidan Stock p. 192 (bottom); The Natural History Museum p. 164; Andrew Walmsley p. 170; Zoonar GmbH p. 152. **Getty Images:** Tahir Abbas p. 177; GlobalP p. 137 (bottom); Sandra Leidholdt p. 148; Windzepher p. 179 (bottom). **Minden Pictures:** Georgette Douwma p. 194 (bottom); Michael Durham p. 195 (bottom); Michael and Patricia Fogden p. 160 (bottom), 160 (top). **National Geographic:** Joel Sartore/Photo Ark p. 141 (top). **Nature Picture Library:** Jiri Lochman p. 172; Plazi p. 155. **Science Source:** ANT Photo Library p. 173; Will Burrard-Lucas/NaturePL pp. 165 (bottom), 165 (top); Tony Camacho p. 187 (middle); Nigel Cattlin p. 191; Suzanne L. Collins p. 190 (top middle left); Dante Fenolio pp. 166, 194 (top), 194 (inset); K H Fung p. 186 (top right); David Kjaer/NaturePL p. 196 (top); C.K. Lorenz p. 144; Dr P. Marazzi p. 185; Loic Poidevin/NaturePL p. 187 (top); Dave Pressland/FLPA p. 145; John Serrao p. 137 (top); Francesco Tomasinelli p. 193; Andy Trowbridge/NaturePL p. 171; Dr. Keith Wheeler p. 182; Jim Zipp p. 186 (bottom). **Shutterstock:** A7880S p. 157; Jose Arcos Aguilar p. 156; bigwa11 p. 176; bravikvl p.159 (top); David Calhoun p. 190 (top right); Paolo Costa p. 168 (top); Dewin ID p. 169 (bottom); dnaveh p. 186 (top left); Gallinago_media p. 179 (top); Gwoeii p. 172 (inset); Harry Collins Photography p. 158 (middle); ImageBROKER on Offset p. 146; Jujubier p. 154; korCreate p. 187 (bottom); Lennjo p. 169 (top right); MarkVanDykePhotography p. 138; PhotocechCZ p. 158 (bottom); Ryzhkov Sergey p. 147; Stegostoma2RR p. 190 (top middle right); Drukpa Tharchu p. 174; Tharuka Photographer p. 159 (bottom); Z-art p. 167. **Wikimedia Commons:** The following image is used under a Creative Commons Attribution CC BY-SA 1.0 License (https://creativecommons.org/licenses/by-sa/1.0/deed.en) and belongs to the following Wikimedia Commons user: Barbod Safaei p. 189. The following image is used under a Creative Commons Attribution CC BY-SA 4.0 License (https://creativecommons.org/licenses/by-sa/4.0/deed.en) and belongs to the following Wikimedia Commons user: Cho M, Neubauer P, Fahrenson C, Rechenberg p. 178. **Public Domain:** David Dehner p. 139 (bottom); Alastair Robinson p. 169 (top middle); Xerces Society p. 141 (bottom).

DESERTS

Alamy: ART Collection p. 204 (bottom); Rick & Nora Bowers p. 213; Cavan Images p. 265; Ken Griffiths p. 251; Robert Harding p. 229; Colin Harris/era-images pp. 260 (right), 263; imageBROKER.com GmbH & Co. KG pp. 222 (bottom), 237 (right), 240; Norm Lane p. 248; Mario Gyß p. 222 (top); Ecolo Pez p. 249 (bottom); RooM the Agency p. 250; shapencolour p. 233; Dan Sullivan p. 225 (top); Dave Watts p. 206 (top middle); Westend61 GmbH p. 253. **AWL Images:** Nigel Pavitt/John Warburton-Lee Photography Ltd p. 201. **Courtesy Use:** Bob Barber p. 204 (top); NPS photo

p. 199; Joe Orman pp. 210–211. **Getty Images:** Roberto Armocida p. 218; Lars Leemann p. 228; reptiles4all p. 245; SinghaphanAllB p. 241; David Steele p. 246; **Minden Pictures:** Robert Valentic p. 252 (bottom middle). **Science Source:** ANT Photo Library pp. 252 (top), 252 (bottom right), 256; Biophoto Associates p. 202; Antoine Boureau p. 235; Dr. John Brackenbury p. 239 (right); Tony Camacho p. 230; Peter Chadwick p. 232; Suzanne L. Collins p. 208 (bottom); John Devries p. 239 (left); Eye of Science p. 262 (top); Bob Gibbons p. 225 (bottom) Francois Gohier p. 260 (left); MerlinTuttle.org p. 211 (bottom); Larry Miller p. 204 (middle); Cordelia Molloy p. 206 (bottom right); William H. Mullins p. 249 (top); Mark Newman p. 206 (top); NHPA/Photoshot p. 236 (top); Michael S. Nolan p. 220; Planetary Visions Ltd p. 261; John Shaw p. 237 (left); Joseph Sohm pp. 204–205 (spread); Sinclair Stammers p. 262 (bottom); Dan Suzio p. 206 (bottom left); svf74 p. 233 (top); B. G. Thomson pp. 243, 252 (bottom left); Francesco Tomasinelli p. 231; Stuart Wilson p. 212; Sara Winter p. 224 (bottom). **Shutterstock:** Brent Coulter p. 209; HelloRF Zcool p. 236 (bottom); Dominic Gentilcore PhD p. 207; Jag_cz p. 208 (paint); Pavel Krasensky p. 238; Cesar Gonzalez Palomo p. 224; Torsten Pursche pp. 236–237; sumikophoto p. 206 (bottom middle); Sara Winter p. 223; You Touch Pix of EuToch p. 252 (top middle). **SuperStock:** Michael & Patricia Fogden/Minden Pictures p. 227.

OCEANS

Alamy: D. Holden Bailey p. 272 (top); Blue Planet Archive p. 318 (bottom); Angelo D'Amico p. 304 (top); imageBROKER.com GmbH & Co. KG p. 304 (bottom); Eric Lafforgue p. 300; Tom Meaker p. 294 (bottom); Nature Picture Library pp. 271, 276; PF-(usna1) p. 281 (bottom); Adisha Pramod p. 320 (top); Science History Images p. 318 (top); Stocktrek Images, Inc. p. 269; Aroon Thaewchatturat p. 284; The History Collection p. 281 (top); The Natural History Museum p. 320 (bottom); Underwater Imaging p. 272 (bottom); Vespasian p. 316; Peter Vrabel p. 294 (top); WaterFrame p. 270; Westend61 GmbH p. 275 (bottom right); WILDLIFE GmbH p. 281 (middle right); Yarr65 pp. 310 (bottom), 310 (top). **Courtesy Use:** Jean Mitchell p. 298 (bottom); NASA image courtesy Jeff Schmaltz, MODIS Land Rapid Response Team at NASA GSFC p. 306; Rebikoff-Niggeler Foundation p. 319 (bottom); Anthony Smith Photography p. 308. **Getty Images:** 4FR p. 299 (top); Yiming Chen p. 299 (middle left); DeeAnn-Cranston p. 315 (inset); Stephen Frink/The Image Bank p. 283; Aleksei Permiakov p. 275 (bottom left); rockptarmigan p. 277. **Nature Picture Library:** Sue Daly/NaturePL p. 298 (middle left); Oscar Dewhurst p. 277 (inset); Jussi Murtosaari pp. 285, 286; Alex Mustard p. 288; Roberto Rinaldi p. 295; David Shale p. 301 (top). **Science Source:** Mark Carwardine/NaturePL pp. 307 (top), 307 (bottom); Peter Chadwick p. 313; Gerald & Buff Corsi/Focus on Nature, Inc. p. 317 (bottom); Dante Fenolio pp. 290 (bottom), 299 (bottom); Francois Gohier p. 302; Daniel Heuclin p. 299 (bottom left); Andrew J. Martinez pp. 274 (bottom), 297; Andrew Martinez p. 298 (middle right); NHPA/Photoshot p. 317 (top); NOAA/Nature Source p. 319 (middle); Michael Patrick O'Neill p. 296; Gregory Ochocki p. 299 (middle right); Alexander Semenov pp. 274 (middle left), 274 (middle right); David Shale/NaturePL p. 319 (top); Wildlife Pictures/Reporters p. 290 (top). **Shutterstock:** Joe Belanger p. 275 (top); Neil Bromhall p. 281 (middle left); Cristina Concepcion Lemes pp. 270 (inset), 298–299 (spread); Sahara Frost pp. 274 (top left), 274 (top right). **SuperStock:** Minden Pictures p. 315; A. E. Migotto/CEBIMar-USP p. 287. **Wikimedia Commons:** The following images are used under a Creative Commons Attribution CC BY-SA 4.0 License (https://creativecommons.org/licenses/by-sa/4.0/deed.en) and belong to the following Wikimedia Commons users: Chong Chen p. 301 (bottom); Himantolophus_sagamius p. 280. The following image is used under a Creative Commons Attribution CC BY-SA 3.0 License (https://creativecommons.org/licenses/by-sa/3.0/deed.en) and belongs to the following Wikimedia Commons user: Christian Ferrer p. 273. **Public Domain:** NOAA p. 311; Peripitus p. 300 (inset).

CITIES

Alamy: AGAMI Photo Agency p. 377 (middle); Keivan Bakhoda pp. 352, 353; Ashton Blackwell p. 341; blickwinkel pp. 332, 340 (bottom middle), 365; Hector Christiaen p. 334; Thomas Cockrem p. 358; Eyepix Group p. 354 (top); FLPA p. 338 (top); Gallo Images p. 357; Lois GoBe p. 327; Jason Smalley Photography p. 351 (bottom); Joe p. 326 (top); Yury Kirillov p. 346; Realimage p. 349 (bottom); reuerendo, p. 323; RGB Ventures/SuperStock p. 380; Mauro Toccaceli p. 333. **Courtesy Use:** Boston Globe p. 336 (top); Lions Of Nairobi National Park p. 355 (top); Carla Rhodes

p. 366. St Lucia South Africa Facebook Page p. 362. **Dreamstime:** Frederick Effendi p. 378 (bottom). **Getty Images:** emranashraf p. 329 (bottom); Goddard_Photography p. 363; Gwenvidig p. 331; heyengel pp. 324–325 (spread); iStockphoto p. 355 (bottom); ljphoto7 p. 340 (top middle); David McGowen p. 376 (bottom middle); Trong Nguyen p. 370; Rich Townsend p. 359 (top); undefined p. 371. **Minden Pictures:** Toshiaki Ida p. 372.
National Geographic: Alejandro Cegarra p. 379. **Science Source:** Anthony Bannister p. 349 (middle right); Phil Degginger p. 349 (middle left); Georgette Douwma p. 330 (top right); Dante Fenolio p. 340 (middle); Adam Fletcher pp. 373 (bottom), 373 (inset), 374 (top); Michael P. Gadomski p. 347; Ian Gowland p. 350 (top); Bertie Gregory p. 329 (top); Richard R. Hansen p. 344; Kenneth M. Highfill p. 338 (bottom); Eric Hosking p. 350 (bottom); Pascal Kobeh p. 330 (top left); Simon D. Pollard p. 376 (top); Robert and Jean Pollock p. 351 (top); Mario Cea Sanchez/VWPics p. 358 (bottom middle); John Serrao p. 340 (bottom right); Millard H. Sharp p. 359 (bottom right top); Peter Skinner p. 359 (bottom right); The Natural History Museum, London p. 330 (bottom); B.G. Thomson p. 359 (bottom right middle); Colin Varndell p. 358 (bottom middle); Jerome Wexler p. 358 (bottom right). **Shutterstock:** 7th Son Studio p. 349 (top); AlecTrusler2015 p. 375; anidaaripin p. 368 (top); ArtifyAnalog p. 361; Jim Cumming p. 336 (bottom); Erni p. 348 (top); Gallinago_media p. 348 (bottom); Nick Greaves p. 377 (top); Tawanda Kapikinyu p. 356; milart p. 368 (bottom); Lakkana Savaksuriyawong p. 376 (bottom left); Rudmer Zwerver p. 340 (bottom). **Wikimedia:** The following images are used under a Creative Commons Attribution CC BY-SA 4.0 License (https://creativecommons.org/licenses/by-sa/4.0/deed.en) and belong to the following Wikimedia Commons users: Agricultural Research Service p. 377 (bottom); Jesse Berry p. 339; Uraspasibo p. 354 (top); WikiPedant p. 343 (bottom). **Public Domain:** Jiri Bohdal p. 340 (top); Albert Froneman p. 360; RCannon992 p. 376 (middle); U.S. Dept. of Transportation p. 343 (top).

ISLANDS

Adobe Stock: Joshua p. 420; Narupon p. 393. **AGE Fotostock:** Michael Nolan p. 418. **Alamy:** Abaca Press p. 395 (right); All Canada Photos pp. 432–433 (spread); Biosphoto p. 415 (bottom); Dordo Brnobic p. 435 (top); Chris Brunskill p. 388; Design Pics Inc pp. 392 (bottom), 417 (top), 423 (bottom); Douglas Peebles Photography p. 413; Moshe Einhorn p. 400 (top); Galaxiid p. 421; Manfred Gottschalk p. 405; Horst Friedrichs p. 392 (top); Chris Howarth/South Atlantic p. 436 (bottom); imageBROKER.com GmbH & Co. KG p. 384; Markus Mayer p. 427 (middle); Nature Picture Library pp. 409, 427 (bottom), 390, 402, 432 (top); Photo Resource Hawaii pp. 412 (middle), 412 (top), 415 (top); Henryk Sadura p. 426 (right); Worawan Simaroj p. 428; Maggie Sully p. 400 (top); Oleg Troino p. 440; Dave Watts p. 406; Kerry Whitworth p. 399 (bottom). **Courtesy of Atlas Obscura Contributors:** Otávio Marquees/Courtesy Instituto Butantan p. 429. **Getty Images:** Aschen p. 431 (top); Guillermo Legaria/AFP p. 395 (left); Jacob Maentz p. 423 (top); V Stokes p. 436 (top). **Minden Pictures:** Neil Lucas p. 404 (top). **Reuters:** Rick Burian/Handout p. 387. **Science Source:** ANT Photo Library p. 401; Oliver Born p. 408; Sylvain Cordier p. 416; Gerald & Buff Corsi/Focus on Nature, Inc. p. 427 (top); Gregory G. Dimijian, M.D. p. 396; Uri Golman/NaturePL p. 442; David Hosking p. 434 (top); Jeffrey Lepore p. 424; Christopher Swann p. 397; The Natural History Museum, London p. 399 (inset); M. Watson p. 407. **Shutterstock:** Agami Photo Agency p. 411; Elif Bayraktar p. 426 (left); BridgetSpencerPhoto p. 389 (bottom); crbellette p. 389 (top); Alina Dely p. 435 (bottom right); Gallinago_media p. 438; Anton Ivanov pp. 426–427 (spread); Natalia Kuzmina p. 419; Little Panda2016 p. 430 (middle); Maridav p. 410; Martin Mecnarowski p. 383; Vladimir Melnik p. 391; photomatz p. 422; Alejandro Piorun p. 434 (bottom); Protasov AN p. 435 (middle); Michal Sarauer p. 435 (bottom left); Richard Susanto p. 430 (bottom); trabantos p. 431 (middle). **Superstock:** Tui De Roy/Nature Picture Library p. 433 (top); Greg Marsh, Founder Member of the Lambay Island Club p. 430 (top). **Wikimedia:** The following image is used under a Creative Commons Attribution CC BY-SA 3.0 License (https://creativecommons.org/licenses/by-sa/3.0/deed.en) and belongs to the following Wikimedia Commons user: Forest & Kim Starr p. 417 (bottom). The following image is used under a Creative Commons Attribution CC BY-SA 4.0 License (https://creativecommons.org/licenses/by-sa/4.0/deed.en) and belongs to the following Wikimedia Commons user: Maui Forest Bird Recovery Project p. 412 (bottom). **Public Domain:** Enno Meyer p. 404 (bottom).

INDEX

tortoises
    desert, 202–203
    giant, 434
    gopher, 18
    Pinta Island giant, 405
Tortula inermis, 200
Totora reed, 153
traffic, avoiding, 343
trap-jaw ants, 58
trashline orb weavers, 7
Tree 75, 43
tree crickets, 49
tree line, Arctic, 109
Tree of Life, 43
trees. *See also individual species*
    network connecting, 30–32
    notable, 43
trench-digging beetles, 230–231
tricolored bats, 334
trilling frogs, 252
Tu BiShvat, 56
tube worms, 310, 318
tucuxi, 11
tufted rock beardless moss,
    175–176
tulip mangrove, 300–301
tumbleweeds, 106–107
túngara frogs, 340
turtle-headed sea snakes, 330
turtles, 60, 292, 396
two-spotted ladybugs, 330

U

Uluru waterfalls, 252
underpasses, 343

V

vampire ground finches,
    432–433
Vellozia, 128–129
velvet mesquite, 206

Venezuelan tepuis, 168
Venus flytraps, 19
verges, 326–327
vicuñas, 156–157
vipers, 429
viruses, 101
Von der Decken's hornbills,
    234
vultures, 130, 196

W

Wabakimi Provincial Park,
    29
wallabies, 430
Wallace's flying frogs, 50
Walleyn, Adam, 436, 437
walruses, 424–425
wapiti, 105
Warlpiri people, 257–258
wasps, 438, 439
water deer, 105
waterwheels, 20
waxcaps, 99
Weddell seals, 264–265
welwitschia, 231–232
Western Ghats purple frogs,
    183
Western glacier stoneflies,
    141–142
western pebble-mound mice,
    255
whale sharks, 292
whales, 96, 292, 293, 319
whiptail lizards, 190
whistling kites, 88–89
whistling thorn acacia trees,
    78–79
white bellbirds, 162
white clover, 364
white-tailed deer, 341
white-throated rails, 437
wild boar, 47

wild camels, 240–241
wild figs, 43
wild tulips, 91
wildebeests, 73–74, 80, 97
Wilson, Kevin, 200
wind-sculpted trees, 304
winghead sharks, 298
wolverines, 142–143
wolves
    Ethiopian, 165
    gray, 47, 97, 146–147
    sea, 420
Wong, Ku'ulei, 412–413
wood frogs, 33–34
wood mice, 100–101
woodpeckers, 17, 123
woolly croton, 90
woolly mammoths, 205
worm lichen, 112–113
wrens, 374–375

X

xenophyophores, 310–311

Y

Yangtze finless porpoises, 11
yellow meranti, 2, 43, 51–53
yellow-crested cockatoos,
    380
yeti, 175
yeti crabs, 310, 318

Z

zebra sharks, 190
zebras, 76, 80
Ziebell's handfish, 273
Zimov, Nikita, 102, 103
zombie fungus, 439
zoomusicologist, 65
zooplankton, 290–291

ABOUT THE AUTHORS

Cara Giaimo lives in Somerville, MA, with her wife, Lilia, two cats, many plants, and uncountable neighborhood rats. A former staff writer at Atlas Obscura, Cara now writes about our fellow species for the *New York Times*, *Fabrikzeitung*, *Bloomberg Businessweek*, and elsewhere. Her first book, *Detector Dogs* (with Christina Couch), was published by MIT Kids Press in 2022. She plays guitar in Sidebody.

Joshua Foer is the cofounder of Atlas Obscura and coauthor of the #1 *New York Times* bestseller *Atlas Obscura: An Explorer's Guide to the World's Hidden Wonders*. His writing has appeared in the *New Yorker*, *National Geographic*, *Esquire*, *Slate*, *Outside*, the *New York Times*, and other publications. His book, *Moonwalking with Einstein*, was an international bestseller published in thirty-seven languages.

Atlas Obscura is widely celebrated for building the definitive community-driven platform for discovering the world's wonders. Atlasobscura.com is the premier destination for the curious, offering fascinating storytelling; award-winning podcasts; a database of unique places, foods, and species; and once-in-a-lifetime trips and experiences.

↔

Also from the authors:
Atlas Obscura and *Gastro Obscura*.

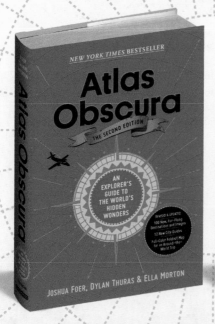
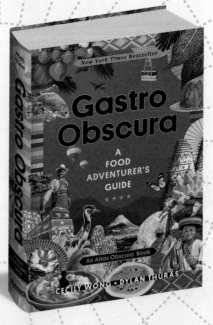

Available wherever books are sold, or visit workman.com.